A MANUAL OF
MODERN GERMAN

BY

FREDERICK J. STOPP, M.B.E., M.A., Ph.D.

LECTURER IN GERMAN IN THE UNIVERSITY OF CAMBRIDGE

UNIVERSITY TUTORIAL PRESS LTD

CLIFTON HOUSE, EUSTON ROAD, LONDON, N.W. 1

Published 1957
Second Edition 1960
Reprinted 1963

PRINTED IN GREAT BRITAIN BY UNIVERSITY TUTORIAL PRESS LTD, FOXTON
NEAR CAMBRIDGE

PREFACE

PECULIAR difficulties beset the path of anyone looking for instruction in the modern German language at both the elementary and advanced levels. No instructional work published during the last fifty years in England could avoid—and none has avoided—being deeply indebted to the scholarly compendium of O. Curme (New York and London, 1905, second, revised edition, 1922), the more so as, during the same period, leading German grammarians have devoted their energies less to recording the facts of their own modern language than to problems of linguistic theory and questions of linguistic politics. How much energy has gone into the argument for and against foreign words alone! Curme is now, however, on many matters, two full generations out of date, and, for the student at least, has the faults of his great virtues: through lack of selection and simplification no clear profile of the language emerges, and moreover the very size of the work conceals some striking omissions, such as the whole field of punctuation.

The result is that, in general, too few writers, in England through lack of incentive, in Germany through lack of desire, have felt the need to stand back a little from the authorities, and to register the facts of modern practice, without undue deference to the evidence adduced by Curme, and without undue respect for the legalistic simplifications of the smaller German handbooks, which are more concerned with determining what should be taught than with registering what is actually said or written.

In England there are signs that the territory long dominated by Curme is being re-entered by scholars. J. Bithell's projected German Grammar, of which one volume, *Pronunciation and Phonology*, has appeared (London, 1952), promises to be as exhaustive as Curme; at the other end of the scale of size, Professor W. E. Collinson's *The German Language Today* (London, 1953) is a remarkable feat of condensation. It is, however, as are *a fortiori* Bithell and Curme, precluded by its general intention from being used as a work of graduated instruction.

It appears, therefore, that there is scope for a manual of the present-day language which seeks to clothe the skeleton of grammatical rule with the flesh and blood of modern practice by liberal quotation from contemporary usage, whether literary, colloquial, or ephemeral, and presents the results in a form suitable for the mature learner. The present work seeks to meet this need. No author of such a work can fail to have learnt much from his predecessors, and this debt is here gratefully acknowledged. But the prime source of the illustrative material given here has been a very large collection of observations of actual practice from about 1890 to the present moment. Not only have the traditional rules of grammar been checked and rechecked against this evidence of practice, and modified where necessary in its light, but, in the sheer proportion of volume by which various usages are represented, such a thesaurus may serve to trace out the changing physiognomy of the language in a way quite different from that open to the normative grammarian. Thus on the one hand certain modern developments, such as the use of the infinitive noun and of the adjectival noun, and in the field of punctuation that of the colon, are here treated at greater length than they could be by one whose concern is merely to formulate a rule and go on his way. On the other hand, certain controverted matters, such as **um . . . zu** with the infinitive, may be treated with the sympathy which they deserve, but which they mostly do not get at the hands of more legalistically minded German writers.

The work accordingly aims at combining the functions of a graded course, suitable for beginners who can call upon the guidance of an experienced teacher, with that of a reference grammar for more advanced students, both in University Departments and in the upper forms of schools. But in so far as it also pursues descriptive aims, it is more properly entitled Manual than simply Grammar or Course.

A list of the main writers of literary standing from whom quotations are made is provided. These must clearly reflect to some extent the predilections of the author, but it is hoped that specialists in the modern literature will regard the selection as not unrepresentative. Quotations have been chosen often as much for their intrinsic interest as for the grammatical point which they illustrate. Almost all the examples quoted have also been translated, though, with long examples, space has often been saved by translating only that part of the quotation relevant to the point under discussion. The translation offered is intended more to elucidate that point than to be itself a model of good English style. Those who do not need or wish to work through the Exercises will find in the Sections marked A a further selection of German examples; these are, increasingly from Chapter XX, and almost entirely from about Chapter XXX, drawn from named German authors.

The Manual is in two Parts. Part One covers all the major grammatical topics except the subjunctive. Part Two treats of the subjunctive, and studies certain selected fields in greater detail. Part One is given a

German—English and English—German Vocabulary, containing all those words needed for working the Exercises, unless such words occur and are translated in the body of the chapter to which the Exercise refers, since it is assumed that the student will maintain and learn his own vocabulary lists. It also gives the meaning of all German words used in the body of the chapters up to Chapter XV, especially in sections on the declension of nouns. Vocabulary has been introduced as needed for the build-up of the grammar, and not with the intention of extending the personal vocabulary of the student in any systematic way. Further, all words are listed and translated only in the sense required in the context in which they occur; the Vocabulary seeks neither to prevent the use of a dictionary as soon as the student is prepared and able to use one, nor does it duplicate information given in a grammatical context elsewhere. In Sections B of the Exercises, square brackets are used to show words to be omitted when translating into German, round brackets for words to be added and any other explanatory comment. When several words are to be rendered by one German word, they are hyphenated in the English.

No Vocabulary is provided for Part Two (*i.e.* from Chapter XLIV), since at this stage the student is expected to have acquired a dictionary, and to have learnt to use it intelligently.

A minimum of matters not susceptible to treatment in the body of the work is presented in Appendices after Part Two. The substance of these has not been incorporated into the final (grammatical) Index, so that information on such important but easily recognisable groups as the strong and irregular verbs must be discovered with the aid of the appropriate Appendix. (For prepositions, see below.) The final General Index, containing both grammatical topics and German words discussed in a grammatical context, has been kept within reasonable bounds, but this is compensated for by liberal cross-reference between different parts of the Manual. This policy seemed indicated by the notorious difficulty experienced by all users of grammars of identifying, under an unfamiliar grammatical heading, a topic as yet imperfectly understood. There seemed therefore no point in multiplying unhelpful headings.

Grammatical nomenclature is itself a difficult point—how difficult in German may be seen by a glance at Appendix E. I have adopted what appeared to be the best modern practice. For the present participle and infinitive with active form, but passive (and modal) force, I have used, though only for want of a better term, Curme's expression 'modal verbal'. It would be helpful if German grammarians would themselves name this construction. I have attempted to introduce order (and some light) into the confusing class of words known variously as pronominals, indefinite numerals, and indefinite pronouns, by distinguishing indefinite pronouns (**man**, etc.) and indefinite adjective-pronouns (**viel**, etc.), and dividing the latter, as explained in § 81, into exhaustives and quantitatives.

The almost invariable practice of grammatical handbooks in the matter of prepositions is to list them alphabetically under the cases they govern, and to illustrate all uses of a given preposition under its one heading. This has always seemed to me to duplicate—inadequately, because of lack of space—the information available in a good dictionary. In deciding to devote space to this important (but only indirectly grammatical) field I was influenced by the fact that, until the projected monumental English and German Dictionary by Mr T. D. Jones appears, no full and reliable dictionary treatment of modern German prepositional usage, against the background of corresponding English usage, exists. It seemed therefore that a genuinely grammatical treatment might be achieved by grouping uses under certain select categories of sense, these being largely the ones traditionally adopted for the classification of certain other forms, especially adverbs, conjunctions, and adverbial clauses. The groundwork of this treatment is explained in § 261, and the special Index of Prepositions enables the student to refer to all uses of a given preposition if required; in the case of fifteen of the commonest, such reference is assisted by a special synoptic table. Prepositions discussed in purely grammatical functions are, however, listed in the General Index.

It seemed to me appropriate and acceptable that a work of this kind should concentrate on the parts of speech (only the interjection and its related exclamatory forms are omitted), their inflection and use, and the groundwork of syntax. Only the main principles of word-order are treated in various sections, but these, I hope, not inadequately. Word-formation is not discussed at all, except in so far as it is relevant to other matters, such as gender, accent, conjugation, etc. On pronunciation and word-stress the Introduction and other sections provide only the minimum of information; but the student is referred to the compendious treatment of this field in W. L. Wardale's *German Pronunciation* (Edinburgh U.P., 1955, 6/-).

In Germany, the successive editions of the reference work known as *Duden*, in four parts (**Grammatik, Stil, Rechtschreibung, Bildwörterbuch**), are widely used and regarded as authoritative; but the student is warned that the volume on Grammar reflects more what its compilers consider practice should be, than what it actually is. The shorter version produced at Leipzig in East Germany (**Kleine Grammatik**, referred to in this Manual as *East German Duden*), is largely, but not entirely, reduplicative of the larger work.

Finally, I am happy to have this opportunity of acknowledging, not in this matter alone, my indebtedness to others, first and foremost to my friend and colleague, Mr T. D. Jones, who originally suggested that I should undertake this work, answered many enquiries from his incomparable knowledge of the language, and read a large part of the final typescript. Dr W. Dellers, formerly Lector in German in the University of Cambridge, checked every statement in this Manual against his own native **Sprachempfinden** and excellent knowledge of regional variants in usage, and made many helpful suggestions. I also thank Miss A. Williamson for valuable assistance with the layout, and Dr Manfred Seidler, of Bonn, for advice generously given over a number of years. I am deeply grateful to my wife for her devoted assistance at all stages of the work.

This Manual is dedicated to the memory of the late H. O. Coleman, most inspiring of teachers.

F. J. S.

NOTE TO THE SECOND EDITION

In the new edition the text has been amended as far as was necessary to eliminate a number of misprints, minor errors, and infelicities of expression. I should like to express my thanks to all those who have very kindly drawn my attention to such points, and especially to Dr H. T. Betteridge, of Glasgow.

F. J. S.

CONTENTS

APPENDICES

LIST OF CHIEF AUTHORS AND SOURCES
QUOTED IN THIS MANUAL

Willy Andreas
Stefan Andres
Ernst Barlach
Gottfried Benn
Werner Bergengruen
Heinrich Böll
Hermann Broch
Heimito von Doderer
Hans Fallada
Theodor Fontane
Romano Guardini
Gerhart Hauptmann
Hermann Hesse
Carl Gustav Jung
Ernst Jünger
Friedrich Georg Jünger
Hermann Kasack
Erich Kästner
Karl Kraus

Ernst Kreuder
Elisabeth Langgässer
Gertrud von le Fort
Heinrich Mann
Thomas Mann
Robert Musil
Rudolf Otto
Will-Erich Peuckert
Theodor Plievier
Hans Reimann
Heinz Risse
Erich Schairer
Edzard Schaper
Wilhelm Speyer
Frank Thiess
Franz Werfel
Bruno E. Werner
Ernst Wiechert
Stefan Zweig

Simplicissimus, Munich (*Simpl.*).
Muttersprache, Lüneburg (*Mspr.*).
Newspapers (newsp.).

LIST OF ABBREVIATIONS

The following abbreviations have been used in secondary parts of the text, and throughout the Vocabulary, Appendices, and Indices:

abbrev.	abbreviation, abbreviated.	insep.	inseparable.
acc.	accusative (case).	interr.	interrogative.
adj.	adjective.	intrans.	intransitive (verb).
adv.	adverb, adverbial, advertisement.	Intro.	Introduction.
		invar.	invariable.
Am.	American.	irr.	irregular (verb).
App.	Appendix.	joc.	jocular(ly).
art.	article.	lit.	literal (sense), literary.
aux.	auxiliary (verb).	m., masc.	masculine.
coll.	colloquial(ly).	mod.	modal (verb).
comp.	comparison.	**Mspr.**	**Muttersprache,** *v.* List of Authors and Sources.
conjn.	conjunction.		
constr.	construction.	neg.	negative.
coord.	coordinating.	newsp.	newspaper.
corr.	correspondent.	nom.	nominative (case).
correl.	correlative.	n., neut.	neuter.
cp.	compare.	obj.	object(ive).
dat.	dative (case).	para.	paragraph.
decl.	declension, declined.	phon.	in phonetic notation.
def. art.	definite article.	pl., plur.	plural.
demonstr.	demonstrative.	pop.	popular(ly).
dist.	distinguish(ed).	poss.	possessive.
Engl.	English.	p. p.	past participle.
esp.	especially.	pred.	predicate.
ex.	example.	pronn.	pronoun.
exc.	except.	pr. p.	present participle
f., fem.	feminine.	refl.	reflexive (verb).
fig.	figurative (sensc).	rel.	relative.
foll.	followed, following.	rev.	review.
Fr.	French.	s.	strong (verb).
gen.	genitive (case).	sep.	separable.
govt.	(case) government.	sing.	singular.
imp.	impersonal (verb).	**Simpl.**	**Simplicissimus,** *v.* List of Authors and Sources.
indecl.	indeclinable.		
indef. art.	indefinite article.	subj.	subject(ive).
Ind.	Index.	trans.	transitive (verb).
indir.	indirect (object).	transl.	translation.
infin.	infinitive.	uninfl.	uninflected.
infl.	inflection, inflected.	**v.**	verb.
		v.	*vide.*

A MANUAL OF MODERN GERMAN

INTRODUCTION

1. General. Vowels (**der Vokal, Selbstlaut**).

(*a*) The German alphabet consists of the same twenty-six symbols as the English, each with a name (*v.* § 7 below), used in reference and for the corresponding noun: **b**, called (phon.) be: (as in **das B, das ABC**). Consonantal groups are referred to by the name of the individual consonants [*v.* § 3 (*e*) below].

It must be remembered that English words quoted below in illustration of German sounds contain mere approximations to the genuine sound, which can be learnt only by observation of the practice of educated natives.

(*b*) Simple vowels (**der einfache Selbstlaut**) are short or long.

(1) PRONUNCIATION.—The long vowels (phon. ɑ e i o u) are like those in *father, eh lad!* (in North), *wheeze, home* (in North), *mood*; they are never diphthongised, as by Southern English speakers (*hay, snow,* etc.), but are pronounced in such a way that they may be continued indefinitely on a constant note.

The short vowels (phon. a ɛ ɪ ɔ ʊ) are like those in *man* (North), or *fun* (South), *let, hit, hot, put*; but short **o** and **u** are more rounded, so that, *e.g.* **Gott** sounds to English ears nearer to long **go-thisch** than to short *hot*. Short **i** is of higher pitch than in English, cp. **ich bin,** *his bin.*

The English flat **a** in *sat, land* (phon. æ) does not occur in German; the nearest approximation for poor speakers of English is ɛ in *set, lend.*

Short, unstressed vowels are not usually indistinct, as often in English; thus **Lóndon** differs from *Lóng Tóm* mainly in the stress, and is not as **Lónd(e)n;** and final **a** in **Sofa, Drama,** is rather like *hookah* than like *sofa, drama.* Unstressed final **-e** in good speech is clearly distinct from **-er,** which is deeper and richer than in English; thus **Butte, finge,** nearer **Mutti,** *hilly,* than **Butter, Finger,** which themselves are more like *attar, Tonga.* In normal speech, however, final unaccented **-el, -em, -en** after a consonant are pronounced as **-l, -m, -n,** thus: **Brennessel,** as in *mussel,* **Atem,** as in *atom,* **landen,** as in *laden.*

(2) SPELLING.—Long and short vowels may be distinguished thus: (i) long from short, by doubling (**Aal, Tee, Boot,** but not **i** or **u**), by adding **-h,** thus called **das Dehnungs-h** (**Rahm, mehr, ihnen, ohne, Schuh**), or by using two letters with a single sound (**Sie,** and in some place-names, as **Soest**); (ii) short from long by doubling a following single consonant, and thus closing the syllable: **schwellen** (**schwel-len,** dist. **schwe-len,**

long), **Schuppen (Schup-pen,** dist. **U-hu,** long); this is of course unnecessary when a consonantal group follows: **schelten.**

(*c*) Three simple vowels may be "modified" (**der Umlaut,** modification, mutation, modified vowel) whether short or long.

(1) PRONUNCIATION.—Ä is open e (phon. ɛ), either short (**hält,** as *melt*), or long (**stähle,** as *me-e-lt*); but some pronounce the latter like normal long e (*i.e.* **stähle** as **stehle**). Ö (phon. ɸ short or œ long) and ü (phon. y short or Y long) are unknown in English; the mouth and tongue is prepared to pronounce close e and i respectively, but the lips are rounded (pursed) as though to pronounce o or u: **Hölle, Höhle,** similar to French *pieu* (closer than *heure*); **Hülle, Mühle,** similar to French *vue*. Avoid the temptation, with ö, to unround the lips, producing a slack, indeterminate vowel: **Hölle** not like *hurler*; or, with ü, to allow the tongue to conform to the rounded lips: **Mühe** not like *mooer*.

Y, only in foreign words, is normally long or short ü: **Typ, Mystik;** but occasionally, especially in words of English origin, it is long or short i: **Willy, lynchen.**

For the modified diphthong **äu,** *v.* (*d*) (2) below.

(2) SPELLING.—Long and short modified vowels may be distinguished [as in (*b*) (2), above], thus: (i) long from short by adding **Dehnungs-h** (**stähle, Höhle, Mühle**), though not otherwise; (ii) short from long by a following double consonant or consonant group: **schwöm-me, Hüt-te, gäl-ten** (distinguish **Tö-ne, Hü-te, Sä-le**). Double vowels become single when modified: **Saal, Säle; Boot, Bötchen.**

(*d*) Diphthongs (**der Diphthong, Doppellaut, Zwielaut**): **au, ei, eu.**

(1) PRONUNCIATION.—Phon. au, ai, ɔʏ; similar to English *house, nice, boy,* but **au** has as first sound that in *father,* is thus nearer to *Mau-Mau.*

(2) SPELLING.—This is normally as given above: **Haus, Bein, heulen;** but **ei** may appear as **ai,** as in **Hai,** or as **ay, ey,** in proper names, thus **Bayern, Meyer, Mayer;** and **eu** very commonly appears as the modified diphthong **äu,** as in **Säule** (**Umlaut** sign over *first* vowel).

Note.—Other diphthongal sounds are found with i as component: **Blödián, Família** (but only unaccented, thus **studieren** is long and simple), **Millión, Sanguíniker** (but distinguish the falling diphthong in some exclamations, **pfúi, húi**).

2. Consonants (**der Konsonant, Mitlaut**), I. Single letters and sounds.

(*a*) Plosives (**der Verschlußlaut**): **b p d t g k.**

(1) PRONUNCIATION.—As in English, voiced or unvoiced (as in *bad, pat, gag, kick*), except that all voiced stops become unvoiced before an

unvoiced consonant (**Habsburg,** as **Hapsburg,** an occasional alternative spelling, **Stadt** as **statt**), or at the end of a word (**Hub,** as *hoop*), or of a word in compound, even when followed by a voiced consonant (**Endsieg,** as **entsiegeln,** but cp. **bugsieren,** voiced).

G often becomes a fricative [*v.* 3 (*b*) below, phon. ç or x] in parts of North Germany, either finally (**Tag,** as **Dach**), or medially (**sagte,** as **sachte, vergnügt,** as **kriecht**). In Standard German this is the rule only with the ending **-ig** (**willig,** as **Drillich,** but not if followed by a vowel, **l** or **r,** thus **königlich** is as **wirklich**). Original pronunciation is retained in some foreign words, thus **Genie** (phon. ʒ), as in *usual*, but **genial** is normal.

(2) SPELLING.—All plosives are double after short vowels: **Kladde, Egge, Lappen, Stadt** (dist. **Fla-den, E-ger, Hu-pe, Ste-te**); but double **k** appears as **ck** until separated (**Bäcker,** for **Bäk-ker**), *v.* § 543 (*a*).

(*b*) Fricatives (**die Frikative, der Reibelaut**): **f v w.**

(1) PRONUNCIATION.—**F** is as in English. **V** is not voiced, so **vier** as *fear*, but is voiced in some foreign words: **Vase, Violine, Alkoven,** as English *vase, violin, alcove.* **W** is the corresponding voiced consonant, thus **weiß,** as *vice*, **Iwan,** for *Ivan.*

For the two palatal fricatives represented by **ch,** *v.* 3 (*b*) below.

(2) SPELLING.—Neither **v** nor **w** is ever found doubled.

(*c*) Liquids (**die Liquida, der Schmelzlaut**): **l m n r.**

(1) PRONUNCIATION.—The nasals **m, n** are as in English. **N** moves back and loses its dental quality before **k** and **g,** as in English (phon. ŋ), but before **k** it is always two sounds (**danke,** as *thanks*), while before **g** it is always only one, **singe,** as *singer*, *v.* 3 (*b*) below.

L remains liquid in all cases, and does not have the "dark" sound, approaching **w** as, *e.g.* in the Cockney *milk* ($mi^w k$). Thus **alt** sounds to English ears near to **eilt,** and may be practised by inserting a slight **i** (a^ilt).

R has no equivalent in Southern English, and especially the form with protruded lips (as *run*) is unknown. Either of the trilled forms may be used, *i.e.* that with the point of the tongue, **das Zungenspitzen-r** (as in Scotland, thus in Southern Germany and Austria, and standard use for actors, phon. r), or that with the uvula, **das Zäpfchen-r** (as in France, thus in North Germany, phon. R). The sound is usually heard after a vowel in a closed syllable, thus **Horn,** not lengthened as in English *horn*; and after **a** it is sharply articulated, sounding to English ears like a guttural fricative: **hart,** near to **Macht, ihr fahrt,** near to **ihr facht.** But this is less so in final **-er,** which, together with leading **ver-** (in verbs) is often transmuted to a short, sharp **a,** thus **vergeben,** as *aha!* [cp. also 1 (*b*) (1)].

(2) SPELLING.—Liquids double, as plosives: **Schall, glimme, Henne, Herr.**

(*d*) Sibilants (**der Sibilant, Zischlaut**): s ß, and *v.* also **sch z tz** and **sp st** below (§ 3).

(1) PRONUNCIATION.—Single **s** is normally voiced or unvoiced as in English: **Rast,** as *haste,* **Hase,** as *loser;* but it is also voiced initially (except in the South), thus **Sohn** is as *zoo,* **singen** as *Zingari,* not as *sing.*

(2) SPELLING.—S doubles as do other consonants (**hassen,** as *massive*), but in cases where the group would not be separated on syllabification (*v.* § 543), the symbol **ß,** the only character now retained from the former Gothic alphabet (and called es-tset, *i.e.* **sz,** and also **scharfes s**), is used. This therefore happens after a long vowel (**Mu-ße**), before a third consonant (**muß-ten**), or at the end of a word (**Haß**) or prefix (**Mißlaut**). In the third group, **ß** does not indicate whether the preceding vowel is short or long, cp. **Haß,** short, but **Fuß,** long; but the plural may assist, cp. **Maße** (pl. of **Maß**), **Masse** (f. sing.).

(*e*) Other single sounds: **h j.**

H is pronounced, as in English, in the initial position (**Hut,** as *hat*), but never elsewhere (**Mohn, sehen**), except in dictation wherever it begins a syllable (**Mü-he**).

J, which only occurs initially, is pronounced as English *y* (its name is as *yacht,* *v.* § 7 below), though with more friction. In words from French, it is as in that language (**Journal,** phon. ꝫ).

3. Consonants, II.   Groups of letters and sounds.

(*a*) The following single consonants have double sounds:

X, pronounced **ks,** as in **Haxen,** a sound otherwise spelt **chs,** as in **Achse,** English *axle*; but if the s is part of an ending, the group is two sounds, thus **näch-st, höch-st** (cp. § 117).

Z, pronounced **ts,** as in **zirpen, Scherz, heizen;** but after a short vowel (*i.e.* when doubled), it appears as **tz: Hetze** (cp. also **c** below).

(*b*) The following consonantal groups have each a single sound:

Ch, in German words a guttural (back) or dental (front) fricative (phon. *x,* ç). The former, as in **Bach,** is as Scottish *loch.* The latter may be pronounced by exaggerating the initial aspiration of *Hugh,* or by aspirating the first sound of *you.*

Back **ch** is used after the back vowels **a o u au** (**Schmach, Buch,** etc.); front **ch** after the front vowels **e i ei eu ä ö ü** (**Scheich, rächen, röcheln,** etc.), and after the liquids **l n r** (**Walcheren, Kirche**). But the diminutive suffix **-chen** has also the front sound, which may thus follow a back vowel: **Schuhchen** (distinguish **fluchen,** back).

Ch, initially in foreign words, is pronounced as **k** before back vowels (**Charakter, Chor,** also **Chöre**), but as front **ch** elsewhere by careful speakers (**Chemie**), though informally **k** is often heard here. All words from French have the French sibilant, thus **Chauffeur,** assimilated as **Schofför** [cp. § 130 (*d*)].

The letter **c** occurs not separately pronounced in the groups **ck, ch, chs, sch;** in foreign words, alone and initially, it is hard (**Couleur,** cp. **Kühler**), or soft (**circa,** cp. **zirpen**).

Ph in foreign words, as **f**: **Phlegma, Sophie.**

Th in foreign words, as **t**: **Theater** (there being no dental fricative, as English *theatre, than*).

Sch, as English *sh,* thus **Schall,** as *shall,* **Asche,** *ash.*

The group **ng** is never a double sound, as sometimes in English: **Wrangel** (name), as *wringer,* not as *wrangle;* **Finger,** as *singer,* not as *finger.*

(*c*) The following groups have differing value in German and English:

Qu, mostly in foreign words, is pronounced as **kw**: **Quantum,** as *ba-ckv-iew;* the same value for **u** occurs occasionally elsewhere: **Biskuit.** But French words have pronunciation of origin: **Maquis.**

Sp and **st,** when initial, are pronounced as if **s** were **sch**: **spinnen,** as *a-shp-an,* **Straße,** as *hu-shtr-ain;* but the unaltered sound is retained in some parts of North Germany (**s-pinnen**). Foreign words, if unfamiliar, also retain pronunciation of origin, thus **S-tratosphäre;** but familiar words are assimilated, thus **Stil, spontan,** as **Straße.**

The group **ti** is pronounced as **tsi** in the common foreign endings **-tion** (as **Nation**), and **-tie** (as **Demokratie**).

(*d*) There are no silent letters in German; thus the group **kn** is always two sounds, even when it leads: **Knie,** as *Ha-ckn-ey,* not as *knee.* This and other initial groups may cause difficulty to English speakers; such groups may be practised in words where they appear medially, and the group then isolated: **Knie,** as *Ha-ckn-ey;* **Pfad,** as **empfangen,** and *cam-pfire;* **Zange,** as **Hetze,** and *ha-ts-on.*

(*e*) Consonantal groups are referred to by the names of their components, as **sch,** es-tse-ha; thus also **ch, ph, qu, th, tz,** etc. A double consonant, thus English double *l,* double *o,* may be **Doppel-l,** or **zwei l.**

4. The Glottal Stop (der Kehlkopfverschlußlaut). This sound (phon. '), which is heard in some Cockney speech (*bottle* rather as *bo'w*), and caused by a momentary closing of the glottis followed by a vigorous release of the following sound, is very common in German, being characteristic especially of standard and formal speech, and reflecting the greater vigour of articulation as compared with English. It should therefore be regarded as a consonant not represented by any letter.

It is heard before any word or part of a word beginning with a stressed vowel: **das 'Amt, ver'achten, Wild'ente.** It must always be given full value between vowels (**be'inhalten, be'obachten**), unless the first one is an inflectional ending which may be elided (**sagt' er**). It is heard less in rapid and connected speech: **das-ist kaum-anzunehmen**, and not at all in fully integrated compounds after a consonant (**Obacht, Interesse**), or in compound particles (**herein, herunter**), especially when -r- has been inserted (*v.* § 33) to facilitate compounding (**darin, worauf**).

5. Word stress.

(*a*) There are two general principles governing German word stress:

(1) Generally, all simple and compound words, and also those derived from other words by prefix and suffix, have a strong stress on the leading syllable: **Líebe, únsere Kátze, (wir) átmeten, régnerisch, únschön, Bácker, Háusfrau, (im) dúnkelsten Áfrika, ánfangen.**

(2) But derivative verbs with inseparable prefixes are accented on the stem of the simple verb: **ergében** (*v.* § 88); and similarly nouns and adjectives derived from these: **die Ergebung**, etc., **ergiebig** [*v.* §§ 193, 448 (*a*)].

(*b*) But certain groups have special stress:

(1) Foreign words, with stressed suffix: **Theoríe, Kinderéi, marschíeren** (*v.* §§ 76, 89 f., 130);

(2) Certain compounds, with stress on a significant component: **das Dreikámmersystem** [*v.* § 448 (*c*)];

(3) Group words, with stress on the last syllable: **das Einmaléins**, [*v.* § 448 (*d*)];

(4) Words with a rhetorical stress on an emotionally toned syllable: **abschéulich**, *disgusting* (but **der Ábscheu**, *disgust*) [*v.* § 448 (*e*)].

Note.—Nominal and adjectival prefixes, with the exception of the collective Ge- [*v.* § 194 (*e*)], are thus normally front stressed: **die Mißehe**, cp. *misfit*. This may mean a different stress from English, thus **únglücklich**, *unháppy*, unless emotional stress causes a change, thus **unglücklich**, cp. **abschéulich** (above).

6. Orthography.   Print and script.

(*a*) Orthography (**die Rechtschreibung**) includes the rules for correct spelling (*v.* a good dictionary), for punctuation (*v.* here Chapter LXIV), the use of capital letters (*v.* §§ 541-2), of the hyphen and apostrophe (*v.* §§ 544-5), etc.

Points of orthography are also introduced gradually, as required; it should be noted now, however, that a capital letter is required in German for all proper names, as in English, but also for ALL NOUNS, or other parts of speech used as nouns.

(*b*) Reform.   There has been extensive discussion recently concerning a possible moderate reform of German orthography, the main proposals being: (1) small initials for all words except proper names (and the beginning of the sentence); (2) simpler spelling for some consonantal groups and long vowels, *e.g.* omission of **Dehnungs-h** [*v.* § 1 (*b*) (2) above]; and (3) German spelling for foreign borrowed words (*e.g.* **Nivo** for **Niveau**, as already **Büro**). It is possible that the suggestions will be generally adopted.

(*c*) Print and script.   In the present century, and especially by Governmental decision in 1941, Roman characters (**die Antiqua**) have replaced Gothic (**die Fraktur**) in printing; but the student must still be familiar with Gothic type, unless he wishes to confine his reading to newspapers and to books published after 1941.   However, the corresponding Gothic cursive hand (**die deutsche Schrift**) is now rare, and is therefore not illustrated in this Manual; but the character ß still remains in script as in type [*v.* § 2 (*d*) above], and should be used.   It is written as printed, but with initial downstroke *ß*, or in the alternative form: *ß*. Typographical signs are as in English except that quotation marks are as follows: „**Haus**“, or sometimes »**Haus**«.

(*d*) The alphabet is given below in Roman and Gothic type, followed by two short texts, the first in Gothic, the second in Roman but using the revised orthography which has been proposed.

7. The Alphabet in German.

Roman	Gothic	Name (phon.)	Roman	Gothic	Name (phon.)
A a	𝔄 𝔞	ɑ:	G g	𝔊 𝔤	ge:
B b	𝔅 𝔟	be:	H h	ℌ 𝔥	hɑ:
C c	ℭ 𝔠	tse:	I i	ℑ 𝔦	i:
D d	𝔇 𝔡	de:	J j	ℑ 𝔧	jɔt
E e	𝔈 𝔢	e:	K k	𝔎 𝔨	kɑ:
F f	𝔉 𝔣	ɛf	L l	𝔏 𝔩	ɛl

Roman	Gothic	Name (phon.)	Roman	Gothic	Name (phon.)
M m	𝔐 m	ɛm	T t	𝔗 t	te:
N n	𝔑 n	ɛn	U u	𝔘 u	u:
O o	𝔒 o	o:	V v	𝔙 v	fau
P p	𝔓 p	pe:	W w	𝔚 w	ve:
Q q	𝔔 q	ku:	X x	𝔛 x	iks
R r	𝔑 r	ɛr	Y y	𝔜 y	ypsilɔn
S s	𝔖 ſ 𝔰	ɛs	Z z	𝔷	tsɛt

initial and medial ſ
in final position 𝔰

Modified Vowels:

Ä ä ɛ:
Ö ö ɸ:
Ü ü y:
Äu äu ɔʏ
(also called a-Umlaut, etc.)

Consonantal Groups:

Ch ch   𝔠ɦ   3 (*e*) above
ß   ß   2 (*d*) above

Gothic Text:

An einem Spätherbſtnachmittage ging ein alter wohlgekleideter Mann langſam die Straße hinab. Er ſchien von einem Spazier= gange nach Hauſe zurückzukehren; denn ſeine Schnallenſchuhe, die einer vorübergegangenen Mode angehörten, waren beſtäubt. Den langen Rohrſtock mit goldenem Knopf trug er unter dem Arm; mit ſeinen dunkeln Augen, in welche ſich die ganze verlorene Jugend gerettet zu haben ſchien, und welche eigentümlich von den ſchnee= weißen Haaren abſtachen, ſah er ruhig umher oder in die Stadt hinab, welche im Abendſonnendufte vor ihm lag.

Theodor Storm, 1849.

Roman text, revised orthography:

In speziallehrgängen werden di luftstewardessen auf íre luftige tätigkeit vorbereitet. Si müssen in 2000 meter höe kleine malzeiten anrichten und auch in der wackligsten situazion libenswürdig serviren können. König ist der fargast und für sein wol haben si zu sorgen, ob es stürmt oder schneit oder gewittert. Ein bisschen kaltblütigkeit wird auch von inen verlangt, denn di luft hat nun mal keine balken.

newsp., 1955.

PART ONE

CHAPTER I

1. There are in German:

three genders: masculine, feminine, and neuter;

two articles: the indefinite and the definite article;

four cases: the nominative, genitive, dative, and accusative.

2. Gender

der Mann, *the man;* **die Frau,** *the woman;* **das Kind,** *the child.*

der Mond, *the moon;* **die Sonne,** *the sun;* **das Schiff,** *the ship.*

The gender of the noun (shown in the German—English vocabulary by *m.*, *f.*, or *n.*) is, in connected language, often indicated by the preceding word, especially the definite article, thus **der Wald.**

In English, sex (*he*, *she*, *it*) determines gender; this is called "natural gender". German, however, also has "grammatical gender"; thus, nouns describing living beings are often masculine or feminine according to sex (**der Mann, die Frau**), but there are many exceptions. Further, nouns describing things are not specifically neuter, but may be of any gender (**der Wald, die Nacht, das Feld**).

Nouns for relations within the family follow natural gender: **der Mann,** *man* or *husband;* **die Frau,** *woman* or *wife;* **der Vater,** *father;* **die Mutter,** *mother;* **der Sohn,** *son;* **die Tochter,** *daughter;* **der Onkel,** *uncle;* **die Tante,** *aunt.*

3. Article

der Wald, *the forest;* **die Nacht,** *the night;* **das Feld,** *the field.*

ein Sohn, *a son;* **eine Tochter,** *a daughter;* **ein Mädchen,** *a girl.*

The definite article in the singular, where present, indicates the gender of the noun. The indefinite article *may*, but does not necessarily, thus **die Mutter** and **eine Mutter;** BUT **der Garten** and *ein* **Garten, das Haus** and *ein* **Haus,** *the (a) garden, the (a) house.*

Kein is the negative of **ein,** and has the same endings: **keine Mutter,** *not a (no) mother,* and similarly, **kein Garten, kein Haus.**

9

4. Case

(*a*) The four cases used in German may be shown as follows:

Nominative: the "who-case".   The man sings.

Genitive: the "whose-case".   The man's hat (hat of the man).

Dative: the "whom-case" (indirect object).   I said to the man, told him.

Accusative: the "whom-case" (direct object).   I praised the man.

The form in which a noun is quoted outside connected speech is always the nominative, see all examples above. The other three cases are often called the "oblique cases".

(*b*) TABLE:

Nom.	der Garten	die Nacht	das Haus
	ein Garten	eine Nacht	ein Haus
Acc.	den Garten	die Nacht	das Haus
	einen Garten	eine Nacht	ein Haus.

Only in the masculine does the accusative differ from the nominative.

Use.   (1) The noun is in the nominative if it is the subject or complement of a verb: **Ich bin der Sohn,** *I am the son.*

Der Mann ist arm, *is poor.*   **Er ist der (ein) Vater,** *he is the (a) father.*

Die Frau ist schön, *is beautiful.*   **Sie ist die (eine) Mutter,** *she is the (a) mother.*

Das Haus ist groß, *is large.*   **Es** (*it*, neuter) **ist kein Schiff,** *it is not a ship.*

(2) The noun is in the accusative if it is the direct object of the verb: **Ich habe einen Garten,** *I have a garden.*   **Er hat ein Haus,** *he has a house.*

5. Verbs and Order

sein, *to be;* **ich bin,** *I am;* **er (sie, es) ist,** *he (she, it) is.*

haben, *to have;* **ich habe,** *I have;* **er (sie, es) hat,** *he (she, it) has.*

A simple question may be asked in German, as often in English, by placing the appropriate verb form first, followed by the subject (inversion of the subject):

Q. **Ist das Kind gut?**   *Is the child good?*

A. **Ja, das Kind ist sehr gut.**   *Yes, the child is very good.*

Q. **Hat der Sohn einen Garten?**   *Has the son a garden?*

A. **Ja, er hat einen Garten.**   *Yes, he has a garden.*

6. Adjectives

An adjective predicated of the subject is used in the simple, uninflected form in which it is given in the dictionary:

Der Vater ist jung, gut und intelligent, *young, good and intelligent.*

Der König ist reich, stark und ehrlich, *the King is rich, strong and honest.*

An adjective is "predicated of the subject" when it forms the complement of a verb of being [**sein**, *v.* § 9 (*c*)], becoming [**werden**, *v.* § 15 (*b*)], remaining [**bleiben**, *v.* § 9 (*c*)], or appearing (**scheinen**, *to seem*).

EXERCISE I

A. Translate into ENGLISH:

1. Der Bleistift ist rot, aber (*but*) die Tinte ist blau.   2. Zeit ist Geld.   3. Hans hat ein Buch, eine Feder und einen Gummi.   4. Inge ist ein Mädchen, aber intelligent.   5. Hans ist faul wie (*as*) der (= *his*) Vater, aber Inge ist eitel wie die Mutter.   6. Hier ist ein Schiff; es ist groß und sehr schön.   7. Ist die Sonne ein Planet? Nein (*no*), die Sonne ist kein Planet.   Die Erde ist ein Planet, und auch (*also*) der Mond.   8. Die Tante hat eine Tochter.   9. Hat der Onkel einen Sohn?   10. Der Vater hat einen Garten und ein Feld.

B. Translate into GERMAN:

1. The night is black as (**wie**) ink.   2. Is the moon beautiful?   3. The newspaper is dull.   4. The pencil is not (**nicht**) black, it is blue.   5. I have a house and a garden.   6. Is the father honest?   7. The sun is hot.   8. Is Hans rich? No, he is poor.   9. The forest is cool and green.   10. Inge has a sister, but no brother.

CHAPTER II

7. Gender

(*a*) There is no short cut to a knowledge of genders (though there are some useful principles, given in Chapter LIX); each noun must be learnt with its gender right from the beginning.

It may, however, be noted that for all inanimates (= names of things), and for many animates (= names of animals and humans), form and sense play some role in determining gender.

(*b*) Gender by sense:

(1) Family relations follow natural gender (*v.* § 2).

(2) Many names of animals follow natural gender:
der Wolf, *wolf;* **der Fuchs,** *fox;* **der Löwe,** *lion;* **der Bär,** *bear;* **die Gans,** *goose;* **die Ente,** *duck;* **die Stute,** *mare;* **die Sau,** *sow.*

It will be seen that in some cases the noun for the male or female of the species has been applied in both languages to the species as a whole: **der Fuchs,** *fox;* **die Ente,** *duck.*

(*c*) Gender by sense and form.

Certain suffixes (end-syllables) either indicate or require a specific gender:

(1) Masculine animals or persons:
-(e)rich: der Enterich, *drake;* **der Gänserich,** *gander;* **der Wüterich,** *ruthless man, tyrant.*

(2) Feminine animals or persons:
-in: die Königin, *queen;* **die Lehrerin,** *woman-teacher;* **die Löwin,** *lioness;* **die Füchsin,** *vixen.*

(3) Diminutive suffixes, indicating the young or small of any species, or a small form of a thing, make a noun neuter:
-chen: das Mädchen, *girl* (from **die Magd,** *maid, maiden*); **ein Wäldchen,** *a little wood, copse.*
-lein: ein Söhnlein, *a little son;* **das Schifflein,** *little (miniature) ship.*
Note.— **-lein** is rather less common than **-chen** (*v.* § 24).

The vowel of any monosyllable mutates [or modifies, *i.e.* receives the **Umlaut** sign, *v.* Introduction, § 1 (*c*)], if possible, when any of the above prefixes are added, cp. **Gänserich, Füchsin, Söhnlein, Mädchen.**

(*d*) The gender of compound nouns is that of their second component:
der Großvater, *grandfather;* **die Großmutter,** *grandmother.*

(*e*) In a conflict between grammatical and natural gender, a following pronoun may agree with either:
Das Mädchen ist müde, *is tired;* **es (or sie) ist müde.**

8. Pronouns

(*a*) There are in German, as in French, two forms for the second person *you*, depending on the relation between the speaker and the person addressed. These are:

(1) The "familiar" form: **du,** singular, **ihr,** plural, for use between intimates and members of the same family.

(2) The "polite" form: **Sie,** singular and plural, for use between all other persons. This is actually the third person plural, **sie,** *they*, written with a capital.

(*b*) The personal pronouns are:

(1) Nom. **ich,** *I;* **du,** *you* (cp. *thou*); **er (sie, es),** *he (she, it);* **wir,** *we;* **ihr,** *you* (cp. *ye*); **sie,** *they;* **Sie,** *you.*

Note.—**ich,** differing from English *I*, has no capital.
sie, *they*, differing from French *ils, elles*, does not distinguish between the genders.
wir, *we*, as in English, may mean *I* and any other(s): *you, he, she, they.*

(2) Acc. **mich,** *me;* **dich,** *you* (cp. *thee*); **ihn (sie, es),** *him (her, it).*
uns, *us;* **euch,** *you* (cp. *ye*); **sie,** *they;* **Sie,** *you.*

(*c*) In accordance with the requirements of gender, *he* and *she* are translated **er** and **sie,** but may also be **es** when standing for a neuter noun:
Es (= das Mädchen or Söhnchen) ist schön, stark, munter.

But natural gender may reassert itself:
Das Mädchen hat einen Apfel and eine Orange; sie ist froh.

Conversely, **er** and **sie** may mean *it* when referring to an inanimate designated by a masculine or feminine noun:
Er (= der Garten) ist groß. Sie (= die Nacht) ist warm.

(*d*) There is an indefinite personal pronoun **man,** accusative **einen,** meaning *one, a person or persons in general* (cp. French "on"), and often translated by *we, you,* or *they:* **Man sagt . . .,** *They say . . .* (cp. On dit . . .).

9. Verbs

(a) The form in which all verbs are given in the dictionary is the infinitive: **lachen,** *to laugh;* **singen,** *to sing.*

The infinitive consists of two elements:

(1) The infinitive ending, which is **-en** for most verbs (cp. **lachen, singen**), but **-n** for a few, as **sein,** *to be;* **tun,** *to do;* and those in **-eln, -ern,** *v.* (*b*) below.

(2) The stem, which is obtained by removing the **-en** or **-n** of the infinitive, and from which all other forms and tenses are obtained by various changes and additions. But for **haben, sein,** *v.* (*c*) below.

Thus **lach-en,** *to laugh;* **sing-en,** *to sing;* **mach-en,** *to make;* **kauf-en,** *to buy;* **find-en,** *to find;* **sag-en,** *to say;* **tu-n,** *to do.*

(b) The present tense is formed from the infinitive stem, with the addition of the following endings, and, in the majority of German verbs (called "weak" verbs), no further change:

Lach-en, *to laugh.*

ich lach-e, du lach-st, er (sie, es) lach-t; *I, you, he,* etc., *laugh(s);*
wir lach-en, ihr lach-t, Sie lach-en, sie lach-en; *we, you, they laugh.*

For convenience of pronunciation, when the stem ends in certain consonants and consonantal groups,

(1) an **-e-** is often inserted before the endings **-st** or **-t,** as:

du bet-e-st, *you pray;* **er red-e-t,** *he speaks;* **er zeichn-e-t,** *he draws;* **ihr fisch-e-t,** *you fish;*

(2) an **-e-** is omitted, either in the stem or the ending, before **-e** or **-en: ich hand(e)le,** *I act;* **sie handel(e)n,** *they act;* **wir wander(e)n,** *we wander, tramp.*

Cp. Appendix B for the full rules.

(c) Present tenses of **haben** and **sein:**

Haben, *to have:*

ich habe, du hast, er (sie, es) hat; wir haben, ihr habt, Sie haben, sie haben; *I have,* etc.

Sein, *to be:*

ich bin, du bist, er (sie, es) ist; wir sind, ihr seid, Sie sind, sie sind; *I am,* etc.

The complement of **sein** is in the nominative [*v.* § 4 (*b*) (1) and cp. § 6].

10. Use of Present Tense.

(*a*) German has only one simple present tense to translate the three English forms:

(1) The simple present: *I sing*.

(2) The progressive form of the present: *I am singing*.

(3) The *do* form, commonly used in emphatic positive statements (*I do sing*), negative statements (*We do not sing*), and questions (*Do you sing?*).

All these forms are in German: **Ich singe** (positive), **Wir singen nicht** (negative), **Singen Sie?** (question).

(*b*) There are, however, certain other ways of expressing progressive force in the verb [*v.* § 67 (*a*)], and an emphatic positive statement can always be expressed with the aid of an adverb:

I do love him, **Ich liebe ihn sehr.**

I do like pancakes, **Ich esse sehr gern Pfannkuchen** (lit. *I eat very willingly*, i.e. *with pleasure*).

11. Adverbs

(*a*) There is in German no specific suffix, like the English -*ly*, or the French -*ment*, which marks the adverb, or makes an adjective into an adverb. Normally, any adjective can be used in its uninflected form as an adverb: **er lacht laut** (*loudly*), **sie singt furchtbar** (*frightfully*). **-lich** (corresponding to English -*ly*) is itself a common adjective ending: **Das Kind ist munter und fröhlich** (predicative adjective). **Der Vogel singt fröhlich** (adverb).

(*b*) If its sense permits, an adverb may become a degree adverb without further formality: **Sie singt furchtbar schlecht,** *frightfully badly.* **Ich liebe sie sehr** (or **besonders**), *I love her very much (especially).* **Sie singt sehr schön** (or **besonders schön**), *she sings very well (especially well).*

A. Translate into ENGLISH:

1. Der Bär tanzt schön; ich sehe ihn im (*in the*) Zirkus. 2. Der Papagei lacht und er spricht (*speaks*) gut Deutsch. 3. Die Großmutter backt Pfannkuchen; sie schmecken gut. 4. Der Lehrer und die Lehrerin essen sie sehr gern mit Zucker und Zitrone. 5. Das Kind kauft ein Schiffchen und bringt es heim (*home*). 6. Der Schauspieler lacht laut, die Schauspielerin weint leise. 7. Er ist immer fröhlich, sie ist oft traurig. 8. Peter kauft ein Rad und Klaus auch (*also*); sie machen

eine Radtour.   9. Das Mädchen sucht das Spielzeug; aber es findet es nicht.   10. Der Deutsche singt gern ein Lied und er spielt die Guitarre.

B. Translate into German:

1. I hear a lion and a lioness; they are in the circus.   2. They are roaring frightfully; they are hungry and they see me.   3. Do you love Annemarie?   She loves you (sing.).   4. Peter and Klaus play the guitar; they play it well and they sing cheerfully.   5. They swim very quickly and they catch a fish.   6. Fruit makes us healthy.   7. Are you (polite form) a teacher (fem.) or a student (fem.)?   8. You (sing.) are not lazy; you are learning German quickly.   9. Are you (polite form) laughing? No, I am weeping.   10. A summer-night is short, a winter's-day is long.

CHAPTER III

12. Cases: Genitive and Dative

(a) The genitive case expresses the possessive relationship and translates the sense *of the*:

Die Tür des Wagens ist offen, *the door of the car is open.*
Heute ist der Geburtstag der Mutter, *today is (my) mother's birthday.*

(b) The dative is the case of the indirect object (the object of *giving to* or *taking from*) and translates the idea *to the* or *from the*:

Ich schenke dem Mädchen den Hund, *I give the dog to the girl.*
Ich nehme dem Schüler das Messer, *I take the knife from the schoolboy.*
Ich sage dem Onkel die Wahrheit, *I (shall) tell (my) uncle the truth.*

(c) The case of a noun is determined by its grammatical role in the sentence, not by any words which may precede it; thus specific words, such as *of* or *to* are often absent in English (e.g. *my mother's birthday*, *I tell my uncle*), yet the genitive or dative rule still applies.

13. The Four Cases. Table and Notes

(a)	der Onkel	die Tante	das Mädchen
Nom.	der (ein) Onkel	die (eine) Tante	das (ein) Mädchen
Gen.	des (eines) Onkels	der (einer) Tante	des (eines) Mädchens
Dat.	dem (einem) Onkel	der (einer) Tante	dem (einem) Mädchen
Acc.	den (einen) Onkel	die (eine) Tante	das (ein) Mädchen

(b) The indefinite article has the same endings as the definite article, except in the three cases: masculine nominative, neuter nominative, neuter accusative, where it is defective (*i.e.* has no ending).

Both in the feminine and neuter, the nominative of both article and noun is the same as the accusative, but *not* in the masculine.

The feminine noun undergoes no change throughout the singular.

(c) The great majority of masculine and neuter nouns have "oblique cases" (*v.* § 4) as follows:

(1) Genitive with **-s** (or **-es** after certain sounds, *e.g.* **-b, -d,** the sibilants, a vowel or diphthong, or the cluster **-mpf: des Lobes, Todes, Hasses, Fisches, Taues, Krampfes**).

(2) Dative with optional **-e** after monosyllables: **dem Hause, Felde** (but not normally after a vowel: **dem Tau**).

(3) Accusative as nominative.

This is described as the "strong" declension of masculine and neuter nouns, as distinct from the "weak" (*v.* § 34) and "mixed" (*v.* § 52) declensions. The terms "strong" and "weak" are also used for adjective inflections and verb conjugations; they are purely terms of convenience.

14. Dative of the Personal Pronouns

(*a*) **mir, dir, ihm (ihr, ihm); uns, euch, Ihnen, ihnen.**
to or *from me, you* (*thee*), *he* (*her, it*); *us, you, you, they.*

(*b*) The indefinite personal pronoun **man** has dative **einem**. For the genitive of the personal pronouns *v.* § 190.

15. Present Tense of Strong Verbs

(*a*) The following classes of verbs are distinguished according to the manner in which they are conjugated:

(1) Strong verbs, which form tenses by varying the stem vowel, cp. English we s*i*ng, we s*a*ng, we have s*u*ng.

(2) Weak verbs, which form tenses by adding an ending only, cp. English we kill, we kill*ed*, we have kill*ed*.

(3) Irregular verbs, as **haben,** *to have;* **sein,** *to be;* **werden,** *to become.*

For the present tense of weak verbs, and of **haben, sein,** *v.* § 9.

(*b*) Present tense of **werden:**

Werden, *to become:*

ich werde, du wirst, er (sie, es) wird; wir werden, ihr werdet, Sie werden, sie werden; *I become,* etc.

The complement of **werden** is in the nominative [cp. §§ 4 (*b*) (1), 6]: **Die Prinzessin wird ein Reh,** *the Princess becomes* (*is turned into*) *a deer,* cp. **sie ist eine Gans,** *a goose* (*foolish*).

(*c*) Present tense of strong verbs.

(1) Some are regular, thus: **ich singe, rufe, schneide, schließe,** *I sing, call, cut, shut;* **du singst, er singt,** etc. (*v.* § 9).

(2) But in the second and third persons singular (**du** and **er** forms), some change **-e-** to **-i-** or **-ie-,** and most of those with the vowels **-a-, -au-** or **-o-** mutate these to **-ä-, -äu-** and **-ö-** respectively.

        ich schenke, du schenkst, er schenkt, *I give,* etc.

but: **ich spreche, du sprichst, er spricht,** *I speak,* etc.

        ich gehe, du gehst, er geht, *I go,* etc.

but: **ich sehe, du siehst, er sieht,** *I see,* etc.

        ich schaffe, du schaffst, er schafft, *I work,* etc.

but: **ich schlafe, du schläfst, er schläft,** *I sleep,* etc.

ich **haue,** du **haust,** er **haut,** *I hit,* etc.

but: ich **laufe,** du **läufst,** er **läuft,** *I run,* etc.

ich **komme,** du **kommst,** er **kommt,** *I come,* etc.

but: ich **stoße,** du **stößt,** er **stößt,** *I push, shove* [*v. (d) (2) below*].

Thus each strong verb should be learnt from the list at Appendix D and C (where a summary of these vowel changes is given) as soon as it is met.

(*d*) Euphonic -e- in the present tense of strong verbs.

(1) Those which do not change or mutate the vowel follow the model of weak verbs [*v.* § 9 (*b*) (1)], thus:

du **schließest** (also du **schließt**), *you shut;* er **schneidet,** *he cuts;* ihr **leidet,** *you suffer.*

(2) If vowel change or mutation takes place, no vowel is inserted:

du **hältst,** *you hold;* du **trittst,** *you step;* du **fichtst,** *you fight.*

But certain incidental modifications may take place to ensure pronounceability (cp. Appendix B for the full rules).

16. Verbs with Direct and Indirect Object

(*a*) A large number of verbs, expressing the ideas of giving and saying, are followed by a direct object (of the thing given, said, etc.), in the accusative, and an indirect object (of the person to whom something is given, said, etc.), in the dative:

Er schenkt der Schwester eine Blume, *he gives his sister a flower.*

Ich leihe ihm das Geld, *I lend him the money.*

Sie sagt der Mutter das Geheimnis, *she tells her mother the secret.*

Some of these verbs are:

(1) Giving: **bringen,** *to bring;* **geben,** *to give;* **lassen,** *to leave (to);* **leihen,** *to lend;* **liefern,** *to deliver;* **reichen,** *to hand;* **schenken,** *to give* (as a present); **schicken** and **senden,** *to send;* **zahlen,** *to pay.* Also the verbs of deprivation, i.e. *taking (from)*: **nehmen,** *to take;* **stehlen,** *to steal.*

(2) Saying: **flüstern,** *to whisper;* **melden,** *to report;* **sagen,** *to say (tell);* **schreiben,** *to write (communicate);* **zeigen,** *to show.*

(*b*) Order of direct and indirect objects.

(1) It will be seen from the above examples that, with the normal case of two noun objects, the dative precedes the accusative, as in English when no preposition is used: He gives his sister a flower, but: He gives a flower to his sister.

(2) When one object is a pronoun, this precedes whatever its case, while in English either order is possible, but a following dative, as noted in (1), must have *to*:

Ich leihe ihm das Geld, *I lend him the money, the money to him.*
Er schenkt sie seiner Schwester, *He gives it to his sister, his sister it.*

(3) When both objects are represented by pronouns, the accusative precedes, *i.e.* the rule is the opposite of (1), while in English either order is possible, and a following dative may have *to*:

Ich leihe es ihm, *I lend it (to) him, I lend him it.*

Er schenkt sie (= **die Blume**) **ihr** (= **der Schwester**), *He gives it (to) her,*
her it.

Note.—English *to* here is purely a function of the dative and must not be translated (cp. § 12).

MNEMONIC : **DAPNAD,** *i.e.*

Nouns:	**D**ative, **A**ccusative.
Mixed:	**P**ronoun, **N**oun.
Pronouns:	**A**ccusative, **D**ative.

EXERCISE III

A. Translate into ENGLISH:

1. Die Farbe des Rades ist rot. 2. Er nimmt dem Schüler das Buch und gibt es seinem Bruder. 3. Der Dieb stiehlt uns das Geld und das Kind stiehlt der Mutter die Schokolade. 4. Nimmst du lieber (*rather*) Tee oder Kaffee? Ich gebe ihn dir mit Kuchen und Schlagsahne. 5. Es regnet und wir leihen dem Onkel einen Regenmantel; er schickt ihn uns später (*later*). 6. Klaus hört den Motor des Flugzeugs und sieht es im Flughafen. 7. Er läuft schnell und ruft: „Peter, es kommt!" 8. Du stößt die Tür und schließest sie. 9. Klaus und Peter spielen ein Tanzlied; Manfred hört es und wird fröhlich. 10. Wie ich dir, so du mir (prov.).

B. Translate into GERMAN:

1. Peter and Klaus find the inn of the village, they call the host (innkeeper) and he gives them hock. 2. He gives it to them and they pay him the money. 3. The dog of the house runs round (**herum**) and barks loudly. 4. It is (the) father's birthday; we give him a (gramophone) record of a piano-concerto. 5. He takes it and lends it to a friend. 6. I write a letter to my sister and send it to her. 7. He sees us and shuts the door. 8. You (polite form) swim and run and play tennis; you get (= become) tired and sleep well. 9. The child shows me the way. 10. They bring mother a knife and she cuts bread-and-butter.

CHAPTER IV

17. Plural of Nouns (1). Masculine and neuter monosyllables.

Note.—Refer to the vocabulary for the meanings of all nouns mentioned.

(*a*) The nominative plural of the definite article for all genders (singular, **der, die, das**) is **die.** But there is no almost universal form of plural ending of the noun, as -*s* in English and French; the form of the noun changes in the plural in various ways:

(1) by the addition of an ending: **die Mond-e, Sonne-n, Kind-er;**

(2) by mutation of the root vowel: **die Väter, Mütter, Klöster;**

(3) by a combination of both (1) and (2): **die Wäld-er, Häus-er;**

(4) or there is no change at all: **die Lehrer, Ufer.**

Almost all nouns add **-n** or **-en** in the dative plural: **den Kinder-n.**

[For exceptions, *v.* §§ 92 (*b*), 130 (*a*), 131.]

TABLE. Plural of **das Haus:**

die Häuser, der (*of the*) **Häuser, den** (*to the*) **Häusern, die Häuser;**
cp. **das Haus/Häuser** (and **die Maus/Mäuse**) with English *mouse/mice.*

As with genders, the form for each noun must be learnt as soon as the word is met. Certain broad classes of noun declension may, however, be distinguished, and will be described in successive chapters. As a beginning, some notes on monosyllables follow.

(*b*) Masculine monosyllables.

(1) Those whose vowels cannot mutate, add **-e:**

> **der Brief, Dieb, Dienst, Feind, Fisch, Freund, Weg.**
> Plural: **die Briefe, Diebe, Dienste,** etc.

(2) Of those which can mutate, *i.e.* with vowels **-a- -o- -u-** or **-au-,** most do so, also adding **-e,** but some do not.

Mutate:

der Arzt, Band (*volume*)**, Baum, Fall, Fuchs, Fuß, Gast, Gruß, Hahn, Hals, Knopf, Kopf, Krug, Platz, Rock, Sack, Sohn, Stock, Strom, Stuhl, Topf, Wolf, Zahn, Zug.**
> Plural: **die Ärzte, Bände, Bäume,** etc.

Do not mutate:

der Arm, Grad, Huf, Hund, Laut, Mund, Punkt, Ruf, Schuh, Stoff, Tod.
> Plural: **die Arme, Grade, Hufe,** etc.

(3) But a few add -er, mutating if possible:

der Geist, Gott, Leib, Mann, Schi, Strauch, Wald, Wurm.

Plural: **die Geister, Götter,** etc.

Also **der Ort** in special senses (v. Appendix A).

(c) Neuter monosyllables.

(1) Most add -er, mutating if possible:

das Amt, Bad, Bild, Buch, Dorf, Ei, Feld, Glas, Haus, Huhn, Kalb, Kind, Lamm, Land, Loch, Nest, Rad, Schloß, Tuch, Volk, Weib.

Plural: **die Ämter, Bäder, Bilder,** etc.

(2) A few add -e and do not mutate:

das Boot, Haar, Heft, Jahr, Pferd, Schaf, Schiff, Schwein, Spiel, Werk.

Plural: **die Boote, Haare, Hefte,** etc.

(d) Feminine monosyllables (v. § 40).

18. Prepositions (1). Dative, Accusative

(a) As in English, prepositions as well as verbs may govern nouns and pronouns; though in English an oblique case is shown by a pronoun but not by the noun, cp. *for him, for the boy; to her, to the woman.*

German prepositions are distinguished according to the case they govern: genitive, dative, accusative; but there is also a fourth group which governs the dative or accusative according to sense.

(b) The following are the commoner prepositions which take:

(1) The dative: **aus,** *out (of);* **bei,** *by, beside, near;* **mit,** *with;* **nach,** *to* (place), *after* (time or goal); **seit,** *since;* **von,** *of, from;* **zu,** *to.*

(2) The accusative: **durch,** *through;* **für,** *for;* **gegen,** *against, towards;* **ohne,** *without;* **um,** *round (about);* **wider,** *against.*

Er geht aus dem Haus. Sie steht bei dem Baum. Er kommt ohne den Vater. Das Wasser fließt durch die Stadt.

Note.—Distinguish **gegen** and **wider.**

Gegen is of physical opposition, including the figurative sense:
Der Wagen fährt gegen einen Baum. Er kämpft gegen Feinde.

Wider is of internal opposition, repugnance, *against* the feelings, etc.:
Er macht es wider seinen Willen.

19. Contractions of Preposition and Definite Article

(a) Certain prepositions combine with certain forms of the definite article to form contracted words; these forms are the three of the dative singular **dem, der, dem,** and the neuter accusative **das.** Some examples of the various possibilities are:

beim Haus, beim Baum (= **bei dem**), *at* or *near the house, tree;*

durchs Wasser, durchs Dach (= **durch das**), *through the water, roof;*

ums Haus, ums Lager (= **um das**), *round the house, camp;*

vom Lehrer, *of* or *by the teacher;* **zum Dorf,** *to the village.*

Only **zu** may combine with feminine dative **der** to form **zur: zur Bahn,** *to the station;* **zur Mutter,** *to mother.*

The contracted article is represented by the last letter: **-m, -r, m-, -s,** and **von** is the only preposition to undergo change. No contractions are possible in the plural.

(*b*) Such contractions are largely optional, are commoner in speech, especially colloquial, than in writing, and are frequent in many simple idioms: **zur Bahn fahren, zur Schule gehen, beim Bäcker kaufen, zehn vom Hundert** (abbrev. **v.H.**), 10%; **Zucker zum Tee nehmen,** *to take sugar in one's tea* (*v.* § 303 for full account of these contractions).

20. Verbs with Dative Object

A certain number of verbs take a single object in the dative.

(*a*) Verbs in which the object, usually a person, is not directly acted upon, but is someone for whose benefit some act or action is undertaken: **danken,** *to thank;* **dienen,** *to serve;* **folgen,** *to follow;* **glauben,** *to believe;* **helfen,** *to help;* and **gehören,** *to belong,* expressing a state which is to the advantage of the owner.

(*b*) Verbs of saying (cp. § 16), in so far as they are used without their direct object, but with an indirect object, may be considered as analogous in a wider sense: **sagen, schreiben, telefonieren,** etc.

Ich danke Ihnen, *I thank you;* **das Heer folgt der Fahne,** *the army follows the flag;* **das Rad gehört mir,** *this bicycle belongs to me;* **ich schreibe ihm morgen,** *I* (*will*) *write to him to-morrow.*

21. Es gibt and es ist (sind)

Both these expressions mean either *there is* or *there are,* but they are distinct both in grammar and sense.

(*a*) GRAMMATICAL USE.—Es gibt never changes and is followed by its own direct object in the accusative:

Es gibt einen Gasthof an der Ecke der Straße, *there is an inn* (*public house*) . . .

Es gibt Elefanten in Afrika, *there are elephants* . . .

But **es ist** points forward to a following subject in the nominative, and becomes **es sind** when that subject is in the plural:

Es ist Besuch da, *a visitor has come.*

Es sind zwei Männer da, *two men are at the door.*

Thus the role of **es** in **es ist (sind)** is purely anticipatory, standing for the real subject which follows, cp. the wider English use of *there* in *there appeared a policeman.*

(*b*) MEANING.—The two expressions are often interchangeable but may be distinguished. **Es ist (sind)** directs attention beyond the subject to some attendant circumstance: **Es sind zwei Polizisten im Zimmer und sie rauchen Zigarren.** **Es gibt** affirms the existence or otherwise of something: **Es gibt Elefanten in Africa.** Thus it is always used to say what *there is* to eat: **Es gibt Fleisch zum Mittagessen; es gibt nachher** (*afterwards*) **Kaffee and Kuchen.** This is clearer still where es gibt cannot be translated by *there is* (*are*), as when a child, who dislikes her uncle and wishes he did not exist, reflects: **Aber es gibt ihn eben** (E. Langgässer), *but he does exist!*

22. Word Order

(*a*) Both in English and German the natural order for an independent declaratory statement is: subject—finite verb—predicate. **Das Ruderboot gehört dem Onkel,** *the rowing-boat belongs to my uncle.* But when an element other than the subject is given leading position English retains the same relative order, while German maintains the second position of the verb and the subject has to follow (is "inverted", cp. § 5, *v.* § 50).

Der Onkel schenkt mir das Boot; jetzt gehört es mir.
Uncle gives me the boat; now it belongs to me.

(*b*) Both **es gibt** and **es ist (sind)** suffer inversion when an adverb or other element leads, or the verb leads in a question; but with **es gibt** the impersonal subject follows, while with **es ist (sind)** the anticipatory **es** disappears:

An der Ecke der Straße gibt es (gibt's) einen Gasthof. Gibt es einen Gasthof . . . ?

Im Zimmer sind zwei Polizisten mit Hunden. Sind die zwei Polizisten noch (*still*) da?

Among the elements which may lead is the noun anticipated by **es ist (sind).** Thus **zwei Polizisten sind im Zimmer** may be translated as *two policemen are in the room* or *there are two policemen in the room.*

23. Numerals to Twenty

First dozen: eins, zwei, drei, vier, fünf, sechs, sieben, acht, neun, zehn, elf, zwölf.

The 'teens: dreizehn, vierzehn, fünfzehn,
se*ch*zehn, sie*b*zehn (these two contracted),
achtzehn, neunzehn, zwanzig.

Note.—(1) eins, zwei, drei . . . when counting, but the indefinite article is: ein Mann, eine Frau, ein Kind.

(2) zwei becomes zwo to distinguish it from drei in telephone conversations, especially in military language (artillery), and its popularity is spreading in ordinary speech.

EXERCISE IV

A. Strong Verbs are listed at Appendix D. Look up and practise the present tenses, noting the meanings, of: essen, fahren, fallen, fressen, geben, gehen, halten, heben, helfen, lassen, laufen, lesen, nehmen, saugen, schlafen, schlagen, sehen, sprechen, stehen, sterben, tragen, treten.

Distinguish gehen and fahren; essen and fressen.

B. Translate into ENGLISH:

1. Der Wirt geht mit den Gästen durch den Garten. 2. Klaus ißt das Butterbrot, Lämmer fressen das Gras und der Löwe frißt die Lämmer. 3. Nach dem Konzert gehen die Freunde mit mir durchs Städtchen. 4. Der Schüler hat einen Traum: siebzehn Polizisten mit zwölf Hunden stehen beim Baum an der Ecke. 5. Der Wagen fährt aus der Garage um die Straßenecke und gegen das Meer. 6. Es gibt Erdbeeren mit Schlagsahne zum (*for*) Nachtisch. 7. Es sind drei Boote am Ufer. 8. Sie liest zwei Bände Novellen des Schriftstellers Thomas Mann. 9. Die Ärzte helfen dem Schifahrer; beide (*both*) Füße sind wund. 10. Sie tragen den Mann vom Berg herunter (*down*); es gibt viel Schnee und die Wege sind glatt mit Eis.

C. Translate into GERMAN:

1. On the kitchen table there are sixteen mice and no cheese. 2. Are there eggs for breakfast? 3. I am writing for (the) mother with a fountain pen; she reads the letter with a pair of spectacles. 4. He is acting against the advice of the doctor. 5. The horses' hooves beat (**schlagen**) against the ground. 6. The child runs round the trees and plays with friends (masc.). 7. There are sheep near the river. 8. The guests from (**aus**) the town help (the) mother with the chickens. 9. The ghosts visit the place every (**alle**) seven years. 10. I thank you (sing.) for the letter and for the books.

CHAPTER V

24. Plural of Nouns (2). Masculine and Neuter with no plural ending.

(*a*) Masculine and neuter nouns in -el, -en, -er, and neuter nouns in -chen, -lein, -sel, add no ending in the plural, but masculine nouns normally modify.

(*b*) Masculines:

der Engel, Bissen, Lehrer. Plural: **die Engel, Bissen, Lehrer.**

(1) Most of those which can mutate, do: **der Apfel, Bruder, Garten, Graben, Hammer, Mantel, Nagel, Ofen, Schwager, Vater, Vogel.** Plural: **die Äpfel, Brüder, Gärten,** etc.

(2) Some do not: **der Balken, Haken, Knochen, Kuchen, Schuster, Spaten.** But a prominent feature of South German usage is to mutate some which normally do not mutate: **die Böden, Bögen, Kästen, Krägen, Mägen, Wägen.**

Note.—A few are differentiated in sense in the plural, according to whether they are mutated or not, thus: **der Laden,** *shop, shutter;* **die Läden,** *shops;* **die Laden** (or S. German, **Läden**), *shutters* (*v.* Appendix A).

(*c*) Neuters:

das Becken, Kissen, Lager, Rätsel, Ufer, Wasser, Zeichen, Zimmer.

Plural: **die Becken, Kissen,** etc.

Only one neuter noun mutates, **das Kloster/Klöster,** but sometimes also **die Läger,** and -wasser in compounds, as **die Abwässer,** waste-water(s).

(1) The diminutive suffixes -chen and -lein [cp. § 7 (*b*)], when added to a word of any gender, cause mutation and the word becomes neuter: **die Magd, das Mädchen; der Hund, das Hündchen, Hündlein,** *puppy.*

(2) The suffix -sel is also largely restricted to neuter words, and often carries the sense of something petty or insignificant: **das Überbleibsel,** *remnant* (lit. *something remaining over*).

25. Possessive Adjectives

(*a*) The possessive adjectives corresponding to the personal pronouns (shown in brackets) are:

mein (ich), dein (du), sein (er, es, man), ihr (sie, sing.), **unser (wir), euer (ihr), Ihr (Sie), ihr (sie,** plur.).

They take throughout the singular the endings of the indefinite article, and in the plural those of the definite article:

TABLE:

	mein (cp. ein) Garten	unsere (cp. die) Gärten
Nom.	mein (ein) Garten	unsere (die) Gärten
Gen.	meines (eines) Gartens	unserer (der) Gärten
Dat.	meinem (einem) Garten	unseren (den) Gärten
Acc.	meinen (einen) Garten	unsere (die) Gärten

Thus also: **deine Katze, sein Haus, Ihre Bücher.**

Note.—As shown above, the possessive *one's* is **sein**, referring back to a preceding subject **man**:

Man hat seine Sorgen, *one has one's troubles.*

But when not referring back, it must be translated otherwise: *One's troubles never come singly,* **Die Sorgen kommen einem** (dative, cp. § 14) **immer haufenweise** (*in heaps*).

(*b*) The possessive adjectives take the gender appropriate to the noun to which they refer, thus note especially:

(1) *its* may be **sein** or **ihr**:

der Staat und seine Macht, *the State and its power.*
die Behörde und ihre Pflicht, *the* (*public*) *authority and its duty.*
das Volk und seine Herrscher, *the people and its* (*their*) *masters.*

(2) A neuter noun standing for a person may entail a possessive adjective with grammatical, but more often with natural, gender:

das Mädchen nahm seinen Hut, more often **ihren Hut.**

26. Interrogative Pronouns: Wer

The basic interrogative pronouns are **wer?** *who?* and **was?** *what?*. **Wer?** has the four cases: **wer, wessen, wem, wen.**

(*a*) **Wer?** *who?* (nom.), though clearly masculine singular in form (cp. **der**) is used in general informatory questions whatever the gender or number of the expected answer: Q. **Wer ist da?** A. **Ich . . ., Deine Tochter . . ., Der Bäcker . . ., Die Eltern Ihres Schülers B.**

Introducing specific questions, it may similarly be the predicate for either gender or number: **Wer ist die Dame? Wer sind die Leute?**

(*b*) **Wessen?** *whose?* (gen.), is also not influenced by the gender or number of the expected answer. The expression *whose fountain pen is this?* may be translated in three different ways: **Wessen Füller ist das? Wessen ist der Füller? Wem** (dat.) **gehört der Füller?**

(c) **Wem?** (*to*, etc.) *whom?* (dat.) is used:

(1) As the indirect object of a verb: Q. **Wem** (*to whom*) **schenkt er die Blume?** A. **Seiner Schwester** (cp. § 16).

(2) After certain prepositions: Q. **Mit wem** (*with whom*) **geht er ins Theater?** A. **Mit seiner Schwägerin** (cp. § 18).

(d) **Wen?** *whom?* (acc.) is similarly used:

(1) As the direct object of a verb: Q. **Wen meint er?** *Whom does he mean?* *To whom is he referring?*

(2) After certain prepositions: Q. **Durch wen bekommt er die Stelle?** *Through whom . . .?* **An wen schreiben Sie?** *To whom . . .?*

Note.—Any preposition governing the interrogative must precede in German (*v.* dative and accusative examples). The end position sanctioned (grudgingly) in English idiom, and the resulting uncertainty about the case of the interrogative (*who are you writing to?*, etc.), is not possible.

27. Interrogative Pronouns: Was. Interrogative Adverbs

(a) **Was?** *what?* has theoretically the four cases: **was, (wessen), (wem), was**; but the genitive and dative are seldom used, as they are liable to confusion with the corresponding forms of **wer** (*v.* §§ 195 and 223).

Though formally neuter singular (cp. **das**), **was?** is the general interrogative used in informatory questions irrespective of the gender and number of the expected answer:

Q. **Was ist das?** A. **Ein Heft . . ., Eine Schachtel mit Bleistiften . . ., Zwei Kätzchen.** But if a plural answer is expected, the verb may be attracted into the plural, even with **das** following:

Q. **Was sind das?** A. **Das sind meine Hefte** (cp. § 480).

Was? may be asked of a person, when asking after his occupation:

Q. **Was ist er eigentlich?** *What actually does he do?* A. **Er ist Lehrer, Sportlehrer, Rechtsanwalt,** etc.

The accusative is the same as the nominative: **Was meint er?** *What does he mean?*

(b) **Wer** and **was** are interrogative pronouns and expect a noun or pronoun in answer. Other interrogatives requiring an answer of an adverbial nature (time, place, manner, etc.) are called interrogative adverbs. The simplest are: **wann?** *when?;* **wo?** *where?;* **wie?** *how?;* **warum?** *why?*.

28. Order with Interrogatives

Two classes of question may be distinguished:

(*a*) The order in English and German is the same when the interrogative pronoun is the subject of the verb and in all questions with the verb *to be*:

Wer nimmt meine Pflaumen? *Who takes (is taking) my plums?* **Wer ist sein Klavierlehrer?** *Who is his pianoforte teacher?* **Was ist das?** *What is that?* **Was (wo, wie) ist ihr Mann?** *What (where, how) is her husband?*

(*b*) In all other cases both English and German have inversion of the subject, but English uses the progressive or the verbal form *does*, while German may only use the simple verb form:

Was schreibt er Ihnen? *What does he write to you?* **Wem gibt der Staat die Macht?** *To whom does the State give power?* **An wen telefonieren Sie?** *To whom are you telephoning?* **Wann arbeitet er eigentlich?** *When actually does he work?* **Wo liegt das Haus?** *Where does the house lie?*

29. Statements of Time (1). Clock Time

(*a*) **Wieviel Uhr ist es? Wie spät ist es?** *What is the time?* **Es ist ein Uhr, zwei Uhr ... zwölf Uhr (Mittag, Mitternacht),** *one o'clock ... twelve o'clock (noon, midnight).* **Ein Uhr** (invar.), but **eins** when standing alone, as: **es ist eins, zehn Minuten nach eins. Es ist fünfzehn Minuten vor vier.**

Er kommt um vier Uhr, um Viertel nach vier (or **Viertel fünf**), **um halb fünf, um Viertel vor fünf** (or **dreiviertel fünf**), *he is coming at four o'clock, four fifteen, four thirty, four forty-five.*

Note.—When **vor** (*to*) and **nach** (*past*) are used, the hour number is as in English; when these do not appear (**Viertel fünf, halb fünf, dreiviertel fünf** above), the sense is *on towards the next hour*, and the figure is one higher than in English. Distinguish English *half four* (used by some speakers for 4.30) from German **halb vier** (= 3.30).

(*b*) Distinguish **zwei Uhr** (invar.), *two o'clock* (time when), from **zwei Stunden** (plur. of **die Stunde**, *hour*), *two hours* (time how long). The quarters are: **eine Viertelstunde** (sometimes **viertel Stunde**), **eine halbe Stunde, eine Dreiviertelstunde** (sometimes **dreiviertel Stunde**).

Die Uhr (plur. **Uhren**) is *clock, watch.* **Die Armbanduhr,** *wristlet-watch;* **Stoppuhr,** *stop-watch;* **Weckuhr** (or **der Wecker**), *alarm-clock.* **Meine Uhr geht vor (nach),** *my watch is fast (slow).*

Clock time is **die Uhrzeit,** while the hour is normally **die Stunde,** both specifically (**die Stunde schlägt,** *the hour strikes;* **die Uhr schlägt halb/voll,** *the clock strikes the half/the hour;* **der Wecker rasselt** is used for an alarm-clock striking), and also descriptively, as in **früher/später Stunde,** *at an early/late hour,* and in the proverb **Morgenstund** (for **-stunde**) **hat Gold im Mund,** *it's the early bird that catches the worm.*

Eine Stunde is also *a lesson,* as **die Musikstunde, Zeichenstunde,** *music lesson, drawing lesson.*

(c) In Germany the 24-hour clock is used for official purposes (administrative, railway, military). **Abfahrt um 17.15 (um siebzehn Uhr fünfzehn),** *departure at 5.15 p.m.* Also with abbrev. **h.** (= Lat. *hora,* **die Stunde**), as **17,15^h** or **17^{15}h.**

The 12-hour clock is, however, usual in everyday life, with the addition, where necessary, of **morgens** (or **vormittags**), *in the morning* (*a.m.*), **nachmittags,** *in the afternoon,* and **abends,** *in the evening* (both *p.m.*), and even **nachts,** *at night* (cp. also **tags,** *during the day,* and *v.* further Chapter XII).

Er kommt immer um 10 Uhr vormittags (abbrev. **vorm.**), *at 10 a.m.*

Ich komme um zwölf Uhr mittags (or um Mittag), . . . um Mitternacht, *at 12 noon, midnight.*

30. Prepositions (2).   Dative or Accusative

(a) Certain prepositions may govern either the dative or the accusative according to the sense of the statement, thus:

(1) The accusative when the sense is that of motion, and of change of relative position between the objects or persons, thus:

Er geht in das Zimmer und hängt das Bild an die Wand, *he goes into (enters) the room and hangs the picture on (to) the wall.*

(2) The dative when the relative position is not changed:

Er bleibt in dem Zimmer; das Bild hängt an der Wand, *he remains in the room; the picture hangs (is hanging, remains hanging) on the wall.*

Note.—Movement, but without change of relative place, is still dative: **Sie tanzen in dem Zimmer,** *they are dancing in the room.*

(b) These prepositions express different forms of spatial relationship: **an,** *on* (in contact with); **auf,** *on* (on top of); **hinter,** *behind;* **in,** *in;* **neben,** *beside;* **über,** *above;* **unter,** *under(neath);* **vor,** *in front of;* **zwischen,** *between.*

Distinguish **auf,** in contact with the upper surface, and **an,** in contact with a side surface or approximate to:

Das Essen liegt auf dem Tisch, und wir sitzen am Tisch (cp. § 318).

Spieglein, Spieglein an der Wand, wer ist die Schönste im ganzen Land? *Mirror, mirror on the wall, who is the prettiest of them all?* (from Grimm's *Fairy Tales*, **Schneewittchen**, *Snow White*).

Note.—The dative/accusative rule only applies to this group, and must not be applied to those taking dative only, thus:

Sie tanzen in das Zimmer (*into*, motion, acc.) **und wieder aus dem Zimmer** (also motion, but dat.).

(*c*) Certain contractions of prepositions and definite article are possible, varying in frequency (cp. § 19).

(1) Common are those with **an, auf, in**, as **am, ans, aufs, im, ins:** **Zell am See** (place-name), **aufs Land gehen, ins Kino gehen.**

(2) Less common are those with **hinter, über, unter, vor**, as **hinterm** and **hinters: hinterm Wald, hinters Licht führen**, *behind the forest, to lead " up the garden path ".*

In each group the dative contractions are commoner than those with the accusative. **Neben** and **zwischen** are hardly ever combined.

The contracted articles are represented by **-m, -s (dem, das)**. **An** and **in** undergo change. There are no contractions in the feminine or plural.

EXERCISE V

A. Learn the prepositions taking the dative and accusative and compare in meaning and use with those taking the dative only, and the accusative only (*v.* § 18).

B. Translate into ENGLISH:

1. Wo sind die Engel? Sie sind nicht auf der Erde, sie sind im Himmel. 2. Wir hängen unsere Mäntel auf den Nagel an der Wand. 3. Dein Hütlein ist sehr schick. Kommt es von dem Laden hinter der Kirche? 4. Klaus und Peter stehen auf der Rheinbrücke und sehen auf das Wasser unter ihren Füßen. 5. Der Fluß fließt zwischen den Ufern in das Meer, und es gibt Schiffe und Boote auf dem Wasser. 6. Was hört man plötzlich? Ein Hubschrauber fliegt über die Brücke und landet auf einem Sportplatz neben dem Lager. 7. Wem gehört das Gold unter dem Boden der Erde? Es gehört dem Staat. 8. Wieviel Uhr ist es, Annemarie? Es ist halb elf und wir essen erst (*only*) um eins. Ach, meine Uhr geht vor und ich bin so hungrig! 9. Es schlägt Mitternacht vom Kirchturm und der Mann auf dem Pferd reitet in den Friedhof. Wessen Gespenst ist es? 10. Was tut man nachmittags im Winter?

Man bleibt in seinem Zimmer, man arbeitet im Büro, oder man geht in
das Kino vor der Stadt.

C. Translate into GERMAN:

1. It is six o'clock and the birds in the forest are sleeping.   2. There
are three convents in the town and one cinema.   3. Whose music-lesson
is it at half-past two in the afternoon?   4. My drawing-lesson is at a
quarter-past six in the evening.   5. Here are three riddles: What stands
on four legs in your room and is not an (kein) animal?   (The chair.)
What stands on two legs in the garden?   (The chicken.)   What stands
on one leg on the bank of the river?   (The stork.)   6. You (sing.) go
with your dog to the river, you throw his ball into the river, and he swims
behind the boat.   7. Our house is next to the shop and behind the theatre.
8. The mirror is on the table in front of the window and beside the wall.
9. What does one do in the evening in this village?   One goes to (= in)
the inn, one dances with the girls and sings songs.   10. Whom do you
see between the two stoves in the kitchen?   It is the cook with his cap
on his (= the) head.

CHAPTER VI

31. Past and Perfect Tenses of Weak Verbs

(*a*) After the present, German has one other simple tense, the past (also called "imperfect", "preterite"), cp. English *I went*.

All other tenses, such as the perfect [*v.* (*c*) below, English, *I have gone, I have been going*] and the future (*v.* § 63, English, *I shall go*), are compound tenses in German.

Note.—(1) There is nothing corresponding to the two simple past tenses in French, *j'allais* (past indefinite, *I was going*), and *j'allai* (past definite, *I went*). There is also, as was seen in the present tense, no progressive form in the past, cp. English, *I was going*, though this can be expressed by an adverb: **Ich spazierte eben . . ., als . . .**, *I was going for a walk, when . . .*

(*b*) The simple past of weak verbs is formed by the addition of the following endings to the stem (obtained as given in § 9):

ich lach-te, du lach-test, er (sie, es) lach-te, *I*, etc., *laughed.*

wir lach-ten, ihr lach-tet, Sie lach-ten, sie lach-ten, *we*, etc., *laughed.*

Note.—Euphonic **-e-**, (*d*) below.

(*c*) The perfect (or compound past) tense of weak verbs is formed from:

(1) the present tense of **haben (ich habe,** etc.), or **sein (ich bin,** etc.);

(2) and the past participle of the verb, obtained by prefixing **ge-** and adding **-(e)t** to the stem:

ich habe gelacht, du hast gestraft, er hat gehört, wir haben gerettet;
ich bin gestürzt, etc.

Note.—(1) The rules for the choice of **haben** or **sein** as auxiliary are given with the past and perfect of strong verbs (§ 44). Until then, only weak verbs taking **haben** will be used in exercises.

(2) Certain verbs do not add **ge-** in the past participle:
Verbs of foreign origin ending in **-ieren** (all weak):

wir haben studiert, du hast das gut arrangiert, er hat mich blamiert, *we studied, you arranged that well, he has let me down.*

Verbs with unaccented prefixes, as **be-, ver-,** etc. [cp. § 88 (*a*) (2)]:

wir haben geweint, *wept;* but **wir haben ihn beweint,** *mourned him.*

er hat das Buch gekauft, *bought;* but **er hat den Wagen verkauft,** *sold.*

(3) Euphonic **-e-** in past participle at (*d*) below.

(4) When the sentence or clause contains independent elements apart from the verb and its subject, the past participle stands at the end:

Der Hund hat das Kind aus dem Wasser gerettet, *saved the child from* . . .
     Er hat auf der Universität Heidelberg Medizin studiert,
                    studied medicine at . . .

(*d*) Euphonic -e- is inserted between the stem and the ending, whether -te, etc., of the past, or -t of the past participle, in the cases where this would happen before -t of the present tense ending (cp. § 9 and Appendix B). Thus: **ich atmete, habe geatmet; redete, habe geredet; rettete, habe gerettet; zeichnete, habe gezeichnet; wir begegneten ihm, sind ihm begegnet.**

32. Demonstratives

There are demonstrative adjectives and demonstrative pronouns.

(*a*) The demonstrative adjectives are **dieser**, *this*, and **jener**, *that*, declined like the definite article (**-es** for both **d-as** and **d-es**):

Jener Garten mit den Blumen ist bunt und schön (cp. der Garten).
Wer kauft dieses Haus? (cp. das Haus) . . . jene Wälder? (cp. die Wälder).

Note.—Like these also **jeder**, *each*:

Vor jeder Tür liegt eine Fußmatte (cp. vor der Tür), *before every door* . . .
Vor der Tür jedes Hauses liegt ein Hund an der Kette (cp. des Hauses),
                before the door of every house . . .

(*b*) When used not preceding a noun (*this one, that one,* etc.), **dieser** and **jener** become pronouns, but with the same endings, and agree with the noun to which they refer in gender and number:

Dieser ist mein Bleistift, jener gehört Ihnen, *this is . . . that one* . . .
     Das ist das Haus meines Großvaters—dieses, nicht jenes.

Das and **dieses** are commonly used, especially in speech, as general demonstratives (pronouns), with a neutral sense between *this* and *that,* and unaffected by gender or number of the word to which they refer:

     Was ist das? Das ist mein Bleistift, *this/that* . . .
Das sind meine Federn, *these are* . . .*;* **Dieses sind unsere Blumen.**

Note.—**Dieses,** both as adjective and pronoun, is often shortened to **dies: Dies ist das Haus meiner Tante. Dies Haus gehört meiner Tante.**
Jener is often replaced in speech by various forms of local indication:
     Das Haus da, der Mann drüben, *there, over there.*

(*c*) German often uses **das** for back reference, where English has *this* or *that:*

Present: **Du schenkst mir den Hund; das** (*that*) **ist nett von dir.**

Past: **Er kaufte zehn Stück Seife; das** (*this*) **amüsierte mich.**

For contrasted reference back, **dieser** (*the nearest*, i.e. *the latter*) and **jener** (*the furthest*, i.e. *the former*) are used:

Hans und Klaus waren Freunde; dieser (pronoun) **war achtzehn Jahre alt, jener war zwanzig.**

Dieser and **jener** are often used to indicate something notorious, or known to the person addressed:

Was ist eigentlich diese Olympiade? *What is this Olympic Games (that they are all talking sbout)?*

Er hat jene Aussprache des Berliners, *the* (*well-known*) *accent of the Berliner.*

Note the idiom: **Wir erwähnten dieses und jenes,** *various things;* **er fragte mich nach diesem und jenem,** *questioned me about this and that.* **Dieser und jener besucht uns von Zeit zu Zeit,** *various people visit us . . .*

33. Adverbial Compounds of Prepositions and Pronouns

(*a*) Personal Pronouns. The dative and accusative of the personal pronoun when referring to things [*it*, cp. § 8 (*c*)] is not usually used after the commoner prepositions because of possible confusion with persons, but is replaced by an adverbial compound formed by prefixing **da-** (before vowels **dar-**) to the preposition:

Ich habe einen Füller und schreibe immer damit, *with it.*

Da- is actually a demonstrative adverb (*with that*, etc.), cp. the English terms (less common) *therewith, thereafter, thereupon.*

This construction is used with the following common prepositions:

an, auf, aus, bei, durch, für, gegen, hinter, in, mit, nach, neben, über, unter, um, von, vor, wider, zu, zwischen.

The accent is normally on the preposition, thus there is often elision of the vowel of **dar-** before vowels: **drin, drüber, drum,** etc.

The compound can be used for persons if understood collectively:

Eine Menge Soldaten waren da, darunter einige von jeder Waffengattung, *a large number of soldiers were present, among them some of each arm.*

Note.—Normally **in** becomes **darin** for dative (*e.g.* **in dem Zimmer, darin**), but **darein** for accusative (*e.g.* **in das Zimmer, darein**); no other compound varies with the case originally represented. With **nach** both **danach** and **darnach** occur.

For compounds of **hier-** with similar senses *v.* §§ 138 (*b*), 225 (*a*).

(*b*) The interrogative pronoun **was?** *what?* is similarly compounded with these prepositions (but not usually with **hinter, wider, zwischen**), to form the compounds **wobei, worin, worüber, worum,** etc. (cp. English *wherewith, whereto,* etc.).

Wovon sprechen Sie? *What are you speaking of?* **Worüber schreibt er sein Buch?** *What is he writing his book about?* **Womit kann ich dienen?** (in shops). *What can I do for you?*

These compounds are current in both written and spoken German, but sometimes colloquially the compound is resolved, **was** being used for any case: **Für was hält er mich?** *What does he take me for?* **Nach was schmeckt das?** **Nach nichts!** *What does it taste of?* *Nothing!*

Note.—(1) **Was** combines with **um** also in the altered form **warum?** *why?* cp. this with **worum,** *around what?* **Worum läuft er? Um den Park? Warum?**

(2) German *never* places the preposition at the end of the statement as in English informal order above, *What does it taste of?* etc. (cp. further Chapter XXIX, especially § 226).

EXERCISE VI

A. Translate into ENGLISH:

1. Wir haben eine Landkarte gekauft und haben damit im Rheinland eine Radtour gemacht. 2. Der Major redete mit dem General, und beide lachten herzlich. 3. Was hat sie amüsiert? Worüber haben sie gelacht? Wovon haben sie erzählt? Das war gewiß sehr komisch. 4. Was hat dir deine Frau zum Geburtstag geschenkt? Eine Füllfeder, zwei Pfeifen und dieses und jenes. 5. Hier ist der Stuhl, und zwei Mäntel liegen darauf; dieser gehört Ihnen, jener gehört mir. 6. An der Ecke jeder Straße wartete ein Detektiv. 7. Das ist mein Wirt; sein Sohn hat in England studiert. 8. Sind Sie für jene Politik der Regierung? Nein, ich bin sehr dagegen und leide darunter. 9. Wozu hast du jenen Spazierstock gekauft? Jener Filmstar, Kurt Freundlich, hat einen Spazierstock und hat damit Furore gemacht. 10. Alles geht drunter und drüber. 11. Glück und Glas, wie bald bricht das (prov.).

B. Translate into GERMAN:

1. I visited (simple past) my friend in the afternoon and we played (compound past) every record in her house. 2. We meant (s.p.) those records by (**von**) Mozart. 3. Why did you laugh (c.p.)? What is funny about-this (**bei**)? 4. They heard an aeroplane and a helicopter; the former landed (s.p.) at (**in**) the airport, the latter (gender!) landed in a field. 5. This is the sea and that is the mountain of the short-story and between-them are fields and forests. 6. Did you buy (c.p.) that newspaper? I see your aunt with-it. 7. What was he talking (s.p.) about (**von**)? About nothing. 8. Why did he (c.p.) let down his general? 9. The king punished (s.p.) him for-it; every boy learnt (s.p.) this at (**in**) school.

CHAPTER VII

34. Weak Nouns (Masculines)

(a) Groups of masculine and neuter nouns earlier described (v. §§ 17, 24) have been "strong" [cp. § 13 (c)]; distinct from these is a group of masculine nouns described as "weak", since they do not have the characteristic endings of the genitive [-(e)s] and dative [-(e)] singular, but end, in all oblique cases of the singular, and in all cases of the plural, in -(e)n:

TABLE:

	Singular: *the boy*	Plural: *the boys*
Nom.	der Junge	die Jungen
Gen.	des Jungen	der Jungen
Dat.	dem Jungen	den Jungen
Acc.	den Jungen	die Jungen

They all stand for human or other living beings, and include both original German words, and words of foreign origin.

(b) Weak masculines of German origin have a single syllable stem, with or without a following unaccented -e:

(1) With -e:

der Affe, Bote, Bube, Drache, Hase, Junge, Knabe, Löwe, Neffe, Ochse, Rabe.

This group includes, in fact, all masculine monosyllables plus -e, except **der Käse (des Käses)**.

Here belong also, though not necessarily German in origin or single-syllable stems, all nouns indicating nationalities, in so far as they end in -e:

der Chinese, Däne, Franzose, Preuße, Russe, Schotte, Schwede, Türke (v. § 35).

(2) Without -e:

These are usually human beings: **der Ahn, Christ** (*Christian*), **Fürst, Graf, Held, Herr, Mensch, Narr, Prinz, Tor**; but a few animals: **der Bär.**
Two regional names are also weak: **der Bayer, der Pommer.**

Note.—Distinguish words for *boy*: **der Knabe,** formal and literary; **der Junge,** general and North German; **der Bub** (not **Bube**), South German; **der Bube,** general for *rogue*.

Der Prinz, a *Prince* by birth; **der Fürst,** a *Prince* by creation, *e.g.* **Fürst Bismarck. Der Herr, des Herrn, die Herren**; but **der Narr, des Narren, die Narren.**

(c) Many nouns, of recent foreign origin, both for human beings and animals, and with characteristic non-German endings and accentuation (cp. § 76), with or without final -e, are weak masculines: **der Elefant, Geologe, Soldat, Student.**   The nationality word: **der Asiat.**

35. Names of Nations, Peoples, Tribes

(a) Most of the names of masculine members of a national or tribal group are either weak (as above, § 34) or strong, ending in **-er,** especially when derived from countries in **-land,** thus **der Engländer, der Grönländer,** but also **der Amerikaner, der Italiener, der Japaner.**   As such they follow the rules for inflection of their appropriate classes.

But a few with exotic endings may, as often with proper names of time [v. § 57 (c)] and of place (v. § 221), drop the genitive **-s**:

der Eskimo, des Eskimo(s); der Zulu, des Zulu(s).   For plurals v. § 130.

(b) Feminine members of these groups are indicated by the feminine ending **-in** for the two main groups (replacing **-e** if present in weak nouns):

die Dänin, die Engländerin, die Amerikanerin;   die Schwäbin and **Französin,**
with mutation;   **die Schottin,** without.

For the exotics a compound would be used: **eine Eskimofrau.**

Note.—**Der Deutsche, die Deutsche** is the only noun of nationality which is inflected as an adjective [cp. § 144 (a)].

36. Weak Adjective Inflection

(a) Adjectives in German are:

(1) declined when used attributively before the noun:

Der arme Vater! Ich gab meinem jungen Sohn ein dickes Buch;

(2) but not declined when used predicatively: **Mein Vater ist arm. Mein Sohn ist jung;**   or in apposition following a noun: **Der Junge, bleich wie der Tod.**

(b) When used attributively, the adjective has endings which vary according to the gender, number and case of the noun with which it is associated.   Such endings follow two main patterns, described as "strong" and "weak" inflection.   For strong inflection v. § 46.

Weak inflections are used whenever a word is present which adequately marks the case of the noun, such as:

(1) The definite article: **der rote Wagen, das dicke Buch;**

(2) A word with endings like the definite article, *e.g.* the demonstratives **dieser, jener,** or the indefinite **jeder** (v. § 32):

diese schöne Frau, jedes dicke Buch, jene schwülen Nächte.

(c) The weak endings are -en throughout eleven of the sixteen possible cases, and -e in the remaining five cases, all of the singular, *i.e.* the three nominative cases and the feminine and neuter accusative.

TABLE:

der rote Wagen, *the red car.*   **diese schöne Frau,** *this beautiful woman.*

Nom.	der rote Wagen	diese schöne Frau
Gen.	des roten Wagens	dieser schönen Frau
Dat.	dem roten Wagen	dieser schönen Frau
Acc.	den roten Wagen	diese schöne Frau

jedes dicke Buch, *each fat book.*   **jene schwülen Nächte,** *those sultry nights.*

Nom.	jedes dicke Buch	jene schwülen Nächte
Gen.	jedes dicken Buches	jener schwülen Nächte
Dat.	jedem dicken Buch(e)	jenen schwülen Nächten
Acc.	jedes dicke Buch	jene schwülen Nächte

Note.—Two or more adjectives take the same inflection:

das schöne, alte, baufällige, aber dennoch sehenswerte Haus, *the fine old house, tumbledown, but still worth a visit.*

37. Present Participle (1). In the Predicate

(a) The present participle of any verb is formed by adding **-end** to the infinitive stem, cp. English *-ing:* **gehend, singend, lachend,** *going, singing, laughing.* It may be predicated of a noun or pronoun, or accompany a noun as a normal inflected, attributive adjective (*v.* § 38).

(b) The present participle may only be used after the verb **sein** if it has acquired a genuine adjectival sense, thus:

das Kind ist reizend, *charming;* **der Film war ganz unterhaltend,** *entertaining;* **seine Argumente waren nicht überzeugend,** *convincing;* **das Wetter ist heute furchtbar drückend,** *oppressive;* **mein Großvater ist leidend,** *poorly;* **ich bin nicht unvermögend,** *quite well-off;* **wir waren wütend,** *fuming.*

Note.—This is *not* the translation of the English present progressive *the clock is striking,* **die Uhr schlägt** (cp. § 10), which describes an event or action, whereas the German adjectival participle after **sein** describes a noun or pronoun, **der Film, das Wetter, wir,** etc.

(c) The present participle may be used as objective predicate after transitive verbs, *i.e.* predicated of the object, either:

(1) in the adjectival sense, as (b):

das Kind findet das Püppchen entzückend, *thinks the doll delightful;* **seine Antwort nenne ich empörend,** *call his answer outrageous;*

or (2) in the verbal sense:

man findet die Kinder schlafend, *the children are found sleeping (asleep);*
ich sehe sie jetzt beim schwachen Lichte der Abendsonne strickend, *I can see her knitting in the* . . .

The corresponding simple statement would, in (1), require the verb *to be* (**das Püppchen ist . . .**), in (2), a verb of activity (**sie strickt . . .**).

(*d*) The present participle may be predicated of the subject of a verb with adjectival force, or more commonly with adverbial force.

(1) Adjectival: **er lag träumend im Bette; sie kam lachend aus dem Hause; einige Studenten stiegen singend in die Straßenbahn.**

(2) Adverbial:

Der Schaffner . . . legte salutierend die Hand an die Mütze (Th. Mann), *with a salute.*

Eigentlich hatte er mehr als dreißig Jahre . . . einzig hier an diesem viereckigen Tische lesend, vergleichend, kalkulierend verbracht (S. Zweig), *reading, comparing, calculating.*

Objects and adverbial phrases associated with the present participle precede it, and the whole construction is, when following a verb, usually placed parenthetically between commas:

Rat und Aufklärung suchend stellte Eduard bei Gelegenheit seine Schwester zur Rede (Th. Mann), *seeking advice and information.*

F. trat, das Taschentuch in den Händen knetend, (ins Zimmer). (S. Andres), *screwing up his handkerchief.*

(*e*) None of the above constructions are as wide or as general as the corresponding English forms. English especially often uses the participle for two concomitant actions of equal importance, where German [in spite of examples such as those at (*d*) (2) above] prefers to use a separate verb: *The whole day he sat in the library reading.* **Er saß den ganzen Tag in der Bibliothek und las.** Cp. also §§ 275-8 for other means of translating the English participle.

38. Present Participle (2). In the Attributive Position

(*a*) As distinct from its use in the predicate (§ 37), the participle as attributive adjective is used as widely in German as in English:

das schlafende Kind, *sleeping;* **ein unterhaltender Begleiter,** *entertaining;*
eine drohende Gewitterwolke, *threatening;* **eine wartende Taxe,** *waiting;*
eine wohltönende Rede, *eloquent.*

am laufenden Bande, lit. *at the production line;* fig. *without intermission;*
ein dienendes Glied, lit. *a serving link, humble member of society.*

(*b*) Maintaining its verbal force, the attributive participle may take a dative or accusative object, adverb, or prepositional phrase, all such adjuncts preceding.

(1) Accusative object:

die Blumen pflückenden Kinder, *picking flowers;* **die Schach spielenden Herren,** *playing chess.*

(2) Dative object:

eine der Sache dienende Maßnahme, *appropriate to the cause;* **ein der Firma gehörendes Lastauto,** *belonging to the firm.*

(3) Other adjuncts:

die lustig singenden Kinder, *singing merrily;* **eine mit einem Ball spielende Katze,** *playing with a ball.*

Note.—Such constructions with dependent nouns are not normally used in speech, and in written German their excessive use is regarded as bad style. English uses the adjectival present participle, but more commonly requires a relative clause (*the children who were picking flowers*), or a following participle in apposition (*a lorry belonging to the firm*).

(*c*) The participle and a simple noun object may be written as a compound if the activity is felt as habitual, or natural, to the agent:

der feuerspeiende Berg, *volcano,* but **meine Flammen sprühende Wirtin,** *belching flames;* **die ackerbautreibende Bevölkerung,** *rural,* but **die Unfug treibenden Studenten,** *causing a bother;* **die radfahrenden Passanten,** *passing cyclists,* but **eine Auto fahrende Dame,** *a lady driving a car.*

39. Present Participle (3).   As Degree Adverb

The present participle may occur as an uninflected degree abverb, in either of the positions above mentioned:

(*a*) In the predicate: **ich fühle mich ausnehmend wohl,** *I feel exceptionally well;* **die Beleuchtung war wohltuend mild,** *the lighting was agreeably soft;* **die Tischplatte war glänzend poliert,** *the table-top was brilliantly polished;* **er kam überraschend früh,** *he came surprisingly early.*

(*b*) With an attributive adjective: **eine auffallend elegante Erscheinung,** *a person of strikingly elegant appearance;* both positions occupied by a participle: **ein wohlhabend aussehender Mann,** *a prosperous looking man;* **ein glänzend gehendes Exportgeschäft,** *an export business which is doing excellently.*

EXERCISE VII

A. Translate into ENGLISH:

1. Der Hund des alten Soldaten liegt schlafend neben seinem Herrn in der warmen Sonne. 2. Die Kinder gehen in den zoologischen Garten und geben dem lustigen kleinen Affen eine ihrer Bananen zu fressen. 3. Der Fleiß des Japaners, die Sparsamkeit des Schotten und die Musikliebe des Österreichers sind wohlbekannt. 4. Jeder gute Christ verzeiht die bösen Taten seines Feindes. 5. Jener große Baum fällt krachend in den schnellfließenden Strom. 6. Klaus und Annemarie kommen, den Walzer tanzend, in die kleine Küche der Mutter. 7. Die ihre goldenen Haare kämmende Lorelei sitzt auf dem hohen Felsen am Rhein. 8. Die hungrigen Mäuse lieben den starken Geruch des Käses. 9. Das Reich der Japaner und das Land der Chinesen liegen im Fernen Osten. 10. Die bunte Mütze des Narren liegt vor dem Prinzen auf dem glänzenden Boden.

B. Translate into GERMAN:

1. The geologist gives the young student his big books and (a) good counsel. 2. My young nephew's book (= the book of . . .) has pictures of Russians, Turks, Japanese, and of Eskimo boys and Zulu women. 3. We travel in our fast new grey car through the sleeping village. 4. This little monkey is charming; it collects money in a red cap for the old soldier. 5. The American's quick answer is entertaining, and the Frenchman's logical answer is convincing. 6. The elephant at (**in**) the zoo steals the bottle with his thick trunk and drinks the cooling beer. 7. The count who is playing chess (= chess-playing count) hears the significant words of the messenger. 8. The young messenger is a pale-looking Italian. 9. I see a German who is riding a cycle (cp. 7). 10. My landlady has a big white cat and it sits howling in the garden in front of my window.

CHAPTER VIII

40. Feminine Nouns: Plural

(*a*) As feminine nouns have no case endings in the singular, the distinction between strong and weak made for masculine nouns (*v.* § 34) does not apply. But in the plural we may distinguish:

(1) Weak feminines, adding **-(e)n.**

(2) Strong feminines, adding **-e** and mutating the vowel.

(*b*) Weak feminines, adding **-(e)n.** These are:

(1) All those with **-e** in the nominative singular, as

die Biene, Blume, Düne, Eiche, Farbe, Fliege, Katze, Kirche, Kirsche, Lerche, Lilie, Linde, Nase, Pflaume, Rose, Schule, Schwalbe, Stimme, Straße.

Plural: **die Bienen, Blumen, Dünen,** etc.

(2) All those ending in the feminine suffixes:

-ei: die Bäckerei;
-heit, -keit: die Aufmerksamkeit, Neuigkeit, Schönheit;
-schaft: die Grafschaft, Landschaft;
-ung: die Bemerkung, Hoffnung.

Plurals: **die Bäckereien, Schönheiten, Grafschaften, Hoffnungen,** etc.; while those ending in **-n**, especially the common feminine personal suffix **-in**, double this in the plural: **die Königin-nen, Gräfin-nen.**

(3) The vast majority of those ending in a consonant, apart from those in (2):

die Schlacht, Tat, Uhr, Zahl, Zeit. Plural: **die Taten,** etc.

(*c*) Strong feminines, adding **-e** and mutating the vowel:

(1) A group of monosyllables:

die Angst, Bank, Frucht, Gans, Hand, Kuh, Kunst, Maus, Nacht, Stadt, Wand.

Plural: **die Ängste, Bänke, Früchte, Gänse.**

Distinguish: **die Bank, Bänke,** *bench;* **die Bank, Banken,** *bank* (*firm*).

(2) Two words mutate without adding an ending: **die Mutter, Tochter.** Plural: **die Mütter, Töchter.** Cp. the masculine plurals **die Väter, Brüder** (§ 24), but **die Schwester, die Schwestern,** as (*b*) (3) above.

(3) A few words with the uncommon suffixes **-nis** and **-sal** add **-e** without mutating; they are more commonly neuter, and sometimes fluctuate between feminine and neuter [*v.* § 194 (*b*)]:

die **Bedrängnis, die Bedrängnisse** (note doubling of -s-); die **Mühsal, die Mühsale; die Drangsal, die Drangsale.**

41. Numerals (2)

(*a*) Cardinals to 100 (*v.* § 23). The "decades" after ten are:
> **zwanzig, dreißig, vierzig, fünfzig,**
> **sec***h***zig, sie***b***zig** (these two contracted),
> **achtzig, neunzig, hundert.**

The intervening numerals have the integers first, and the whole numeral is normally compounded: **einundzwanzig** (not **einsund-**), **vierundfünfzig, achtundneunzig.** Cp. the older English (still in clock-time): *five and twenty* (*minutes to four*).

Note.—Until recently telephone numbers were officially (and generally) spoken in groups of two digits: 347582 was **vierunddreißig—fündundsiebzig —zwoundachtzig** (for **zwo,** *v.* § 23). But by a ruling (1953) of the Federal Postal Administration they are now spoken in simple figures as written and dialled: **drei vier sieben fünf acht zwo.**

(*b*) Ordinals are formed by adding **-t** to cardinals as far as 19, and **-st** from 20, the whole being treated as a normal adjective: **die zwei-te Frau, das zwölf-te Kind, das dreißig-ste Haus.** But note: **der *erste* Mann der *dritte* Schüler. Siebent-** is sometimes contracted to **siebt-.** When figures are written for ordinals, the distinction from cardinals is preserved by placing a full stop (of abbreviation) after the figure [*v.* (*c*) below].

Der (die, das) zwote is sometimes used for **zweite,** on the analogy of the cardinal **zwo** for **zwei** (cp. § 23); but it is incorrect, since no confusion could arise with **der (die, das) dritte.**

Note.—Ordinals may occur isolated:
Bitte eine Fahrkarte dritter (= gen., **dritter Klasse**) **nach Köln,** *a third-class ticket to Cologne, please.*
Ich wohne Hauptstraße 68III or **achtundsechzig dritte** (= **Etage**), **dritter** or **dritten** (= **Stock**), *I live at Hauptstraße 68, third floor.*

(*c*) Ordinals in dates. This is, of course, one of the commonest uses for ordinals. The gender is masculine, since **Tag** is understood:
Der wievielte (lit. *the how many-th*) **ist heute?** (**Welches Datum haben wir heute?**) **Heute ist der zweite Januar, der dritte März, der einund-dreißigste Juli. Wir haben heute *den* zweit*en* Januar,** etc.

In figures the date is written with a stop (of abbreviation) to distinguish it from the corresponding cardinal: **Es ist der 31. Juli,** *the 31st July;* but the full ordinal is spoken, as in English. As a letter-heading the date stands in the accusative (of definite time): **Freitag, den 8. April,** spoken: **Freitag, den achten April;** with place-names also **am: Berlin, am 8. April.** [*v.* § 58 (*a*), and § 57 for the names of days and months.]

A literary use is: **Wir schreiben den 20. Augst,** *it is* . . . (G. Hauptmann). **Bereits schrieb man späte Tage des September,** *it was already* . . . (Th. Mann).

The ordinal is thus abbreviated also in titles: **Georg VI.** (= **der Sechste), Elisabeth II.** (= **die Zweite).**

Note.—**Das Datum** and "the date".

Das Datum (plural, **Daten,** which also means *data, v.* § 91) is only used for the calendar date, and in a few associated phrases: **der Brief ist ohne Datum,** *undated,* or **ohne Datumsangabe,** *without indication of date;* **sein Anzug ist nicht gerade neuesten (jüngsten) Datums,** *of recent date* (*cut*); **die wichtigsten Daten der deutschen Geschichte,** *the most important dates.*

Elsewhere other words are used: *To learn dates,* **Jahreszahlen lernen.** *What was the date of* (*the battle of*) *Waterloo?* **In welchem Jahr war (die Schlacht von) Waterloo?** *Let's fix a date,* **eine Zeit, den Zeitpunkt.** *What is the final date?* **der Termin,** an officially fixed date. *I've a date with* . . ., **eine Verabredung** (appointment). Often a compound of **Tag** is required: **der Eröffnungstag,** *date of opening;* **der Erscheinungstag,** *date of publication.* *To-day's the date!* **Heute ist der (große) Tag!** *Up-to-date,* **neuzeitlich, modern.**

(*d*) The complex numeral derived from **das Mal,** a *single time* or *occasion,* may be:

(1) A compound cardinal meaning "number of times", thus: **einmal, zweimal, dreimal** . . . **zwanzigmal,** *once, twice, thrice* . . *twenty times* (lit. *on one,* etc., *occasion*). This serves two purposes:

(i) Repetition (called an "iterative", **Wiederholungszahl**), as in **zweimal am Tage, in der Woche, im Monat, im Jahr,** *twice a day, week, month, year;* **x-mal** (pronounced eeks-**mal**) or **zigmal** [cp. **zwan-zig** and example at § 154 (*b*)], *umpteen times.*

(ii) Multiplication (called a "multiplicative", **Vervielfältigungszahl**), as in **zweimal zwei ist** (or **macht) vier,** *twice two are four* (note the number of the verb).

(2) An ordinal, not usually compounded: **das erste, zweite, dritte** . . . **hundertste Mal,** *the first, second, third, hundredth time;* **das letzte Mal,** *the last time.* **Zum ersten Mal,** as at the auctioneer: **Zum ersten, zum zweiten, zum dritten Mal!** *For the first,* etc., *time,* or: *going, going, gone!*

Exercise VIII

A. Translate into English:

1. Die entzückenden Töchter des Hauses singen zweistimmig das sentimentale Liedchen: „In einer kleinen Konditorei, da saßen (past of sitzen) wir zwei bei Kuchen und Tee". 2. Unter den Bänken an den Wänden sitzen Mäuse und ängstigen die Schülerinnen. 3. Bitte, dreißig Fahrkarten zweiter Klasse nach München für den Mütterverein. 4. Klaus hat heute, am achtundzwanzigsten März, eine Verabredung mit Annemarie; sie spielen dreimal in der Woche Tennis. 5. Der wievielte ist morgen? Morgen ist der vierte August; dieser Tag ist bedeutend in der Weltgeschichte. 6. Zehnmal sieben macht siebzig. Wieviel ist viermal zwölf? Achtundvierzig. 7. Heute kommt die dreiundzwanzigste Köchin; sie bleiben nie mehr als sieben Tage. 8. Er telefonierte dreimal die Nummer sechs neun vier sieben; beim ersten und zweiten Mal keine Antwort; beim dritten Mal hörte er die Stimme seiner Freundin. 9. Wir haben heute zum x-ten Mal Pflaumen zum Nachtisch. September hat dreißig Tage und täglich Pflaumen! 10. Ich lese ein altes Buch; es heißt: „Einige Bemerkungen eines reisenden Deutschen über die Landschaft der östlichen Grafschaften Englands". Die Jahreszahl auf der ersten Seite ist vom achtzehnten Jahrhundert. 11. Proverbs: In der Nacht sind alle Katzen grau. Eine Schwalbe macht noch keinen Sommer.

B. Translate into German:

1. The swallows fly round (**um**) the three old lime trees near the school. 2. The flowers in your hands are lilies, roses and cornflowers. 3. Bees and flies visit them a hundred times a day in the month [of] June. 4. Where does one buy cakes? I tell you for the (**zum**) third time: at (**in**) the baker's. 5. What is the date to-day? It is the 27th [of] July. 6. Two third-class tickets to Vienna, please. We have a date with two Austrian girl-friends. 7. We live in a little house on (**auf**) the dunes and we swim twice a day. 8. The two young countesses were great beauties in olden times. 9. The date of publication of my seventh book is January 31st. 10. To-day my grandmother celebrates her ninetieth birthday.

CHAPTER IX

42. Past and Perfect Tenses of Strong Verbs

(*a*) The simple past of strong verbs is formed by the addition of certain endings to the past tense stem, which is the infinitive stem with certain vowel changes (*v.* § 43), thus:

singen, *to sing;* stem of infinitive and present: **sing-**, of past: **sang-**:

ich sang, du sang-st, er (sie, es) sang; *I,* etc., *sang.*

wir sang-en, ihr sang-t, Sie sang-en, sie sang-en; *we,* etc., *sang.*

Note.—The first and third persons are alike, having no ending. For omission of **-e-** of the ending in certain verbs *v.* (*b*) (2) below.

(*b*) The perfect (or compound past) tense of strong verbs is formed from:

(1) the present tense of **haben** (ich habe, etc.), or **sein** (ich bin, etc.).

(2) and the past participle of the verb, obtained by prefixing **ge-** and adding **-(e)n** to the past participle stem, which may or may not have the same vowel as the present and past stems:

singen, *to sing;* **ich sang,** *I sang;* **ich habe gesungen,** *I have sung.*

sehen, *to see;* **ich sah,** *I saw;* **ich habe gesehen,** *I have seen.*

bleiben, *to remain;* **ich blieb,** *I remained;* **ich bin geblieben,** *I have remained.*

gehen, *to go;* **ich ging,** *I went;* **ich bin gegangen,** *I have gone.*

The prefix **ge-** is omitted before the past participle of verbs which already have an inseparable prefix, thus:

erfahren, *to learn, experience;* **Ich habe gestern seinen Tod erfahren.**

verlesen, *to read (out);* **Der Rechtswalt hat das Testament verlesen,** *the lawyer read out the will.* [Cp. § 88 (*a*).]

Note.—After past and past participle stems ending in **-ie-**, the **-e-** of the ending **-en** may be omitted:

schreien, *to cry (out);* **ich schrie,** but **wir schrie(e)n, du hast geschrie(e)n.**

speien, *to vomit;* **das Geschütz spie Tod und Verderben,** *spat death and destruction,* but **die Geschütze spie(e)n . . ., haben . . . gespie(e)n.**

(3) When the sentence or clause contains independent elements apart from the verb and its subject, the past participle stands at the end. Cp. examples above.

(*c*) The main facts about the conjugation of strong verbs are given in most dictionaries, and may be obtained at a glance from Appendix D: List of Strong (and Irregular) Verbs. They fall into two groups:

(1) The vowel changes which (may) take place in the second and third persons singular of the present tense [*v*. § 15 (*c*)], the simple past and past participle.

No rules can be given, but memorisation is assisted by grouping strong verbs into classes according to the pattern of vowel change (*v*. Appendix C).

(2) The auxiliary (**haben** or **sein**) required in the perfect tense.

Some rules, for verbs whether weak or strong, are given at § 44.

(*d*) Some verbs are also, or commonly, conjugated weak, and there may be differentiation of sense between strong and weak forms (*v*. Chapter LXVI).

Note.—Only the infinitive form of strong verbs will be found in the Vocabulary. Reference to the List of Strong Verbs will easily establish that *e.g.* **schwammen** and **geschwommen** are forms of **schwimmen,** *to swim*.

43. Vowel Changes (Gradation Classes) in Strong Verbs

(*a*) The changes of vowel in the past and past participle of strong verbs (and the associated changes in the present) are called "Gradation", thus the groups into which such verbs may be arranged in respect of these vowel changes are called "Gradation Classes". These are given summarily at Appendix C. The division into classes there is according to the pattern of vowel change (thus: **a/u/a**, as **schaffen, schuf, geschaffen**); that into sub-classes is either by vowel change or by distribution of long or short vowels within the same vowel change (thus ă/ū/ă, as **schaffen; ā/ū/ā** as **fahren, fuhr, gefahren**).

Regular changes of vowel and mutations in the present tense and in the past subjunctive are grouped elsewhere for convenience (*v*. § 15, Appendix B and § 272), but these changes are noted for each individual verb at Appendix D.

Verbs with inseparable prefixes, as well as simple verbs, are mentioned in the Classes; for these *v*. §§ 87 f.

The verbs given under each Class as "Examples" should be learnt now and referred to as types of their class of vowel change.

(*b*) Certain consonantal changes require comment:

(1) A very few verbs change the last consonant of the stem as well as the vowel, thus:

-**d** to -**t**: **sieden, sott, gesotten** (cp. English see*the*, so*dd*en);

-**h** to -**g**: **ziehen, zog, gezogen;**

-**s** to -**r**: (**wesen,** now obsolete), **war, gewesen** (cp. English wa*s*, we*r*e).

(2) All other apparent consonantal changes are due to the requirements of orthography, thus:

A single consonant must be doubled after a short vowel:

greifen, griff, gegriffen, and those changing **-d** to **-t** [(1) above]:

leiden, litt, gelitten; schneiden, schnitt, geschnitten.

A double consonant becomes single after a long vowel:

kommen, kam, but **gekommen; treffen, traf,** but **getroffen.**

The double consonant **-ck-** (= **-kk-**) in this case becomes **-k-**:

backen, buk, but **gebacken; erschrecken, erschrak,** but **erschrocken.**

The double consonant **-ss-** or **-ß-** alternates in various positions according to its own rules [*v.* Introduction, § 2 (*d*)]:

beißen, biß, gebissen; messen, maß, gemessen.

44. Auxiliaries and their Use

(*a*) **Haben** and **sein** are named "auxiliaries of tense" to distinguish them from the "auxiliaries of mood" ("modal auxiliaries", *v.* Chapters XIII and XIV).

Basic rules for their use with verbs strong and weak are:

(1) **haben** is used with all transitive verbs, *i.e.* those which take a direct object in the accusative: **Wir haben das Lied gesungen.**

(2) **sein** is used with certain (senses of) intransitive verbs expressing the idea of change of state, or of movement towards or from a place:

Er ist gestorben, *has died.* **Die Blumen sind verwelkt,** *have faded.*

Er ist nach Hamburg gereist, *went to . . .,* **von London gekommen,** *has come from,* **nach Hause gelangt,** *arrived home,* **über den See geschwommen,** *swam across the lake.*

(3) **haben** is used with all those (senses of) intransitive verbs which do not require **sein.**

These basic rules may be expanded as follows:

(*b*) **Haben** forms the perfect of all verbs with an accusative object:

(1) This includes those with reflexive pronoun as object:

Ich habe mich auf das Bett gelegt, *I lay* (*laid myself*) *down* [*v.* § 179 (*b*)].

Note.—Avoid the false analogy of French use: Je me *suis* couché.

(2) Close synonyms may thus be grammatically different:

Ich habe ihn getroffen, but: **Ich bin ihm begegnet,** *met him.*

Es hat so was nie gegeben, *no such thing has ever happened;* but:

So was ist nie gewesen, ist nie geschehen.

(3) All exceptions to this rule, *i.e.* verbs apparently with accusative object and **sein,** are either only apparent or due to false analogy; thus certain compound verbs, as **einen Hafen anlaufen,** cognate and adverbial accusatives: **Gefahr laufen, einen Weg gehen** (*v.* § 378), a pronoun apparently in accusative, but actually in genitive: **ich bin es gewahr geworden,** *I noticed it* (*v.* § 192).

(*c*) **Sein** forms the perfect with:

(1) The three verbs: **sein,** *to be;* **werden,** *to become;* **bleiben,** *to remain:*

Er ist arm gewesen, reich geworden, aber bescheiden geblieben. *He was poor, became rich but remained modest.*

(2) Intransitive verbs, or uses of intransitive verbs, in which the subject undergoes some change through:

(i) Passing from one state or condition to another:

eine Saite, die Fensterscheibe ist gesprungen; *a violin string broke, the window-pane cracked,*

der Schnee, sein hartes Herz ist geschmolzen; *the snow, his hard heart melted.*

(ii) Motion to a goal, or from a place of departure:

Er ist schon gegangen, *has left already.*

Wir sind aufs Land gefahren, *went into the country.*

Er ist ins Zimmer gestürzt, *burst into the room.*

(*d*) Comparison between **sein** and **haben.**

Haben directs attention to the action for its own quality, **sein** directs interest to the event which is the result of the action, to the impact on the outside situation. Thus:

(1) Verbs expressing duration or repetition of an act require **haben:**

Duration: **ich habe (lange) gewartet, gehofft, gezögert, gewußt, um ihre Hand geworben,** *waited, hoped, hesitated, known, been a suitor for her hand.*

Repetition: **ich habe (wiederholt) geklopft, gefragt, reklamiert,** (*repeatedly*) *knocked, asked, complained.*

And especially those verbs which express continuing positions of the body: **wir haben gestanden, gesessen, gelegen.**

Note.—**gelegen** may be used with **sein** as a predicative adjective:

Die Stadt ist in einem lieblichen Tälchen gelegen, *the town lies in, is situate(d) in a charming valley.*

In the absence of specific adverbs of time (once, often, during the performance, etc.), the English progressive form may be tested on such expressions; its suitability is a clear indication of the need for **haben**: *I have been waiting, knocking, hoping, asking*, etc.

(2) Verbs expressing the inception or ending of an action do not in themselves require **sein,** but they may do so if either by sense or by form they convey a sense of destination or change of state, thus:

Das Konzert hat schon begonnen, *the concert has begun;* but **er ist schon gefahren,** *he has already left (for a destination),* and **sie sind gestartet,** *they (the runners) have started (moved off).*

Note.—**Er hat seine Mutter nach Hause gefahren,** *he took* (transitive) *his mother home.*

Er hat lange geredet und hat dann geschwiegen, *spoke long, then was* (or *became*) *silent;* but **er ist dann verstummt,** *fell silent,* since the inseparable prefix **ver-** has perfective force.

45. Auxiliaries. Pluperfect Tense

(*a*) Past tense and participles of **sein, haben, werden**:

ich war, du warst, er (sie, es) war, wir waren, etc., *I was,* etc.

ich hatte, du hattest, er (sie, es) hatte, wir hatten, etc., *I had,* etc.

ich wurde, du wurdest, er (sie, es) wurde, wir wurden, etc., *I became,* etc.

seiend, *being*	**habend,** *having*	**werdend,** *becoming*
gewesen, *been*	**gehabt,** *had*	**geworden,** *become*

(*b*) Pluperfect Tense. The past tense of **sein** or **haben** is used with the past participle to form the pluperfect tense:

er war gestorben, *had died;* **ich hatte ihn getroffen,** *had met him;* **wir waren aufs Land gefahren,** *had gone;* **sie hatte sich gesetzt,** *had sat down;* **ich hatte wiederholt um ihre Hand geworben,** *had been a suitor.*

(*c*) Use of the pluperfect, *v.* § 134 (*a*).

A. Translate into ENGLISH:

1. Der Zug ist im Bahnhof geblieben und ist erst (*only*) am nächsten Tag gefahren. 2. Die Lerche flog hoch in den Himmel und fiel dann plötzlich zur Erde. 3. Das Schiff glitt geräuschlos durch den Hafen und gewann die offene See. 4. Peter ist zweimal von seinem Rad gefallen; er erschrak und floh nach Hause. 5. Ich habe den ganzen Vormittag in der Nähe des Landungsstegs geschwommen; dann bin ich über den Fluß geschwommen, und bin am anderen Ufer gelandet. 6. Ich bin

sehr geeilt, bin aber nicht zur rechten Zeit gekommen. 7. Ist er nach Bonn gereist? Ist er mit dem Zug gefahren oder mit dem Flugzeug geflogen? Mit dem Zug; geflogen ist er noch nie in seinem Leben. 8. Der Dieb stieg durch das Fenster in das Geschäft, man hat ihn aber bei frischer Tat (= *in the act*) ertappt; er log und lügt noch, aber es hilft nichts. Er hat schon einmal gesessen (= *served a term*). 9. Der berühmte Musiker Suszewski starb im Alter von 66 Jahren; man widmete ihm in der Zeitung einen warmen Nachruf. 10. Wir sind am frühen Vormittag auf den Berg gestiegen, und sind abends erst (*not till*) wieder heim gekommen.

B. Put sentences 2, 3, and 9 into the perfect tense, and sentences 1, 5, 6, and 10 into the pluperfect.

C. Translate into GERMAN:

1. They went to the inn and drank (simple past) hock. 2. We ran to the station and met (compound past) our friends. 3. The soldier threw (s.p.) the dice. "You have lost", he cried excitedly. 4. I spoke (s.p.) seriously to (**mit**) my son and said: "You have told a lie (lied)". You had swum near the harbour and that was very dangerous. 5. Annemarie helped (s.p.) her mother in the kitchen; she cut the beans, she baked cakes, she washed the dishes. 6. He came home and got (became c.p.) cross. 7. He gave her fruit and she put (placed c.p.) it on the table. 8. We travelled (s.p.) to Vienna in the evening; our friends had already gone in the afternoon. 9. We have been hoping for (**auf,** acc.) fine weather. 10. Peter threw (s.p.) his ball into the air and caught it cleverly. I saw (c.p.) him at once.

D. Put sentences 1, 2, 5, 7, and 10 into the pluperfect tense.

CHAPTER X

46. Strong Adjective Inflection

Revise weak adjective inflection (§ 36).

(*a*) When the attributive adjective is not preceded by a word showing the case, this function falls to the adjective itself, which then takes the endings of the definite article (with one exception, *v.* below), called in this connection strong adjectival inflection:

armer Junge, cp. **der arme Junge; dunkles Bier,** cp. **das dunkle Bier.**

This requirement occurs:

(1) When no adjective precedes, as above, or a numeral:

zwei kleine Mädchen, cp. **die kleinen Mädchen.**

(2) When the indefinite article **ein,** or another word declined like it (**kein, mein,** etc.), precedes in one of the three cases in which these are defective of ending (*v.* § 13):

mein armer Junge! Kein dunkles Bier, nur helles?

An exception occurs when an adjective stands alone before a strong noun in the masculine or neuter genitive, since the noun itself then marks the case with its ending **-(e)s.** Here the adjective may, and usually does, revert to the weak ending **-en,** thus:

ein Glas guten (for **gutes**) **Weines; eine Flasche dunklen Biers.**

This, as these examples show, is common in expressions of measurable quantities of a material commodity.

(*b*) TABLE:

	alter Wein, *old wine.*	helles Bier, *light beer.*	frische Milch, *fresh milk.*	dunkle Augen, *dark eyes.*
Nom.	alter Wein	helles Bier	frische Milch	dunkle Augen
Gen.	altes/-en Weins	helles/-en Biers	frischer Milch	dunkler Augen
Dat.	altem Wein	hellem Bier	frischer Milch	dunklen Augen
Acc.	alten Wein	helles Bier	frische Milch	dunkle Augen

Note.—Two or more adjectives in the same position take the same inflection: **dein schöner, alter, zottiger Hund.**

47. Notes on Adjective Inflection

(*a*) INFLECTION.—The unaccented suffixes **-el, -en, -er,** when followe l by certain weak or strong endings, namely, **-e, -em, -en, -er,** tend to elide the **-e-** of the suffix, less commonly that of the ending:

-en only elides the suffix -e-:

die offne Tür, ein wollner Stoff, bei offnem Fenster.

-el elides the suffix -e- by preference:

die edle Frau, ein edler Mann, der edlen (or edeln) Frau, mit edlem (seldom edelm) Wein.

-er sometimes elides the suffix -e-:

muntre Buben, mit munterm (or muntrem) Gesang, muntres Singen, die heitern (or heitren) Kinder.

This form occurs particularly in speech reproduced in print, since it renders the natural elisions of spoken language.

(*b*) NON-INFLECTION.—In a few cases the attributive adjective, whether in a weak or strong position, is invariable, *i.e.* takes no endings, thus:

(1) A few foreign adjectives of colour in -a:

auf rosa Briefpapier, ein lila Hemd; also prima, *first-class:* prima Waffeln, das prima Bier.

(2) Adjectives derived from a place-name, especially that of a town or city, by the addition of -er:

Göttinger Würste. Das Münchner (for Münchener) Bier schmeckt ausgezeichnet.

This invariable ending should not be confused with the strong ending -er, thus:

ein neue*r* Wagen and ein Berline*r* Wagen;

but: ein zweit*es* Bier, Berline*r* Bier.

For further notes on adjective inflection *v.* §§ 280 f.

48. Past Participle (1), in the Predicate, in Apposition

(*a*) Apart from its function in forming compound tenses of the verb (*v.* §§ 31, 42), the past participle, like the present participle (*v.* §§ 37-9), may be used in various other syntactical roles, both adjectivally and adverbially.

(*b*) Past participle in the predicate.

(1) After the verb sein to express a state or condition:

die Tür ist geöffnet, *is open;* die Fensterscheibe ist gebrochen, *is broken;* der Mann ist unglaublich gelehrt, *incredibly learned;* seine Nase war leicht gebogen, *slightly curved;* die Tapeten des Zimmers waren dunkel geblümt, *had a dark flower-pattern;* das Museum ist seit 1. d.M. (= des Monats) wegen Reparatur geschlossen, *closed for repairs.*

This use is equivalent to the normal predicative use of the adjective.

Note.—Such past participles are quite distinct from the past participle as part of a compound verb; in some few cases the participle is not derived from a verb at all, but forms with an adjective (adverb) a descriptive compound, as often in English, thus **dunkel geblümt** (Th. Mann), cp. English *long-legged.*

(2) After transitive verbs as objective predicate.

(i) In the adjectival sense, as (1):

ich fand meinen schönen Blumentopf zerbrochen, *found . . . broken;* **ich halte ihn für verrückt,** *consider him mad.*

(ii) Occasionally the past participle is a genuine predicative extension of the sense of the verb: **er nahm den Feind gefangen,** *took the enemy prisoner.* Sometimes it is difficult to distinguish from (i), thus:

ich brachte ihr die Puppe in bunter Tracht gekleidet, *in colourful national costume* = adjectival [cp. (*c*) below].

er führte den alten Vater unter dem Arm gefaßt, *brought him along, holding him by the arm* = predicative extension of the verb.

The construction in (ii) may translate the passive: *the enemy was taken prisoner; the old father was brought . . .* [*v.* § 437 (*a*) (1)].

(*c*) Past participle in apposition to noun or pronoun.

Er trug immer ein halbes Dutzend Bleistifte, wundervoll gespitzt, in der Tasche, *a half-dozen pencils, finely pointed.*

Frisch gewaschen sind diese Leintücher blendend weiß, (*when*) *freshly washed these sheets are . . .*

Der alte Mann, an allen Gliedern gebrochen, schleppte sich durch das Dorf, *weary in all his limbs, dragged himself . . .*

Der Lehrer, durch diese Antwort empört, schickte den Schüler aus dem Zimmer, *indignant at this answer.*

Liebe eisgekühlt, *Love in a Cold Climate* (book title in translation).

Adjuncts of the past participle precede (**frisch gewaschen**), and the whole construction, unless short and immediately preceding its noun of reference, is usually placed parenthetically in commas, thus in the last two examples above, after **der alte Mann, der Lehrer.**

49. Past Participle (2), as Attributive Adjective, Degree Adverb

(*a*) As inflected attributive adjective:

ein gekochtes Ei, *boiled egg;* **eine geschlagene Stunde,** *whole hour;* **gesprochenes Deutsch,** *spoken German;* **ein gewendeter Rock,** *a turned skirt;* **ein belesener Mann,** *well-read man;* **die weißgetünchte Wand,** *white-washed wall;* **die (gründlich) gemischten Karten,** (*well*) *shuffled* *cards;* **der empfangene Brief,** *letter received;* **unverschuldetes Unglück,** *undeserved misfortune.*

The past participle as attributive adjective still has verbal force, and may be preceded by an adverb of manner: **die langsam gekochten Kartoffeln schmecken sehr gut,** *cooked slowly;* this may in fact be a predicative adjective of result: **die weich gekochten Eier,** *lightly boiled eggs.* As with the present participle, this use may correspond to other constructions in English, thus a relative clause (*the potatoes, which we had cooked slowly; the letter, which had been received*), or a following appositional construction, as described in § 48 (*c*) (**die wieder geöffnete Tür,** *the door, again opened . . .,* **der von mir bezahlte Betrag,** *the sum paid by me*).

(*b*) As uninflected degree adverb:

(1) In the predicate: **eine unverhofft schöne Gelegenheit,** *an unexpectedly good opportunity;* **eine gerieben schlaue Antwort,** *a wily, sly answer;* **ein ausgesprochen sportlich aussehender Mann,** *a man with a decidedly sportsman-like look.*

(2) With an attributive adjective: **die Antwort kam unerwartet schnell,** *the answer was unexpectedly prompt.*

(*c*) Compound past participles.

(1) The past participle, when not forming a compound tense, is negated by means of the adjectival prefix **un-,** thus examples above, and: **eine unerwartete, unverhoffte, ungewollte Begegnung,** *an unexpected, unlooked for, and undesired meeting.*

(2) Other extensions of the sense may, as with the present participle [*v.* § 38 (*c*)], be compounded if simple and common, cp. examples above: **ein weich gekochtes Ei,** but **eine leichtgebogene Nase,** and **die weißgetünchte Wand.**

das neugeborene Kind taufte man auf den Namen Hans,

or if the combination incorporates an abbreviated form of statement:

Liebe eisgekühlt (above) = **Liebe, auf Eis gekühlt.**

50. Order of Words (1). General

The rules for word order which have been learnt may be summarised and extended.

Word order is much less variable in German than in English; there is a fairly strict basic pattern from which limited variations are possible for the purpose of emphasis, style, euphony, etc.

(*a*) The Noun and its Adjuncts.—The general pattern is as in English, *i.e.* article (or limiting adjective, **kein, dieser, mein**), attributive adjective, noun.

(1) A preceding dependent genitive used to be common, especially in elevated language: **des Tempels hohes Dach** ("Saxon genitive"); but this is now rare except for certain common nouns which approach the status of proper names: **Vaters Wagen, Mutters Kleid** (and earlier: **Kaisers Geburtstag,** *the Emperor's birthday*). Otherwise a dependent genitive must always follow: **die Liebe der Eltern.** An objective genitive must always follow: **der Ausbau der Untergrundbahn,** *extension of the underground.*

(2) Certain descriptive adjuncts, such as short adverbial or prepositional phrases, may follow: **seine Liebe zu ihr,** *for her;* **ein Ellbogenstoß in die Seite,** *elbow dig in the ribs;* **die Tür daneben,** *the next door;* **die Wacht am Rhein,** *the Watch on the Rhine.* But this construction is much more limited in German than in English.

(3) Descriptive participial phrases may precede or follow, in the English translation often following: **eine Gruppe Studenten, als Seeräuber gekleidet,** *dressed as . . .;* **drei Mandoline zupfende alte Kerle,** *three old men playing . . .* (*v.* fully, Chapter VII).

(*b*) The Sentence.—Sentence order is built round the finite verb, whether the sentence (clause) is a main (independent) statement, or a subordinate statement (subordinate clause with adverbial function; relative clause with adjectival function; clause with noun function). Subordinate order is considered later (*v.* §§ 113 f.).

A main statement has:

(1) The finite verb, or in compound tenses the auxiliary, in the second position, with or without inversion of the subject (*v.* § 22).

(2) The past participle, separable prefix or dependent infinitive at the end [*v.* §§ 31, 63 (*d*), 88 (*a*), 107 (*b*)].

Note.—End-position is also characteristic of:

(i) Participles in phrases of descriptive apposition (*v.* §§ 37 and 48).

(ii) Infinitives in all infinitive constructions (*v.* Chapter LV).

(iii) Predicative adjectives in many statements:
Die Dänin ist in der Regel blond. Die Kinder sind vor dem Essen hungrig.

51. Adverbs of Time

Dann, *then;* **jetzt** and **nun,** *now;* **nie,** *never;* **immer,** *always;* **schon,** *already;* **noch,** *still;* **erst,** *only* (in time expressions).

(a) **Dann** is more often an event in sequence than general past time:
Erst wägen, dann wagen, *first weigh the act, then risk it!*
Die Uhr schlug zwölf, dann kamen die ersten Kinder aus der Schule, *the clock struck twelve, and the first children appeared . . .*
    Damals is often used for *then*, in the sense *at that time:* **Vor zwanzig Jahren hatte ich einen Wagen; damals hatten wir noch Geld,** *we still had money then.*

(b) **Jetzt** is only temporal, **nun** has the force of the present as conditioned by the past and conditioning the future:
Jetzt schlägt die Uhr zwölf, nun kommt er nicht mehr, *the clock is striking twelve, he will not come now (after all this time).*
    Von jetzt an koche ich mein eigenes Mittagessen, *from now on . . .*
Von nun an kümmere ich mich nicht mehr um ihn, *from now on I shall stop bothering about him* (new resolution).
Zwischen jetzt (not **nun**) **und nächster Woche.** **Nun gut!** *all right then!* **Was nun?** *What now?* **Nun?** *Well?* **Nun, nun!** *Come, come!*

(c) **Nie** and **niemals** are forms for the opposite of **immer,** while **nimmer,** which seems so suitable in this meaning, is only used in a few set expressions, as **nie und nimmer!** *never! never more!*
Besser spät als nie, *better late than never.* **Er spart immer und hat doch nichts,** *he's always saving and (yet) has nothing.*
    Immer and **noch** reinforce each other, *v.* **noch.**

(d) **Schon** has a much wider use than the strictly temporal *already.* **Er ist schon gekommen,** *has already come,* but also: **Er kam schon am Dienstag,** *he was there as early as (already by) Tuesday.* **Schon der Anfang des Briefes ist genug,** *the beginning is quite enough (by itself).* **Schon das Gesicht ist komisch,** *his face is funny enough (without looking for anything else).* **Schon gut!** *all right!*
    Schon weakly asserts a positive content in argument, and often prepares to restrict such a statement, thus:
Hat er die Arbeit nicht gut verrichtet? **Schon, aber . . .** *Yes, but . . .*
    Thus it may, like **doch,** oppose a negative, though less forcefully:
Er hat nie richtig gearbeitet! **Doch!** *Oh yes, he did!* **Schon, aber . . .** *Well yes, he did, but . . .*

(e) **Noch,** *yet, still.* **Wir haben noch Geld, Zeit, Obst,** *some . . . left.* **Wir sind noch nicht am Ende,** *not yet.* **Noch kein Brief?** *No letter yet?*
    Like **schon** and **nun, noch** is used in time and other contexts where English has no word, or another: **Ich tue das noch heute,** *I will do that*

(*no later than*) *to-day.* **Zehn Pfund ist noch nicht genug,** *ten pounds is not* (*by itself*) *enough.* **Noch sein Vater trug einen Vollbart,** *his father* (*was still of the generation which*) *wore a beard.* **Noch eins,** *one more* (*for the road*). **Noch eine Tasse Tee?** *Another cup?*

Noch nicht, *not yet.* **Noch nie,** *never* (*yet*). **Ist er immer noch** (or **noch immer**) **nicht gekommen?** *Has he not come yet?*

(*f*) **Erst** is used for *only* in time statements: **Es ist erst 10 Uhr,** *only 10 o'clock;* and in both past and future contexts for *not before, not till:* **er kam erst vorige Woche,** *only came* (*did not come till*)*;* **er kommt erst nächste Woche,** *is only coming* (*will not be here till*).

Also with other time expressions: **erst dann aßen wir zu Mittag,** *it was only then that . . .;* **erst jetzt höre ich davon,** *I have only just heard of it.* Also with expressions not of time, but which occur in a time sequence: **Erst im Theater sah ich ihn wieder,** *it was not till I got to the theatre that . . .;* **ich habe erst** (or **nur, bloß**) **10 Seiten geschrieben,** *I have only written ten pages.*

Note.—Double forms. **Nie und nimmer!** *Never* (*again*)*!* **Jetzt oder nie!** *Now or never!* **Immer und ewig,** *for ever and a day.* **Dann und wann,** *now and then.*

(*g*) Prepositions governing adverbs.

The expressions for *before* and *after* past and present time are difficult in both languages; in German **dann** is not usually used here [cp. (*a*) above].

Before then: **vor jener Zeit; vorher.** *After then:* **nach jener Zeit; nachher, danach.**

Up till now: **bis jetzt.** *From now on:* **von jetzt (nun) an.**

The special sense *before now* is **schon einmal:**

Das ist leider schon einmal (in dieser Woche) passiert, *that has unfortunately happened before now* (*once before this week*).

Thus **vor** and **nach** are not used with adverbs of time, but only with expressions of time, *e.g.* **vor dem Mittagessen, nach Mitternacht.**

EXERCISE X

A. Translate into ENGLISH:

1. „Kleiner Mann, was nun?" ist der Titel eines guten Buches von Hans Fallada. 2. Zu Hause bei der Mutter gibt es immer eine gute, starke, süße Tasse indischen Tees. 3. Vier pechschwarze, muntre, kleine Negerkinder standen am Ufer und winkten mit roten Fähnchen. 4. Edler, neuer Wein in alten Flaschen war schon immer gefährlich.

5. Die Wiener Küche ist weltberühmt. In Wien bekommt man köstliche Torten und herrlich schmackhaftes ungarisches Gulasch. 6. ,,Londoner Polizisten sind einfach wunderbar", sagte ein reizendes amerikanisches Fräulein. 7. Erst jetzt ist dein vor zehn Tagen geschriebener Brief gekommen. 8. Hier hast du ein neues rosa Kleidchen für deine Puppe. Lila ist keine schöne Farbe für ein Püppchen mit dunklem Haar. 9. Ein neugereinigter brauner Anzug kam eben erst von der chemischen Reinigung. 10. Mehr braucht man nicht im Leben als schwarzes Brot, frisches Obst und funkelnden Wein. 11. Proverbs: Offne Hand, offnes Herz. Graue Augen, schlaue Augen. Frisch gewagt, ist halb gewonnen.

B. Translate into GERMAN:

1. Dark houses are never popular with good housewives. 2. Young girls sometimes write long letters on pink or mauve note-paper. 3. A lively little horse jumped over a low fence into the well-kept garden. 4. Strong black coffee, freshly made for each customer, is a speciality of many Viennese cafés. 5. I still have some (etwas) money, but from now on I am saving. 6. Twenty years ago I was only a young student at (in) Tübingen. 7. Your old brown suit is cleaned now and has already come from the shop. 8. Six young Hungarian dancers in [regional] costume danced through the open door on to the beautifully decorated stage. 9. Frankfurt sausages, well boiled, and new potatoes, freshly cooked, make a first-class meal for hungry boys. 10. His song was funny enough but his dance was still more-comical (komischer).

CHAPTER XI

52. Masculine and Neuter Mixed Nouns

(*a*) A few nouns have a strong singular [with genitive -(e)s], and a weak plural [ending -(e)n].

(1) Masculines: **der Dorn, Mast, Muskel, Nerv, Schmerz, See** (*lake*), **Staat** (political unit), **Strahl, Vetter.**

Plural: **die Dornen, Masten, Muskeln,** etc.

Note.—**der Ahn, Bauer** (*peasant*), **Nachbar,** vary between a strong and weak singular: **des Bauers** or **des Bauern,** etc.

Distinguish **der Bauer,** *peasant,* and **das Bauer,** *bird-cage;* **der Staat,** *state* (political), and **der Staat,** *state* (*finery,* no plural); **der See,** *lake,* and **die See,** *sea,* plural of both **die Seen.**

(2) Neuters: **das Auge, Bett, Ende, Hemd, Herz, Insekt, Interesse, Kleinod, Ohr.**

Note.—**das Kleinod, des Kleinods; die Kleinod*ie*n;**
das Herz, des Herze*ns*, dem Herze*n*, das Herz; die Herzen.

(*b*) Certain strong masculine nouns, ending in **-en** (*v.* § 24), have also, and even more commonly, a form in the nominative singular which has shed the **-n;** they therefore appear to be mixed, with a combination of weak and strong endings in the singular, and an apparently weak plural:

TABLE:	SINGULAR	PLURAL
Nom.	der Haufe(n)	die Haufen
Gen.	des Haufens	der Haufen
Dat.	dem Haufen	den Haufen
Acc.	den Haufen	die Haufen

Thus also: **der Friede, Funke, Gedanke, Glaube, Name, Same, Wille.**

Note.—**der Gefallen** is now never without **-n** in nominative singular, and thus belongs to § 24; **der Buchstabe** is always with **-e** in nominative singular. Distinguish **der Drache,** weak (**des Drachen, die Drachen**), *dragon;* **der Drachen,** strong (**des Drachens, die Drachen**), *kite, a "dragon"* (*human*).

53. Numerals (3). Cardinals to the Highest Numbers

hundert, *100;* **tausend,** *1,000;* **eine Million** (plural **-en**), *a million;* **eine Milliarde** (plural **-n**), *a milliard;* **eine Billion** (plural **-en**), *a billion.*

hundert(und)eins, *101;* **zweihundert(und)zwei,** *202;* **tausendzweiundzwanzig,** *1,022;* **zehntausend,** *10,000;* **siebenhundertausendsiebenhundert(und)-vierzig,** *700,740.*

(*a*) By rule, all numbers less than a million are compounded; they are, however, if written out at all, often broken at convenient points, thus (above) 700—740. The copula **und** is optional.

(*b*) **Ein** may precede the figure if the numeral is *one* followed by ciphers:

Etwa dreiviertel der rund einhunderttausend Studenten . . . haben . . . weniger als einhundert Mark im Monat zur Verfügung (newsp.), *about three-quarters of the rough total of 100,000 students (in Germany) have less than 100 DM a month at their disposal.*

And in compounds it may be necessary to prevent ambiguity:

eine Bombe . . ., zwei Tote . . . Einmetertiefe Löcher! (S. Andres), *holes a metre deep* (**metertief,** *several metres deep*).

(*c*) Numerals [except as noted in (*f*) below] are not a specific part of speech, and thus may have either adjectival or nominal function.

As adjectives they are plural in sense, but invariable in form, and have a small initial:

vierhundert Menschen; meine hundert Bäume; einige (= *some*) hundert- zehn Bücher; die vielen hundert Schulstunden.

Da liegen nun Franzosen, Engländer, Deutsche in der Nacht (= im Felde, *at the front*). **Von hunderttausend keine hundert ganz freiwillig** (S. Andres), *among 100,000 not a hundred volunteers.*

Von 165 000 Mädchen meldeten sich ganze vier! (newsp.), *no more than four girls volunteered (to be trained as air-hostesses).*

And in their collective sense may even take an ordinal:

die Umsiedlung der zweiten (plural) **300 000 Heimatvertriebenen** (newsp.), *the resettlement of the second 300,000 refugees.*

For **einige,** with numerals, *v.* § 102.

When the noun is understood, capitals may be used, but still without nominal inflection: **die oberen Zehntausend,** *the upper ten (of society).*

(*d*) **Hundert** and **tausend** become full nouns when:

(1) the numeral indicates a common unit of commerce:

(ein)hundert Zigaretten, but **ein Hundert Zigaretten,** *a box of 100.*

(2) or is followed by a noun in the partitive genitive:

Hunderte von Menschen (or alter Männer) waren auf dem Platz. **Tausende glänzender Lichter füllten den Saal.**

Note.—A very common mistake in newspapers is to confuse adjective and noun: **tausende Menschen, Tausende Lichter.**

(*e*) The round numerals from **eine Million** upwards, as also **die Null** (plural **Nullen**), *nought, the cipher,* and the collectives **das Paar** (plural **-e**), *pair,* and **das Dutzend** (plural **-e**), *dozen,* are genuine nouns: **Er ist eine Null,** *a cipher,* or **eine Niete,** from the sense *"non-winning" number* in a lottery.

(*f*) The years are normally as in English: **neunzehnhundertsechs-undfünfzig,** *1956;* but *1066* is **tausendsechsundsechzig.** The phrase *in 1956* is either **im Jahre** (abbreviated **i.J.**) **1956,** or the simple numeral used adverbially: **1789 begann die Französische Revolution,** but even this sentence would commonly be spoken as **Im Jahre . . .** Seasons are also sometimes used as uninflected adverbs: **Er ging Herbst 1933 ins Ausland** (= **im Herbst**), cp. § 59 (*b*).

54. Numerals (4). Cardinals as Nouns

Cardinals may be used as nouns, with the gender (as it happens, commonly feminine) of the noun understood.

(*a*) The figure itself (**die Zahl, Ziffer**): **eine römische Vier,** *a Roman four.* **Die Eins ist Anfang und Ende aller Dinge** (W. Andreas), *the figure one is the beginning and end of all things.* **Der große Zeiger der Kirchenuhr stand knapp vor der Drei** (H. Böll), *just before (the figure) three.*

(*b*) A (tram) route: (**die Linie, Straßenbahn**): **Die Acht ist eben angekommen.** *The No. 8 has just arrived.* But: **Ich nahm die Linie zwölf, stieg am Tuchhoffplatz in die Zehn und fuhr bis Endstation** (H. Böll).

(*c*) A (terminal) mark or report (**die Note**): **Clemens hat im Latein eine Zwei. Der Lehrer gab den Kindern eine Vier im Betragen,** *a four for behaviour.* (The scale in German schools is 1 to 5, or 1 to 6.)

(*d*) *A team* (**die Mannschaft**): **Die Mannschaft nützte die Verwirrung der gegnerischen Elf aus und schoß das ersehnte Tor,** *took advantage of the confusion of the opposing eleven and shot the much needed goal.*

(*e*) A measure, especially of beer, as in Bavaria: **eine Halbe Helles** (= **eine halbe Maß helles Bier; Maß** otherwise is neuter, *v.* Appendix A); but elsewhere one asks for **einen Halben,** or **ein Halbes** (= **Liter,** masculine or neuter).

(*f*) Personal ages, *v.* § 94 (*f*).

Note.—In some of the above groups, a numeral noun with ending **-er** occurs (*v.* § 94).

55. Numerals (5). Ordinals

(*a*) ADJECTIVES.—Tausend follows **hundert** (*v.* § 41) in forming its ordinal with **-st**:   **der hundertste Mann, jeder tausendste Soldat;** but **Million** varies: **der million(s)te Stern.**

Nächst, *next* [*v.* § 117 (*c*)], and **letzt,** *last,* may be regarded as ordinals.

(1) The ordinal **erst** has a capital letter when it stands for the first in rank rather than in a series:

> **Er war der erste, kam als erster,** *was the first (to come);*

but: **Er ist der Erste im Staat,** *the first person in the State.*

or the first of the month:

Vergangenen Ersten trat unsere neue Köchin ihre Arbeit an, *our new cook began work on the first of last month.*

(2) The ordinals *first, next,* and *last* when standing alone are in English exclusive, *i.e.* can indicate only one thing, e.g. *the first day.* In a more general sense they must be combined: *one of the first days.* German can use either the indefinite article or the plural in an indefinite sense here:

Es war ein erster Oktobertag des Jahres achtundvierzig (Th. Mann), *one of the first days of (an early day in) October . . .*

Thus also: **ein nächster Satz,** *one of the next few sentences;* **erst** is also often used in this manner for quality (*first class,* **erstklassig**):

eine Kochkünstlerin, die keinem Chef eines ersten Hotels nachsteht (F. Werfel), *an artist in cookery, not inferior to the chef of a leading hotel.*

Mamsell Jungmann (in *Buddenbrooks,* Th. Mann) could distinguish socially **haarscharf zwischen ersten und zweiten Kreisen,** and was proud to have grown grey **im Dienste der ersten Kreise,** *leading families of the town.*

With *last,* priority is not so keenly contested, thus: **ein letzter Kuß, letzte Abschiedsgrüße,** *a (one) last kiss, last (final) farewells;* but the adjective-noun **ein Letztes** (*v.* § 143) requires the firmer *one:* **Und jetzt nur noch ein Letztes, meine Herren!** *One last point, gentlemen!*

(*b*) ADVERBS.—The ordinal adverbs, *firstly, secondly,* etc., are formed by the addition of **-ens** to the ordinal stem: **erstens, zweitens, zwanzigstens.**

Note.—As in the English, this seldom survives far up the scale; an alternative in enumeration is to use **Punkt** with cardinals: *sixteenthly* (= point 16), **Punkt sechzehn.**

56. Order of Objects and Adverbs

(*a*) Direct and indirect objects of the verb (*v.* § 16).

(*b*) Adverbs:

(1) Of the same kind. Several adverbs, each of time, place, etc., are normally arranged in order from the more general to the more specific; this is often the reverse of the English order:

Wir fanden draußen im Garten unter einem Haselnußstrauch einen großen Frosch, *we found a large frog under a bush out in the garden . . .*

Wir fahren morgen um fünf Uhr, *at five o'clock to-morrow.*

(2) Of different kinds. The normal order is: time, manner, place:

Er fuhr gestern mit dem Schnellzug nach Berlin.

But particularly manner and place are liable to inversion:

Er hat heute auf der Straße laut gelacht.

Adverbs of cause, when present, commonly precede all others, and adverbs of result (purpose) usually follow.

Wir haben durch einen Zufall heute im Garten zu unserer großen Freude meinen goldenen Ring wieder gefunden.

Ich werde aus Pflichtgefühl morgen mit meinem Bruder nach London zur Beerdigung fahren.

(3) Several adverbs of the same kind, but not of different kinds, may precede the verb without breaking the second-position rule:

Draußen im Garten unter einem Haselnußstrauch fanden wir . . .

but: **Gestern fanden wir draußen . . .**

(*c*) Adverbs and Objects:

When both adverbial and objective elements are present:

(1) A direct noun object commonly follows adverbs:

Ich habe gestern für meine Eltern ein Haus gekauft.

Wir haben vor einigen Tagen im Büro einen netten Einfall gehabt.

while an indirect noun object or any pronoun object precedes:

Ich habe es gestern gekauft. Wir haben sie vor einigen Tagen auf der Straße getroffen, or **wir sind meiner Schwester . . . begegnet** [cp. § 44 (*b*) (2)].

But a prepositional phrase, whether it is regarded as objective or adverbial, and includes a pronoun or noun, follows adverbs and precedes a direct noun object: *v.* **für meine Eltern,** above, and:

Ich habe gestern für sie ein Haus gekauft, es gestern für sie gekauft.

(2) It follows that an indirect and direct noun object should "bracket" the adverbs:

Ich habe meiner Mutter gestern ein Buch gegeben.

Wir haben dem Vater vorgestern zu seinem Geburtstag eine goldene Uhr geschenkt.

But if the bracket becomes too long, adverbs are grouped before the noun objects:

Er hat heute in der Stadt zu meiner Überraschung einem armen Mann einen Schilling geschenkt.

(But with pronoun objects: **Er hat's ihm heute in der Stadt . . . geschenkt.**)

(*d*) General Principles:

The above rules are subject to many conflicting principles of style, rhythm and emphasis. Thus:

(1) Balance requires that a series of adjuncts should be lightened by placing one before the verb, thus [in (*b*) (2) above]: **Zu unserer großen Freude haben wir heute . . .; Morgen werde ich . . .;** and that parts of speech which are shorter and lighter [thus pronoun objects in (*c*) (1) above] should precede those which are heavier and longer.

(2) Sense often requires the leading position to be occupied by an element linking the statement to a preceding one:

Ein König im Osten hatte einen geliebten Sohn. Diesem Sohne sagte er einmal . . .

(3) Emphasis requires certain elements to stand either in front or in the end-position:

Eine goldene Uhr haben wir ihm geschenkt, *it was a gold watch which* . . .
Er fährt um fünf Uhr *heute,* *wir* **fahren um dieselbe Zeit morgen,** *he* . . . *to-day, we . . . to-morrow.*

Thus adverbs of degree, even though short, are often reserved for the end:

Schön war das Mädchen nicht. Ich liebe Erdbeeren mit Schlagsahne sehr.
Der Schifahrer läuft am Hang des Berges schneller.

The answer to a question is often given emphasis; thus the last statement above might be the answer to: **Warum läuft er am Hang, und nicht im Tal?** while the question **Wo läuft er schneller?** would require: **Der Schifahrer läuft schneller am Hang des Berges** (or: **Am Hang des Berges läuft er schneller**).

EXERCISE XI

A. Translate into ENGLISH:

1. Die silbergrauen Möwen flogen um die Masten des Schiffs auf hoher See. 2. Eine Vier und eine Zwölf bogen um die Ecke; ich stieg in die Vier und fuhr bis Endstation. 3. Ich habe gekauft: erstens hundert Zigaretten, zweitens ein Dutzend Schachteln Streichhölzer,

drittens und letztens zwei Aschenbecher. 4. Unsere Elf hat dieses Jahr unerwartet (degree adverb) gut gespielt. 5. Die Frau des Nachbarn fordert von ihrem Mann den ganzen Lohn. 6. Das ist auch ihr gutes Recht; er säuft furchtbar. 7. Er gab seiner Frau eine kürzlich gekaufte, schön gearbeitete Briefmappe aus dunkelgegerbtem Schweinsleder. 8. Vierhundert von meinen Bäumen sind durch den Frost zugrunde gegangen. 9. Die Jahreszahl am steinernen Torbogen ist kaum noch sichtbar; ich sehe eine Vier und eine Null, aber nichts mehr. 10. Herr Wirt! Ein Glas eisgekühlten Wein mit frischgebackenem Schwarzbrot! 11. Proverbs: Keine Rosen ohne Dornen. Ende gut, alles gut. Herz und Hand kommt durch das ganze Land. Kein Funken ohne Feuer.

B. Translate into GERMAN:

1. The food of the German peasant is still very simple; he eats rye bread, a pile of (von) potatoes and vegetables. 2. Sometimes he takes firstly meat or sausage, secondly cheese, thirdly eggs. 3. The muscles of the heart are very strong. 4. Hundreds and even thousands of birds reach our island in the third or fourth month of the year. 5. We got into the 115; a dozen people were already in the bus. 6. The business of my German cousin is full of interest; he has a toy factory and he sells hundreds of toys every month, and thousands every year. 7. The peace of Westphalia did not come unexpectedly. 8. Great ships with tall masts navigate the lakes of North America. 9. A is the first letter of the alphabet and Z is the last. The letter V can also be a Roman five. 10. London has eight million inhabitants.

CHAPTER XII

EXPRESSIONS OF TIME

57. Nouns of Units of Time

(a) The day and its divisions:

Almost all expressions for days or parts of the day are masculine, since they are largely either compounded with or presuppose **der Tag** (*v.* § 439, and dates § 41):

Der Vormittag (Morgen), Mittag, Nachmittag, Abend, but **die Nacht** and **die Mitternacht;** *morning, noon, afternoon, evening, night, midnight.*

Der Wochentag, Arbeitstag, Feierabend, Feiertag, Ruhetag, freie Tag, but **die Woche;** *weekday, working day, free evening after work, holiday, rest day, day off, week.*

Der Sonntag, Montag, Dienstag, Mittwoch, Donnerstag, Freitag, Samstag (Rhineland and South), **Sonnabend** (Central Germany and North); *Sunday, Monday,* etc.

Meals are mainly formed from compounds of **das Essen,** *meal,* and are all neuter: **das Frühstück, Mittagessen, Abendessen,** *breakfast, midday meal, evening meal.* **Der Tee** may be used by extension for the tea meal (**Wir nehmen den Tee um vier Uhr**), usually, however, it is **der Kaffee** (Austrian: **die Jause**). The names of the meals are not, as in England (lunch, dinner) socially differentiated, but **das (einfache) Abendbrot** is used (with the very faintest moral note) for a less substantial evening meal. **Das zweite Frühstück** is sometimes used for a mid-morning snack, rather more substantial than "elevenses" (cp. Austrian **das Gabelfrühstück**).

(b) The year and its divisions:

Again, most of these are masculine, the months because **der Monat** is understood; but all compounds of **das Jahr** are (*v.* § 7) neuter. **Der Mónat, die Mónate** (N.B.—accent). They are (with abbreviation in brackets): **der Januar (Jan.), Februar (Febr.), März, April, Mai, Juni, Juli, August (Aug.), September (Sept.), Oktober (Okt.), November (Nov.), Dezember (Dez.).**

Distinguish **Augúst,** the month, and **Áugust** the Christian name.

Die Jahreszeit, *season.* They are: **Der Frühling, Sommer, Herbst, Winter.**

Das Jahr, Vierteljahr, Schuljahr, Schaltjahr, *year, quarter, school-year, leap-year.*

Das Jahrzéhnt, *decade,* **Jahrhúndert,** *century;* and even beyond: **das Jahrtáusend,** *thousand years, millenium,* and **Jahrzéhntausend,** etc.

(c) Grammatical use of days, months, seasons:

When these are subject or object of a verb (and in many adverbial phrases, v. below), the definite article:

(1) may be used with the names of days;

(2) is usually taken by the names of months and seasons;

(3) is always taken by common nouns indicating other divisions of time, that is, within the limits of the use of the article in general (v. later chapters).

(Der) Montag ist für mich immer ein schlimmer Tag; dagegen freue ich mich immer auf (den) Samstag.

Der Januar war schön und trocken, dagegen hatten wir einen sehr regnerischen Februar.

Dieses Jahr habe ich den August frei, *I have August free.*

Die weitaus beste Jahreszeit ist der Frühling, *by far the best* . . .

Der Abend kommt mit leisem Schritt, *comes soft-paced.*

Apart from dates, where it is never used (**am 1. Januar,** v. § 41), the genitive -(e)s is falling into disuse with the names of months, but is still commoner with the "long" months than with the others: **in den ersten Tagen des Juni, März, Dezember(s).** With these latter it is still used in emphatic contexts: **die schweren trüben Nebeltage des Novembers.** Also sometimes omitted, though this is still considered incorrect, with the days: **in den späten Nachmittagsstunden des Mittwoch.**

(d) Feasts:

The following feasts were originally dative plural: **Weihnachten,** *Christmas;* **Ostern,** *Easter;* **Pfingsten,** *Whitsun.* They have now taken neuter gender by analogy (with **das Osterfest,** etc.), or are sometimes treated as feminine plural, and from this latter the new short singular feminine form **die Weihnacht** has been created. Otherwise the short form only occurs in compounds: **das Pfingstfest, Ostermontag, ein Weihnachtsgeschenk.**

Weihnachten ist da. Ostern fällt dieses Jahr früh. Zu or an Ostern, Weihnachten, Pfingsten.

das Fest der Freude, das grünende, blühende, jauchzende, jubilierende Pfingsten (W. Raabe), *Whitsun, feast of joy* . . .

„Langweilige Ostern waren das bei uns", klagte sie (F. Werfel), *we had a very boring Easter.*

In everyday use, the compounds are invaluable: (1) for wishes: **ich wünsche ein gesegnetes Osterfest, fröhliche Weihnachtsferien;** (2) in reference to the actual days: **Weihnachtsabend gingen wir heim. Am**

ersten (zweiten) Weihnachtstag, *on Christmas* (*Boxing*) *Day.* **Am zweiten Osterfeiertag,** *on Easter Monday.*

58. Adverbial Phrases of Time

The translation into German of adverbial phrases expressing time sometimes causes difficulty. As a general rule it may be said:

(*a*) Definite time, *i.e.* "time when" and "time how long" are translated by a noun in the accusative, or a prepositional phrase:

(1) Time when:

er kam voriges Jahr, diesen Morgen; er kommt nächsten Sommer; er geht jeden (*every*) **Abend ins Kino; er ging schon den Abend vorher** (*the evening before*).

Prepositions: compare the following with English usage:

um for point-time: **er kam um Mittag (Mitternacht),** *at;*

an for shorter divisions and masculine words: **er kommt am Abend, am Tag, am Dienstag,** *in, on;*

in for larger divisions and feminine words: **er kam in der Nacht, in der Woche, im Monat Mai, im Winter, im Jahre 1954,** *in.*

(2) Time how long:

er blieb eine Stunde, einen Tag, zwei Monate.

Prepositions:

Er kam auf (*for,* prospective) **zwei Tage, und blieb für** (*for,* completed) **ganze zwei Monate** (or, less conversational: **blieb zwei Monate,** acc.).

For the omission of the definite article in expressions of definite time *v.* § 59 below.

Note the following idioms:

The ***other*** *day* (*week*) is **vor einigen Tagen (Wochen). Den (am) *anderen* Tag** is (*on*) *the next day,* as is also **den (am) nächsten Tag. *Last* month** is ***vorigen* Monat, letzt** being only used for the last of a series (*v.* **ander-** in § 105).

Morgen (Dienstag) über acht Tage, in acht Tagen, *to-morrow* (*Tuesday*) *week;* **heute in einem Monat, in zwei Jahren,** *to-day month, two years from to-day.*

Gestern (Montag) vor acht Tagen, *a week* (*ago*) *to-morrow* (*on Monday*).

Every Tuesday (*summer*) may be **jeden Dienstag (Sommer),** but *every March* is **Jedes Jahr im März,** as also *every 13th October,* **Jedes Jahr am 13. Oktober.**

(*b*) Indefinite time, *i.e.* "sometime when" and "time how often", and a few expressions of relative time, are translated by a noun in the genitive or a prepositional phrase:

(1) Sometime when:

The genitive is common after **ein** in shorter divisions: **eines Morgens, Tages, Montags,** *one morning, day, Monday,* and also in the expressions: **dieser Tage,** *recently,* **jederzeit,** *at any time.*

Prepositional uses are analogous to those for definite time: **an einem Tag,** *one day;* but **in einer Nacht, in einem Jahr,** or **einmal in der Nacht, im Sommer,** *one night, year, summer.*

(2) Time how often:

mittags, abends, tags, *at midday, in the evening, by day;* also **des Tages,** and, by false analogy with these masculine forms, **nachts,** or even **des Nachts,** *by night.*

dienstags, *on Tuesdays,* and sometimes **sommers (winters),** *in the summer (winter),* but for the other two seasons only prepositions: **im Frühling, Herbst.**

Prepositional uses are as for "definite time when".

(3) Relative time:

There are a few expressions in the genitive: **ander(e)n Tag(e)s, anderntags** (or **tags darauf**), *next day;* **anfangs,** *at the beginning (of)* [*v.* § 59 (*b*)]; **letzten Endes,** *in the last resort;* **mittlerweile,** *meanwhile;* but also with prepositions: **am nächsten Tag, den Tag darauf.**

59. Adverbs of Time

(*a*) Many expressions of time were originally nouns, and have become widely used in adverbial phrases, or even as adverbs by themselves. As nouns they require a capital and inflection, as adverbs a small letter and need not be inflected. This causes some uncertainty.

(1) Primary adverbs always have small initial: **heute,** *to-day;* **morgen,** *to-morrow;* **gestern,** *yesterday;* and in association with nouns of divisions of time they cause the latter to become adverbial, with small initial: **heute abend,** *this evening;* **morgen nachmittag,** *to-morrow afternoon.*

Note.—*Last night* is either **gestern abend** (*evening*), or **gestern nacht (in der Nacht)** (*after bedtime*). *To-morrow morning* is **morgen früh** or **morgen vormittag.**

Similarly, even when alone, nouns of division of time become adverbs when used in the genitive: **abends, tags, nachts.**

(2) Divisions of the day when associated with other adverbs are uninflected, as **Mittwoch abend** [and **gestern vormittag,** as in (1)], or

inflected with times and dates, as **um sieben Uhr abends, am 10. Oktober nachmittags.**

(3) Names of days, when associated with parts of the day, retain the capital for the uninflected form: **Sonntag nachmittags** (one or several occasions), but shed it when inflected: **sonntags nachmittags** (an indefinite, and usually repeated occasion).

Note.—In general, the short genitive forms suffer from lack of clarity, thus **er kam abends** means both *in the evening* (once), *i.e.* **am Abend,** and *of an evening* (repeated), *i.e.* **des Abends.**

(*b*) Certain nouns become adverbs while retaining their capitals:

(1) Days of the week: **Ich werde Sonntag (abends) verreisen.**

Seasons: **Sommer 1919 kam er endlich nach Hause. Herbst letzten Jahres fuhr er ins Ausland** (often spoken: **im Sommer,** etc.).

But *not* the months: **Er macht sein Examen erst im Juni.**

(2) The nouns **der Anfang, die Mitte, das Ende;** and in their company even months may shed their article. Thus **Anfang August** [= **am Anfang des (Monats) August], Mitte März, Ende Februar.**

Note.—Sometimes **Anfangs** (or **anfangs**) and **Ausgangs** (**Juli,** etc.) are found, especially with seasons: **Ausgangs des Sommers = am Ende des Sommers.**

(3) The nouns **der Schlag, der Punkt,** for point-time, *on the stroke of, on the dot:* **Punkt sieben Uhr; Schlag Mitternacht.** Cp. also **pünktlich um** (*punctually at*). Radio: **Beim Gongschlag ist es zehn Uhr fünfzehn.**

(*c*) Order of Adverbs of time [cp. § 56 (*b*) (1)].

General before specific: **Er verreist nächsten Montag um 10 Uhr abends** (also: **abends um 10 Uhr**), *he is leaving at 10 p.m. next Monday.*

Exercise XII

A. Translate into English:

1. Sonntags gleich nach dem Frühstück machen wir gewöhnlich einen Ausflug aufs Land und kommen erst zum Abendessen nach Hause. 2. Jeden Sonnabend im Winter gehe ich zum Fußballspiel. 3. Am 21. März ist Frühlingsanfang; von jenem Zeitpunkt an wird das Wetter besser. 4. Jedes Jahr, Ende August und im September, verlassen viele Tausende von Singvögeln unser Land und ziehen nach dem Süden. 5. Der Montag ist im allgemeinen Waschtag—also kein Ruhetag für die Hausfrau. Zum Mittagessen gibt es dann kalten Braten und geröstete Kartoffeln. 6. Vorigen Mittwoch um sechs Uhr abends hatten wir ein

schweres Gewitter. Gottseidank war es nicht nachts. 7. Vor einigen
Monaten, kurz vor Weihnachten, besuchte mich mein Vetter auf vierzehn
Tage. 8. Eines Tages—vielleicht sogar schon nächstes Jahr—besuche
ich ihn in seiner Heimat in Süddeutschland. 9. Zu Pfingsten fahren wir
an die Ostsee. 10. Proverbs: Heißer Sommer, guter Wein. Es ist nicht
alle Tage Sonntag. Maxim: Tages Arbeit, / Abends Gäste, / Saure
Wochen, / Frohe Feste (Goethe).

B. Translate into GERMAN:

1. Christmas is the children's feast. On Christmas Eve they have
(get) many presents and a Christmas tree with candles, nuts and apples.
2. At noon the other day the telephone rang for a long time (= long)
and I did not answer. 3. She visited her mother every Wednesday
afternoon at tea-time. It was her day off. 4. Last Friday was Monika's
birthday. The next day she went to (= into) the opera and heard
"Lohengrin". 5. I water the flowers once a day in the summer, especially
in the dry month [of] August. 6. It did not rain [for] two months last
spring. 7. Last night I found an exciting detective story and I read till
midnight. 8. At the beginning of October the leaves turn (= become)
yellow and brown. It is autumn. 9. Monday week is a holiday. It is
the Monday after Easter. 10. This evening I am visiting my parents.
They are expecting me punctually at eight o'clock.

CHAPTER XIII

60. Indefinite Pronouns (1). Persons

Certain words such as "someone", "everyone", "something", "nothing" are pronouns, since they refer to persons or things, but are indefinite compared with *e.g.* the personal pronouns, since they do not specify the person or object of reference. Those relating to persons are: **man, jemand, niemand, jedermann,** and sometimes **manchermann.**

(*a*) **Man,** the most indefinite personal pronoun (cp. §§ 8, 14).

Man geht nach Hause. *People* (*they*) *are going home. The party is breaking up.*

Das macht einem viel Freude. *One likes to see that. That gives one* (*everyone, us all*) *real pleasure.*

In the nominative, **einer** may also be used:

„**Nun seh' mal einer diesen Krischen Buddenbrook!**" **sagte Konsul Döhlmann mit seiner breiten Aussprache** (Th. Mann), *now look at . . .* (pres. subj.).

(*b*) **Jemand,** *someone.*

Usually inflected as the definite article, but dative and accusative are also found uninflected:

> **jemand, jemand(e)s, jemand(em), jemand(en).**
> **Ich gab jemandem meinen Hut und trat in den Saal.**

in einem Variété-Theater, wo . . . ein Zauberkünstler jemandes goldene Uhr in einem Mörser zerstampfte (Th. Mann), *pounded up someone's gold watch in a mortar.*

Also as a noun:

Ich blieb stehen und drehte mich um. Der Jemand hinter mir blieb auch stehen (F. Werfel), *whoever it was behind me . . .*

And to a child or friend, in a rather coy tone:

Ein gewisser Jemand wollte die Suppe nicht essen, *someone didn't want to finish his soup.*

When followed by an adjective or other limiting word:

(1) **Jemand** may be declined or not, and **ander-** may be a neuter invariable (**anders**), or inflected as a strong masculine (**anderer,** etc.); and any combination may occur:

jemand anders (anderer)	no genitive.
jemand(-em) anders (anderem)	**jemand(-en) anders (anderen)**

the masculine endings standing for both masculine and feminine sense.

(2) The neuter ending of **anders** has, by incorrect analogy, become the rule and the practice with other adjectives:

Die Leute sahen alle vor sich hin . . . Nur wenn jemand Frisches sich an die Reihe der andern anstellte . . . (H. Fallada), *only when someone new joined the queue . . .*

But there is also a general tendency to inflect masculine:

Wir sollen ihm also jemand Vertrauenswürdigen empfehlen (H. Fallada), *someone who inspires confidence.*

die Einrichtung (= ein Telephon-Apparat) war für stehendes Sprechen gedacht und zwar für jemand ganz überaus Kleinen, nämlich für E.P.s Mutter (H. v. Doderer), *for someone quite small . . .*

Irgend (indecl.) may be prefixed to **jemand** [and to **etwas**, *v.* § 61 (*a*)], to emphasise its indefiniteness, *someone* (*or other*):

Wer hat geklopft? Irgend jemand, ein Hausierer . . . *Someone* (*or other*), *a hawker* (*I think*).

Irgend jemand may be replaced by:

(1) **irgend einer (irgendeiner)** or **einer**:

Hat irgend einer unter euch einen Bleistift? *Has anyone of you . . .?*
Weiß denn einer, was mit ihm los ist? *Does anyone know . . .?*
Ich versteh' alles, ich kann 'nen Geldschrank knacken mit 'nem Schneidbrenner, wie nur einer (H. Fallada). *I can crack a safe with anyone.*

(2) **irgendwer** or **wer**, both colloquial:

Den hat wer in die Pfanne gehauen. Der schiebt Arrest (H. Fallada), *he's been split on by somebody; he's under arrest.*
Wie könnte ich in meiner Situation ein seriöses Urteil über irgendwen oder irgendwas fällen? (F. Werfel), *a serious judgment on anyone or anything?*

Somebody when emphasised (= somebody important) may be:

(1) **wer**, as above:

Es hat seinen Stolz für immer geknickt, die Einbildung, er wäre wer (H. Fallada), *his idea that he was somebody.*

(2) **wunder was (wunderwas)**:

Er hält sich für wunderwas, *he thinks himself no end of a chap.*

(*c*) **Niemand**, *no one.*

Inflected as **jemand**: **niemand, niemand(e)s, niemand(em), niemand(en)**.
Niemand sagt mir ein Wörtchen Wahrheit, *no one tells me a word of truth.*
S. war unbestechlich, er hatte zwar Feinde, war aber selbst niemandes Feind (H. Böll), *the enemy of no one.*

(d) **Jedermann,** *everyone.*

Jedermann kauft Geschenke zu Weihnachten, *everyone buys presents at Christmas.*

Only the genitive is inflected:

war ich denn nicht längst weit genug entfernt vom Leben jedermanns, vom Dasein und Denken der Normalen? (H. Hesse), *far enough removed from the life of everyone?*

61. Indefinite Pronouns (2). Things

(a) **Etwas,** *something;* abbreviated, **was.**

Wünschen Sie etwas, mein Herr? *Would you like something, sir?*

Ist heute was mit der Post gekommen? *Has anything come with the post?*

As with **jemand, irgend** may be prefixed to emphasise indefiniteness (*v.* examples there and):

Er murmelte irgend etwas durch die Zähne und schloß die Tür, *mumbled something or other and . . .*

Indefiniteness may assume other shades of meaning:

(1) Concessive: **was immer.**

Und Sie glauben . . . daß eine Menschheit zu was immer gelangen kann, die ihr Herz an den Augenblick hängt? (H. Risse), *can achieve anything?*

(2) Grudging:

Das ist doch wenigstens etwas! *that's something at least!*

(3) An unspecified thing:

Aus der Sache wird schon etwas, *something (good) will come out of it, develop from it.*

Haben Sie etwas für Halsschmerzen? *can you give me something (a remedy) for a sore throat?*

Etwas may be further qualified in various senses:

(1) Descriptive, by a following neuter adjectival noun:

Steht etwas Interessantes in der Zeitung heute? [*v.* § 147 (*b*)].

(2) Partitive, commonly **etwas an** [*v.* **an,** § 487 (*e*)].

Bei jeder solchen Erschütterung meines Lebens hatte ich am Ende irgend etwas gewonnen, das war nicht zu leugnen, etwas an Freiheit, an Geist, an Tiefe (H. Hesse), *gained something in freedom . . .*

(3) Comparative, commonly **etwas wie,** *something of . . .*

Er ist so etwas wie ein Zigeuner (so'n halber Künstler), *he's something of (a bit of) a gipsy (an artist).*

Note.—**Etwas** may also be used as an adjective (**etwas Milch, Zucker**), or a degree adverb (**die Milch ist etwas sauer**). Cp. also the Quantitatives, Chapter XXI.

(*b*) **Nichts,** *nothing.*

Nichts may be qualified rather like **etwas**:

Es ist heute nichts (nichts Interessantes, descriptive; **nichts von Bedeutung,** partitive) **mit der Post gekommen.**

Comparative: **Ich brauche sonst nichts als Abspannung,** *nothing but* (*only*) *relaxation.*

Compare also:

Sein Verhalten war nichts anders als frech, *could only be described as impudent.*

Diese Mitteilung wirkte geradezu wie das Platzen einer Bombe, *was nothing less than a bombshell.*

Der D-Zug ist lange (bei weitem) nicht so bequem wie der F-T-Wagen (Ferntriebwagen), *the normal express is far less convenient than the express Diesel railcar.*

Note.—**Nichts weniger als** implies a negative comparison, i.e. *anything but* rather than *nothing less than*: **Die Wäsche ist nichts weniger als billig** = **die Wäsche war teuer.**

62. Indefinite Pronouns (3). General Notes

(*a*) All these pronouns have **sein** as possessive adjective:

Man tut sein Bestes, *one does one's best.*

Jedermann kauft seine Geschenke erst einige Tage vor Weihnachten, *people buy their presents . . .*

Niemand sagte seine Meinung, *no one ventured an opinion.*

(*b*) Negative statements. English statements negating a positive, as *not any* (*some*) *thing*, *not any* (*some*) *one* should be translated by a negative pronoun rather than a positive pronoun negated:

Haben Sie nichts (niemand) gesehen? *Didn't you see anything (anyone)?*
Man schaut doch nichts Langweiliges jeden Tag ein paar Stunden an? (S. Andres). *One surely doesn't look at boring things for hours a day?*

Cp. § 82, **keiner.**

(*c*) Intensifying the positive. **Irgend** is used [cp. above 60 (*b*), 61 (*a*)] as an adjunct, to intensify any pronoun of indefinite (**jemand, etwas**) or general (**was, wer**) reference, or any pronominal compound (**wohin,**

woher, etc.).   It is sometimes used as a degree adverb (of manner) in the sense of **irgendwie:**

diese Augen schienen schon alles irgend erdenkliche Leid gelitten zu haben (H. Hesse), *seemed to have experienced all suffering that could possibly be imagined.*

(*d*) Intensifying the negative.   **Gar** with negative pronouns corresponds to **irgend** in the positive: **gar nichts (niemand),** cp. **gar nicht (gar kein);** all these combinations except **gar niemand** are also found compounded: **garnichts.**   Also **absolut, ganz und gar, überhaupt nichts,** etc.

Note.—**Jedermann** is less commonly intensified, *e.g.* **einfach jedermann.** Neither **irgend** nor **gar** may be used.

63. The Simple Dependent Infinitive (1).   Future Tense and Modal Verbs

(*a*) The simple dependent infinitive is used in German, (1) to form the future tense, and (2) after certain verbs called "modal auxiliaries".

(*b*) The future tense is formed from:

(1) The present tense of **werden** (normally = *to become*), *v.* § 15.

(2) The infinitive of the verb:

Ich werde kommen, du wirst gehen, er wird singen, *I shall come,* etc.

For the use of the future tense *v.* § 68.

Similarly, the future perfect is formed from the present of **werden,** and the "perfect infinitive", *i.e.* the infinitive auxiliary **sein** or **haben** and the past participle of the verb:

Ich werde gekommen sein, er wird gesungen haben, *I shall have come,* etc. **Er hat 10 Seiten gelesen, wird 10 Seiten gelesen haben,** *will have . . .*

Note.—The future and future perfect also render the corresponding English progressive forms: I shall be coming . . ., he will have been reading . . .

(*c*) The simple dependent infinitive is used after certain other verbs, of which the commonest are the "modal verbs" (also "modal auxiliaries", "auxiliaries of mood", as distinct from the "auxiliaries of tense", **haben** and **sein**).

These six verbs form a group, in that:

(1) They all express a certain mood or attitude rather than a specific interior or exterior state or action.   They are:

VERB	IDEA	SENSE	KEY WORD
dürfen	permission	*to be allowed to*	*may/might*
können	capability (possibility)	*to be able to*	*can/could*
mögen	inclination (possibility)	*to like to*	*may/might*
müssen	necessity	*to have to*	*must*
sollen	obligation	*to be expected to*	*shall/should/ought*
wollen	volition	*to want (wish) to*	*will/would*

Many shades of meaning are expressed by these verbs, both in English and German, and familiarity can only be acquired gradually. For further uses *v.* §§ 476-9. Note in the English forms the lack of correspondence between the modal "key word" (*can*, etc.) and the infinitive form (*to be able*, etc.). German is here more regular.

(2) Their conjugation (and like them that of **wissen,** *to know*) is in some respects different from that of the normal strong or weak verb.

(*d*) The simple dependent infinitive, whether in the future tense or after the modal verbs, always stands at the end of the sentence:

Ich werde morgen mit meinem Vater ins Theater gehen.

Wir müssen von dem uns geschenkten Gelde auch unserem Bruder seinen Teil geben, *we (shall) have to give . . .*

And in the future of the modal verbs the modal infinitive follows its dependent infinitive:

Wir werden . . . auch unserem Bruder seinen Teil geben müssen.

64. Present Tense and Use of Modal Verbs

(*a*) The present tense of modal verbs is:

(1) like a strong past tense, in that the first and third persons singular are the same, but

(2) different from the present-day form of the past strong tense in that there is one vowel for the singular, another for the plural.

TABLE: **dürfen,** *to be allowed.*

Singular: **ich darf, du darfst, er (sie, es) darf,** *I may,* etc.

Plural: **wir dürfen, ihr dürft, Sie dürfen, sie dürfen,** *we may,* etc.

Similarly: **kann/können,   mag/mögen,   muß/müssen,   soll/sollen, will/wollen,** and **weiß/wissen.**

(*b*) The addition of **nicht** may with **müssen,** and sometimes with **sollen,** either negate or only modify the sense, thus:

ich muß nicht gehen = *I must not go* (negative command) or *I do not have to go* (absence of compulsion).

(c) The dependent infinitive may be replaced by:

(1) **Es,** standing for its sense content:

Können Sie schwimmen? Nein, ich kann es (or **das**) **nicht.**

(2) A noun or pronoun object:

Können Sie Spanisch? Ja, ich kann Spanisch (or **es, das**).

or (3) it may be omitted; thus the first example could be continued:

Aber man kann, wenn man will, *one can* (*do something*) *if one wants.*
or: **Aber man muß können,** *but one has to be able* (*to do such things*).
Muß ich das tun? Sie müssen nicht, aber Sie können (es), *you do not have
to* [cp. (*b*)], *but you can* (*if you like*).

Exercise XIII

A. Translate into English:

1. Soll man jemand anders mit den Kindern schicken? Hans ist zu
jung. 2. Was kann dieses rote Signal auf dem Berg bedeuten? Vielleicht
irgend ein Unglück? Es mag wohl sein. 3. Man darf nicht ohne
Führer ins hohe Gebirge gehen, denn das ist etwas sehr Gefährliches.
4. Heute will mir niemand im Garten helfen; so etwas kann man bei
dieser Hitze kaum erwarten. 5. Der Vater schreibt an seinem Buch und
nichts darf ihn stören. Also Ruhe, Kinder! 6. Ich werde in diesen
Tagen gar niemanden einladen, denn er soll ruhig arbeiten können.
7. Im Winter werde ich tüchtig heizen müssen in diesem kalten Haus,
sonst frieren wir. 8. Dürfen wir rauchen? Nein, nur im Raucherabteil.
9. „Nein, meine Suppe mag ich nicht!" rief der schlimme kleine Junge.
Seine Mutter wird böse sein. 10. Wir können nicht alles wissen, sagte
irgend jemand, müssen aber doch fleißig lernen. 11. „Sechs Wörter
nehmen mich in Anspruch jeden Tag: / Ich soll, ich muß, ich kann, ich
will, ich darf, ich mag." (Friedrich Rückert.) 12. Kein Mensch muß
müssen (Lessing).

B. Translate into German:

1. Someone or other must help me with the gardening. 2. One does
one's best, but one can't do everything alone. 3. They will go home in
their car, and they will go (**fahren**) through the Black Forest. 4. You are
not to read that book. 5. I don't like any (**kein-**) milk and sugar in my
tea. 6. Everyone wants to learn a foreign-language. 7. Do you want to
telephone [*to*] him before or after supper? 8. Is there anything new in
that book? 9. You will have heard the news. 10. We may not visit
anyone (use negative pronoun) at the hospital before 3 p.m.

CHAPTER XIV

65. Demonstratives (2). Der, die, das

(*a*) The definite article was originally equivalent to a light demonstrative: **das** Haus, *the house* = *this one, the one of which I am speaking.* This use is now uncommon, since other demonstrative forms (as **dieser, jener,** etc., *v.* § 32) are more convenient. It still occurs, however, if the definite article is accented, sometimes with the noun placed in a position of emphasis (*v.* § 50). The emphasis is shown in print by spacing the article, and in speech by lengthening the vowel in some forms (**dēm, dēn, dēr**):

D a s Haus interessiert mich gar nicht! *that house doesn't interest me at all* (to an estate agent).

D e m Jungen gebe ich nichts, *I won't give anything to that boy.*

The demonstrative force may, however, be in the sense, and need no emphasis:

Ich habe die Nacht kein Auge zugemacht (E. Kästner), *I didn't close an eye all (last) night* (**die Nacht** is adverbial accusative).

(*b*) The pronominal form is much commoner; standing alone it is clearly demonstrative in force and is less often marked by spacing.

(1) Masculine and feminine: **Die hat Glück gehabt!** *She's lucky.* **Dem geht's gut!** *He's all right!*

„**Der?**" **sagte der Knecht verächtlich** . . . „**Der hört nichts. Der ist taub wie ein Stock. Vor dem könnt ihr alles sagen**" (E. Langgässer), *Him? He . . . He's . . . In front of him . . .*

Der may replace **dieser** [*v.* § 32 (*c*)] in the sense *the latter*:

Er hatte kein Wort gesagt, das ein Mensch dem anderen zu sagen hat, wenn der seine Mutter verliert (H. Risse), *not a word of what a man should say to another when he (the latter) loses his mother.*

(2) Neuter forms are much used to refer collectively to things or persons, irrespective of number or gender [cp. § 32 (*b*)]:

Wer ist die Dame in der Ecke? Das (*that, she*) **ist meine Tante.**

Das war eine Szene! Dem konnte man kaum in Ruhe zusehen! *That was a scene! One could hardly look on calmly.*

Nichts als Tränen, Vorwürfe und Beschwerden! Das ist nun schon seit sieben Tagen so. *It's been the same for . . .*

(3) The neuter pronominal is commonly combined with **alles** in a variety of forms: **das alles, alles das, alldas, dem allem, alldem,** etc.:

Das alles kenne ich Takt für Takt (F. Werfel), *I know the whole thing*
(i.e. *an opera*).

Ich hörte alldem nur mit halbem Ohre zu (Th. Mann), *I listened to all this*
with only half my attention.

(*c*) The comments in (*b*) apply to those forms in which the demonstrative force of the pronominal is shown only by stress, with or without vowel lengthening. In five cases, however, emphasis has caused a lengthened form to develop:

(1) Dative plural: **denen.**

Denen muß man immer die Wahrheit sagen! *Those people must always be*
told the frank truth!

Hat einer von denen allen uns nur ein freundliches Wort gesagt? *Has one*
of the lot of them ever given us a friendly word?

(2) The four genitive cases are:

Masculine: **dessen.** Feminine: **deren.** Neuter: **dessen.** Plural: **deren.**
Deren Vater war ein ausgedienter General, *her father was a retired general.*
Ich bin dessen ganz sicher, *I am quite sure of that.*

(*d*) The above examples show this demonstrative to be fairly indeterminate in its reference, in respect of the demonstrated thing (person or object), or the demonstrated place (this one here, that one there).

This is seen in the genitive, where there are two broad uses:

(1) The isolated pronominal, with adjectives and verbs governing the genitive [*v.* § 195 (*a*)], where **dessen** stands for little more than the unused genitive of **es,** *v.* example with **sicher** above.

(2) The pronominal preceding a noun, *v.* **deren Vater,** above. Here the genitive not only emphasises, like the other cases, but also, and more importantly, refers back to a person just mentioned; thus:

Des Mannes erinnere ich mich; dessen Vater hat niemals Mangel an Geld gehabt, *I remember the* (*that*) *man; his father* (not *of that father*) *was never short of money.*

Thus as **dessen** in (1) comes to be used for the genitive of **es,** so **dessen,** etc., in (2) comes to be used for the genitive of the personal pronouns, and even to replace the possessive adjectives (*his, her,* etc.). Grammarians have prevented the indiscriminate use of the genitive demonstrative for the possessive adjective, and restrict it to the genuine demonstrative force of *the latter*:

Not: **Die Schmidts und deren Kinder waren auch da,** *Smiths and their children,* but: **Die Schmidts und ihre Kinder . . .**

Correct: **mein Onkel, mein Bruder, und dessen Frau,** *and the latter's wife.*

Note.—Compare § 95 for demonstrative force of relative pronoun and § 229 for genitive of demonstrative for possessive adjective.

66. Past and Perfect Tenses of Modal Verbs

(*a*) The past tense of modal verbs is formed:

(1) with regular weak past tense endings (*v.* § 31), but

(2) in several cases from a stem differing from that of the infinitive. Thus: **ich wollte, sollte;** but: **ich durfte, konnte, mochte, mußte.**

TABLE:

ich durfte, du durftest, er (sie, es) durfte, wir durften, etc., *I,* etc., *was allowed.*

(*b*) The perfect tense is formed from **haben,** and the past participle, derived from the past tense stem on regular weak principles (§ 31), thus: **gedurft, gekonnt, gemocht, gemußt, gesollt, gewollt.**

But (1) This past participle is used only when the modal verb has no dependent infinitive [cp. § 64 (*c*)]:

er hat (es) gekonnt, *he could (do it);* **wir haben gemußt,** *we had to.*

(2) When, as is usual, a dependent infinitive is present, it precedes the modal past participle [cp. § 63 (*a*)], which takes a form identical with that of the infinitive:

sie haben gehen können (zahlen müssen), *they were (have been) able to go (obliged to pay).*

wir haben kommen wollen, aber nicht dürfen, *we wanted to come, but were not allowed to* (dependent infinitive understood in second part).

(*c*) The pluperfect tense is formed on analogous lines:

ich hatte gemußt, ich hatte zahlen müssen, *I had had to (pay).*

(*d*) Actual and envisaged modality. These perfect and pluperfect forms translate the normal past of the sense represented by the English infinitive, thus:

we were (had been) able, allowed, expected to go, etc.

we (had) wanted, liked, had to pay, etc.

When in English the modal key word [*v.* § 63 (*c*)] precedes the perfect infinitive of the verb, *he could have come, would have sung, ought to have paid,* etc., the force is that of a possibility envisaged but not actually realised, and is therefore translated into German by the (pluperfect) subjunctive [**er hätte kommen können,** etc., cp. § 309 (*b*)].

67. The Use of the Present Tense

The present tense in German, as in English, is used not only for present time, but also for acts and states which are general and universal, or even already past or still in the future.

(*a*) Present time.   An action (state) now happening (existing).

Die Sonne scheint; Blumen und Menschen sind froh.
Der Schnee fällt; die Menschen sind nicht mehr zufrieden.

While an action is taking place, English uses the "progressive" form of the present: I am painting (**ich male**), someone is knocking (**jemand klopft**).   This may be rendered, more closely than with the simple present:

(1) By one or more adverbs, such as **gerade, eben** (*just now*), and/or a preposition with the infinitive noun [*v.* § 205 (*c*)]:

Gerade geht er, *he is* (*just*) *going.*   **Er telefoniert eben,** *he is telephoning.*
Sie ist eben gerade am (beim) Kochen, Jäten, Schreiben, *she is at the moment cooking, weeding, writing.*

(2) By **an, bei, in, mit,** in a prepositional phrase, and sometimes with the past participles **begriffen, beschäftigt,** *engaged* (*in, with*):

Er ist bei der Arbeit.   Er ist in der Arbeit begriffen.   Sie ist mit Aufräumen beschäftigt.   Ich bin am Telefon.

(*b*) General or universal time.   The present may describe:

(1) A habit, custom or quality:

Abends besuche ich ihn immer zwischen 8 und 9 Uhr, *I always call on him …*
Sie singt himmlisch, *she sings* (*can sing*) *magnificently.*
Er schreibt sehr ungern Briefe, *he doesn't like writing.*

(2) A truth:

Die englische Verfassung ist ungeschrieben. Der Brocken liegt in Deutschland.   Eine Schwalbe macht noch keinen Sommer.

(*c*) Past/present time.   To show that an action or state, begun in the past, has continued, and is continuing in the present, English uses the (progressive) perfect: We have been (staying) here for 10 days; German (with French) uses the present: **Wir sind nun schon 10 Tage hier.**

The continuous time relation is usually further underlined by:

(1) an adverb: **bereits, schon, erst, lange, nun schon** (*v.* above);

(2) and/or the preposition **seit.**

Er ist bereits (schon, erst) vierzehn Tage (or seit vierzehn Tagen) von zu Hause weg. *He has been away from home* (*now*) *for* (*only*) *14 days.*

Lange is usually made explicit by adding **schon** (positive) or **nicht mehr** (negative):

> **Ich bin lange schon da,** *I have been* (*waiting*) *here for a long time.*
>
> **Er wohnt lange** (or **schon lange**) **nicht mehr in dieser Straße,** *he has not lived in this street for a long time.*

But if the verb negated is less expressive of a continuous state or action, German sometimes uses the perfect:

> **Er hat seit vielen Jahren nicht mehr geschrieben.**
>
> **Ich habe seit Jahren keine Gelegenheit zum Malen gehabt.**

Note.—German and English sometimes have different views about the relevance of present and past to a situation: **Ich komme wegen der Annonce,** *I have come about the advertisement.* **Ich habe seinen Namen vergessen,** *I forget his name.* **Wissen** with **noch** or **nicht mehr** is *to remember,* or *to have forgotten:* **Ich weiß die Nummer nicht mehr. Wissen Sie noch, wie damals . . .?** *Do you remember how . . . that time . . .?* **Ist die Post schon da?** *Has the post come?* **War die Post schon da?** *Has the post been?*

(*d*) Past time. In lively style, the "historical present" is used in both languages to narrate past events:

> **Dann überfallen plötzlich die Räuber den Wagen und schleppen die Geldsäcke weg,** *the robbers suddenly attack . . .*
>
> **Ich reiß' die Tür auf, sage ihm: „Du Hund!" und schmeiß' ihm seine Banknoten vor die Füße,** *I tear open the door . . .*

(*e*) Future time. The present tense shades off into the future:

(1) In statements of intention, with or without a specific temporal indication: **Morgen reisen wir,** *we are off to-morrow.* **Wann geht der nächste Zug nach Hamburg?** *When does the next train leave . . .?* **Sobald sein Gemälde fertig ist, geht er nach Amerika.** *As soon as his picture is ready he will be leaving . . .* (cp. subordinate clauses, § 113).

(2) In instructions (as to children and servants):

> **Du gehst zum Markt, kaufst Gemüse und Fleisch, und kommst sofort zurück,** *you are to go . . .* [cp. imperative, § 248 (*c*)].

This may be considered as a vivid narrative future (of anticipation) corresponding to the historical present as the form of the vivid narrative past:

> **Sie fahren jetzt weiter, kommen an einem Warenhaus vorbei, gehen links ab, und nach weiteren zwei Minuten sind Sie am Ziel.**

Note.—Present tense for future time in certain subordinate clauses (*v.* § 135).

68. The Use of the Future Tense

(*a*) The future tense indicates a foreseen event, or an intention to be realised in the future:

Er wird morgen mit dem neun Uhr Zug kommen, *he will arrive* . . .

Ich werde ihn morgen um neun Uhr vom Bahnhof holen, *I shall meet him at* . . .

In neither case is there any simple German form for the English progressive: he will be arriving.

Note.—**Wollen** often translates the anticipatory form *to be about to* used with any tense, especially the past [cp. § 478 (*f*)].

(*b*) The future tense often suggests a probability or likelihood, without specific reference to future time; the assumption is often supported by the particles **wohl,** *probably,* or **schon,** *already*:

Er wird wohl schon zu Hause sein, *I suppose he is back home by now.*
Es wird schon werden (reassuringly), *It'll come right* (*in the end*).

(*c*) The future tense may be used in instructions (to children):

Du wirst morgen dein Zimmer reinigen, *I want you to clean* . . .

and in question form, with greater urgency:

Wirst du deine Suppe (sofort) essen? (Sofort wirst du deine Suppe essen!) *Will you finish your soup?* [cp. imperative, § 248 (*c*)].

Note.—Present tense for future time in certain subordinate clauses (*v.* § 135).

EXERCISE XIV

A. Translate into ENGLISH:

1. Der kann nicht reden! Der hat ja selbst seinen Militärdienst nicht machen wollen! 2. Ich wollte nicht so viel für den Fernsehapparat bezahlen. 3. Aber ich habe ihn kaufen müssen, denn meine Frau will immer etwas Neues haben. 4. Der Schauspieler war eben mit der Erlernung einer neuen Rolle beschäftigt und hat nicht auf Urlaub fahren können. 5. Die Kinder suchten gerade Erdbeeren im Walde; da kommt plötzlich ein Gewitter. 6. „Kinder!" ruft die Mutter ängstlich, „sofort werdet ihr ins Haus kommen!" 7. Die Kinder haben schnell laufen müssen und haben gerade noch rechtzeitig nach Hause kommen können. 8. Er arbeitet nun schon zwei Monate im neuen Büro. 9. Wer kann denn so (*such*) eine alberne Geschichte glauben? Das ist ja kindisch! 10. „Ich will rasch den Arzt rufen," sagte die Krankenschwester, „das wird nicht so schlimm sein".

B. Translate into GERMAN:

1. He could not understand her story. Naturally; *he* has always been rich. 2. In those days the public was allowed to visit the house and the park (use successively simple and compound past). 3. We did not want it. 4. The soldiers had to march thirty kilometres in the heat. It (= *that*) was a dreadful day. 5. They have been abroad for several months now. 6. "Will you be going to the Bavarian Alps this year?" 7. He was picking fruit in the orchard and suddenly he heard a cry-for-help. 8. He ran towards the river but he could not see anything (simple and compound). 9. I have been learning German for quite a-long-time now. 10. My brother had to pay a lot for his new car; he is having to buy it on the hire-purchase.

CHAPTER XV

69. Coordinating Conjunctions. General

(a) A conjunction is a word used to connect (conjoin) two words, phrases or clauses: **Georg und ich; nicht im Zimmer, sondern im Garten; er kam, aber ich war nicht zu Hause.**

Those German conjunctions which are described as "coordinating" connect units of equal importance, without subordinating one to the other, either in sense or grammatical construction: **und,** *and;* **oder,** *or;* **aber, allein** and **sondern,** *but;* **denn,** *for.* Being essentially links, when they join clauses they stand outside the order structure of both clauses and do not affect either: **Der Vater sang/und/die Mutter las.**

German uses conjunctions and associated particles much more profusely than does English. Thus conjunctions may be doubled (**oder aber**), or used with adverbial conjunctions (*v.* § 74), as in **aber doch, oder doch, außer aber, trotzdem aber, wie auch, aber auch, daher auch, besonders auch, so doch,** etc. Examples are given later passim.

(b) Note that a strict conjunction is not necessary to join parallel units, even clauses. They may be joined by:

(1) Simple juxtaposition without explicit link: **Sie kam, ich ging. Sie müssen gehen, ich will Sie nicht behalten. Beruf, Stadt, Vaterland bedeuteten für ihn alles.**

(2) Explanatory phrases not strictly conjunctions and not belonging to either clause: **Er konnte mir kein Geld geben, das heißt er wollte nicht** (cp. § 112).

(3) An element of the second sentence, usually an adverb:

Es regnet nicht mehr, trotzdem gehe ich nicht aus (cp. § 74).

(c) Coordinating conjunctions may be single, introducing the second half of the statement, or double, introducing both halves. They may be set out as follows:

SINGLE COORDINATING CONJUNCTIONS

Copulative:	**und, sowie**	*and, as also*
Adversative:	**aber, allein, sondern**	*but, however*
Alternative:	**oder**	*or*
Causal:	**denn**	*for*

DOUBLE COORDINATING CONJUNCTIONS

Copulative:	**sowohl . . . wie/als (auch)**	*both . . . and . . .*
	nicht nur . . . sondern auch . . .	*not only . . . but also . . .*

Alternative:	**entweder ... oder ...**	*either ... or ...*
	weder ... noch ...	*neither ... nor ...*
Partitive:	**bald ... bald ...**	*now ... now ...*
	teils ... teils ...	*partly ... partly ...*

For double coordinating conjunctions *v.* § 111.

70. Copulative Conjunction: **und,** *and.*

Mutter und Kind; er kam und ging nicht wieder; zu Fuß und mit dem Zug.

Synonym: **sowie. Mädchen sowie Jungen pflegen heutzutage den Sport.** Also: **wie (auch), ebenso wie.**

(*a*) Elements common to both sentences may be omitted:

Gestern ging er und (gestern) kam (er) nicht wieder.

If the subject is to be repeated, the second sentence should revert to normal order, preferably without the copulative:

Gestern ging er, er kam nicht wieder.

(*b*) It is perhaps the misreading of sentences such as the example above which led to the practice, once common, especially in business letters, of inverting after **und:**

Es ist nach Gottes willen ein Mädchen, und finde ich keine Worte zu sagen, wie freudig bewegt ich bin (Grünlich to his father-in-law, in *Buddenbrooks,* Th. Mann).

Note.—This error now imparts roughly the same flavour as the pseudo-polite English form *and oblige.*

71. Adversative Conjunctions: **aber, allein, sondern,** *but.*

Aber has a general function, **allein** and **sondern** are specialised.

(*a*) **Aber. Er ist klug, aber faul. Er hatte Karten fürs Kino besorgt, aber ich wollte nicht gehen (or ich wollte aber nicht gehen).**

(1) Like French *mais,* and unlike English *but,* **aber** often introduces minor phrases: **Aber doch! Aber sicher! Aber nein! Aber kommen Sie!**

(2) Like many adverbial conjunctions, but unlike the coordinating conjunctions proper, **aber** often comes later in the clause:

Sein Vater war schon siebzig, seine Mutter aber noch ganz jung.

(*b*) **Allein** has the same sense as **aber,** but is more emphatic:

Ich wollte so gerne gehen, allein es ging einfach nicht.

(*c*) **Sondern,** after a negative, implies a contrast which is a contradiction: **Er ist nicht klug, sondern dumm,** *but (on the contrary) ...*

(1) It is not sufficient that a negative should precede, thus in **er ist nicht klug, aber auch nicht dumm,** the first assertion is negated and limited, but not contradicted.   Thus also:

Dein Vater wird seine Pläne aufgeben . . . Sein Sohn wird nicht Minister werden, aber Nachfolger in seinem Geschäft (H. Mann), *his son will not become a Minister, but he will become his successor in the business.*

(2) It follows from this that, for **sondern** to be used, a contrast must be between things strictly comparable, thus:

Wer erschien, war nicht Georg, sondern Franz.

Wer nicht erschien war Georg, aber sein Vater kam für einige Minuten vorbei, *George (admittedly) didn't appear, but . . .*

(3) Other terms used in the limiting sense are **wohl aber** (stronger) and **nur** (weaker):

Zehn Pfund kann ich nicht hergeben, wohl aber neun, *but I can produce nine pounds.*

Mein Vater hat Einfluß, er ist nicht reich, nur sehr wohlhabend (H. Mann), *he is not rich, (but) only well off.*

72. Alternative Conjunctions: **oder,** *or.*

Heute oder morgen muß ich das tun.   Er konnte nicht, oder wollte nicht, ich weiß nicht welches.   Sofort aus dem Wagen, oder wir schießen! Morgens muß ich Kaffee trinken, oder (= *otherwise*) **ich kann nicht arbeiten.**

(*a*) **Sonst** (with inversion, § 74) may replace **oder** in the sense *otherwise*:
Du machst sofort deine Arbeit, sonst kriegst du Strafe.

(*b*) **Oder** may be used alone as a truncated threat or question:
Sofort aus dem Wagen—oder! *or else . . .!*
Du gehst doch nicht heute ins Kino—oder? *or are you?*

(*c*) The sense *and/or, or, as the case may be* is rendered concisely by **beziehungsweise** (abbreviated, **bzw.**) or **respektive** (**resp.**):
Der wachthabende Offizier bzw. Unteroffizier muß das erledigen, *the officer or N.C.O. on guard . . .*
but both have the flavour of officialdom.

73. Causal Conjunction: **denn,** *for.*

Denn is equivalent to a weak explanatory particle:
Den Zug kannst du nicht kriegen, denn er fährt schon um neun.

As such it hardly competes successfully with the method of simple juxtaposition, since the sense of a weak inference is the easiest logical relation for the mind to supply [cp. §§ 69 (*b*) (1) and 201 (*b*)]. It is, however, also used as a conjunction of comparison (*v.* § 121).

74. Adverbial Conjunctions. General

(*a*) *And* and *or, but* and *for* are basic and universal conjunctive senses, and there are many adverbs which broadly correspond:

(1) *and* and *or*: **auch,** *also;* **außerdem,** *as well;* **namentlich,** *more particularly;* **besonders,** *especially;* **sonst,** *otherwise.*

(2) *but:* **dagegen,** *however;* **übrigens,** *moreover;* **trotzdem,** *nevertheless;* **dennoch,** *but;* **vielmehr,** *rather.*

(3) *for:* **darum, deshalb** or **daher,** *therefore;* **so,** *thus;* **folglich,** *for that reason;* **also,** *so, thus.*

(*b*) These differ from genuine conjunctions, in that, though used to join statements, they remain adverbs, so that:

(1) When leading the clause they cause inversion;

(2) They may occur elsewhere in the clause without ceasing to supply the conjunctive sense, linking the two statements:

Sie hatte kein Geld, daher mußte sie per Anhalter fahren,
so she had to get lifts.
mußte daher per Anhalter fahren.

Ich bringe die Briefe sofort auf die Post, sonst kommen sie zu spät,
or they will arrive late.
sie kommen sonst zu spät.

(*c*) **So** has many uses as a conjunction, coordinating and subordinating (*v.* Index), but the sense of a weak synonym of *thus, therefore,* so common for English *so,* is rare in German, which usually prefers the more firm **daher** (cp. English, *hence*), or **darum** (cp. **warum,** *why*):

. . . **der Engländer war noch nicht erschienen, so erhob ich mich, reichte ihm die Hand und ging davon** (F. Thiess), *so I got up* . . .

(*d*) Synonyms of **denn** are **ja** and **doch** used only after the verb, **ja** with the special force of *you know*:

Ich kann schon kommen, ich habe ja nicht viel Arbeit, *I have after all not much work on hand.*

While **doch** has the special force of *haven't I?* etc.:

Sicher komme ich, habe ich doch immer solche Veranstaltungen für sehr nützlich gehalten, *have I not always* . . .?

Ich verstehe diese Angst. Hege ich sie zuweilen doch selbst (Th. Mann), *I understand this fear; after all I sometimes experience it myself.*

Doch is much over-used in this sense by indifferent writers.

75. Abverbial and Coordinating Conjunctions

(*a*) A few adverbial conjunctions fluctuate between the role of conjunction (with pure linking function), and adverb (requiring inversion). They include especially the important contrasting adverbs **doch, jedoch, indessen** or **indes,** *however;* also **zwar,** *it is true* (concessive); **im Gegenteil,** *on the contrary* (contrasting); and **bloß** or **nur,** *but* (restrictive).

(*b*) **Doch, jedoch, indessen,** *but, however.*

Ich habe ihn seit drei Tagen nicht gesehen, doch glaube ich (or **doch ich glaube) nicht, daß er schon gefahren ist.**

Ich konnte ihm nicht helfen, jedoch gab ich (or **jedoch ich gab) ihm gute Ratschläge.**

Thus also **indessen.**

(1) **Doch** is probably more commonly followed by inversion than **jedoch/indessen,** and cannot be used later in the sentence without acquiring a slightly different sense [*v.* § 74 (*d*)].

Note.—**Doch** shows its adversative force by being used to contradict a negative presumption: **Sie werden also nicht dabei sein? Doch!** *Yes, I shall be* (cp. § 51). But **doch** cannot affirm a positive statement: **Sie kommen doch?** *You are coming, aren't you?* **Jawohl.** *Yes, indeed I am.*

(2) **Indes** is a rather less common form than **indessen. Indessen** when, as often, followed by a colon, must not invert [*v.* (*c*) below]:

Indessen: er hat das überhaupt nicht gesagt.

Indessen with inversion often means *meanwhile,* though it is seldom possible to isolate clearly the adversative and temporal force of this conjunction (cp. § 123):

Indessen sprach die Mutter weiter mit dem Kinde, *But (meanwhile) the mother went on speaking . . .*

(3) Other conjunctions:

Er hat es mir mehrmals gesagt, bloß ich glaube es nicht.

Ich würde sehr gerne mitkommen, nur habe ich kein Geld.

Zwar bin ich (Ich bin zwar) nicht sicher, ich glaube es aber.

Er machte kein Geheimnis daraus, im Gegenteil er sagte es jedermann.

(*c*) The question of inversion or non-inversion after these and many other coordinating conjunctions of mixed nature is a matter of usage and subtle variations of sense. One thing is certain: any leading conjunction followed by a mark of punctuation is immediately isolated parenthetically from what follows, and cannot influence the order of the rest of the statement. Thus especially with comma, colon:

Ich kann nicht kommen, ich habe keine Zeit; außerdem, ich habe auch kein Geld . . . *and anyhow I have no money.*

Die Preise sind nicht gefallen, im Gegenteil, sie sind gestiegen.
Er war sehr nett, z.B. (= zum Beispiel) wollte er mir Bücher geben.
But: . . . z.B., er wollte mir . . .
Wir haben alles versucht, trotzdem ging es nicht. But: trotzdem: es
ging nicht.

EXERCISE XV

A. Translate into ENGLISH:

1. Nachmittags machte der alte Herr ein Schläfchen oder er saß und rauchte friedlich auf der sonnigen Bank im Garten. 2. Im hohen Gebirge findet man sowohl Enzian als auch Edelweiß, aber nicht Wiesenblumen, sondern Heidekraut. 3. Bäume wachsen hoch oben nicht, denn es ist zu kalt und der Boden ist auch zu steinig. 4. Von der Mosel kommt Weißwein sowie auch Rotwein; trotzdem aber ist der weiße Moselwein mehr geschätzt. 5. Friedrich ist arm aber ehrlich, Hermann ist nicht ehrlich sondern ein Dieb. 6. Aber machen Sie doch keine Geschichten, mein Lieber, denn dazu haben wir ja keine Zeit. 7. Ich kann noch nicht gut Französich, daher gehe ich diesen Frühling nach Paris. 8. Das Fleisch ist sehr teuer, außerdem können viele Leute es nicht verdauen, trotzdem aber ißt man es zwei- oder dreimal am Tag. 9. Schwimmen kann ich gut; jedoch reiten habe ich nie gelernt. 10. Des Nachbars Kinder lärmen heute im Garten, doch habe ich gut arbeiten können.

B. Translate into GERMAN:

1. Either he has gone to town or he is still somewhere in the house. 2. The shop is not in the narrow little street but in (auf) the market place. 3. The concert will be broadcast (use man) but not on (von) all stations. 4. We must go quickly, otherwise we shall miss the train. 5. Two policemen jumped into the car and held him because (= for) he was dangerous. 6. He was ill; in spite of this, however, he wanted to go to the cinema. 7. We have no money, so how can we pay for a trip to (nach) Germany? 8. After a week she went to Berlin, yet she did not see her friend. 9. I saw him on the other side of the street and I ran; but meanwhile he had got into a bus. 10. The man with the beard pulled a revolver from (aus) his pocket; he did not shoot, it is true, but I was, nevertheless, afraid.

C. Proverbs and Sayings. Supply the conjunction understood and translate into ENGLISH:

1. Ländlich, sittlich. 2. Ländlich, schändlich. 3. Jugend vergeht, Tugend besteht. 4. Vorsicht, bissiger Hund! 5. Der Mensch denkt, Gott lenkt.

CHAPTER XVI

76. Foreign Nouns (1).   Strong and Weak Declensions

(*a*) Numerous nouns have been received from other languages into German in (mainly recent) historical times.   In so far as these have been assimilated in accent and endings to German declension classes, they no longer constitute a separate declensional group, thus **die Familie (-n), das Kloster (-ö-), der Match (-e).**

In so far as they are still, in one respect or another, not assimilated, two groups may be distinguished:

(1) Those with German endings, strong or weak, but with the end-accent of their foreign origin (*v.* below).

(2) Those assimilated to the strong singular declension, while the plural still provides difficulties, and is therefore either:

(i) Weak (*v.* §§ 89 f.).

or (ii) Foreign (*v.* § 130).

Both these sub-classes, with strong singular and weak or foreign plural, are therefore examples of the mixed declension (*v.* § 52).

(*b*) Nouns with foreign end-accent.

A large number of words, especially from French, are accented on the last syllable, or last but one if ending in **-e**:

der Apparat, *camera;* **der Offizier,** *officer;* **das Kostüm,** *costume;* **der Komparse,** *film-extra;* **der Statist,** *stage-extra;* **der Student,** *student.*

They are masculine and neuter nouns, and among the masculines both animates and things are represented.   About forty foreign endings occur, of which some of the commonest are: **-al, -an, -ant, -ast, -at, -ent, -et, -ier, -ist, -it, -ph.**   They include strong and weak nouns.

(*c*) Strong end-accent class: genitive **-(e)s,** plural **-e.**

These are masculine and neuter, and include both animates and things.

der Admiral, Chauffeur (Schofför), Granit, Monsun, Offizier, Tribut.
das Kostüm, Stativ, Transparent, Ventil.

(1) Mutation.   A few masculines modify the last vowel:

der Altar, General, Kanal, Palast, Tenor.

Plural : **die Altäre,** etc.

But there is a tendency to move towards the (larger) unmodified group, thus **die Generale** is common, and **die Altare, die Tenore** are sometimes found.

(2) Accent. There is a tendency for these words to adopt native front-accent, *e.g.* always now: **der Bíschof, die Bíschöfe; das Mámmut, die Mámmuts** (or **-e**); **der Altar** and **der Pastor** sometimes have front accent in the singular (not plural); **der Charákter** shifts accent in plural to **die Charaktére.**

Note.—**Der Pastor** has normally weak plural, thus belongs to § 90; but also (N.G.) **Pastore,** and (pop.) **Pastöre.**

Distinguish **Das Regiment,** *régime, regiment;* **die Regimente,** *régimes,* **die Regimenter,** *regiments.*

(*d*) Weak end-accent class: singular oblique cases **-(e)n**, plural **-(e)n**. This is a large class, all masculine, almost all animates, and in fact containing most end-accent words standing for animates. A very few have the end **-e** characteristic of many German words of this class (cp. § 34).

der Apostat, Assistent, Athlet, Autokrat, Demokrat, Doktorand, Inserent, Jesuit, Kamerad, Kandidat, Passant, Philosoph, Polizist, Proselyt, Poet, Reflektant, Soldat, Statist, Student, Veteran.

(1) A few animates in **-e**: **der Experte, der Komparse;** compounds of **-loge** (= *-loger, -logian, -logist*), as **der Philologe,** and of **-mane** (= *-maniac*), as **der Kleptomane, Monomane** (but distinguish **der Veteran**).

(2) A few names of peoples or nations: **der Bulgar(e), Kosak, Tatar,** and **Ungar** accented as **Bayer** [*v.* §§ 34 (*b*) and 35 (*a*)].

(3) A few, without **-e**, denote things: **der Automat, Diamant, Komet, Konsonant;** but **Photograph** is the person, as is now also **Telegraph.**

(4) In so far as their senses allow, these words may take the feminine suffix **-in**: **die Assistentin, Doktorandin, Studentin, Komparsin, Bulgarin.**

Note.—**Der Papagei, des Papageis** (or **-en**), **die Papageien** (or **-e**).

77. Irregular Weak Verbs

A group of weak verbs, apart from adding the normal endings of the part and past participle, also change the vowel of the stem. There are two groups:

(*a*) **brennen,** *to burn;* **kennen,** *to know* [personally, *v.* § 476 (*c*) (3)]; **rennen,** *to run* (*race*)*;* **senden,** *to send;* **wenden,** *to turn.*

Example: **brennen.**
Present: **ich brenne,** etc.   Past: **ich brannte,** etc.
Perfect: **ich habe gebrannt,** etc.

Note.—**Senden** and **wenden** are also conjugated weak, thus **senden** in the sense *to broadcast* (cp. **der Sender,** *broadcasting station*), **wenden** in the sense *to turn* (a coat, etc.), and also when used intransitively: **das Flugzeug wendete . . .** In general, literal senses of **wenden** are more often weak than figurative senses.

Der Rundfunk sendete von morgens um sechs bis abends um zehn. Der Schneider hat mir (*for me*) den alten Rock gewendet. Das Schiff wendete gegen Süden. Der Bauer wendete den Pflug. Ich habe nur reinste Butter zum Kuchen verwendet.

Er wandte sich an das Amt, *he applied* (reflexive, *v.* § 179) *to the authorities.*

Er sandte ein Paket an seine Mutter, *he sent his mother a parcel.*

Thus past participles used in an applied sense as adjectives (or adjective-nouns, *v.* § 143) are commonly strong: **gewandt,** *skilful;* **ein Gesandter,** *ambassador* (**ein gewandter Gesandter!**); **die angewandte Mathematik,** *applied mathematics;* **ein Eingesandt** (lit. *sent in*) *a letter to the Editor.* But: **ein gewendeter Anzug,** *a turned suit.*

(*b*) **Bringen,** *to bring;* **denken,** *to think.* Both these verbs change the stem vowel, and the following consonantal group to **-ch-:**

Present: **ich bringe, ich denke,** etc.   Past: **ich brachte, ich dachte,** etc.
Perfect: **ich habe gebracht, ich habe gedacht,** etc.

78. Other Irregular Verbs

(*a*) For **haben, sein** and **werden** *v.* §§ 9, 15, 45.

(*b*) **Tun** is strong, but irregular:

Present: **ich tue, du tust, er (sie, es) tut;** *I do,* etc.
            wir tun, ihr tut, Sie tun, sie tun; *we do,* etc.
Past: **ich tat, du tatst, er (sie, es) tat;** *I did,* etc.
            wir taten, ihr tatet, Sie taten, sie taten; *we did,* etc.
Present part.: **tuend,** *doing.* Past part.: **getan,** *done.*

(*c*) Minor irregularities occur in many other strong verbs, for which reference should be made to the List at Appendix D.

79. Numerals (6). Fractions

(*a*) Formation:

(1) *Half* is, as a numeral: **ein halb;** as a noun: **die Hälfte.**
sechseinhalb (6½), **zweieinhalb Milliarden, er gab mir die Hälfte seines Apfels,** *half his apple.*

(2) All other fractions are formed by adding **-tel** (a vestigial form of **der Teil,** *part,* thus, e.g. *the fourth part of*) to the ordinal stem (formed as

in § 41), but with the absorption of -t- into that stem, thus: **ein (das) Drittel, Viertel, Fünftel, Zwanzigstel** (for **Dritt-tel, Viert-tel,** etc.). (**Ein Zweitel** has theoretical existence.)

(*b*) Copula: The copula **und** is optional in vulgar fractions: **ein-(und)einhalb, drei(und)dreiviertel, neun(und)zweifünftel.** Those who omit **und** often separate a complicated fraction: **zweieinhalb,** but **zwei dreiviertel.**

(*c*) Capitals and compounds:

(1) Fractions may be adjectival or nominal. The second figure of a fraction is small when followed by a noun of time, size, weight, measurement: **drei viertel Stunden, zwei fünftel Meter, sieben achtel Kilogramm.** The second figure has a capital if the fraction is alone or followed by a noun of material: **ein Viertel, ein Achtel Butter.** Thus in time: **es ist drei Viertel vier.** But as a compound: **dreiviertel vier.**

(2) **halb** is the only adjective numeral which is inflected, but many are compounded: **eine Viertelstunde, eine halbe Stunde, ein halbes Pfund (Halbpfund), fünf viertel Stunden (Viertelstunden).**

(*d*) Number of Verb. Fractions of which the first figure is not **ein** and those over one normally take a plural noun [except in so far as the invariable singular is used, cp. § 241 (*a*)]: **drei viertel Stunden, eineinhalb Scheiben,** but with **halb** the inflected form may be compounded, with a singular noun: **einundeinhalbe Stunde.**

(*e*) An older form of counting by halves has left the vestigial form **anderthalb,** *one and a half* (lit. *the second half*). Cp. also the forms **selbander,** etc. [§ 155 (*e*)].

80. Numerals (7).   Other Expressions

(*a*) Decimals:

Null, zero (*nought*); **die Null,** *cipher.* The decimal point is called and is in fact, a comma, **Komma;** it may not, as in English, begin the decimal fraction, even in speech, thus:

$0.3 = $ *point three* $= \mathbf{0,3} = $ **nullkommadrei.**
$0.03 = $ *point nought three* $= \mathbf{0,03} = $ **nullkommanulldrei.**

(*b*) Equations:

$6 \times 3 = 18$:   **sechs mal drei ist (ist gleich, macht) achtzehn.**
$6 - 4 = 2$:   **sechs weniger (minus) vier ist (——) zwei.**
$6 \div 2 = 3$:   **sechs durch zwei ist (——) drei.**
$6 + 8 = 14$:   **sechs und (plus) acht ist (——) vierzehn.**

(c) Powers:

2^4 is **zwei hoch vier**, or **zwei zur vierten Potenz**, and 16 is **die vierte Potenz** (*the fourth power, degree*) **von zwei**, or **zwei zur vierten Potenz erhoben** (infin. **erheben**, *to raise to*). **'Das Quadrat**, *square;* **der Kubus**, *cube.* **Zwei im Quadrat ist vier**, *two squared.* The idiom: (**ein Narr**, etc.) **in höchster Potenz**, is (*a fool*) *of the first water.*

(d) Percentages:

Das Prozent (plur. **-e**), *percent(age)*, abbrev. **p.c.**, **%**, **v.H.** (= **vom Hundert**). Even in the singular it has a plural verb, since the Latin sense (per hundred) makes the preceding numeral the real subject of the verb:

Auf alle steuerpflichtigen Getränke werden 10% (spoken: Prozent) Getränkesteuer erhoben und von sämtlichen Getränken werden 10% Bedienungsgeld . . . (official notice), *on all drinks liable to tax 10% tax is levied, and on all drinks a 10% service charge is levied.*

Von diesen rund 73 000 Personenkraftwagen verblieben 81 v.H. (= einundachtzig vom Hundert) innerhalb Europas, 11 v.H. kamen nach Afrika und 5 v.H. wurden nach Amerika . . . verschifft (newsp.)

The plural may mean *tips*:

die Prozente von Speis und Trank aufgemunterter Gäste (R. Musil), *the tips from guests made cheerful by food and drink.*

EXERCISE XVI

A. Translate into ENGLISH:

1. Die tapfere Handlung des Offiziers rettete das Leben der Hälfte seiner Soldaten und erntete ihm das Lob seines Generals. 2. Über siebzig Prozent (also fast dreiviertel) der Kanäle Englands sind durch die Entwicklung anderer Transportmethoden überflüssig geworden. 3. In Deutschland kann man in manchen Lokalen belegte Brote, Obst, Kuchen usw. aus Automaten bekommen. So spart man die Bedienungsprozente. 4. Viele Veteranen des ersten Weltkrieges haben auch noch im zweiten Krieg ihre Pflicht getan. 5. Sie brachten ihre Erfahrung, und die Offiziere der neugeformten Regimenter und sogar die Generäle schätzten ihre Dienste sehr. 6. Mit der Hilfe seines guten Apparats machte der erste Photograph des Städtchens ausgezeichnete Aufnahmen von dem berühmten Poeten. 7. Der Schweif des Kometen brannte feurig am nächtlichen Himmel. 8. Zum Erntefest legen die Bauern reife Ähren und Brot auf die blumengeschmückten Altäre der Dorfkirchen. 9. Man brachte das Resultat des großen Matches auf allen Sendern, und Zeitungsverkäufer rannten durch die Straßen. 10. Die Pastoren und

Bischöfe der Staatskirche in den Skandinavischen Ländern haben im
Krieg viel für ihr Volk getan und großes Leid gekannt. 11. Proverbs:
Jung gewohnt, alt getan.   Gut gekaut ist halb verdaut.

B. Translate into GERMAN:

1. The language of the Hungarians is difficult, even for good philo-
logists. 2. $3\frac{1}{2}\%$ is not enough.   You can get more, perhaps even a
third more. 3. Peter was saying his tables: twice two are four, three
times three are nine. 4. He could say the numbers up to (**bis**) hundred
and knew (**kennen**) his tables quite well. 5. "What are you doing?"
the policeman asked the passer-by. 6. "I haven't done anything,"
answered the passer-by and then he ran off (**weg**). 7. The edge of a
diamond is very hard, almost as hard as (**so . . . wie**) the sharp edge of
granite. 8. "Do you know (**kennen**) my niece?   She has brought her
violin.   We shall have a little concert to-night." 9. The banks of the
canal were cool and shady with willow trees. 10. He ran (**rennen**)
swiftly; the roof of the house was burning.   He thought of (**an, acc.**)
his children.

CHAPTER XVII

INDEFINITE ADJECTIVE-PRONOUNS (1). EXHAUSTIVES

81. General. Exhaustives

(*a*) Certain words of an adjectival nature express an indefinite amount, number or quantity: *some, any, both, many, much, each, every, all, few,* etc. They may be used both adjectivally and pronominally, and are thus more general than the indefinite pronouns (§§ 60-2). They are often called pronominals, because of their common use as pronouns; or indefinite numerals (the definite numerals being the cardinals and ordinals).

(*b*) For convenience of grouping, the indefinite adjective-pronouns will here be set out under the headings:

(1) Exhaustives, *i.e.* words which in some way exhaust the class to which they refer: **kein,** *no* (*one, thing*), *none;* **all-,** *all* or *every;* **jed-,** *each* or *every;* and their synonyms and related forms.

(2) Quantitatives, *i.e.* words which express an (incomplete) quantity, number or amount of the class to which they refer: **wenig (wenige),** *a little* or *few;* **einig-** and **welch-,** *some* or *any;* **viel (viele),** *much* or *many;* and their synonyms and related forms.

These words are described in the present chapter (Exhaustives) and in Chapter XXI (Quantitatives). In both their adjectival and pronominal functions there occur cases both of inflection and non-inflection. Details are given under each word, and §§ 145-7 summarise the inflectional problems they present, and describe also their pronominal and nominal uses.

(*c*) Exhaustives. The first group includes all those which exhaust the class to which they refer, whether negatively (**kein-**), positively (**all-**) or distributively (**jed-**).

82. Kein-, *no* (*one, thing*), *not any, none.*

Inflection as indefinite article (*v.* § 13).

As **ein Baum** when negated becomes **kein Baum, etwas** becomes **nichts** (§ 61), and **jemand** becomes **niemand** (§ 60), so also the pronoun **einer, -e, -es,** when negated is **keiner, -e, -es.** English retains the choice of the negated positive or a negative form: *not a* (*no*) *tree, not anything* (*nothing*), *not anyone* (*no one*), *not one* (*none*).

Mit Bewußtsein verachtete er den Bourgeois und war stolz darauf, keiner zu sein (H. Hesse), *was proud not to be one.*

Cp. § 62 (*b*), indefinite pronouns.

83. Jed-, *each* or *every*.
Inflection as definite article (-es for both **d-as** and **d-es**).

(*a*) In the positive exhaustives, not limited to any number, English distinguishes between *each* and *every*, in which:

(1) *Each* considers the individual items on their own, without necessarily regarding them as in all respect equal, while

(2) *Every*, regarding all items as equal, takes them as a totality.
Cp. England expects *every* man to do his duty. The country expects *each* man to know what his duty is, and to carry it out.

As German does not make this distinction, **jed-** translates both *each* and *every;* but there are certain emphatic forms which incline to one sense, thus: **ein jeder** (*each, each and every*), and **jeder einzelne** (*each*):

**Der Schutz, den die Polizei ohne Ansehen der Stellung einem jeden zuteil
werden läßt . . .,** *provides for each and every person.*

(*b*) **Jed-** and **all-** are in a sense complementary, referring respectively to singular and plural ideas, but:

(1) **all-,** in the sense *every*, is common in the singular: **wir hatten
alles Recht,** *every right;* **die Lage hatte jeden Vorteil,** *every advantage.*
But where English *every* precedes successive groups in a series (every few months, second week) German has **all-** with plural: **alle paar Wochen,
zwei Monate, 12 Stunden,** or **jed-** with the ordinal and singular: **jeder
dritte Monat, jede zweite Minute.**

(2) **jed-** is not impossible in the plural, especially with **Ferien:**

In jeden Ferien verbrachte er einige Wochen in Italien.
**Beim Beginn jeder Ferien schnürte Hans seinen Ranzen mit hoher
Freude zur Fahrt nach der Heimat** (W. Raabe), . . . *each holiday*, or
. . . *the holidays, Hans always* . . .

(*c*) **Jed-** is not limited, as is *each* and *every*, to things which can be enumerated, and often precedes general and abstract words, especially those with negative force, in the sense *any;* **all-** may usually also be used:
ohne alle Begleitung, ohne jede Anrede, (*she went*) *without any companion,*
(*he began*) *without any form of address.*

Es lohnt jede Mühe, einen solchen Plan zu verwirklichen, *it is worth any
effort to . . .*

Sie verschmähte jedes Liebäugeln mit dem Publikum (Th. Mann), *any
form of making up to the public.*

ein größeres (Erdbeben), als jedes, dessen sich Menschen entsannen
(H. Risse), *worse than any within human memory.*

(*d*) **Jed-**, pronoun, may be used in apposition, as in English *each, every-one*, in a partitive sense, without affecting the plural number of the verb:
Wir leben jeder so abgesondert wie vor hundert Jahren, ehe Dampfschiff und Bahn und Flugzeug und Post erfunden waren (S. Zweig), *we all of us live . . ., everyone lives . . ., we live—everyone of us— . . .*
Cp. § 483, agreement of number.

From this sense should be distinguished the use of **je ein**, *one of each*, etc.; this is a genuine distributive:
Vor kurzem ging ich durch die öffentlichen Anlagen . . . Je ein Pflanzenkind einer Gattung trug auf einem geschmackvollen Schildchen auch seinen Namen (corr. in Mspr.), *one of each species bore . . .*
Cp. § 241 (*c*), for the distributive *each*, **je**, **à** or **pro**.

(*e*) **Jeglich-** is occasional (and lit. style) for **jed-**, and is useful when a heavy term is required:
eine Lebensweise, ohne jeglichen Anflug höherer Kultur, *a way of life without a touch of* (*completely innocent of*) *any cultured interests.*

84. Beid-, *both, the two.*
Strong or weak adjectival inflection (*v.* §§ 36, 46).

(*a*) **Beide** and *both* may precede the noun, or follow the verb:
Beide Handwerker waren schon da, die Handwerker waren beide schon da, *both the workmen . . ., the workmen were both . . .*
Similarly in the pronominal form:
Beide waren da, sie waren beide da, *both were there, they were both there.*
But there are two cases where the order in English and German is different:

(1) **Beide** may *not* come between pronoun subject and verb:
We both thank you for your letter, **beide danken wir dir für deinen Brief.**
unless the pronoun subject is stressed:
Wir beide gehen auf jeden Fall, *we two* (*at least*) *shall be going.*

(2) But **beide** *may* come between the definite article (demonstrative or possessive adjective) and the noun: **die beiden Jungen, diese beiden Bücher, ihre beiden Augen,** *both the . . ., both these . . ., both her . . .*

(*b*) In (2) above, care should be taken to notice whether the German intends to convey the emphatic sense of the English *both*, or merely that of *the two* (*the two boys*, etc.):
Wo sind meine beiden Bleistifte hingekommen? *What has happened to my two pencils?*

The emphatic sense of *both* may be **alle beide:**
Ihr seid Schurken, alle beide! *You're rascals, both (the two) of you!*

(*c*) *Both* is only one of several words used in English to refer to two persons (things); there are also: *either* (positive), *neither* (negative), *whether* (of two possibilities). Cp. conjunctions for *whether* [ob, § 114 (*c*)], and for *either* (*neither*) . . . *or* (*nor*) (§ 111).

German uses compound forms for:

(1) *Either* (i.e. *of them*) *can do that for you,* **Einer von beiden** (unemphatic) . . ., or **Jeder von beiden** (emphatic) **kann das für Sie tun.** (Cp. **in beiden Fällen,** *in either case.*)

(2) *Neither* (i.e. *of them*) *was there on time,* **Keiner von beiden war zur Verabredung pünktlich da.**

These are both pronominal and agree with the noun referred to. Cp. §§ 147 (*a*) (1), 493 (neuter as collective).

85. All-, *all, every.*

(*a*) Inflection.

Singular uninflected: **all sein Vermögen, all die Sehnsucht, bei all dieser Aufregung,** *all his fortune, this yearning, with all this excitement.*

Singular (strong) inflection:

aller Ruhm und Glanz seines Namens, *all the fame and lustre* . . .
Alle meine Kochkunst konnte ihm nicht helfen, *all my skill in cooking* . . .
Dieser Staatsmann hat alle Jugend für sich, *the whole of the youth (of the country)* . . .

Plural uninflected: **all meine Gedanken, all die vielen Hausfrauen,** *all my thoughts, the many housewives.*

Plural (strong) inflection:

Alle die Schüler, die ins Theater gehen wollen, sollen sich bis 10 Uhr melden, *all those boys who . . ., should report by . . .*

Note that **all-** may be inflected without the definite article, or uninflected with it, but the combination of **all-,** inflected, *and* definite article is uncommon except in the plural where the article has demonstrative force or is antecedent to a relative [cp. **alle die Schüler** (above) and]: **es** (= *this experience*) **hatte seither, durch alle die öden Tage, hin und wieder aufgeglänzt** (H. Hesse), *through all those empty days (which were to follow)* . . .

(*b*) **Alle,** plural, may follow the verb, especially when referring to a pronoun: **Sie waren alle schon da,** *they had all arrived.*

But it is not possible for both a pronoun subject and **alle** to precede the verb (cp. also **beide**); one must precede and one follow: *Then they all went home*, **sie gingen dann** (or **dann gingen sie**) **alle heim.** For a similar reason **alle** may not precede a relative pronoun (cp. English *all of whom*): **diese paar Stammgäste, die ich vom Sehen alle kannte** . . . **alle waren sie ziemlich schweigsam, und alle waren sie Trinker und saßen gleich mir lieber vor einem halben Liter Elsässer als vor einer Damenkapelle** . . . (H. Hesse), *all of whom I knew by sight* . . ., *were all silent drinkers* . . .

(*c*) Distinguish the above uses from the predicative use of **alle** (invariable) idiomatically, for *used up, exhausted*: **der Kuchen, das Brot, mein Geld is alle (geworden); Die Dummen werden nicht alle,** *there's never an end to the fools in the world;* and *all* as adverb: *the house is all clean now,* **das Haus ist ganz (volkommen) sauber.**

Cp. § 83 (**all-** and **jed-**), and § 148 (neuter pronouns).

86. Other Exhaustives

(*a*) **Ganz,** *all, the whole,* may be used as an adjective (inflected or uninflected), or as an adverb, in a sense close to that of **all-: mein ganzes Geld, ganz** (or **das ganze**) **Deutschland, ganz gut**; but in the plural it is replaced by **sämtlich-** [*v.* (*b*) below], except when used before numerals in the sense *no more than* [cp. § 53 (*c*) (**ganze vier,** *four in all*)].

(*b*) **Sämtlich,** *all, the whole,* an inflected adjective (plural only), or adverb: **seine sämtlichen Werke,** *collected works;* **die sämtlichen Anwesenden,** *all those present;* **sie waren sämtlich erschienen,** *they all came.*

(*c*) **Lauter,** *nothing but, sheer, all,* invariable.

Er hielt eine lange Rede, lauter Unsinn! *Sheer nonsense!*

Das sind lauter Ausreden, *all excuses.*

Distinguish from **lauter,** a normal descriptive adjective meaning *pure,* cp. **lauter** (invariable) **Unsinn,** *pure nonsense,* and **die lautere Wahrheit,** *the pure (unsullied) truth.*

Eitel is used similarly:

Bei seinem ersten Auftreten war er schwarz gekleidet, und dennoch ging eitel Glanz von ihm aus (Th. Mann), *yet he radiated sheer glamour.*

EXERCISE XVII

A. Translate into ENGLISH:

1. Die Luft war sehr klar und man konnte jeden einzelnen Berg am blauen Horizont erkennen. 2. Er klebte alle neuen Briefmarken in sein neues Album. 3. Dieser kleine Spaziergang in den Bergen ist

ohne alle Gefahr. 4. „Hier habt ihr je eine Mark, Kinder", sagte Onkel Rudolf, „ihr könnt euch etwas Schönes damit kaufen". 5. Die Kinder waren beide entzückt und die beiden kleinen Spielzeuge waren schnell gekauft. 6. Alle sechs Monate zahle ich meine Steuern; jedesmal bekomme ich eine Quittung. 7. Der Philosoph widmete diesem Problem seine ganze Aufmerksamkeit. 8. Im Schwimmbad waren heute lauter Kinder—wir hatten keine einzige ruhige Minute. 9. Dieser Schüler hat eine schlechte Übersetzung geschrieben—lauter Fehler; der Lehrer hatte allen Grund zur Klage. 10. Sämtliche Passagiere auf dem dritten Deck haben nur ganz kleine Kabinen. 11. Proverbs: Ende gut, alles gut. Er sieht den Wald vor lauter Bäumen nicht. 12. Ich verließ das Städtchen in aller Frühe und ohne jedes Gefühl der Reue. Kein Mensch, der mir gute Reise wünschte! 13. Eines Mittags . . . fand ich den Laden leer, und zwar leer nicht nur von Besuchern, sondern auch von jedem bedienenden Personal (Th. Mann). 14. Selling lottery tickets: „Hier ist das Monte Carlo der armen Luder! Keine Mark, keine halbe Mark, sondern einen Groschen!" (E. Kästner).

B. Translate into GERMAN:

1. There were ancient monuments on (zu) either side of the cathedral. 2. The whole of England has had an excellent summer. 3. They (man) have made an edition of his collected short stories. They are all very funny. 4. He went home at once, and without any [good] reason, said his friends. 5. The child made these drawings without any help. 6. She was sad at the (am) end of every holiday. 7. They each drank five whole bottles [of] beer. 8. Neither of the two could walk home. 9. I have to weed the garden every seven days, else it is nothing but weeds. 10. They both saw the same play but each thought differently about it (darüber).

CHAPTER XVIII

COMPOUND VERBS, SEPARABLE AND INSEPARABLE

87. General

(*a*) There are in German many compound verbs, consisting of a simple verb and a prefix; the prefixes may be:

(1) Separable: **Ich wache um 10 Uhr auf,** *I wake up at ten.*

(2) Inseparable: **Er bedeckte den Tisch mit Blumen,** *he covered* (cp. *bedecked*) *the table with flowers.*

(3) While some are separable or inseparable with different verbs, or with the same verb in different senses:

Separable: **Der Fährmann setzte ihn über,** *the ferryman took* (lit. *put*) *him across.*

Inseparable: **Er übersetzte das Buch,** *he trans-lated the book.*

It will be seen that English has elements analogous to the German prefixes, the major difference being that a German separable compound verb, when standing as infinitive, participle, or finite verb in the end-position, is reunited with its prefix in the order: prefix, simple verb:

Ich werde um zehn Uhr aufwachen, *I shall wake up at ten.*

Der Fährmann hat ihn übergesetzt, *the ferryman took him across.*

(*b*) Every compound verb in German, like every simple verb, is either transitive or intransitive (or both), and may be followed by an object in any oblique case, or a prepositional phrase, or any combination of these:

Er fiel um, *he col-lapsed;* **er umging die Stadt,** *he avoided* (*circum-vented*) *the town;* **zwei Zivilisten kamen um,** *two civilians were killed;* **er sprach dem Weine zu,** *he ap-plied himself to the wine;* **ich legte ihm eine schwere Arbeit auf,** *I im-posed a difficult task on him;* **wir belegten zwei Sitzplätze,** *we oc-cupied two seats;* **er versprach ihr die Stelle,** *he promised her the job;* **man bewarf ihn mit Schnee,** *they threw snow at him;* **die Mutter setzte ihm seine Mütze auf,** *his mother put his cap on him.*

(*c*) Thus every care must be taken to find out the exact construction following a German compound verb, and especially:

(1) not to confuse prefix and preposition, even if the same word appears in both functions,

(2) or to assume that an English preposition must be translated by a German preposition, and not by a prefix:

Er ging *an* dem Hause vorbei, *he went past the house;* cp. er ging an das Haus, *he went (up) to the house.*

Ich klopfte *bei* ihm an, *I knocked at his door* (fig. *touched him for a loan);* but Er bettelte *mich* an, *he begged (off me);* Du bettelst *mir* eine (= Ohrfeige) ab! *You're asking for a clip on the ear!* (lit. *you are begging something off me).*

Der Hilfeschrei durchfuhr mich, *went right through me;* Wir fuhren durch die ganze Stadt hindurch, *right through the town*—in this example the prefix could be omitted, but *not* the preposition.

Er verzichtete auf seinen Gewinn, *he gave up (for-went) his winnings;* Er gab alle Hoffnung auf, *he gave up all hope;* but Er gibt nicht viel auf (= prep.) seine Chancen, *he doesn't give much for his chances.*

(*d*) It is clear from the above examples that:

(1) German compound verbs can express every shade of literal or figurative sense, cp. [(*a*) above] übersétzen and übersetzen (and cp. English *I put him across, I put it across on him);* thus:

Angehen may have the following uses:

Ich ging ihn an, *I tackled (approached) him;* Die Musik ging an, *the music started (up);* Das geht ihn nichts an, *that doesn't concern him;* Das geht nicht an, *that is not possible.*

(2) Superficial analogies with English usage can be quite misleading. Thus: ein Gefühl überkam ihn, *came over him;* but: *overcame him* is überwältigte ihn. Bekommen is *to receive, to become* is werden. Besprechen is *to discuss, to bespeak* is bestellen. Vergeben is *to for-give,* but versagen is not *to fore-tell,* but *to deny,* and the (different) prefix in *fore-tell* is translated vorher-sagen.

(3) A verb may mean very different things when used as a simple verb, when variously compounded or used with objects of different case and with differing prepositional adjuncts.

Cp., for the characteristic use and force of certain separable prefixes, § 173.

Meanwhile, the basic rules governing compound verbs may be stated.

88. Statement of Rules

(*a*) Position:

(1) Separable prefixes always stand at the end of the sentence (or phrase):

(i) Alone in the finite forms of the verb:

Ich kam gegen 10 Uhr in Berlin an, *I arrived.*

(ii) Compounded with the verb in the

Infinitive:	**Ich werde gegen 10 Uhr ankommen.**
Past part.:	**Ich bin gegen 10 Uhr angekommen.**
Present part.:	**Das Buch aufmachend, las er rasch einige Seiten.**

and when the present participle is used as attributive adjective:

Die einschlagende Bombe machte uns große Angst, *the bomb frightened us greatly when it fell.*

(2) Inseparable prefixes always precede the verb, wherever it stands, when compounded, and in the past participle the prefix **ge-** is *excluded*:

Finite forms:	**Ich bekomme (bekam) einen eingeschriebenen Brief,** *I receive (received) a registered letter.*
Infinitive:	**Ich werde hoffentlich morgen den Brief bekommen,** *I shall, I hope, receive . . .*
Past part.:	**Ich habe heute den Brief bekommen** (no ge-).
Present part.:	**Den Blumentopf zerschlagend, verschwand der Junge,** *breaking the flower-pot, the boy disappeared.*

and when the present participle is used as attributive adjective:

Sie gab ihm einen verzeihenden Blick, *a forgiving look.*

(*b*) Accent. Separable prefixes are always accented, inseparable never:

Ich muß mein Geld in Wertpapieren ánlegen, *invest in securities.*

Ich habe das Buch leider verlégt, *afraid I have mislaid.*

In the end-position of the finite forms, and always in the infinitive and present participle, the accent is the only means by which those few prefixes which may be either separable or inseparable may be distinguished in their various senses:

Im Sommer will ich Frankreich durchréisen, . . . *travel through (about in) France.*

Ich bleibe nicht lange in Paris, ich will nur dúrchreisen, . . . *only travel (straight) through.*

(*c*) List of Prefixes.

(1) The following prefixes are always inseparable: **be-, ent- (emp-** before **-f-), er-, ge-, miß, ver-, zer-,** thus: **beschlagen,** *to shoe (horses);* **entkommen,** *to escape;* **empfehlen,** *to recommend;* **erhalten,** *to receive;* **gestehen,** *to confess;* **mißhandeln,** *to ill-treat;* **vergeben,** *to forgive;* **zerschlagen,** *to break into pieces;* **wider-** as in **widerlegen,** *to refute,* is usually inseparable.

Inseparable prefixes were originally significant words, but have long lost their separate meaning (but *not* their characteristic force); their number thus cannot be increased.

(2) Separable prefixes, on the other hand, cannot possibly be fully listed, since:

(i) They include most of the common prepositions and adverbs, as: **ab, an, auf, aus, bei, bevor, da** (and compounds), **durch, empor, fort, entgegen, entzwei, heim, hin** and **her** (and compounds), **hinter, los, mit, nach, nieder, ob, über, um, unter, voll, vor** (and compounds), **weg, weiter, wider, wieder, zu, zurück, zusammen.**

(ii) New compounds are constantly being formed, both from these, and through the compounding of predicative adjectives (**totschlagen,** *to kill*), noun objects (**standhalten,** *to resist*), and prepositional phrases (**nachhausegehen,** *to go home*).

(3) The following separable prefixes are also used inseparably: **durch, hinter, über, um, unter, voll, wider** [*v.* (1) above], and **wieder.** There is usually differentiation of sense (or at least of force) between the same verb compounded separably and inseparably.

Note.—v. also §§ 472-5, especially § 472 (plurality of prefixes, **miß-, ob-**).

(*d*) Formation of new compounds. The striking situation described in [(2) (ii) above] derives from the fact that, apart from most prefixes of prepositional origin, the majority of prefixes would stand towards the end of the sentence when used in their autonomous function. They are regarded as prefixes, and the verb as a settled compound, from the moment when their frequent association leads to a fusion of sense, with the emergence of a new (sometimes only a slightly changed) meaning. This is represented orthographically by writing the two elements together in the infinitive, and end-position generally: **Er kam wieder** = *he came again* (adverb), or *he returned* (prefix). **Er wird wieder kommen** (adverb), or **wiederkommen** (prefix).

Gott wird ihn tot schlagen; Die Gangster haben ihn halbtot geschlagen, *strike him dead, half killed him* (both predicative adjectives).

Man hat ihn totgeschlagen (prefix).

Thus the grammar and orthography of compound verbs is one indivisible problem with their meaning, and a small initial letter is usually the outward and visible sign that a noun object, for example, has become a prefix:

Der Unteroffizier kommandierte Kehrt, und die Mannschaft machte kehrt, *the N.C.O. gave the right about order, and the men wheeled right about.*

Similarly: **er hielt stand,** *resisted;* **der Junge stand kopf,** *stood on his head;* **das Konzert findet statt,** *takes place;* and with more complex structures several forms may be in current use, as **nach Hause gehen, nachhause gehen, nachhausegehen.**

Other idioms seem hardly less deserving of being compounded, but usage has not yet reached the point of regarding them as special new senses distinct from the component parts, thus: **er schlug Feuer,** *struck a match;* **er fing Feuer,** *became enthusiastic;* **ich hörte bei ihm Kolleg,** *I went to his lectures;* **der Schneider nahm weiter Maß,** *went on measuring.*

(*e*) Conjugation:

(1) Both strong and weak verbs conjugated directly with a separable and inseparable prefix have forms like the simple verb; but inseparable verbs omit the **ge-** of the past participle: **erschießen, erschoß, erschossen; verreisen, verreiste, verreist.** Strong verbs should therefore be looked up under their simple forms in the List of Strong and Irregular Verbs (Appendix D).

(2) But the auxiliary of the simple verb may or may not be that of the compound, since the use of **haben** or **sein** depends on the sense and transitive or intransitive force of the verb (*v.* § 44).

EXERCISE XVIII

A. Translate into ENGLISH:

1. Der Direktor stellte eine neue Sekretärin an. 2. Er hat vorige Woche einen zweiten Buchhalter angestellt. 3. Er will auch noch eine Stenotypistin anstellen. 4. Ich mußte meine geplante Deutschlandreise aufschieben, denn ich hatte noch nicht genug Geld verdient und aufgespart. 5. Ich habe meinen „Reiseführer durch die bayrischen Alpen" weggelegt, denn ich kann erst nächstes Jahr hinfahren. 6. Unser General wollte erst bei Tagesanbruch vorgehen, aber der Feind griff schon kurz vor Mitternacht an. 7. „Jetzt klopft er an der Türe", dachte sie; aber die Straße war leer und wahrscheinlich hatte niemand angeklopft. 8. Manche Leute machen täglich vor dem Frühstück einen Spaziergang und das verdient unsere Achtung. 9. Wir machen es aber nicht nach, denn wir ziehen die Langschläferei vor. 10. Meine Kenntnisse in der deutschen Sprache nehmen jetzt täglich zu. 11. Das arme Kind hat Keuchhusten gehabt und hat in den letzten Wochen sehr abgenommen. 12. Die Schweden haben das Dorf mit Feuer und Schwert zerstört. 13. Ich habe heute früh ein eingeschriebenes Paket von meinen Freunden in Kanada bekommen. 14. Es hat mich freudig überrascht. Was mag es wohl enthalten? 15. Er hat die Adresse eines Hotels in Berlin für mich aufgeschrieben.

B. Translate into GERMAN:

1. After his long journey he fell asleep at once. 2. You can count on me; I will not leave the house. 3. When will he come back from (aus) Italy? I have forgotten. 4. The number of students at German universities is still increasing. 5. They employ a gardener for the heavy work. 6. At last they discovered a house in that lonely forest and they knocked at (an) the door. 7. He picked up a shining object from the ground and recognised his own gold watch. 8. Why do you not write down the name of that book? One forgets so easily. 9. Closing (up) the book the pastor stepped down from the pulpit. 10. One day he went away from (von) the district and he never came back.

CHAPTER XIX

89. Foreign Nouns (2). From Classical Languages

(*a*) Words from classical languages have long resisted inflectional assimilation, partly because of a genuine difficulty in attaching German endings (*e.g.* genitive -s to **der Kaktus**; plural ending to **das Album, das Drama**), and partly because of a reluctance to relinquish the opportunity of showing learning (*e.g.* **das Thema**, plural **die Themata**). A compromise has been reached by declining many such words with a strong singular and weak plural, thus according to the mixed pattern [cp. §§ 52, 76 (*a*)], though with minor variations. There are still some words of this group with an un-German stress accent. In some cases the classical plural is still possible or even the only form (**die Stigmata**), or it may be combined with the German weak ending (**die Atlanten**). This is the only large declensional group in which the choice of a form markedly reflects the cultural outlook of the speaker.

(*b*) Most of these words are, however, still undergoing further assimilation along lines which are summarised at § 92.

90. Masculine Nouns of Classical Origin

These may end in **-or, -ismus, -us.**

(*a*) Singular **-or** (short, unaccented), plural **-óren** (long, accented).

Example: **der Áutor, des Áutors, die Autóren.**

Also: **der Doktor, Professor, Pastor.**

Distinguish from this accented **-or** which is strong, thus **der Tenór,** and often **der Pastór** [*v.* § 76 (*c*)].

(*b*) Singular **-ísmus,** plural **-ísmen.**

Example: **der Katechismus, des Katechismus(ses), die Katechismen.**

Also: **der Absolutismus, Despotismus, Internationalismus.**

The genitive ending is often omitted, and some seldom need a plural.

(*c*) Singular **-us,** plural **-en.**

Example: **der Globus, des Globus(ses), die Globen (Globusse).**

This was once a large group, with no genitive singular **-s,** and the plural weak **-en,** but has now gone over almost entirely to the strong declension as shown.

Der Radius, Rhythmus, Typus still retain the former inflection: **des Radius, die Radien.** Thus also: **der Anónymus** (plural **Anónymi** or **Anonýmen**), and **der Káktus** (plural **die Kaktéen**). But two have developed a shortened form which is simpler to handle: **der Typ,** normal strong, and **die Kaktée,** normal weak.

Some are still uninflected in the singular, though strong in the plural: **der Fokus, Fidibus, Krokus, Kubus, Spiritus.**

91. Neuter Nouns of Classical Origin

These may end in -a, -as, -is, -os, -um, -on, -ium, etc.

(*a*) Singular -a, plural -en.

Example: **das Drama, des Dramas, die Dramen.**

Also: **das Dogma, Thema.** The three plural forms available are shown by **das Schema,** which has them all: **Schemas, Schemen, Schemata. Das Klima** and **Komma** have plural -s, **Thema** has also **Themata, Stigma** has only **Stigmata,** while **Klima** has also a curious popular form **die Klimáte.**

(*b*) Singular -as, -is, or -os, plural -en, sometimes with change of stem.

Der Atlas, *a volume of maps,* has also meanings in mythology, geography, architecture, anatomy, textiles. An *atlas* is **der Atlas, des Atlas, die Atlanten,** but it is also strong (**des Atlasses, die Atlasse**), and there is a variant weak form, from the plural stem (**der Atlant, des/die Atlanten**).

Die Dosis, Dosen, *dose;* **die Basis, Basen,** *basis, base.*

Das Epos, die Epen and **der Heros, die Heroen,** *epic* and *hero,* each have unchanged genitive.

The strong forms compete, especially in -as endings, thus **Atlas**; also **das Rhinozeros,** and proper names, where there are no classical modals for the plural: **die (verräterischen) Judasse, die (ungläubigen) Thomasse.**

(*c*) Singular -um, plural -en.

Example: **das Museum, des Museums, die Museen.**

Also: **das Evangelium, Faktum, Individuum, Medium** (including spiritualist), **Plenum** (in Parliament, etc., *the whole House*).

Many have also a plural in **-a: das Datum, Fixum** (*fixed element in a salary*), **Charakteristikum, Maximum, Pensum, Quantum, Vakuum.**

A few others are popularly given an **-s** plural: **das Album,** also **das Pensum.**

Words of Latin origin in **-um,** often with the **-a** plural, are common in the field of learning and education, thus in the fields of geography and history (**das Baltikum, Neolithikum**), education (**das Kolloquium, Praktikum, Physikum**), and medicine (**das Drastikum, Sensorium**), in grammar (**das Kompositum, Verbum**), printing and the book trade (**das Ineditum, Rarum**—which may be **Rarissimum** and even **Unikum**—and the plural **Judaica**).

The Greek ending **-on** is cognate: **das Lexikon, Rhododendron,** plural **Lexika, Rhododendra.**

(d) Singular **-ium**, plural **-ien.**

Many words are accompanied by or have been replaced by singular forms which have shed the Latin nominal (or adjectival) ending **-ium,** or adjectival neuter **-e,** while retaining the plural form **-ien,** corresponding in both cases to an original **-ia;** often also the shedding of the singular ending opens the way to a new strong plural.

Thus: **das Konzil(ium), die Konzile, Konzilien; das Partizip(ium), die Partizipien; das Prinzip, die Prinzipe, Prinzipien; das Fossil** and **Mineral, die Fossilien** and **Mineralien; das Stimulans, die Stimulantia.**

Some exist only in the plural: **die Realia** or **Realien,** *concrete aids to teaching;* **die Personalien,** *personal details;* **die Quisquilien,** *things of minor importance*—with which word it is appropriate that this section should close.

92. Summary of Assimilation of Classical Nouns

(a) An inflection which would appear out of place in normal prose may be preserved in special contexts; this applies especially to:

(1) Grammatical terms, which often follow the original declension: **das Imperfektum, des Imperfekti; das Partizipium Präsentis, das Partizipium Perfekti,** with adaptation to German orthography, unless indeed the term is treated as a complete foreign body: **die consecutio temporum** (cp. Appendix E).

(2) Terms of religion, especially proper names, thus: **Herz-Jesu-Bild, Mariä** (or **Maria) Himmelfahrt, der Name (das Wort) Christi,** and the terms for *B.C.* and *A.D.*: **vor (nach) Christi Geburt.**
Earlier, all cases were shown, now only the genitive.

(b) Assimilation of the above groups proceeds along lines of convenience.

(1) Genitive singular **-s** is added throughout, if pronounceable; but dative plural **-n** cannot be added where the plural ending is clearly foreign. Thus: **des Pensums, Dramas,** but **den Themata.**

(2) Assimilation to the strong declension is mainly in words ending in **-us** (**-usses, -usse**) and **-as** (**-asses, -asse**), but:

(i) **-um** words are occasionally given plural **-s: die Albums, Pensums,** and **das Faktotum** is always **die Faktotums,** while

(ii) loss of endings makes possible immediate assimilation: **die Konzile, die Partizipe.**

(c) Pending assimilation there is a noticeable tendency to accept the foreign word in the singular, but to use the plural of a German synonym:

der Atlas, die Kartenwerke; der Kasus, die Fälle (grammatical case); **das Komma, die Beistriche; der Musikus, die Musiker** (for **Musizi**).

93. Numerals (8). Inflection

Numerals as such are not inflected, but certain special cases call for notice:

(a) **Ein** is both indefinite article (v. § 13) and numeral.

As a numeral:

(1) It is invariable as a numeral proper (**von *eins* bis zwanzig zählen**), in clock times (**nach ein Uhr, zehn Minuten nach *eins***), in fractions (**zwei durch ein halb macht vier**). When a noun follows a fraction or collective numeral in apposition, the numeral may or may not be inflected: **in ein viertel Butter, mit einem halben Brot, mit ein(em) Dutzend Eiern,** but it is invariable when part of an indefinite adjective-pronoun: **mit ein bißchen Geduld, in ein paar Wochen** [v. § 101 (b) and (c)].

(2) When preceding a noun it is not distinguishable from the indefinite article (**ich habe nur einen Apfel**), unless made significant by spacing or by a capital (**nur e i n e n** or **Einen Apfel**).

(3) When preceded by the definite article or a limiting adjective, it is strong or weak according to normal adjectival rule: **sein ein*es* Glas, mein ein*er* Sohn, die ein*e* Frau, vor dem ein*en* Mann.**

(4) When standing alone as a pronoun it has strong endings: **Ein*er* von diesen Herren,** *one of* . . . **Wieviele Häuser haben Sie heute gesehen? Nur ein(e)s.**

(b) **Zwei** and **drei** in the genitive and dative plural, when not preceded by a word showing the case, sometimes in literary style take the strong adjective endings; a following second adjective is usually strong: **Es war nicht schwierig, sich in das Vertrauen zwei*er* alter Frauen einzuschleichen!** (H. Broch), *to worm one's way into the confidence of two old women.*

For further inflection of numerals beyond one v. § 155 (d).

94. Cardinal Nouns in -er

(a) The cardinals may be converted into full masculine nouns (as distinct from § 54 where the cardinal bears the capital for a noun understood), by the addition of **-er**, which then designates a group consisting of that number (**eine Fünfergruppe**, *group of five*), or a person or thing associated with the number (**ein Sechser**, pop., *a 5-pf. piece;* **ein Sechziger**, *a man of sixty*). These forms, not all of the same origin, occur in simple and especially compound words, and occasionally [v. (e) below and cp. § 281] even as invariable adjectives.

(*b*) The units, tens and hundreds of the numerals themselves are **die Einer, Zehner, Hunderter** [distinguish **die Eins, die Zehn, die Hundert** (*v.* § 54), the names of one figure only: *the figure* 1, 10, 100]:

Bei den deutschen Zahlwörtern werden die Einer vor den Zehnern genannt, also dreizehn, vierzehn bis neunundneunzig, *the integers are named before the tens.*

(*c*) Group numerals: **eine Fünferserie,** *a set of five* (*postage stamps*); **ein Neunerpakt,** *nine-nations pact;* **eine Zwanzigerpackung,** *packet of 20* (cigarettes, etc.); **eine Sechzehnergruppe,** *group of 16* (singers, etc.).

Der vorbeijagende Viererzug gehörte Korff (W. Bergengruen), *sledge and four.*

Zweierreihen bilden, Abmarsch! (H. Broch), *March off in double file!*

(*d*) Descriptive numerals, especially with denominations of currency, etc., as: **eine Zwanziger,** *stamp of 20 pf.;* **ein Zwanziger, Hunderter,** *note of 20, 100* (*marks, francs,* etc.), conveniently short for **eine Zwanzigpfennigmarke, ein Hundertmarkschein.**

Ein schlechter Bauer, hat getrunken, hat sein Grundstück gekauft, damals, so im Fünferjahr . . . (F. Werfel), *about the year '05.*

Die Münchener Bevölkerung hat die Neunhunderttausendergrenze überschritten (Munich newsp.), *passed the 900,000 mark.*

(*e*) The first component of a descriptive or group numeral may appear as an (invariable) adjective, thus: **die zwanziger Lebensjahre, in den dreißiger Jahren dieses Jahrhunderts, eine Flasche dreiundzwanziger (23er) Rotwein,** or **Dreiundzwanziger, eine fünfzehner Birne,** *the twenties, thirties of this century, a bottle of '23, a 15-watt bulb.*

(*f*) As may be expected, there is considerable overlap with other (*e.g.* feminine, *v.* § 54) numeral nouns, especially in the following fields:

(1) Numerals proper: -er nouns are common in the case of **der Einser,** and of *one* to *four* as used in school marks (reports): **er schrieb geschwind einen Einser, bekam einen Vierer;** but also for tram-numbers: **die Sechzehn, der Sechzehner.** Feminine nouns are general in the North, -er nouns in the South; but the latter use is also partly due to uncertainty about the plural of normal cardinals:

Selbst mit zehn ,,Vierern" wird künftig ein Schüler in Bayern in die nächste Klasse versetzt (newsp.), *pupils are certain of moving up even with low marks in all subjects.*

(2) Personal age:

A person has always the -er form: **ein behäbiger Vierziger, ein reservierter Fünfziger, eine lebendige Sechzigerin.**

The decades generally have the unaltered plural form: **er mochte Mitte der Dreißig sein, war in der zweiten Hälfte der Vierzig.** Occasionally: **eine Frau in den Dreißigern** (H. Broch), **er stand in den Vierzigen** (H. Hesse). Year with ordinal: **Ich bin über mein fünfzigstes** (= **Jahr) hinaus** (S. Andres); **Ins Einundsiebzigste geht sie seit Gründonnerstag** (F. Werfel), *her 71st year.*

EXERCISE XIX

A. Translate into ENGLISH:

1. Die Stadt bereitet für die berühmten Professoren einen großartigen Empfang vor. 2. Man kann die Museen der Stadt Paris mit keinen anderen der Welt vergleichen. 3. Welches Thema haben Sie für Ihren Aufsatz gewählt? Die Themen waren dieses Jahr ziemlich schwer. 4. In katholischen Ländern feiert man das Fest Mariä Lichtmeß am zweiten Februar. 5. Meine Tante, eine rüstige Siebzigerin, hat eine Sammlung von wundervollen Kakteen in ihrem Wohnzimmer. 6. Der Würfel fiel und es war ein Sechser; ich hatte gewonnen. 7. Jede Fabrik liefert ein gewisses Quantum Arbeit im Monat ab. 8. Die Erde enthält vielleicht noch viele unentdeckte Mineralien. 9. Nicht alle Medien in spiritistischen Kreisen sind Schwindler. 10. Die Epen der europäischen Dichtung sind nach dem Muster des griechischen Epos von Homer geschrieben. 11. Wieviele Hunde haben Sie? Das ist ja ein furchtbares Gebell! 12. Nur einen, aber unser Hund macht genug Lärm für zehn. 13. Das vierjährige Kind konnte schon ganz gut in Zehnern und Hundertern zählen. 14. In Deutschland kann man Zigaretten einzeln kaufen, nicht nur in Zehner-, Zwanziger- oder Fünfzigerpackungen [cp. § 544 (*a*)] wie in England.

B. Translate into GERMAN:

1. How did you like life in tropical climates? Did you find it strenuous? 2. (The) comedy is and always has been the weak point of German drama. 3. You must look up the position of this town in one of my big atlases. 4. One of these birds is a thrush, the other is a blackbird; you can recognise them by (**an**) their song. 5. In the early centuries councils of Christian bishops used to assemble and discuss common problems. 6. They served an excellent wine with the lunch; it was a 1937 Liebfrauenmilch. 7. Professors are usually forgetful but our professor never forgot his discussion class on Thursday morning. 8. During (**in**) the war, the treasures of many museums were safely hidden far from (**von**) the towns. 9. In the twenties of this century fashions for ladies were very strange. 10. Was Luther the originator of the catechism in its present form?

CHAPTER XX

95. The Relative Pronoun and Clause

(*a*) The relative pronouns standing for *who, which, that*, are:

TABLE:	Masc.	Fem.	Neut.	Plur.
Nom.	**der**	**die**	**das**	**die**
Gen.	**dessen**	**deren**	**dessen**	**deren**
Dat.	**dem**	**der**	**dem**	**denen**
Acc.	**den**	**die**	**das**	**die**

These will be seen to be the same forms as those of the demonstrative described at § 65, *i.e.* the definite article emphasised, with consequent lengthening of the -e- vowels of **der, dem, den** (in any gender), and extension of the four genitive forms and dative plural. This emphasis is also the reason why no demonstrative or relative pronoun may be *contracted* with a preposition (as can the definite article, §§ 19, 30), thus:

> **Das Haus, in das er ging, gehört seinem Vater.**

> Cp. **Er ging *ins* Haus, das seinem Vater gehörte.**

> **Das Zimmer, in dem er arbeitete, nannte er sein Studierzimmer.**

> Cp. **Er arbeitete *im* Zimmer, das er sein Studierzimmer nannte.**

Note.—But the relative may, like the demonstrative, *combine* with prepositions to form the adverbs described in § 33, *v.* § 227.

The function of the relative pronoun is to link two statements which have as common factor a noun or pronoun, thus in the above example:

> **Er ging in das Haus.   Das Haus gehört seinem Vater.**

One of these two statements is regarded as of secondary interest, and is linked to the noun or pronoun of the main statement through the relative. Thus the relative has relations within its own clause [an adjectival clause, one of the class of subordinate clauses, *v.* §§ 113, 114 (*b*)], and also outside its own clause, to the "antecedent" noun or pronoun to which it refers.

(*b*) The relative pronoun introduces a relative (or adjectival) clause, which as a subordinate clause is marked by having the finite verb at the end:

> **Ich verlangte das Buch, das man mir empfohlen hatte.**

> **Mein Onkel, der als Kavallerist gedient hatte, trug einen langen, herabhängenden Schnurrbart.**

Note.—As suggested in (*a*), the relative developed out of the demonstrative; an old form of relative statement with main clause order is preserved in the traditional openings of many fairy-tales (**Märchen**):

Es war einmal ein König, der hatte zwei schöne Töchter. *There was once a king, who* (= *he*) *had* . . .

The relative pronoun follows as closely as possible on its antecedent; it is thus normally first in its own clause. But:

(1) A governing preposition must precede the relative within the relative clause:

> **In dem Haus, vor dem wir stehen, wohnt ein Kunde von mir.**

(2) Parts of speech (verbs, prefixes, etc.), which by rule have end-position, must follow the antecedent in the main sentence:

> **Der Kunde, der in dem Hause wohnt, vor dem wir stehen** . . .

The relative clause must be separated off from the main clause or another following clause by punctuation; thus a comma precedes the relative or governing preposition, and a comma or other stop follows the verb at the end (*v.* examples above).

English *may* omit the relative when it is the object of the verb, however governed: the man I want (direct object), the man I wrote to (indirect object), the house we moved from (prepositional object). German may never omit the relative: **der Mann, den ich brauche . . ., dem ich schrieb . . . ; das Haus, von dem wir weggezogen sind** . . .

(*c*) The antecedent and its associated relative clause is regarded as one unit for the purpose of the order in the main statement. Thus when the main verb follows an interpolated relative clause [*v.* examples in (*b*) and § 96 (*a*)], it may be greatly delayed without ceasing to occupy its proper second place.

96. Agreement of Antecedent and Relative: Gender, Number, Person

(*a*) The relative pronoun agrees with its antecedent in gender and number, but *not* in case:

Der Junge (nom.), **dem** (dat.) **ich das Buch gab, hat es verloren.**

Dem (dat.) **Jungen, der** (nom.) **mir die richtige Antwort sagt, gebe ich ein Buch.**

The case of antecedent and of relative is dictated solely by their respective functions within their own clauses; thus the agreement of cases in the three examples in § 95 (*b*) above was entirely fortuitous.

(1) English reserves *who* for persons and uses *which* or *that* for antecedents other than persons. German has only the one form, which is used solely in accordance with the gender of the antecedent:

> **Das Haus, dessen Fenster weit offen waren** . . .

> **Der Bauer, in dessen Hause die Fenster weit offen waren** . . .

(2) English has, in the genitive, *whose* for persons, but *of which* for non-persons, while German uses the simple genitive form for both, cp. above: *The house, the windows of which . . . The farmer, whose house.* Note that in both languages the simple genitive form involves omission *of the article* of the associated noun: **dessen [die] Fenster,** *whose [the] house.*

(*b*) Person. The relative pronoun, developing out of the demonstrative (*he, she, it; that one, person, thing*) is grammatically third person. When the antecedent is a first or second person pronoun or a noun in the vocative a conflict may arise, since when the relative is the subject in its own clause, it and the antecedent will both seek to determine the person of the verb: **ich, der dein Vater (?bin ?ist).** This is solved in English by assimilating the verb to the antecedent: You who hope (*not* hopes) . . . I who am (*not* is) . . . German adopts the alternative course of repeating the appropriate pronoun in the relative clause, with which the verb then agrees:

Ich, der ich dein Vater bin, wünsche für dich das Beste.

Vater unser, der du bist im Himmel, geheiliget werde dein Name [opening of Lord's Prayer, with main clause order, after Luther's Catechism, cp. § 95 (*b*) Note.]

(1) This rule is not always observed:

Nun aber hatte ich schon eine Portion Leber in mir, aparter Genuß für mich, der selten Fleisch ißt (H. Hesse), *an unusual pleasure for me, who rarely eat meat.*

(2) And cases must be distinguished where it does not apply:

Ich bin es, der das Zeichen zum Lächeln zu geben hat (Th. Mann), *It is I who have to give the sign to smile* (apposition to **es**).

Blutiger Laie, der ich bin . . . (F. Werfel), *greenhorn that (as) I am . . .* (third person relative is predicate of the first person subject).

97. Verbs with Dative Object

(*a*) A certain number of verbs take their object in the dative. They may be said to express the personal attitude in its relation to the world, and thus either the subject or the dative object is almost always a person; in many cases both are:

Ich diene dem König, *I serve the King;* **er half mir bei der Arbeit,** *he helped me in my work;* **sie telefonierte ihm gestern,** *she telephoned him yesterday;* **der Anzug paßt ihm wie angegossen,** *the suit fits him perfectly;* **er erlag der Schwindsucht,** *he succumbed to consumption.*

It is convenient to consider here only simple and inseparably compounded verbs with the dative, leaving other dative verbs for later treatment (*v.* §§ 171 f., 179 f., 243 f.).

(b) Dative verbs express commonly some form of communication, co-operation, suitability or similarity obtaining between the person or thing which is the subject and that which is the object; or the relation may be the opposite, *i.e.* non-cooperation, dissimilarity, etc.

(1) Between persons:

Ich schrieb, antwortete, erwiderte ihm, *I wrote, replied to him.*

Ich folgte, glaubte, traute ihm, *I followed, believed, trusted him.*

Ich widerstehe, kündige, trotze ihm, *I resist, give notice to, defy him.*

Er schadet, droht, mißtraut mir, *he harms, threatens, mistrusts me.*

(2) Between persons and things:

Der Anzug steht, paßt, sitzt mir gut, *the suit suits, fits, becomes me.*

Die Sache liegt, ziemt mir; das Essen schmeckt mir, *the matter is congenial to, appropriate for me; the food tastes good* (*I like*).

Das gehört mir, *that belongs to me;* **er unterlag dem Fieber,** *he succumbed to the fever;* **er widerstand dem Feinde,** *he resisted the enemy.*

Note.—The underlying note of personal advantage or disadvantage causes a number of these verbs to form contrasted pairs, thus:

erlauben (verweigern), *to allow* (*deny*); **befehlen (gehorchen),** *to command* (*obey*); **trauen (mißtrauen),** *to trust* (*mistrust*); **gefallen (mißfallen),** *to please* (*displease*); **helfen (widerstehen),** *to help* (*resist*).

Foreign words, as received into the language, are used with a dative object on the analogy of German verbs of similar sense:

telefonieren, *to telephone;* **gratulieren,** *to congratulate;* **imponieren,** *to impress, overawe.*

98. Use of Verbs with Dative Object

(a) All verbs taking a dative object alone are intransitive, and all have the auxiliary **haben,** except the two verbs of motion (cp. § 44) **begegnen,** *to meet,* and **folgen,** *to follow.*

Such verbs are often described as taking the dative object "to complete the meaning". The following should here be noticed:

(1) Many such verbs are often not noticeably incomplete without the object: **ich schrieb (ihm), ich glaubte (ihr).** But the dative object is necessary to express the peculiar sense of the dative verb, thus:

ich glaube, *I believe* (*have faith*); **ich glaube ihm,** *I believe him* (*give credence to*); **ich schreibe,** *I write* (*am writing*); **ich schreibe ihm,** *I write* (*communicate*) *to him.*

Thus also: **er steht, lebt,** *he stands, lives;* but: **er steht seinem Feind,** *stands up to . . .;* **er lebt seiner Arbeit,** *lives only for . . .*

Wir wollen, daß alle Menschen ohne Vorrecht miteinander konkurrieren können und daß dem Verdienste seine Krone wird! (Th. Mann), *we want everyone to be able to compete without privileges, so that the prize shall fall to the lot of merit!*

(2) The dative object, however, may be omitted without change of meaning if it is clearly understood [cp. § 377 (*c*) Note]:

(ich) Danke schön! *thank you!* **Verzeihen Sie (mir)! Gestatten Sie (mir)!** *excuse me, allow me.*

Höflichkeit schadet (einem) nie, Scheiden tut (einem) weh, *politeness doesn't hurt, partings are sad.*

(3) Conversely, even with the dative object, the sense may allow or need further completion by a prepositional phrase, infinitive construction, or subordinate clause, often adding the substance (content) of the action or the reason for it:

Ich gratulierte ihm / zu seinem Geburtstag, *I congratulated him on his birthday* (prep. phrase of reason).

Er verhalf ihm / zu einer großen Karriere, einem Vermögen, *he helped him towards (to acquire) a great career, a fortune* (prep. phrase of result).

Der König dankte dem Offizier /, daß er ihm so treu gedient hatte, *the King thanked the officer for having served him so faithfully* (subord. clause of reason).

Er befahl ihm /, das Haus zu räumen, *he commanded him to leave the house* (prep. infin. construction of purpose).

(4) Many verbs of communication may, apart from their strict dative use, also take an accusative of the content communicated: **Sie telefonierte ihm / die Nachricht,** *she telephoned / the news,* and in this use are analogous to the verbs of giving and saying, etc., with dative and accusative objects (cp. §§ 16, 99).

Equally, many dative verbs may convert the dative into a prepositional object, with little change of meaning or force:

Ich schreibe meinem (or an meinen) Bruder, *write to my brother.*

Er vertraut seinem (or auf seinen) Freund, *trusts in his friend.*

Some dative verbs appear to take an accusative object, which is in fact an adverbial accusative of extent or amount:

Das hilft etwas, schadet nichts, *that will help a little, do no harm.*

Many verbs regularly take a prepositional object rather than the dative when the sense changes from person to thing:

Sie telefonierte ihrem Mann, but **ins Büro,** *to her husband, the office.*

Both objects: **Er schrieb seiner Mutter nach Rom,** or, with different order: **Er schrieb nach Rom an seine Mutter.**

Lastly, a dative verb may take an accusative in an entirely distinct sense:

Er befahl ihm, seine Seele Gott zu befehlen, *he commanded him* (dat.) *to commend his soul* (acc.) *to God.*

(*b*) Intransitive verbs with the dative, like many other intransitive verbs, may often take an accusative if another construction, usually a prepositional phrase, is also present, describing the result or designating the action as having effected the required purpose:

Er rief ihm, *called to him;* **rief ihn aus dem Zimmer,** *called him out.*
Er befahl ihm, *commanded him;* **befahl ihn zu sich,** *fetched him along.*

Note.—It is characteristic of the greater indirectness of **helfen** and its compounds, that, even with an indication of result, the dative object remains: **er half ihr aus dem Wagen,** *helped her out of the car* [cp. example in (*a*) (3) and § 386 (*b*)].

99. Compound Verbs with Direct and Indirect Object

(*a*) Many compound verbs express the basic senses of giving (lending, selling, depriving, etc.) and saying (telling, explaining, promising, etc.) which were seen (*v.* § 16) commonly to take a direct and indirect object in the accusative and dative respectively. In many cases the relationship between verb and dative object is not significantly different from that described for the dative verbs proper (§ 98). Separable compounds are reserved for treatment with similar dative verbs (§§ 171 f.). Among inseparable compounds in these senses are:

(*b*) Verbs of giving, etc.:

bewilligen and **gewähren,** *to grant;* **überlassen,** *to hand over* (*to*); **überweisen,** *to send, remit* (money, etc.); and especially those with the prefixes:

(1) **ver-** in the senses both of giving and denying: **verdanken,** *to owe* (*be indebted to someone for*); **versprechen,** *to promise;* **verkaufen,** *to sell;* **verweigern,** *to deny;* **verhehlen,** *to conceal* (*from*).

(2) **ent-** almost always with the force of denial: **entführen, entnehmen, entziehen, entwenden,** all in the various senses of *to take* (*from*), *deprive* (*of*).

(*c*) Verbs of saying, etc.

erklären, *to explain;* and especially those with the prefix **ver-,** mainly in the sense of denying information: **verheimlichen,** *to keep secret* (*from*); **verschweigen,** *to conceal* (*from*).

Exercise XX

A. Translate into English:

1. Das Opernhaus in Dresden, in dem ich zuerst „Die Zauberflöte" von Mozart hörte, ist jetzt zerstört. 2. Sie verbrachten die Sommerferien in einem Landhäuschen, das ihnen gehörte. 3. Das Häuschen, dessen Garten sehr schön war, stand in einem sonnigen, stillen Gebirgstal. 4. Die Briefmarken, die er seinem Sohn versprochen hatte, waren von Südamerika. 5. Gestern sah sie die Kinder, denen sie damals bei ihren Schulaufgaben geholfen hatte, und die ihr so schön gedankt hatten. 6. Die jungen Männer, deren Motorräder schnell und gut fahren, sind stolz und glücklich. 7. Eine Hausfrau, deren Küche sauber glänzt, ist auch stolz und glücklich. 8. Der Matrose, der betrunken war, folgte dem Soldaten und drohte ihm mit der Faust. 9. Dieser aber hatte keine Angst; er trotzte ihm und verweigerte ihm nicht den Kampf, den er verlangte. 10. Die Vögel, die wir eben sahen, waren Schwalben, die nach Süden ziehen. 11. Wieviele Millionen lauschen täglich dem Rundfunk: den Nachrichten, Vorträgen, Hörspielen! 12. In den Ecken hockten Spieltische, an deren einem zwei Hofräte oder Professoren Schach spielten (S. Zweig). 13. Große krakelige Schriftzeichen bedeckten die Postkarten, deren jeder Buchstabe so groß war wie die Buchstaben auf Zigarrenkisten (H. Böll). 14. Er lebt nun schon die Jahre seit seiner Rückkehr und Niederlassung einzig Geschäften (H. Mann).

B. Translate into German:

1. The old woman who sells fruit in the market place has an interesting face. 2. An artist to whom she had sold grapes did an excellent picture of (von) her which was exhibited (use man) at an art gallery. 3. Rembrandt, whose pictures we all admire, painted many such (solch-) types. 4. The workers to whom the manager had given notice were in [a] revolutionary mood. 5. He recognised the song; it was the melody they had heard together in a mountain valley in Spain. 6. In the museum of (von) which you have heard so much there is a large diamond from (aus) India. 7. The cake belongs to the lady who guesses its correct weight. 8. I, who was in the last row, could not see the stage well. 9. He wrote to the student he had met in [the] Tyrol and the student answered him by return.

CHAPTER XXI

INDEFINITE ADJECTIVE-PRONOUNS (2). QUANTITATIVES

100. General

(*a*) The second group of indefinite adjective-pronouns (*v*. Exhaustives, Chapter XVII) includes all those which refer to a (small, medium or large) quantity, number or amount of the class they describe, but without exhausting that class. We may thus distinguish quantitatives of :

(1) Small reference: **wenig (wenige)**, *a little* or *few;* also **ein bißchen** and **ein paar.**

(2) Medium reference: **einig-** and **etlich-,** *some,* and the terms for *a number;* **welch-** and other terms for *some* or *any*; and others with partitive force: **ander-, genug, mehr,** *other, enough, more,* etc.

(3) Large reference: **viel (viele),** *much* or *many, a lot* (*of*); and similar expressions.

(*b*) The inflection is described summarily under each word, and in detail at §§ 145-7. In general, if inflected at all, they follow the (strong or weak) pattern of the normal descriptive adjective.

101. Wenig, ein bißchen, ein paar

(*a*) **Wenig,** *little;* **ein wenig,** *a little;* **wenige,** *few.*

The singular is normally uninflected [**wenig Milch, ein wenig (Brot), mit wenig Mühe**], but is usually inflected after the definite article (**die wenige Milch, das wenige Brot**); the plural must be inflected (**wenige Menschen, die wenigen Häuser**).

As in English, a distinction is made between positive force with the indefinite article: **ein wenig,** *a little,* and negative or restrictive force with the definite article: **das wenige Geld,** *the (that) little money;* **die wenigen Menschen,** *the (those) few people.*

Mit (ein) wenig Geld kommt man durch die Welt, *with little (a little) money one can travel far* (suggested motto for hitch-hikers).

But, for the plural positive sense (*a few*), **wenige (Bücher,** etc.) is too restrictive, and **einige,** *some* (*v*. § 102), or **ein paar** [*v*. (*c*)] may have to be used.

Wenig as an adjective-noun (*v*. § 143):

Die Wenigen, die etwas davon verstehen, *the few who understand anything about that . . .*

Das Wenige, was ich Ihnen darüber sagen kann . . ., *what little I can tell you about it* [**was** as an indefinite relative, *v.* § 177 (*b*) (1)].

(*b*) **Ein bißchen,** *a little,* much used for **ein wenig** in speech.

Mit ein bißchen Verstand kommt man durch Stadt und Land, *with a little common sense one can travel far* (alternative suggested motto for hitch-hikers).

Ein bißchen may be abbreviated or amplified:

(1) Abbreviated to **'n bißchen,** and often to **bißchen:**
> **Bißchen kalt hier?** *bit cold here?*

Bißchen mehr Haltung auch in solchen Äußerlichkeiten kann nicht schaden, *bit more discipline can't hurt . . .*

(2) Amplified, *e.g.* **das bißchen Geld,** *that bit of money;* **ihr bißchen Habe,** *her bit of property;* **kein bißchen Talent,** *not a spark of talent.* (But: *Not a bit of it!* **Bitte schön! Nein, gar nicht!**)

Man muß ihr doch das bißchen Abwechslung gönnen, *one must grant her her little bit of change.*

Wieviel nützt mir nicht mein bißchen Studium der Natur! (Goethe), *How valuable was my small amount of nature study!*

Ein bißchen is normally indeclinable, especially when followed by a noun (*v.* first example above), but it may be declined when standing alone: **man muß mit einem bißchen vorliebnehmen,** *put up with (a) little,* and the definite article (or possessive adjective, etc.) replacing **ein** must, of course, be declined: **mit dem (ihrem) bißchen Energie . . .,** *with that (her) bit of go . . .*

Bißchen is actually a diminutive from **der Bissen,** *bit* or *bite;* and this may still be used in this sense:

Ich genoß wie ein verhungerter Hund den Brocken Wärme, den Schluck Liebe, den Bissen Anerkennung (H. Hesse), *this crumb of warmth, mouthful of love, and scrap of recognition.*

(*c*) **Ein paar,** *a few* (indecl.).

Mit ein paar Worten ist die Sache erledigt, *the matter can be settled in a few words.*

Like **ein bißchen, ein paar** may be abbreviated or amplified:

(1) Abbreviated to **'n paar,** or, more commonly, **paar:**
> **War paar Tage unterwegs,** *been away a few days.*

(2) Amplified, *e.g.* **die paar Kleider im Schrank,** *the (those) few clothes in the cupboard;* **die paar Mark Verdienst!** *that little bit of profit!*

Ein paar, like **ein bißchen,** is normally indeclinable, only a word replacing **ein** being declined: **in diesen paar Tagen.**

Note.—The definite article or limiting adjective preceding **bißchen** is neuter, and does not agree with the following word (**mit dem bißchen Energie,** above); while that preceding **paar** agrees with, and is inflected in association with the noun (**in diesen paar Tagen,** above).

Ein paar derives from **das Paar,** *pair,* a fully inflected noun:

Ich stand vor dem grotesken Paar und lachte, *before the grotesque pair;* **ein Paar Handschuhe,** *pair of gloves;* **mit dem Paar Schuhen** (but: **in den paar Tagen . . .**) **kann man nichts anfangen,** *we can't do anything with . . . (in . . .);* **das Pärchen,** *a pair (of lovers).*

Note.—**paar oder unpaar,** *even or odd* (mathematics and gambling), lit., *making* (or *not making*) *a pair.*

102. Einig-, etlich-, mehrer-, and manch-

(*a*) **Einig-,** *some,* is the general term of indefinite medium number, in the sense *a few, a certain amount (number):* **einige Männer, Brötchen, Bäume;** followed by another indefinite word: **einige wenige,** *some few;* **einige andere,** *some others.*

(1) Sometimes in the singular, with abstract terms: **nach einiger Zeit,** *after some time;* **in einiger Entfernung,** *at some distance;* **mit einiger Menschenkenntnis,** *with some knowledge of human nature.* Distinguish from this the sense *of one will* (**sie wurden einig,** *they agreed*— *e.g.* on a price); *one and indivisible* (**der einige Gott,** Biblical).

(2) In the plural when modifying a numeral, **einige** is ambiguous, suggesting either an approximation (**einige zwanzig Bücher,** *some twenty books*), or a multiplication (**einige hundert Meilen,** *several hundred miles*). The context usually suggests the appropriate sense.

(*b*) The terms translating the sense of *a number* may be placed in rising order as follows:

(1) **einige,** *some* in general, *a few* [v. (*a*)].

(2) **mehrere,** *several, a (small) number:*

Mehrere Soldaten traten vor und meldeten sich zum Absprung, *a number of soldiers volunteered for the parachute jump.*

(3) **manch, manche,** *quite a number, a (fair) number:*

Manche (Manche Leute) sagen einem niemals die Wahrheit, *(there are) quite a number of people (who) . . .*

Uninflected before a singular adjective and noun: **manch guter Mann,** and, in literary style: **mancher Mann, manch ein Mann,** *many a man.*

Manch represents a quantity hardly known in English, corresponding to *many a man,* etc., but not to *many men;* it is definitely a word of medium reference, thus **manchmal** is nearer *sometimes* than *often.*

(4) **viele,** *many, a large number* (v. § 106).

(c) **Etliche** is a regional (especially Rhineland) term of the range of **einige** or **manche: es sind etliche zehn Tage her, daß . . .,** *some ten days ago;* **über . . . hat er mir etliches** (neut. pron., v. § 148) **erzählt,** *he told me some things* (= **einiges, manches**) . . .

103. Welch-

(a) **Welch-** is an indefinite of medium reference standing for *some,* or, in questions or statements with negative force, *any;* it is always used pronominally, both in singular and plural:

Haben Sie Zucker? Ja, ich habe welchen, *I have some,* cp. French *j'en ai.*

Haben Sie übrigens etwas zu schreiben bei sich?—Ja, meinen Füllfederhalter. Aber kein Papier.—Hier ist welches (Th. Mann). *Here is some.*

Als jemand einwarf, es gebe keine Dramatiker, behauptete Strom, es gebe welche (E. Kästner), *that there were some.*

Wir besuchen jetzt weder Gesellschaften, noch geben wir welche . . . (H. Mann), *nor do we give any* (*parties*) *ourselves.*

(b) This sense is under attack from those who consider **welch-** colloquial; but with its strong partitive and indefinite force (*any*) it cannot well be replaced. It is, however, distinctly popular in style when used as subject of a declaratory sentence, rather than as object, complement, or in the sense *any*, as above, thus:

Welche waren anderer Meinung, *there were some who . . .*

The partitive force is strong in conditional statements:

Ein Mädchen, dem die Bedienung der Gäste—falls welche kommen würden—oblag, stand hinter einem Schanktisch (H. Risse), *if any were to come.*

(c) **Solche** is the definite term corresponding to **welche** with indefinite force (v. § 231).

Note.—Appropriately, when the sense of *some* is intensified with **irgend,** it is **welch-** which accompanies as an indefinite adjective:

Der Bürgermeister von Neuyork wurde auf dem Flugfeld—aus irgendwelchen nicht näher bekannten Gründen—von drei Schönheitsköniginnen begrüßt (newsp.), *was greeted—for some reason or other not entirely clear . . .*

Cp. also **welch-** in § 132 (*b*) (interrogative adjective) and §§ 290 f. (relative).

104. *Some* or *any* in other contexts.

(a) These, in English, are both terms of indefinite quantity. But *some* refers to an amount whose existence, though not its actual size, is known: he has some books, I took some thought, have some sweets!

Any refers to an amount indefinite in size, because it is still quite unidentified: have you any matches? ask anyone you like.

(*b*) German thus will be found to use an indefinite, an adjective, or no term at all, in such contexts:

(1) Indefinites for *some, any, v.* **einig-, welch-** above.

(2) Other words:

Ich habe es in irgend einem Buch gelesen, *read it in some book.*

Any emphasised, meaning *any* (*thing* or *person*) *you like* may be:

Jeder: Das wird Ihnen jeder Schuster machen können, *any cobbler will make that for you.*

A phrase: **Die Mitglieder dürfen zwei Bücher im Monat nach Wahl bestellen,** *members may order any two books a month.*

(3) No corresponding term:

Haben Sie Benzin? *Have you got some petrol?* **Wollen Sie noch Kartoffeln?** *Will you have some more potatoes?* **Ist noch Brennholz da?** *Is there any firewood left?* **Geht es ihm besser?** *Is he any better?* **Es kann nicht schlimmer werden.** *It can't get any worse.*

Note the preponderance of questions and negative statements where English uses *some* or *any*, and German no corresponding term.

Tailpiece: *Some car!* **So ein feiner Wagen!**

(*c*) For **etwas** as an indefinite *v.* § 61.

105. Other terms: **ander-,** inflected, and **genug** and **mehr,** neither inflected, may be included under quantitatives of medium reference.

Ander- and *other* are used differently in two important contexts:

(1) Time: *the other day,* etc. (*v.* § 58).

(2) Counting: *another cup of tea* is **noch eine Tasse Tee.**

Cp. **Er hat einen anderen Wagen,** *another car* (replacement), **sie haben noch ein Kind bekommen,** *another child* (addition), **wieder ein Kind?** *what, another one?* (cumulation).

Similarly with *more* in the "additional" sense, above:

May I give you (*some*) *more soup?* **Darf ich Ihnen noch Suppe geben?** and in answer: **Gern! Noch ein wenig.** *Thank you! a little more.*

106. Viel (viele)

(*a*) **Viel (viele),** *much* or *many, a lot* (*of*), is used with both singular and plural, inflected and uninflected, but an uninflected singular and an inflected plural are the combinations usually preferred:

Viel Plage, *much worry;* **viel Vergnügen!** *have a nice time;* **viel Glück!** *good luck;* **viel Damengekicher,** *much tittering from the ladies.*

Da seine Klienten viel Geld und viele Prozesse hatten, hatte auch er viele Prozesse und viel Geld (E. Kästner), *many cases and much money* (a fashionable defence counsel).

Singular inflection is popular in the masculine accusative: **Das hat nicht viel Sinn,** *there's not much sense in that;* but **Vielen Dank!** and **in dem sie Trost und Ausgleich fand für vielen Verzicht** (Th. Mann), *found consolation for much self-denial.*

But after the definite article **viel** behaves as a normal adjective:

Ach Gott, das viele Obst! *What a lot of fruit!* **Die vielen Bücher, die er in seinem Zimmer liegen hat,** *all the books he has lying around . . .*

Distinguish between two senses of *much, a lot*: (1) pronominal: **er hat mir viel geholfen,** *he helped me a lot* (amount); (2) adverbial: **das hat mir sehr geholfen,** *a lot* (degree). Thus **essen, weinen, schreien** require **viel**; **lieben, hoffen,** and **glauben** require **sehr.**

(*b*) **Viel** appears in many compounds of which the orthography is uncertain; normally a pronominal (uninflected) form is compounded, an adjectival (inflected) form not: **wieviel? wie viele Eier? zuviel Geld, zu viele Menschen, soviel Angst, so viele Sorgen.** Similarly with **allzuviel. Viel mehr** is *much more*, **vielmehr** is *rather*. But, apart from this last example, it is often a matter of personal taste.

EXERCISE XXI

A. Translate into ENGLISH:

1. Zu einem guten Paar Frankfurter Würstchen ißt man gern ein bißchen Senf und ein wenig Brot. 2. Mit einiger Erfahrung kann man kleine Reparaturen am eigenen Wagen machen. 3. Nehmen Sie noch ein Schlückchen Wein? Vielleicht eine andere Sorte. 4. Mit ein wenig Geschick und viel Geduld kann man manch schönes Kleidungsstück stricken. 5. Man hat ein paar alte Kleidungsstücke im Schrank gefunden, sonst war das Zimmer leer. 6. Die Ferien im Gebirge haben den Kindern sehr gut getan und auch den Eltern viel Freude gemacht. 7. Proverbs: Viel Geschrei und wenig Wolle. Genug ist nicht genug. 8. „Kleine Sängerin, großes Talent, keine Beschäftigung. Kann sämtliche Opern auswendig. Bißchen laut auf die Dauer" (E. Kästner). 9. Vermutlich war es ihm völlig unbekannt, daß es vor und außer Jazz auch noch einige andere Musik gegeben hatte (*that there had been*) (H. Hesse). 10. „Unanfechtbare Wahrheiten gibt es überhaupt nicht, und wenn (*and if*) es welche gibt, so sind sie langweilig" (Th. Fontane).

B. Translate into German:

1. Have you any matches? Yes, here are some.   2. I have a few cigarettes which we can smoke.   3. There are not many, but enough for a few hours.   4. Good clothes cost a lot [of] money.   5. Will you [have] another piece [of] cake? Or a little more coffee? Oh, I'm afraid (**leider,** adv.) there is none left.   6. Too many people have to take their holidays in August.   7. He has quite a large collection of postage stamps; he owns one of the few genuine Cape of Good Hope stamps.   8. Anyone can criticise but only a few can do the work properly.   9. We have recently seen several foreign films; not a bit of fun in any of them. 10. In winter we must enjoy the bit of sunshine we get.

CHAPTER XXII
INFINITIVE CONSTRUCTIONS

107. The Prepositional Infinitive

(a) The infinitive preceded by **zu** (cp. English *to* go, *to* come) is used in certain grammatically dependent relations:

(1) In apposition after many nouns and adjectives:

Seine Art, den Hut zu lüften, finde ich ganz entzückend, *I think his manner of raising his hat is quite delightful.*

(2) As the direct object of many verbs:

Ich versuche, dem Leser den Infinitiv zu erklären, *I am trying to explain the infinitive to the reader.*

(b) The construction of the dependent prepositional infinitive statement is as follows:

(1) Infinitive in end-position preceded by **zu,** written separately with simple and inseparably compounded verbs: **zu gehen, zu verkaufen,** but compounded in the manner of the past participle [v. § 88 (a) (1)] with separably compounded verbs: **aufzufassen, anzukommen.** Note examples here and in § 108.

(2) All adjuncts of the infinitive precede it.

(3) The whole construction is preceded by a comma if any further adjuncts beyond the **zu** of the infinitive are present, but not otherwise:

Das ist die beste Art zu kochen; but: **die beste Art, Spargel zuzubereiten,** *the best way of cooking, of preparing asparagus.*

Ich hoffe zu gewinnen, but: **Ich hoffe, morgen zu gewinnen.**

(c) Infinitive dependent on noun, etc.

Noun:	**Ich hatte keinen Grund zu schreiben,** *no reason to write.*
	Deinen Vorsatz, in die Türkei zu fahren, kann ich nicht billigen, *your intention of travelling to Turkey . . .*
Pronoun:	**Es ist lächerlich, über so was den Mut zu verlieren,** *it is ridiculous to be discouraged by . . .*
Adjective:	**Ich bin bereit, Ihnen das Haus zu einem angemessenen Preis zu verkaufen,** *ready to sell you the house at a fair price.*
Adj. Part.:	**Sie war geneigt, andere Meinungen als Opposition aufzufassen,** *inclined to take other opinions as opposition.*
	Ich bin überzeugt, ihn gestern auf der Straße gesehen zu haben, *convinced that I saw him . . .*

(*d*) Infinitive dependent on verb.

The prepositional infinitive is the general rule for the infinitive dependent on a finite verb, and applies to all verbs other than the specific classes which require a simple infinitive (*v.* §§ 109, 110, 215, 216, etc.).

Ich verbot dem Jungen, auf die Straße zu gehen, versprach ihm aber, ein Stück Schokolade nach Hause zu bringen, *forbade the boy . . . but promised him to bring . . .*

Note.—Apparent synonyms may require a different infinitive construction; thus **können** and **wollen,** as modal verbs, take a simple infinitive, but **vermögen** and **wünschen,** with similar senses, require **zu**:

Vor lauter Schlaf vermochte er nicht, aus den Augen zu sehen, *he could not see out of his eyes for sleep* (but: **konnte er nicht . . . sehen**).

(*e*) Comparison with English.

English also makes wide use of the dependent prepositional infinitive, but idiom varies in detail; thus:

(1) After nouns the gerund is often used, cp. (*c*) above: **Vorsatz zu fahren,** *intention of travelling.*

(2) After verbs, a subordinate statement introduced by *that* [**daß,** *v.* § 114 (*c*)] often corresponds to the prepositional construction in the other language.

This is especially so after verbs indicating certain mental processes (to think, know, etc.), or actions associated with these (to say, pretend, etc.), which make wide use of the prepositional infinitive:

Er glaubte, behauptete, war überzeugt [cp. last example in (*c*)], **das Ungeheuer vom Loch Ness (Simpl.) gesehen zu haben.** *He believed, insisted, was convinced **that** he had seen . . .*

Der Junge gestand, das Fenster entzweigeschlagen zu haben, *the boy admitted **that** he had (confessed to having) broken the window.*

But with a double object (pronoun and infinitive) the situation is reversed: *I expect him to come this evening,* **ich erwarte, daß er heute abend kommt** [*v.* § 369 (*b*)].

(*f*) Subject of the prepositional infinitive. Only finite verbs may have a grammatical subject, but the prepositional infinitive, like any non-finite verb, has an inferred or logical subject. This is usually indicated by the context, and is either a general subject [*v.* (*b*), (*c*) above: **zu kochen, den Mut zu verlieren**] or specific, in which case it is the subject of the main statement (*ich* **hatte keinen Grund zu schreiben**), or indicated by the noun to which the infinitive refers (*deinen* **Vorsatz . . . zu fahren**). But it is clear that a number of dative verbs, as [(*d*) above] **verbieten,** also **befehlen,**

erlauben, must by their very sense transfer the logical subject of the prepositional infinitive to the dative object of the main verb [cp. **verbieten** with **versprechen** in first example of (*d*)], *v.* more fully § 370.

108. The Prepositional Infinitive with um

(*a*) Some form of intention is implicit in many prepositional infinitive constructions [*e.g.* in § 107 (*c*), **Deinen Vorsatz . . .**]. Such intentional force can, especially when not clearly present in the sense of the governing verb, be made explicit by introducing the whole construction with the preposition **um** (called here the **um . . . zu** construction):

Ich verließ das Haus, um einige Besorgungen zu machen, *I left the house (in order) to make a few purchases.*

No categorical rule can be given as to when **um,** in addition to **zu** and the infinitive, is desirable or necessary. Views on what, in any context, constitutes good, or even correct usage, vary widely; thus only indications of general practice can be given (*v.* further, §§ 371-5).

The construction of the **um . . . zu** statement is the same as that of the prepositional infinitive statement, with **um** following immediately upon the initial comma, which must always be present, as **um** constitutes an extension of the prepositional infinitive [*v.* § 107 (*b*) (3)].

(*b*) The **um . . . zu** construction is normally used (even though the sense of *in order to* is not prominent) after expressions stating what is adequate, desirable, or necessary to achieve a given object, *e.g.* **genug,** *enough;* **genügen** and **ausreichen,** *to suffice;* **brauchen** and **bedürfen,** *to need;* and in certain statements dependent on modal verbs (*v.* § 373):

Eine Zigarre genügt vollkommen (ist vollkommen genug), um einen Schüler krank zu machen, *one cigar is enough to . . .*

Die Summe reicht kaum aus, um ein Gartenhaus zu bauen, *is hardly sufficient to . . .*

Man braucht nur einen Blick in das Buch zu tun, um seinen Wert zu erkennen, *one only needs to glance into the book to recognise . . .*

(*c*) With many verbs and adjectives indicating (1) intention, inclination (**bereit, gewillt, geneigt**), or (2) adequacy, sufficiency [**genügen,** etc., as in (*b*)], the sense of an objective is supported by the prepositional compound **dazu** standing in the main clause:

Ich bin dazu bereit, Ihnen das Haus . . . zu verkaufen [cp. § 107 (*c*)].

Die Summe reicht kaum dazu aus, um . . . zu bauen [cp. (*b*) above].

The "pointer" **dazu** (a prepositional adverb, cp. § 33, meaning *to that end*) points forward to the following infinitive construction with which it is in apposition; for clarity it should thus stand as late in the main statement as possible, close to the construction to which it points:

Ich bin von morgen ab nach Möglichkeit dazu bereit, Ihnen bei den Verhandlungen beizustehen, *I am ready to assist you* . . .

Its presence is grammatically even less obligatory than that of **um**; it occurs with both **zu** and **um** . . . **zu** constructions (*v.* examples above).

109. Quasi-auxiliary Verbs with Simple Infinitive. Verbs of Motion

(*a*) The simple infinitive is used in the predicate after a number of verbs:

(1) **werden,** in the normal future tense, *v.* § 63.

(2) The six auxiliaries of mood, *v.* § 63.

(3) **gehen, fahren,** and certain other verbs of motion.

(4) **bleiben, lernen,** and colloquially, **brauchen, tun.**

In some cases, an alternative construction with **zu** is possible. These verbs are, in other constructions, largely intransitive.

(*b*) Verbs of motion, especially **gehen**, may be followed by the simple infinitive of a generalised activity, especially **spazieren**:

wir gingen, fuhren, ritten spazieren, *we went for a walk, drive, ride.*

wir gingen spazieren, schwimmen, rudern, Fußball spielen, *we went for a walk, swim, row, game of football.*

The simple infinitive corresponds to an English present participle (*swimming*) or prepositional phrase (*for a ride*), and, as in English, the verb *to be* may be substituted in a statement of the immediate past (but not the past proper, or the present) for the verb of motion: **ich war eben schwimmen,** *I have (just) been for a swim.*

Occasionally also in transitive sense: **er führte seinen Hund spazieren,** *took his dog for a walk.*

This use is restricted, in both languages, to a generalised activity (thus English *swimming*), which may be intentional, but must be habitual. Thus:

(1) It is limited to **gehen** and its synonyms, and the complementary sense of **kommen: Kommen Sie schwimmen! Die Damen kamen Tee trinken.**

Sie wandte sich an Zerline, die inzwischen das Abendbrot melden gekommen war (H. Broch), *who had just come to announce supper.*

(2) A specific intention requires **zu**:

Ende des Monats muß ich wieder stempeln gehen, *go card-stamping again* (euphuism for *go on the dole*); but:

Ich ging, die Karte stempeln zu lassen, *to have my card stamped.*

Sie ist einkaufen gegangen, *she has gone shopping;* but:

Marie ist wohl noch einmal dies oder jenes einzukaufen gegangen (H. v. Doderer), *gone to buy this or that.*

Mit solchen Steuern können wir bald betteln gehen, *with taxes at this level we shall soon be able to* (*have to*) *go begging for our living;* but:

Er ist wieder gekommen, mich anzubetteln, *he has come to touch me for a loan again.*

(*c*) Compound of simple verb and dependent infinitive.

The simple dependent infinitive is (apart from prefixes, etc.) one of the recognised first elements in potential compound verbs. The criterion for a new compound is (*v.* § 88) the emergence of a new meaning for the compound as distinct from its parts. Thus **baden gehen** and **schlafen gehen,** *to have a bath, go to bed,* are still considered distinct; but all forms of *going for a . . .,* are compounded, as **spazierengehen, spazierenfahren,** etc.

110. Simple Infinitive with bleiben, lernen, brauchen, tun

(*a*) **Bleiben,** *to stay, remain.*

er blieb stehen, sitzen, liegen, *he remained standing, sitting* (*seated*), *lying.*

Distinguish, with the English participial form, the two senses of:

(1) Continuation in a place, *to remain —ing,* examples above, and the idiomatic senses of **bleiben . . . hängen, sitzen, stecken,** generally meaning *to remain stuck in a place, not to make any advance:*

Da und dort blieb ich in einer Kneipe hängen, dann jagte es mich weiter (H. Hesse), *occasionally I got caught up in a pub . . .*

Sie ist sitzengeblieben, *she is still "on the shelf".*

Die Versuche, (diese Grundsätze) methodisch in die Kindererziehung hineinzutragen, pflegten steckenzubleiben (W. Bergengruen), *such attempts . . . usually came to nothing.*

In **stehenbleiben,** *to stop, halt,* either of a person or a watch: **Meine Uhr ist stehengeblieben bei dem Anprall** (H. Risse), the sense of remaining in a place is transferred figuratively to the sense *to halt.*

(2) Continuation in an activity *to go on —ing,* must be translated otherwise:

sie redete in einem fort, *went* (*kept*) *on talking;* **die Uhr fiel hin, aber sie tickte ruhig weiter,** *just went on ticking* (cp. example above); **er hört nicht auf, zu rauchen,** *he won't stop smoking.*

Note.—In **Das bleibt zu sehen,** *that remains to be seen,* the infinitive is active in form, but, as the English shows, passive in force, *v.* § 249 (*a*).

(*b*) **Lernen,** *to learn.*

A short simple sentence, or one in which the dependent infinitive precedes the form of **lernen,** has simple infinitive:

ich lernte tanzen, gut tanzen, die Leute kennen, *I learnt to dance, to dance well, I got to know those people.*

Mit jedem Tage habe ich dieses Land mehr lieben gelernt (S. Zweig), *learnt to love this country more every day.*

A longer sentence, or one in which the dependent infinitive follows the main statement, requires **zu**:

Ich habe allmählich gelernt, zuzuhören und mit meiner eigenen Meinung zurückzuhalten.

(*c*) **Brauchen,** *to need.*

Normally **brauchen** is always followed by **zu** and infinitive, but colloquially it may take the simple infinitive, especially in negative statements, rather like English constructions after *need*:

Ich brauche ihn bloß (gar nicht) an(zu)rufen, *I only need to phone him . . ., do not need to . . .;* but: *need not phone him.*

Note.—In both languages the model is that of the modal verbs: *I must not . . . need not . . .,* **ich muß nicht . . . brauche nicht . . . gehen.** Besides *need, dare* also is used in this way: I dare not come; German has no simple equivalent: *I dare not say,* **ich wage es nicht zu sagen;** *how dare you (show your face . . .)!* **wie können Sie so unverschämt sein . . .!** *I dare say . . .* **ich glaube schon . . .**

(*d*) **Tun,** *to do.*

This verb is followed by a simple infinitive only in popular and dialect use:

er tut nicht kommen; arbeiten tu' ich schon, *he's not coming, I am working,* and expressions such as these are the nearest in German to the English progressive form [cp. § 67 (*a*)]. But some related expressions are accepted, though distinctly colloquial: **sie tut den ganzen Tag nichts als weinen,** *she does nothing but cry* (cp. § 367).

(*e*) Compound verbs may arise from the simple dependent infinitive as noted at § 109 (*c*). Thus cp. for **bleiben** and **lernen**:

Verb	Separate	Compound
stehen / bleiben	*to remain standing*	*to stop*
sitzen / bleiben	*to remain seated*	*to be "left on the shelf"*
lesen / lernen	*to learn to read*	
kennen / lernen		*to get to know, "meet"*

Exercise XXII

A. Translate into English:

1. Die hübsche junge Dame, die nebenan wohnt, geht täglich mit mehreren weißen Pudeln spazieren. 2. Viele Leute sehen sie an, und mancher Passant bleibt sogar stehen. 3. Was werden Sie mit den vielen Ansichtskarten anfangen, die Sie auf Ihrer Reise gesammelt haben, um sie nach Hause zu bringen? 4. Seinem Rat, nicht allein in dieses Viertel der Großstadt zu gehen, bin ich gefolgt, und er war notwendig. 5. Er hat versprochen, auf mein Haus aufzupassen. 6. Schon lange wünschte sie, diesen alten blinden Musikanten wieder einmal auf der Straße zu sehen; aber er war verschwunden. 7. Ein Päckchen Blumensamen reicht aus, um ein ganzes Beet im Garten anzusäen. 8. Der Arzt empfahl ihm, weniger zu arbeiten, und starken Kaffee und Tee gänzlich zu vermeiden. 9. Sie hatte genug Verstand, um die Gründe des Rechtsanwalts vollkommen einzusehen und zu billigen; er schlug vor, den Prozeß endlich aufzugeben. 10. Sie hat ihr Fahrrad einige Minuten lang an der Ecke gelassen und ging einkaufen. Für so kurze Zeit brauchte sie es nicht abzuschließen.

B. Translate into German:

1. The horse tried to swim across the river, but the current was too strong and it had to turn back. 2. He wished to read a manuscript at (in) the University Library, and to compare it with the printed text. 3. A nap of half an hour after lunch was enough to refresh her. 4. On Saturdays the landlord came to fetch the rent. 5. I learned to talk very softly, so as not to disturb the professor at (bei) his work. 6. You need only look at that dog and it begins to bark furiously. 7. He had too little patience to teach small children and to play with them. 8. In the morning she often went swimming, and in the afternoon she went riding on the firm sand by (an) the seashore. 9. He went to (nach) Austria with a friend in order to collect folksongs. 10. He was ready to take her to (führen in) the theatre the other day, but she wanted to stay at home to sew a new dress.

CHAPTER XXIII

CONJUNCTIONS

111. Coordinating Conjunctions. Double Forms

A number of conjunctions bind the two halves of the statement by a link introducing either part: **entweder . . . oder,** *either . . . or;* **weder . . . noch,** *neither . . . nor,* etc. (cp. § 69).

(*a*) Copulatives:

(1) **sowohl . . . als / wie (auch),** *both . . . and.*

Sowohl sein Vater wie (auch) sein Großvater waren Landpfarrer, *both his father and grandfather . . .*

Sowie, wie (als) auch, are also used as single conjunctions, **der Vater sowie der Großvater,** but if the full double form is not required, it should be considered whether simple **und** is not enough.

(2) **nicht nur . . . sondern auch,** *not only . . . but also.*

Nicht nur sein Vater, sondern auch seine Mutter war dem Trunk ergeben, *not only his father, but also his mother . . .*

Also: **dazu noch seine Mutter;** single conjunction: **Seine Mutter nicht weniger als sein Vater . . .**

This form, not (1), must be used if clauses are to be linked:

Nicht nur ist er ein Schuft, sondern er will auch alle anderen zu Schuften machen, *not only is he* (inversion) *a rascal, but he wants* (main order) *to make . . .*

(*b*) Alternatives:

(1) **entweder . . . oder,** *either . . . or.*

Das werden Sie entweder beim Bäcker oder in einer Konditorei kaufen können, *either at the baker's or at a cake-shop . . .*

When clauses are introduced, **oder** is always followed by main order, but **entweder** without inversion is more emphatic than with it:

Entweder kommt er oder er kommt nicht, die Sache ist sehr einfach, *either he comes or he doesn't . . .*

Entweder er kommt oder ich gehe, einfacher kann's (kanns) nicht sein! *either he comes or I go . . .*

(2) **weder . . . noch,** *neither . . . nor.*

Zeiten, die weder Haus, noch Pflug, noch Webstuhl kannten, *times which knew neither house, nor plough, nor loom.*

139

Introducing clauses, the leading position of the conjunction gives a strong negative assertion:

Weder konnte er länger bleiben, noch wollte er schon gehen—die Situation war ausweglos, *he could neither stay nor did he want to go.*

and a position after the verb for **weder,** with **noch** unchanged, is usually felt to combine rhythm and sense to best advantage:

Meine Mutter malte weder, noch zeichnete, noch schrieb sie, aber sie war herrlich empfänglich für alle Wirklichkeit (E. Barlach), *she neither painted, nor drew, nor wrote . . .*

(3) Other negatives with **noch.**

Strictly, other negatives should be followed by other second terms, thus: **er hatte kein Geld, auch keine Zeit; ohne Fleisch und (oder) Fisch; er ist nicht schlimm, auch nicht dumm.**

But many writers use **noch** after these and other expressions with negative implications:

Es fehlt nicht an Begabung noch an gutem Willen (R. Musil), *neither talent nor goodwill was lacking.*

Besonders der Zylinder . . . war ohne Stäubchen noch Rauheit (Th. Mann), *the top-hat especially was smooth and without a speck of dust.*

bis er nicht Schmerz noch Durst mehr fühlte (H. Hesse), *till he felt neither pain nor thirst.*

Ich, weiß Gott, war leider kein Historiker noch sonst ein gelehrter Kopf (F. Werfel), *neither a historian nor in any sense learned.*

These constructions may be considered as a double negative rather less emphatic than **weder . . . noch.**

(*c*) Partitives:

(1) **bald . . . bald,** *now . . . now.*

Er schwankte—bald wollte er, bald wollte er nicht, *sometimes he wanted to, sometimes not.*

Bald so, bald so, *now this way, now that way.*
Also (coll.): **mal so, mal anders.**

(2) **teils . . . teils,** *partly . . . partly.*

Er arbeitet nicht gut: teils ist es Unfähigkeit, teils aber Mangel an gutem Willen, *partly through incapacity, but partly through . . .*

(3) Others.

Halb zog sie ihn, halb sank er hin,
Und ward nicht mehr gesehen. (Goethe).

Partly she drew him, partly he sank towards her . . . (*The Fisherman and the Mermaid*).

Einerseits verdient man weniger, ander(er)seits kostet alles mehr Geld, *on the one hand . . ., on the other hand . . .*

112. Exemplifying Conjunctions

(*a*) **Als, wie,** and certain other coordinating conjunctions, are used to introduce exemplifying passages, which may be:

(1) Explanatory, *i.e.* purely illustrative of what has preceded, in the sense, *such as*, etc.

(2) Intensifying, *i.e.* either extending or restricting what has been said, in the sense, *especially*, *let alone*, etc.

(*b*) Explanatory conjunctions. They mainly connect words and phrases rather than clauses.

Als and **wie** are used interchangeably:

Dort sah ich die Güter der schmückenden Industrie . . . als: Kunstgemälde, Tonwaren . . ., Statuen . . . (Th. Mann), *I saw the products of the decorative industries . . . such as . . .*

allerlei exotische Blumen, wie Orchideen, Kakteen . . ., *all kinds of exotic flowers, such as . . .*

Als may be followed by **da sind . . .** in a phrase which, with its old-fashioned air, is admirably suited to irony:

Kunsterzeugnisse der alten Meister, als da sind Dürer, Rembrandt . . . *products of old masters, such as . . .*

Die Spiritisten, als da zumeist sind alte, jumperstrickende Damen (F. Werfel), *spiritualists, usually old ladies of the jumper-knitting variety.*

Also: **nämlich,** *namely, to wit* (distinguish **namentlich,** *especially*); **zum Beispiel** (abbrev. **z.B.**), or **etwa,** *for example;* **und zwar, das ist** or **das heißt** (abbrev. **d.i., d.h.**), *that is* (*i.e.*). (Now often abbreviated without stops: **zB, zb, dh**).

As regards following order when linking clauses, **etwa** and **und zwar** usually require inversion, **das ist, das heißt** are followed by main order, **zum Beispiel** by either order [*v.* § 75 (*c*)].

(*c*) Intensifying conjunctions.

Namentlich, *particularly;* **selbst,** *even;* **geschweige (denn),** *to say nothing about . . .* (an old first person singular, **ich** understood).

113. Subordinating Conjunctions.   General

(*a*) A subordinating conjunction is, as its name implies, any word which links ("conjoins") a secondary statement (the dependent or "subordinate" clause) to the main statement of a sentence:

Ich kann es tun, wenn ich die Zeit dazu finden kann, *if I can . . .*

The signs of the subordinate nature of such a clause are:

(1) The conjunction at the beginning, which is in most cases the point of "junction" between subordinate and main statement (but a relative pronoun may be preceded by a governing preposition, *v.* § 95).

(2) The finite verb at the end, after all other non-finite forms which normally stand there [subordinate clauses with main clause order are (apparent) exceptions, *v.* § 271 (*c*) and *v.* § 153A].

(3) The separating off of the subordinate clause from the main, or another subordinate clause, by punctuation; in the absence of any other mark a comma must precede the conjunction and follow the end verb.

Ich ging gestern aus , *weil* ich etwas Luft schnappen *wollte*. *I went out yesterday because I wanted to get a breath of fresh air.*

(*b*) The subordinate clause both makes a statement itself and plays a role within a wider statement; in both examples above, the conjunctions introduce adverbial clauses of the main statement, of condition (**wenn**) or of reason (**weil**). Thus an adverbial clause may precede the main verb, causing inversion, just as a single word adverb may:

Adverb:	Main Verb and Predicate (incl. Second Adverb):
Gestern	**ging ich aus, weil ich etwas Luft schnappen wollte.**
Weil ich etwas Luft schnappen wollte,	**ging ich gestern aus.**

With a preceding clause, it is quite clear why, in the interests of elementary comprehension, a comma must separate **wollte** and **ging**.

114. Subordinate Clauses. Classification

Within the structure of all but the simplest statements there are in German numerous occasions for the introduction of subordinate clauses, stamped as such by the signs noted in § 113. Such clauses may be classified by the conjunction introducing them, of which the main groups are relatives, interrogatives, and adverbs. Before these groups are discussed in detail, it may be useful to set them out summarily with the minimum of explanation, but with references to where they are more fully treated.

(*a*) Relatives, which may be:

(1) Normal relative pronouns or adjectives introducing a relative (adjectival) clause:

Ich wohne immer noch im Hause, in dem ich geboren wurde, *I am still living in the house in which I was born.*   (Chapter XX)

Man gab mir eine goldene Uhr, welches Geschenk mich außerordentlich erfreute, *I was given a gold watch, which present pleased me greatly.*   (*v.* § 290)

(2) An adverb acting as a relative after nouns of time, place, etc., and introducing an adjectival clause, but with adverbial function:

Im Augenblick, als (da, wo) ich ins Zimmer trat, geschah etwas Furchtbares, *at the moment when I entered the room something terrible happened.*

(Chapter XL)

(3) An interrogative adverb acting as a relative, and introducing an adjectival clause:

Das Haus, wo ich wohne, ist mein Geburtshaus, *the house where . . .*

Die Feder, womit er schreibt, ist eine Füllfeder, *the pen with which . . .*

(*v.* §§ 227, 228)

(4) An interrogative pronoun acting as an indefinite or general relative and introducing a noun clause:

Wer das sagt, spinnt, *whoever (anyone who) says that, is imagining things.*

Was der sagt, ist nur Angeberei, *what(ever) he says is swank.*

(Chapter XXXII)

(*b*) Interrogatives, which, in addition to their direct function of asking questions (**Wer sind Sie? Wann kommen Sie?**) may, as interrogative pronouns, adverbs, or adjectives, introduce:

(1) A noun clause as subject of a verb [*v.* (*a*) (4) above].

(2) A noun clause as object of a verb, usually known as an indirect question, whether the statement is an explicit question or not:

As Interr. Pron.:   **Ich fragte ihn (ich weiß nicht), wer er war.**

As Interr. Adj.:   **Ich fragte ihn (ich weiß nicht), welches Haus er kaufen wollte.**

As Interr. Adv.:   **Ich fragte ihn (ich weiß nicht), wann er kommen wollte.**

(3) Occasionally, an adverbial clause:

Wo ich zu Hause bin, da wachsen keine Reben, *where I live the vine does not grow.*   [*v.* § 141 (*c*)]

(*c*) The adverbs **daß** and **ob**, introducing a noun clause, as subject or object of a verb, commonly in the form of an indirect statement, question, or command; these constructions come under the general heading of "reported speech" (Chapters XLVI, L, LIV).

Ich sagte, daß (fragte, ob) er mitkommen wollte (subj.).

Ich sehe, daß (weiß nicht, ob) er mitkommen will (indic.).

Ob er morgen kommt, ist mir noch unbekannt.

(*d*) Many adverbs introducing adverbial clauses of time, place, cause, result, condition, concession, manner, and means. The subordinate verb (like that in all forms of indirect speech) may be in the indicative or subjunctive, and the two moods are discussed separately:

(1) Indicative, *v.* § 116 and Index.

(2) Subjunctive, *v.* Index.

115. Notes on the words introducing subordinate clauses.

(*a*) As the normal relative (**der, die, das**) was derived from the demonstrative (*v.* § 95), so, for other forms of relative statement, interrogative forms have been heavily drawn upon [cp. § 114 (*b*)].

(*b*) The scope of simple interrogatives is limited, whether in direct or indirect questions or the related relative statements.

(1) Simple questions may be framed with the interrogative pronouns (**wer, was**), adverbs (**wann, wo, wie**), or adverbial compounds (**warum,** reason; **wozu,** purpose; **womit** or **wodurch,** means).

(2) But for many more specific questions, phrases with the interrogative adjective **welch-** are used: **in welcher Absicht,** *with what intention;* **zu welchem Zweck,** *to what purpose;* **mit welcher Folge (mit welchem Erfolg),** *with what result (success);* **mit welchen Mitteln,** *by what means.*

(*c*) Apart from the role of **daß, ob,** and the interrogative adverbs (**wo,** etc.), in reported speech, the great field of the adverb as conjunction is in adverbial clauses proper. But great care is needed to distinguish between related but different forms of adverbs (and prepositions), when used in their primary role, and as conjunctions (cp. § 128).

(*d*) Although all words introducing a subordinated statement are strictly conjunctions, it is those introducing adverbial clauses which are (and will here be) commonly referred to under this term.

116. Subordinating Conjunctions (Adverbial)

The following are certain common adverbial subordinating conjunctions, classified by the types of clauses they introduce. References are given to fuller treatment in later chapters.

(*a*) Time: **als, wenn, indem,** *when* (*v.* Chapter XXV).

(*b*) Place: **wo** and its compounds **woher, wohin,** (*from, to*) *where(ever)*:

Wo des Menschen Herz ist, da liegt sein Vaterland, *where a man's heart is, there is his country.*   [*v.* § 141 (*c*)]

(*c*) Reason: **da, weil,** *as, because, since;* cp. **denn** (coord.), *for.*

These three have respectively approximately the degree of emphasis of English *as, because, for*:

Da es spät wurde, ging ich nach Haus, *as it was getting late . . .*
**Ich ging früh nach Hause, weil ich mich für den Ausflug am nächsten Tage
gut ausschlafen wollte,** *I went home early because I wanted to have a good
sleep before . . .*
Cp. **Ich ging früh nach Hause, denn es blieb mir nichts anderes übrig,** *I went
home early, for I had no choice.*   (Chapter XXXVI)

(*d*) Result: **so daß,** *so that.*
Ich arbeitete den ganzen Sommer, so daß ich den Preis gewann, *I worked
the whole summer, with the result that . . .*

Distinguish **so daß** from the sense of purpose (so that I *should* . . .),
which in German is:

(1) **damit,** usually with subjunctive or similar form:
. . . damit ich den Preis nicht verfehlen sollte, *so that I should not . . .*

(2) **um . . . zu** construction (*v.* § 108), provided the subjects of both
statements are the same:
. . . um den ersten Preis nicht zu verfehlen, *so as not to . . .*
(Chapters XXXIV, LIV, LV)

(*e*) Condition: **wenn,** *if.*
Wenn er kommt, werde ich ihm meine Meinung sagen, *if he comes I shall
give him a piece of my mind.*

Conditions are either:
(1) Open, *i.e.* likely to be fulfilled, thus **wenn** with future force (above)
can also mean *when* (*v.* § 122 and Chapter XLI); or

(2) Unreal, *i.e.* a condition expressed speculatively, with the subjunctive (*v.* Chapter LVIII).
Cp. English *if he comes . . .* (open), *if he were to come . . .* (unreal).

(*f*) Concession: **obgleich** or **obwohl,** *although, even if.*
Obwohl ich tüchtig arbeitete, bekam ich doch nicht den Preis, *although I
worked hard . . .*

Distinguish this from a negative condition: *unless*, **wenn nicht:**
Wenn man nicht arbeitet, hat man keine Hoffnung auf einen Preis . . .,
unless one works . . . (if one does not work . . .).

Concessive clauses, like conditional clauses, are also partly indicative
clauses (Chapter XLI), partly subjunctive (Chapter LVIII).

(*g*) Manner, means: **indem,** *as,* or a present participial or gerundial
construction. **Indem** links two events, associated in time with the special
force of:

(1) Manner (attendant circumstance); this use, though widespread, is now regarded as bad style:

Indem ich Ihnen nochmals herzlich danke, verbleibe ich . . ., *thanking you once more, I remain,*

and is replaced by simple coordination:

Ich danke Ihnen nochmals herzlich und verbleibe . . .

(2) Means:

Ich versuche gesund zu bleiben, indem ich viel Milch trinke, *I try to keep well by drinking plenty of milk.*

Cp. §§ 123 (*b*), 276 (*b*), 314, 315.

EXERCISE XXIII

A. Translate into ENGLISH:

1. Entweder müssen Sie Ihre Grammatik und die Vokabeln fleißig lernen, oder Sie werden in der deutschen Sprache wenig Fortschritte machen. 2. Man weiß, daß Rembrandt viel im jüdischen Viertel von Amsterdam verkehrte, um interessante Modelle für seine biblischen Bilder zu finden. 3. Man kann nicht nur Obst, sondern auch verschiedenes Gemüse für den Winter einwecken. 4. Wir haben in Bayern sowohl Bier mit Weißwürsten, wie auch Wein mit Pastetchen verzehrt. 5. Ob ich nächstes Jahr nach Spanien reise, weiß ich noch nicht, weil bis dahin so Vieles geschehen kann. 6. Da Friedrich der Große im persönlichen Verkehr immer nur Französisch sprach, schrieb er auch seine Bücher französisch. 7. Er hatte nicht Mensch noch Tier in Todesnot gesehen (E. Wiechert). 8. Ich sah nirgends ein Pianoforte, noch irgendein anderes Musikinstrument, auch kein mechanisches, kein Grammophon, kein Radio (F. Werfel). 9. Das Fatale daran war bloß, daß er weder wußte, wie man einer wird, noch was ein bedeutender Mensch ist (R. Musil). 10. A traveller in party novelties:

An der anderen Wand standen zwei grobe Holztische . . . mit jenen an der Tür erwähnten Juxartikeln für fröhliche Geselligkeit, als da sind Zigarren, die explodieren, Zigarettenschachteln, aus denen ein Teufelchen springt, Knallbonbons, magische Zündholzer, Masken, Papierhüte und dergleichen mehr (F. Werfel).

B. Translate into GERMAN:

1. Either you can go by (with the) train or you can take a bus. 2. She was neither clever nor pretty, yet everyone liked her. 3. On the one hand he understood the position well, but on the other he did not want to give in. 4. There were all sorts of trees in the forest, for example, beeches,

oaks, and ash-trees.   5. Albrecht Dürer was a painter as well as an engraver.   6. It is not certain whether the conference will take place, because the delegates from (**aus**) a certain country do not want to come. 7. As he has suddenly fallen (auxiliary!) ill, the Swedish runner cannot take-part in (**an**) the race.   8. Some people can only work if the wireless is on (is running).   9. Others hate all forms of noise and can only work if everything is quiet.   10. [On] the day on which he went into (**zu**) the army he burnt all his literary efforts.

CHAPTER XXIV

COMPARISON

117. Comparison of Adjectives and Adverbs. Forms

(*a*) The forms for the comparison of adjectives and adverbs are very similar to those in English, but usage shows some points of considerable divergence.

As most German adjectives may be used without change of form as adverbs, so in the comparative and superlative they have the same inflectional endings, **-er** and **-(e)st,** but the superlative of the adverb differs in construction from that of the adjective:

(1) Adjective:

Sie ist reich, reicher als . . ., die reichste (im ganzen Lande), *she is rich, richer than . . ., the richest (in the country).*

(2) Adverbs:

Sie singt schön, schöner als . . ., am schönsten in Konzerten, *she sings well, better than . . ., best in concerts.*

and the predicative adjective when the basis of the comparison is adverbial:

Der See ist malerisch, malerischer, am malerischsten gegen Abend, *the lake is picturesque, more picturesque, most picturesque towards evening.*

Am in this use is *always* contracted (cp. § 162).

The statements on form and use in (*b*) and (*c*) below apply therefore without distinction to the adjectival and adverbial senses.

(*b*) The inflectional endings of comparison are **-er** in the comparative and **-(e)st** in the superlative, cp. English fin-er, fin-est; and in addition, the adjective *may* modify the root vowel.

(*c*) Modification of the root vowel.

(1) Only monosyllables modify [exc. **gesund,** *v.* (4)].

(2) Of these, many of the commonest modify, as:

alt, arm, groß, jung, kalt, kurz, lang, oft, scharf, stark, etc.

Note.—**hoch** becomes **höh-er,** but **höch-st.**

nah(e) becomes **näh-er,** but **näch-st** (= *nearest, next*).

groß becomes **größer,** but **größ-t** (for **größ-est**).

(3) Others do not, thus: **froh, knapp, stolz, voll, zart;** and no words in **-au** modify: **flau, schlau** [but *v.* (4) *Note*].

148

(4) With some, both forms are common: **bange, fromm, naß**; while with **blaß, glatt, schmal,** and the one disyllable which is capable of modification: **gesund,** the unmodified form is preferred.

Note.—Modification is strongly affected by dialectal and personal speech habits. Modification is, in general, characteristic of the South rather than the North, spoken rather than written style, and a humorous rather than a serious tone:

Gestern war die bewußte Firma gut . . . Heute ist sie flau, und B. Grünlich ist fläuer-am-fläuesten . . . Das ist doch klar? (Th. Mann), *and the firm of B.G. couldn't be in a slacker state!*

(*d*) Insertion of euphonic -e- in superlative, -(e)st:

(1) The euphonic -e- is inserted after an accented syllable which ends in one of the sibilants -s, -sch, -ß, -st, -x, -tz, -z, and preferably also after -d, -t, a diphthong, or a vowel lengthened by -h:

die präziseste Bedeutung, das süßeste Kind, am stolzesten;
der fremdeste Blick, am gesündesten, bunteste Farben;
der freieste Wille, die genaueste Beachtung, frühestens.

But: **größt,** for **größ-est,** *v.* (*c*) (2). And modern usage, especially in speech, accepts omission of -e- after accented diphthongs and long vowels: **die genauste Beachtung, frühstens.**

(2) This means that all monosyllables with these endings will or may have euphonic -e-, but not polysyllables unless they have end accent, thus the following always have **-st:**

(i) Polysyllables with the common ending **-isch: praktisch, typisch, malerisch, malaiisch; der praktischste Vorschlag.**

(ii) Present and past participles (when they may be compared, *v.* § 119): **der blendendste Vorschlag, der ausgezeichnetste Mann.**

Note.—Adjectives ending in **-el, -en,** or **-er** omit the -e- of suffix or ending: **der edle Mann, der edlere Mann, der edelste Mann.**

(*e*) Not all words may take the above forms; among those which may not, certain special groups may be distinguished:

(1) Words or senses refractory to inflection, and forming comparisons with the periphrastic forms **mehr, am meisten,** *v.* § 118.

(2) Words or senses which can only to a limited extent be compared at all, *v.* § 119.

118. Periphrastic Comparison with **mehr, am meisten,** etc.

(*a*) English has the alternative comparative forms *more* and *most,* and uses them generally when an adjective is longer than a disyllable, and always with adverbs in -*ly*: *more punctual, most efficient, more prettily, most quickly.* The corresponding German forms **mehr, am meisten** are used, not for long words (thus **interessanter, am unglaublichsten**) but in cases where inflection is not possible.

(*b*) Certain kinds of words which cannot take an inflection:

(1) Adjectives or adverbs derived from other parts of speech, especially nouns; thus **schuld**, *guilty* (*to blame*), from **die Schuld**, *guilt*:

Er war schuld, mehr schuld (als ich); am meisten schuld daran war Karl,
    to blame, more to blame, most to blame.

But **weh**, adverb from interjection, is now regarded as an adjective (**das mir allerdings weher tat als . . .**, Th. Mann).

(2) Adjectival phrases: **mehr der Mühe wert**, *more worth while;* but these phrases are few, and the tendency is to compare the adjective: **des Schreibens kundiger (als des Lesens)**, *more skilful at writing*, or to form a compound: **lesenswerter**, *more worth reading* (cp. § 164).

(*c*) Certain senses which resist inflection:

(1) A comparison which indicates preference rather than gradation (cp. English *rather . . . than*): **mehr dumm als faul**, *more stupid than lazy;* **mehr müde als friedfertig**, *more tired than really agreeing;* and the corresponding negative contrast: **weniger faul als dumm.**

„**Es kommt nicht auf das Aussehen an, mein Herz ist deutsch!**"—**Verzeih, aber . . . du wirkst auf mich mehr komisch als deutsch!**" (S. Andres),
    you seem to me more comical than German.

Mehr . . . als can compare other parts of speech: **es war mehr Dummheit als Faulheit** (cp. above), and:

von einem Lächeln, das aber dieses Geheimnis mehr hütete als es verriet
    (Th. Mann), *a smile which rather kept than disclosed the secret.*

(2) A comparison indicating a relative position:

Die am meisten (am weitesten nach) links stehenden Mädchen konnten nicht gut hören, *the girls standing furthest to the left.*

Forms: **mehr rechts, weiter (nach) rechts;**
    am meisten rechts, am weitesten nach rechts [cp. § 166 (*b*) (2)].

(3) A comparison indicating a choice or greater probability, especially with **möglich** and its synonyms, requires **eher, am ehesten** (comparative of **bald**, *v.* § 120), *rather, most likely*:

Es ist eher möglich, daß er es vergißt, als daß er zu spät kommt, *it is more possible (likely) that he should forget than that . . .*

der am ehesten durchführbare Vorschlag, *the most practicable suggestion.*

Bei solchen Festessen wird man eher des Redens satt als des Essens und Trinkens, *at these dinners you are more likely to get tired of . . .*

For compounds of **möglich,** *v.* § 164 (*a*) (3).

119. Limited Degree of Comparison

(*a*) Present and past participles.

(1) Participles in which the verbal sense is still active may not be compared, but only those (senses) which have become primarily adjectival. No general rule can be given. The verbal sense precludes comparison in, *e.g.* **der angehende Offizier, rufende und schreiende Kinder, die geöffnete Tür;** the adjectival sense allows it in, *e.g.* **der blendendste Witz, der geriebenste Schurke.**

An adjective may be comparable in one sense but not in another: **der ausgezeichnetste Mann,** *this most excellent man,* but **der (vom König) ausgezeichnete Offizier,** *the officer decorated by the King;* **die schreiendsten Farben,** *most garish colours,* but **die schreienden Möwen,** *screaming sea-gulls.*

Comparison may be "by special licence":

Der Pfarrer sah sie fragend an. Sie aber erwiderte seinen Blick noch viel fragender, wenn mans so ausdrücken darf (F. Werfel), *but she looked at him even more questioningly . . .*

(2) Past participles of intransitive verbs are never compared (**ein vielgereister Mann, eine sehr verwelkte Blume**), but an exception is **gelungen: der gelungenste Witz,** *a superb joke.*

(*b*) Vast numbers of words are precluded by their sense from being compared: **dreieckig, doppelt, jährlich.**

(1) But metaphorical senses are more amenable to comparison than literal senses: **das leerste Gesicht, der schwärzeste Undank.**

(2) Terms which already express a high degree of selection should not be compared, thus not: **der einzigste Mann,** *the only man;* **der unbedingteste Gehorsam,** *absolute obedience;* but **weitgehendst** (*the highest degree of*), and **hauptsächlichst** (*chief* or *main*) are tolerated: **die hauptsächlichsten Teile des Satzes** (East German Duden), *the main elements of the sentence.*

In general, good taste should protect the writer from the multiplication of inappropriate superlatives, such as the description of a film-actress of intentionally "primitive" appeal as **die ungekämmteste Frau Italiens** [*v.* further, § 162 (absolute superlative)].

(*c*) But humour makes its own rules: **Mai, Meier, am meisten; in keinster Weise. Bei ihm ist die Nase am vornedransten,** *he has a most "advanced" nose.*

120. Irregular Comparison

Certain words have irregular forms in the comparative and/or superlative.

(*a*) **bald** and **gern.**

Positive	*Comparative*	*Superlative*
bald (adv.), *soon.*	**eher,** *sooner, rather.*	**am ehesten,** *soonest.*
gern (adv.), '*like*'.	**lieber,** '*like more*'.	**am liebsten,** '*like most*'.

Ich esse gern Äpfel, lieber Pflaumen, aber am liebsten Erdbeeren, *I like apples, but prefer plums, and most of all I like strawberries.*

(1) Both **eher** (**am ehesten**) and **lieber** (**am liebsten**) are used to state preference, the former also to express a higher probability:

Eher (lieber) Tod als Schande, *rather death than dishonour.*

Ich würde ihn lieber morgen als heute empfangen, *I would rather see him to-day than to-morrow.*

Ich würde ihn eher heute als morgen erwarten, *I would expect him rather to-day than to-morrow.*

(2) **früh** (adj./adv.) is regular: **früher, früh(e)st,** and **früher** (adv., also **ehemals**) means *formerly.* For **baldigst** *v.* § 163 (*a*).

(3) **ungern** (adv.), the opposite of **gern,** is regular: **ungerner, am ungernsten;** but the simple negation of **gern** is possibly preferred: **nicht gern, weniger gern, am wenigsten gern.**

(*b*) **gut** (adj.), *good.*	**besser,** *better.*	**best,** *best.*
gut (adv.), *well.*	**besser,** *better.*	**am besten,** *best.*

But **wohl** (adv.) is often used for *well* of mental and bodily comfort or health, and is regular: **eine halbe Stunde später war ihm wohler,** *he felt better;* **fern von der Hauptstadt fühle ich mich am wohlsten,** *I feel best far from the capital.*

(*c*) In general, adverbs can be compared only if they are also adjectives. **Oft** is an exception:

oft (adv.)   **öfter,** *more often, oftener*   **am öftesten,** *most often, oftenest.*

The sense of *frequent(ly)* is rendered by:

(1) Adjective **oftmalig,** *repeated,* or **häufig,** *frequent:* **seine oftmaligen (häufigen) Besuche waren mir nicht erwünscht.**

(2) Adverb **öfters,** an absolute comparative [*v.* § 161 (*b*)] common in speech for **oft,** with a parallel form in officialese, **des öfteren:**

Er kommt öfters zu Besuch, *he often comes on a visit,* but:

Er kommt öfter (comp.) als ich ihn gerne sehe, *he comes more often than I like to see him.*

(*d*) **viel** (adj.), *much, many.*   **mehr,** *more.*   **meist,** *most.*

    viel (adv.), *much.*   **mehr,** *more.*   **am meisten,** *most.*

    Er ißt viel, mehr im Sommer, das meiste im Winter.

Englisch macht mir viel Mühe, Französisch mehr Mühe, Deutsch macht mir aber am meisten Mühe, *but German causes me most bother.*

The double comparative **mehrer-** (adj.) is used mainly in the plural, but in the singular in the set expression: **ein mehreres,** cp. § 148 (*b*).

(*e*) **wenig** (adj.), *little* (amount), plur., *few.*   **weniger,** *less, fewer.*

                                          wenigst, *least, fewest.*

    wenig (adv.), *little* (degree).   **weniger,** *less.*   **am wenigsten,** *least.*

    Er braucht wenig Schlaf, weniger Schlaf als sein Bruder.

Die Wenigsten haben mehr als 1000 DM Einkommen im Monat, *very few people have more than 1000 DM monthly income.*

Seine Vorwürfe betrafen mich am wenigsten, ihre eher, *his reproaches affected me least, hers rather more.*

(1) There is also the form **minder, mindest,** mainly used in the adverbial sense (. . . **betrafen mich am mindesten**), sometimes in the singular of the adjectival sense (**minder Schlaf, nicht der mindeste Laut kam von ihm**). Note **wenigstens (mindestens),** *at least;* **nicht im wenigsten (mindesten),** *not in the least;* but **zum mindesten,** *at the very least;* **am wenigsten,** *least of all.*

(2) These two forms are the basis of the so-called "descending comparison", expressing the opposite of the normal comparison:

Diese Pflaumen sind gut, die anderen weniger (minder) gut, *less good.*

The descending comparison has only the adverbial form of the superlative, since when preceding an adjective it becomes a degree adverb:

Compare: **In jenem Haus waren wir am glücklichsten,** *happiest,* or **am wenigsten glücklich,** *least happy.*

Degree Adverb: **Der am wenigsten Schläfrige soll zuerst Wache stehen,** *the one who is least sleepy is to take first watch.*

(3) **Wenig** (like **viel**), though used with adjectival inflection in the positive (*v.* indef. adj.-pronouns, § 101), is strongly partitive in force, so that the comparative **weniger** (like **mehr**) cannot be inflected: **ich habe weniger (mehr) Einkommen, als Sie,** *I have less (more) income than you.* But **minder,** which is the comparative, not only of **wenig** but also of **klein, gering,** may be inflected: **ich habe das mindere Einkommen,** *the lesser income* (*of the two*).

121. Conjunctions of Comparison, als, wie, denn

These conjunctions are used to introduce a comparison after adjectives, adverbs, and similar parts of speech, meaning *as, than* (or *but*).

(*a*) **Als** is used in expressions of inequality or dissimilarity:

(1) An ascending or descending (*v*. § 120) comparison:

kleiner als, nasser als, mehr besucht als, weniger angenehm als.

Note the analogous use to introduce a clause of comparison after **zu** and an adjective, expressing degree:

Er kam zu spät, als daß wir etwas hätten anfangen können (with subjunctive), *too late for us to be able to do anything* [*v*. § 360 (*a*)].

(2) After words expressing dissimilarity through negation (**nicht, niemand,** etc.), otherness (**anders,** etc.), or opposition (**entgegengestzt, umgekehrt**):

Niemand (anders) als er, nichts als weinen, nirgends als zu Hause; Was hat er die ganze Zeit anderes (sonst) getan als kritisieren? *What has he done the whole time but criticise?*

Er tat es umgekehrt als man es ihm gezeigt hatte, *in the opposite manner to that which he had been shown.*

(3) After certain expressions with **so** [*v*. (*c*) below].

(*b*) **Wie** is used primarily to express equality or similarity:

(1) After the positive of the adjective (adverb): **so alt wie Sie, hart wie Eisen,** and in conjunctions: **ebenso wie er, so wie sein Vater** (*v*. §§ 70, 111). If **so** is retained, the expression may be modified to produce substantial *dis*similarity but will still require **wie: nicht (beinahe, halb) so alt wie . . .**

(2) Colloquially, but incorrectly in written style, **wie** is used in all senses of **als** listed in (1), (2) above (exc. clauses of comparison): **er ist größer wie sein Vater; nichts wie Arbeit den ganzen Tag.**

(*c*) **Als** versus **wie** after **so**-forms.

Strictly, therefore, **wie** should follow all forms with **so**; but:

(1) Many subordinating conjunctions are formed from adverbial compounds of **so** and **als,** thus:

Time: **sobald, sooft, solange . . . als,** *as soon, often, long as . . .*

Degree: **sofern, soviel . . . als,** *as far, as much as . . .*

though in modern usage these have largely shed the **als** and are used simply as subordinating conjunctions [*v*. § 125 (*c*) (time), § 313 (*b*) (degree)].

(2) The double (coordinating) conjunction **sowohl . . . als** (*v*. § 111) may take **wie** less formally, especially when followed by **auch:**

Sowohl der Fürst, als (wie auch) sein Erster Minister waren anwesend, *both the Prince and his First Minister were present.*

Similarly before **möglich: so bald als (wie) möglich,** *as soon as possible.*

(3) After multiplicatives as **drei-, viermal so (groß, alt)**, it seems to many speakers that the basic sense is rather one of *inequality*, and **als** is often heard: **er ist zweimal so alt wie (als) seine Frau,** *twice as old as* . . .

(*d*) **Denn** is an older (literary) form for **als,** and is still used in a few set expressions: **mehr denn je,** *more than ever;* and also to replace **als,** and thus avoid a harsh construction, when a second **als** follows in the sense *in the function of*:

Er ist bekannter als Musiker denn als Chirurg, *better known as a musician than as a surgeon.*

But here again **wie** is used in conversational style:

Als Firmenchef behandelt er seinen Sohn besser wie als Vater, *as a boss he treats his son better than as a father.*

For further uses of **als** and **wie** *v.* § 311.

Exercise XXIV

A. Translate into English:

1. Die größten Kinder sind nicht immer die gesündesten. 2. Die Amsel sitzt auf dem höchsten Zweig des Tannenbaums und singt ein immer hinreißenderes Lied. 3. Sie werden diesen Reisebericht interessanter finden als jeden Roman. 4. Die Beschreibung der hohen Gebirgswelt in Indien, höher als irgendwo anders, wird Sie am meisten anziehen. 5. Er ging lieber in die Gemäldegalerie als in Museen, denn dort konnte man am besten seine Sorgen vergessen. 6. So arm wie dieser Musikant war wohl keiner, aber er war lustiger als alle anderen Bettler in der Stadt. 7. Diesen Herbst war das Wetter viel schöner als im vorigen Jahr. 8. Sie ging lieber nicht zu ihrer Tante, denn da gab es nichts als sehr einfache Kost zu essen. 9. Sein Leben in der Großstadt war noch einsamer als seine Kindheit auf dem Land, denn er hatte dort wenig Freunde und keine Verwandten. 10. Proverbs: Hunger ist der beste Koch. Ob Ost, ob West, zu Haus das Best. 11. Ich empfand die Tätigkeit solcher Leute wie Zola und Ibsen als Flickwerk an den Ruinen einer mehr und mehr einstürzenden Welt (H. Risse).

B. Translate into German:

1. The river is much fuller after the heavy rains we have had, but it is fullest in winter. 2. You will find this chapter easier than the next. 3. She went to visit her more often after her illness and she liked her better than before (**vorher**). 4. It was the hottest summer they had had for (**seit**) some years, and the harvest was more plentiful than ever (**je**).

5. It was warmest in the month [of] July and temperatures were highest
(adv.).   6. Which boy had the most luck at (in) the examination?
The boy who knew most!   7. She was more popular but less fortunate
than her more intelligent sister.   8. I prefer to spend (spend rather)
my holiday in a big town than in the country.   9. Children have fewer
problems than adults, but they often feel them more deeply.   10. He
ran more quickly than anyone else, and he reached the goal in-the-
fastest-time (adv. superl.).

CHAPTER XXV
ADVERBIAL SUBORDINATE CLAUSES OF TIME

The adverbial conjunctions of time, and the clauses they introduce, may be divided, according to the time-relations indicated, into the groups: time when, during, before and after, since and till, etc.

122. Clauses of Time When, als and wenn, *when.*

(*a*) **Als** is used for a single event in the past, or in the historic present:

Als er das Buch fertiggelesen hatte, ging er ins Bett, *when he had finished reading . . .*

Als er endlich ankommt, findet er das Lager verlassen, *when he finally arrives . . .*

(*b*) **Wenn** is used:

(1) For repeated events in the past, *whenever:*

Wenn er seine Tante besuchte, pflegte er ihr immer Geschenke mitzubringen, *when he visited his aunt, he always . . .*

(2) In the present and future, for both single and repeated events:

Wenn du fertig bist, sollst du ins Bett gehen, *when you have finished . . .*
Wenn er eine neue Idee hat, will er sie jedermann mitteilen, *when(ever) he has a new idea . . .*

Note.—**Wenn** is also conditional (*if*) without distinction of tense [*v.* § 116 (*e*)]. The time sequence of the verbs may indicate which is intended (especially in the past), but not always. Thus **wenn du fertig bist** (above) could also be a condition.

(*c*) In adverbial clauses which also have a relative aspect, *i.e.* in which *when* refers to a preceding noun or adverb of time (**Zeit, Tag, Jahr, nun, jetzt, damals,** etc.), it is translated variously by **als, wenn, wo, da, daß,** *v.* fully, § 228. There may be a difference in sense between: **Jeden Tag, wenn ich ins Büro fahre, sehe ich ihn,** and: **Jeden Tag, da ich ins Büro fahre . . .,** cp. *every day when . . ., every day that . . .*

(*d*) **Wann** is used to introduce questions, direct or indirect, but not adverbial clauses (*v.* §§ 114-15).

123. Clauses of Time During Which
Während, indem, indessen, indes, *as, while.*

Two actions may be (1) fully contemporaneous, or (2) one occurring at a point of time within the other: (i) while she worked she sang, (ii) while she was working she pricked her finger.

(*a*) **Während** is the commonest conjunction, in both these senses, for any time:

Während sie arbeitete, sang sie / stach sie sich mit der Nadel in den Finger, *while she worked she sang / pricked* . . .

Während du kochst, mache ich die Post schnell fertig, *while you are cooking I will quickly get the post ready.*

Further emphasis on contemporaneity may be achieved by using:

Die ganze Zeit, während [or wo, *v.* § 122 (*c*)] **ich las, trommelte er mit den Fingern,** *during the whole time that I was reading* . . .

(*b*) **Indessen,** also **indes,** is literary usage:

Er saß, indes er den Totenschein ausfüllte, an dem Tisch in unserer Wohnstube (H. Risse), *while filling up the death certificate* . . .

(*c*) Derived senses of **während, indessen.**

Expressions of time "during which" may easily develop the force of logical contrast, especially:

(1) Adversative force.

They work while (= *during* and *but*) we play.

This often develops when **während** (sometimes more specifically **wogegen**) and **indessen** introduce a following clause:

Ich fuhr mit dem Zug, während er seinen eigenen Wagen hatte, *I went by train, while he had his own car.*

Sie empfing die Gäste, indessen ihr plötzlich erwachter Mann mit unrasiertem Gesicht Befehle durch das Haus schrie, *she received the guests while her husband (did nothing but)* . . .

Indessen is a kind of afterthought, and never leads the sentence, and thus is always close to the adversative sense; it is a fully developed adversative when used as adverbial conjunction (*v.* § 75, *but*).

(2) Concessive force:

Der Neurastheniker klammert sich an seine fixe Idee, während (or indessen) er zu gleicher Zeit darunter leidet, *the neurasthenic person holds tight to his idée fixe, while (though) suffering* . . .

This sense is common where **während** is supported by another adversative **doch, jedoch, dennoch,** etc.

(*d*) **Indem** is used:

(1) Occasionally in sense (2) (ii) above, § 123, meaning *as, while*:

Indem sie sprachen, erschien auf dem gegenüberliegenden Hügel ein einzelner Reiter, *as they were speaking there appeared* . . .

(2) Commonly, but now incorrectly, to introduce an event roughly contemporaneous with the main event (attendant circumstance):

Indem er seinen Hut aufsetzte, bat er seinen Besucher, ihn zu begleiten, *putting on his hat he asked his visitor . . .*

Re-stated: **Er setzte seinen Hut auf und bat den Besucher . . .**

Note the imprecise time sequence of the English participle, and compare the greater definiteness and change of subject in the example in (1). For **indem,** correctly used for means, *v.* § 315.

(*e*) **Wie,** *as,* especially in colloquial use and present tense:

Wie ich mir die Sache überlege, fällt mir ein anderes ein, *thinking over the matter, there occurs to me . . .*

124. Clauses of Time Before and After

Bevor and **ehe,** *before;* **nachdem,** *after;* **sobald,** *as soon as.*

(*a*) **Bevor** and **ehe.**

Bevor wir den Antrag annehmen, sollten wir ihn doch überprüfen, *before we accept the motion we should examine it.*

Ehe is more select diction and may indicate preference:

Ehe ich diesen Antrag annehme, lege ich mein Amt nieder, *before I accept this motion I will retire from office* (*rather than . . . I would . . .*).

Before following a negative may be:

(1) **nicht . . . bevor:**

Die Ware wird nicht geliefert, bevor die halbe Kaufsumme erlegt ist, *goods will not be delivered before half the purchase price has been paid.*

Or, in more elevated style, **nicht eher . . . (als) bis:**

Dem Sünder wird nicht eher vergeben, als bis er voll gesühnt hat, *the sinner is not forgiven before he has fully atoned.*

(2) *v.* also the forms for *not . . . till,* § 125 (*b*).

(*b*) **Nachdem.**

Nachdem sie alles gestanden hatte, brach sie in Tränen aus, *after* (*when*) *she had fully confessed she burst into tears.*

The sense of *immediately after* is rendered, if not by some similar form (**gleich nachdem, kurz nachdem**), by:

(1) One of the compound conjunctions **sobald** (**solange,** *v.* below):

Sobald ich meine Arbeit fertig hatte, ging ich auf Urlaub, *immediately on finishing my work . . .*

Ich werde Sie sofort benachrichtigen, wenn der Brief kommt, *I will let you know directly on arrival of the letter.*

(2) One of the constructions discussed in § 126.

Note.—All conjunctions of time tend to develop some logical force; thus **weil,** once temporal, is now fully causal, and compare **während** (above) and **seitdem** (below). **Nachdem** in time contexts thus often has secondary causal force (= **da**), especially in the sense *now that* (**Nachdem er nun gekommen ist** . . . = **Da er jetzt** . . ., *v.* **nun** below). Popularly (especially in Austria), but incorrectly, **nachdem** is used with pure causal force, outside time contexts:

Nachdem das Wetter schön war, machten wir einen Ausflug, *as the weather was fine . . .*

125. Clauses of Time Since and Until

Seitdem (seit), *since;* **bis,** *till, until, by (the time);* **solange,** *as long as;* **nun,** *now that.*

(*a*) **Seitdem** (also **seit**).

Seitdem ich vegetarisch esse, lebe ich viel gesünder, *since I have been (become) a vegetarian, I enjoy much better health.*

This example illustrates two points of usage:

(1) German present for English perfect in time sequence starting in the past and continuing in the present, as with **seit** (prep.), *v.* § 67 (*c*).

(2) Secondary causal force, *v.* Note at end of § 124.

(*b*) **Bis.**

Ich kann warten, bis er kommt, *I can wait till . . .*

Können Sie die Arbeit bis Freitag fertig haben? *by Friday?*

Bis er sein Examen bestanden hat, sind wir alle Graubärte, *by the time he passes his examination, we shall all be old men.*

Till following a negative may be a simple negation, thus:

Ich kann nicht warten, bis er kommt, *I cannot wait till . . .*

But if it looks forward to a positive and expected event, it is:

(1) **erst** (= *only,* cp. § 51) followed by the appropriate *when* conjunction:

Erst als ich ihn sah, fühlte ich mich völlig zu Hause, *it was not till I saw him that . . .*

Der Hirte kommt erst, wenn die Sonne untergegangen ist, nach Hause, *the shepherd does not return home till . . .*

Ich komme erst dann zurück, wenn du mir vergeben hast, *I shall not come back till . . .*

(2) *v.* also the forms for *not before,* § 124 (*a*); and those under **solange.**

(*c*) **Solange.**

Solange er in die Schule ging, blieb dieses Gefühl der Unterdrückung, *as long as he went to school he retained* . . .

As with English *as long as*, **solange** may, especially in the present and the negative, have secondary conditional force:

Solange er sich nicht bei mir entschuldigt, will ich ihn nicht sehen, *as long as he does not apologise* (*unless he apologises*) . . .

Note on conjunctions compounded with **so-**. These have developed in two stages:

(1) **Solange** as adverb in main clause, followed by the subordinate clause introduced by a conjunction proper, *i.e.* **als, als nicht** [*v.* § 121 (*c*)], for a parallel event, **bis** for a following event:

Ich bleibe solange, als er mich gerne da sieht,
als er mich nicht wegschickt,
bis er mich wegschickt.

(2) The construction was simplified, and the distinction between parallel and following events preserved, by omitting **als** after **solange**, which then moved forward to the conjunction position: **Ich bleibe, solange er mich gerne da sieht (nicht wegschickt),** and by omitting **solange** before **bis** (though both are sometimes still met): **Ich bleibe, bis er mich wegschickt.**

Der Krug geht (solange) zum Brunnen, bis er bricht, *the jug goes to the well until it breaks.*

Ich bleibe, solange bis man mich wegschickt, in meinem eigenen Hause, *I shall remain, until I am sent away* . . .

(*d*) **Nun.**

In literary style **nun** is used as a subordinating conjunction, *now that*, by the same process of omission of the original conjunction as was described for **solange**, etc. [*v.* (*c*) above], thus **nun, da** . . . [*v.* § 122 (*c*)] = . . ., **nun:**

Die Kabine war, nun das Schiff sich stärker bewegte, ein problematischer Aufenthalt (G. Hauptmann), *life in the cabin presented problems, now that the ship was rolling more.*

126. Time Link in Vivid Statement

(*a*) English *when* in narrative style often introduces a clause which is:

(1) in close succession to the main statement (which is often therefore introduced by *hardly*), and

(2) no less important in the narrative context than the main statement, sometimes more so:

Hardly had he left the house (first event), when it received a direct hit (second event).

There are similar forms of statement in German.

(*b*) Subordination of second event.

Corresponding to *hardly . . . when* German may have **kaum** (or **noch . . . nicht**) **. . . als:**

Kaum hatte er das Haus verlassen, als es hinter ihm einstürzte, *when it collapsed behind him.*

Noch hatte er den Bahnhof nicht erreicht, als er die heulende Sirene hörte, *when he heard the siren whine.*

Kaum or **noch** may come later in its own clause:

Der Blinde saß kaum, als er zu sprechen begann (H. Risse), *hardly was the blind man seated, when . . .*

But subordination of the second event, even if only technical, does not satisfy the need for narrative vividness; so there are two more stages:

(1) The second event becomes a main clause.

(2) The first event is subordinated to the second.

(*c*) The second event has main clause order and is linked by:

(1) The copula **und:**

Es dauerte nicht lange und ich erfuhr, warum er sitzen geblieben war (F. Thiess), *it was not long before I learnt . . .*

(2) More commonly an adverbial conjunction with inversion:

So: Kaum hatte ich einen Schluck Elsässer genommen, so spürte ich, daß ich heute noch nichts gegessen hatte (H. Hesse), *hardly had I taken a sip of the wine when I noticed . . .*

Da: In solcher Weise verging die Zeit, da empfing U. einen Brief seines Vaters (R. Musil), *when one day . . .*

Dann: Nicht lange, so überlegte das Kind, dann würde wieder der Flieger über den Himmel ziehen . . . (E. Langgässer), *it would not be long before . . .*

(3) In vigorous style, even the adverbial conjunction disappears and some form of parataxis (juxtaposition without join) results:

Kaum hatte die Alte diesen Laut vernommen, hob sie mit einer leidenschaftlichen Gebärde die Arme und rief (S. Andres), *hardly had the old woman heard this sound when she . . .*

Wie leicht wird ein Koffer gestohlen. Kaum dreht man sich um, fort ist er (E. Kästner), *hardly has one turned round when . . .*

(*d*) The first event is subordinated to the second, and introduced by **kaum daß** (or even **kaum,** cp. **nun** § 125):

Kaum daß sie die Vögel im Rücken hatte, fiel der Hahn plötzlich über die Henne her (E. Langgässer), *hardly had she passed . . .*

Often the second **then** leads:

Leiden Sie an der Seekrankheit?—Ich bin jedesmal, kaum daß ich das Schiff betreten habe, eine Leiche (G. Hauptmann), *from the moment of setting foot on board . . .*

127. Other Constructions for Subordinate Time Clauses

Many other constructions correspond, often obliquely and in an abbreviated manner, to subordinate clauses of time. It is usually necessary for both parts of the sentence to have the same subject, otherwise a subordinate clause is needed.

(*a*) A preposition and noun construction, thus:

Bevor er starb . . . = Vor seinem Tode . . .

Nachdem er sich verheiratet hatte . . . = Nach seiner Heirat . . .

Seitdem er weggefahren ist . . . = Seit seiner Abreise . . .

Ich bleibe hier, bis er kommt = . . . bis zu seiner Ankunft.

Während (solange) er in die Schule ging . . . = Während seiner ganzen Schulzeit . . . (prep. with gen., *v.* § 188).

(*b*) Past participle constructions often express preceding time (*v.* §§ 347 f.) and thus correspond to a clause with **nachdem,** thus:

(1) In related apposition:

Von meiner Krankheit erholt, ging ich wieder an die Arbeit, *having recovered from my illness, I went to work again.*

(2) In unrelated constructions:

Die Arbeit erledigt, wendete ich mich dem Vergnügen zu, *work finished, I turned to pleasure.*

(3) In verbless absolute constructions:

Kaum gedacht, schon getan, *no sooner thought of, than done.*

(*c*) A single word or phrase, all verbal forms being understood:

Krank (= **geworden**)**, wollte er Mönch werden; gesund** (= **geworden**)**, dachte er nicht mehr daran,** *when ill . . ., when well . . .*

Cp. example from Langgässer [§ 126 (*c*) (2)]: **Nicht lange, so überlegte das Kind . . .**

(*d*) A temporal clause may constitute a condition (in time), and may thus omit the conjunction and invert the verb [cp. § 236 (*b*)]:

Der (= **der Baum**) **fällt nicht um . . . kommt seine Zeit, da steigen die Säfte ihm doch** (Th. Mann), *when its time comes the sap will again start to rise* [cp. § 126 (*c*) (2)].

Kommt Zeit, kommt Rat, *time brings counsel.*

128. Conjunctions, Adverbs, and Prepositions of Time Compared

As these are often confused, they are here set out summarily:

(*a*) Time when. **Als** and **wenn,** conjns.; (**wann,** interr. adv.); **dann** and **damals,** adv.; **zur Zeit, im Augenblick,** etc., with gen. phrase following.

(*b*) Time during which. **Während, indem** and **indessen,** conjns.; **währenddem, währenddessen,** and **indessen,** adv.; **während,** with gen. (or dat.), prep. (§ 188).

(*c*) Time before. **Bevor** and **ehe,** conjns.; **vorher** and **eher,** adv.; **vor,** prep.

(*d*) Time after. **Nachdem,** conjns.; **nachher,** adv.; **nach,** with dat., prep.

(*e*) Time since. **Seit** and **seitdem,** conjns.; **seither** and **seitdem,** adv.; **seit,** with dat., prep.

(*f*) Time until. **Bis,** conjns.; **bisher,** *hitherto,* adv.; **bis,** with acc., and **bis zu,** with dat., prep.

Distinguish especially the **-dem** forms [*v.* § 225 (*c*)]; some are adv. (**währenddem**), others conjns. (**indem, nachdem**); only **seitdem** and **trotzdem** (*v.* § 238) are both adv. and conjns.

129. The Interrogative Adverb Wann

(*a*) **Wann** may introduce:

(1) A direct question: **Wann kommt er? Wann gehen Sie?**

(2) An indirect question: **Ich will wissen, wann er kommt. Sagen Sie mir, wann Sie gehen** (cp. §§ 114, 115).

(*b*) In either case, but especially in direct questions, it may be governed by the prepositions **seit** and **bis** for retrospective (since when), and prospective (till when) time:

Seit wann hat er einen neuen Wagen?   Bis wann bekomme ich meinen?
Since when has he had a new car?   By when shall I have mine?

These correspond to the use of the directional particles **hin** and **her** with the interrogative adverb **wo**? (cp. § 141).

Exercise XXV

A. Translate into English:

1. Nachdem das Lied verklungen war, trat eine feierliche Stille ein.
2. Nun wir das Schlimmste überwunden haben, können wir vertrauensvoll in die Zukunft blicken. 3. Kaum war ich ins Wasser gesprungen, so hörte ich einen verzweifelten Hilferuf. 4. Den Tag, als er zuerst die herrliche alte Kathedrale betrat, konnte er nicht vergessen. 5. Und wo er hinkam, da verließ er glücklichere Menschen und mutigere Herzen. 6. Wenn man immer büffelt und niemals ausspannt, hat man schließlich keine Freude an der Arbeit mehr. 7. Seitdem in Edinburg die berühmten Festspiele stattfinden, ist es jeden Sommer ein internationales Touristenziel. 8. War das Licht abgeschaltet, so begann er mit leiser Stimme Gespenstergeschichten zu erzählen. 9. Indem die Weihnachtsglocken zu läuten anfingen, zündete sie die Kerzen am geschmückten Tannenbaum an. 10. Der Professor brach mitten im Satze ab, und zögerte so lange mit der Fortsetzung seiner Darlegungen, bis die Studentin ihren Platz eingenommen hatte. 11. Die Neugierigen standen . . . mauerfest auf gespreizten Beinen, entschlossen, nicht eher von der Stelle zu weichen, bis sie alles wußten (L. Frank). 12. Falsches Geld, Banknoten höheren Wertes, geschickte Fälschungen, die erst entdeckt wurden, nachdem sie vielmals den Besitzer gewechselt hatten . . . (E. Wiechert).

B. Translate into German:

1. Hardly had he whistled when the dog leapt up to fetch the stick. 2. They went to the Greek islands because they wanted to help the victims of the earthquake. 3. As she was reading she completely forgot the time. 4. As soon as the elephants appear in the circus the children begin to clap. 5. I will peel the potatoes and prepare the vegetables if you will cook them. 6. While she drove off in her little red sports-car which makes so much noise, I tried to pacify the old couple next door. 7. As (**indem**) she was opening the door she heard the sirens. 8. When you have time you should visit the old lady and bring her some flowers. 9. Since they had seen that film they had wanted to emigrate to (**nach**) Canada. 10. Now I have read the paper I am ready to listen.

CHAPTER XXVI

130. Foreign Nouns (2). From Modern Languages

(*a*) A large group of foreign nouns from modern languages has -(e)s in genitive singular, and the foreign (French and English) -(e)s throughout the plural, with no -n in the dative plural; but German endings are steadily being introduced.

This group contains a large number of masculine nouns, many neuters but only few feminines:

(1) Masc. **Der Bestseller, Cant, Cutter** (film), **Gag, Lift, Match, Nonsens, Slogan, Slum, Snob, Song, Whisky** (and **Scotch**).

(2) Neut. **Das Komitee, Team, Taxi.**

(3) Fem. **Die Bar** (legal and alcoholic).

Many masculine and neuter nouns have passed through this class, and achieved strong status, though still end-accented, *v.* § 76.

There is much uncertainty in genders and inflection; some terms are chaotic, thus **der, die,** or **das Dschungel; der Túnnel,** plural **die Túnnels,** but in S.G. **das Tunnéll,** plural **die Tunnélle.**

Assimilation presents many problems: gender, pronunciation, spelling; all are included under the general term **Eindeutschung (eindeutschen,** *to assimilate;* to do so *partially* is **andeutschen**).

(*b*) Gender is whimsical and uncertain, but governed remotely by the principles explained in Chapter LIX, *i.e.* gender of origin, or of analogy of sense or form.

(1) Gender by origin. Words of French origin in **-e** and of Latin origin in **-a** are feminine and have plural in **-en: die Chance, Charge, Nuance, Patience; die Chancen,** etc.; **die Runda, Suada, Villa; die Runden,** etc. **Fata Morgana** has **Fata Morganen** (or **Morganas**).

(2) Gender by analogy of sense. **Der Lift (Aufzug), der Dreß (Anzug),** and of course the personal words **der Clown, die Miß,** etc.

Analogy of form with the neuter infinitive noun (*v.* §§ 404 f.) is perhaps the reason why words in both **-ing** and **-ment** are neuter: **das Training, Camping** (activity and place); **das Amüsement, Bombardement, Enjambement, Ressentiment, Revirement** (especially in diplomacy, the "new look").

Some obscure analogy of form may explain why certain French final consonantal clusters incline to neuter: **das Double** (*film double*), **Ensemble** (in music), **Timbre, Renkontre.**

(3) Gender by convenience must surely explain why some end-sibilants have become feminine, the German plural -en ending being much more pronounceable: **die Box, Kautsch,** plural **Boxen, Kautschen.**

(c) Pronunciation. The natural home of these words among German inflections is the -e plural for masculine and neuter nouns, and the -en plural for feminines. Whether they reach this goal depends partly on successful assimilation of pronunciation and spelling.

Final French nasals resist assimilation so long as even a colourable imitation is current [e.g. as in English (pop.) "nong" for non]. Thus **der Salon** (an old borrowing) and **das Bassin,** with the nasal, have -s, while **das Bataillon,** with German -n, has -e. This is shown clearly by **der Balkon,** which takes either plural according to pronunciation.

Feminine pre-final nasals present no such problem, thus **Chance** and **Nuance** may become **Chancen, Nuancen.** But the word from English *lorry* meaning a *station trolly* is **die Lori,** plural **Loris,** or **die Lore,** plural **Loren.**

The occasional omission of genitive -s is caused less by problems of pronunciation (**des Matches, Kekses**), than by analogy to its increasing omission in quasi-proper names (cp. §§ 235 f.), thus in national and tribal groupings of exotic form: **des Zulu, Eskimo.**

(d) Spelling. An approximate German spelling (as **der Charme** = **der Scharm**) is the usual prerequisite to assimilation to a German plural class. Thus English *clown*, which is universally **der Clown,** plural -s, is now listed as **der Klaun, die Klaune** (Duden); formerly all said (and wrote) **alle Couches im Hause,** but now **die Kautsch** has been devised for plural **Kautschen.** But it is not essential. Thus **Chauffeur** and **Friseur** had the -e plural before they became **Schofför** and **Frisör**; and **Match** may have it without (yet) having become **Matsch.**

English final -ss becomes -ß, as in **der Dreß,** (*sports*) *dress*, especially **Sportdreß, Turnerdreß,** and **die Fairneß** (analogy to -heit). **Die Stewardeß** (plural -ssen), *stewardess* and *air-hostess*. Confusion between French and English here provides sometimes a plural **Stewardesse** and a singular **Baroneß** (= **Baronesse**).

French close -u- occurs without the expected modification in **Nuance,** but takes it in endings: **Allüre, Attitüde.**

(e) Final assimilation often leaves (for a time) both endings in currency, thus the masculine nouns **der Lift, Match, Scheck, Sketch, Streik,** plural **Lifte** and **Lifts.** **Der Keks** (a proprietary biscuit), is now **die Kekse.**

(f) Finally, mention must be made [cp. § 92 (c)] of a tendency to make the best of both worlds by using foreign singular, but German plural: **das Baby, Foto, Motto; die Säuglinge, Lichtbilder, Sinnsprüche.**

131. -s Plurals in German Words

There is also an indigenous German -s plural, used especially in North German colloquial, and applied to certain special groups of nouns not suited to the normal endings; but in some groups an unchanged or strong plural is regarded as preferable.

(*a*) Standard nouns:

Persons: **die Kerls, Jungs** or **Jungens** (a double plural), **Fräuleins** (cp. S.G. **Mädels**), **Militärs: die Fräuleins in den Reisebüros** (W. Bergengruen, playfully); diminutives, **die Hänschens.**

Other (N.G.) terms: **das Deck, Haff, Wrack,** plural **die Wracks,** etc., but **-e** plurals also exist.

(*b*) Proper names, and these and onomatopoeic words when ending in a vowel: **Schmidts, Försters** (*the forester and his family*); **die Muttis, Papas, Hannas; die Wauwaus,** *bow-wows,* and **die Uhus,** *owls.*

Abbreviations: **die LKWs (Lastkraftwagen),** *lorries, M.T.*

(*c*) Some nouns from other parts of speech, especially nonce formations:

Das Hoch and **das Tief** in all senses (*vivat, sea-deep, high and low pressure area*) become **Hochs** and **Tiefs: Drei Hochs auf seine Gesundheit!** and **drei Lebehochs** (but **Er lebe dreimal hoch!**).

Die Wenns und Abers (*If ifs and ans were pots and pans* . . .), **die A.s,** and, as Th. Fontane wrote to a publisher who had amended his MS.:

Ich opfere Ihnen meine „Punktums", aber meine „Unds", wo sie massenhaft auftreten, müssen Sie mir lassen! *you must leave me my "ands".*

But for occasional nouns from other parts of speech [cp. § 447 (*a*)] the unchanged form is preferred.

132. Interrogative Adjectives

(*a*) Interrogatives may be pronouns (**was? wer?**), adverbs (**wann? wo?** etc.) or adjectives, in the sense *which, what* (*kind of*). German has the two interrogative adjectives **welcher, -e, -es** (as definite article) and **was für ein, -e, ein** (as indefinite article). These are used both in direct and indirect questions, and analogously as exclamations (*what a . . .!*). They each have a pronominal use (*which of* . . ., etc.) with inflections as the definite article.

(*b*) **Welcher, welche, welches.**

(1) As adjective, *which? what? what* (*a*)*!*

Inflected: **Welches Buch meinten Sie?** *which book did you mean?*

Von welchem Bahnsteig fährt der Zug nach . . .? *From which platform . . .?*

Mit welcher Begeisterung hat er sich an die Arbeit gemacht! *With what enthusiasm did he tackle his work!*

The uninflected form **welch** (cp. **manch, solch**) is as good as limited to exclamations: always before the indefinite article [**Welch ein (kompletter) Unsinn!**]; sometimes before an adjective (**Welch furchtbarer Hohn!**); and occasionally before a noun (**Welch Glück!**); *what (complete) nonsense! what dreadful mockery! what luck!;* but usually: **Welches Glück!** and always **Welcher Hohn! Welche Seligkeit!** *what bliss!*

Note.—Sometimes in a question: **Welch** (or **Was**) **ist der Unterschied . . .?   Wie schade!** *What a pity!*

(2) As pronoun, *which (one or ones)?*

Welcher ist der Sohn, und welcher der Vater? *Which is the son . . .?*

Welches war das Haus, in dem er wohnte? *Which was the house . . .?*

The neuter pronoun **welches** is also used in an undifferentiated ("neuter") sense in asking a question, whatever the gender of the following word; this is more common with things than persons, and especially when a choice is indicated:

Welches ist länger, der Bleistift oder die Feder? *Which is longer . . .?*

Welches ist der richtige Ausdruck? *Which is the correct expression?*

Welches waren die leitenden Grundsätze seines Handelns? *Which were the guiding principles of his action?*

But a following partitive expression requires gender agreement:

Welcher von den beiden Ausdrücken ist der richtige? *Which of the two?*

(*c*) **Was für ein, eine, ein,** *what (kind, sort of)?*

This is a traditional combination in which **für** has no effect on the following case. It is used:

(1) Adjectivally, usually followed by the indefinite article:

Was für ein komischer alter Herr das ist! *What a comical old man* (nom. case, complement of **ist**).

Mit was für einem Hut ist sie gekommen? *What kind of a hat . . .?*

But also with a noun, either an abstract idea: **Was für Dummheit!** or a material: **Was für Papier haben Sie?** or in the plural: **Was für Leute sind das?** With a preposition: **Mit was für Mitteln will er das versuchen?** *With what means . . .?*

(2) Pronominally:

Er kam in einem Wagen. In was für einem? *In what kind of car?*

If the indefinite article is omitted, the pronominal sense is supplied by **welch-** (cp. § 103):

Was für welches? (= **Papier**).   **Was für welche?** (= **Leute**), *what kind,*
sort? (of paper, people).

(3) In the nominative and accusative (only) **was** and **für** may, and often are, separated, adopting a position which was the original one:

Er tat mir leid, aber was war das auch für ein trostloses, verlorenes und wehrloses Leben, das er führte! (H. Hesse), *what a melancholy, forsaken, and unprotected life was his!*

Einen Hund will sie haben?   **Was will sie aber für einen?**   *What kind does she want?*

(*d*) Both these terms ask the double question *what* (of a thing not yet known), or *which* (of a class of things known); they may, however, differ among themselves and against **was** in these senses: **Was war Ihr Buch?** *what was your book?* **Welches war Ihr Buch?** [... **Ihre Zeitung?**—(*b*) (2)], *which book (newspaper) was yours?* **Welchen Hut soll ich nehmen?** *which?* (of several available) **Was für einen Hut** (or **welche Art Hut**) **soll ich kaufen?** *what kind of?* (of all the types available).

Was für ein Landsmann ist er? *what is his nationality?* (**Von**) **welcher Nationalität ist er?** (dat. or gen.).

(*e*) In indirect questions (only) *what a,* followed by an adjective, may, apart from the above expressions, be translated by **ein** (**eine, ein**) **wie** ...

Man sieht aber aus solchen Schriften, ein wie stark entwickeltes Bewußtsein der eigenen Bedeutung in den Städten lebte (W. Andreas), *what a strongly developed sense of* ...

or, with a preposition:

Jetzt erst begriff ich, an ein wie einzigartiges Wunder von Gedächtnis ich bei Jacob Mendel geraten war (F. Werfel), *what a unique memory I had run across in* ...

= **welch** (**was für ein**) **stark entwickeltes Bewußsein; an welch ein** (**was für ein**) **einzigartiges Wunder von Gedächtnis.**

133. Use of Past and Perfect Tenses

(*a*) The past tense is used to describe an action (event) in the past:

     Er starb im Alter von 74 Jahren, *he died aged 74 years.*

Such an event is primarily unrelated to the present, though its results may still be with us; it is thus the appropriate tense for historical narrative:

Die Mönche bauten im 15. Jahrhundert die Abtei, deren verwitterte Ruine noch den Berg krönt, *built the abbey, the ruins of which* ...

Kolumbus entdeckte Amerika im Jahre 1494, *Columbus discovered America in 1494.*

But it may be related to another action in the past; and the two time stages are more often related by an adverb than in English:

Als die Mönche ihre Abtei bauten,

> (i) **stand ihr Orden noch in voller Blüte,** *their order was (still) in full vigour.*

> (ii) **stand die Reformation schon vor der Tür,** *the Reformation was imminent.*

The simple past has to be supplemented to render the force of the English progressive past:

When I came in she was sewing, **saß sie bei ihrem Nähen** [infinitive noun, cp. § 67 (*a*), § 205 (*c*)].

He was always going off to Italy in the vacation, **während der Ferien pflegte er immer nach Italien zu fahren.**

(*b*) The perfect tense describes an action (event), completed in the past, but whose effects are related to the present situation:

Gutenberg hat die Buchdruckerei entdeckt (cp. **Kolumbus,** above), *Gutenberg discovered printing* (was the originator of a present art).

Die Westminster Abtei hat man im 12. Jahrhundert gebaut, *Westminster Abbey was built . . .*

Ich habe heute meine 20 Seiten Russisch gelesen, *I have read . . .* (event not yet superseded by to-morrow's stint).

Progressive: *What have you been doing with your clothes?* **Was um Himmels willen hast du mit deinen Kleidern angestellt?**

The past is often linked with the present in continuous time:

(1) By the force of adverbs: **wiederholt, mehrmals:**

Ich habe Spanien mehrmals (wiederholt) von Norden bis Süden durchreist, *I have several times (repeatedly) travelled through Spain . . .*

or in the negative:

> **Ich habe nie (nur einmal, kaum jemals) mit ihm gesprochen.**

and in statements of common experience:

Solche Leute hat es immer gegeben, aber die Welt hat sie abgelehnt, *there have always been such people, but the world has rejected them.*

(2) But if the past continues *unchanged* into the present, then the present tense is required, cp. § 67.

Note.—In S.G. speech the perfect is common as a narrative tense (cp. French), the imperfect having virtually disappeared: **Dann bin i'** g'gangen und hab' ihm meine Meinung g'sagt, und dann hat er mich hauen wollen, aber da ist der Seppi g'kommen . . .

(c) The past and perfect tenses compared.

Whether an event is recent or remote in time does not in itself determine the choice between these two tenses; but the past directs attention to an originating action, the perfect to its result in the present. Thus the examples in (a) direct the mind to certain historical actions of Columbus, and of the monks; those in (b) to book printing and Westminster Abbey, both of which are still with us, and about which also certain historical statements are made.

Events in the immediate past, however, are normally reported in the perfect, since their prime results are still with us, so in newspapers:

Der Premierminister ist nach Amerika geflogen, hat einen Vertrag unterzeichnet, ist im Wagen verunglückt, hat seine Demission gegeben, *The Prime Minister has flown to America, signed a Treaty, had a car accident, resigned.*

But a fashion, now perhaps waning, decreed that the simple past, which was felt to be more vivid, should be used in such headlines:

Premierminister flog nach Amerika, gab seine Demission, etc., and especially in reports of deaths: **Einstein starb im Alter von 75 Jahren.** The corresponding vivid form in English would be the historical present: *P.M. flies to America, retires; Einstein dies, aged 75.*

134. Use of Other Compound Tenses

The following are used broadly as in English, and with no greater degree of frequency:

(a) The pluperfect tense (*v.* § 45):

Bevor ich ihm den Teller entreißen konnte, hatte er schon mein halbes Mittagessen verschlungen, *before I could . . . he had . . .*

In continuous time statements, where German would use the present for English perfect (cp. § 67), the past corresponds to the pluperfect:

Ich wartete schon zwei Stunden, da kam sie, *I had been waiting . . .*

(b) The future perfect tense (*v.* § 63):

Bevor du mit deiner Schminkerei fertig bist, wird der Zug schon längst gefahren sein, *before you have finished . . . the train will have . . .*

As the future may suggest a presumption, the future perfect may suggest a presumption relating to the past:

Der Zug wird schon längst gefahren sein, *the train, one must assume, has long since left.*

An imperative in the perfect may be a concealed future perfect:

Bis Mittag hast du dein Zimmer aufgeräumt, *by noon you will have cleared up your room!* (*have your room cleared up by . . .*).

135. Simplification of Tenses in Subordinate Clauses

(*a*) When a statement consists of main and subordinate clause, and one or both tenses are compound (future, future perfect, pluperfect), the indication of the precise tense in one verb is felt to be sufficient in German, as in English, the other verb being reduced to a corresponding simpler form (present, perfect, past). This is especially common in time statements:

Wenn der Minister erscheint, werde ich mein Gesuch vorbringen, *when the Minister appears* (present for future), *I will make my request.*

Als er kam, gingen wir, *when he came* (past for pluperfect), *we went.*

Ich werde warten, bis sie alles abgewaschen hat, *I shall wait till she has washed up everything* (perfect for future perfect).

Note that though the forms are thereby simplified, the tenses may be either assimilated (**kam, gingen,** for **gekommen war, gingen**), or they may be differentiated (**erscheint, werde,** for **erscheinen wird, werde**).

(*b*) Further simplification in the main verb is often not possible because of ambiguity, thus:

Wenn der Minister erscheint, bringe ich mein Gesuch vor, could mean either *when* or *if*. But with more precise (time) conjunctions the further reduction of future to present in the main statement (cp. § 67) is normal:

Sobald der Minister erscheint, bringe ich mein Gesuch vor.

Solange sie noch abwäscht, spiele ich Klavier.

Bis der einen Entschluß faßt, haben wir alles verloren, *by the time he has made up his mind, we shall have lost all.*

These conjunctions are thus especially useful when the main statement has an imperative, which shows no time, or a modal verb, which resists any subtle differentiation of time:

Sobald du etwas erfährst, schreibe mir.

Solange der Vater nicht da ist, darfst du nicht gehen. *As long as father has not returned* (*until . . . has returned*) *. . .*

Note that German is often able to simplify both verbs together more radically than English; and the use of inexplicit present tenses may characterise the German when speaking English.

EXERCISE XXVI

A. Translate into ENGLISH:

1. Schon wieder ein Erdbeben in Japan? Was für eine Katastrophe!
2. „Welch grandioses Schauspiel der Natur!" rief der Professor, indem er in den dunklen Gewitterhimmel blickte. 3. Welche Frage haben Sie am schwersten gefunden in Ihrer mündlichen Prüfung? 4. Nach was für einem Muster hast du dieses reizende Kleid genäht? 5. In was für einem Bett schlafen Sie am besten? In einem altmodischen Federbett, in einem Himmelbett, oder auf einer modernen Kautsch? 6. Mit welch einer starken Stimme las der alte Herr noch jeden Abend ein Kapitel aus der Bibel vor! 7. Welcher Mann hat nicht den geheimen Wunsch gehegt, einmal eine Entdeckungsreise zu machen—in den Tropen, in den arktischen Regionen, oder was es noch für unerforschte Gebiete gibt. 8. Bevor der Schnee aufhört zu fallen, ist der Waldweg schon lange verschwunden. 9. Wenn der Frühling kommt, arbeite ich wieder fleißig im Garten. 10. Proverb: Wage, und du hast gewonnen! 11. Welche Zeiten, in denen wir leben, Zeiten des Sturmes und der Bewegung! (Th. Mann). 12. Ich hatte schon vordem in Wien ab und zu mit Militärs verkehrt (S. Zweig). 13. Ich kann Telegramms nicht leiden. Immer ist einer tot, oder es kommt wer, der besser zu Hause geblieben wäre (subj., *ought to have*) (Th. Fontane). 14. Germany in 1930. Rotfront! Deutschland erwache! Schwarze Schlipse, rote Schlipse. Biergebrüll, Saalschlachten. Tschingbummtrara. Im Schritt und Tritt. Statt der Gewehre (*instead of*, gen.) Knotenstöcke. Was war doch das Militär dagegen für eine saubere Sache! (B. Werner).

B. Translate into GERMAN:

1. With what (sort of) pen do you write? A fountain pen or a ball point? 2. Which book can I lend you? A travel book, a detective story, or a biography? 3. Which are the biggest rivers in Germany? The Rhine and the Elbe. 4. "What funny animals!" cried the little boy as he watched the monkeys at the Zoo. 5. What a wonderful concert! Mozart's Serenade on a warm night in June in the court of the castle-ruins in Heidelberg! 6. What an ideal setting! It must have been a great joy for you all. 7. As long as the sun is still shining I [will] take (**machen**) a snap of you in your new car. 8. From which platform does the 2.45 train go? Which staircase goes (leads) to the right platform? 9. "As soon as the order comes through you will attack the enemy's outposts," said the general. 10. Which of you is prepared to undertake this dangerous work?

CHAPTER XXVII

ADVERBS AND PREFIXES OF PLACE

There are a large number of adverbs expressing the idea of place, whether of location, motion, or direction, and used both in physical and figurative senses. Any of these may enter into compounds with verbs as separable, and some as inseparable prefixes. Certain groups may be distinguished and the commoner senses listed.

136. Original Adverbs

Ab, *down* or *away;* **auf** and **empor,** *up;* **da** and **dort,** *there;* **da** and **hier,** *here;* **fort, los,** and **weg,** *away;* **nieder,** *down;* **weiter,** *further, on;* **wieder** and **zurück,** *back;* **zusammen,** *together;* and the original particles of motion, often not translated into English: **hin** (away from the speaker) and **her** (towards the speaker).

Of the above, the following are derivatives: **weiter, zurück, zusammen;** and there are the derivative adverbs of location: **oben,** *up* (*there*), **unten,** *down* (*there*), **außen,** *outside;* **vorne,** *in front* [*v.* § 166 (*b*)].

Note that none of the above, even when rendered by the same approximate word in English, are synonymous. A few distinctions are given:

(*a*) **Hin** and **her.** **Komm her,** *come here;* **er fuhr hin,** *he went* (*there*); **hin und her,** *backwards and forwards;* (**eine Karte**) **hin und zurück** (*a ticket*) *there and back;* (**eine Rückfahrkarte,** *return ticket*).

Temporal: **es sind zehn Jahre her,** *it's ten years ago.*

Her sometimes loses its relation to the speaker and expresses a continuing relation between two things in motion: **Der Bettler lief neben dem Wagen her,** *ran along beside;* or even in position: **Die Bettler standen neugierig um den Wagen her,** *stood curiously around.*

Hin sometimes loses its relation to the speaker and means *downwards*: **Er taumelte und fiel auf die Erde hin** (= **nieder**), *fell to the ground.*

(*b*) **Hin** and **her** indicate strictly only motion. Thus if goal or origin is to be expressed, a preposition is supplied, **hin** and **her** being retained as secondary elements:

Er bewegte sich auf sein Ziel hin, *he moved towards his goal.*

Ein Zuruf kam von oben her, *a call came from above.*

Thus **hin** and **her** must not be regarded as replacing prepositions corresponding to English *from* and *to* in their genuine noun-governing force. Cp. prepositions, especially § 263 (*e*).

175

(c) **Hin, los,** and **zu.** Instead of a preposition with **hin,** motion towards a goal may be expressed by the adverbs **los** and **zu,** replacing **hin, los** emphasising the start of the action, **zu** the final goal: **Er ging auf der Straße hin,** *along the street,* **nach der Stadt hin,** *towards the town,* **auf den Mann zu,** *up to the man,* **auf sein Ziel los,** *towards his goal.*

(d) **Fort** and **weg. Weg** is *away,* of objects in space, in any direction: **der Wagen fuhr weg,** *drove off.* **Fort** is *away, on,* of time and space, in a continuous direction, thus:

In time, **fort** gives the compounds **fortfahren** (intrans.), and **fortsetzen** (trans.), both *to continue*: **er fuhr mit der Arbeit fort, setzte seine Arbeit fort.**

In space, the distinction between **weg** and **fort** is confused: **er fuhr fort** should mean: *he continued his journey,* actually it usually means: *he left.*

137. Two or More Adverbs in Combination or Compound

(a) Position or rest:

Hier, *here;* **da,** *there;* and the more definite **dort,** *there,* with another adverb, thus:

(1) **hier oben, unten, außen, vorne;** *up, down, out here, here in front.*

(2) **da oben, unten, außen, innen;** *up, down, out, in there.*

Da, with euphonic -r- before vowels, is often contracted to **dr-,** thus: **draußen, drunten;** cp. **droben,** *up there,* with **drüben,** *over there, yonder.*

Hier is not usually contracted, but there are the literary forms: **hienieden,** *here below* (*on earth*), cp. **hie und da,** *here and there;* and **hüben und drüben (standen drohend wartende Gestalten),** *on both sides* (*stood waiting, threatening figures*).

(3) Colloquially, even reduplicative forms appear: **da drüben, da drinnen, da draußen,** *over there,* etc.

(4) Similarly, **dort oben, unten,** and the reduplicatives **dort droben, drunten,** *up there, down there.*

Note.—**Da** and **dort** are distinct, **da** denoting rest or motion in a comparatively undefined space, **dort** rest at some distance. Thus **da** is not always English *there,* but also *here*: **Ist er schon da?** *Is he here* (*there*)? *Has he come?* **Da bin ich!** *Here I am!*

With the participles of motion **da** soon loses its place sense: **dahin, daher** become figurative [*v.* below (b)]; but **dorthin, dorther** become even more clearly defined in their local force.

(*b*) Motion:

The same adverbs as above, with **hin, her**: **hierher** (also **hierhin**), *hither;* **dahin, dorthin,** *thither;* **daher, dorther,** *from there, thence;* **daher** (and sometimes **einher**) is also *along,* with weakened local sense: **Das Schiff segelt daher wie ein Vogel,** *sails along like* . . .

These compounds may appear separated: **Da komme ich her,** *I come from there;* **da gehe ich hin,** *I am going there;* also **dort her, dort hin;** compare English *therefrom, thereto.*

Daher is also the logical *therefore, thus.*

Combinations: **da herauf,** *up there;* **dort hinunter,** *down there,* *v.* below § 138 (*a*). **Von dorther,** *from there.* **Dahin** in the figurative sense, *finished, gone*: **Die letzte Möglichkeit ist dahin.**

(*c*) **Hin** and **her** combine with some other prime adverbs: **hinweg,** *away;* **hinfort, weiterhin,** *henceforth, from now on;* **hinwieder(um),** *again, once more.*

138. Two or More Adverbs and Prepositions in Combination

(*a*) Movement without relation to an object, but specified in its direction to the speaker by compounding with **hin** or **her** many common prepositions: **herab, heraus, herbei, hervor,** etc.; **hinab, hinan, hinaus, hinunter, hinüber,** etc.; **herein** and **hinein** from the preposition **in.**

These are often abbreviated to **'rauf** or **rauf, 'nunter**; in some cases, the shortened form is almost accepted as the normal prefix, as **(he)rausschmeißen,** *to throw out* ("*give the boot*"), **(he)reinfallen,** *to "be had"* (*taken in*); the nouns are **der Herausschmiß,** but **der Reinfall.**

(1) All these compounds, as prefixes, may have a figurative sense: **Er gibt das Geld heraus** (*pays up*), but **Er gibt das Buch heraus** (*publishes*); **Er ließ den Vorhang herab** (*lowered*), but **Er läßt sich herab** (*condescends*); **Er ging hinaus** (*went out*), but **Das geht über den gerechten Preis hinaus** (*exceeds*).

For case after prepositions in figurative senses, *v.* § 265 (*c*).

(2) There are many combined forms, as: **von oben herunter, von unten herauf, oben hinaus** (but **oben hin,** *superficially*).

Note the construction with English double prepositions, as *from under*: **Er kam unter dem Tisch hervor; Er nahm den Koffer von unter dem Bett** [*v.* § 263 (*e*)].

(*b*) Movement or position in relation to an object, rather than relation to the speaker, is expressed by compounding **da-** (before vowels **dar-**) or sometimes, more strongly, **hier-**; the former is sometimes contracted (**drauf,** but only **hierauf**), while **hier-** may appear as **hie-** before consonants (**hiemit** for **hiermit**). **D(a)ran, d(a)rauf, d(a)raus, d(a)runter, davor, dazu; d(a)rein,** *into it,* **d(a)rin,** *in it;* **hieran, hierauf, hieraus, hierunter, hierzu.**

Im Zimmer stand ein Tisch, daran (darauf, darunter) saß ein Männlein. Das Dorf besaß eine kleine Kirche; hierum lief eine alte Mauer. Er erblickte das Wasser, stürzte sich drein und schwamm drin herum.

In these senses, **hier** and **da** have (almost) lost their local force (*here, there*) and acquired the force of demonstrative pronouns (preposition plus *this, that*), and even of simple pronouns (preposition plus *it, them*). As such they quickly acquire figurative sense, and are used in quite abstract contexts: **danebenhauen,** *to make a mistake;* **daran tut er gut,** *he does well to do that;* **hiervon sprechen wir nicht,** *we do not refer to that;* **hierauf verließ er das Zimmer,** *thereupon he left the room;* **was verstehen Sie darunter,** *what do you understand (mean) by that.*

Distinguish **von hier,** *from here;* as: **zehn Meilen von hier;** and **hiervon,** *about that;* as: **hiervon verstehe ich nichts.**

Dort, which is not compounded, retains local force: **er machte sich davon,** *made off* (figurative force), **er begab sich von dort weg,** *went away from there* (local force).

(*c*) **Hin** and **her** follow some prepositions in compound: **hinterher, nachher, nebenher, nebenhin, seither, vorher, vorhin.** They are partly adverbs of place, partly of time.

There are also a few double prepositional compounds: **voraus, vorbei, voran, vorauf, zuvor.**

139. Adverbs of Relative Movement with -wärts

(*a*) Relative movement in the direction of a stated goal, but without relation to a speaker, may be expressed by compounds of the element **-wärts** (cp. English to*wards*) with.

(1) Adverbs: **abwärts, aufwärts, vorwärts,** *downwards, upwards, forwards.*

(2) Nouns: **heimwärts, nordwärts, seitwärts, seewärts,** *homewards, northwards, sideways, seawards.*

Those with adverbs are analogous to **hin** and **her** compounds (**hinab, hinauf**), but express a less complete movement: **Der Weg führte aufwärts** (*upwards*), but, with indication of goal: **Der Weg führte hinauf, auf den Berg hinauf, ganz hinauf,** (*right*) *up* (*to the top*).

Those with nouns correspond to a prepositional phrase with directional particle: **Er neigte den Kopf seitwärts, nach der Seite hin. Die entlassenen Soldaten zogen heimwärts, nach der Heimat hin.**

(*b*) English -*wards* compounds are adjectives as well as adverbs German -**wärts** compounds only adverbs. Thus *a sideward(s) movement of the head* is **eine seitwärts** (degree adv.) **gerichtete Kopfbewegung,** or **eine Kopfbewegung nach der Seite hin.**

(*c*) The use of compounds of -**wärts** for position, not motion, thus **die breite hüftwärts** (= **an der Hüfte**) **getragene Ledertasche** (S. Zweig), *the leather bag carried at the hip*—is Austrian and is regarded as incorrect. Thus **sein seitwärts gescheiteltes Haar** (Th. Mann), should mean *parted* or *brushed towards the side*, not *at the side*.

140. Adverbs of Undifferentiated Position or Movement

Überall, *everywhere;* **rings herum,** *round about;* **umher,** *around.*

(*a*) (**Von**) **überall her,** *from everywhere,* **überall hin,** *to everywhere, from* (**in**) *all directions;* **überall anders, überall sonst,** *everywhere else.* **Überall** also means, in emphatic contexts, *anywhere*: *Look anywhere you like and you will find* . . ., **sehen Sie überall hin, und Sie werden finden . . .,** but (non-emphatic): *Put it anywhere (you like),* **legen Sie es hin wo Sie wollen** (or **irgendwo hin**).

(*b*) Distinguish **rings, umher, herum.**

Rings is a secondary adverb to **um, herum** is of directed movement round, **umher** of undirected movement around:

Die alten Stadtbefestigungen lagen rings um die Altstadt, *all around the old part* . . . (*encircling*).

Der Boxer läuft jeden Morgen einmal um die Anlagen herum, *once round the gardens (completing a circuit).*

Er war die ganze Nacht unruhig und ging dauernd in seinem Garten umher, *walked around in his garden.*

141. Interrogative Adverbs of Place

(*a*) The primary interrogative adverbs of place are: **wo?** *where?* **wohin?** *to where, whither?* **woher?** *from where, whence?*

German distinguishes carefully between questions with positional force (**wo?**) and with directional force (**woher? wohin?**), English using simple *where?* at least for **wohin?**: **Wohin gehen Sie?** *where are you going?* **Woher kommen Sie?** *where do you come from?* or, with the particles in end-position: **Wo gehen Sie hin? Wo kommen Sie her?**

(*b*) The primary interrogatives may be modified by secondary adverbs, thus:

(1) As interrogatives: **Wo gehen Sie überhaupt hin?** *Wherever (Where, anyhow* . . .*) are you going?* **Wo anders sollte er sein, als hier?** *Where else should he be* . . .?

(2) As adverbs: **irgendwo(her, -hin)**, (*from, to*) *somewhere;* similarly: **anderswo(her, -hin)** and **sonstwo(her, -hin), nirgendwo(her, -hin).**

(*c*) Apart from asking direct questions, they may also act as subordinating conjunctions, introducing:

(1) Noun clauses, the object of a verb:

Ich fragte ihn, woher er kam (wo er herkam), *I asked him where he came from.*

Ich weiß nicht, wohin ich das Buch gelegt habe (wo ich das Buch hingelegt habe), *I do not know where I have put the book down.*

(2) Adverbial clauses, meaning *wherever*, or *there, where*, with the appropriate particles of direction:

Wohin ich gehe (wo ich hingehe), da sind ganz andere Menschen als hier, *Where I am going there are quite different people from here.*

As this example shows, the interrogative adverb as conjunction is usually balanced in the main clause by a demonstrative adverb: **da,** also **dort, dahin, dorther,** etc.

142. Some Compound Verbs with Separable Prefixes of Place

Many compound verbs derive their prefixes from adverbs or prepositions expressing motion, direction, or location, whether literal or figurative.

(*a*) Adverbs:

Compound verbs with adverbs of place represent one of the loosest stages of compound verbs, since, as local motion is a basic sense of numerous adverbs (*v.* preceding paragraphs), in the normal position of the verb there is nothing to indicate whether a compound verb is present or not [cp. § 88 (*c*) and (*d*)]:

Er ging, *he went;* **er ging vorbei, hinauf, herum, davon, zurück, weiter,** *he went past, up, round, away, back, on;* or: *he passed, ascended, circled, left, returned, continued.*

Such verbs, being intransitive in force, may not take a direct object, but may complete the sense in relation to any local object by:

(1) A prepositional phrase: **er ging davon, an dem Hause vorbei,** *went away* (*left*), *went past* (*passed*) *the house.* Distinguish carefully between a possible English transitive corresponding to a German intransitive needing a preposition to complete the sense: **hinausgehen,** *to go out* (intransitive); *to leave* (Am. *quit*), transitive, is **aus (dem Hause) hinausgehen.**

(2) A noun in the accusative: **er ging die Treppe hinunter,** *went down* (*descended*) *the stairs.* This is *not* a direct object, but an adverbial

accusative, and is analogous to the accusative *preceding* a few prepositions of local motion, thus:

Er ging mit unruhigen Schritten den langen Saal auf und ab, *with unquiet steps he walked up and down the long room.*

Die Königin reitet langsam die Allee entlang, *the queen rides slowly along (down) the avenue.*

The compound preposition **auf und ab** needs only to be given directional particles to become two adverbs: **hinauf und hinab** [cp. **hinunter,** above and § 264 (*b*)].

(*b*) Prepositions:

Certain prepositions, mainly local in force, follow the nouns they govern (in dat.): **entgegen,** *towards;* **gegenüber,** *opposite;* **gemäß** and **nach,** *according to;* **nach,** *after* (*pursuit*). [Several of these may also precede, cp. § 264 (*a*).]

Seiner Ansicht entgegen muß ich das Haus verkaufen, *in opposition to his opinion I shall have to . . .*

Dem Geschäft seines Bruders gegenüber sitzt die Konkurrenz, *the competitors have established themselves opposite his brother's shop.*

Dem Gesetze gemäß (or **nach**) **muß man das tun,** *according to the law one has to do that.*

Er lief dem Dieb nach, *he ran after the thief.*

Such prepositions easily give rise to compounds governing the same case as the preposition: **entgegenkommen,** *to meet halfway, oblige;* **nachlaufen,** *to pursue;* **nachtun,** *to imitate.*

(1) The compound will normally represent one (joint) sense of the combination, an original, more literal sense being distinguished by continued separation:

Man muß einem Diebe nachlaufen, *pursue;* but: **man muß dem Gesetze nach laufen,** *according to the law one must walk* (*go on foot*).

Ich muß ihm alles nachtun, *I have to imitate him in all he does;* but: **das muß man dem Gesetze nach tun,** *according to the law one must do that.*

(2) The direct object of the simple verb, if any, remains that of the compound verb; thus many verbs thereby acquire two objects:

Ich warf ihm einen Stein nach, *threw a stone at (after) him.*

Ich schickte ihm den Brief nach, *forwarded the letter to him.*

and compare the verbs of giving and saying when thus compounded:

Ich brachte ihm viel Vertrauen entgegen, *I met him with much confidence (was prepared to trust him).*

Ich sagte ihm den Text nach, *I said the words after him.*

and the many verbs synonymous with these two:

Seine Frau plappert ihm seine Binsenwahrheiten nach, *his wife chatters his*
         banalities after him (*thoughtlessly echoes* . . .).

Exercise XXVII

A. Translate into English:

1. Ich sah dem Schifahrer von unten zu: unermüdlich stieg er den
Berg hinauf und sauste dann wieder mit rasender Geschwindigkeit
herunter. 2. So ging es stundenlang weiter, auf und ab, hin und zurück,
bergauf und bergab. 3. „Da oben muß es tüchtig frieren," rief ich ihm
zu. 4. „Keineswegs," kam die fröhliche Antwort von oben zurück.
„Kommen Sie mal selbst herauf. Es ist viel schöner droben bei mir
als drunten bei Ihnen!" 5. Sie ist wieder nach Majorca gefahren. Dort
reist sie im Winter immer hin, denn sie findet es wärmer drüben am
Mittelmeer. 6. Er nahm die Flasche aus der Kiste heraus. 7. „Dafür
brauche ich einen großen Pfropfenzieher," sagte er; „der kleine reicht
nicht dazu." 8. „Die Sterne da oben funkeln heute prächtig," sagte er;
hierauf blickte sie himmelwärts. 9. Er nahm die Puppe weg; da heulte
schon die Kleine (the little girl, *v.* § 143) aus vollen Lungen los. 10. Sie
stöberte rasch in allen Laden herum, aber die Uhr war fort und sie konnte
sie nirgendwo finden.

B. Translate into German:

1. There on the table—that's where I put the book. Perhaps it is
underneath. 2. "Where are you off to (going) so early in (an) the
morning?" "That's my secret. I don't want to talk about it."
3. "Will you come up [for] a moment?" he called from the window
upstairs to the policeman down in the street. 4. The monkey ran to and
fro in its cage; it climbed up and down on the bars and thereupon it
rushed round the cage once more. 5. Slowly the dog crept out [from]
under the table. "Outside with you, bad dog," cried the boy. 6. Up
there on that hill there is a ruined monastery. Long ages ago monks
lived and worked and prayed in there. 7. "Here they are at last!"
"Where? I can't see them!" "Over there!" 8. "They are just
coming down the hill and round our corner. They are hurrying towards
us, don't you see?" 9. The house was large inside and there was a
garden at the back and in front. 10. Where I come from we can't get
return tickets on (auf) the bus.

CHAPTER XXVIII

ADJECTIVES AS NOUNS (1). INFLECTED ADJECTIVE-NOUNS

143. Adjective-Nouns, General. Persons

(*a*) In general, any adjective (or adjectival participle, *v.* §§ 38, 49) may be used as an adjective-noun, and usage is immensely wider than in English. Thus "the good" is a collective concept referring to (good) persons, or the abstract idea (good). But German, for persons, has both genders and the plural (**der Gute, eine Gute, die Guten**), and for things, apart from the definite article use [**das Gute**, *the* (abstract) *good*], has many other modes (**Gutes, ein Gutes, dieses Gute, sein Gutes,** *good things, a, this, his good thing*). In addition, the fact that almost any adjective, and thus any compound adjective, or any participial adjective derived from a compound verb, may form an adjective-noun (**das Ausweglose,** *the element of hopelessness,* **das Unheilbringende,** *that which brings misfortune,* **die Schwergeprüften,** *people who are sorely tried*) means that almost any speaker or writer in the language may create new words, senses and nuances.

(*b*) The adjective-noun is:

(1) Masculine, feminine, or plural, referring normally to persons;

(2) Or neuter singular, referring to a concept or thing:

ein Armer, *a poor man;* **meine Verwandte,** *my* (*female*) *relative;*
die Schlafenden, *sleepers;* **das Schöne,** *the beautiful;* **sein Äußeres,** *his external appearance.*

(*c*) The adjective-noun is characterised grammatically by:

(1) the capital of the noun, and

(2) the inflection of the adjective, which may be weak or strong, according to the usual rules [*v.* §§ 36, 46; but cp. § 144A (*c*)].

Thus **ein Reisender,** *a traveller;* but **der Gesandte,** *the ambassador* (lit. *man sent*); **die Vielen,** *the many;* **sein Äußeres** (above).

A preceding normal adjective is either:

(1) Parallel with the adjective-noun and inflected identically:

der Anblick einiger armer Schlafender, *the sight of some poor sleepers.*

(2) Or uninflected, with the force of a degree adverb:

der Anblick einiger *tief* Schlafender, *of some deep sleepers* (lit. *of some persons sleeping deeply*).

A preceding object of a participial adjective-noun may be compounded: **die Schach Spielenden,** *those playing chess;* **die Skilaufenden,** *those ski-ing, the skiers* (cp. § 38).

(*d*) Persons:

(1) An adjective used as a noun may designate persons in the appropriate gender or number by many criteria, thus: a quality (**der Reiche,** *rich man*), an activity (**der Studierende,** *student,* **ein Handlungsreisender,** *a commercial traveller*), an action of which they are the object (**der Geprellte,** *person swindled, dupe,* **die Betrogene,** *woman deceived*), their number (**die Politik, Opiat für die Vielen,** *opium for the people*), etc., etc.

(2) The adjective-noun may be further modified along lines already partly described [(*c*) above], thus by: a further adjective (**die unerbittliche Schöne,** *la belle dame sans merci*), a (degree) adverb (**ein schwer Kranker,** or **Schwerkranker,** *a man seriously ill*), an object (**die Krachschlagende,** *the lady causing the fuss*), etc.

A modifying adverb may be a genuine adverb not normally used as an adjective (**der angeblich Schuldige,** *the allegedly guilty person*) and preceding adjectives and adverbs must be carefully distinguished (as **ein gemächlich Reisender,** *man travelling by easy stages,* but **ein militärischer Reisender,** *a travelling military man*). Distinguish also **der eingebildete Reiche,** *vain rich man,* and **der eingebildet Reiche** (= **der Reiche in der Einbildung**), *man who believes himself to be rich.*

Other elements may precede which in English may become part of the predicate: **die vom Schicksal Geschlagenen,** *those struck down by fate;* **der Totgeglaubte,** *the man thought to be dead* (*missing man*).

144. The Neuter Adjective-Noun for Things

(*a*) The neuter adjective-noun, except for the field of persons, is almost universal in its manner of reference, since it can range in its force from the most abstract ideas (**das Ferne, Kindliche, Häßliche,** *distance, childlike qualities, ugliness*), through collective concepts (**das Geleistete,** *what we have achieved,* **Wichtiges,** *important things*) to entirely concrete senses (**Gefälschtes,** *forgeries,* **das Liegengelassene,** *what was left on the plates*). Some examples are given, arranged by grammatical categories.

(*b*) The definite article commonly designates a concept both abstract and collective, thus **das Komische** is both the quality of comedy, and all that is comical. With this general force, a preceding adjective cannot easily be distinguished from an adverb, and is often compounded: **das niedrig Komische,** or **das Niedrig-Komische,** *low comedy* (*humour*).

Past participles have indefinite but quite concrete reference, and express often *that which* . . .: **zum Beweise des Gesagten,** *in proof of what was said,* **das unverlierbar Geglaubte,** *what one thought one could never lose.*

(*c*) A characteristic use is as an isolated noun, with no preceding article or other word. The reference is concrete and miscellaneous: **Schicksal teilte mit vollen Händen aus, aber mit keiner Gutes** (E. Barlach), *fate dealt her gifts liberally, but neither hand gave blessings.*

Amtliches, *official business;* **Näheres,** *further details;* **Schweres,** *terrible experiences;* **Irriges,** *false assumptions;* **Unterhaltendes,** *entertaining stories;* **Wichtiges,** *important items.*

Fehlendes läßt sich immer nachschicken, *we can always have sent on anything which we have forgotten to pack.*

(*d*) Equally common are uses with a preceding indefinite article or possessive adjective: **ein Doppeltes,** *a double criterion,* etc., **sein Äußeres,** *his external appearance,* **ihr Erspartes,** *her . savings;* **(er) fand, daß der Vorschlag sein Hübsches habe** (W. Bergengruen), *that there was something nice about the suggestion.*

144A. Stabilised Adjective-Nouns

(*a*) Many of the above nouns have become stabilised in their sense, and are no longer thought of as *the person who* [*thing*(*s*) *which*] *has* (*have*) a certain quality: **ein Bekannter, Deutscher, Gefangener, Gesandter, Heiliger, Industrieller, Verklagter,** *a friend, German, prisoner, an ambassador, a saint, an industrialist, a defendant,* and the corresponding feminines. Thus also neuter terms, especially in idioms, thus: **im Freien,** *out of doors,* **aus Eigenem,** *of one's own resources* (*free-will*), **das Weite gewinnen** (**suchen**), *to get away* (*make off*).

(*b*) Analogous to these are certain nouns standing for things and ideas, not for persons, but feminine as they stand for a feminine noun understood: **die Elektrische,** *tram*(*way*) (**Straßenbahn**), **Moderne,** *modern outlook* (*style*) (**Richtung**), **Rechte,** *right hand* (**Hand**); **eine Gerade,** *straight line* (**Linie**), **Unbekannte,** *unknown quantity* (**Größe**).

(*c*) As a result of the more nominal nature of such words, it is not uncommon, though not always approved, for them to take a weak singular or plural ending where a strong ending is strictly required [cp. § 285 (*c*)]:

(1) Singular: after an adjective (**ein geschlossenes Ganze,** better, **Ganzes**), and in apposition to a pronoun (**mir als Verwandten**).

(2) Plural: in the genitive (**die Hilfe guter Bekannten**), after numerals (**zwei Brünetten, Geraden**), and especially after indefinites (**einige Angestellten, Elektrischen, Parallelen**).

145. Inflection of Indefinite Adjective-Pronouns

For convenience, the various ways in which ·the indefinites (*v.* § 81) can be used are summarised:

(*a*) Adjectival use, either inflected (**einige Häuser, die vielen Bücher**), or uninflected (**wenig Milch, manch guter Mensch**).

(*b*) Adverbial use: **ich kenne ihn genug; das Haus ist wenig anziehend; ich fahre mehr als du; die Milch ist etwas sauer.**

(*c*) Pronominal use:

(1) Inflected, for a noun understood:

       Das wird Ihnen wohl mancher (= **Mann**) **sagen.**

(2) Inflected or uninflected for a general neuter concept:

       viel, *much;* **wenig,** *little;* **genug,** *enough.*

Ich könnte Ihnen manches über ihn erzählen, *much* or *many things.*

(3) A descriptive adjective may follow either form in (2), but especially the uninflected form; such an adjective takes the form of a neuter noun (cp. §§ 143, 144) inflected strong or weak, according to the preceding indefinite pronoun: **viel Gutes (vieles Gute), wenig Interessantes (weniges Interessante), manch Schreckliches (manches Schreckliche),** *v.* § 147 (*b*).

Note.—Not all indefinites have all the above uses. Thus **lauter** is used (invariably) only in the adjectival position (**lauter Gold**), **mehr** and **genug** are also never inflected; **sämtlich** has hardly any pronominal uses; only **manch** may precede an indefinite article or descriptive adjective uninflected (**manch ein Mann, manch guter Mensch,** cp. also **solch** and **welch,** §§ 103, 231); and only **all** may precede the definite article, etc., uninflected (**all das Geld, all mein Geld**).

(*d*) As the indefinite adjective-pronouns occupy a position halfway between adjectives and pronouns, their inflection presents some difficulties, and some points are summarised in § 146.

146. Indefinites.   Adjectival Inflection

(*a*) Two groups of inflections have been described in preceding chapters (*v.* §§ 32, 36, 46):

(1) The articles and the so-called "limiting adjectives", *i.e.* **dieser, jener, kein,** and the possessive adjectives.

(2) The normal descriptive adjective, which is strong or weak according to position.

The indefinites in some respects occupy an uneasy position between these two groups. Three points are selected: (i) the strong genitive,

(ii) the inflection of a descriptive adjective following, and (iii) the relation between indefinites and other *limiting* adjectives present.

(*b*) Strong genitive ending. Alone before nouns, indefinites are, of course, strong: **alle Männer, jedes Haus, andere Leute, beide Mädchen, viele Städte.** But in the genitive masculine and neuter singular, limiting adjectives retain the **-es** of the article (**das Dach jenes Hauses**), while descriptive adjectives revert to the weak **-en** (**ein Glas guten Weines**).

Of the indefinites, which should follow the inflection of the limiting adjectives, **all-, jed-, manch-,** and **viel-** often, and the others always, revert to weak **-en: der Sinn alles (allen) Geschehens,** *the meaning of all which happens;* **Kinder jedes (jeden) Alters,** *children of all ages;* and especially in genitive constructions, as **anderen Sinnes werden,** *to change one's mind,* **allen Ernstes,** *in all seriousness,* after the analogy of such adverbial compounds as **jedenfalls, geradenwegs,** etc.

(*c*) A following descriptive adjective.

Jed- and **kein** are followed by weak adjectives in all cases, singular and plural, except where **kein** is defective [*v.* § 13 (*b*)]; thus also **manch-,** when inflected strong in the singular.

No problem arises therefore in the singular; but in the plural, practice varies, and the following may be a useful generalisation:

(1) The exhaustives are followed by an adjective with weak inflection: **all-** always (**alle guten Männer**), and **beid-** and **sämtlich-** generally (**beide alten Leute, sämtliche guten Werke**).

(2) The quantitatives are followed generally by an adjective with strong inflection: **einige starke Burschen, mehrere stattliche Häuser, wenige lesbare Bücher, viele herzige Tiere,** etc.

But **manch** (together with **solch** and **welch,** *v.* §§ 103, 231) varies in the plural between a strong and weak following adjective: **manche alte(n) Männer;** and cp. § 144A.

(*d*) Indefinites and a limiting adjective [*v.* (*a*) (2)].

(1) **alle** precedes and raises no problem: **alle diese Menschen.**

(2) **einige, mehrere, manche** also precede, but adopt pronominal function, causing a following group to stand in the genitive:

einige, manche, mehrere seiner Werke (dieser Arbeiter).

(3) **beide, sämtliche, viele** must follow, and are weak adjectives: **seine beiden Brüder, meine sämtlichen Werke, diese vielen Leute.**

(4) **viele** and **wenige** may precede or follow, with different senses: **viele (wenige) seiner Werke; seine vielen (wenigen) Werke.**

Note.—**Jed-** obeys the normal adjective rule after the indefinite article: **ein jeder Baum, eines jeden Baumes, einem jeden Baum, einen jeden Baum.**

147. Indefinites. Pronominal Inflection

(*a*) The indefinites may be used as neuter pronouns, standing for a general neuter concept of a collective nature, not excluding reference to human beings: **alles,** *everything* (*everybody*), **beides,** *both* (things, persons), etc. Inflection: **alles, alles, allem, alles.**

alles austeigen! *all change, please!* **beides ist richtig,** *both* (*either*) *of the two* (*alternatives*) *are* (*is*) *true;* **in Ihrem Aufsatz ist einiges falsch,** *some wrong things, mistakes;* **alles war zum Fest erschienen,** *all appeared,* **alles trennt sich in heiterer Eintracht** (W. Bergengruen), *all depart in a good humour.*

(1) These may make joint reference to objects of different gender: **Ich holte Teller und Messer und stellte beides vor ihn,** *put down both before him* (cp. §§ 132, 493).

(2) There is no clear distinction between the uninflected and inflected form of the general neuter concept: **wenig / weniges, viel / vieles.** But the former may suggest amount, the latter variety:

Ich habe vieles zu tun, aber eigentlich nicht viel, *a lot of jobs but not really very much.*

Schließlich habe ich auch fechten gelernt! Ich habe ja so vieles getrieben, so vieles versucht! (W. Bergengruen), *so many things.*

(*b*) The neuter pronouns **etwas** (**was**) and **nichts,** and the neuter indefinites **manch, viel, wenig,** may be followed by an adjective-noun in either their inflected or uninflected form:

etwas Anregendes, *something exciting;* **mit nichts Brauchbarem,** *with nothing useful;* **alles Gute,** *all good* (*wishes*); **manches Unzuträgliche,** *much that was unsuitable;* **viel Fortschrittliches,** *many elements of progress.*

Die Suppe hat etwas Salziges, compare **ist etwas salzig** (adverbial use).

Occasionally two indefinites (pronoun or adjective-pronoun) occur together: **alles beides, alles andere, etwas anderes, etwas weniges, nichts anderes, ein mehreres, ein weniges,** etc.

(*c*) The two indefinite pronouns **jemand** and **niemand,** though their force is personal, are, by custom become rule, followed by a neuter form: **jemand Fremdes, niemand Bekanntes, jemand anders.** But there is an opposing tendency to give the following word masculine inflection (*v.* § 60).

148. Adjective-Nouns in Pronominal Form

On the analogy of many pronominal forms such as **etwas anderes, alles beides,** etc., many adjectival nouns in common use are, despite the general rule [*v.* § 143 (*c*)], written with small letters.

(*a*) After an indefinite: **alles mögliche, alles übrige, etwas derartiges, nichts wesentliches, nichts sonderbares.** There is no clear dividing line between nominal and pronominal status, and some writers go far in the latter direction:

Er fragte mich sachlich etwas auf das Tennis-Spiel bezügliches (H. v. Doderer), *something referring to the game.*

(*b*) Alone or after an article or limiting adjective:

ähnliches (especially **und ähnliches,** *and the like*), **folgendes,** *the following,* **verschiedenes,** *various things.*

(als) erstes, nächstes, letztes, einziges, (as) *the first, next, last, only thing.* **das einzige, das einzig mögliche,** *the only* (*possible*) *thing.*

ein anderes, leichtes, mehreres, übriges, übliches, *something else, simple, extra, more, usual.*

The usual defence of this practice is that such phrases are the equivalent of simple adverbs:

mit klarer, warmer Stimme, die um etliches dunkler klang als ihre Stimme sonst (E. Schaper), *which sounded somewhat darker* (= **etwas dunkler**).

Mein erstes in Paris war, mich nach ihm zu erkundigen (S. Zweig), *the first thing I did . . .* (= **zuerst erkundigte ich mich**).

(*c*) It is important that such words, especially those under (*b*), should be written with their capital as soon as they acquire genuine nominal function:

Ich tue es paragraphenweise, weil ich nicht alles in einem Zuge sagen kann, und mache hier abermals einen Abschnitt, um in dem Folgenden folgendes zu bemerken (Th. Mann), *I make another paragraph here and would comment in the following paragraph as follows . . .*

EXERCISE XXVIII

A. Translate into ENGLISH:

1. Von der bürgerlichen Seite her gesehen war mein Leben eine immer größere Entfernung vom Normalen, Erlaubten, Gesunden gewesen (H. Hesse). 2. Weibliches hat in die Clausur keinen Eintritt! (S. Andres). 3. Das Buch ist für amerikanische Leser geschrieben, die von Luther wenig oder Irriges wissen (bookrev.). 4. . . . wie ein

verprügelter Hund, der weiß, daß er Schlechtes getan hat (S. Zweig).
5. „Du aber, Tetinko, wirst uns Unterhaltliches erzählen können von deiner
Reise . . .“ (F. Werfel).   6.   . . . eine ausgesprochen unglückliche Liebe
(etwas, wie man sich denken kann, zur Zeit äußerst Seltenes) (F. Werfel).
7. Bei all ihrer frauenhaften Anmut hatte sie etwas Burschikoses,
Offenherziges, Unzimperliches, etwas Kameradschaftlich-Zuverlässiges,
ja mitunter Derbes (W. Bergengruen).   8. Hie und da (am See) wächst
ein weniges von Schilf und Binsen auf (Th. Fontane).   9. In dieser
großartigen Vision hat Wagner sein Höchstes geleistet.   10. Die
Geschwister kommen gut miteinander aus, weil jedes das andere gern
hat.   11. „Der letzte Mohikaner“ war das Buch, das ich als letztes las.
12. Heute nachmittag machte ich einen langen Spaziergang, bin aber
niemand Bekanntem begegnet.

B. Translate into GERMAN, using adjectival nouns wherever possible:

1. He ran quickly to the front entrance of the building, but only
found a beggar standing there in the shadow of the doorway.   2. The
poor are always with us. That's something very true, for we don't
know many rich [people].   3. The doctor came to visit the seriously
sick [man].   4. Beauty and ugliness are sometimes close neighbours in
medieval sculpture.   5. I have not heard further-details of the accident.
6. Her external-appearance was always very neat; indeed, there was
something almost spinsterish about (an) her.   7. When he went to town
he heard a lot [that was] new.   8. All good (brav) children obey their
parents, but only a few are really good.   9. She had various-things to
do but nothing really important.   10. You can buy what-is-necessary
at any shop.

CHAPTER XXIX

INFINITIVE CONSTRUCTIONS. THE OBJECTIVE PREDICATE

149. The Objective Predicate. General

(*a*) Many verbs are followed by (i) an object, noun, or pronoun in the accusative, and (ii) a second element which is predicated of the first, and is therefore called the objective predicate; it may be an adjective, noun, phrase, etc.:

Du machst mich verrückt, man nannte ihn Hauptmann, machte ihn zum König, *you make me mad, they called him captain, made him king* (*v*. fully, §§ 433-7).

The second element may be an infinitive, and the first object is then the logical subject of the activity it describes:

Ich ließ ihn kommen, sah den Zug einfahren, hatte Geld auf der Bank liegen, *I had him come* (*sent for him*), *saw the train enter the station, had money* (*lying*) *in the bank.*

(*b*) Only a limited number of verbs take a simple infinitive as objective predicate; they are:

(1) **Lassen,** as a verb of causation.

(2) **Heißen,** *to bid*, **lehren,** *to teach*, and **helfen** (with dat.), *to help,* as verbs of quasi-causation. Also an idiomatic use of **haben.**

(3) **Sehen, hören, finden, fühlen,** and certain other verbs of experience or perception.

(*c*) The infinitive is, as stated, normally simple, but may be with **zu** in the case of certain of these verbs; and it is sometimes alternative to other constructions of the objective predicate [*v*. § 434 (*b*)], especially the present participle (cp. English *I heard him come, saw him coming*).

(*d*) All infinitive forms [cp. examples in (*a*)] are active in force, since they have the preceding noun or pronoun object as logical subject. Analogous constructions in which the infinitive is passive in force, though active in form [*e.g.* **ich hörte ihn rufen,** *I heard him* (*being*) *called*], are reserved for the Passive (§§ 215 and 216).

150. Lassen. Verbs of Causation

(*a*) German has no verb of causation as wide in scope as English *to make.* The most general is **lassen,** but other causative constructions are noted at (*e*) below.

Lassen has a number of simple senses not requiring a following infinitive, thus:

(1) *to leave (off), refrain from*, with accusative:

es war streng verboten, ins Wasser zu fallen; wer es dennoch nicht ließ, bekam Schläge (E. Barlach), *those (of us children) who still fell in were beaten.*

(2) *to relinquish, hand over, grant*, with dative:

Ich lasse Ihnen den Stoff zum Selbstkostenpreis, *I'll let you have the material at the wholesale price.*

Hübsch war sie, das muß man ihr lassen (E. Kästner), *one must grant that she had looks.*

(*b*) **Lassen** with a dependent infinitive expresses a wide degree of causality, from actions almost beyond the subject's control to extreme manifestations of power:

Ich ließ das wütende Tier entkommen, *I allowed the savage animal to escape.*

Hitler ließ Berge versetzen, *Hitler removed mountains* (lit. *caused . . . to be removed*).

But it always conveys the sense of operating through the instrumentality of others; it cannot therefore be used in:

(1) The sense of *to permit*, where the (indirect) object is the primary agent:

Ich erlaubte ihm, mit dem Wagen der Firma in die Stadt zu fahren, *I let him take the firm's car . . .*

(2) The sense of *to make*, where the object is inanimate or an unwilling cooperator:

A passing plane made the windows shake, **ein vorüberfliegendes Flugzeug brachte die Fensterscheiben zum Zittern** [infinitive noun, § 205 (*c*)].

Her illness made her give up her work, **ihre Krankheit veranlaßte sie, ihre Arbeit aufzugeben.**

(*c*) Thus the primary senses of **lassen** as a causative are *to let, leave, have, make*:

Sie ließ ihre Augen auf seinem Gesicht ruhen (E. Wiechert), *she let her eyes rest on his face.*

Er ließ alles im Zimmer stehen und liegen, *he left everything lying just as it was.*

Wir ließen den Schreiner das Schloß reparieren, *we had the carpenter mend the lock.*

Man sollte einen Mann seine Armut nicht fühlen lassen, *one should not make a man feel his poverty.*

Note the present participle in English after *to leave* (*lying*); and in German often a second noun object, of the dependent verb (**Armut, Schloß**), immediately following the first.   Idiom: **ich ließ es gut sein,** *I desisted, made no further attempt.*   *To drop* is **fallen lassen : er ließ die Tasse, den Vorschlag fallen.**   For **lassen** in imperative (*let us go*, etc.), *v.* § 247 (*e*).

(*d*) Verbs with the simple infinitive as objective predicate form with them verbal compounds when a derived sense develops [cp. § 88 (*d*)]. Thus, especially, **lassen** with a number of common dependent verbs: **fahren, gehen, sitzen, stehen :**
Wir müssen alles im Zimmer stehen- und liegenlassen, *we must leave things just as they are.*

Cp. **Der Arzt will ihn zwei Monate liegen lassen,** *the doctor wants to make him lie up for two months.*

This often means in practice that the permissive senses of **lassen** [*to let, leave,* cp. (*c*)] are compounded, but the more causative senses (*to have, make*) are not:
Den Autofahrer, der seinen Wagen auf der Straße stehen- und den Kontaktschlüssel steckenläßt, sollte man nach Haus pilgern lassen (newsp.), *the car driver, who leaves his car in the street with the ignition key in position, should be made to walk home.*

(*e*) Other expressions of causation:

(1) To see that, **aufpassen (sorgen), daß . . .**
Ich werde (darauf) aufpassen, daß er die Sache richtig macht, *see that he does it properly.*
Ich werde dafür sorgen, daß jemand sie vom Bahnhof abholt, *see that there is someone to fetch her.*

(2) **Machen** is seldom used with dependent infinitive, more commonly with a more clear indication of resultant state, thus an adjective, present or past participle: **er macht mich immer nervös, rasend, verrückt,** *he makes me irritable, mad* [cp. § 435 (*b*)].
Machen, daß . . . is often *to arrange that,* especially as a form of peremptory demand: **Mach, daß du herauskommst!** *clear out!*

(3) To make an unwilling or resistent agent act may be, in increasing order of persuasion: **dazu zwingen, bringen, bewegen :**
Ich zwang (brachte, bewegte ihn dazu) mir das entwendete Geld zurückzuerstatten, *made him (persuaded him to) return the stolen money.*

(4) Other constructions:
I made the clock go, **ich setzte (brachte) die Uhr wieder in Gang.**
It made me think of her, **ich mußte an sie denken.**

151. Heißen, *to bid;* **lehren,** *to teach;* **helfen,** *to help;* **haben,** *to have.*
The first three verbs, like **lernen** (*v.* § 110), are followed by a simple infinitive in shorter constructions, but **zu** is added in longer statements.

(*a*) **Heißen,** used similarly to **lassen:**

Sie schenkte mir ein und hieß mich einen Schluck trinken (H. Hesse), *she poured out some wine and told me to drink some.*
Wer hat dich geheißen, die Blumenbeete zu bewässern, *who told you to water the flower-beds?*

Note.—**Heißen,** like **nennen,** is also a verb of "implication", with similar, but not quite identical uses:

Das heißt zuschlagen! Das nenne ich zuschlagen! *That's* (*what I call*) *a real blow* (*energetic action*). Also past participle: **zugeschlagen,** *v.* § 351.
Das nenne (heiße) ich einen Schlag für die Freiheit!

(*b*) **Lehren.**

Ich lehre dich tanzen . . . ich werde dich lehren, zu tanzen und zu spielen und zu lächeln (H. Hesse), *I will teach you to dance . . . play and smile* [cp. also §§ 216, 383 (*e*)].

(*c*) **Helfen.**

Er half der alten Frau ihre Last über die Brücke tragen, or: **der alten Frau, ihre Last über die Brücke zu tragen.**
Ich möchte helfen, die Menschen anständig und vernünftig zu machen (E. Kästner), *help to make people . . .*

(*d*) **Haben** is used with an objective predicate of certain verbs describing the manner in which something is owned, worn, etc.:

Er hat Geld auf der Bank liegen, *he has money* (*lying*) *in the bank.*
Ich weiß ja, du hast irgendwo in der Welt eine Geliebte sitzen (H. Hesse), *I know that somewhere in the world you have a lover* (*waiting*).
Die sieben Mann vom Nachkommando saßen dort; sie hatten Suppe auf dem Tisch stehen und dicke Scheiben Brot und Fleisch daneben (H. Böll), *the seven men of the rear-guard . . . had soup standing on the table and . . .*

The dependent infinitive is normally intransitive, and **liegen, sitzen** and **stehen** are the commonest; but occasionally it is transitive, especially **umhängen,** which is perhaps oblique for **um sich hängen** (intrans.):

Er hatte eine karierte Reisedecke umhängen (E. Kreuder), *he had a checked plaid thrown around his shoulders.*

But with transitive verbs the commoner construction is past participle, as in English [**umgehängt,** *thrown,* cp. § 434 (*d*)]; this is, in both languages, a not uncommon alternative sense of the auxiliary and past participle, the compound tense construction, cp. § 218 (*a*).

152. Verbs of Perception

(*a*) The verbs **hören, sehen, fühlen,** and sometimes **finden** (and **wissen**) are used with a simple infinitive as objective predicate:

Ich hörte mein eigenes Herz klopfen, *heard my own heart beat.*

Wir sahen den Wagen langsam den Berg herauffahren, *saw the car slowly climb(ing) the hill.*

Ich fühlte einen teuflischen Schmerz in mir brennen, *felt a terrible pain burning in me.*

Ich fand zu meinem Erstaunen Herrn Haller beim Absatz der Treppe sitzen (H. Hesse), *found, to my surprise, H. sitting on the landing.*

and also other verbs of similar sense or force:

Ich spürte alles in mir Widerstand leisten (H. Hesse), *I felt everything in me rise up in opposition.*

(*b*) But in some cases another construction is as common or commoner:

(1) A present participle, especially after **finden** (*e.g.* **fand ihn . . . sitzend**), compare English versions above and *v.* § 434 (*c*).

(2) **wie** and a subordinate clause:

Ich sah, wie er mit der Hand winkte, *saw him beckon.*

Er fühlte, wie ihre Arme zitterten, *felt her arms tremble.*

This is common with **sehen** and its synonyms, and must replace the simple dependent infinitive where the main verb takes an object in a case other than the accusative:

Hat irgend jemand beobachtet, wie der Dieb das Haus verließ? *did anyone observe the thief leaving?*

Ich sah ihr zu, wie sie die Wäsche bügelte, *watched her ironing the washing.*

Lange sah ich ihm nach, wie er unter der kahlen Allee davonging (H. Hesse), *watched him walking away along the bare avenue.*

(3) A prepositional phrase, especially with an infinitive noun [cp. § 205 (*c*)]; thus, for first two examples in (2), above:

Hat irgend jemand den Dieb beim Verlassen des Hauses beobachtet?

Ich sah ihr beim Bügeln zu.

153. Infinitive for Past Participle with Certain Verbs

(*a*) The limited number of verbs with dependent simple infinitive, (thus including **lernen,** *v.* § 110, but *not* **haben** as in § 151) have a quasi-auxiliary role analogous to that of the modal verbs. They have thus acquired the practice of modal verbs of taking the infinitive for past participle when preceded by the dependent infinitive in compound tenses:

Nie habe ich ihn (= den Wirt) einen Handgriff tun sehen. Handgriffe sind die Prärogative der Frauen (W. Bergengruen), *never have I seen him do a hand's turn . . .*

Ich habe die großen Massenideologien unter meinem Auge wachsen und sich ausarbeiten sehen (S. Zweig), *I have seen the great mass ideologies grow . . .*

But the past participle is perhaps equally common, and the same writer may use both:

ein ungeheueres altertümliches Billard . . . Ich habe niemanden auf ihm spielen gesehen (W. Bergengruen), *I have never seen anyone play on it.*

Lassen in compounds [cp. § 150 (*d*)] also uses this form, probably in preference to that with the past participle proper:

Sie hat ihn warten lassen, er hat sie daher sitzenlassen, *she kept him waiting, so he threw her over.*

(*b*) It may, therefore, be suggested that the infinitive construction for past participle is: (i) usual for **lassen**, including compound forms, (ii) common for **sehen, hören, helfen, heißen**, (iii) less common for **lehren, lernen,** and (iv) never used for **haben** as in § 151.

153A. Order of Three Verb Forms in Subordinate Clause

(*a*) When in a subordinate clause a finite part of the verb joins two infinitives in end-position, it precedes them rather than following by strict rule [§ 113 (*a*) (2)]; this construction is especially common with verbs in which the past participle may assume infinitive form [*i.e.* modal verbs, § 66 (*b*) (2), and certain others, § 153, above]:

    . . . **weil wir sie haben einladen wollen,** *wanted to invite them.*

    . . . **als ich ihn habe kommen sehen,** *saw him come.*

but occurs also with the normal future tense:

    . . . **wenn wir sie werden einladen können,** *shall be able . . .*

and also, though rarely, with other combinations of finite and non-finite verb forms.

(*b*) The construction is optional, not compulsory; but in the case of the two special classes of verbs mentioned in (*a*) above, the infinitive standing for the past participle must revert to participial form if the auxiliary is to follow: . . . **als ich ihn kommen gesehen habe.**

154. Numerals (9). Compound Cardinals

(*a*) Variatives are formed from numerals and indefinites by the addition of **-erlei** (invar.), in the sense (*three*, etc.) *kinds of,* (*all,* etc.)

sorts of: **einerlei, dreierlei, zehnerlei, allerlei, beiderlei, jederlei, keinerlei, mancherlei, vielerlei,** etc.

Porzellane in allerlei Tiergestalt (Th. Mann), *porcelain products in all kinds of animal forms.*

Sein Leben und er waren zweierlei Dinge (E. Wiechert), *his life and he were two (distinct) things.*

The number of the following noun is usually that which the word with the suffix would require if standing alone: thus numerals after **einerlei** require plural number: **hunderterlei Bäume.** But indefinites (especially **beiderlei,** *e.g.* **beiderlei Geschlechts**) prefer the singular, and the noun itself may not permit a plural: **hunderterlei Obst** [cp. § 444 (*b*) (3)], **auf mehrerlei Weise.**

The majority of variatives with indefinites are no more than emphatic in intention: **mancherlei Bekannte,** *many a friend,* **in beiderlei Hinsicht,** *in both respects,* and cp. **zweierlei Dinge** (above); especially also **einerlei** and **keinerlei:**

Dinge sagen zu lassen, aus denen keinerlei Folgerung gezogen werden kann (H. Risse), *from which no inference at all can be made.*

Pronominal use: **ich habe hunderterlei zu tun,** *a thousand (minor) things.* Nominal: **das ewige Einerlei,** *never-ending monotony.*

(*b*) Multiplicatives, adjectival or adverbial in use, are formed by adding **-fach** to a cardinal in the sense *two-, three-,* etc. *-fold (times)*: **zweifach,** *double;* **dreifach,** *triple;* **zehnfach,** *tenfold;* **einfach,** *simple;* **x-fach** or **zigfach,** *a large number of times:*

Dreifach hält besser (prov.), *threefold insurance is safe.*

Dann platzten Handgranaten . . . Zigfach, sich abschwächend, gaben sie ihr Echo in die Ebene hinunter (H. Böll), *many repeated echoes . . .*

Alternative to **-fach** is **-faltig,** but more of organic variation (i.e. *-fold*) than of sequence in time (i.e. *times*), and thus less common: **ein dreifaches Hoch,** *a triple acclamation,* but **die heilige Dreifaltigkeit,** *the Trinity;* cp. **Mutter und Tochter—dasselbe Gesicht in zweifacher Auflage,** *the same face twice* (contemporaneous but distinct). Sometimes **-fältig** replaces **-faltig: einfältig,** *simple* (derogatory), distinguish **einfach; vielfältig,** *manifold,* besides **vielfach** and **mannigfaltig;** with **zwie-** for **zwei-,** in **zwiefältig,** besides **zwiefach.**

(*c*) Iteratives, formed by adding **-mal** to the cardinal, in the sense *. . . times, v.* § 41. A further formation is that in **-ig,** adjectival use: **eine einmalige Gelegenheit,** *single* (unrepeatable) *opportunity,* **nach zweimaligem Besuch,** *after two visits.* [Cp. the adv. formations in **-mals, damals,** *at that time,* **vormals,** *at an earlier period, v.* § 155 (*c*), below.]

155. Numerals (10).   Compound Ordinals

(*a*) Neuter nouns in **-tel, -stel** for fractions, *v.* § 79.

(*b*) Degrees within the superlative: **der beste Schüler, der zweitbeste, drittbeste,** etc., **Schüler,** *the best, best but one, best but two,* etc.

Er war der drittletzte an der Reihe, *last but two.*

Die zweithöchste Kirchturmspitze Deutschlands, *highest but one.*

(*c*) Iteratives in adjectival and adverbial use, **erstmalig,** *first,* **erstmals,** *for the first time;* but these are hardly necessary in addition to **erst** (adj.), and **zum ersten Mal** (adv.), and few others are found. Note, however, from the adverb **einst,** *formerly,* **einstmals,** also *formerly,* and **einstmalig** (referring to past or future), *one-time* and *future:*

Sie liebte diesen Bruder, in dem sie das einstmalige Familienhaupt erblickte (Th. Mann), *in whom she saw the future head of the family.*

(*d*) Group numerals take the form of phrases with **zu** and the (invar.) ordinal stem, meaning *in a group of,* thus:

auf einem Spaziergang zu viert, *during a walk which four of us took.*

But this form is losing popularity and being replaced by the (less formal) inflected dative plural: **zu zweien, dreien, vieren:**

Wir betraten das Haus zu dreien (H. Risse), *the three of us entered the house.*

Das Déjeuner wurde diesmal nur zu vieren eingenommen (Th. Mann), *only four of us sat down to lunch this time.*

And, certainly from seven onwards, the simple cardinal is quite possible: **zu sieben, zu acht,** etc.

(*e*) An older form of counting has left the vestigial form **anderthalb,** *one and a half* (lit. *the second half*), and the terms **selbander, selbdritt,** *in a group of two, three,* which are still current in dialect, but occur in standard German in the titles (of pictures): **Heilige Maria Selbander,** *The Virgin with the Child Jesus;* **Heilige Anna Selbdritt,** *St Anne with the Virgin and the Child Jesus.*

Exercise XXIX

A. Translate into English:

1. Man hörte jetzt auch schon die Pfeife eines Rettungswagens schrillen (R. Musil).   2. Denn jeder starke Mensch erreicht unfehlbar das, was (*that which*) ein wirklicher Trieb ihn suchen heißt (H. Hesse). 3. Er hatte alle ihre Namen (= der Schüler) in einem Heft stehen, aus den ganzen zwanzig Jahren (E. Wiechert).   4. Nun aber hatte ich eine Portion Leber in mir, und hatte den zweiten Becher vor mir stehen (H. Hesse).

5. Der Bruder Pförtner kam . . . Ich sah, was er noch vom Abendbrot im Schnurrbart hängen hatte (S. Andres). 6. Ein Mädchen hatte mich essen, trinken, schlafen geheißen, hatte mir Freundliches erwiesen, hatte mich angelacht, hatte mich einen dummen Jungen genannt (H. Hesse). 7. Oskar wußte nicht, ob (*whether*) er stehenbleiben oder weitergehen sollte. Beides schien ihm gleich gefährlich (L. Frank). 8. Man kann alles auf mehrerlei Weise ausdrücken (H. Reimann). 9. Als Kinder haben wir einmal im Winter einen toten Wolf im Wald liegen sehen. 10. Manchmal war sie vergeßlich und ließ den Schlüssel in der Tür stecken, wenn sie ausging.

B. Translate into German:

1. She had a delicious salad prepared with six sorts of vegetables: tomatoes, cucumber, carrots, peas, cress, and lettuce. 2. The children left all their toys lying on the grass and I had to help clear them away. 3. The child seemed very frightened and this made him drive the car more slowly. 4. The policeman made him park the car on the other side of the square. 5. She had an umbrella standing about somewhere but she could not find it. 6. The gardener came along the next day with all-sorts-of excuses. 7. On (**bei**) solemn occasions the pope wears a triple crown on his (*the*) head. 8. I will see that the rain doesn't spoil my new hat. 9. The soldiers saw the bridge collapse behind them and heard the river rushing over the falling masonry. 10. He felt the injured bird tremble in his hand as he picked it up from the ground.

CHAPTER XXX

156. Proper Names (1). Personal Names. Inflection

(*a*) Under proper names may be distinguished:

(1) Those of persons, including titles with these, §§ 156-9, 174-5.

(2) Those of geographical and political places and entities, §§ 219-22.

(3) Quasi-proper names, *i.e.* of newspapers, literary works, ships, planets, etc., § 235.

(*b*) Names of persons, being nouns of unique reference, do not take the full singular and plural inflection of common nouns. They present problems of inflection, however, in the genitive singular and the plural.

Both Christian names and surnames, whether masculine or feminine, regularly take **-s** in the genitive singular: **Georgs Fahrrad, Inges Haarzöpfe, die Bestrafung Annas, der Selbstmord Kleists.**

(1) Complex names are regarded as a unit: whether two Christian names (**die Regierung Franz Josefs**), Christian and surname (**die Werke Friedrich Hebbels**), or incorporating **von** or other particle of nobility (**die Novellen Heinrich von Kleists**); but in the last case a following genitive noun may (especially in older names) take the **-s** on the first part, when the surname is felt as a place-name: **die Dichtungen Gottfrieds von Straßburg.**

(2) A well-established practice in written German after sibilants (**s, ß, x, z, tz**), and after feminine Christian names in **-a** or **-e**, is to use a genitive in **-ens**:

Hansens Brief, Felixens Eigenschaften (Th. Mann), **Luisens Verhalten** (S. Andres), **ein Leben wie das Herminens** (H. Hesse), **Fortunens Gunst** (Th. Mann).

In common practice this use has an archaic flavour, and is avoided, especially in speech, in various ways: (i) by ignoring it in feminine words (**Luisas Bemerkung**), and with the sibilant **-sch** (**die Stellung Wilhelm Buschs in der Literatur**); (ii) by the apostrophe (**Demosthenes' Reden, Agnes' Hochzeit**); (iii) but best and simplest by the provision of a preceding inflected word (**das Ei des Kolumbus, die Schulzeugnisse meines Hans, der Ruhm des Dichters Lenz**).

(*c*) The genitive **-s** is omitted from proper names when another inflected element precedes: **die Laufbahn unseres Willi, das Kleid der Anna, die Kriegstaten des Großen Friedrich, die Leiden des Jungen Werther** (title, reflecting Goethe's later usage; early versions have **Werthers**); and cp. (2) (iii) above.

But some would insist on -s if an adjective is present (cp. last two examples): **das Haus des Schmidt,** but: **des alten Schmidts.**

Note.—The genitive inflection of proper names is governed by two principles: (i) economy of ending, thus: **des alten Schmi***dt,* **des Kaiser Wilhel***m***(***s***);** (ii) a genitive -s, even if otherwise omitted, is required at the point of contact between a governed and governing noun: **das Haus *des* alten Schmidt,** but **des alten Schmidts Haus; die Dichtungen *W*olframs von Eschenbach,** but: **Wolfram von Eschenbachs Dichtungen.**

157. Personal Names.   Plural

(*a*) Christian names, when used in the plural, take the nearest form to a corresponding noun declension: **die Dieter, Wilhelme, Agnes, Annas, Ottos, Luisen, Hänschen, Christel.**

(*b*) Surnames, *i.e.* members of the family bearing a name; there are various possibilities:

(1) Good literary use: article and uninflected plural: **die (Brüder) Grimm, die Stifter, die (Angehörigen der Familie) Adenauer.**

(2) Colloquial: -s plural, no article: **Tümmlers und ihre Begleiter** (Th. Mann), **wir waren bei Brauns** (their home) **eingeladen;** also article: **die Brettauers, die ursprünglich ein Bankgeschäft besaßen** (S. Zweig); designation by title of head: **Botschafters, Vater und Tochter** (newsp.), *the Ambassador and his daughter,* **Oberförsters** (Th. Fontane), *Oberförster K. and his wife.*

(3) Popular: -ens plural: **Ihnen Ihren Dreck nachräumen?   Ich bin nur für Seidenzopfens da!** (H. Fallada—Minna, the servant). *Clear up your mess?   I'm only here for the Seidenzopfs!*

(4) Popular and humorous: strict grammatical plural: **Grünebäume** (W. Raabe); **selbst wenn der Fambäche Legion würde, behaupte ich . . .** *even if my opponent Fambach were multiplied a thousandfold I would assert . . .* Also Christian name: **die Nikoläuse** (Simpl.), with punning force.

158. Personal Names.   Use

(*a*) Normally the distinction between proper names and common nouns is that the former refer to one person (in the context), the latter to a class of persons or things.   Thus proper names do not strictly take the articles or plural (except as noted in § 157).   But it is possible for common nouns to be used as proper names, and the reverse, each acquiring some characteristics of the other class.

(b) Certain common nouns are used as proper names because of their unique reference in certain circumstances; they omit the definite article and take genitive -s, even feminines:

(1) **Gott** and compounds has no article in the Christian sense:

Gottes Gnade, die Milde Gottvaters (Gottsohnes); but **eine Statue der Muttergottes** (or **Mutter Gottes, Gottesmutter**).

(2) Family relationships, and others by extension:

Vaters Studierzimmer, Mutters neues Kleid, Kaisers Geburtstag (before 1918), **aus eigenem oder Nachbars Garten, die helle Stimme Bräutigams Io-Do** (F. Werfel).

(3) Noun agents in contexts where they are unambiguous:

Verfasser dieser Zeilen, *the author of these lines;* but **die Ansicht des Verfassers (dieser Zeilen),** cp. § 302 (d).

(c) But the definite article is used with proper names in certain contexts:

(1) When the person is further described or specified:

der Beethoven, der dieses Quartett schrieb, *the B. who wrote,* or: *B., when he wrote . . .*

Der Gott, der Eisen wachsen ließ, der wollte keine Knechte, *the God who caused iron to grow . . .* (War of Liberation poem, 1812).

Friedrich der Große (der Zweite), or **der Große (Zweite) Friedrich.**

(2) Similarly with the plural of **Herr,** etc.: **die Herren A. und B., die Fräulein S.**

(3) In familiar language, when referring to a common acquaintance: **der Langhorn, die Müller**; within the family: **der Vater, die Tante**; more formally when referring to well-known *women* writers: **die Droste, die Lagerlöf.**

(4) For grammatical reasons, to avoid ambiguity: **Dem Hans versprach Luise treu zu bleiben, die Schriften des Paracelsus** [v. § 156 (b) (2)].

(d) The definite article is also used to distinguish:

(1) An author's work from the author: **ich habe den Kleist wieder durchgelesen,** *read through Kleist;* but in genitive normally: **eine Ausgabe von Hebbel; der Mackensen** (*dictionary by*) **fehlt mir noch, der Velasquez in der Nationalgalerie** [cp. § 159 (c)].

(2) Fictitious characters from real persons: **der Laokoon,** *the Laocoon* (group of sculpture), **der Koriolan,** play and character by Shakespeare; but the article stands more commonly for a work than for a character, thus, **der Faust** (or **die Faust-Dichtung**), *Faust* (by Goethe), but **Faust** (the character in this work).

159. Proper Names as Common Nouns

Used, by transferred sense, as common nouns, proper names may take either article.

(*a*) A person of the name (member of the family) of . . .

Ich kannte damals einen Ziehmüller. Eigentlich ist er ein Acton; especially with women's maiden names (= *née*): **Frau Senatorin Möllendorpf, geborene Langhals; eine geborene da Cruz; die geborene da Cruz** (all Th. Mann).

(*b*) A person like . . .

Deutschland brauchte einen Metternich und bekam einen Bismarck; man verlangte einen Bismarck und bekam einen Adenauer.

Dieses Gedächtnis Jacob Mendels war nicht geringer als jenes Napoleons für Physiognomien, eines Lasker für Schachanfänge, eines Busoni für Musik (S. Zweig).

As in English, *a person like* may be indistinguishable from the person himself (cp. first example above); the genitive normally discards the -s [cp. second example and § 156 (*c*)]; the plural is invariable, but sometimes according to the strong inflection [cp. § 91 (*b*)]:

diese „Judasse der Gesellschaft" (E. Wiechert), *these traitors within society.*

(*c*) A person's work, especially artistic: **das muß ein echter Franz Hals sein, die vielen gefälschten Vermeerens** [and cp. § 158 (*d*)]. **130,000 verschiedene deutsche Wörter gibts laut neuem Mackensen,** *according to the new* (*dictionary by*) *Mackensen.*

(*d*) The proper name is permanently transferred to the class of common nouns when it designates an object in the generic sense, after an original product: **der Zeppelin, die Junkers, der Mäzen. Kulissen-Knigge für Schauspieler,** *book of stagecraft hints for actors* (after a famous book of etiquette), etc.

The fully transferred use raises problems of:

(1) Gender: (i) man to man, no problem arises: **der Mäzen;** (ii) man to object, either masculine gender is retained (**der Zeppelin,** and name for a picture, **der Dürer**), or gender is by analogy [**die Junkers = Junkersmaschine,** *v.* § 441 (*b*)]; **der Diesel** from man or **Dieselmotor;** (iii) place to thing, neuter gender of places [*v.* § 219 (*b*)] is retained: **ein zweites Hiroschima will niemand.**

(2) Inflection: full normal inflection is adopted: **der Mäzen, des Mäzens, die Mäzene,** which may be the basis of a distinction between man and product. Thus: **die Leistungen des alten Diesel** (*the engineer*

Diesel), **eines Diesel** (*a man like Diesel*), but **eines Diesels** (*a Diesel engine*).
Die neue Auflage des Dudens (*Duden*, the orthographical handbook).

160. Relative and Absolute Comparison

(*a*) The forms of comparison described in Chapter XXIV are called
"relative" in that they always imply the relation of one thing to another
(adjectival use), or of one state, etc., of the same thing or person to
another (adverbial use).

Hans ist älter als Inge (Hans and Inge compared).

Ich arbeite immer am besten, wenn ich unter Druck bin, *I always work*
best when under pressure (different conditions compared).

In Geschichte ist er immer am besten gewesen, *he was always best at*
history (different performances compared).

(*b*) The same forms, though in different constructions, may also be
used to indicate a fairly high (comparative) or a very high (superlative)
degree or quality, without an explicit comparison with another person,
thing or condition, being made: **eine ältere Dame,** *an elderly lady;* **er gibt**
höchstens tausend Pfund für das Haus, *he will offer a thousand at the most.*
This is called "absolute comparison", and has both an adjectival and an
adverbial use.

161. The Absolute Comparative

(*a*) Adjectival use. **Eine längere Aussprache** (*longish*), **die neuere**
deutsche Literatur (*modern*), **unsere erste persönlichere Begegnung** (*rather*
more personal), **wir müssen uns das Nähere (Fernere) überlegen** (*think over*
the details, next step).

Note.—English often has the positive (*modern*). There may be an
implicit comparison (*more personal*), but the characteristic note of the
absolute comparative is that it falls short of the positive, thus *longish*
is less than *long*, *elderly* younger than *old*. **Ein besserer Mensch** is a
person with some claims (only) to good family, culture, etc. The flavour
may often be hesitant, approximative:

Der Schaffner, schon höher an Jahren, erbat sich die Erlaubnis zum
Eintreten durch sachtes Klopfen (Th. Mann), *getting on in years.*

(*b*) Adverbial use. **Er kommt öfter zu seinen Verwandten herüber**
(*fairly often*), **ich konnte ihn näher kennen lernen** (*quite well*), **ein länger**
dauerndes Verhältnis (*lasting some time*).

162. The Absolute Superlative

(*a*) Adjectival use. This occurs usually in the attributive position:
Liebste Eltern (*dearest*), **Ihr ergebenster** (*very sincerely*), **im höchsten**

Grade (*highest*), **eine erste Familie** (*of the first standing*), **feinste Stickerei** (*of finest quality*). Predicative only: **allerliebst** (*charming*, lit. *nicest of all*). The "highest possible degree" uses forms of the absolute superlative: **durch möglichste Sparsamkeit, die erdenklichste Sorgfalt**, (*by*) *the greatest possible* (*degree of*) *economy, care*.

(*b*) Adverbial use. This uses a form **aufs** (**beste**, etc.), *in the* (*best*) *possible way*, distinct from **am besten**, *best* or *at* (*his*) *best*, for the relative superlative:

Es ist alles aufs beste in die Wege geleitet worden, *everything is excellently in hand*, (*nicely*) *under control*.

As the absolute comparative has a slightly deprecating tone, so the absolute superlative with **aufs** has a slightly self-satisfied tone which makes it suitable for official pronouncements.

Note.—The compound **aufs** may be resolved for emphasis: **auf das**.

163. Intensifiers from Absolute Superlatives

The absolute adverbial superlative has been productive of a number of terms of *high*(*est*) *degree* which have been worn down into simple intensifiers or adverbs of degree.

(*a*) A few adverbs in -st: **möglichst, tunlichst**, *as far as possible;* **baldigst, demnächst**, *soon;* **jüngst**, *recently;* **längst**, *long since;* **äußerst, höchst, meist**, *extremely, highly, mostly;* **höflichst, innigst**, *politely, lovingly;* and **gütigst, freundlichst, gefälligst**, three terms used to support a courteous request which may consort well with a note of irony or irritation:

Machen Sie sich freundlichst nicht die geringste Hoffnung, *please do not entertain the slightest hopes.*

Lassen Sie mich gefälligst in Ruhe! *Leave me alone, if you please!*

As intensifiers, many are re-used as degree adverbs: **äußerst grob, höchst unangenehm, möglichst schnell, tunlichst bald**.

(*b*) A few adverbs in -ens: **bestens** and **schönstens**, *nicely;* **frühestens** and **spätestens**, *at the earliest, latest;* **höchstens, wenigstens, mindestens**, *at the most, least;* **meistens**, *usually;* **längstens**, *long since;* **nächstens**, *in the near future*. **Danke bestens!** *many thanks. At best* is **bestenfalls**.

(*c*) A few adverbs with **im**, usually in negative phrases:

(**nicht**) **im geringsten, mindesten, leisesten, entferntesten**, (*not*) *in the least, slightest, remotest.*

164. Comparison of Compound Adjectives

(*a*) In a combination of adjective and degree adverb, the latter is usually compared:

(1) Comparative: **leichter verkäuflich,** *easier to sell, more easily sold;* **rascher vergänglich,** *more evanescent;* **innerlicher beschäftigt,** *more deeply involved* (*occupied*).

(2) Superlative: **die schlechtest bezahlte Arbeit,** *worst paid work,* but in the predicate the correct adverbial form is common: **die Arbeit ist am schlechtesten bezahlt von allen,** unless the superlative is absolute: **die Arbeit ist miserabelst bezahlt,** *wretchedly paid.*

Here belong also comparative forms of the past participle, not usually compared, in the repetitive sense: **der meist bestiegene Berg,** *the most* (*often*) *climbed mountain,* and in descending comparison (*v.* § 120), **die wenigst gelesenen Bücher,** *least read books.*

(3) The words for *possible, imaginable* vary:

Möglich behaves as above: **ein möglichst langer Spaziergang,** *as long as possible;* **er soll möglichst bald kommen,** *as soon as possible.* But **denkbar** remains unchanged and transfers the ending to the adjective: **in den denkbar kleinsten Portionen,** *the smallest* (*imaginable*) *portions;* **den denkbar schlechtesten Dienst leisten,** *to serve someone in the worst manner* (*imaginable*).

(*b*) A compound adjective is compared either in the first or second part, depending on the degree of unity of the sense:

(1) **der meistgebotene Preis, die nächstgelegene Ortschaft, die best-bewiesenen Tatsachen.**

(2) **ein fortgeschrittenerer Staat, die altmodischste Aufmachung.**

If the first part takes the comparative ending, the compound is separated: **ein zarter besaiteter Jüngling,** *more sensitive youth.* Many words may be compared in either way; and the best practice is to avoid such words or phrases, unless they are well established.

(*c*) A word should not show a double comparison, thus not: **die größtmöglichste Vorsicht.** The only (apparent) exceptions to this rule are ordinal compounds (cp. § 155): **das zweitkleinste Kind, die zweitwichtigste Erfahrung meiner Reise.**

165. Orthography of Forms of Comparison

(*a*) The adverbial contractions **am** and **aufs** [*v.* § 162 (*b*)] are never resolved, and the following adjective or adverb with the superlative inflection has always a small letter, since the whole phrase is adverbial in force:

Es ist am besten (das beste), immer ehrlich zu sein, *it is always best to be honest.*

Er hat uns aufs schlimmste hintergangen, *he deceived us disgracefully.*

(*b*) From these constructions must be distinguished similar ones which incorporate a genuine (adjectival) noun, thus, cp. with the examples above:

Das Beste ist, offen und ehrlich zu sein, *the best* (*line of action at the moment*) *is to be frank and honest.*

Ich bin aufs Schlimmste gefaßt, *I am prepared for the worst* (i.e. *news*).

166. Defective Comparison

(*a*) **Erst** and **letzt,** *first* and *last,* are themselves superlatives, but may form new comparatives **erster-** and **letzter-** in the derived senses *the latter, the former,* with the article (as in English), but also without. They are, however, repetition forms, and the same sense can be expressed by **der erste, der letzte,** or **jener, dieser.**

(*b*) Certain adverbs express relationships of position: **außen, innen, hinten, oben, unten, vorne,** *outside, inside, at the back, top, bottom, front* (cp. § 136). They may be compared in various ways:

(1) Adjectival use. Example: **außen,** *outside.* Comparative: **äußer-,** *outer, exterior.* Superlative: **äußerst,** *outermost, extreme.* **Die äußere Mauer, der äußerste Stadtring, die äußerste Energie.**

Similarly: **inner-, hinter-, mittler-, ober-, unter-, vorder-.**

The comparative **mittler-** reverts in the superlative to **mittelst-,** not strictly logical, since "middle" can hardly be made into "middlemost":

Sie belegte einen Eckplatz im mittelsten Wagen (E. Kästner).

Äußerst has become a new adverb of degree [*v.* § 163 (*a*)].

(2) Adverbial use.

mehr (weiter) außen, *further out;* **am meisten (weitesten) (nach) außen,** *furthest out.*

Ich bestellte Plätze in der am weitesten (nach) oben liegenden Sitzreihe, *took seats in the uppermost row* [cp. § 118 (*c*) (2)].

(3) Adverbial superlative, with **zu** and the superlative as in (1), as: **zuerst, zuletzt, zumeist, zunächst, zuvorderst,** *first, last, most*(*ly*), *next, foremost;* and the following which may also be separated: **zuhinterst, zuinnerst, zuoberst, zuunterst,** *right at the back, inside, top, bottom.*

Note.—The above converted to a preposition:

Die Sternenaugen des Hausherrn zuoberst der kleinen Tafel blickten . . . (Th. Mann), *at the top end of the small table, the host's eyes* . . . (= **oben an der Tafel**).

(c) The choice between alternatives above is often a matter of greater or lesser complexity of style: **zuhinterst** (literary), **am weitesten (nach) hinten** (good normal), **ganz hinten** (speech).

EXERCISE XXX

A. Translate into ENGLISH:

1. „Meine liebe Mama, tausend Dank für Deinen Brief, in dem Du mir Armgard von Schillings Verlobung mit Herrn von Maiboom auf Pöppenrade mitteilst" (Th. Mann). 2. Erst als wir alle drei die Treppe zum Dachboden hinaufstiegen, konnte ich den Mann genauer ansehen (H. Hesse). 3. Die eigene Aufgabe liegt einem immer am nächsten. Man kann seine Pflichtbereitschaft immer am Nächsten beweisen. 4. Die am dichtesten besiedelten Industrieländer fangen an, einen stärkeren Mangel an Rohmaterial zu empfinden. 5. „Eine Tasse schwarzen Kaffee!" rief der Offizier mit erhobener Stimme, „und möglichst schnell, wenn ich bitten darf!" 6. Er hatte seine Sammlung von chinesischen Seidenmalereien aufs schönste eingerahmt. 7. Die Regierung Maria Theresiens brachte Österreich mancherlei Segen, aber auch vielerlei internationale Schwierigkeiten. 8. Er hat seinem alten Kunden, der nun arm war, in großzügigster Weise die Schulden bezahlt. 9. Nun bekommt man in den Geschäften endlich eine vielseitigere Auswahl von Käse und Fleisch als in den Nachkriegsjahren. 10. Meine Kakteensammlung gedeiht am besten in einem Zimmer mit regelmäßiger Temperatur. 11. „Der brave Mann denkt an sich selbst zuletzt" (Fr. Schiller).

B. Translate into GERMAN:

1. The Müllers and I saw an excellent performance of *Hamlet* at (**auf**) the open air stage at (**zu**) Elsinore. 2. Eduard's son has gone on (**auf**) an expedition to the Sahara desert. 3. The pen-name of Friedrich von Hardenberg, the greatest of the German Romantic poets, was Novalis. 4. He was an elderly little man, and he was speaking to the detective in a rather loud, excited voice. 5. They can deliver the machine next spring at the earliest. They are not hurrying in the least. 6. The most carefully-planned garden yields the best possible variety of flowers at (**zu**) every season. 7. The best-thing about (**an**) a holiday is the moment of one's (the) return, say the cynics. 8. It is most interesting to read periodicals as soon as they appear. 9. The outermost islands of Scotland lie directly in (**an**) the path of great bird-migrations from the Arctic regions.

CHAPTER XXXI

167. Informal and Formal Address: Du and Sie

(*a*) The whole field of direct address is divided up between **Sie** and **Du,** the so-called polite and familiar forms respectively, as follows:

(1) **Du** is used among members of a family, intimate friends, and in all poetic and higher diction.

(2) **Sie** is used in the language of all ordinary social intercourse outside the bounds of **Du.**

Du is therefore both more formal (elevated) and informal (straightforward) than **Sie,** which is restricted to the middle reaches of human relations. It is easier, therefore, to list the **Du** uses.

(*b*) **Du** is used in elevated language, *i.e.*

(1) Addressing God and in the solemn language of the Church and of prayer generally:

Vater unser, der Du bist im Himmel, geheiliget werde Dein Name, *Our Father, Who art in Heaven, hallowed be Thy Name.*

(2) In lyrical poetry:

Sausewind! Brausewind! / Dort und hier! / Deine Heimat sage mir! (Mörike, *Lied vom Winde*).

(*c*) **Du** is used in intimate address, *i.e.*

(1) Within the family, thus between parents, children and relatives; and between persons on terms of intimate friendship.

Note.—The pronoun of intimacy, unless intimately assumed, must be formally proposed, not informally drifted into, the proposal coming strictly from the person senior in age or status. It is more carefully circumscribed than the use of Christian names in England. Idioms: **jemandem das Du anbieten, wir duzen uns seit sechs Monaten, mit jemandem (einander) per Du (auf dem Duzfuß) sein; wir siezen uns, sind immer noch seit Jahren per Sie.**

But in the Army (other ranks), the world of entertainment, in academic "corporations", and, conversely, among tramps, drunks and gaol-birds, **du** is used between equals without previous formal proposal.

Note.—**Ihr** may be used to several persons of mixed **Du** and **Sie** status, thus from a wife to her husband and his personal friends.

(2) When addressing someone or something outside polite society, as animals, objects (**Du, mein altes Vaterhaus!**), children, and schoolchildren

to the age of 15/16 [while the child returns the **Sie**, unless on **Du** terms according to (1)]; but *not* from employer to servant except in peasant and patriarchal surroundings.

Teacher addresses schoolboy: **Bist du noch Untersekundaner, oder sind Sie schon Obersekundaner?** *are you Lower Fifth or Upper Fifth?* (quoted by H. Reimann).

(3) When addressing oneself by internal monologue, etc.

(*d*) **Du** is used in general and indefinite address to members of the public, imaginary opponents, and in the simulated language of thought. Thus it is widely used in advertisement:

Hast Du deine Weihnachtsgeschenke schon eingekauft? *Have you bought your Christmas presents?*

Die Hilfsgemeinschaft „Tu Dein Bestes" sorgt für die soziale Eingliederung ehemaliger Tuberkulose-Kranker, *the organisation "Do your Best" looks after the social after-care of T.B. patients.*

Niemand ergreift, was er nicht von Geburt besitzt, und was dir fremd ist, kannst du nicht begehren (Th. Mann), *and what you know nothing about you can feel no desire for.*

168. Formal Address and Reference

(*a*) **Du,** as the mode of address in elevated language and invocation, is in a peculiar sense more "formal" than **Sie**. It is thus used with a capital in any elevated context [cp. (*b*) (1) above], and this practice persists in the use of the capital in correspondence for all forms of **Du** and **Dein.**

(*b*) Analogous to this is the use of **wir,** with singular reference, as the plural of solemnity, in the context of formal pronouncements, editorial, Royal or Papal. In the last two contexts, again as in English, all related forms (**Wir, Uns, Unser**) have capitals.

(*c*) **Ihr,** with capital, is often used for polite address, with both singular and plural reference, in country speech:

(Die) alte Frau . . . sah mich an und nickte dann: „Ihr seid da!" (S. Andres) *. . . and nodded: "So you've come!"*

(*d*) The third person plural number was used, until quite recently, with a noun of address, in certain social contexts: (1) to a social superior: **Wissen Herr Konsul das Neueste?** (Th. Mann); (2) to ladies: **„Dann sind Gnädigste entschuldigt," erklärte von Pfaff** (H. Mann);

(3) in the Army to superior officers (and even in some regiments,
N.C.O.s): **Wünschen Herr Major eine Tasse Kaffee?**

Analogous to this is the still common use of the third person *singular*,
with noun of address, by shopkeepers: **Was wünscht der Herr? Was
bekommt die Dame?** or simply: **Die Dame?**

(*e*) In other cases, the third person address may be the degree of
distance appropriate to convey irony or a threat, as when a schoolmaster
receives a late pupil, and grasps the cane:

,,**Ist man da?" fragte die Stimme, ,,Ist man angelangt? Ist man ein-
getroffen?"** (E. Wiechert), *well, and so we've come, have we?*

169. Other Pronoun Forms

(*a*) **Sie** and **du** may be compounded in abbreviation with a preceding
verbal form to render colloquial elisions of speech:

,,**Passense auf!" schrie der Polizist** (E. Kästner), "*Look out!" shouted
the policeman.* (= **Passen Sie auf!**)

Denkste! (Simpl.).   *That's what you think.*   (= **Denkst du!**)

**und dann saust der Wind, haste was kannste, aus einer ganz anderen Ecke
daher** (Simpl.), *and then the wind veers and comes in at a cracking speed
from another direction.*

(*b*) **Selbst** and **selber**, -*self*, is a strongly stressed indeclinable adjective-
pronoun much used to reinforce pronouns, whether personal, relative, or
reflexive (*v.* § 181), or nouns. **Selbst** may precede or follow the pronoun
(noun) or come later in the sentence; **selber** may not precede. English
terms are -*self* or (when **selbst** precedes) *even*:

Ich selber will das unternehmen, ich will das selber unternehmen, *I myself
will do that, I will do that myself* (or **selbst**).

Selbst ich kann das nicht verstehen, *even I cannot understand that* (but not
selber).

The position may be material to the sense:

Ich mußte ihm das Geld selbst geben, *I had to give him the money myself.*

Ich mußte das Geld ihm selbst (selber) geben, *I had to give the money to
him* (not another person).

Note that English:

(1) Only uses -self to reinforce the subject or complement:
I myself . . ., He said I must be myself; but not (except as an Irishism)
the direct or indirect object: I saw himself, gave it to himself. But
German **selbst** may reinforce the object (*v.* example above).

(2) Places the pronouns in an oblique case in compound with -self: myself, himself (and yourself). German **selbst** does not affect the case of the pronoun:

Er wurde mehr und mehr er selbst; man muß man selbst sein, *he became more and more himself; one must be oneself.*

(*c*) *v.* § 60 for uses of **man;** *v.* § 197 for compounds of pronouns with certain prepositional forms, **-wegen, -willen, -halb;** *v.* § 234 for invariable pronominal compounds with **-gleichen, -einer.**

170. Possessive Pronouns

Revise § 25, possessive adjectives.

The possessive pronouns are used in three related forms:

(*a*) Uninflected in the predicate as the complement of certain verbs (**sein, werden, bleiben**), and occasionally as the objective complement (*v.* § 149) of certain others (**nennen**):

der Hut ist mein; das Geld bleibt dein; sie wurde mein; ich nannte sie mein, *the hat is mine; the money remains yours; she became mine; I called her my own.*

This use is very limited, being now not possible for the forms **ihr** (*her, their*), and **Ihr** (*your*). They may only be used in the general sense of belonging; if the intention is to distinguish one object of possession from another, the full form in (*b*) is used:

Hier ist mein Buch—wo ist deines (das deine)?

(*b*) Inflected in the normal sense of *mine, yours,* etc. There are two forms:

(1) With strong (definite article) endings:

mein Haus und seines, aus meinem Garten in ihren, der Sinn meines Lebens und seines . . .; *and his . . ., into hers . . ., and of his.*

Ein Junge, der so alt war wie ihrer, saß am Klavier und klimperte lustlos (H. Böll), *a boy who was as old as hers . . .*

(2) With the definite article and weak endings:

mein Haus und das seine, or the lengthened form: **das seinige,** *my house and his.*

Similarly: **das unsere** (or **unsre**), **das unsrige, das Ihre, das Ihrige,** etc.

(*c*) The forms in (*a*) and (*b*) also exist as nouns with capitals:

(1) Uninflected they represent a collective reference to the possessions of a person, or the title to possession, but only in set expressions, thus:

Das Kind muß lernen, zwischen Mein und Dein zu unterscheiden, *the child must learn to distinguish between its own things and those of others.*

(2) Inflected, in the plural, for the family, relatives and friends, etc.: **Ich zählte acht Jahre, als ich und die Meinen einige Sommerwochen in dem benachbarten L. verbrachten** (Th. Mann), *when I and my family . . .* especially in greetings in letters: **Herzliche Grüße an Dich und die Deinen;** or in the neuter singular for property, sometimes for duty (cp. *to do one's bit*):

Die Espressomaschine bringt ächzende, auch wohl klagende Geräusche hervor, und dennoch tut sie unverdrossen das Ihre (W. Bergengruen), *the coffee-machine produces groaning and complaining sounds, but cheerfully continues to do its bit.*

(*d*) All forms of the possessive pronoun are written with a capital when referring to the person addressed in a letter: **Du hast sowohl mein Leben gerettet als auch Deines,** *mine and yours.*

171. Separable Compound Verbs with Dative and Dative/Accusative Objects

(*a*) Many separable compounds take a dative object, usually of a person concerned, and may, if transitive, also take an accusative object. The senses common with this construction are analogous to those earlier described for this group of verbs (*v.* §§ 97-9), *i.e.*:

(1) Verbs of advantage and disadvantage, etc.:

er geht mir ab, *I miss him* (lit. *he is lacking to me*), cp. **er fehlt mir.**

das kommt mir zu, *that is in my field* (*responsibility*), cp. **das gehört mir.**

er hörte mir zu, *he listened to me,* cp. **er lauschte mir.**

er trat (stand) dem Verein bei, *he joined* (*helped*) *the society,* cp. **er diente (half) dem Vereine.**

er schwörte dem Rauchen ab, *he gave up* (*forswore*) *smoking,* cp. **er trotzte dem Feinde.**

(2) Verbs of giving and bringing:

er brachte mir großes Vertrauen entgegen, *showed great confidence in me* (lit. *met me with . . .*).

er führte die Verhandlungen einem glücklichen Abschluß zu, *he brought the negotiations to a successful conclusion.*

and the reverse, denial, and deprivation:

er hat mir das Gesuch abgelehnt, *he refused my application.*

ich habe ihm das Amt weggenommen, *I deprived him of his office.*

(3) Verbs of communication:

er spielte mir das Klavierstück vor, *he played the piece over to me.*

sie lächelte mir freundlich zu, *she smiled at me in a friendly way.*

and the reverse, denial or withdrawal:

ich habe ihm meinen Besuch abgesagt, *I cancelled my visit to him.*

(*b*) The dative, with or without the accusative object, may be governed by compound verbs incorporating:

(1) Many common prefixes, from prepositions or adverbs, as:

ab, an, auf, bei, ein, entgegen, gegenüber, nach, unter, vor, zu.

(2) Some prefixes derived from other parts of speech, as adjectives (**fern, nahe, gleich, leicht**), nouns (**stand, wort, not**), and phrases (**zustatten, abhanden**) [*v.* § 173 (*b*)].

172. Force of Separable Compounds with Dative

(*a*) The general sense of such verbs is indicated by the groups distinguished, and examples given, at § 171. As earlier noted (§§ 97, 99), many such verbs fall naturally into contrasted pairs, thus:

(1) Contrasted prefixes:

absagen, *to refuse* (*invitation,* etc.), **zusagen,** *to accept, grant.*

nachlaufen, *to pursue, run after,* **weglaufen,** *to run away from.*

nachsprechen, *to say something after someone,* **vorsprechen,** *to speak something to someone* (as a model).

nahestehen, *to be associated with,* **fernstehen,** *to remain at a distance from.*

(2) Contrasted senses:

beistehen, *to support;* **entgegenwirken,** *to use one's influence against;* **zusprechen,** *to set to* (*eating,* etc.); **abschwören,** *to forswear.*

(*b*) The full force of such verbs depends on the combined force of the dative (of interest, advantage, or the opposite, or of motion to or from, etc.), and of the prefix itself. Thus the same simple verb may often take the dative alone, or a prefix and the dative, or a preposition alone, all in related but distinct senses. Usually it is the compound which has the more figurative sense. Thus:

(1) Simple and compound verb compared:

er winkte dem Kellner, *signed to the waiter* (to give an order).

er winkte ihr freundlich zu, *waved to her* (as a pure gesture).

(2) Preposition and prefix compared:

er stand bei mir, *stood near me,* **er stand mir bei,** *stood by me* (*supported me*).

er spielte das Stück vor dem König, *before the King* (who may have been asleep).

er spielte das Stück seinem Lehrer vor, *played it over to his teacher* (who was listening critically).

(3) Simple verb, preposition and prefix compared:

der Anzug steht ihm, *suits him;* er steht zu mir, zu seinem Wort, *stands by me, by his word;* das steht mir zu, *that is one of my rights.*

(*c*) It follows that the dative after the separable compound, having some force of personal interest or otherwise, is often not used with a non-personal object, which requires a prepositional phrase:

sie setzte dem Sohne die Mütze auf, setzte ihm das Essen vor, *she put his cap on her son's head, put his meal in front of him.*

sie setzte das Essen auf den Tisch, vor den leeren Stuhl, *she put the meal on the table, in front of the empty chair.*

173. Force of Certain Prefixes in Compounds with Dative

The particular force of certain prefixes in this group may be suggested; for examples *v.* § 171 and the Exercise.

(*a*) Adverbial and prepositional prefixes:

Ab- has the force of *to deny* in this and similar verbs: **absprechen**, *to deny* (*a right*, etc.), **absagen**, *to decline* (*an invitation*, etc.), **abschwören**, *to forswear*. In relation to property it has the force of acquiring from someone else, **abkaufen**, often furtively, or against the will of the dative object, thus **abknöpfen** and **abzwacken**, *to wrest from, get* (*money*, etc.) *out of*, and **abgucken** or **absehen**, *to see furtively*, e.g. *to copy in school.*

An-, together with **auf-** and **ein-**, indicates the imposition, perhaps against the will of another, of something extraneous. Thus **anhängen**, *to pass off a thing on a person*, **andichten**, *to impute something* (falsely); **aufgeben**, *to give a person a task* (**die Aufgabe**, which may be acceptable, even honourable, as in the sense of a *commission*, or neutral, as *homework* in school), but **aufbürden, aufladen, aufhalsen** are all *to impose* an unwanted burden, load; **einpauken**, *to cram* (*a pupil*) *with*, **einflößen**, *to inspire with* (*e.g.* courage, perhaps Dutch courage).

Bei- indicates an action or gesture of support, as **beitreten**, *to join;* **beistehen**, *to support;* and **beipflichten**, *to agree.*

Nach- and **vor-** are complementary prefixes indicating that something is done in imitation of another or as a demonstration to another, thus **vorlesen**, *to recite*, and analogously: **vorsingen, vorpielen**; and **nachsingen**, *to sing* (*after*, **nach jemandem**, but also *in imitation*, **jemandem nach**). **Nachmachen**, *to imitate* (generally).

Zu- indicates an action or gesture towards, but is less strong than **bei-,** as **zuhören,** *to listen to,* **zulächeln** and **zuwinken,** *to smile, wave to,* **zutrinken,** *to drink a person's health.*

(*b*) Other prefixes:

Fern and **nahe** form verbs of close association or the opposite, thus **es liegt mir fern, nahe,** *it is far from, near to my mind.* These prefixes [as explained § 172 (*b*)] are always analogous to, but much more figurative (immaterial) in force than, the literal sense of the adjectives.

Gleich, as in **jemandem gleichtun,** *to imitate a person.*

Stand, as in **standhalten,** *to resist, stand up to.*

Not, as in **nottun,** *to be necessary to.*

Wort, as in **worthalten,** *to keep (one's) word to.*

Note that when nouns become prefixes they lose their capital initial [cp. § 88 (*d*)].

Zustatten, as in **zustattenkommen,** *to come in handy,* means (literally) *in the right place.*

Abhanden, as in **abhandenkommen,** *to get lost,* means (literally) *away from the hands.*

EXERCISE XXXI

A. Translate into ENGLISH:

1. Selbst der Schaffner mußte mir zugeben, daß er nicht rechtzeitig geklingelt hatte.   2. Er kann diese Arbeit nicht selber bewältigen; wir müssen ihm beistehen.   3. Wir haben nicht oft einen Wagen gesehen, der so alt ist wie unserer (der unsrige).   4. ,,Du sollst es nicht immer dem schlimmsten Jungen in der Klasse gleichtun," sagte der Vater ernst zu seinem kleinen Sohn.   5. Er folgte dem Kaiser, seinem Vater, nach. Er folgte seinem Vater auf dem Thron.   6. Sie brachte ihm Geschenke. Sie brachte ihm ihre Gründe vor.   Sie brachte ihm ihr volles Vertrauen entgegen.   7. Der Verkäufer hat mir einen schlechten Wagen angehängt. 8. Es liegt mir fern, an seiner Ehrlichkeit zu zweifeln.   Es liegt einem solchen Manne nahe, an der Ehrlichkeit anderer zu zweifeln.   9. Etwas Abspannung tut uns allen not, sagte der Mannschaftsführer.   10. Das Geld haben wir nicht verschwendet, irgendwie ist es uns aber abhanden gekommen.   11. In dieser Not kam die finanzielle Hilfe des Onkels der Familie sehr zustatten.   12. ,,Nicht weglaufen sondern standhalten müssen wir jetzt," flüsterte er seinem Freunde rasch zu.   13. Sage mir (*tell me*) mit wem du umgehst, und ich sage dir wer du bist (Prov.). 14. ,,Alt Heidelberg, du feine, / Du Stadt an Ehren reich, / Am Neckar und am Rheine / Kein' andre kommt dir gleich" (Scheffel).   15. *Give yourself*

a treat. „Du solltest (*ought*) sie dir wirklich gönnen, die kostenlose Freude der Lektüre des 240-seitigen Photohelfers, der interessante Photo-Ratschläge und herrliche Farbbilder bringt" (Simpl., adv.).

B. Translate into GERMAN:

1. Even he had not the patience to repair that old clock. 2. She herself decided to visit her aunt and explain the situation to her. 3. The car is yours and you must take full responsibility for the accident. 4. The house remains his as long as he lives. 5. My sister and his went for a holiday together last summer. 6. He respected his father very much and wanted to imitate him in everything. 7. He held revolutionary meetings at street corners until they withdrew his office. 8. You must join the music club when you get to this little town. 9. Won't you read your essay to me? I will listen carefully to you, and two heads are better than one, so they (**man**) say. 10. He dictated a letter [to] his secretary in which he promised to keep-his-word.

CHAPTER XXXII

174. Titles of Profession, Rank, and Occupation, etc.

Revise §§ 156-9, proper names.

The genitive inflection of titles is a little difficult.

(*a*) When no article precedes, title and name are felt as a unit, and the latter only takes the inflection:

das Haus Professor Lehmanns, Graf Wilhelms Tod, nach Lehrer Schmidts Ankunft, Onkel Hermanns Hunde, der Verlobte Fräulein Köpkes, das Angebot Präsident Eisenhowers.

Note.—But **Herr** is always declined: **Herrn Schmidts Stellung, an Herrn Öhme;** also when **von** follows: **ihre Verlobung mit Herrn von Maiboom. Kollege** (and **Genosse**) should also be declined, but are often used without inflection, following the main rule: **Kollege(n) Kohns Antrag, ich hörte von Kollege(n) Kohn.**

(*b*) When the article or other modifying word precedes, the title and not the name takes the inflection:

der Antrag des Rektors Lehmann, im Beisein unseres Lehrers Schmidt, der Sohn des Pastors Wieler, das Haus des Professors Kuckuck, die Rede unseres verehrten Präsidenten Eisenhower.

Titles which are purely occupational should have the article and follow this rule: **die Rede des Betriebsführers Holland.**

Cp. for (*a*): **scharfe Stellungnahme Kardinal Innitzers** (newsp.), and for (*b*): **Tag und Nacht ziehen Tausende am Katafalk des Kardinals Fauhaber vorbei** (newsp.).

Note.—Double Titles. **Herr** preceding is inflected: **der Vorschlag des Herrn Direktors Kuhn,** but any other title following may be inflected or not: **die Rede des Ministerialdirektors Professor(s) Dr. Kuhn.**

(*c*) But a practice is growing increasingly common of regarding the whole title and name after the definite article as a unit and not inflecting, on the analogy of proper names [cp. § 156 (*c*)], thus:

die Rede des Herrn Professo*r* Schmi*dt*, das Büro des Rechtsanwa*lt* Mülle*r* on the analogy of **die Mütze des Heinrich.**

This is still regarded as incorrect, and in any case the genitive -s is always required at the point of contact between governed and governing noun [cp. § 156 (*c*)], thus: **des Rechtsanwalt Müller*s* Büro.**

(d) **Dr.** (= **Doktor**), an academic title, not a medical qualification, is regarded as part of the name, and never inflected under any circumstances: **Dr. Schmidts Haus, das Haus (Herrn) Dr. Schmidts,** etc.

(e) An appended title is always inflected:

die Regierung (Herzog) Karls des Kühnen, *of* (*Duke*) *Charles the Bold.*
die Thronbesteigung Eduards des Siebenten, *accession of Edward VII,*
or: **des Königs Eduard des Siebenten.**

175. The Courtesy Titles: Herr and Frau

(a) The courtesy titles **Herr** and **Frau** usually precede all names, titles, including those of aristocratic families, but not royal or similar titles (**Fürst, Prinz**), in direct address, on envelopes and letter headings (in the oblique case **Herrn**), and in polite third person reference:

Guten Morgen, Herr Professor! Herr Oberregierungsrat Kühne läßt bitten. Herrn Amtsgerichtsrat Müller a.D., Göttingen, Lohbergweg 17.

Note.—Letter addresses to the lower nobility in some parts still preserve a more involved style than the simple address which is adequate for personal relations (**Herr Baron, Frau Baronin**), and it is wise to take advice on this.

(b) An earlier practice, now less common, allowed married women to assume the title of their husbands: **Frau Professor (Georg) Müller.** Thus a title in the form **Frau Dr. Wertheim, Frau Professor Hardenberg** would probably *now* indicate that the lady holds the office or title in her own right; but *not*, however, that she is married, since unmarried professional women of a certain age adopt **Frau** as a courtesy title. Thus **Fräulein Dr. Schmidt** would be quite common, but only **Frau Professor Müller.**

Note.—In addresses of letters, **Herrn und Frau Dr. Wesel** (transferred title, cp. above), may become **Familie Dr. Wesel,** if the writer is on informal terms. Opening formula: **Liebe Familie Wesel.**

(c) **Herr, Frau,** and **Fräulein** are also commonly prefixed to names of relationship for courteous reference when addressing the relative:

Ihr Herr Vater, Ihr Herr Gemahl, Ihr(e) Fräulein Schwester, Ihre Frau Mutter, *your father, husband, sister, mother.* There are three degrees of formality when referring to a husband or wife; very formal: **Ihr Herr Gemahl, Ihre Frau Gemahlin;** normal polite: **Ihr Gatte, Ihre Gattin;** informal friendly: **Ihr Mann, Ihre Frau.** The last two never take **Herr** or **Frau.**

176. Wer and Was as General and Indefinite Relatives

(*a*) The interrogative pronouns **wer** and **was** (case-forms, *v.* §§ 26, 27) are used as relatives with indefinite or general reference, *i.e.* combining the role of relative and antecedent (cp. § 95), and referring to:

(1) Persons, whether masculine, feminine, or plural, in the sense *somebody who, whoever, (he) who*—**wer.**

(2) Things, whether singular or plural in the sense *something that, whatever, (that) which, what*—**was.**

Wer Bücher liest, lebt doppelt, *those who read books live twice over* (slogan at book-fair).

Was ich nicht weiß, macht mich nicht heiß, *what the eye doesn't see the heart doesn't grieve over* (prov.).

(*b*) The normal rules for relative clauses (end-position of verb, punctuation, etc., *v.* § 95) apply to clauses introduced by general relatives. Although almost all such clauses are noun clauses (subject, object, or complement of a verb), while normal relative clauses are adjectival, the same distinction is made between:

(1) internal case government, which determines the form of the general relative, as in the above examples:

wer (subject)—**Bücher** (object)—**liest** (verb, subject **wer**).
was (object)—**ich** (subject)—**weiß** (verb, subject **ich**).

(2) and external case government, *i.e.* the role played by the clause introduced by the general relative, as a whole, thus:

wer Bücher liest (subject)—**lebt** (verb)—**doppelt** (adverb).
was ich nicht weiß (subject)—**macht** (verb)—**mich nicht heiß** (object, etc.).

Thus the case of the general relative and that of the clause as a whole may be quite different [cp. § 96 (*a*) antecedent and relative]:

wer (above) is both nominative and introduces a subject clause, but **was** (above) is accusative and introduces a subject clause, thus also:

Wen E.S. führt, ist gut geführt (rev. of guide-book), *those who entrust themselves to the guidance of E.S. are well guided.*

(*c*) When the general relative clause precedes, it may be immediately followed by a demonstrative in the main clause, referring back to and summing up the preceding clause; thus in the above examples:

Wer Bücher liest, der lebt doppelt, (*he*) *lives twice over.*

Was ich nicht weiß, das macht mich nicht heiß, (*that*) *does not . . .*

Wen E.S. führt, der ist gut geführt, (*he*) *is well guided.*

Note (1).—The demonstrative has the case required by the role of the relative clause within the main clause [cp. (*b*) (2)]; and (2).—It precedes the main verb without breaking the second-place rule [cp. §§ 50 (*b*), 95 (*c*)] as it is in apposition to the preceding clause.

(*d*) **Was** may be used for persons in a collective or representative sense [cp. **das**, § 32 (*b*)].

Was sich liebt, das neckt sich, *lovers will always tease each other* (prov.).

This is often implicitly *all those who*, and the **was** equals **alles, was** [cp. § 147 and § 177 (*b*) below]:

Aber es kamen nicht nur die Maler (= **zur Ausstellung**) **und nur die Fremden und was man so Publikum nennt. Nein, alle kleinen Leute waren gekommen** (W. Bergengruen), *those who are known as the public.*

(*e*) Concessive force. **Wer** and **was** are already general in sense, rendering the sense *whoever, whatever*, but for them to have truly concessive force further emphasis is supplied by the adverbs **auch, immer, auch immer, auch nur, nur immer,** etc. (*it doesn't matter who . . . what . . .*), which may follow the relative immediately or at a distance:

Nietzsche, Dostojewski oder wen immer sie gerade gelesen hatten, mußten sich bescheiden, auf der Erde oder dem Bett liegen zu bleiben (R. Musil), *or whoever it was they had been reading, had to be content . . .*

Was auch immer in dem Buch enthalten sein mag, Schund bleibt's doch (or: **Was in dem Buch auch immer . . .**), *whatever is contained in the book, it is still trash.*

Compare concessive clauses, § 239.

177. Was as Indefinite Relative

(*a*) The use of **was** as general relative described above, § 176, dispenses with a specific antecedent; the clause is a noun clause. **Was,** however, is also used (instead of **das,** the normal neuter relative) after certain specific antecedents of an indefinite or neuter nature. The antecedent may be explicit, or implicit in the sense of the statement.

(*b*) **Was** follows certain *explicit* antecedents of indefinite or collective meaning:

(1) The neuter indefinite pronouns **etwas** and **nichts** (*v.* § 61), the general demonstrative **das** (*v.* § 65), and the indefinite adjective-pronouns (*v.* §§ 81, 147) when used in the indeclinable, or neuter inflected forms, as: **alles; eins, einiges, solches, manches, mehreres, viel(es), wenig(es), genug; das einzige, das wenige, das bißchen; mancherlei, allerhand,** etc.

In der Zeitung gibt's etwas, was Sie interessieren würde, *something which would interest you.*

Das einzige, was ich tun kann, ist radfahren, *the only thing I can do is ride a bicycle.*

Es gibt mancherlei, was diesen Verdacht in mir bestätigt, *there is much which confirms this doubt in me.*

(2) Superlative adjectives used as nouns:

Das Erste, was ich in München unternahm, war ein Museumsbesuch, *the first thing I did in Munich . . .*

Das ist das Letzte, was man mir zumuten darf, *that is the last thing which can be expected of me.*

Das Schlimmste, was einem dabei passieren kann, ist eine kleine Geldstrafe, *the worst which can happen to one . . .*

Note.—The boundaries of **das** and **was** after indefinite antecedents are fluctuating. **Was** is often extended, especially in North Germany, to analogous cases to those in (1) and (2), such as adjectival uses (**das wenige Geld, was ich besaß . . ., das kostbarste Gut, was wir besitzen . . .**), or adjective-nouns, not superlatives (**das Gute, was man tut, überlebt einen . . .**). More important is the gradual use of **das (welches)** for **was** in the contexts described in (1) and (2), *v.* § 227 (*b*).

(*c*) **Was** follows an antecedent of indefinite nature which is *implicit* in the sense:

(1) An adjective or noun referred to in its general rather than specific sense:

Mein Bruder ist gesellig gewandt, was man mir nie vorwerfen könnte, *my brother is provided with social graces, something of which I could never be accused.*

Mein Vater ist Rechtsanwalt, was mir nie eingefallen wäre (subj.) **zu werden,** *a lawyer, which it would never have occurred to me to become.*

For **was, welches** may be used. In each case **was** could be replaced by **und das . . .,** showing that the reference is to the fact of being (socially acceptable, a lawyer), rather than the quality or function itself.

(2) The general trend of the preceding statement rather than any actual word:

Dieses Wort (Fortschritt) umschließt, was inzwischen auch schon den Minderklugen bekannt ward, eine arge Illusion (F. Werfel), *the word Progress involves a grievous illusion, a fact which has since become known to even the less intelligent.*

Good writers interpolate (as above) this **was**-clause; in a following position it drags, and is criticised as **weiterführender Nebensatz** (*spinning out the sentence*):

Ich bin nicht in der Lage, Ihrer freundlichen Einladung Folge zu leisten, was ich sehr bedauere, *I am not able to accept your kind invitation, a fact which I much regret.*

Correct: **Ich bin leider (bedauerlicherweise) nicht in der Lage . . .**

(*d*) **Was** introduces a general relative clause in apposition to the impersonal **es** (cp. §§ 343 f.):

Es ist nicht alles Gold, was glänzt, *all is not gold that glitters.*

Es war ein entzückendes kleines Palais, was er da besaß (R. Musil), *it was a charming little residence that he had there.*

Es war nicht bloß Altersschwäche, was die alte Mme A. B. an einem kalten Januartag . . . darniederwarf (Th. Mann), *it was not just old age that made old Mme A. B. take to her bed.*

Note that this is in fact a return to the pattern of the examples in § 176, since such statements can be reversed, the **was**-clause becoming subject, and the **es** disappearing:

Was glänzt, ist nicht alles Gold.

178. External Case Government of the General Relative Clause

(*a*) When the relationship between internal and external case government is not of the simplest, as in some short proverb sayings:

Wer wagt, gewinnt, *he who dares, wins* [and examples in § 176 (*a*)].

then grammar may be satisfied, but style and clarity may suffer:

Wen E.S. führt, ist gut geführt [example in § 176 (*b*)].

Further, when the general relative clause is externally governed in the dative, or by a preposition, even grammar is not satisfied without further clarification; thus the following two statements cannot possibly be linked without further elaboration:

(1) **Wen Wir lieben**—*those whom* (*whomever*) *we love.*

(2) **wir schenken (ihm) Vertrauen**—*we trust in* (*them*, dat.).

or   **wir setzen Vertrauen (in ihn)**—*we trust in* (*them*, prep. acc.).

There are two possibilities for this, a literary and proverbial form, and a simple common form.

(*b*) Literary form of resolution of external case government:

Wen wir lieben, dem schenken wir Vertrauen.
Wen wir lieben, in den setzen wir Vertrauen.

The **was**-clause is resumed in the form of a demonstrative pronoun in apposition, which reflects the external case government (here dative or accusative after preposition) of the clause. The summarising demonstrative is quite common in proverbial statements, even when it is not fulfilling this grammatical role [cp. § 176 (c)]:

> **Wer probt, der lobt,** *testing is the best judge.*

In this use, the demonstrative in the dative is often that used with parts of the body, a form of the dative of the person to whose (dis)advantage something happens (cp. § 171, and fully §§ 382, 384-5):

> **Wer die Hand gegen die Eltern erhebt, dem wächst sie aus dem Grab,** *he who raises his hand against his parents, his hand will grow* (lit. *to him it will grow*) *out of the grave* (precept said to have been inculcated into German children).

(c) Simple form of resolution of external case government:

> **Wir schenken Vertrauen dem, den wir lieben.**
> **Wir setzen Vertrauen in den, den wir lieben.**

The general relative **wer** is itself resolved into the double form, antecedent and relative, **der, der** (*he, who*), and the antecedent reflects the external case government [cp. § 96 (a)]. This is commonly the form taken in statements where the person referred to is specific, though either not mentioned or not yet ascertained:

> **Ich gebe das Buch dem, der mir zuerst die richtige Antwort sagt,** *I'll give the book to whoever gives me the right answer first.*

> **Ich denke nicht mehr an den, der mir das Buch gab,** *I no longer think of the person who gave me the book.*

Cp. also § 292 (correlatives).

The general relative **was** is resolved in such cases into **das, was** [in accordance with § 177 (b)]:

> **Für das Glück kommt es sehr wenig auf das an, was man will, sondern . . .** (R. Musil), *for happiness it is very little a question of what one wants, but . . .*

This demonstrative is never contracted with a governing preposition (v. § 95).

(d) **Was,** popular.

Was is sometimes, in popular language, added to or substituted for the normal relative:

> „**Frau Baronin werden sich am Ende noch krank machen mit dieser Unruhe, die was keinen Sinn und Zweck hat**" (H. Broch), *you will make yourself ill with all this worry, which has no sense* (servant speaks).

(*Note.*—Third person plural address as § 168, courtesy title as § 175.)

EXERCISE XXXII

A. Translate into ENGLISH:

1. Der Tod seiner Hoheit des Kronprinzen Ruprecht von Bayern kam nicht ganz unerwartet. 2. Darf ich fragen, ob Ihr Herr Vater noch diese Woche verreisen wird? 3. Seine Antwort war wohl das Witzigste, was man an jenem Abend gehört hatte. 4. Ja, liebes Kind, in der Zeitung steht eben allerhand, was du noch nicht verstehen kannst. 5. Wer auch immer es gesagt hat, ich kann dieser Nachricht keinen Glauben schenken. 6. Der Mann ist ein fabelhaft guter Lehrer; es gibt einfach nichts, was er einem nicht erklären kann. 7. In der Stube eines Tiroler Gasthofs fanden wir folgenden Spruch an der Wand: „Iß (imperative) was gar ist; trink was klar ist; sprich was wahr ist." 8. „Wer am Wege bauet, der hat viele Meister", schrieb Luther über die Kritiker seiner Bibelübersetzung. 9. Wer die Wahl hat, hat die Qual. Was zu tun ist, tue (do) bald. 10. Wer einmal lügt, dem glaubt man nicht, und wenn er auch die Wahrheit spricht. 11. Wem Gott will rechte Gunst erweisen, / Den schickt er in die weite Welt. (Eichendorff.)

12. Troubles of a German Teacher.

Luise schob verächtlich die Lippen vor: „Kennen Sie ‚Die Kuh‘, Herr Studienrat?"

„Herrschaften!" der Deutschlehrer prallte ein wenig zurück. „Himmel, Donnerwetter, welche Kuh in aller Welt meinen Sie?"

„Die von Friedrich Hebbel—die Novelle, was er so nennt . . ."

„Was er so nennt? . . . So! Sie meinen: die er so nennt!"

(S. Andres.)

B. Translate into GERMAN:

1. The child ran to Mr Brown's shop and fetched me (dat.) a bundle of [fire]wood. 2. Dr Smith's boy was not allowed to join the football club as he was too wild and excitable. 3. I do hope that your (= formal) sister has had a pleasant journey and that your mother's health is very much better now. 4. Those-who do not save, rarely have enough money for holidays. 5. What you are forgetting is that no one saw him yesterday. 6. Whoever saw him did not tell us about it. 7. The first-thing that happened was that the light suddenly went out and we were (order!) left in complete darkness. 8. He who answers first will get the prize. 9. Is there nothing that will silence your aunt? 10. The last-thing she will do is to listen quietly to other people.

CHAPTER XXXIII
REFLEXIVE VERBS

179. Reflexive Verbs.   General

(a) Many German verbs take, or may take, their subject as the object of the action, as also in English: **ich wasche mich,** *I wash (myself).* But a German reflexive verb may correspond to an intransitive use in English: **ich setze mich,** *I sit down* (and *wash,* above); or to another idiom: **er schneuzt sich,** *he blows his nose.* It is seldom that an English reflexive is not reflexive in German.

Most verbs which usually are used reflexively govern the accusative of the relative pronoun, as above quoted. But some others govern the dative: **er schadet sich dabei, er gefällt sich sehr.** And a large number may be used with the "dative of interest" (*v.* § 382), analogous to that of personal advantage in all dative verbs (cp. §§ 97, 171): **er baut sich** (dat. *for himself*) **ein neues Haus.** This dative is often used in actions to parts of the body, where English has the possessive adjective: **er wäscht sich** (dat.) **die Hände,** *his hands* [*v.* §§ 184 (*d*) (3), 384 (*a*)]. A few govern the genitive: **er spottet seiner selbst,** *he mocks at himself* (cp. § 191).

The reflexive also follows a preposition closely associated with the verb to whose subject it refers: **er arbeitet nur für sich; jeder für sich,** *every man for himself.*

(b) Reflexive Pronouns:

TABLE:

	SINGULAR			PLURAL		
	1st pers.	2nd pers.	3rd pers.	1st pers.	2nd pers.	3rd pers.
Gen.	(*v.* §§ 190-1).					
Dat.	**mir**	**dir**	**sich**	**uns**	**euch**	**sich**
Acc.	**mich**	**dich**	**sich**	**uns**	**euch**	**sich**

It will be seen that the only distinct form for the reflexive is **sich,** standing for all English forms with -self in the third person singular, all genders (incl. **man**), and the plural, both in the dative and accusative. It has no capital, even when standing for **Sie** in letters. All other persons and cases use the appropriate form of the normal personal pronoun. The reflexive has of its nature no nominative.

(c) The reflexive pronoun is normally placed immediately after the main verb, and in subordinate clauses after the conjunction. In the subordinate clause and in the main clause when there is inversion, a pronoun subject precedes the reflexive, but a noun subject follows:

Haben Sie sich weh getan?   Hat sich der Junge weh getan?
Als sich meine Frau gestern einen neuen Wagen kaufen wollte . . .   (Als
sie sich gestern . . .).

(*d*) A few verbs are used predominantly or entirely as reflexive verbs; they are mainly concerned with immediate personal actions and reactions: **sich erkälten,** *to catch cold;* **sich schämen,** *to be ashamed;* **sich schneuzen,** *to blow one's nose;* **sich sehnen,** *to yearn.*

A very few may be used intransitively or reflexively without distinction of meaning: **(sich) eilen,** *to hurry,* **(sich) irren,** *to make a mistake,* **(sich) lohnen,** impersonal, *v.* §§ 221 f., *to be worth* (*while*).

Apart from these, the reflexive use constitutes a distinct additional sense of which a large number of verbs are capable, and it can be adapted to a variety of idiomatic uses.

180. Idiomatic Uses of Reflexive Verbs

The scope of the reflexive is wider in German than in English; thus a German reflexive may correspond, in English, apart from a parallel reflexive idiom [cp. § 179 (*a*)], to:

(*a*) An intransitive verb: **das Fenster (die Tür) öffnet sich,** *is opened;* **das Zimmer füllt sich,** *becomes full;* **ich beeile, freue, langweile, schäme mich,** *I am in a hurry, pleased, bored, ashamed.*
Der Geruch kam von dem großen Holzhof der Firma Sandberg, wo sich Bretter und Balken in offenen Hallen schichteten und stapelten (H. Kasack),
where planks and beams stood in piles . . .
A common idiom: **(eine Sache) arrangiert sich, macht sich, tut sich:**
Die Roggenangelegenheit mit van Henkdom und Comp. arrangiert sich
(Th. Mann), *the rye deal with . . . is going through.*
Wie geht's Geschäft?   Danke, es macht sich. *Not so bad.*

(*b*) A transitive verb and noun object: **sich erkälten,** *to catch a cold,* **sich schneuzen,** *to blow one's nose,* **sich ausschweigen,** *to hold one's peace,* **sich bescheiden,** *to moderate one's demands;* and many compounds of motion in the form **sich hindurch . . .,** *to . . . one's way,* as **sich hindurch- drängen, -schlagen, -tappen,** *to press, break, grope one's way through.*

(*c*) An adjective and dependent prepositional infinitive:
Das sagt sich leicht, und es hört sich wohl auch leicht an. Aber . . . *That is easy to say, and quite plausible to listen to. But . . .*
Es sah und hörte sich furchtbar an (Simpl.), *it was terrible to hear and look at* (*a terrible sight and row*).

Thus also the special use **sich**—adjective, infinitive—**lassen:**

Alleen, in denen es sich so angenehm lustwandeln läßt (Th. Mann), *avenues in which it is so pleasant to walk.*

In some few cases, English may use a normally transitive verb with intransitive or passive force:

These shoes wear well, **diese Schuhe tragen sich gut.**

Häßlichkeit verkauft sich schlecht, *badly presented goods sell badly* (advertising slogan).

But this is generally only with *well* and *badly;* the German reflexive use extends to other common terms, as **leicht** and its synonyms, in which cases English reverts to the standard adjective and infinitive:

Mit dem neuen Kühler fährt sich's äußerst bequem, *motorists will find it easy to drive* (or: *driving easy*) *with the new radiator.*

Cp. also § 249 (*c*) (modal verbal).

(*d*) A reflexive verb with objective predicate (of result) is possible in both languages: **sich müde gehen,** *to walk oneself off one's feet* [*v.* § 385 (*c*)].

181. Selbst (Selber) Supporting the Reflexive

(*a*) The reflexive pronoun naturally refers to the subject of the verb of which it is the object: **sie kleidete sich an,** *dressed herself.* This raises no problem in the singular since only one person is involved. But in any of the plural persons the statements: **wir loben uns, sie loben sich, Sie loben sich,** *may* stand for any of three senses: (1) each himself, (2) each the (an)other, (3) each all of us (them). Discarding (3) as in practice identical with (1), we have to distinguish a "reciprocal" sense (2) from the ordinary reflexive sense (1).

(*b*) The reflexive sense proper may be distinguished from another sense by adding the supporting word **selbst (selber): Wir loben uns selbst (selber),** *we praise ourselves.*

The forms in *-self* constitute in English the reflexive pronouns proper, while in German **selbst (selber)** are but reinforcements to the reflexive sense, as is *-self* in English with the *non*-reflexive verbs (you must read the book yourself), or with verbs which do not need the reflexive to convey reflexive meaning (I washed; I washed myself from head to toe).

Thus in German **selbst (selber)** is used:

(1) In non-reflexive contexts, to emphasise the subject (**Sie müssen selber das Buch lesen**), but also any other word:

Er war die Höflichkeit selber, *courtesy itself.*

Es war der Direktor selber, der erschien, *the manager in person . . .* (*v.* fully, § 169).

(2) In reflexive contexts to emphasise the identity of subject and reflexive object, thus distinguishing from the reciprocal [v. (a)], usually by emphasising the object (**jeder rette sich selber,** *let every man look after himself;* **der Starke hilft sich selbst,** *places reliance on himself*), but also sometimes the subject (**die Kinder sollen sich selbst waschen**—no one else will wash them).

Selbst is also used where a second reflexive follows the first:

Ich wünsche . . . nicht durch eine Reisekur, wie man sie mir verordnet, mich mir selbst zu entfremden und Zaza zu vergessen (Th. Mann), *to become a stranger to myself.*

After a preposition the introduction of **jeder** may be sufficient without **selbst**: **sie arbeiten jeder für sich,** *each for himself.*

182. The Reciprocal Reflexive

(a) The more specific expressions of reciprocity are as follows, in order of commonness:

(1) **einander,** *one another* (*each other*), replacing **sich**: **sie lobten einander.**

(2) **gegenseitig,** *mutually,* added to **sich**: **sie lobten sich gegenseitig.**

(3) **einer (jeder) den anderen,** or other case as required, *each other,* replacing **sich,** but without affecting the number of the verb: **sie lobten jeder den anderen.**

Einander is invariable for case, but if the verbial construction requires a preposition, it is compounded: **sie tanzten miteinander,** *they danced* (*together*). Thus also **aufeinander (folgen), ineinander (verliebt), füreinander (arbeiten),** and:

vom Mitgefühl geleitet, das Betrunkene füreinander haben (H. Broch), *impelled by that sympathy which drunks have for one another.*

Einander, representing **sich,** dative or accusative, may be followed by a prepositional phrase indicating action to the body (cp. § 385):

Sie schrieen einander Beleidigungen ins Gesicht, *they shouted insults at each other('s faces).*

(b) **Einander** is strictly not fully reciprocal, as is shown by such expressions as: **die Schachteln waren ineinander verschoben, die Redner folgten einander am Redepult;** its force is that it expresses "one to one working", and thus permits the sense of reciprocity in suitable contexts (**ineinander verliebt**). **Einander** does not distinguish the active agent from the passive, and means *one another* as often as *each other.* The fully reciprocal sense needs (**sie lobten**) **jeder den anderen,** or (**sie lobten sich**) **gegenseitig.**

(c) Distinguish **gegenseitig,** *mutual,* and **gemeinsam,** *common* (adjective and adverb), as in English:

ihre gegenseitige Liebe, ihre gemeinsame Liebe (zu einem Dritten).

Der Wagen gehört den beiden Brüdern gemeinsam, *in common.*

Our Mutual Friend (Dickens, incorrectly), **Unser Gemeinsamer Freund.**

Thus **gemeinsam** has no reciprocal, and, of course, no reflexive sense.

(d) The possessive adjective may be subject to similar ambiguity:

Die Bürger waren jederzeit bereit, ihren Vorteil zu wahren, *the citizens were always prepared to further their advantage.*

Diese Schichten lebten in ihren eigenen Kreisen, *these classes lived in their own circles.*

The above expressions may be used for greater clarity:

(1) **eigen, gegenseitig, gemeinsam,** etc.:

Die Bürger waren bereit, den eigenen Vorteil, ihren gemeinsamen Vorteil, ihren Vorteil gegenseitig (untereinander), ihren Vorteil gegeneinander zu wahren.

(2) But **jeder** without changing the number of the verb (cp. § 483) is the only means of excluding any form of reciprocity:

Alle diese Schichten lebten jede in ihrem (sing.) eigenen Kreise und sogar in eigenen Bezirken (S. Zweig), *each class lived in its own social circle and area.*

183. Contexts of Reciprocity

There are many contexts which so clearly bear reciprocal (as against normal reflexive) force, that the reflexive pronoun may be used without further clarification:

(a) Plural subject; the sense of the context may be:

(1) Promiscuous conflict: **sich schlagen, hauen, balgen, raufen, streiten,** and by extension, senses of pushing and shoving, **sich drängen, reißen (um):**

Im Warenhaus rissen sich die Menschen um die verbilligten Waren.

(2) Mutual: **sich begegnen, treffen, sehen, wiedersehen, trennen, begrüßen, schreiben, küssen:**

Mitunter schrieben sie sich, aber wiedergesehen hatten sie sich nicht (W. Bergengruen), *they exchanged letters, but had never met again.*

These are characteristically the cases where English omits the reflexive: we met, parted, wrote, kissed; but with a preposition the reflexive re-enters:

Die Eheleute saßen sich beim Essen gegenüber, *husband and wife sat opposite one another.*

Note.—On being introduced, *we have met* is **wir kennen uns schon,** but otherwise **einander** is as common:

Wir kannten einander nur so, wie eben Zimmernachbarn in einem Mietshaus sich kennen (H. Hesse), *we knew each other the way lodgers in neighbouring rooms do.*

(3) Distributive: **sich teilen in** (acc.), *to share out equally:*

Die Herren Offiziere teilten sich kameradschaftlich in die Beute (W. Bergengruen), *shared out the loot.*

Note.—**Man** may be used to indicate any number, according to the context. Thus it could replace any of the subjects in (1), (2), (3) above, and the reflexive **sich** would have the same reciprocal implication: **man riß sich, schrieb sich, teilte sich . . .**

(*b*) Singular subject.

The reflexive with reciprocal force can even be used with a singular subject (**er duellierte sich,** *he fought a duel*); the opponent may be introduced after the preposition **mit:**

P. dachte daran, sich mit K. zu schießen (W. Bergengruen), *P. thought of challenging K. to a duel.*

Immer noch hatte er ein wenig Angst vor B., obwohl er sich mit ihm seit zwei Wochen duzte (H. Böll), *although he had been on 'du' terms with him for a fortnight.*

184. Case Government of Reflexive Verbs, etc.

The simpler possibilities of case government in reflexive verbs may be set out schematically as follows:

The reflexive pronoun is:

ACCUSATIVE	DATIVE
(*a*) One object, the reflexive:	
sich ärgern	**sich widersprechen**
to be annoyed.	*to contradict oneself.*

(*b*) Two objects, the reflexive and a second:	
sich einem Ziele nähern	**sich einen Luxus erlauben**
to approach a goal.	*to allow oneself a luxury.*

(*c*) The reflexive and a prepositional infinitive construction:	
sich weigern, für den Schaden aufzukommen, *to refuse to pay for the damage.*	**sich geloben, eine Auslandsreise zu machen,** *to promise oneself to make a journey abroad.*

(*d*) The reflexive, with the subject, is impersonal:

es lohnt sich nicht   **es ziemt sich nicht**
it is not worth while.   *it is not seemly (proper).*

Note.—Reflexive statements of the nature of sich (dat.) **einen Luxus** (acc.) **erlauben** are of three fairly dissimilar classes:

(1) The reflexive sense is an integral part of the verbal meaning: **sich einen Luxus erlauben; sich Mühe geben,** *to take trouble;* **sich eine Arbeit aufbürden,** *to assume the burden of a work,* etc.

(2) The reflexive sense is explicitly that of "advantage" (cp. earlier statements on the dative object), and corresponds to *for oneself*: **sich einen Mantel kaufen,** *to buy oneself a coat;* **sich eine Zigarette anzünden,** *to light a cigarette;* **sich ein Haus anschauen,** *to have a look at a house.*

(3) The reflexive sense corresponds to the possessive adjective with a part of the body [cp. § 384 (*a*)]: **sich das Haar kämmen,** *to comb one's hair;* similarly with a prepositional phrase: **sich in den Finger schneiden,** *to cut one's finger.*

EXERCISE XXXIII

A. Translate into ENGLISH:

1. Die Läden öffnen sich auf schmale, hochgelegene Lauben, aus denen man in das Menschengewimmel der engen Gäßchen heruntersieht (G. Hauptmann). 2. Er horchte auf die Radiomusik. Die spielen Tänze. Es hört sich nicht schlecht an, aber es ist schlecht (H. Fallada). 3. Überall duftete es nach Blumen und Thymian um die Steinmassen, die sich im wohltätigen Scheine der Morgensonne warm anfühlen (G. Hauptmann). 4. Sie gingen schweigend und taten sich und einander leid (E. Kästner). 5. Die Tertianer hatten sich noch eben gewaltig gestritten (W. Speyer). 6. In der Altstadt belebten sich die Straßen, Kinder spielten auf dem Pflaster, Bekannte begrüßten sich, redeten miteinander (H. Kasack). 7. Wir waren einander wie Tag und Nacht geworden, die sich im grauen Dämmern treffen (S. Andres). 8. Die Tapeten zeigten umfangreiche Landschaften . . . Idylle im Geschmack des 18. Jahrhunderts, mit nett bebänderten Schäferinnen, die sich mit zärtlichen Schäfern küßten (Th. Mann). 9. „Was haben Sie denn gemacht, Menschenskind?"—„Ich hab' mich geprügelt mit einem," sagte K. (H. Fallada). 10. In Tetas Gepäck befanden sich wahrhaftig keine Kostbarkeiten, sondern nur das Armselig-Übliche, das sich im Leben einer Dienstmagd ansammelt (F. Werfel). 11. Er fühlte sich

einsam im fremden Land und sehnte sich unendlich wieder in die Heimat zurück. Die Rückreise aber ließ sich einfach nicht bezahlen.

B. Translate into GERMAN:

1. After he had cleaned his shoes he washed his hands and brushed his hair [*v*. § 184 (*d*) (3)].   2. He prepared himself carefully for (**auf,** acc.) this meeting, and had longed for it for many weeks.   3. "Did you enjoy yourself at the (**im**) theatre?"—"No, I was terribly bored."   4. Can this child button up her own coat? She is hardly old enough.   5. If we help one another we shall finish much more quickly.   6. They met outside (**vor**) the station and went for a long walk together.   7. We wrote to one another regularly and arranged-a-meeting every month.   8. I sat down at (**an,** acc.) my desk and wrote many pages of my new novel; it was coming along nicely [*v*. § 180 (*a*)].   9. He had a powerful voice and he liked to hear himself talk.   10. She rejoiced-in her returning health and was able to rely on-it more and more.

CHAPTER XXXIV

185. Adjective-nouns (2). **Uninflected and Inflected**

(*a*) Certain groups of adjectives may be used as nouns:

(1) In a rudimentary nominal form, with the capital, but otherwise uninflected or seldom inflected: **Alt und Jung,** *old and young;* **das Rund des Himmels,** *the orb of the sky;* **das Braun,** *brown* (*colour*).

(2) If they acquire full nominal (inflected) status they may be strong nouns (**das Recht,** *right,* **der Stolz,** *pride*), neuter adjective-nouns [**das Deutsche,** *German* (*language*)], or feminine abstract nouns (**die Weiße,** *whiteness*).

(*b*) Prominent among these groups are collective concepts, languages, and colour nouns. Their force is in varying degree concrete, collective and abstract.

Languages may here be mentioned briefly:

(1) Uninflected: **er lernt Deutsch, spricht Spanisch mit starkem Akzent, spricht ein schönes Italienisch, schreibt ein elegantes Latein;** adverbial: **auf deutsch, englisch, französisch.**

(2) Inflected: **er übersetzt das Buch vom Deutschen ins Englische, das Wort Tinte heißt im Französischen (auf französisch)** encre; **heutzutage versteht jedermann Amerikanisch** or **das Amerikanische.**

186. Adjectives, commonly uninflected, whose sense inclines towards descriptive, collective or abstract force:

(*a*) Descriptives:

das Rund des Himmels, des Platzes (H. Broch), **der Arena** (Th. Mann); **das doppelte Halbrund der Säulenhallen** (F. Werfel), *the double semi-circular colonnade* (of Bernini, at Rome).

das salzige Naß (F. Werfel), *tears,* **das edle Naß** (joc.), *wine, tea.*

das Tief, das Hoch [most senses, *v.* § 131 (*c*)], and sometimes in compounds: **das Achtflach** (also **der Achtflächner**), *octahedron.*

All these have acquired (strong) nominal status: **des Rund(e)s, die Runde; des Tiefs, die Tiefs; des Nasses,** no plural. But they demonstrate their adjectival and concrete nature in comparison with related feminine abstracts, etc., thus **das Tief,** *deep* (*place*), *area of low pressure,* **die Tiefe,** *depth;* **das Rund der Arena,** *the circle of the arena,* **das Runde der Arena,** *the roundness* . . ., **die Runde,** *the round* (*of drinks,* etc.).

(*b*) Collectives:

Hoch und Nieder kam bei dieser Kunstgattung auf seine Rechnung (W. Andreas), *this genre met the needs of both educated and popular taste.*

Jenseits von Gut und Böse, *Beyond Good and Evil* (title of book by Nietzsche).

Gleich und Gleich gesellt sich gern, *Birds of a feather flock together.*

Reich und Reich gesellt sich gern, *Birds whose nests are feathered flock together* (sub-title of a play by B. Brecht).

or, with representative force, for persons with this quality:

ein huldvolles Lächeln und Nicken von Hoch zu Nieder (Th. Mann), *as from a superior to an inferior.*

Thus also: **Alt und Jung,** *old and young* (*people*), **Richtig und Unrichtig,** (*what is*) *correct and incorrect.*

Words of this group are invariable, being used without the article, and very close to adjectives, with which they show their affinity in sometimes reverting to small letters, as:

(1) In collective doublets: **der Abstand von arm und reich,** *the distance between rich and poor* (quoted from O. Curme); and, indeed, many adjectival doublets, as **von nah und fern,** *from near and far,* **durch dick und dünn,** *through thick and thin,* **schwarz auf weiß,** *in black and white,* are hardly distinguishable from them.

(2) Singly, in the predicate:

Und obwohl Gut immer gut bleibt, und Böse bös; obwohl Ehre Ehre bleibt ... (Guardini), *although good remains good, evil evil, and honour honour.*

Note that a full noun (**Ehre**) can predicate itself.

(*c*) Abstracts:

Many nouns of abstract force have acquired nominal status through the stages described in (1) and (2), the descriptive or collective force having weakened with time: **das Gut,** *good,* **Heil,** *salvation,* **Leid,** *suffering,* **Licht,** *light,* **Mittel,** *means,* **Recht,** *right,* **Übel,** *evil.* They are still capable of use with medium collective force, since they are often situated between a more abstract use (as **das Gute,** *what is good*), and a more concrete use [as **das Gut,** plural **die Güter,** *a* (*concrete*) *good, country estate*]. Two are now masculine: **der Stolz,** *pride,* **der Gehorsam,** *obedience.*

Like nouns in (2) they are often used with small letters in the predicative position, thus especially **Recht** and **Unrecht,** which are:

(1) Nominal in senses still closely connected with (in)justice; thus **das Recht,** *right, law,* **im Recht sein,** *in the right,* **Recht sprechen,** *to give a judgment,* **zu Unrecht,** *wrongly,* **Unrecht leiden,** *to suffer injustice.*

(2) Adverbial in senses associated with correct, incorrect: **das ist recht,** *right;* **Sie haben recht (unrecht),** *you are right (wrong);* **ich muß ihm recht (unrecht) geben,** *I think he is right (wrong).*

187. Colour Nouns

(*a*) Names of colours are primarily neuter, with genitive -s and no plural, but a strong plural is found: **das Grün, des Grüns, (die Grüne); das Grau, des Graus, (die Graus,** *v.* example below). Some analogous adjectives (especially **das Dunkel,** and compare **das Sternklar** in example below) are treated similarly:

bei dem Eingang eines der Tunnels oder Schutzdächer—der schwarze Mund stand wie Samt in dem Weiß und Sternklar der Nacht (H. v. Doderer), *in the whiteness of the snow and the clearness of the stars.*

(*b*) But there are two other forms:

(1) The neuter adjective-noun, usually with concrete sense: **das Schwarze,** *bull's-eye,* **das Weiße in den Augen,** *the whites of the eyes;* or in prepositional phrases: **im Dunklen,** *in the dark,* **ins Grüne hinausfahren,** *to take a trip into the country.*

(2) The feminine abstract in **-e**; strangely this is common, almost preferred, for the light colours, especially white (**die Puderweiße des feisten Gesichtes,** Th. Mann), and for blue (**die unbegreifliche Bläue des Meeres,** S. Andres), but not for other colours. Cp. **das Dunkel,** but **die Helle.**

Note the following description of the disillusionment of demagogues:

Jeder hat das Blaue vom Himmel heruntergelogen, nun macht ihnen der Himmel klar, daß seine Bläue geblieben ist (H. Kasack), *they all promise the sky, but find out later that the sky has remained where it was.*

188. Prepositions Governing the Genitive

(*a*) There are a very large number of prepositions and prepositional phrases which take the genitive. Some of the commoner are: **anstatt** or **statt,** *instead of;* **infolge,** *as a result of;* **trotz,** *in spite of;* **um . . . willen** (bracketing the genitive object), *for the sake of;* **unweit,** *not far from;* **während,** *during;* **wegen,** *because of, on account of.*

(An)statt eines Photoapparats kaufte er sich ein neues Fahrrad, *instead of a camera he bought himself a new bicycle.*

Infolge der schlechten Ernte verteuerten sich die Lebensmittel, *as a result of the bad harvest the foodstuffs went up in price.*

Trotz des unlängst geschlossenen Friedens behandeln sich die Menschen immer noch wie Feinde, *in spite of the recent conclusion of peace people still treat each other as enemies.*

Um seines Vaters willen nahm er sich vor, sich zu verbessern, *for his father's sake he resolved to turn over a new leaf.*

Unweit der Schule stellte sich eine Obstfrau auf und verkaufte Pfirsiche, *not far from the school a fruit-seller set up her stand and sold peaches.*

Unweit von Frankfurt überschlug sich ein Wagen; alle drei Insassen kamen um, *near Frankfurt a car turned over; all three occupants were killed.*

Während der Sommermonate ergehen sich Tausende von Sommerfrischlern auf dem Strand am Meer, *during the summer months thousands of summer guests disport themselves on the sea-shore.*

Wegen dringlicher Umbauarbeiten wird das Geschäft während des ganzen Monats August geschlossen bleiben, *on account of urgent rebuilding the store will remain closed for the whole of August.*

(*b*) **Trotz, während,** and **wegen** are also used, colloquially (and especially popularly), with the dative. **Unweit** may take **von** (and the dative) before place-names. For further grammatical notes, especially on case, *v.* Chapter XLV (§§ 266-7), and for the use of each preposition consult the Index.

189. Verbs Governing the Genitive

(*a*) A certain number of verbs take a genitive object. The group is dwindling, and such constructions are normally found in literary or poetic style, in traditional set expressions, or in contexts requiring an old-fashioned or ironical flavour. Almost all of them can be used in modern style with other constructions.

The senses are closely grouped round certain ideas:

(1) To use or otherwise: **genießen,** *to enjoy;* **hüten, pflegen, schonen,** and **walten,** various senses of *to care for, devote oneself to;* **entbehren, entraten,** and **ermangeln,** various senses of *to be (do) without.*

(2) To devote attention to, or otherwise: **erwähnen,** *to mention;* **gedenken,** *to bear in mind;* **vergessen,** *to forget;* **lachen** and **spotten,** *to laugh* and *mock (at);* **zürnen,** *to be angry with.*

(3) To need or expect: **bedürfen,** *to need,* **begehren,** *to desire;* **harren** and **warten,** *to wait for;* **hoffen** and **leben,** *to hope for, live on (hope, etc.).*

(*b*) Only a dictionary can do justice to the appropriate senses. Note however:

(1) Those known now only in set expressions:

Man harrt der Dinge, die noch (or da) kommen sollen, *awaits the things which are to come.*

Man pflegt der Ruhe, *one takes one's ease.*

Vergiß mein(er) nicht! (cp. § 190) **das Vergißmeinnicht,** *forget-me-not.*
Man waltet seines Amtes, *carries out the duties of one's office.*

(2) Their use for ponderous humour:

mein Wirt Laemmle, ein schwächlicher Mann, der häufig von seinem Weibe geschlagen wurde, nun aber an ihrer Seite friedlich des Sonntags genoß (F. Thiess), *but now peacefully took his Sunday's ease at her side.* ·

(3) **entbehren** and **spotten** still retain the genitive for the figurative sense as against the literal:

Seine Argumentierung entbehrt jeder logischen Grundlage, *is without* (not: *does without*) *any basis in logic.*

Die Wohnverhältnisse spotten jeder Beschreibung, *living conditions are beyond* (not: *mock at*) *all description.*

(*c*) The modern constructions which have replaced the genitive are:

(1) The direct accusative for, *e.g.,* **begehren, entbehren, genießen, schonen, vergessen.**

(2) Prepositional constructions for other verbs, especially **auf** (of expectation, *for,* cp. § 401), for **harren, hoffen, warten;** and **über** (of occasion, *at,* cp. § 454), for **lachen, spotten, zürnen.** .

But **bedürfen, ermangeln,** and **gedenken** are still used (when not replaced by *e.g.* **brauchen, denken an,** etc.) only with the genitive:

Sie schlief schon wieder. Des Schwans aber gedachte sie noch öfter in den folgenden paar Wochen, seines blutroten Schnabels, des schwarzen Schlags seiner Schwingen (Th. Mann), *but her thoughts often dwelt on the swan, its beak, pinions.*

190. The Genitive of the Personal Pronouns

(*a*) TABLE

	SINGULAR			PLURAL		
	1st pers.	2nd pers.	3rd pers.	1st pers.	2nd pers.	3rd pers.
Gen.	**meiner**	**deiner**	**seiner** (masc.) **ihrer** (fem.)	**unser**	**euer** **Ihrer**	**ihrer**

me, of me, etc.

These have not previously been introduced, partly because they are restricted in use, partly because they are so easily confused with the possessive adjective.

(*b*) They are used:

(1) When a verb, preposition, adjective (*v.* § 192) or noun require a following object in the genitive:

Er bedarf meiner, *he needs me;* distinguish: **er bedarf meiner Hilfe,** *he needs my help* (poss. adj. with ending).

Und wir würden uns das Recht nehmen, Dostojewski zu deuten trotz seiner (Guardini), *we would claim the right to interpret D. in spite of himself.*

(2) In certain partitive constructions; usually third person plural **ihrer**:

Es gibt in allen Ländern der Welt Fußgänger, aber in Deutschland gibt es ihrer am meisten (Simpl.), *but in Germany there are most.*

And especially in constructions before the indefinites **beid-** and **all-**: **ihrer beider Stimmen, unser aller Garten,** *both their voices, the garden of all of us* (gen. of the pron., invar., followed by gen. plur. strong adj. ending).

Distinguish this clearly from the possessive adjective : **der Laut ihrer Stimmen,** *of their voices;* **unser Garten** (nom. sing.), *our garden* (cp. §§ 487-8).

(*c*) **Seiner** is probably only used as the genitive of **er.** For **es,** the demonstrative form **dessen** is common [cp. § 195 (*a*), and *v.* also § 192, genitive object of certain adjectives].

(*d*) The genitive of the personal pronoun (with **selbst**) provides this case for the reflexive (*v.* § 191).

Note.—Under the influence of **ihrer, Ihrer,** a lengthened form of the other two plural forms has developed: **uns(e)rer, eu(e)rer,** but this has absolutely nothing to recommend it.

191. Proper Reference of Third Person Reflexive

(*a*) The genitive of the reflexive pronoun [cp. § 197 (*b*)] is the same as that of the personal pronoun (*v.* § 190), with the addition, in the third person singular and plural, of **selbst;** these forms are used when verbs taking the genitive are used reflexively (*v.* § 189), and in certain other idioms:

ich spotte meiner selbst, du spottest deiner selbst, er spottet seiner selbst,
                    I mock at myself, etc.

Distinguish: **er spottet seiner, sie spotten ihrer,** which may mean, *he mocks at him* (*another*), *they mock at them* (*others*).

Note.—This case should be distinguished from the commoner case in which an accusative reflexive is followed by a further object in the genitive: **er erinnerte sich seines Auftrags,** *remembered his commission* [*v.* § 383 (*b*)]; this is what is usually meant by "reflexive verb taking the genitive".

(*b*) **Selbst** is also added, whether needed for clarity or not, in non-verbal constructions requiring the genitive:

Wenn ich will, bin ich stets Herr meiner selbst, *in control of myself.*

jene Seelen, welchen nicht mehr die Vollendung ihrer selbst als Lebensziel erscheint, sondern . . . (H. Hesse), *to whom the perfection of their own personalities no longer appears as a suitable aim in life, but . . .*

192. Adjectives Governing the Genitive

(*a*) Certain adjectives require the genitive of a noun or pronoun to complete the sense. The commoner are: **bar,** *bare, free of,* **bedürftig,** *in need of,* **bewußt,** *conscious of,* **eingedenk,** *mindful of,* **fähig,** *capable of,* **froh,** *pleased about,* **gewahr,** *conscious of,* **gewärtig,** *ready for,* **gewiß,** *sure (certain) of,* **gewohnt,** *used to,* **kundig,** *skilled in,* **los,** *free from,* **mächtig,** *capable of,* **müde,** *tired of,* **satt,** *sated with, tired of,* **schuldig,** *guilty of,* **sicher,** *sure (certain) of,* **teilhaftig,** *sharing in,* **überdrüssig,** *surfeited with, tired of,* **verdächtig,** *under suspicion of,* **verlustig,** *(by loss) deprived of,* **voll** (also **voll von**) and **voller,** *full of,* **wert,** *worth,* **würdig,** *worthy of,* **zufrieden,** *satisfied with.*

(*b*) It is common practice, and never incorrect (except with **voller** and **voll von,** *v.* below), for such words to follow the genitive expression: **er ist der Tat fähig, der Sache kundig, einer Sprache mächtig, des Verbrechens schuldig,** *capable of the deed, skilled in the matter, able to speak a language, guilty of a crime.*

But a number, especially **bar, froh, müde, wert** may also precede:

aller Mittel und jeder Hilfe bar (F. Werfel), *deprived of all means or help.*

bar jeden Rechts, jeder Logik und jeder Humanität (newsp.), *without the shadow of right, reason or humanity.*

(*c*) Other constructions are now common, but without replacing the original genitive to the same extent as has happened with verbs (*v.* § 189). As most may be used with **sein, werden,** a construction with an older genitive **es,** identical with nominative and accusative, was common:

Ich bin es gewohnt, müde, satt, zufrieden (geworden), *I am (became) used to, tired of, satisfied with it.*

Er wurde es gewahr, los, *he noticed, got rid of it.*

and this was assumed to be accusative and that case extended to other noun and pronoun objects:

Wie leicht kann man sein Geld los werden, wie schwer wird man einen Irrtum gewahr, *how easily one can lose one's money, how difficult it is to notice one's mistakes.*

Note.—A new genitive of **es**, where required, is now formed from the demonstrative: **dessen** [cp. § 65 and § 195 (*a*)].

With **wert** this process was assisted by the uninflected nature of *e.g.* **viel, wenig, nichts, wieviel (Wieviel ist das Haus wert?)**, and by the analogy of the adverbial accusative of measure:

Der Arbeiter ist seines Lohnes wert, *worthy of his hire,* but: **meine Arbeiter sind keinen Schuß Pulver wert,** *not worth a farthing.*

Satt commonly replaces **sein** by **haben,** with the same result:

Ich bin seiner satt (geworden), habe ihn nun endlich satt, *I am (now, at last) tired of him.*

On the other hand, those idioms using other synonyms for **werden** are still constructed with the genitive:

Er ging seines schönen Eigentums verlustig, *he lost his very attractive property.*

Er machte sich des Mordes verdächtig, *he incurred suspicion of having committed the murder.*

Schuldig, *guilty of* (gen., cp. also **schuld** in Index), is now quite distinct from **schuldig sein,** etc. (acc.), *to owe* (*i.e.* to be in debt to the extent of):

Ich bin Ihnen den Betrag von . . . schuldig, muß Ihnen den Betrag schuldig bleiben, *owe you, must continue to owe you.*

(*d*) Some of these adjectives may have alternative prepositional constructions, often corresponding to the English use: **fähig zu (zu allem fähig), froh über** (acc.), **schuldig an** (dat.), **zufrieden mit, gewohnt an** (acc.).

But distinguish **müde der Arbeit,** *tired of work,* and **müde von der Arbeit,** *tired from (tired out by) work;* **des Erfolges sicher,** *sure of success,* and **vor Angriffen sicher,** *safe from attack.*

(*e*) A number may be followed by a subordinate construction, either:

(1) A prepositional infinitive:

Ich halte ihn für fähig, eine solche Aufgabe durchzuführen, *I consider him as capable of undertaking such a task.*

Ich bin (es) müde, immer wieder Nein zu sagen, *I am tired of always having to say No.*

or (2) A **daß**-clause:

Er ist (es) nicht wert, daß man ihm immer nachläuft, *he is not worthy of being run after.*

(*f*) **Bewußt** usually takes an additional dative of the reflexive pronoun, since it refers to an entirely interior process:

Ich bin mir bewußt, in dieser Sache versagt zu haben, *of having failed in this matter.*

Ich bin mir hier eines persönlichen Fehlers bewußt, *conscious of a personal fault.*

(*g*) **Voll** and **voller** (an old inflected form, now invariable) are both followed by a genitive, **voll** being perhaps preferred with either article: **ein Blech voller gelber Plätzchen** (H. Böll), *full of yellow biscuits:* **Augen voll eines weichen Schimmers** (Th. Mann), *full of a soft light;* **voll Kultur, voller Atmosphäre;** the genitive singular noun unaccompanied often omits the -s: **voll Lobs,** *of praise,* **voll Lärm,** *of noise.* Some would distinguish the more literal **voll** from the more figurative **voller**: **ein Korb voll Blumen,** *full of;* **ein Korb voller Blumen,** *a profusion of.* But practice does not bear this out, and rhythm appears to exert the stronger influence.

EXERCISE XXXIV

A. Translate into ENGLISH:

1. Das Rund des Himmels spiegelt sich im Rund des Platzes, das Rund des Platzes spiegelt sich im Kreise um das Monument, der Gesang der Engel spiegelt sich im Gesang, der aus der Kirche heraustönt (H. Broch). 2. Gutes Deutsch, ein Führer durch Falsch und Richtig (title of book by E. Engels). 3. Dieser Boden treibt alle Formen und Farbentönungen hervor, Blumen und Rasen, Sonnenplätze und Schattengänge, Smaragd- und Schwarzgrün, Grau, Blau und Weißgrün (W. Bergengruen). 4. In der Bäckerei war alles grau und weiß, alle Abstufungen zwischen dem Schwarz des Kuchenblechs, dem Schwarz der Kohlen und der Weiße des Mehls gab es: Hunderte von durcheinanderschimmernden Graus, nur selten einmal Rot oder Gelb; das Rot von Kirschen, das milde Gelb einer Zitrone oder das sanfte der Ananas (H. Böll). 5. Eine Stunde täglich, das ist ein Zwölftel des bewußten Lebens, und sie genügt, um einen geübten Leib in dem Zustand eines Panthers zu erhalten, der jedes Abenteuers gewärtig ist (R. Musil). 6. Meine Eltern wollen in aller Liebe und Fürsorge einen Gefühlsmord begehen. Sie werden scheitern, ich bin dessen so sicher wie meiner selbst (Th. Mann). 7. Durch die Hilfe seines alten Freundes ist der Bankdirektor großer Sorgen und Verlegenheiten endlich los und ledig geworden.

B. Translate into GERMAN:

1. He has been learning Italian for a year now and can already translate quite well from English into Italian. 2. The returning spring sunshine made everyone happier; young and old were out in the streets

enjoying its warmth.   3. She is right; blue suits her much better than green.   4. He went swimming in the river in spite of his friend's warning. 5. As a result of this action he nearly lost his life.   6. When I was in Spain I took a siesta like everyone else during the hottest part of the afternoon.   7. Every year in November there is a service at which (**wo**) we commemorate those who fell in the war.   8. She is grown up now and no longer needs the advice of her parents; at least, that is what she says. 9. It is forbidden to smoke during the performance.   10. The French language [*v.* § 185 (*a*)] is much more elegant than northern languages; in spite of this fact it does not lack a certain forcefulness.

CHAPTER XXXV

193. Accent of Nouns Derived from Verbal Stems

(*a*) Many masculine and feminine nouns are derived from the stems of compound verbs, both inseparable and separable.

Normally these nouns have the same accent as their parent verbs, thus providing some exceptions from the general rule that all nouns are front-accented [Intro. § 5 (*a*)]: **ábfahren, die Ábfahrt; vórschreiben, die Vórschrift, éintreten, der Éintritt; verschíeben, der Verschúb.**

But prefixes with fluctuating accent (*v.* § 88) are stressed in the noun-derivative: **übergében,** but **die Übergabe; unterríchten,** but **der Únterricht.**

(*b*) Derivative verbal nouns, *i.e.* those direct from the infinitive, and those with the suffix **-ung** (*v.* §§ 489-90), corresponding generally to the English gerund or abstract verbal noun, retain the verbal stress in all cases. **Das Übergében,** *surrendering;* **das Unterríchten, die Unter-ríchtung,** *instructing, instruction.*

194. Final Noun Plurals, especially Verbal Derivatives

(*a*) It is clear from earlier sections on noun declensions that the broadly characteristic features of the three genders in their formation of plurals are:

(1) Masculine, **-e** with (sometimes without) vowel mutation.

(2) Neuter, **-er** with (sometimes without) vowel mutation.

(3) Feminine, **-(e)n** weak, but also **-e** and vowel mutation, strong.

Lists of declensional groups can hardly ever be complete, but a further and last survey of certain groups is given here, dealing especially with disyllables, and nouns with nominal suffixes, or derived in some way from verbal compounds. (Revise first §§ 17, 24, 40.)

(*b*) Strong **-e** plural, without mutation:

(1) Masculines include:

    (i) some with unaccented verbal prefixes:
        der Besuch, Erfolg, Erlaß;

    (ii) unaccented nominal suffixes:
        der Früh-ling, Hab-icht, Kön-ig, Mon-at, Rett-ich, Wege-rich
        (though many of these are not now recognised as such);

(iii) thus also foreign nominal suffixes which have, in the process of assimilation, shifted the accent forward (cp. § 76):

der Alkoh-ol, Blöd-ian, Plur-al.

(2) Neuters include:
some with unaccented nominal suffixes:
das Spül-icht, das Ereig-nis (-nisse), das Schick-sal.
Words in -nis and -sal are shared with the feminine (*v.* § 40).

(*c*) Strong -e plural, with mutation.

This is a largely masculine declension, to a lesser degree feminine (*v.* § 40); for neuter *v.* Note (below).

The vast majority of disyllables derived from compound verbs, whether with accented or unaccented prefixes, belong here. Some may here be given under the second component, corresponding to the simple verb:

-dacht, from **denken,** as **der Verdacht.**
-laß, from **lassen,** as **der Anlaß, Einlaß, Nachlaß [Erlaß,** *v.* (*b*)].
-stand, from **stehen,** as **der Abstand, Bestand, Vorstand.**
-trag, from **tragen,** as **der Antrag, Beitrag, Vertrag.**
-wand, from **wenden,** as **der Einwand, Vorwand.**

Two groups of derivatives have been differentiated by mutation of the plural, influenced by the verb from which they appeared to be derived:

-druck, from **drücken,** *to press, imprint:* **der Abdruck, Ausdruck, Eindruck, Händedruck,** plurals **die Abdrücke,** etc.

-druck, from **drucken,** *to print:* **der Abdruck, Nachdruck, Neudruck,** plurals **die Abdrucke,** etc.

Note.—Neuters only **das** (also **der**) **Floß,** *float,* **die Flöße.** Distinguish: **das Chor, die Chore,** *choir* (part of church), *chancel;* **der Chor, die Chöre,** *choir* (singers), *chorus* (singers or song).

(*d*) Strong -er plural, with mutation.

All nouns with the suffix **-tum;** they are all neuter (**das Besitztum,** etc.), except two: **der Irrtum, Reichtum.**

A few foreign words: **das Regiment** [cp. § 76 (*c*)]; **das Spital**—but **das Hospital,** the same word and sense, has now also **Hospitale.**

(*e*) Neuters, etc., with the form: **Ge . . . (e).**

This very common prefix is used to form nouns (with or without the -e ending) from verbal stems; such nouns are:

(1) Predominantly neuter, mostly with -e plural: **das Gesetz, Geräusch, Gespräch;** but: (i) a considerable number end in -e, -el or -er, and are

unchanged: **das Gebäude, Gewinsel, Gelichter** (cp. § 24), and (ii) a few add **-er** and modify if possible: **das Gemach, Gemüt, Geschlecht, Gesicht, Gespenst, Gewand.**

(2) But some are (i) masculine, with **-e,** and mutation if possible: **der Gebrauch, Genuß, Geruch, Gewinn,** etc.; (ii) feminine, with weak plural: **die Gebärde, Geburt, Gefahr, Geschichte,** etc.; but **die Geschwulst, Geschwülste.**

Distinguish **das Gehalt, Gehälter,** *salary;* **der Gehalt, Gehalte,** *contents.*

(*f*) Feminine compounds derived from verbal stems are commonly strong with mutation and **-e** (the only strong form open to a feminine noun), but a sufficient number are weak to confuse the situation, and some, of their nature, do not (normally) take a plural: thus **die Macht, Mächte,** and thus also **die Großmacht,** but **die Ohnmacht** and **Vollmacht** are weak, **die Ohnmachten.** Arranged by simple verb stems, some are:

-fahrt, from **fahren,** weak: **die Fahrten, Ausfahrten, Einfahrten.**

-flucht, from **fliehen,** strong: **die Ausflüchte,** but **Zuflucht,** no plural.

-kunft, from **kommen,** strong: **die Auskünfte, Einkünfte,** but **Zukunft,** no plural.

-sucht, from **siechen** (*to be sick,* earlier also *to yearn*), strong: **die Süchte, Sehnsüchte,** but **Eifersucht** and **Schwindsucht,** no plural.

195. Genitive of Certain Pronouns (1).   Neuter Singular

The following may be added to what has been said on the genitive singular of the neuter of certain pronouns:

(*a*) The demonstrative pronoun (*of that*).

There is a shorter (older) form **des,** and a longer form **dessen.**

(1) **Des** is now found only in Biblical texts:

Wes das Herz voll ist, des gehet der Mund über (after Luther), *out of the abundance of the heart the mouth speaketh* (Matt. xii, 34), lit. *of what the heart is full, of that the mouth overflows.*

And occasionally in adverbial compounds with prepositions:

indes, *meanwhile;* **deshalb, deswegen,** *therefore, for that reason.*

(2) **Dessen** is the normal form for the genitive of es, **das,** when governed by verbs, adjectives: **dessen erinnere ich mich ganz genau, ich bin dessen so sicher wie meiner selbst,** and by prepositions in most of the adverbial compounds: **stattdessen,** *instead,* **währenddessen,** *meanwhile,* **infolgedessen,** *therefore,* **dessenungeachtet,** *in spite of this,* **dessenunbeschadet,** *without prejudice.*   Cp. § 65 and § 192 (*c*).

(*b*) The interrogative and general relative [*of what? of* (*that*) *which*].

Wessen may be used, in questions, with verbs or adjectives governing the genitive: **Wessen ist er schuldig?** *of what is he guilty?* But it is limited to common uses because of the ambiguity with **wessen,** from **wer,** and is normally avoided after prepositions; thus **aus welchem Grunde?** for **wegen / infolge (wessen?)** *for what reason? why?* As in English, such forms as **wegen was?** (*because of what?*) may occur colloquially in questions asked to establish a point not clearly heard:

Er konnte nicht kommen wegen . . .—Wegen was?—Wegen des Wetters.

Wessen has a limited use as a general relative:

Wessen er bedurfte, um sein Werk auszuführen, das und noch mehr gab ihm der Starost (W. Bergengruen), *the Starost gave him what he needed and more . . .*

but a simpler form would normally be available with **was** or **das, was.**

There are short forms **wes** in traditional statements [*v.* the Biblical example in (*a*)], and in the adverbial compounds **weshalb, weswegen,** *for what* (*which*) *reason, why* (*?*). Cp. § 197.

Note.—There are similar short and long forms for the masculine genitive: **des, dessen, wes, wessen.**   Cp. § 26, and § 229 for **dessen** used for the possessive adjective.

196. Genitive of Certain Pronouns (2).   Plural

(*a*) The demonstrative pronoun **die** (feminine singular, all plurals) has a general form **deren** used in most contexts, especially (1) standing for a possessive (**Herr Schmidt, seine Frau und deren Schwester,** *and her/ their sister,* cp. § 65), or (2) in the plural partitive sense [**es waren deren nur wenige da,** *few—of them—were present,* cp. § 229 (*a*) (1)].

(*b*) But the slightly more emphatic form **derer,** plural, is used *for persons only* when the demonstrative is followed by a determinative phrase or clause.   This occurs especially:

(1) Before a relative clause:

die Tapferkeit derer, die mit ihrer Furcht fertig werden (W. Bergengruen), *of those who overcome their fear.*

(2) Before a family name of the **von** type:

der Landsitz derer von Wallenstein, *the estate of the W. family.*

(*c*) The form **derer** is sometimes used in other contexts, *e.g.* as a relative, but incorrectly.

197. Pronouns Compounded with Um . . . Willen, -halb, -wegen

The preposition **um . . . willen,** *for the sake of* (*v.* § 188), and the prepositional particles **halb** and **wegen,** both meaning *on account of,* enter into compounds with certain governed pronouns:

(*a*) **Um . . . willen,** is normally used for persons, and forms certain corrupt compounds with intrusive **-t-**:

(1) Relatives:

um . . . dessentwillen, masculine and neuter, and **um dere(n)twillen,** feminine and plural, *for the sake of whom* (*which*).

Sein Vater war's, um dessentwillen er den Posten annahm, *it was his father, for the sake of whom he took the job.*

Zu den vielen Dingen, um derentwillen ich das tessinische Land liebe, gehört sein Glockengeläut (W. Bergengruen), *among the many things for the sake of which I love . . .*

(2) Personal pronouns:

The intrusive **-t-** replaces, or in the case of **unser, euer,** is added to, the genitive of the pronoun (*v.* § 190):

> **um meinetwillen, deinetwillen, seinetwillen, ihretwillen;**
> **um unsertwillen, euertwillen (or euretwillen), Ihretwillen.**

(3) Interrogatives and general relatives:

The form **um wessentwillen** is probably little used.

(*b*) Compounds with **-halb** and **-wegen** are commonly used for things:

(1) Relatives: **dessentwegen, deretwegen:**

Die Angelegenheit, deretwegen ich ihn aufgesucht hatte, *the matter about which I had called on him . . .*

Note that for persons **wegen** is not compounded:

Der Dienstbote, wegen dessen ich mit den Behörden Streit bekam, ist wieder gegangen, *the servant, on whose account . . .*

(2) Personal pronouns:

meinethalben, meinetwegen, and corresponding forms for the other pronouns, are hardly distinct in sense from **um . . . meinetwillen,** etc. **meinetwegen** has also the special sense: *If you like* (*I don't mind*).

(3) Demonstratives:

deshalb and **deswegen,** *on that account, for that reason, therefore.*

Wir haben in der Inflation unser ganzes Geld verloren; deshalb (or deswegen) ging es uns in den nachfolgenden Jahren so schlecht, *that was the reason why . . .*

(4) Interrogatives and general relatives:

weshalb? *for what reason?* is often used for **warum?** *why?*

Weshalb kommt er noch immer nicht? Er ist wohl verhindert. *Why does he not come? He has probably been prevented.*

The general relative, referring to the thought of the statement as a whole, is **weshalb** or **weswegen:**

Er kam immer besoffen an, weshalb (weswegen) ich ihm am Ende das Haus verbieten mußte, *for which reason . . .*

The word **der Grund,** *cause* or *reason,* since its sense is identical with the following relative, may be followed by either a general or specific relative:

Der Grund, weswegen er nicht erschienen ist, ist mir unbekannt. *The reason why he has not appeared . . .*

Der Grund, dessentwegen . . . [*v.* (1), above, cp. § 198 (*c*)].

Note.—In most cases in which **-halb** and **-wegen** are alternatives, the **-halb** compound is in fact rather commoner.

198. The Use of Warum, Weshalb, etc., for Why?

(*a*) The interrogative adverb **Warum?** *why?* asks a question which, as in English, may have:

(1) Retrospective force to the reason (motive or cause):

Warum ist er nicht gekommen? *Why did he not come?*

(2) Prospective force to the purpose (aim):

Warum will er ausgerechnet morgen kommen? *Why is he coming to-morrow of all times?*

Greater distinction between the two senses may be achieved by using the two specific expressions:

Aus welchem Grunde ist er nicht gekommen? *What is the reason . . .?*
Zu welchem Zwecke will er ausgerechnet morgen kommen? *What is his object in . . .?*

or by using, in the same contrasted sense, the interrogative adverbs **warum?** and **wozu?**

The answer to question (1) is then a statement of cause (**weil,** etc.). That to question (2) one of purpose [**damit,** etc., §§ 202 (*b*), 356; or (**dazu**), **um . . . zu,** §§ 371 f.].

(*b*) Some would restrict **warum?** to question (1) above, and require **weshalb?** for question (2), the answer in each case being introduced by their appropriate adverbs **darum** and **deshalb:**

Warum kam er heute? Darum, weil . . . *Why . . .? Because . . .?*
Weshalb kommt er morgen? Deshalb, um . . . *Why . . .? (So as) to . . .*

But this distinction is not observed in practice, and **warum** is used for all cases [as in example in (*a*)]; while **weshalb** is used widely by some writers (*e.g.* E. Wiechert) in open questions where no one knows which answer will be returned, the intention being to confer distinction of style.

Further, only **weshalb** is used (in the sense **aus welchem Grunde**) as a general relative referring back to the thought of the sentence, a case which would clearly appear not to concern purpose:

Ich habe ihn seit Jahren nicht leiden können, weshalb es mir völlig unmöglich sein würde, ihn einzuladen, *for which reason . . .*

eine Verabredung (zwischen S. und K.), die dieser nicht einhalten konnte, weshalb er früher als vorgesehen erschienen war . . . (F. Thiess), *for which reason . . .*

But the distinction is so far operative as **weshalb** is avoided for a purely causal statement:

Warum (not **weshalb**) **war er am Kommen verhindert?** *Why was he prevented from coming? What prevented him . . .?*

and the adverbs **darum** and **deshalb** are closely associated with their respective appropriate conjunctions, etc.:

Er kam darum, weil ich ihn kommen ließ.

Er tat es deshalb, um zu Geld zu kommen.

Er bleibt schon deshalb weg, damit er sein Geld nicht auszugeben braucht, *he will stay away, if for no other purpose, so that he need not . . .*

(*c*) **der Grund** and **die Ursache,** *reason, cause.*

(1) The sense of **der Grund** is indeterminate between motive and purpose, thus both **warum** and **weshalb** are used as following relatives. But while **aus dem (einfachen) Grund, weil . . .** is *for the (simple) reason that . . .*, a distinct note of purpose would need **mit dem (einfachen) Zweck, . . . zu** (infin.); and **der Zweck** takes the relative **wozu**.

(2) The sense of **die Ursache** is clearly cause; it is thus followed by **warum.** There is no simple expression for *for no other cause than . . .*, cp. **durch die einfache Ursache bedingt, daß . . .**

EXERCISE XXXV

A. Translate into ENGLISH:

1. Bei verschiedenen Anlässen, wie z.B. bei einem Staatsbesuch der Königin, schließen alle öffentlichen Stellen der Stadt.   2. Die Chöre der großen deutschen Kathedralen haben manchmal hübsche Namen; die Sängerknaben vom Regensburger Dom heißen z.B. die „Regensburger Domspatzen".   3. Die Preise steigen dauernd und deshalb auch die

Gehälter; so kommt es langsam zur Inflation. 4. Er spottete derer, die ihn auf die Gefahr aufmerksam machten. 5. Während Rom in Flammen stand, ließ Nero die Geigen aufspielen. 6. Wessen hat man ihn beschuldigt? Er hat anscheinend eine Unterschrift gefälscht. 7. Die Namen derer, die im Krieg gefallen sind, befinden sich auf einer steinernen Tafel im Eingang der Halle. 8. Sein jüngster Sohn war noch in der Schule, und um seinetwillen blieb er noch zwei Jahre in der Heimat anstatt auszuwandern. 9. Als Kind lebte der Bischof am Meer, weshalb er auch jetzt noch, als alter Mann, gerne dorthin zurückkehrt. 10. Das ist auch die Ursache, warum er früher immer Matrose werden wollte, denn die Eindrücke der Kindheit sind sehr stark.

B. Translate into GERMAN:

1. He left home for her sake and never returned. 2. The reason for which the regiment plundered the deserted farms was not difficult to understand: the men were just hungry. 3. The fate of those who stayed in the town is still uncertain. 4. Why do you not take (**machen**) a photograph of these new buildings? 5. Because I think they are ugly, and that's why I will not waste a film on (**auf,** acc.) them. 6. His impressions of this journey were most vivid. 7. He left his wealth [to] his younger brother whose salary had always been very small. 8. Whose books are these? (translate in two ways). 9. The child on whose account I wrote to you is now in a home. 10. A man whom he could not remember at all addressed him and called (**nennen,** v. irr.) him by (**bei**) his Christian-name.

CHAPTER XXXVI

CLAUSES OF CAUSE AND RESULT

199. Causal Clauses

(a) The causal conjunctions are: **weil** and **da** (also pop. **wo**), *as, because, since;* **daß,** *that.* Other conjunctions with secondary causal force are: **indem** (manner), *in that, as* (*v.* §§ 314-15); **nun** (time), *now that* (*v.* § 125); in Austria **nachdem** (time), *since, as* (*v.* § 124). Cp. also **denn,** coordinating conjunction (*v.* § 73).

(b) **Weil, da,** and **wo** [cp. § 116 (c)].

Weil is the most widely used causal conjunction; it adduces a (new) reason not previously known, whereas **da** draws attention to a fact known to the hearer:

Da ich arm bin, muß ich mich in meinen Ausgaben einschränken, *as I am poor I have to limit my expenditure.*

Ich muß mich beschränken, weil ich mir solche Ausgaben einfach nicht leisten kann, *because I just cannot afford . . .*

This is the reason why **da** often leads, but **weil** follows (as above); why **da** has a secondary, but very distinct sense of *seeing that*:

Aber was fange ich mit der Macht an, da ich nicht mächtig zu sein wünsche? (E. Kästner), *since I have no desire to be powerful?*

and, lastly, why **da** is often supported by modal particles asserting the patentness of the fact adduced (**da doch, da ja, da nun einmal**), which seldom occur with **weil.**

Note.—**Wo,** pop., is close to the *seeing that* sense of **da:**

Und eine Stellung kriege ich auch nicht so leicht, wo die fünf Jahre in meinen Papieren fehlen (E. Kästner), *with those five years (in prison) not shown in my papers.*

(c) **Daß** and **weil.**

Many **daß**-clauses derive secondary causal force from the fact that they stand in apposition to a preceding demonstrative adverb whether present or understood:

Ich bin (dessen) froh, daß ich nun über das Schlimmste hinaus bin, *I am pleased that I am now past the worst, pleased at being . . .*

Der König dankte dem Offizier (darum), daß er ihm so treu gedient hatte, *thanked the officer for having . . .*

This is in fact the standard method in German for dealing with the English gerundial construction governed by a preposition, *at being, for having* [*v.* § 278 (*f*)].

252

A preceding genitive (dessen) may be omitted, and daß then has full causal force; thus also if darum is omitted, cp. examples above. But darum explicitly stated is now usually followed by weil, which is felt to represent the causal sense generally:

Mein Urteil über ihn mußte schon darum revidiert werden, weil Hermine ihn so gern hatte (H. Hesse), *had to be revised for the simple reason that . . .*

Similarly, though less suitably, after deshalb (and deswegen):

Und ich habe gedacht, daß viele Menschen es nur deshalb schwer haben, weil andere es leichter haben (E. Wiechert), *have a worse time for the same reason that others . . .*

Cp. fully, § 198 (and there **aus dem einfachen Grunde, weil . . .**).

(*d*) Negation of a Cause:

A causal statement may be negated in two ways:

(1) Definitely, often with counter-statement of the real cause:

Ich sage es nicht, weil ich Ihnen davon abraten will, sondern . . . *I am not telling you because I want to advise you against, but . . .*

(2) Tentatively, while introducing a positive statement as a modification (English: *not because . . ., not that . . .*):

Nicht daß (or nicht etwa weil) ich Ihnen abraten möchte, sage ich das; ich muß aber . . . *it is not that I want to . . . but I must . . .*

Note that (2) usually requires the subjunctive (**möchte**), and that the distinction is exactly that between **sondern,** and **aber** as a limited denial (cp. § 71).

200. Abbreviated Causal Statements

Many causal clauses, if the subject is the same in main and subordinate clauses, may be stated more briefly through:

(*a*) A prepositional infinitive:

Ich bin froh, ihn los zu sein, *to be rid of him* [cp. § 199 (*c*)].

But as **weil** may introduce a statement of motive as well as of cause, the prepositional infinitive may require **um** and become purposive:

Ich sage es nicht, um Ihnen davon abzuraten . . . [cp. § 199 (*d*)].

(*b*) A participial phrase, especially any present participle with the sense . . . *ing as it does:*

Die Handlung, in hundert Szenen und Höllen führend, ist unmöglich (K. Kraus), *the action, taking place in a hundred different . . .*

But the present participle often retains a causal conjunction:

Die Gruppe hat, da in den Anfängen stehend, noch sehr zu kämpfen, *the group, having only just been founded, is finding it difficult* . . .

der erste entscheidende Appell zur Verbrüderung, wirksamer, weil breitere Massen erreichend, als . . . (S. Zweig), *more effective, in that it reached wider masses* . . .

The past participle construction often precedes:

Durch die Absage entmutigt, gab er das Stellungssuchen auf, *discouraged by the refusal he gave up looking for a post.*

(*c*) Many prepositions have causal meaning (cp. §§ 517-23, **infolge, wegen,** etc.), but these or a converted conjunction (*because of,* etc.) may not be used, as in English, to govern a verbal noun and thus abbreviate the causal statement: *Because of* (*owing to, on account of*) *his having refused the post* . . . Cp. § 278 (*d*) and (*f*).

201. Other Constructions with Causal Force

(*a*) In numerous cases a noun or adjective in apposition has causal force (. . . *as I was*), though the transition to the opposite, concessive force (. . . *though I was*) is very easily made:

Sie ließ sich, selbst gütig, gern gütig behandeln, zum Lachen bereit über die eigene Herzenseinfalt (Th. Mann), *kind as she herself was, she liked to be treated kindly.*

Ein phantastisches Kind, gab ich mit meinen Einfällen und Einbildungen den Hausgenossen viel Stoff zur Heiterkeit (Th. Mann), *imaginative child as I was* . . .

But concessive:

Der beste Franzose, war er zugleich der leidenschaftlichste Anti-Nationalist (S. Zweig), *a fine patriot, he was at the same time* . . .

The literal translation of *as I was,* **wie ich war,** is similarly poised between cause and concession:

Müde wie ich war, konnte ich unmöglich zum Kongreß fahren, *tired as I was I found it quite impossible* . . .

Müde wie ich war, wollte ich den Kongreß doch nicht versäumen, *tired though I was I did not want to miss the Conference.*

(*b*) Many paratactical statements [cp. § 126 (*c*) (3)], whether consisting of full clauses or of verbless fragments, have implicit causal force:

Ich kann nicht zum Kongreß fahren, ich habe soviel Arbeit.
Achtung! Schule! Vorsicht, bissiger Hund! *Beware of the dog!*

202. Consecutive Clauses (Clauses of Result)

(*a*) The consecutive conjunctions are: **so daß, daß,** *so that, that, with the result that;* **als daß** (after a comparative statement), *for . . . to;* and with negated results: **(an)statt daß,** *instead of,* **ohne daß,** *without.*

(*b*) **So daß,** in German, like *so that* in English, is the most widely used conjunction of result; **so daß** may stand at the head of the subordinate clause, or **so** may precede in the main clause, with a perceptibly closer linking of the sense:

Das Kindermädchen ist schon wieder da, so daß wir gehen können, *the nursemaid is back, so that we can now go.*

Sie kam so früh nach Hause, daß wir den Abend auswärts verbringen konnten, *she came home so early that we could go out for the evening.*

The separated form may have a distinct flavour of purpose:

Er machte seine Kunststücke so, daß jedermann sie sehen konnte, *he did his tricks in such a way that everyone could see them.*

But as long as the sense is that of manner (*in such a way*), **so daß** may be used; a distinct sense of purpose, however, though in English also expressed by *so that,* needs in German **damit,** often with the subjunctive (*so that . . . should, in order that . . . might*), *v.* §§ 356 f.:

Ich kaufe eine neue Feder, damit er meine Handschrift lesen kann, *so that he can read . . .*

Ich schrieb ihm sofort Bescheid, damit er keine Ausrede habe (subj.), *I wrote to him straight away, so that he should have no excuse.*

(*c*) Clauses of result require the indicative of the verb if the result has actually happened, the subjunctive if it is only entertained as a possible result from certain circumstances. Only the indicative is exemplified here, for the subjunctive *v.* §§ 356 f.

(*d*) **So** replaced by other intensifiers.

The basic sense of the consecutive statement is *of such a nature* (or *in such a manner*) *that* (a certain result ensued). This embodies the force of both manner and degree, both implicit in **so** in the main clause; **so** may there be replaced by specific intensifiers:

(1) Manner: **solch, von (in) einer Art, ein,** etc.:

Er sprach mit solcher Überzeugung, daß die Spottenden betroffen schwiegen, *with such conviction that the mockers . . .*

Er sprach mit einer Überzeugung, daß man ihm alles glauben konnte, *with a conviction such that one could believe all he said.*

(2) Degree: **genug, hinreichend, hinlänglich,** *enough*, etc.:

Wir haben hinreichend Lebensmittel gekauft, daß wir auch bei ungünstigster Witterung den ganzen Winter davon leben können, *we have bought food in such quantities that . . .*

(3) Comparative degree: **zu (viel) . . . als daß,** *too much . . . (for) to . . .*:

Ich war im Augenblick zu überlastet (hatte zuviel zu tun, etc.), als daß ich zum Kongreß fahren konnte [or subj., **könnte,** cp. § 360 (*a*)], *I was at the time too full up with work to be able to go to the Conference.*

(*e*) Intensifiers omitted.

In certain vivid statements the sense is enough to dispense with specific intensifiers of manner or degree in the main statement, and the result, which is usually an imagined one, descriptively entertained rather than factually asserted, follows with **daß:**

(1) Descriptive statements:

Sie schlug den Klavierdeckel zu, daß das Instrument jammerte (E. Kästner), *slammed the piano lid and drew complaining sounds . . .*

Der Schlag knallte, der Kutscher schnalzte, die Pferde zogen an, daß die Scheiben klirrten (Th. Mann), *the door slammed, the coachman clicked his tongue . . . and the windows trembled.*

Immer ist Blütezeit, daß einem Hören und Sehen vergeht vor dem Duft (F. Werfel), *there is always such blossom that the fragrance causes the senses to swoon.*

(2) Inferred consequence:

The first statement is inferred, incredulously, as the only possible explanation of the second, and the surprise conveyed often by a rhetorical question:

War er besoffen, daß er uns so beleidigen konnte? *Was he drunk, to have insulted us in that manner?*

Ich muß von Sinnen gewesen sein, daß ich das Angebot annahm, *I must have been out of my senses to have accepted that offer.*

(*f*) Negative results, *i.e.* events which do not occur, are introduced by **(an)statt daß, ohne daß,** which are never separated:

Anstatt daß er tüchtig arbeitet, gibt er sich die ganze Zeit mit Politik ab, *instead of working he is always involved in politics.*

Ohne daß wir ein Wort wechselten, drückten wir uns die Hand, *without exchanging a word we pressed each other's hand.*

But **ohne daß** may also assert absence of reason for a given result:

Man gratulierte ihm zum Erfolg, ohne daß er einen Handgriff dazu getan hatte, *he was congratulated on his success without having done a hand's turn towards it.*

203. Abbreviated and other Statements of Result

(a) Many consecutive clauses, if the subject is the same in the main and subordinate statements, may be abbreviated to a prepositional infinitive, usually with **um** (cp. examples above in § 202):

> . . . **hinreichend Lebensmittel, um . . . davon leben zu können,**
> . . . **zu überlastet, um zum Kongreß zu fahren,**
> . . . **von Sinnen gewesen sein, das Gebot anzunehmen,**

Er hatte ein Lachen, um die ganze Stadt zu erschüttern, *he had a laugh powerful enough to shake the town.*

Sie haben wahrhaftig nicht so viel Zeit mehr, um auf unnütze Reisen zu gehen (F. Werfel), *that you can go . . .*

(b) Similarly, negative results may be stated, when the subject is the same throughout, with the prepositions **ohne, anstatt,** and the prepositional infinitive, but without the conjunction **daß**:

> **Ohne ein Wort zu wechseln, drückten wir uns die Hand,**
> **Anstatt tüchtig zu arbeiten, gibt er sich . . . mit Politik ab.**

But when the participle develops gerundial force, with a possessive adjective enabling it to change the subject, the subordinate clause is needed in German; thus compare the last example in § 202 (*f*), which could be in English: *we* congratulated him . . . without *his* having done . . .

(c) After the verb **sein,** an idiom allows an **um . . . zu** statement, or **zu** with the infinitive noun, expressing an anticipated result:

> **Es ist zum Heulen,** *enough to make one weep.*
> **Es ist, um verrückt zu werden,** *enough to drive you mad.*

Cp. § 252 (*b*).

(d) Various forms of parataxis and simple coordination may have consecutive force, with or without an expression of degree in the first section:

Es genügt ein Riß, und die ganze Bude fällt ein (E. Kästner), *one crack is enough* (*in the German economic system*) *for the whole crazy structure to collapse.*

Er brauchte nur die Hand zu heben, zu jenem abgenutzten Glockengriff, das Tor sprang auf, und . . . (E. Wiechert), *he need but raise his hand to the bell-handle and the door would* (conditional) *fly open . . .*

Ohne Fleiß kein Preis (prov.), *toil not, reap not.*

Note.—The common expression *will you be so good as to . . .* is translated according to either (*a*) or (*d*):

> **Wollen Sie so gut sein, mich an den Bahnhof zu begleiten?**
> **Wollen Sie so gut sein, und mich an den Bahnhof begleiten?**

Exercise XXXVI

A. Translate into English:

1. In Frankreich jammern die Weinbauern, daß die Ernte gut gerät. Stellen Sie sich vor! Die Menschen sind verzweifelt, weil der Boden zu viel trägt! (E. Kästner). 2. Pastor Hirte gebot über die Kunst, die Lippen in den Mund zu klemmen und sie wieder hinauszuschnellen, in einer Art, daß es knallte wie ein springender Champagnerpfropfen (Th. Mann). 3. Der Schlag knallte, der Kutscher schnalzte, die Pferde zogen an, daß die Scheiben klirrten (Th. Mann). 4. Nun stand aber zwischen Kufstein und Rosenheim der Zug fast eine Stunde still, so daß ich erst nach elf Uhr in München ankam (G. Keller). 5. Ein sehr berühmter hiesiger Gelehrter suchte meine Bekanntschaft, weil seiner Frau meine Bilder so außerordentlich gefallen haben (H. Thomas). 6. Kein Faden ist so fein gesponnen, es kommt doch endlich an die Sonnen (old sing.). 7. Ländlich, sittlich.—Ländlich, schändlich. 8. Sie war ins Zimmer gekommen, ohne daß ich ihren Eintritt bemerkte. 9. „Warum gehst du denn nicht weg?" fragte er. „Du bist doch mündig." „Aber das geht doch nicht," widersprach sie heftig. „Wo Vater hier Meister ist, und . . . wo mich hier alle kennen!" (H. Fallada).

B. Translate into German:

1. As you are going to Munich, which is a town of artists, you will probably be taking your paints and brushes. 2. He found that he had to walk slowly and carefully as the roads were icy and very slippery. 3. The doctor scolded him for having gone out when the wind was so cold. 4. He did not pass his examination, and not only for-the-reason that he had been lazy. 5. The river, flowing as it does right through the capital, adds considerably to the beauty of the town. 6. Inconsiderate as he was he made a great deal of noise at night when he came home late. 7. The artist worked so hard at (an) his picture that it was finished by the end of the month. 8. The old lady preferred to do the work herself instead of making a scene with the lazy servant girl. 9. Can you not come without your family knowing about it? 10. He took books enough to be able to while away the dullest evening. 11. Instead of going to his nine o'clock lecture he stayed in bed and read a detective novel. 12. There was far too little furniture for her to arrange the room in an attractive way. 13. The old car made a noise fit to wake the dead. 14. She only had to lift the telephone and they would deliver all she wanted from the shop. 15. How can I go to the theatre when I can't afford to buy a ticket?

CHAPTER XXXVII

THE INFINITIVE NOUN

204. The Infinitive Noun, General

(a) The infinitive may be used as a (neuter) noun, *i.e.* as the subject or object (direct, indirect, prepositional) of a verb:

Das Reisen erfreut den Geist, *travelling rejoices the spirit,*
Er lernt Zeichnen, *he is learning drawing (to draw),*
Die Fäulnis dient neuem Leben, *decay serves new life.*

Von (vom) Fasten wurde niemand dick, *no one ever put on weight through fasting.*

Durchs Lesen verdirbt man sich die Augen, *reading damages the eyes.*

General comments may be divided into: (1) form, (2) accent, (3) sense, (4) force, and (5) tense.

(b) FORM.—The infinitive noun has its normal infinitive ending **-(e)n,** has a capital, neuter gender, strong declension, and a plural if the sense allows. The article and adjectival modifiers precede, and any other adjuncts follow:

Das unaufhörliche Verschlingen von Romanen bei künstlichem Licht verdirbt den Geschmack und die Augen, *incessant consumption of novels in artificial light spoils the taste and the eyes.*

(c) ACCENT.—The infinitive noun retains the accent of the parent verb: **das Empfángen, Áusreiten, Unterríchten** (but: **der Únterricht,** cp. § 193).

(d) SENSE.—The infinitive noun, so far as its primary and universal sense is concerned, refers to the activity of the parent verb in a general, abstract manner. It may thus correspond to the English prepositional infinitive (to travel), the gerund (travelling) or a noun of activity (travel); but in acquired concrete senses (cp. § 208) it may correspond to any concrete noun. It is one of the two "verbal nouns" in the language, the other being the feminine noun in **-ung,** which also designates an activity, but more often a single, present or concrete action. The sense of the infinitive noun must thus in many cases be distinguished from related forms of the action, thus:

schreiben, *to write;* **(das) Schreiben** (*process of*) *writing;* **die Schreibung** (*actual*) *writing* (*e.g.* **die Schreibung eines Wortes,** *the correct way of writing a word*), **die Schreibe** (*general result of*) *writing, what is written,* **die Schrift** (*specific result of*) *writing,* e.g. *handwriting, a written product* (*book,* etc.).

Similarly with many other words, as **schneiden, die Abschneidung, die Schneide, der Schnitt, die Schnitte.**

Note.—Not all verbs have the same group of verbal and derivative nouns, nor need such nouns bear precisely the same sense-relationship. Many verbs, especially simple verbs (*e.g.* **schneiden**), have no form in **-ung.**

(*e*) FORCE.—The infinitive noun has neutral force; though usually active it may be reflexive or passive without change of form:

(1) Reflexive force: **das Ankleiden, Benehmen, Erbarmen, Erschrecken,** from the corresponding reflexive verbs, and:

Seine Majestät gab durch Erheben vom Sitze das Zeichen zur Beendigung des Empfanges (Th. Mann), *by rising from his seat.*

(2) Passive force; this is less usual generally:

(eine) Vase, in der Blumen aufs Wegwerfen warteten (E. Kästner), *a vase in which flowers were waiting to be thrown away.*

But it is common in the idiomatic use of the infinitive noun with **zum** (*v.* § 252): **Geld zum Ausgeben,** *money to be spent;* **einen Anzug zum Kunststopfen geben,** *to take a suit to be invisibly mended.*

A verb which has active force has intransitive or transitive force according to the sense of the infinitive: **das Weinen, das Skatspielen.**

(*f*) TENSE.—The infinitive noun is also neutral in tense; thus it often corresponds to a perfect participle (gerund) in English:

Ich kenne ihn vom Sehen, weiß das nur vom Hörensagen, *know him by sight (from having seen him), know that by hearsay (from having heard it said).*

Meine Sachen waren ja alle hin vom langen Liegen (H. Fallada), *my clothes were all useless from having lain so long in storage.*

205. Infinitive and Infinitive Noun Distinguished

The infinitive has many nominal functions (as subject, object of a verb), and may even be governed by a preposition, and the infinitive noun, when it has no adjuncts, is not clearly distinguished.

(*a*) Many uses of the infinitive noun might well use the infinitive:

Denn Dreinstolpern war nie meine Art, eine ernste Sache in Angriff zu nehmen (Th. Mann), *it was never my habit to tackle a serious matter by stumbling into it.*

Jungsein, Frischsein und nicht mehr Würdigtun wurde die Parole (S. Zweig), *our motto (after First World War) was: be young, alert and cut out the dignified airs* [cp. infin. as imperative, § 248 (*d*)].

Especially subjects of study are indeterminate: **er hat Lesen, Schreiben und Rechnen (or lesen, schreiben und rechnen) gelernt.**

(b) The infinitive noun becomes distinct from the infinitive when syntactical relations develop:

(1) An adjective, limiting or descriptive, or article:

Gegen drei starke Männer gibt es kein Kämpfen (R. Musil), *there's no (it's no use) fighting against . . .*

Metzgen, essen, trinken, gesundes Ausarbeiten der Glieder im Spiel, im Kampfspiel zumeist, war für griechische wie für germanische Männer der Inbegriff jeder Festlichkeit (G. Hauptmann), *butchery, eating, drinking and healthy physical activity . . .*

(2) A direct object:

Dies erblicken und handeln war für den Spanier eins (Simpl.), *the Spaniard acted without a moment's delay.*

would require an objective genitive after the infinitive noun [cp. § 207 (b) and (c)]:

Das Erblicken seines Vorteils und seine (*its*) Wahrnehmung war für ihn eins, *he saw his advantage and grasped it at once.*

(3) A governing preposition:

Er sagte, ich würde nach solchem Weglaufen nie wieder eine Anstellung finden (Th. Mann), *after having thus run away.*

But the infinitive is also found here if no adjective is present:

mit essen fertig (Th. Mann), **mit arbeiten anfangen** (H. Fallada).

(c) With a preposition and definite article [note: always contracted, v. § 303 (b)] the infinitive noun develops full participial or gerundial force:

(1) Intransitive:

Im Vorübergehen, beim Fortgehen vom Hause, nach mehrmaligem Hinblicken, *while going past, when leaving (as we left) the house, after looking several times.*

(2) Transitive, with objective genitive:

„Ihre Phantasielosigkeit im Ausfinden einer Gelegenheit," sagte sie, **„ist recht kläglich"** (Th. Mann), *in devising an opportunity . . .*

(3) Intransitive, with subjective genitive:

Im Weitergleiten des Schiffes erfüllte mich nur noch der eine Gedanke (G. Hauptmann), *as the ship glided on . . .*

The following prepositions are especially associated with the infinitive noun: **an, bei** or **in,** of activity in progress: **am Überkochen,** *boiling over,* **am Platzen,** *about to burst,* **beim Anziehen,** *getting dressed,* **im**

Stehen (*while*) *standing;* and **zu**, of purpose or suitability: **Zeit zum Nachdenken,** *for thought,* **das Signal zum Aufstehen,** *for getting up,* **ein schöner Morgen zum Spazierengehen,** *for going for a walk.* Cp. § 67 (*a*) (progressive tense), and § 527 (**zu**, prep.).

(*d*) The infinitive noun often corresponds to a dependent prepositional infinitive construction:

Der Mensch ist des Denkens nicht in hohem Maße fähig (H. Hesse), *not capable of a high degree of thought* (**fähig, zu denken**).

bei der Witwe H., die das Vermieten früher nicht nötig gehabt hatte (E. Kästner), *had formerly not needed to let rooms* (**nötig gehabt hatte, zu vermieten**).

Es gibt Tage, wo J. nur liest, ohne Aufhören, ohne Bewußtsein der Welt (E. Wiechert), *without ceasing* (**ohne aufzuhören**).

206. Certain Fields of Infinitive Nouns

The primary force of the infinitive noun is the abstract statement of the process of *any* verb for its own sake:

(Ich fühle mich) eins mit dem Sprossen, Keimen und Blüten rings um mich her (G. Hauptmann), *with the sprouting, burgeoning and blossoming going on all around me.*

In the light of this definition and such an example, it may seem senseless to speak of "fields" of the infinitive noun. But there are certain classes of statement which find the generalised force of the infinitive noun apposite.

(*a*) Basic human activities and the expressions of human experience, especially in proverbs and traditional formulas:

Reden ist Silber, Schweigen ist Gold; Essen und Trinken, Wohnen und Reisen; Zeichnen, Malen und Schreiben; das Tun und Lassen, *acts and omissions;* **Einkaufen macht Spaß; Rauchen (ist) gestattet; Arbeiten ist gesund; Bitten ist keine Schande; Zögern ist sinnlos.**

(*b*) Human actions and relations:

das Anerbieten, Ansehen, Betragen, Gebrechen, Selbstvertrauen, Wohlgefallen, *offer, standing* (*reputation*), *behaviour, disability, self-confidence,* (*sense of*) *satisfaction.*

(*c*) Concepts of philosophy and functions of psychology:

das Dasein, Denken, Denkvermögen, Fühlen, Schaffen, Wissen, Verstehen, *existence, thought, faculty of thought, feeling* (*artistic*), *creation, knowledge, understanding.*

(*d*) Actions by the body:

das Atmen, Blinzeln, Hinken, Husten, Kopfschütteln, Lachen, *breathing, blinking, limping, coughing, shaking the head, laughing.*

Schimpfen, Lachen und Schwatzen drang durch mehrere Türen (Th. Mann).

das Schwanken und Stolpern von Betrunkenen (W. Bergengruen).

Many of these correspond to an English concrete noun, thus: wink, limp, cough, laugh, etc. The following noun (of the part of the body concerned) as in: to nod the head, nod of the head, usually requires in German the same preposition with both verb and noun: **nicken (Nicken) mit dem Kopf; klatschen (Klatschen) in die Hände,** or **Händeklatschen,** *to clap* (*a clap*); **scharren (Scharren) mit den Füßen,** *to scrape with* (*a scraping of*) *the feet;* but an involuntary action is followed by a (subjective) genitive: **das Zucken der Augenlider,** *twitching of the eyebrows.*

(*e*) Sports, Games and Pastimes:

das Boxen, Baden, (Pferde-)Rennen, Schwimmen, Tauziehen, *boxing, bathing,* (*horse-*)*racing, swimming, tug-of-war.*

Er erzählte ihnen Geschichten, spielte Fangen mit ihnen (W. Bergengruen), *played catch with them.*

Einige Kinder spielten Hüpfen (H. Böll), *hop-scotch.*

207. The Infinitive Noun and Other Nouns from Verbs

(*a*) No universal rule can be given for the distinction between various kinds of nouns from verbs, *e.g.* **das Schreiben, die Schreibung, die Schrift,** beyond the general statement that these represent process, action and result respectively [cp. § 204 (*d*)]. O. Curme (p. 282) illustrates this distinction with the following example:

Das Unterscheiden ist nicht leicht, denn der Unterschied zwischen zwei Dingen ist oft so versteckt, daß die Unterscheidung des einen von dem andern kaum möglich ist, *process of distinguishing . . . difference . . . distinction . . .*

Further, it is usually considered that an infinitive noun should not stand before an objective genitive if (as is not always the case) a verbal noun in **-ung** is available; thus **das Schneiden des Apfels,** but only **die Führung der Gruppe** [but *v.* (*b*) (2), below, and § 489 (*a*)].

(*b*) There is at present, however, a tendency for the infinitive noun to invade the field of the verbal noun in **-ung,** especially in its more concrete senses and with a subjective genitive following:

(1) Concrete senses:

Wir waren einander wie Tag und Nacht geworden, die sich im grauen Dämmern treffen (S. Andres), *which meet in the grey dusk.*

Thus also: **Bemerken, Begegnen, Erinnern, (wider) Erwarten, Meinen** are becoming common for **Bemerkung,** etc., and **das Unternehmen,** *an economic activity, business, firm,* seems to be fast replacing **die Unternehmung.**

(2) Objective genitive:

Dieses Vernichten der Persönlichkeit und Brechen des Willens nun war bei diesem Schüler nicht gelungen (H. Hesse), *the destroying of the personality and breaking of the will had not succeeded . . .*

(3) Subjective genitive:

schuldig am Entstehen des Krieges (H. Hesse), *the outbreak of war.*

Gamler erkundigte sich nach dem Erscheinen des Sandbergschen Katalogs (H. Kasack), *asked about the (date of) publication.*

mit einem leichten Anschwellen ihrer Armmuskeln (Th. Mann), *with a slight swelling of her arm muscles.*

The expansion of the infinitive noun with the subjective genitive is striking, and enables words in **-ung** to concentrate on more concrete senses, as: **eine Erscheinung, Neuerscheinung,** *a (new) publication, phenomenon, (person of striking) appearance;* **eine Anschwellung** (*an actual*) *swelling.*

(*c*) Only slightly less striking is the use of infinitive nouns for verbal nouns of various other derivations: **das Erleben (das Erlebnis), ein Unterkommen (eine Unterkunft), in schlaffem Genießen (Genuß), durch das Mitnehmen Zazas (die Mitnahme), ein Seufzen (ein Seufzer).**

An example of the correct distinction of the three forms of verbal derivative:

Es hat nicht eine, sondern drei Urzeugungen gegeben: das Entspringen des Seins aus dem Nichts, die Erweckung des Lebens aus dem Sein und die Geburt des Menschen (Th. Mann), *three primary creative acts . . . the emergence of being from nothing, the awakening of life out of being, and the birth of man.*

(*d*) Possessive Adjective:

When the two kinds of verbal noun still have their verbal force, a preceding possessive adjective without any following genitive is understood as:

(1) Subjective genitive with the infinitive noun:

Sein Bleiben nach dem Unterricht war zur stehenden Einrichtung geworden (Th. Mann), *it had become an accepted thing that he should stay . . .*

Thus also: **die Schnelligkeit seines Eintreffens,** *of his arrival;* **Gründe für sein Ausbleiben,** *for his absence.*

Note.—Objective genitive following: **das Hassen seiner selbst, Selbsthaß** (H. Hesse).

(2) Objective genitive with the verbal noun:

Luther pries seine Verwaltung (= die Verwaltung Nürnbergs) als ein Paradies (W. Andreas), *its administration, the way it was governed.*

Note.—Subjective genitive only when objective genitive follows: **seine Verwaltung der Stadt.**

208. The Infinitive Noun Particularised

The infinitive noun in its primary force may be modified descriptively (**das langsame Wachsen**), but it can hardly be individualised or multiplied, unless in a transferred sense (a growth, growths). With increase in its concrete force this may, however, happen.

(*a*) Singular. **Bei jedem Vorübergehen,** *each time he passed,* **nach dem dritten Klingeln,** *after his third ring,* **ein Einsehen haben,** *to show consideration,* and:

Diese unerquickliche Abendstunde war für mich ein letztes Mißlingen und Davonlaufen (H. Hesse), *a final occasion of failure and flight.*

(*b*) Plural. (1) Many infinitive nouns are completely nominalised and form simple plurals (declension § 24): **kurze Antwortschreiben, meine weiteren Reisevorhaben, das kranke Römische Reich mit all seinen Gebrechen, seine sämtlichen Anliegen,** *answers, plans, disabilities, requirements.*

(2) Others may form a plural from another ending; **das Bestreben, die Bestrebungen,** *efforts;* **das Vergnügen, die Vergnügungen,** *pleasures.*

(3) A few, such as **Leben,** require compounds: **Menschenleben,** (*human*) *lives; every human soul contains many potential lives,* **trägt viele Lebens- und Daseinsmöglichkeiten in sich.**

209. Idiomatic Uses of Infinitive (Noun) with Haben, Geben, Sein

Certain idiomatic uses of the infinitive or infinitive noun after **sein, es gibt,** and **haben,** may be grouped here. They express respectively a firm denial or assertion of the possibility of an action, and have thus modal force.

(*a*) Denial, with **kein** and an infinitive noun.

(1) **Jetzt ist kein Halten mehr** (W. Bergengruen), *there is no holding them;* cp. **auf ihn ist (kein) Verlaß,** *one can trust (there is no trusting) him.* **Auf solchem Boden ist kein Spazierengehen, hier ist ein wahrhaftes Lustwandeln, ein holdes Irren, ein liebenswürdiges oder gedankenvolles Glück**

(W. Bergengruen), *here (in the parks of Geneva) there is no question of walking, there is only delighted wandering, sweet sauntering* . . .

(2) **Und dennoch gab es kein Fortlaufen** (F. Thiess), *there was no question of running away,*

Er hätte sofort trachten müssen, zu entwischen, denn gegen drei starke Männer gibt es kein Kämpfen (R. Musil), *there can be no question of resistance.*

(*b*) Assertion, with **gut** and an infinitive.

(1) **Hier ist gut sein,** *it is good to be here,* and

Er sah einen Glückspilz in mir, mit dem zusammen gut arbeiten sein würde (Th. Mann), *he saw in me someone with a lucky touch, with whom collaboration would be profitable.*

(2) **Sie haben gut reden,** means primarily, *it is easy for you to talk,* thus also: **Sie haben leicht fragen;** from this derives the sense *you talk in vain* (cp. French vous avez beau parler):

Sie haben gut sich ergeben! Aber ich kann es nicht (Th. Mann), *it's all very well for you to give in, but I can't!*

Note.—For the expression: **es ist zum** and infinitive noun, *v.* § 205 (*c*), and § 252.

EXERCISE XXXVII

A. Translate into ENGLISH:

1. Die Mutter war meistens irgendwohin: zum Kartenspielen, zum Friseur (zum Aufblonden), zum Schneider oder in die Geschäfte (S. Andres). 2. Er suchte in dem Holz nach einem Scheit zum Nachlegen (E. Wiechert). 3. Er ist hilfsbereit bis zum Selbstvergessen. Das fremde Dasein und dessen Not lebt er bis zum Versinken (R. Guardini). 4. Sind denn Ideale zum Erreichen da? (H. Hesse). 5. Borgen macht Sorgen. Probieren geht über Studieren. 6. Arbeiten ist gesund . . . Verhungern ist Geschmacksache . . . Sogar stehlen will gelernt sein (E. Kästner). 7. (Die weiße Katze) liegt unbeweglich da, und das Blinzeln ist ihre Gymnastik (W. Bergengruen). 8. Mit einem schrägen Zurückwerfen des Kopfes, einem leichten Ausbreiten der Hände deutete er seine Überraschung, sein Vergnügen an (Th. Mann). 9. Im Etschtal ist es zur Zeit der Traubenlese noch gut sein, obwohl die Gipfel rund um Meran schon weiße Hauben aufhaben (newsp.). 10. A Servant's Life. Es war immer dasselbe: Erwachen, Ankleiden, Morgenmesse, Feuermachen, Frühstückkochen, Aufräumen, Einkaufengehen, Mittagessen zubereiten, Geschirrwaschen, Tee oder Kaffee am Nachmittag,

die verausgabten Summen zusammenrechnen, Abendessen richten, Geschirrwaschen, die Küche säubern, Schlafengehen. Teta beklagte sich keineswegs über diesen eintönigen Wandel. Sie arbeitete gern (F. Werfel).

B. Translate into GERMAN, using infinitive nouns where possible:

1. I felt a complete stranger in this society, different in my feeling and thinking. 2. Writing is speaking without anyone interrupting you. 3. I found her mending socks and listening to the wireless. 4. The importance of his action became frighteningly (bis zum, infinitive noun) clear to him. 5. "You are not here for pleasure to-day. This is a dancing lesson and it's a serious affair." 6. I now felt how tired I was after hours of (stundenlang, adj.) wandering-about, and I remained seated. 7. Sleeping is like eating and drinking; when you have been without it for some time you can't go on working. 8. With the passing of time he forgot the dreadful-thing that had happened. 9. It was easy for him to laugh; it wasn't his hat that had fallen into the river. 10. This town is an unfriendly place and it is not good to be here. 11. My pleasure in those days was hiking. Now I have many so-called pleasures and I enjoy none of them. 12. Laughing and crying are not so very different as people sometimes think. 13. Only the continual questioning of the scientist has wrested nature's secrets from her. 14. Early rising in the morning, early going to bed at night, keep you in good health, so the doctors say.

CHAPTER XXXVIII

THE PASSIVE VOICE

210. The Passive. General

(*a*) A verb is placed in the passive voice when the object of the action is made the grammatical subject of the verb: *I was asked*. English uses the verb *to be* as passive auxiliary, German the verb **werden** (whose sense elsewhere is *to become*) with the past participle of the verb:

ich werde (wurde) gefragt, *I am* (*was*) (*being*) *asked*.

ich werde gefragt werden, *I shall be asked* [*v*. (*b*) (2) below].

ich würde gefragt werden, *I should be asked* [*v*. §§ 426 f., conditional].

ich bin (war) gefragt *worden*, *I have* (*had*) *been asked* (*v*. note below).

Note.—The past participle of **werden** as passive auxiliary is **worden**, not, as in other senses, **geworden**.

Der Student der Medizin ist geprüft worden, und darauf Arzt geworden, *the medical student was examined, and then became a doctor.*

(*b*) Tenses and tense forms:

(1) The special aspect of the passive brought out by the English progressive form *being* may be rendered in various ways, not only with the passive:

The house is being built. **Das Haus wird *eben* gebaut, ist im Bau begriffen, befindet sich im Bau.**

(2) The future passive (*v*. above) uses **werden** in two distinct auxiliary functions; it is, however, uncommon, as the present passive is usually adequate to indicate future sense (cp. § 67), especially:

(i) When intention is expressed:

Das Haus wird nächste Woche verkauft, *is going to be sold . . .*

(ii) In the future infinitive:

ihre positive Religiosität und die Zuversicht, dort drüben einst für ihr schwieriges und glanzloses Leben entschädigt zu werden (Th. Mann), *confidence that she would be* (*was going to be*) *recompensed beyond the grave.*

But distinguish, in verbs in which past participle and infinitive appear identical:

sie werden empfangen = (i) future active: *they will receive;*

(ii) present or future passive: *they are* (*being*) *received, will be received.*

(3) The perfect passive is often equivalent in force to a present state resulting from a past event:

> **Das Haus ist verkauft worden,** *has been sold.*
> **Das Haus ist verkauft,** *is (now) sold.*

Thus the latter is often substituted for the former, and it is said that **worden** has been omitted. It is always omitted in this tense with **geboren,** past participle of **gebären,** *to bear.*

> **Ich bin am 14. Juli 1911 geboren,** *I was born on 14 July 1911.*

Similarly with the pluperfect.

(*c*) An English passive does not necessarily require a German passive; thus especially accidental events are often expressed in the active:

> *The letter was lost in the post,* **der Brief ging auf der Post verloren.**
> *He had a car accident and was killed,* **er verunglückte mit dem Auto und kam dabei ums Leben.**

A passive may in fact often be an Anglicism, as **wurde getötet,** now often found in examples as that above, and:

> **In diesem bedeutenden Hause gab es eine Figur, die der „Beständige Gast" gerufen wurde** (F. Werfel), *who was called the "Permanent Guest".*

(*d*) In certain impersonal constructions there is no person (thing) which is represented as being acted upon:

> **Es wurde viel geplaudert,** *there was a lot of chatting (going on),* v. § 246.

211. The Statal Passive

(*a*) The English passive with *to be* combines two aspects:

(1) Event: the house was (being) built on the hill
  (= statement of action in progress).

(2) State: the house was built on the hill
  (= description of house in existence).

Even when the event is a repeated one, it still does not become a state: The bell is rung every time there is a funeral—but only when the completed event leaves a distinct and changed situation.

The normal German passive with **werden** (v. § 210) describes an event and is thus called the "actional passive" [and is unsuitable for certain statements in § 210 (*c*)]; but **sein** may be used as auxiliary to describe a state, this being the "statal passive":

> **Das Haus wurde auf dem Berg gebaut** = actional passive.
> **Das Haus ist auf dem Berg gebaut** = statal passive.

(*b*) The statal passive is often not clearly distinguishable from:

(1) The perfect actional passive, with **worden** omitted:

> **Das Haus ist auf dem Berg gebaut (worden),** *was built on the hill.*

(2) **sein** with the past participle as adjectival predicate:

Das Haus war zerstört, total beschädigt, ausgebombt, *destroyed, a complete loss, bombed out;* cp. **Das Haus war weg, lag in Ruinen.**

(3) **sein** in the perfect (active) of an intransitive verb where the past participle may also be transitive:

Sein Herz ist verdorben, *is corrupt* = *has become corrupt* (intrans.)
= *has been corrupted* (trans.).

(c) The following gradation of uses represents a decrease in (actional) passive force:

(1) Actional passive, present progressive:

Die Hauptstadt wird eben von einem feindlichen Fliegerverbande angegriffen, *is being attacked by an enemy formation.*

(2) Actional passive, past event:

Das Haus wurde gebombt und total zerstört, *bombed and destroyed.*

(3) Full statal passive, with agent:

Obwohl ich sie nicht jeden Tag sah, war ich doch stets von ihr gesehen, geleitet, bewacht, begutachtet (H. Hesse), *I was always in her sight, under her guidance and guard, and under observation by her.*

(4) Diminished statal passive, equivalent to a perfected actional passive:

Der Streik muß morgen früh beendet sein (H. Mann), *the strike must be finished (over) by to-morrow morning.*

(5) Diminished statal passive, descriptive context:

Die schmalen Pfädchen waren mit ockergelbem Kies bestreut (L. Frank), *the narrow paths were strewn with ochre-coloured gravelly sand.*

Am Ende des Steges war ein Boot mit einer dünnen Kette befestigt (H. Risse), *was secured by a thin chain.*

(d) The statal passive often demonstrates its vigour, and is distinguished from the descriptive past participle [v. (b) (1) above] by taking the accusative with dative/accusative prepositions:

In die Erlen waren verdeckte Sitze wie Krähennester eingebaut (E. Jünger), *concealed seats (for shooting) like crows' nests.*

And this use extends also to the past participle used in appositional constructions:

Auf der letzten Anhöhe stand der Bauer, auf seinen Stock gestützt (E. Wiechert), *the peasant, leaning on his stick.*

212. Actional and Statal Passive Contexts

Some uncertainty may be felt in distinguishing between the actional and statal passives in non-physical contexts.

(*a*) The actional passive does not necessarily require an overt action, but may be used in contexts involving:

(1) An active relation:

Sie glich einem Irrwisch, der von der Knabenschar im Halbkreis umstanden wurde (E. Langgässer), *surrounded by a group of* (*curious*) *boys.*

(2) A relation of the will:

Von jedem wird erwartet, daß . . ., *every man is expected to . .*

Er, der Arzt, ist der Vertreter jener Welt, die von den betriebsamen Ameisen (= *Nazis*) **beherrscht wird** (H. Risse), *that world which is controlled by the busy ants.*

(3) Mental operations:

Das Dreieck ABC wird durch die Linie XY in zwei gleiche Teile getrennt, *is separated by . . .*

Die Stadt wird durch einen schmalen Kanal mit dem offenen Meer verbunden, *is connected with . . .*

(*b*) The statal passive is often used in grammatical categories which emphasise completion, thus:

(1) Always in the imperative:

Sei gegrüßt, du liebes Kind! (lit.) *be greeted, dear child!* [*v.* § 273 (*d*)].

(2) In the infinitive:

Womit nicht gesagt sein soll, daß . . ., *by which I do not mean that . . .*

Wo es so schwer ist, zu sprechen, da will gefragt sein (Th. Mann), *where it is so difficult to speak, a sympathiser may put questions.*

(3) In the past participle:

Daß ich an der Universität studieren sollte, war im Rate der Familie von je beschlossen gewesen (S. Zweig), *had always been agreed . . .*

But the wide, and increasing use of the statal passive in non-physical contexts does not permit classification.   Examples:

Zwischen den Menschen sind Schranken gesetzt, *there are barriers between human beings.*

Ich werde erklären, was mit diesem Urteil gemeint ist, *I shall explain what is the sense* (*intention*) *of this judgment.*

Wem ist damit gedient? *who is served thereby?*

Mit der Versetzung eines Jungen in eine andere Schule ist seine ganze Ausbildung in Frage gestellt, *his whole training is endangered.*

Newspaper headlines particularly confuse the two forms of the passive, by omitting the distinguishing verb form:

Über Helgoland-Anschluß ist abgestimmt (sc. **worden**), *Heligoland plebiscite completed.*

Bau des neuen Gästehauses gefährdet? (sc. **Ist / wird der . . .**) *New guest-hotel project endangered?*

213. Actional Passive with Objects not in Accusative

(*a*) Only an object in the accusative may become the subject of the actional passive construction in § 210: **Man fragt mich oft, ich werde oft gefragt.**

Verbs governing a genitive, dative, or prepositional object must use in the passive a construction with the impersonal subject **es**:

(1) Genitive:

Active: **Der Direktor spottete seiner in offener Versammlung.**

Passive: **Es wurde in offener Versammlung vom Direktor seiner gespottet.**

(2) Dative:

Active: **Man befahl ihm, den Gefangenen wegzuführen.**

Passive: **Es wurde ihm befohlen, den Gefangenen wegzuführen.**

(3) Prepositional:

Active: **Man spricht gut von ihm.**

Passive: **Es wird gut von ihm gesprochen.**

(*b*) Notes on the **es** construction in the passive:

(1) The personal object governed in the dative or genitive or by a preposition remains unchanged: **seiner, ihm, von ihm** (above).

(2) The subject takes the form suitable for the agent of an action: **vom Direktor;** but **man** disappears, as *they* in English: They laughed at him.   He was laughed at.

(3) With inversion, **es** may and often does disappear as well:

Ihm wurde befohlen . . . Von ihm wird gut gesprochen . . .

Distinguish this from genuine impersonal idioms, as

Es bedarf seiner Hilfe, *his help is needed,*

which are not in the passive, cannot be put into the passive, and cannot omit their impersonal subject:

Jetzt bedarf es mehr noch seiner Hilfe, *needed even more.*

(*c*) English makes no distinction between a personal and an impersonal passive: *he was laughed at, ordered to . . ., spoken well of.* Thus, in translating from the English special care must be taken to detect verbs which govern oblique cases in German, especially dative: *I was told, commanded, contradicted,* etc., must become: **Es wurde mir gesagt, befohlen, widersprochen,** etc., or **Mir wurde gesagt,** etc.

(*d*) But it is the sense rather than the grammatical construction which must be translated. So verbs governing oblique cases will often require a construction other than the impersonal passive, as:

(1) **man** and the active, cp. examples above, (*a*).

(2) A verb taking the accusative in the normal passive:

Thus *he was told* =   (i) **es wurde ihm mitgeteilt, erzählt, gesagt,**
                        (ii) **er wurde benachrichtigt.**

Thus *he was laughed at* =   (i) **es wurde seiner gespottet,**
                             (ii) **er wurde verspottet.**

Thus *he was spoken of* =   (i) **es wurde von ihm gesprochen,**
                            (ii) **er wurde besprochen, erwähnt.**

(3) A compound verb taking the accusative with a prefix corresponding to the governing preposition:

He was spoken to (*in the street*), **er wurde angesprochen.**
He was passed over, **er wurde übergangen.**

(*e*) A verb taking a direct object *may* be used in the impersonal passive, *v.* § 246 (*c*). But when the accusative object is one of two, the normal passive must be used except in the common combination of dative / accusative:

Eine rohe Soldateska erleichterte ihn seiner Uhr und seiner Schuhe, *the brutal soldiery relieved him of his watch and shoes* (acc., gen. obj.).

Er wurde durch eine . . . seiner Uhr . . . erleichtert, *he was relieved of . . .*

Man schenkte ihm eine goldene Armbanduhr, *he was given a gold wristlet watch* (dat., acc. obj.).

Eine goldene . . . wurde . . . but also: **Es wurde ihm eine . . . geschenkt.**

214. Other Verbs as Passive Auxiliaries

Certain verbs other than **werden** (or **sein**) may, in conjunction with the past participle, form genuinely passive constructions:

(*a*) Verbs of receiving, **bekommen, erhalten, kriegen,** with the past participle as predicative complement (objective predicate, *v.* that); in ordinary speech these constructions conveniently avoid the clumsy impersonal form of the passive with dative verbs:

Meine Mutter war eine gute Frau . . . wer hausieren kam, hatte die Chance, etwas abgekauft zu bekommen (H. Böll), *a pedlar always stood a chance of having something bought off him.*

**Die stellvertretenden Vorsitzenden erhielten einstimmig ihr Mandat wieder
zugesprochen** (newsp.), *the Vice-Chairmen were re-elected unanimously to
their offices.*

Der kriegt von mir die Meinung gesagt, wenn er so weiter macht, *he will get
a piece of my mind, if he goes on like this.*

(*b*) The verb **gehören** in conversational usage, often with a prepositional
phrase of direction, which may lead to the past participle being omitted
as unnecessary:

Das Kind gehört ins Bett (geschickt), *the child should be sent to bed, ought
to be in bed.*

Note.—As shown by the English (should, ought), the idiom may be
paraphrased by a modal (past subj.) and a passive infinitive:

Das Kind sollte ins Bett geschickt werden.

Gehören does not eliminate the dative, as do **bekommen,** etc.; it is in
fact often used with the dative, which may have possessive force:

Dem gehört die Wahrheit gesagt, *he ought to be told the truth* (*a few home
truths*).

corresponding to the modal forms: **Dem sollte (müßte) einmal die
Wahrheit gesagt werden.**

Dem gehört der Kopf gewaschen, *he needs a good talking to* (lit. *his head
washed*).

An analogous use with **bekommen:**

**Die Z. haben den Schatz der Sprache in reichlichem Maße in die Wiege
gelegt bekommen** (E. Wiechert), *the Z's (family) received the gift of
eloquence in **their** cradle.*

Note.—Similarly, sometimes with **haben,** *v.* § 218 (*c*).

215. The Simple Active Infinitive with Passive Force after Lassen

(*a*) The simple dependent infinitive used after certain verbs may
have either active or passive force, though active in form:

Er saß am Fenster und ließ sich von der Sonne kitzeln (E. Kästner), *he sat
at the window and let himself be warmed by the sun.*

These are the verbs of causation and perception discussed in §§ 149-53,
and occasionally verbs of knowing and believing (**wissen, glauben**). The
development of this idiom may be shown by examples with **lassen.**

(*b*) **Lassen,** apart from its use with the direct object and infinitive
objective predicate (**ich ließ ihn kommen,** *v.* § 150), may be used with the
logical subject of the dependent infinitive implicit in the context:

Das volle schwarze Haar ließ heute, ohne Hut, denn doch Silberfäden wahrnehmen (Th. Mann).

Such a sentence may be construed in two ways:

(1) With generalised subject of the dependent infinitive: allowed (people) to see the streaks of grey hair.

(2) With noun object and active infinitive with passive force: allowed streaks of grey hair to be seen.

When the object of the dependent infinitive is the same as the subject of **lassen,** the statement has the force of (2) above, thus:

Er ließ sich (durch den Chirurgen) operieren, *he had himself operated upon by the surgeon.*

The extent of divergence of such statements from the normal objective predicate (example and reference above) is shown by (i) the use of the reflexive **sich** for a personal pronoun **ihn,** (ii) the passive force of the infinitive, (iii) the introduction of the logical subject of the dependent infinitive, here *the surgeon,* in the agent form, **durch den Chirurgen.**

(*c*) The dependent infinitive may require constructions other than the simple accusative, and these are reflected in the case and form of the noun or pronoun object following **lassen:**

(1) Prepositional object:

Meine Mutter und Schwester machten auf der Promenade durch Übertreibungen in der Form ihrer Hüte von sich reden (Th. Mann), *made people talk about them, got themselves talked about.*

(2) Dative with accusative object:

Dennoch ließ er sich (dat.) **nichts anmerken,** *yet he did not show anything (of his feelings),* lit. *let anything be seen in himself.*

Er geht hinein und läßt sich (dat.) **einen Schnaps geben,** *he goes in and orders (has himself given) a brandy.*

(3) Dative and prepositional phrase (of part of body):

Der alte Robinson war ein entschlossener Mann und als solcher nicht gesonnen, sich von seinem Sohne auf dem Kopf herumtanzen zu lassen (Simpl.), *allow his son to lord it over him (the father).*

(*d*) **Lassen** with dative **sich** and dependent infinitive is widely used in the common idiom *to have (something) done (for oneself):*

Ich ließ mir das Buch binden, den Katalog schicken, einen Smoking machen, *I had a book bound, a catalogue sent, a dinner jacket made.*

the dative "of interest" (cp. § 382) being often omitted in English.

(e) In the few cases in which the context does not make clear whether a following accusative is subject or object of the infinitive, a further elucidatory object may be added:

Er ließ ihn untersuchen, *had him examined, had him examine* (*someone else*).
Er ließ ihn den Patienten untersuchen, *had him examine the patient.*

(f) **Lassen** with a following reflexive is used in many idiomatic senses, especially in the more passive sense, *to allow, let* (cp. § 150):

Das läßt sich (leicht) sagen, *that is easy to say.*
Warum ließ er sich das gefallen? *why did he put up with it?* (lit. *allow it to please him,* dat.).
Man kann sich damit sehen lassen, *It* (e.g. *a suit*) *is not so bad at all* (lit. *one can let oneself be seen with it*).
Mein Mann läßt sich entschuldigen, *my husband presents his excuses.*
Sich sagen lassen is often simply *to be informed*; analogously:
F. ließ sich inzwischen, nicht ganz freiwillig, von M. über kurzfristige Anleihen aufklären (E. Kästner), *meanwhile F. was being instructed by M., not entirely willingly, on short term loans.*

(g) **Lassen** should only form a passive when the force of the dependent infinitive is active:

Ich bin fünfundzwanzig Jahre alt, und von zwei Männern wurde ich stehengelassen . . . wie ein Schirm (E. Kästner), *and have already been jilted by two men.*

Even then the use is limited; thus *not* **er wurde kommen gelassen,** *but* **man ließ ihn kommen.**

216. The Simple Active Infinitive with Passive Force after Hören, etc.

(a) **Hören** may have similar constructions to those described for **lassen** (v. § 214):

(1) Dependent infinitive with generalised implicit subject:

Es ist eine Ausnahme und sehr wohltuend, einmal zugunsten der guten Sache gut und gewinnend sprechen zu hören (Th. Mann), *to hear someone speak well of,* or: *to hear the good cause spoken well of . . .*

(2) The same with dative or accusative object:

Ich will freudig anerkennen, daß mir von mehreren geschätzten Seiten die Genugtuung zuteil geworden ist, Deine Leistungen (acc.) **loben und Dir** (dat.) **eine aussichtsreiche Zukunft zusprechen zu hören** (R. Musil), *the satisfaction of hearing people praise your merits and predict for you a promising future,* or: *to hear your merits praised . . .*

(b) Similar uses with other verbs, and those with a reflexive pronoun object, are much rarer than corresponding expressions with **lassen**. But a few reflexive idioms, followed by a past participle of a verb which commonly takes the dative, are often defended with the argument that the construction is analogous to the dependent infinitive, and that the reflexive is actually a dative [cp. § 434 (b)]:

Er fühlte sich geschmeichelt, *felt himself flattered.*

Er glaubte (wußte) sich gefolgt, *believed (knew) himself to be followed.*

(c) In the few cases of ambiguity, the passive force of the dependent infinitive may be clarified by using the past participle or subordinate clause:

Er hörte sich rufen, *heard himself call.*

Er hörte sich rufen, or, less ambiguously: **hörte sich gerufen,**
  hörte, wie er gerufen wurde,
  heard himself called.

(d) **Hören** should only be used in the passive when the force of the dependent infinitive is active: **Er wurde rufen gehört,** *he was heard to call out.* But, as with **lassen** [§ 215 (g)], this use is limited, and **man hörte ihn rufen** is preferred.

Except in the case of the two type verbs **lassen** and **hören,** it is better to avoid such constructions entirely and translate by the active or by other forms of the passive:

Man hieß ihn gehen, *he was told to go;* **man hörte ihn sagen,** *he was heard to say;* **man fühlte den Boden schwanken,** *the ground was felt to move.*

Er wurde für krank gehalten, *he was thought to be ill.*

The passive of **lehren** is felt especially to be a "paper construction", and for e.g. *I was taught swimming,* another verb should be used: **Ich wurde im Schwimmen unterrichtet (unterwiesen),** *instructed in . . .*

217. Further English Passive Idioms

The passive is used in English in many cases where German uses the active, reflexive or some other form.

(a) Verbs of instructing, stating, perceiving, believing, where English may have one or both verbs in the passive; German commonly uses active forms:

His condition is stated to be improving, **man berichtet, daß sein Zustand . . .,**
  sein Zustand soll . . .

I consider him to have been deceived, **ich halte ihn für betrogen.**

I believe the picture to have been sold, **ich glaube, daß . . . worden ist.**

He is held to have been led astray by . . ., **man ist der Ansicht, daß er . . . wurde.**

(*b*) Reflexive constructions for English *to get*:

    So ein kleines Ding verliert sich leicht, *easily gets lost.*

    Das wird sich irgendwie machen, *that will get done somehow.*

    Cp. also **lassen,** § 215 (*f*).

(*c*) Intransitive verbs for English *to be* . . . :

ertrinken (ersaufen), *to be drowned;* **erschrecken,** *to be frightened;* **heißen,** *to be called;* **sollen,** *to be said* (*expected*) *to* . . .; **dürfen,** *to be allowed to* . . .

(*d*) The "modal verbals" (cp. §§ 249 f., 279) for English passive infinitive.

    Das Haus ist zu verkaufen, *is to be sold* (*for sale*).

    Das zu verkaufende Haus, *the house to be sold* (*for sale*) . . .

218. Haben, with Past Participle

(*a*) Two special idiomatic senses of **haben** are relevant here, and may be approached through the normal sense of the past participle. The statement: **ich habe den Schrank repariert,** *I have repaired the cupboard,* may be said to have a double force:

(1) A completed action, as in the normal perfect tense.

(2) The possession (**haben**) of an object (**den Schrank**) in a repaired, *i.e.* changed state (**repariert**).

(*b*) Thus in certain contexts, especially when modal verbs underline the sense of expectation, **haben** and past participle may have a force analogous to **lassen** and the infinitive:

Wir müssen den Kamin bis Ende des Monats gefegt haben, *we must have* (*had*) *the chimney swept by the end of the month.*

Ich möchte diesen Löffel versilbert haben, *I should like to have this spoon silvered.*

(*c*) The same construction may even, in this sense, have a force analogous to **bekommen** and the past participle [cp. § 214 (*a*)], and thus be a variant of the passive with dative verbs:

Die Weine wollte er (= **der Wirt**) **nicht bezahlt haben** (B. Werner), *the landlord did not want to be paid* (dat.) *for the wines.*

EXERCISE XXXVIII

A. Translate into ENGLISH:

    1. Auf einem Reklameplakat ist eine dreiteilige Platte mit Braten und Kartoffeln in Gesellschaft eines schäumenden Steinkrugs dargestellt (newsp.). 2. Die Rückseite (= des Schulhauses) war gegen einen steil

ansteigenden, eng bewaldeten Berg gelehnt (W. Speyer). 3. Er unterschied nur drei Arten von Menschen: Offiziere, Frauen und Zivilisten;
letztere eine körperlich unentwickelte, geistig verächtliche Klasse, der
von den Offizieren die Frauen und Töchter abgejagt wurden (R. Musil).
4. Sie haben die Gewißheit, daß es wirklich etwas Einmaliges ist, was Sie
geliefert bekommen (adv.). 5. In ihrem Salon mit den schönen Groß-
väterbildern und Großvätermöbeln bekam ich Tee vorgesetzt (H. Hesse).
6. Er war der kleinste von allen im Schulstaat. Er bekam deshalb auch
stets die lächerlichsten Aufgaben zugewiesen (W. Speyer). 7. Ein alter
Herr schiebt sich an den Schalter (= eines Wohnungsamtes), möchte
eine Wohnung zugewiesen erhalten (Simpl.). 8. Das Buch gehört auf
den Schreibtisch des Lehrers und des Schülers, des Geschäftsmannes und
des Büroangestellten (adv.). 9. Er (= *the new lodger*) ließ sich über
Heizung, Wasser, Bedienung und Hausordnung unterrichten (H. Hesse).
10. Er ließ sich gern was vorplaudern und plauderte selber gern (Th.
Fontane).

B. Translate into GERMAN:

1. When the letter is written, the envelope is addressed and the stamps
are usually stuck in the right-hand corner. 2. After the letter has been
posted it is sorted at the office and it will finally be delivered by the postman. 3. A fence has been placed round (**um,** acc.) the pond and continued as far as (**bis an,** acc.) the road. 4. Children ought not to go
(use **gehören**) to films of this kind. 5. The position of the temple is
delightful; it is built on a hill-top and surrounded by dark olive trees.
6. The journey in the boat was very uncomfortable as we were wedged
in a small space behind a pile of luggage. 7. I had (**bekommen**) the door
banged in my face. 8. We went into a shop together and looked at
gramophones and had records played over to us. 9. This matter was
brought up at the next meeting and discussed. 10. He had his books
sent regularly from a lending library in the town. 11. He was told to
deliver the beer-bottles at once. 12. She had her hair dyed black in order
to appear younger. 13. When she got to the shore she suddenly felt
herself being lifted up and carried into the boat. 14. He wanted to have
the book bound in red leather. 15. A bell is rung for meals and everyone
is expected to appear punctually.

CHAPTER XXXIX

219. Proper Names (2). Place-Names

(*a*) A large number of proper names, not personal, are themselves common nouns, and, therefore, have a recognisable gender, and may be used with article and inflection:

(1) Nations, parties, dynastic families, and similar collective groups: **der Däne, Italiener, Deutschnationale, Bourbone, Habsburger,** *v.* § 35.

(2) Months, days, seasons: **der Januar, Mittwoch, Frühling,** *v.* § 57.

(3) Place-names, *i.e.* natural, political, and administrative divisions of the earth's surface: **die Donau, das Rheinland, der Schillerplatz,** *v.* below.

(4) Quasi proper names, *i.e.* names of stars, ships, newspapers, books, works of art and scholarship: **der Uranus, die „Washington", das „Hamburger Tageblatt", der „Prinz von Homburg", der Apollo Belvedere, die Iliade, „Der Untergang des Abendlandes",** *v.* § 235.

Many of these present problems of gender, use of article, and inflection.

(*b*) Natural divisions:

(1) Names of islands and continents are neuter and take no article: **Europa, Asien, Kreta, Madagaskar.**

(2) All others take the article, which is masculine for all mountains [**der Brocken,** but *v.* § 439 (*a*)], and for some German and most foreign rivers (**der Inn, Main, Neckar, Rhein; der Amazonas,** after **der Strom**); but many German rivers are feminine (**die Ruhr, Weser**), as are also those foreign rivers which have (apparently) feminine endings (**die Wolga, Seine, Themse**), *v.* § 439 (*a*).

(*c*) Political Divisions:

(1) Major political divisions, as countries, regions, cities, do not as a rule take the article, and are neuter: **Deutschland, China, Libyen, Pakistan, Kapstadt, Köln.**

(2) But one city (**der Haag**) and a considerable number of regions, especially in Europe, take the article, and have various genders, often determined by the second element in a compound:

(i) Masculine: **der Sudan,** and compounds in **-gau,** as **der Rheingau, (Freiburg im) Breisgau;** but **-gäu** compounds, as **das Allgäu,** are neuter.

(ii) Feminine: **die Schweiz, Pfalz** (Palatinate), **Bretagne, Riviera;** words in **-ei,** as **die Türkei,** or **-au,** as **die Wachau;** compounds of **-mark,** as **die Altmark,** and the older term for Austria, revived by the Nazis: **die Ostmark.**

(iii) Neuter: **das Banat, Elsaß**; some compounds of **-land,** as **das Vogtland,** and (plural) **die Niederlande,** *the Netherlands;* but **Deutschland** takes no article [as (1) above].

220. Place-Names, Articles, and Plural

(*a*) All the above place-names take the definite article when modified, even if they do not do so normally: **das wieder erstandene Deutschland, das alte Köln, das nördliche München, das Berlin der Gründerzeit, das verhandlungsbereite China; das Europa, in dem er zu leben gezwungen war.**

Note.—**im Niemandsland,** *in No-man's-land.*

(*b*) The use of the place-name both unmodified and modified is commoner than in English:

(1) Local reference by common noun: in town, down by the river, up the mountain, is less common than: **wir waren heute in München, er wohnt direkt am Neckar, wir machten einen Ausflug auf den Venusberg,** even when the common noun reference would be quite clear.

(2) Modification by adjective or a following genitive phrase being commoner than in English, the uninflected proper name use is less common: **das China der Nachkriegszeit,** *China in the post-war years;* **das besetzte Berlin,** *Berlin under the occupation;* **das neuzeitliche Bolivien,** *Bolivia in the modern age;* **das sommerliche Italien,** *Italy in the summer* (or even, *summer in Italy*).

(*c*) The place-name, used in the plural, figuratively, is unchanged: **die zwei Amerika, die beiden Wien, das alte und das neue;** but in practice a compound is often used: **die beiden Englandgesichter,** *the two Englands* (lit. *faces of* . . .).

221. Place-Names, Genitive Inflection

(*a*) All those which are masculine or neuter, whether normally used with or without the article, also take the genitive **-s** when standing unmodified: **die Industriegebiete Deutschlands, die Bewohner Kölns, die Wirtschaft Bayerns, die Einwohner des Sudans.**

But no **-s** is added when a noun in apposition precedes and can take the genitive government: **der Verkehr der Großstadt Köln, die Erschließung des Erdteils Afrika, die Politik des Kantons Bern.**

(*b*) Between these two groups usage is uncertain:

(1) Place-names with unfamiliar endings *may* omit the genitive **-s: an den Ufern des Kongo, im Schatten des Vesuv.** But objection is raised to the extension of this practice to familiar names: **die beiden Ufer des Rhein.**

(2) Place-names of all kinds are often used without the genitive **-s** when preceded by an inflected adjective, though against strong opposition: **der Wiederaufbau des zerstörten Dresden, eine Ahnung des wirklichen England.**

Note.—Inflection of a sibilant is avoided by using **von** or a noun in apposition: **die Straßen Hamburgs,** but **von Paris,** or **der Stadt Olmütz.**

222. Administrative Divisions of Cities, Towns, etc.

(*a*) Areas and suburbs which have developed from independent names of villages, etc., are analogous to general place-names without the article, and are neuter: **Schwabing, das intellektuelle Schwabing; Wedding, das Wedding der Kommunisten.**

(*b*) Compounds of **-straße, -platz, -viertel,** etc., behave as normal nouns, as distinct from English, where they retain place-name status: **die Schellingstraße,** *Schelling Street;* **der Rathausplatz,** *Town Hall Square;* **das St. Pauli-Viertel,** *St Paul's.*

But when used adverbially such terms are largely stripped of their attributes: **ich wohne in der Schillerstraße,** but **ich wohne Schillerstraße 5; ich besuche einen Freund in der Nähe des Kriegerdenkmals,** but **Sie müssen Kriegerdenkmal** (stopping place) **aussteigen. Wir fahren bis Uhlandallee.**

223. Dative of Certain Pronouns

(*a*) The dative of certain neuter pronouns, as **dem** (demonstrative), and **wem** (interrogative, and indefinite relative), is commonly avoided, owing to possible confusion with the corresponding masculine forms (cp. § 195, genitive). When they are used, ambiguity is not far off:

Demonstrative and interrogative:

„Sie können doch nicht einfach fortgehen und mich dem überlassen." — **„Wem überlassen?"** — **„Dem, was dann kommen würde..."** (H. Risse), ... *abandon me to that?—To what?—To what will then come.*

Indefinite relative:

Wem Tante Alix in den Weg trat, das war wohl nicht einmal unsere Reiterei, ... nein, es war ... (W. Bergengruen), *but that to which Aunt Alix was opposed was not our riding, but ... (what ... disapproved of ...).*

(*b*) Such pronouns are thus commonly restricted to certain recognisable contexts, as for the demonstrative: the combination—**alldem, dem allem** [*v.* § 65 (*b*)]; idioms as **wie dem auch sei,** *whatever the truth may be in the matter;* **dem ist nicht abzuhelfen,** *there is nothing that can be done in this matter;* and **dem** when acting as back reference to an earlier statement:

Sie (= die Hirten) lebten wie in Zeiten, die weder Haus, noch Pflug, noch Webstuhl kannten . . . Dem entsprachen auch ihre Sitten (E. Jünger), *their habits were according (to this condition).*

and *v.* § 225 (*c*) for compounds of **dem,** of which **dementsprechend,** from contexts similar to the above example, is one.

224. Pronominal Adverbs (1) from Personal Pronouns

(*a*) It was noted in § 33 that, after certain prepositions, the personal and interrogative pronouns, when standing for things, form adverbial compounds, analogous to forms not unknown, though less common, in English: *therein,* **darin,** *wherewith?* **womit?**

These are called pronominal adverbs; the rules for compounding may now be given in greater detail and extended to other classes of pronouns.

(*b*) Prepositions other than those listed at § 33 do not enter into compounds with pronouns of non-personal reference, but take the full pronoun or borrow a demonstrative: **ohne den Schlüssel, ohne ihn; ohne das, infolge dessen;** *without* or *as a result of it (this).* These may, however, be *simply* compounded to *e.g.* **ohnedas, ohnedies,** *moreover,* and **infolgedessen,** *therefore.*

(*c*) Even those prepositions which commonly form pronominal compounds are often, perhaps increasingly, resolved into their component parts.

(1) In some cases clarity may be said to be assisted:

Auf dem Tisch lag eine rote Samtdecke und auf ihr stand eine Porzellanschale mit Birnen (H. Risse), *and on the latter stood . . .*

(2) Or a point of grammar requires the compound to be resolved:

Das Buch füllt eine durch es selbst erst fühlbar gewordene Lücke aus (book-review), *a gap which has been revealed by its own publication (= emphasis).*
und das Gnädige sah mit immer seltsameren Blicken auf es (W. Raabe), *looked with ever stranger glances at it (= a child,* **das arme Wesen).**

(3) But for others no specific reason can be adduced:

Sie zeigten sich als Männer, die ihren Beruf liebten und in ihm eine bewundernswerte Tüchtigkeit besaßen (R. Musil), *and showed admirable competence in it.*

Der Infinitiv nennt das Verb schlechthin. Aus ihm wird die substantivierte Verbform geleitet (East German Duden), *from it* (the infinitive) *is formed the infinitive noun.*

225. Pronominal Adverbs (2) from Demonstratives

(*a*) The compounds in **da(r)-** serve for both personal and demonstrative pronouns:

Ich kann nichts damit anfangen, *I can't do anything with it.*

Damit kann ich was anfangen, *I can do something with that.*

Demonstrative force is indicated in speech by accenting the first syllable (**dámit**), and the compound often takes the leading position. Thus accented, **darin, darunter,** etc., cannot be elided to **drin, drunter,** etc.

Compounds of **hier-** may be regarded as the specific pronominal adverbs from demonstratives (preposition and **dies-**), also with front-accent and not elided; but these are largely restricted to non-physical (legal and logical) contexts: **Hierunter verstehe ich . . ., Hiervon spreche ich noch nicht . . ., Hierin hat er recht . . .** *By this . . ., of that. . . ., in this . . .*

(*b*) The resolved form (preposition plus demonstrative) is preferred:

(1) Always when followed by a determining phrase:

Die Tische hatten weiße, leichtgeäderte Marmorplatten; auf der vor ihm stand ein Glas dunkles Bier (H. Broch), *on the one before him stood . . .*

(2) Commonly when followed by a determining clause:

Für das Glück kommt es sehr wenig auf das an, was man will, sondern nur darauf, daß man es erreicht (R. Musil), *happiness depends much less on what one wants than on one's achieving it.*

Note.—The compound is resolved before the determining clause **was . . .,** but retained before the gerundial clause **daß . . .** [cp. § 278 (*e*)].

(3) Increasingly in other contexts to retain the specific force of the demonstrative:

Er ging nach der Mahlzeit mit dem Mantel um die Schultern auf und ab und beschloß, sich vom dem heute nacht nicht mehr zu trennen (E. Schaper), *resolved not to part with the coat at least . . .*

(*c*) *Simple* compounds of demonstrative and preposition are widely used as standard adverbs: (i) genitive: **deshalb** and **deswegen,** *therefore;* (ii) dative preceding: **dementsprechend, demgemäß, demnach, demzufolge; dementgegen, demzuwider,** *according to* or *against that; thus* or *however;* (iii) dative following, including many conjunctions: **nachdem, seitdem, trotzdem, zudem, währenddem** (also **währenddessen**), cp. § 128, etc.

Note that these are all from neuter demonstratives; thus an apparently identical combination with different force may have to stand separately, thus:

Dem (= **dem Manne**) **gegenüber saß seine Tochter,** *opposite him,* but **demgegenüber,** *on the other hand.*

Der Plan, dem zufolge die Bergwerke wieder in Betrieb genommen werden sollen, *according to which the mines are to be put into commission again,* but **demzufolge,** *accordingly.*

226. Pronominal Adverbs (3) from Interrogatives

(*a*) Direct Questions, cp. § 33.

Womit (wozu) hat er das Haus gekauft? *with what? to what purpose?*

But colloquially, **was** is often used without distinction of case:

Ich habe ihn nicht gehört, über was hat er gesprochen? *what did he speak about?*

Was hat nichts mit was zu tun?   Title of a short excursion into popular (incorrect) etymology (H. Reimann).

Zu was die ganze Schererei? *what's all the trouble about?*

(*b*) Indirect Questions.

Man wird schon verstehen, worauf ich hinaus will, *what I am aiming at.*

Also **weshalb, weswegen,** cp. § 198.

In the indirect question, resolution of the accusative occurs, but not of the dative:

Ich konnte zunächst nicht entdecken, um was es sich handelte, *what it was all about.*

Es ist belanglos, worin das Verbrechen des jungen Menschen bestand (H. Risse), *it is irrelevant what the crime of the young man consisted of.*

Es ist mir noch nicht klar, wonach Sie mich fragen wollen, *not yet clear to me what you are asking me about.*

227. Pronominal Adverbs (4) from Relatives

(*a*) The normal relatives **der, die, das.**

An earlier general practice was to use the interrogative pronominal adverb also for relatives governed by prepositions:

Interrogative: **Ich weiß nicht, womit er das Haus gekauft hat,** *what ... with.*

Relative: **Das Geld, womit er das Haus gekauft hat,** *with which ...*

Though this is still considered standard practice, such compounds are increasingly avoided in favour of:

(1) The informal resolution into original preposition and relative:

wie (er) plötzlich von seinem Schemel auffuhr, auf dem er eine Zeitung lesend gesessen hatte (S. Andres), *on which he had been sitting ...*

des Vaters Grab, an das er niemals hatte denken wollen, und an das er nun doch denken mußte (H. Broch), *of which he had never wanted to think . .*

(2) The more formal and literary use of corresponding demonstrative compounds in **da(r)-**:

Manches, daran er sich noch erinnerte, kam ihm wie aus fremdem Munde gesprochen vor (E. Schaper), *much which he still remembered . . .*

das Gebiet, darin er die Gewalt erstrebte (E. Jünger), *in which he aimed at seizing power.*

(*b*) The general relative **was.**

(1) After the neuter adjective-pronouns as antecedents.

The general practice until recently was to use the interrogative pronominal adverbs with prepositions as a corollary to the use of **was** when no preposition is present:

Alles, was ich geglaubt hatte . . .   Alles, woran ich geglaubt hatte . . . (hat sich als falsch erwiesen).

However, **was** is being increasingly displaced by **das** after **alles, etwas, nichts, das einzige,** etc. (but not after **das,** *v.* below), and the two forms alternate even within the same writer with little but sound and rhythm to indicate a preference.

In prepositional uses, this results in the increasing use of the two forms illustrated in (*a*) (1) and (2), thus:

Alles, an das ich geglaubt hatte . . . or Alles, daran . . .

Some writers, however, while substituting **das** for **was** in simple forms, prefer the **wo-** compounds to the **da-** compounds:

Und ist Arbeit bloß etwas, worunter man schmachtet und das man ungern tut und wofür man unzureichend bezahlt wird? (H. Broch), *something under which . . . and which . . . and for which . . .*

And there is general agreement that **das, was** is preferable to **das, das,** but that if pronoun and relative are separated, the interrogative form [cp. § 177 (*b*) (1)] should not be used:

Nichts von dem, *um das* die Leute sich streiten, hat Bedeutung. Wo ist denn noch ein Unterschied zwischen dem, *was* man konservativ nennet, und dem, *was* sich für fortschrittlich hält? (W. Bergengruen), *that which people fight about . . . what people call . . . and what is considered . . .*

(2) But where there is no explicit antecedent [cp. §§ 176, 177 (*c*)] **wo(r)-** compounds must be retained:

General relative:

Sie wird sich installieren können, wonach ihr der Sinn steht (Th. Mann), *she will be able to fit up her home as she wishes.*

Wozu einer Veranlagung hat, das sieht man am besten aus seinem Spiel, *where a man's talents lie is best seen in his choice of pastimes.*

Referring to sense of preceding passage; here **wobei,** *in which, where,* and **worauf,** *whereupon,* are common:

Durch das Tälchen schlich ein kleiner Bach, wobei das Wort Bach zu viel Ehre für diesen mäßigen Wasserlauf ist (F. Werfel), . . . *but the word stream is too much honour for . . .*

And similarly in book titles after the older English model:

Zweites Kapitel

Worin ich meinem Freund B.H. begegne (F. Werfel), *Chapter Two, in which . . .*

EXERCISE XXXIX

A. Translate into ENGLISH:

1. Gott hat uns die Erde gegeben, um sie zu beherrschen und auf ihr glücklich zu sein (H. Risse). 2. Die Lampe auf dem Tisch, an dem ich tagsüber zu sitzen pflegte, brannte; ein Buch war vor sie gestellt (H. Risse). 3. Er sprang auf und ging mit großen Schritten um den Arbeitstisch, darauf das Modell der Festung stand (S. Andres). 4. Im Umgang mit dem rauhen Volke lernte man auch das Gute kennen, das ihm zu eigen war (E. Jünger). 5. Das, wodurch man sich verdient macht, ist das Verdienst; *der* Verdienst ist das, was man verdient (auch wenn man es manchmal nicht verdient, so viel zu verdienen), (quoted from E. Schairer, *Funf Minuten Deutsch*). 6. Wovon uns erzählt wird, daß es um Franziskus (= von Assisi) geschah, ist nicht „Legende", sondern Wirklichkeit (R. Guardini). 7. Aber nicht Wissen und Verstehen war es, was mir not tat, wonach ich mich so verzweifelt sehnte, sondern Erleben (H. Hesse). 8. Ist dein Leben nicht so fest in ihr verankert, daß du nichts tun kannst, an dem sie nicht teil hat? (W. Bergengruen). 9. Etwas muß in mir sein, das ihn anzieht, etwas, das ihm ähnlich, vertraut ist. Oder das Gegenteil, auch das ist möglich, etwas, das er entbehrt (S. Andres). 10. Es war darin (= in seiner Art) etwas beinahe Rührendes, etwas wie Flehendes, wofür ich erst später die Erklärung fand, das mich aber sofort ein wenig für ihn einnahm (H. Hesse).

B. Translate into ENGLISH, using pronominal adverbs where possible:

1. Switzerland remained neutral during the last war. 2. The source of the Elbe is now behind the Iron Curtain. 3. Eighteenth century Germany was not a political unity. 4. He told us not to visit him, and accordingly we refrained (from it). 5. A house is no longer a home when one gives up living in it. 6. With what (translate two ways) do you polish your furniture? 7. What is ink made of? I can't really answer (to) that. 8. I didn't understand where I was to go. 9. What are you two laughing about? 10. Nothing that you have once learnt can disappear completely from your mind—it only seems like-it (so).

CHAPTER XL

228. Special Relatives in Certain Contexts

(*a*) Certain relative clauses, when following an antecedent noun which expresses place, time, manner, or degree, may function as adverbial clauses. In these cases certain adverbial conjunctions or compounds take the place of, or are sometimes alternative to, the normal relative forms.

(*b*) Place: **wo, woher, wohin,** *where, from where, to where.*

die Gegend, wo wir uns befanden, *the area, in which we were* . . .

die Stadt, wohin ich übersiedelte, *the town, to which I moved* . . .

der ländliche Ort, woher meine Familie kam, *the place in the country, from which my family came.*

and in figurative contexts: **Fälle, wo . . .,** *cases, in which . . .,* or after an adverb of place: **unten, wo . . . dorthin, wo . . .**

The normal relative is also used: **die Gegend, in der . . .;** but less commonly when motion to or from is described (cp. examples above); and never when the antecedent is a place-name:

Berlin, wohin ich am Anfang des Krieges meine Familie brachte . . ., *Berlin, to which I took my family . . .*

The particle may be prefixed to the verb in less formal usage:

die Stadt, wo ich herkomme, *from which I come.*

A more emphatic form for **wo,** with an antiquated air, is **woselbst:**

im Eßsaal, woselbst die Einsegnung stattfand (Th. Mann), *in the dining-room, where the funeral service took place.*

In accordance with the use described in § 227 (*a*) (2), a more elevated style might have **daher, dahin** for **woher, wohin.**

(*c*) Time: **da, wenn, als, wo, daß,** *when, in* (*on*) *which.*

Da is by far the commonest conjunction after nouns and adverbs of time: **in dem Alter, da . . . zu einer Zeit, da . . . die Tage, da . . . in dem Augenblick, da . . . Nächte, da . . . in der Sekunde noch, da . . .; nun, da . . . jetzt, da . . .** (both *now that*); **unlängst, da . . .** (*recently when . . .*).

Wir dachten auch an die lichten Tage, da der Arno stahlfarben erscheint (W. Bergengruen), *those bright days when . . .*

The resolved relative is also often found with nouns:

die Zeit, in der . . . Stunden, in denen . . . seit dem Tag, an dem . . .
Ich kann sogar den Zeitpunkt angeben, in dem (das Gefühl) auftrat (H. Risse), *I can even give the moment in which . . .*

288

Compared with these two constructions, **wo,** earlier common, has greatly receded, reflecting perhaps the success of purists who have strongly opposed the mixing of place and time, so that **in dem Alter, wo . . . die Zeit, wo,** etc., are now comparatively rare.

The success of **da** is measured by the fact that it is now invading contexts of place:

das Land, da keinem Rittmeister zu begegnen ist (W. Bergengruen), *the country where there are no captains of horse.*

The time conjunctions **wenn** and **als** are equivalent to relatives when the clause they introduce follows immediately on an adverb of time, thus:

Jedesmal, wenn er ankam, spielten seine Freunde Klavier (R. Musil), *every time he came . . .*

im Jahre 1935, als ich in Heidelberg studierte . . . *in 1935, when . . .*

Daß may be used in certain cases, especially after **Mal, Zeit,** but is less common than other words: **das letzte Mal, daß (als) . . .; die Zeit, daß (während, in der);** and **da** may be used in all these cases.

(*d*) Manner and Degree:

Manner: **die Art und Weise, wie . . .** (or **in der**), *the way in which . . .*

Degree: **in gleichem Maße, als . . . in dem Maße, wie . . .,** *to the same degree in which . . .*

229. Demonstratives. The Genitives Dessen, Deren

(*a*) Prominent among the uses of the genitive forms **dessen** (masc. and neut.) and **deren** (fem. and plur.), *v.* §§ 65, 195-6, are those in which the demonstrative acts as a simple reference back to person(s) or thing(s) previously mentioned. It is usually an alternative to other pronominal forms:

(1) Partitive sense, with a numeral following:

Der Leser wird sich wundern, statt keines oder eines Motto deren sechs zu finden (W. Bergengruen), *the reader will be surprised to find, instead of one dedicatory motto or none at all, six (of them)* (**ihrer sechs**).

(2) Possessive sense, with a noun following:

Engelke, noch um ein Jahr älter als sein Herr, war dessen Vertrauter geworden, aber ohne Vertraulichkeit (Th. Fontane), *had become his (the latter's) confidant, but without intimacy* (= **sein Vertrauter**).

(*b*) The grammatical value of **dessen, deren,** in (2) above, is that they refer to the last mentioned person, and not, as would the possessive, to the subject of the sentence, and thus have the sense *the latter*, avoiding ambiguity:

Er brachte den Gast und dessen Frau an den Bahnhof, *the guest and his* (*the guest's*, not **seine,** which could mean *the host's*) *wife.*

Most agree with the critics that the excessive use of **dessen** in legal, etc., language is to be condemned:

Die Schrift ist mit der Unterschrift des Klägers oder dessen Stellvertreters zu versehen, *the document must be signed by the plaintiff or his representative* (= **seines Stellvertreters**).

But many reputable writers use this form in circumstances which make it technically correct but unnecessary:

Er haßt und verachtet den Vater und wünscht dessen Tod (R. Guardini), *and wishes his father's death* (no ambiguity).

Oft sind die Bezeichnungen Aktiv und Passiv oder deren deutsche Übersetzung Tätigkeitsform und Leideform nicht zutreffend (East German Duden), *the terms active and passive or their German versions* . . . (desire to avoid **ihre** for things).

The student is advised to avoid this use completely unless definite ambiguity would result.

230. Demonstratives (3).   Derselbe, etc., *the same, the latter.*

(*a*) **Derselbe (dieselbe, dasselbe),** *the same,* is a definite article and weak adjective (**derselbe Mann**), also used pronominally in emphatic contexts (**derselbe,** *the same, that person, he*); it is perhaps due to its pronominal use that it is written as a compound, even when functioning adjectivally.

(1) Adjectivally:

Sie hat jeden Tag denselben Hut auf, *wears the same hat every day.*

A preposition which contracts with the definite article (*v.* § 30) may do so with **derselbe** provided the compound is resolved into its parts: **im selben Tonfall, im selben Maße, am selben Tage.** Some prefer to retain the compound and preposition separately: **an demselben Tage.** Accusative contractions are rare:

Doch das gehört auf ein anderes Blatt—Nein, aufs selbe (H. Broch), *that's another matter—No, the same.*

Other limiting adjectives are not compounded with **selb-:**

„Kapitulation ausgeschlossen!" sagte dieser selbe Chef jetzt (Th. Plievier), *said this same commander now.*

(2) Pronominally:

The commonest use, for *the latter*, is an incorrect one and should be replaced by a pronoun or possessive:

Ich bekam seinen Bericht und las denselben sofort, *and read it immediately* (= **ihn**).

Er interessierte sich für alles, was die Stadt und die Verwaltung derselben anging, *everything which concerned the town and its administration* (= **ihre**).

The latter, genitive use, is parallel with the incorrect use of **dessen, deren,** for the possessive, *v.* § 229 (*b*).

A justified use is to render the dignity of royalty:

Seine Majestät hörte das sichtlich gern. Dieselbe saß bequem zurückgelehnt (Th. Mann), *His Majesty* (fem. reference) *sat back comfortably* . . .

(*b*) **Derselbe,** compounded and meaning *one and the same*, is now seldom correctly distinguished from **der** (etc.) **gleiche,** *the same* in the meaning *similar*: **wir sind am selben** (not **am gleichen**) **Tag geboren.**

Thus H. Kasack has:

Etwa zu der gleichen Stunde saß Sandberg (= **zu derselben**). **Auch Lukas war des gleichen Vergehens beschuldigt worden** (= **desselben,** or, if intended, **eines ähnlichen Vergehens,** *a similar crime*).

231. Demonstratives (4). So, solch-, etc., *so, such* (*a*), etc.

(*a*) The demonstratives of manner, corresponding to English *so, such* (*a*), etc., are (i) **so,** as adverb, *so, like this* (*that*), and (ii) **so** or **solch-** in a variety of contexts before nouns and pronouns, and in pronominal use. They may be purely demonstrative in force (pointing out), or may express quality or intensity of degree, often in an exclamatory manner.

(*b*) **So,** the demonstrative adverb of manner, corresponds less to *so, thus* in English, than to *like this* (*that*), *in this way* (*manner*), *of this kind* (*nature*):

So muß man die Sache in die Hand nehmen, *that is how one must tackle the job.*

So sind eben die Menschen, *that's just how people are.*

v. also § 202 (**so daß, so . . . daß**), and § 232 below.

(*c*) **Solch-** is used as an adjective or pronoun.

Adjectivally it is inflected like the indefinite **manch** (§§ 102, 145-6) and the indefinite and interrogative **welch** (§ 132), *i.e.*:

(1) Uninflected always before **ein** (**solch ein schlechter Mensch**), and sometimes before a descriptive adjective (**solch hübsche Bilder**).

(2) In other contexts inflected strong or weak as a descriptive adjective: **ein solcher Unsinn, solche Menschen, das Empörende solcher Sitten, ich bin kein solcher Schuft, solcher Mut, solche Härte!.**

Note.—Like the indefinites it may take the weak or strong form when standing alone before a noun in the masculine or neuter genitive [cp. § 146 (*b*)]: **müde solches (solchen) Arbeitens.**

(3) Usually strong after indefinites: **einige solche Leute;** but **viele solche** or **solcher** (gen.) **Bücher;** a following descriptive adjective is strong or weak: **solche nette(n) Menschen.**

(*d*) **Solch-** is used pronominally, especially in the plural, **solche,** followed by a determining genitive or relative clause, in the sense of *ones, those*:

eine Menge von Beispielen, darunter solchen absonderlichster Art . . .,
a mass of examples, including some of the most peculiar type, kind.
Die alte Fehde zwischen denen, die auf Schusters Rappen reiten, und solchen, die das nicht nötig haben (Simpl.), *those who go on Shanks's pony, and those who do not have to.*

Solche here is a definite pronoun corresponding to the indefinite **welche** (*v.* § 103), from which it is distinguished by its use with a following determining statement. It may be replaced by other terms, as *e.g.* **einige** (first example above), or the compound **diejenigen** (second example), and the latter [cp. further, § 292 (*a*)] commonly stands for **solch-** in the singular:

Die Mundart des Nordens ist ganz verschieden von derjenigen des Südens, *is quite distinct from that of the South.*

232. Demonstratives (4). So for solch-

Solch- forms are often replaced in informal language by various combinations of **so.**

(*a*) **So** and the indefinite article; adjectivally: **so ein Mann, so'ne Frau, mit so'nem schönen Wagen;** and pronominally: **So eine redet Sie in zehn Minuten verrückt,** *a woman like that would talk you out of your mind in ten minutes.*

Various nuances implicit in all demonstratives of manner are well shown in the use of so for **solch-,** *e.g.*:

(1) Pointing out (demonstrative proper):

Ich möchte so ein (so'n) Dings haben, zum Büchsenöffnen . . ., *I want one of those things you open tins with . . .*

(2) Approximation:

Ich habe so ein (so'n) Gefühl, daß da alles nicht ganz in Ordnung ist, *I have a kind of feeling that . . .*

(3) Exclamation:

So ein schlimmer Bubi! *What a naughty boy!* (cajoling).

Thus distinguish **So eine freche Miene!** *Such an impertinent look!* from **Eine so freche Miene, daß ich nichts mehr sagen konnte,** *such an impertinent look that . . .*

The plural often occurs in senses (1) and (2):

Überall im Hause hatte sie so kleine Nippsachen liegen, *all over the house she had trinkety kinds of things lying around.*

(*b*) **So etwas, so was** stands for the neuter pronoun **ein solches,** *such a thing*:

So etwas kommt nicht alle Tage vor, *it's not every day that such a thing happens.*

So was muß immer mir passieren, *things like that always have to happen to me.*

In a derogatory and collective sense for persons:

„Und so etwas will Journalist werden," **stöhnte Münzer** (E. Kästner), *and this is what we are supposed to make a journalist of.*

So etwas, like **etwas,** may be followed by an adjective-noun, as **so etwas Ähnliches,** *something (rather) similar.*

(*c*) **So etwas, so was** followed by the partitive **von** becomes a further (colloquial) equivalent for **solch-** with a noun:

So was von Frechheit, Gemeinheit, Unsinn! *What impudence, vulgarity, nonsense!*

So etwas von Kreuzgang ist mir noch nicht vorgekommen (Th. Mann), *I have never seen such a (fine specimen of a) cloister.*

In this sense it is often associated with its opposite, **nichts von,** *not* or *no*:

Der (Palazzo) hätte bis zum Jüngsten Tag ausgehalten—nichts von Einsturzgefahr—bei sowas von Mauern (S. Andres), *no danger of collapsing with walls like that.*

233. Demonstratives (4). The translation of *such as.*

(*a*) The expression *such as* combines a demonstrative and a relative: A sunset, such as one only sees in Mediterranean countries (= of a kind which . . .).

German uses **wie,** *as,* with repetition of a pronoun standing for the antecedent in the subordinate clause:

(1) Subject and object: the third person pronoun:

Hütten aus grobem Schilf, wie sie zur Entenjagd errichtet werden (E. Jünger), *huts of coarse reeds such as are set up . . .*

ein Sonnenuntergang, wie man ihn nur am Mittelmeer erlebt, *such as . . .*

(2) Complement: the pronoun **einer, eine, eines:**

Ich bin kein Sportsmann, wie mein Bruder einer war, *I am not a sportsman, (such) as my brother was.*

usually with **auch** added after a positive:

Er wurde Rechtsanwalt, wie sein Vater auch einer gewesen war, *as his father had been before him.*

(*b*) Other forms are sometimes found:

(1) A demonstrative of quality or degree in the first part:

Es gibt ziemlich viele Menschen von ähnlicher Art, wie Harry einer war, viele Künstler namentlich gehören dieser Art an (H. Hesse), *there are many people like Harry . . .*

(2) The invariable pronoun **dergleichen** (*v.* § 234) in the second part:

Auf der Brücke standen Handwerkerbuden, wie man dergleichen sonst nur in östlichen Ländern sieht, *such as one otherwise sees only . . .*

Note.—Distinguish *such as* from *such that,* as **er schreib einen solchen** (or **derartigen,** *v.* § 234) **Unsinn, daß . . .,** *such nonsense, that . . .*

234. Stereotyped Pronominal Compounds

There are a certain number of stereotyped pronominal compounds which have quasi-demonstrative force, and because of their origin are often used undeclined in the adjectival position. They mostly express the general sense of *the like.*

(*a*) **-gleichen** (invar., cp. English, *the likes of . . .*) combines with the genitive forms of certain pronouns, etc.:

(1) Possessive adjective, thus **meinesgleichen,** *one of my kind, type:*

„Still!" befahl sie. „Ihresgleichen schwört kalten Blutes sogar vor Gericht" (E. Wiechert), *one of your stamp would swear in cold blood even before a law court.*

(2) Demonstrative pronoun: **desgleichen** (sing.), but more commonly **dergleichen** (plur.), used by extension for all cases singular and plural, *of such a kind (nature), such like, the like,* etc.:

Dergleichen Menschen gehören doch ins Gefängnis, *people like that ought to be in prison.*

Cp. § 233 (*b*), in the sense *such as.*

Note.—Also with the two prepositions **ohne** and **sonder** (older form), *without*, in the sense *without an equal*: **eine Frechheit ohnegleichen, eine Last sondergleichen,** *an unparalleled impertinence, burden.*

(*b*) Other compounds. **Derlei** and **derart,** both with the genitive demonstrative, are used like **dergleichen: derlei Menschen, derart Eltern,** *such people, parents.* For -**lei** compounds, *v.* § 154. **Derart,** from **der** (gen.) **Art,** *of that kind,* as **ein Mann der Art (von der Art, von solcher Art),** *a man of such a kind,* has several uses:

(1) Adverbially: **das Kind hat derart geschrieen, daß . . .,** *the child screamed so much, that . . .* (= **so, so viel,** etc.).

(2) Pronominally, after **etwas, nichts,** etc., or alone:
etwas (nichts) Derartiges (or derart), *something (nothing) of that kind (sort).*
Derart wäre noch manches auszuführen (R. Guardini), *one could add many more details of this kind.*
derartiges [small initial, *v.* § 148 (*b*)], as in **Gefälligkeiten und derartiges,** *compliments and such like.*

(3) Adjectivally in the lengthened and inflected form **derartig,** with the sense of **solch-** (or **so ein**):
Er schrieb einen derartigen Unsinn, daß ich den Aufsatz nicht zu Ende lesen konnte, *he wrote such nonsense that . . .*

(*c*) **Unsereins** (invar.), *a person like me (us),* compounded of **eins** and the genitive pronoun; but more commonly in the masculine form and declined: **unsereiner, mit unsereinem,** (*with*) *people like us.* Note that **unsereiner** never has the literal sense *one of us* (= **einer von uns, unter uns**).

EXERCISE XL

A. Translate into ENGLISH:

1. Der Schüler Christian Buddenbrook durfte eines Abends mit einem guten Freunde das Stadttheater besuchen, woselbst „Wilhelm Tell" von Schiller gegeben wurde (Th. Mann). 2. Es hatte damals schon die Zeit begonnen, wo man von Genies des Fußballrasens oder des Boxrings zu sprechen anhob (R. Musil). 3. Zum wirklichen Leiden, zur Hölle wird das menschliche Leben nur da, wo zwei Zeiten, zwei Kulturen und Religionen einander überschneiden (H. Hesse). 4. . . . vorbei waren die glorreichen Zeiten, da die Esterhazys einen Haydn beherbergten (S. Zweig). 5. Übrigens habe ich in Genf kein Stammcafé gehabt, wie in Florenz, sondern deren ein kräftiges Dutzend (W. Bergengruen). 6. Es war auch von ihrem Neffen die Rede, und sie zeigte mir in

einem Nebenzimmer dessen neueste Feierabendarbeit, einen Radio-
apparat (H. Hesse). 7. Die Wissenschaft des fünfzehnten Jahrhunderts
ist eine solche des Bewährens und Tradierens, keine eines eignen neuen
Schaffens (W.-E. Peuckert). 8. Die Klause stand am Rande der Marmor-
Klippen, immitten einer der Felsen-Inseln, wie man sie hier und dort das
Rebenland durchbrechen sieht (E. Jünger). 9. „No, wie gehts?"—„Wie
es unsereinem eben jetzt gehen kann, in dieser Zeit . . ." (L. Frank).
10. Alles ging ihm so selbstverständlich von der Hand wie einem Tier
das Laufen; sogar seine schlechten Manieren hätte unsereiner sich nicht
erlauben dürfen (= *could not have* . . .), ihn kleideten sie (F. Thiess).

B. Translate into GERMAN:

1. The town to which he was going was quite unknown to him.
2. We fear the days when the air-force station sends jet-planes out on
practice flights. 3. There were many long hours when he battled against
his mood of despair. 4. The first time (add relative) I saw her she was
running to catch a train. 5. There were a lot of pets of this kind on (**auf**)
the farm, especially cats; I believe there were eight of them. 6. Twins
often wear the same [*v.* § 230 (*b*)] clothes, which makes it difficult for
people-like-ourselves to distinguish them. 7. It is (an) unparalleled
stupidity to marry such a girl. 8. I'm very sorry that a thing-like-that
has happened to such an intelligent man. Such people are often unlucky
in marriage. 9. I should like one of those [*v.* § 232 (*a*)] new reading-lamps.
10. He showed courage such as is rarely seen. 11. She had a Christmas
(-feast) of unclouded happiness such as she had not experienced since
her childhood. 12. He found it hard to make friends with people of his
own type [*v.* § 234 (*a*)].

CHAPTER XLI

235. Proper Names (3). Quasi-Proper Names

Certain difficulties are presented by personal names and common nouns applied as names or titles to planets, ships, newspapers, books, plays, etc.; these are here referred to as quasi-proper names.

(*a*) Planets are masculine, and are used with or without the article: **(der) Mars, (der) Saturn, (der) Uranus**; but the article is required in oblique cases: **gibt es Menschen auf dem Mars?**

(*b*) Ships are, by recent practice derived from English usage, feminine: **die „Washington", die „Kassel", die „Deutschland"**; but the article may be omitted. The verb is always singular, whatever the apparent number of the name: **die „United States" ist Träger des Blauen Bandes** (newsp.). In an oblique case, a descriptive noun is often added in apposition, thus: **Eisenhower konferiert an Bord der „Helena"** (newsp.), but the dispatch was headed: **An Bord des Kreuzers „Helena".**

An older practice was for the name to have natural gender (neuter for place-names, etc.): **der „Panther", der „Albatros", die Ankunft des „Cap d'Ancona"**; or the analogy of **der Dampfer, das Schiff,** may be invoked to explain such occasional deviations.

(*c*) Names of newspapers have gender and number according to the (apparent) sense of the title; but a singular verb is often used for a plural subject: **die „Welt", das „Stuttgarter Tagblatt"; „Die Times"** (or **„Times"**) **schreiben ... (schreibt ...); der „Simplicissimus", der „März".**

(*d*) With books, plays, etc., there is often uncertainty whether title or construction should be preserved in its integrity, thus: **eine Aufführung des „Hauptmanns von Köpenick"**, or **von „Der Hauptmann von Köpenick"**?

(1) It is correct to inflect such names, leaving a definite article in an oblique case outside inverted commas (if placed): **ein Leitartikel im „Neuen Journal", Thomas Manns Stil in den „Buddenbrooks".** It is felt as particularly objectionable to preserve the title against the construction by causing a nominative to follow a preposition, especially in speech where inverted commas are not perceptible; thus not: **Sie hören nun die Ouvertüre zu „Der Zigeunerbaron".**

(2) But the following compromises are accepted:

Title in accusative if form is same as nominative:

    Ich habe Wassermanns „Das Gänsemännchen" gelesen.

Reversion to nominative if an appositional noun is inserted:

Der Mann, dem ich den Namen „Der letzte Rittmeister" gegeben habe . . .
(W. Bergengruen), *the man to whom I have given the name "The Last Captain of Horse"* (title of book).

in dem Lustspiel „Die Soldaten"; eine Aria aus der Oper „Der Barbier von Sevilla".

(3) If the author's name precedes in the genitive, a definite article in the title should be omitted: **Schillers „Räuber", in Mozarts „Zauberflöte".**

(*e*) The omission of the genitive -s which was noted with names, especially those with titles (*v.* §§ 156, 221), is spreading, against opposition, to quasi-proper names, such as: ships (**die Ankunft des „Cap d'Ancona"**, above), business names (**die Aktionäre des „Norddeutschen Lloyd"**), and newspaper names (**Chefredakteur des „Badischen Tagblatt"**).

236. Conditional Clauses

(*a*) The commonest conditional conjunction is **wenn,** which is followed by a verb in

(1) The indicative for "open conditions", *i.e.* those which have already or are likely to come about:

Wenn ich gekommen bin, so nur, um dich sofort wegzuholen, *if I have come it is only to . . .*

Wenn er kommt, werden wir zusammen den Ausflug machen, *if he comes we shall go on the excursion together.*

(2) The (imperfect) subjunctive (or a modal verb as substitute) for "unreal conditions", *i.e.* those whose materialisation is improbable or in doubt:

Wenn er käme (kommen sollte), würden wir zusammen . . ., *if he were to come we should . . .*

Note.—Both main and subordinate clause must have the same mood, indicative or subjunctive. For conditional subjunctive *v.* §§ 429 f. Only indicative statements are considered here.

(*b*) Possible variants in conditional and main statement:

(1) A conditional clause may omit the conjunction, taking front position of the verb (question order), and

(2) A main clause following the condition may be introduced by an adverb (**so** or **dann**):

Kommt er, so (or **dann**) **werden wir zusammen ausgehen.**

Note.—The order is here: first, conditional clause; second, main verb **werden**; linking adverbs do not affect the order.

(*c*) Possible variants for **wenn.**

Wenn with present indicative for present or future time also means *when, whenever* [*e.g.* example in (*a*) (1), *when he comes we shall . . .*]. Thus other conjunctions for conditional statements are often to be preferred; they emphasise some aspect of the condition:

(1) Contingency, *in case*, **falls, im Falle** (or **im Falle, daß . . .**), **für den Fall, daß . . .** (the last only following the main clause):

Falls (im Falle, daß) er verreist ist, schicke ich ihm den Brief nach, *in case he has gone away I will send the letter on.*

Ich schicke ihm eine Postkarte für den Fall, daß wir ihn nicht mehr zu Hause antreffen, *I will send him a P.C. in case we . . .*

(2) Provision, *provided that*, **vorausgesetzt, daß . . .**, *on condition that*, **unter der Bedingung (Voraussetzung), daß . . .**

Vorausgesetzt, daß Sie damit einverstanden sind, unterschreibe ich den Vertrag, *provided you are agreed I will sign the contract.*

(3) Assumption, *granted that, supposing that*, **angenommen, (daß),** **unter der Annahme, daß . . . :**

Angenommen, er hat das Geld gestohlen, was tun wir dann? *Supposing he did steal the money, what do we do then?*

(4) Sole condition, **nur wenn, bloß wenn,** *only if*:

Nur wenn die Unterlagen in Ordnung sind, kann ich ihn entlasten, *I can only give him his discharge if the books are in order.*

Note.—*Only when* is **erst wenn**, *v.* § 125 (*b*).

(*d*) Negative conditions are introduced by **wenn nicht,** or **außer wenn,** *unless*, the latter usually following:

Wenn er nicht bis morgen da ist, müssen wir allein vorgehen, *unless he is here by to-morrow we must proceed alone.*

Ich bin sicher bis vier Uhr da, außer wenn es regnet, *I shall be there* (*here*) *by four for certain, unless it rains.*

(*e*) An English gerund after *in case of* needs a full clause in German:

In case of his arriving too soon . . . **Im Falle, daß er . . .**

On condition of her completing the work . . . **Unter der Bedingung, daß sie . . .**

237. Other Constructions with Conditional Force

(*a*) The conditional clause may be replaced by other statements with conditional force:

(1) The imperative (*v.* §§ 247 f.):

Sag das noch einmal, so kriegst du Haue, *say that once more and I'll smack you.*

(2) Conditional prepositions, such as **bei, unter,** etc., *v.* § 528.

(3) A participial construction in apposition:

Allzu straff gespannt, zerspringt der Bogen, *bent too far, the bow breaks* (or: *it's the last straw that breaks* . . .).

(*b*) Many clauses introduced by a general relative contain a concealed condition:

Wer gut schmert (= **schmiert**), **der gut fährt,** (lit.) *if you want to travel in comfort you must grease the wheels* (*i.e.* bribe your way).

(*c*) A condition precedent is often expressed by a time statement, *not before, only when,* etc.; cp. especially **bevor** (§ 124) and **bis** (§ 125).

(*d*) Many abbreviated statements, especially proverbial in nature, which express a consequence, may also be regarded as conditional in force:

Ende gut, alles gut. *All's well that ends well.*

Viele Brüder, schmale Güter. *Many mouths make small portions.*

Verrohte Eltern—verwahrloste Kinder (newsp. headline), *vice in the parents makes for neglect of the children.*

238. Concessive Clauses

The concessive clause has two forms: (1) a milder form with **obgleich,** *although,* etc.; (2) a firmer form, with terms corresponding to English compounds of -*ever.* Only the former is properly "concessive", the latter is more aggressive in tone.

(*a*) The milder concessive statement.

Obgleich, *although,* is the commonest concessive conjunction, and has many synonyms: **obwohl, obschon, wenngleich** (or separated: **wenn er gleich** . . .), **wenn auch, selbst wenn,** *even if*:

Obgleich sein Vater es ihm verboten hatte, ging er ins Kino, *although his father had forbidden it, he went to the pictures.*

Selbst wenn ich das kann, werde ich es doch nicht für ihn tun, *even if I can, I shall not do it for him.*

Trotzdem is an adverb from **trotz dem**, *in spite of that*, as is **seitdem** from **seit**, and **nachdem** from **nach** (*v.* § 128), and is thus used as an adversative adverbial conjunction:

Sein Vater verbot es, trotzdem ging er, *but he went all the same*.

It is also now widely used, though against opposition, as a subordinating conjunction with concessive force, elbowing out **obgleich** by reason of its stronger tone:

Trotzdem sein Vater es verboten hatte, ging er ins Kino.

(*b*) As with the conditional statement [*v.* § 236 (*c*)] certain variants are possible in concessive and main clause:

(1) A concessive clause may omit the conjunction **obgleich**, and especially **wenn** (but leaving **auch**), taking question order, and

(2) A main clause following the concession may be introduced by **so** or strengthened by the adversative adverbs **doch, dennoch, trotzdem, gleichwohl**, etc., in a later position:

Hat es der Vater auch verboten, so werde ich doch (dennoch, etc.) hingehen.

(*c*) An English gerund after *in spite of* needs a full clause in German:

In spite of his having arrived late . . . **Obgleich er** . . .

(*d*) Clauses with **obgleich, trotzdem**, etc., take the indicative, but those with **wenn auch, selbst wenn**, being strengthened conditions, take the subjunctive if the supposition is unreal:

Selbst wenn ich das könnte, würde ich es doch nicht für ihn tun, *even if I could (even were I able), I would not* . . . [*v.* 429 (*b*)].

239. Concessive Clauses. The Firmer Concessive Statement

(*a*) The firmer concessive statement involves a strengthening of both concessive and main statement. The force is one of disjunction rather than conjunction, so that the speaker, far from wishing to minimise the sense of opposition, has every reason to emphasise it:

Milder: Although his father had forbidden it, he went to the pictures.
Firmer: Whatever my father says afterwards, I shall go to the pictures.

(*b*) The concessive statement is strengthened by using an interrogative with the generalised force noted under general and indefinite relatives (*whoever, whatever, v.* § 176), supported by the adverbs **auch** or **auch immer**:

Was ich auch sagen wollte, er blieb unerbittlich, *whatever I said, he would not be persuaded.*

**Er sagte nichts, aber wo man sich auch versteckte im Raum, von überall
sah man seine Augen** (E. Wiechert), *wherever one hid in the room, one
always saw his eyes.*

Two kinds of concession have special conjunctions:

(1) Degree: *however* with adjective or adverb (*however ugly he may
be . . . well she may sing . . .*) may have the generalised interrogative
wie . . . auch (immer), but **so (soviel,** etc.) is also common:

Wie häßlich der Hund auch sein mag, sie liebt ihn, *however ugly the dog
may be . . .,* or: **So häßlich er auch ist . . .**

**Diese Andeutungen, so dunkel sie klangen, waren doch jedermann
verständlich** (E. Wiechert), *these hints, no matter how mysterious they
sounded . . .*

Soviel ich mich bemühte, seine geistreichen Interpretationen aufzufassen . . .
(F. Thiess), *no matter what efforts I made to understand . . .*

(2) Alternatives: *whether . . . or* may only be **ob . . . ob (oder):**

Ob Ost, ob West, zu Haus das Best, *East, West, home's best.*

**Ob fremde Herren kamen oder gingen, immer blieb das Volk bei Sitte und
Gesetz** (E. Jünger), *whatever strange masters came or went . . .*

(*c*) The main statement is emphasised by taking main order without
inversion, in spite of the preceding concessive statement, thus achieving
the force of disjunction [cp. (*a*)]; see all above examples. This is possible
with **wenn auch** (**auch** being the outward sign of the firmer concessive
statement), but is otherwise rare with concessive statements in the milder
form:

Rare: **Obwohl bloß ein Mietshaus, es war eines von aristokratischem
Gepräge** (H. Broch), *though only an apartment house, it had
an aristocratic air.*

Common: **Aber sie haben Geld, und wieviel ich auch verlange, sie zahlen.
Und wenn sie vorher ihre Ehemänner bestehlen sollten, sie
kommen** (E. Kästner), *however much I ask, they pay; even if
they have to steal from their husbands, they come.*

(*d*) The subjunctive often supplies the necessary emphasis for the firmer
concessive statement, *v.* § 429 (*c*).

240. Abbreviated and other Concessive Statements

(*a*) A concessive clause in the milder form may be abbreviated to
conjunction and appositional phrase:

**Obgleich (wenn auch) klein von Gestalt, gewann er durch seine leuchtenden
blauen Augen,** *though small of stature he made up for this . . .*

(*b*) Abbreviated, by omission of the conjunction, to a simple appositional construction (**klein von Gestalt**), a statement such as that above would cease to have concessive and acquire causal force; thus statements with concessive force will be looked for in vain among (present and past) participial constructions, cp. §§ 201, 276, 347.

But with apposition of a noun, concessive force is common, almost the rule, especially when a simple adversative adverb (**doch**, etc., *v.* §§ 74-5) is added in the main statement. Thus:

Causal: **Ein zarter Knabe, wurde er immer von Krankheiten befallen.** *Delicate as he was, he was always assailed . . .*

Concessive: **Ein zarter Knabe, war er doch immer in allen gesunden Kinderspielen in erster Reihe.** *Delicate though he was . . .*

(*c*) Other constructions with concessive force:

Relative:

Frau B. räumte wutentbrannt die Stube auf, die tadellos in Ordnung war (L. Frank), *set furiously about clearing up the room, although . . .*

Verbless and proverbial statements:

Bitter im Mund, im Herzen rund, *though sharp of tongue, sound of heart.*
Ob arm, ob reich, vorm Tode gleich, *whether rich or poor, all are equal before death* [cp. § 239 (*b*)].

Prepositions: *v.* § 471 (**trotz**).

241. Statements of Weight, Measure, Extent, etc.

These present several problems: (1) of number, (2) of case in apposition, and (3) expressions of distribution.

(*a*) Number.—Expressions of weight and measure, including collective numerals, normally retain the unchanged singular form with plural sense:
zwei Glas Bier, drei Faß Wein, 15 Grad Fahrenheit, 30 Pfennig, 10 Mark, 4 Stück (Orangen), eine vier Mann starke Abordnung, zwei Paar Schuhe, vier Dutzend Eier, zweihundert Bäume.

But the following require the normal plural form:

(1) All feminine words except **Mark** (coin):
zwei Flaschen Bier, drei Portionen Leber, vier Tassen Tee, acht Millionen.
For compounds of **Hand**, *v.* below, § 242.

(2) Units of time, of whatever gender, seldom take the singular of measure: **acht Tage, zwei Wochen, sieben Jahre.**

(3) A preceding definite article usually requires the plural: **er zählte mir die zehn Pfennige, die zwei Fässer sind schon verladen;** but not when the

article can link up with a following noun: **die zwei Dutzend Eier, die vier Paar Schuhe.**

(4) Any unit of measure when used with individualising force: **ich trank zwei Gläser Mineralwasser** (emphasis on the number), **ungefähr zwanzig Paare tanzten auf der Tanzdiele** (an approximation individualises); **Die Sekundanten maßen eine Entfernung von zehn Schritten** (paces are measured one by one).

Pfennig has a strong tendency towards the plural:

pro Stunde 60 Pfennige, abends 5 Pfennig extra.

Note.—The singular of measure applies only to the noun of measure, not to the objects measured, as in English. *A basket of fish,* **ein Korb (voll) Fische.**

(*b*) Case.—The case of a noun following a unit of measure is not uniform:

(1) A singular noun stands in caseless (nom.) apposition whatever the case of the preceding noun:

zwei Glas Bier, der Preis eines Liters Wein, mit einem Stück Seife, er verlangte eine Portion Leberkäs.

(2) A qualified singular noun or unqualified plural noun takes the case of the preceding word:

er bekam ein Stück mageren Käse, in einer Art dankbarem Staunen, er holte eine Flasche alten Chianti, mit einem Dutzend Haarnadeln, er saß vor einem Haufen Geldscheinen.

Note.—Thus many expressions in apposition to measures of time:

75 Jahre katholischer Kirchenchor „Cäcilie" (newsp. headline), *Catholic Church choir celebrates its 75th birthday.*

Diese Handlung besiegelte zweihundert Jahre alten Irrtum (newsp.), *this action confirmed an error of 200 years' standing.*

(3) A qualified plural noun after a numeral or collective is in the genitive:

eine Menge kleinerer Fahrzeuge, vier solcher Arbeitsplätze, von einem Dutzend fauler Birnen, ein Strauß duftender Rosen.

(4) A qualified singular noun is occasionally, in literary style, found in the genitive, whatever the preceding case:

bei einem Glas(e) kühlen Weines.

(*c*) Distributive expressions (*v.* also § 423).

There are two distributive prepositions, **pro,** *per,* and **à,** *at,* with accusative: **die Äpfel kosten 20 Pf. pro Stück, eine Briefmarke à 10 (Pf.).**

They are subject to criticism because of their foreign origin and commercial flavour. Alternative forms are **zu** for **à** (**zu 10 Pf.**, above), and for **pro** a direct apposition in the accusative (of measure): **die Äpfel kosten 20 Pf. das Stück**, or **Stück 20 Pf.**

Bananen, die im Einkauf die Tonne soviel kosteten (H. Böll), *so much per ton.*

ein Taschenmesser—aber eins vom Jahrmarkt, Stück einen Groschen (E. Wiechert), *a penknife from the fair, one Groschen each.*

There is a distributive particle **je**, *each*: **die Kisten enthalten je 50 Stück**, *50 (items) each.*

242. Compound Nouns of Measure

(*a*) The nouns **Hand, Fuß, Löffel**, etc., are compounded:

(1) With the adjectives **breit, voll**, to form adjectives and nouns.

(2) With the nouns **Breite, Tiefe, Länge**, to form compound nouns.

(*b*) Compounded with an adjective they retain their own gender, stand in the accusative of measure; and in the plural are either unchanged or are resolved into their proper plural; thus:

Der Fußbreit, (lit.) *a foot's breadth*, (fig.) (*not*) *an inch.*

Der alte König weicht keinen Fußbreit, gibt keinen Fußbreit Landes her, *the old king won't stir an inch, give up an inch of land.*

Der Weg war kaum einen Fuß breit, or as adjective: **war kaum fußbreit.**

Die Handvoll, *handful.* **Zwei, mehrere Handvoll; beide Hände voll.**

Der Löffelvoll, *spoonful.* **Drei Löffelvoll Zucker.**

(*c*) Compounded with feminine nouns, as in **die Haaresbreite, Handtiefe, Mannslänge**, etc., they present no problem except that of distinguishing **ein Haarbreit** [neut., as in (*b*)] from **die Haaresbreite.** They are common in adverbial phrases: **(nicht) um Haaresbreite**, or **um eines Haares Breite, in Handtiefe** (*at a hand's depth*, in water), **kaum eine Mannslänge weiter.**

A. Translate into ENGLISH:

1. Als erstes deutsches Schiff nach dem Kriege hat der Frachter „Kassel" der Hamburg-Amerika-Linie Peru angelaufen; die „Kassel" traf Mitte Februar in dem peruanischen Callao ein (newsp.). 2. Sein Lieblingsunterricht bestand darin, in der Gesangstunde das schöne Lied „Der grüne Wald" üben zu lassen (*consisted in practising*, Th. Mann). 3. Dramen in Blankversen und in griechischen Kostümen, selbst wenn

von Sophokles oder Shakespeare, sind nicht geeignet, auf der realen Bühne „Kassa zu machen" (S. Zweig). 4. Es ist wirklich nichts leichter, als einen Lift zu bedienen. Allein, ein Kinderspiel an und für sich, ist dieser Dienst, wenn man ihn mit kurzen Unterbrechungen von sieben Uhr morgens bis gegen Mitternacht zu versehen hat, recht sehr ermüdend (Th. Mann). 5. Wer einmal lügt, dem glaubt man nicht, und wenn er auch die Wahrheit spricht (prov.). 6. Regnet's am Johannistag, ist's der Haselnüsse Plag' (prov.). 7. Ohne Fleiß kein Preis. 8. The Conscientious Schoolmaster: Er wich nicht um Haaresbreite vom Pensum ab, der Schulordnung, der Dienstanweisung (E. Wiechert). 9. Daß stille Wasser tief sind, ist eine Grundüberzeugung, die jeder hat. Aber man hat sich auch aufmerksam über welche gebeugt, die in kaum Handtiefe nur gewöhnliche Kiesel am Grunde sehen ließen (*showed*, H. v. Doderer). 10. Georg stürzte auf ein kleines Café zu, dessen Wirt gerade eine Konservenbüchse mit einem Strauß rosa Nelken auf einen weißgedeckten Tisch stellte (B. Werner).

B. Translate into German:

1. Wherever we went we saw nothing but tourists. 2. Another word and you go to bed! 3. Many Germans can recite Schiller's "Das Lied von der Glocke" by heart. 4. If you laugh again I shall be very cross with you (in two ways). 5. He can only travel when his passport is ready (two versions: only ... when ...; only ... if ...). 6. Although she was a child psychologist she could not handle her own daughter properly. 7. Whatever I said I was (use **man**) misunderstood. 8. Though very plain the food we got in Iceland was nutritive and wholesome. 9. I had to take a teaspoonful [of] medicine three times a day. 10. We gave the children some fruit—an orange and a banana each.

CHAPTER XLII
IMPERSONAL USES OF THE VERB

243. General

(*a*) The term "impersonal verbs" should be more strictly "impersonal uses of the verb", since there is not a special group of verbs which may only be used impersonally. Subject to this proviso, however, it is possible to distinguish impersonal uses of the verb from uses of **es,** the impersonal subject, in functions required rather by grammar than by meaning.

(*b*) Impersonal uses of the verb include:

(1) Impersonal verbs of perception, especially natural phenomena, which are always used with the **es** subject except when predicated metaphorically of a person:

es regnet, blitzt, donnert, *it is raining, lightning, thundering.*
Er donnerte sein Machtwort in den Saal hinein, *he thundered a command into the room.*

(2) Impersonal verbs of sensation, especially human feelings of body and mind, which are commonly used impersonally, but may occur with a personal subject:

es tut mir leid, *I am sorry;* **er tut mir leid,** *I am sorry for him.*
es fehlt mir an Mut, *I lack courage;* **er fehlt mir,** *I miss him.*

(*c*) Functional uses of the impersonal pronoun **es:**

(1) "Situation **es**", where **es** stands as a shorthand summary of a general situation or inexplicit content:

Hat er das Haus schon gekauft? Ja, ich glaube es, *I think so* (= *that he has already bought the house*).

(2) "Appositional **es**", where **es** stands in apposition to a noun, phrase, or clause (usually **daß** or prepositional infinitive construction), and has thus a purely grammatical role:

Es ist schwer, den rechten Mann zu finden, *it* (i.e. *to find the right man*), *is difficult.*

(*d*) The impersonal **es** is always the subject in (*b*), but may be subject or object in (*c*). Each group has its own rules (and practice) concerning when **es** must, may, or must not be omitted. The four groups are discussed at §§ 244, 245, 343-6.

For **es gibt** and **es ist (sind)** distinguished, *v.* § 21.

244. Impersonal Verbs of Perception

More elemental perceptions may be registered with any verb [*v*. (*a*)], but time and weather statements are made with **sein** and **werden** [*v*. (*b*) and (*c*)].

(*a*) Natural and indistinctly perceived phenomena.

(1) Natural phenomena.

Atmospheric:

es regnet, donnert, blitzt, hagelt, schneit, lichtet sich, klärt sich auf, *it is raining, thundering, lightning, hailing, snowing, lifting, clearing.*

Other phenomena, especially water:

es braust, brodelt, rauscht, sprudelt, strudelt, *it roars,* etc., or *there is a roaring, bubbling, rustling, swirling, eddying.*

Figurative statements may apply natural phenomena to man, or attribute human actions to natural phenomena:

Es blitzte mich plötzlich durch und durch (S. Zweig), *in a flash (of insight) it occurred to me . . .*

Es keuchte und schnaubte hinter den Bergen, als rollte jemand eine ungeheuere Last (S. Zweig), *there was a panting and snorting . . . as if . . .*

(2) By extension, **es** is used to report indistinct perceptions, or those of uncertain, including human, origin:

Es klopfte an der Tür, *there was a knock(ing) at the door.*

Im Saale ging es lebhaft zu, *there was quite a commotion . . .*

Es rumorte in der Tiefe unten, *down below (in the stalls) there was something of a hubbub.*

(3) In both these cases, **es** is retained with inversion or in the subordinate clause: **Gestern hat es den ganzen Tag geschneit, . . ., weil es den ganzen Tag geschneit hat.**

Note.—The English use of the present participle or verbal noun, with *it* or *there*: *it is thawing, there was a rustling . . .*

(*b*) Time and weather statements with **sein.**

Es ist (jetzt) zehn Uhr Mittag, es ist (heute) Sonntag, es war (gestern) der siebente März, es wird (morgen) mein Geburtstag sein, es ist (heute) gutes, schlechtes, veränderliches Wetter.

When **es** is displaced from leading position, it may often be omitted:

(1) After a leading adverb of time, especially **heute, morgen, gestern:**

Heute ist Montag, gestern war Sauwetter, morgen ist Gründonnerstag, übermorgen wird schönes Wetter sein.

Der wievielte ist heute? *What is the date to-day?*

Immer ist Blütezeit, daß einem Hören und Sehen vergeht vor dem Duft (F. Werfel), *it is always blossom-time* . . .

Figurative:

Bei ihrem Erscheinen war sofort Hochspannung, *as soon as she appeared the atmosphere became electric.*

(2) After a leading adverb of place, with weather statements:

Draußen war herrlichstes Oktoberwetter, heller Sonnenschein.

Figurative:

Im Büro ist momentan Hochdruck, *we are working under pressure at the office at the moment.*

(3) But most other statements, especially those of time, retain **es**: **Wie spät ist es? Wieviel Uhr ist es? Ist es schon Mittag? Zehn Uhr ist es schon. Noch war es erst sieben. Schon war es zu spät. Scheußliches Wetter ist es. In Amerika ist es jetzt schon Sonntag.**

(*c*) Time and weather statements with **werden.**

Es wird Tag, Nacht, Abend. Jetzt wird es schon Tag, Nacht, Abend. Und Gott sprach: Es werde Licht. Und es ward Licht (Gen. i. 3). **Und so ward es Abend; so ward es Morgen**—**der erste Tag** (after Gen. i. 5). **Es begann schon der Tag. Der Tag begann schon.**

Der Tag, der es werden will, kann mein letzter sein, *the day which is now beginning may be my last.*

Es is retained in all such cases with **werden,** since **Tag,** etc., cannot, for two reasons, be made into the subject:

(1) The predicate **Tag** does not exist till the verbal action, of which **es** is the subject and impelling agent, is completed: **es wird Tag, es beginnt (entsteht) der Tag,** but only **der Tag beginnt.** Cp. **Die Lage wurde heikel,** *became ticklish;* but **eine heikle Lage entstand** (not **wurde**).

(2) The noun **Tag** is predicative and not fully nominal, lacking the article. It could thus be replaced by an adjective: **es wird Tag, Licht, hell, licht,** analogous to **es hellt sich auf** [*v.* (*a*) (1)]; or by a verb **es tagt,** analogous to **es blitzt, donnert.**

[*v.* further, Karl Kraus (*Die Sprache*, pp. 74-81), who calls this use of **es: „Das stärkste Subjekt, das es im Bereich der Schöpfung gibt".**]

(*d*) Statements of perception with **es** as subject are always exposed to loss of descriptive impact through familiarity, but their elemental force can be revived:

Als es nämlich in der vergangenen Nacht zur Mette geweckt hatte, meinte ich im Traume . . . (S. Andres), *when the rising bell went for recital of the office* . . . (adapted from: **es läutete**).

Ich schrie auch nicht selbst, es schrie, es war eine heilige Ekstase der Schmerzen (Th. Mann), *I did not cry out, something cried within me.*

245. Impersonal Verbs of Sensation

(*a*) Generalised Sensations.

There are a large number of expressions, mainly taking the dative of the person concerned, which describe states of the mind or body:

es ist (wird) mir nicht gut, schlecht, schwindlig, schwül, *I don't feel well, feel bad, giddy, oppressed.*

  es war mir ganz eigentümlich zu Mute, *I had a peculiar sensation.*

es geht mir gut, schlecht, mittelmäßig, *I am well, not well, in average health.*

(1) Case.—A few take accusative: **es dürstet, friert, hungert, verlangt, wurmt mich,** *I am thirsty, frozen, hungry, desirous of . . ., annoyed.*

(2) Some may also take as their subject the person registering the sensation: **ich dürste (nach), fror, schauderte (vor), verlange (nach),** *I thirst (for), was cold, recoiled (from), yearn (for).*

It is less common, but still possible, for such verbs to take a personal (or third person) subject and an object of the person registering the sensation:

jenes blühende Lupinenfeld, das mich einstmals so gejammert hatte (E. Langgässer), *field of lupins which I had once been so sorry for.*

Darum weine ich ja auch, weil ich mir so leid tue (H. Fallada), *that is why I am weeping, because I am so sorry for myself.*

(3) Practice varies as regards omission of **es** on inversion:

    es geht . . ., retains **es: Heute geht es mir sehr schlecht.**

    es ist (wird) . . . omits **es: Mir ist schlecht, schwindlig.**

But an external, more objective reaction may retain **es**, which then approaches the status of "situation **es**" (*v.* § 345):

    Mir wird schlecht, *I am feeling sick,* but:

  Mir ist es hier zu kalt, warm, heiß, *it is too cold,* etc., *for me here.*

Similarly with the full verbs, in which **mich dürstet, hungert, friert, mir ekelt vor ihm,** register subjective reactions, while **mich schaudert's vor ihm,** though still subjective, creates an exterior source for the feeling.

Thus **es zieht mich** and **es verlangt mich** may both mean *I am drawn,* but the former is more externalised, posits an outside (elemental) force:

So zog es mich, später in der Nacht, in ein Wirtshaus hinein (H. Hesse), *thus later in the night I was drawn into an inn* (the will being passive).

Mich verlangte nach keiner Beschäftigung, keiner Lektüre (Th. Mann), *I felt drawn to no activity or reading* (the feelings being dominant).

(*b*) Localised Sensations.

The sensations may be localised in a part of the body. The use of the es subject may be analogous to the perception of natural phenomena (1), or to its use in the grammatical function of anticipation (2).

(1) The part of the body is in a prepositional phrase:

es brannte in mir, es kochte ihm im Herzen, es summte mir im Kopfe, es fror mich an den Händen.

Es is retained with inversion:

mir summte es im Kopfe, mir tat's im Rücken weh.

(2) The part of the body is the (postponed) subject:

es tun mir die Augen weh, es brummt mir der Schädel, es klopft mir das Herz, es fallen mir die Haare aus.

Es is omitted when the indirect object (**mir**) or postponed subject comes first:

mir tun die Augen weh, die Augen tun mir weh.

(*c*) Verbs of Advantage, etc.

Many verbs which take a dative object of the person to whose advantage, etc., something happens are often (though not necessarily) used with an impersonal subject, and may be included here:

es gefällt (mißfällt) mir . . ., cp. **sein Benehmen gefällt mir nicht,** *I am pleased (displeased), his behaviour does not please me.*

es ist mir egal (einerlei) . . ., cp. **was er geantwortet hat, ist mir einerlei,** *it (what he answered) is all the same to me.*

es reicht (genügt, langt) uns zu einem einfachen Abendessen, nicht mehr, cp. **das Geld reicht uns . . .,** *it (the money) is enough for . . . but no more.*

Cp. § 97, etc., dative verbs. Many of these uses occur in contexts in which es is either anticipatory or situation es [*v.* § 243 (*c*)], *e.g.*

es gedieh mir nichts, *nothing (I attempted) was successful* (anticipatory es).

es schadet uns nichts, *it* (what has been spoken of) *will do us no harm* (situation es).

246. Impersonal Passive Constructions

(*a*) An impersonal use of a verb, with subject **es,** may not be put into the passive, since the impersonal subject, even when taking a direct (accusative) object, is not sufficiently defined to be regarded as the author or agent of an action; hence

es wurmt mich, daß . . ., *I am annoyed, that . . .*

could only take another construction (intransitive, reflexive), if **mich** is to become **ich,** subject, translating (literally) *I am annoyed*: **ich ärgere mich, daß . . .,** etc.

The English equivalent of an impersonal expression of sensation is often a statal passive: *I am annoyed, frozen, starved, dazed;* but it is also often a predicative adjective: *sick, dizzy, sorry, angry,* etc.

There are, however, conversely, a number of impersonal constructions derived from various active or passive uses of the verb.

(*b*) An intransitive verb or a transitive verb with no object may assume the impersonal passive form to indicate the activity in general, without reference to any special agent, or with implicit reference to the pronoun **man:**

Der Kommandeur besichtigte sein Regiment, und dann wurde wieder gewartet, gefroren und geflucht (W. Bergengruen), *and then again there was nothing but waiting, freezing, swearing.*

Am Morgen des Abgabetermins wurde um fünf Uhr aufgestanden (R. G. Binding), *on the morning when it* (a school essay) *had to be given in, it was a case of getting up at 5 a.m.*

Es is omitted, as above, when (as commonly) displaced from leading position (**es wurde gewartet . . ., es wurde . . . aufgestanden**).

This use supplies in the present an imperative locution (*v.* §§ 248 f.), and even in other tenses may have quasi-imperative force: *last possible date; up at seven!*

When intransitives are thus used in a construction, the passive, normally only associated with transitives, the sense is sharply outlined, and the effect may be one of irony:

Schätzungsweise alle zehn Seiten einmal wird geweint, „haltlos geschluchzt", getobt, zusammengebrochen (book review by H. E. Holthusen), *about every ten pages someone weeps, "sobs uncontrollably", raves, collapses.*

Und mit der Weltanschauung verhält es sich genau so. Da wird gemeint und auf Standpunkten gestanden, aber angeschaut wird nicht (W. Bergengruen), *people have opinions and points of view, but no genuine beliefs* (**anschauen** suggested by **-anschauung**).

(*c*) A transitive verb governing a direct object may, and one governing an indirect (gen., dat., prepositional) object must, be given an impersonal form in the passive:

Ein Haus wurde an der Ecke gebaut. Es wurde an der Ecke ein Haus gebaut.

Both forms become the same on inversion: **An der Ecke wurde ein Haus gebaut.** This use of **es** is anticipatory [cp. § 243 (*c*)]. For full account, *v.* Passive, Chapter XXXVIII, esp. § 213. Note that this form is not possible if the direct object is a pronoun:

Sein Vater züchtigte ihn, *his father chastised him,*

may only become:

Er wurde von seinem Vater gezüchtigt, *he was chastised . . .*

But cp. **es wurde ihm anläßlich der Feier eine goldene Uhr überreicht,** *he was presented with a gold watch on the occasion,* where the direct object of the action is a noun (**Uhr**).

(*d*) The direct noun object of the active form may appear in two differing roles in the impersonal passive:

Man baute Häuser. Es wurden Häuser (nom., delayed subject) **gebaut.**

Man spielte Karten. Es wurde Karten (acc., object of verb) **gespielt.**

In rendering such expressions into the passive, the decision must be made whether what is being transposed is the normal nominal object [**Häuser,** as in (*c*) above], or the verb/noun object group [**Karten spielen,** as in (*b*) above]. It may be either of these:

Es wurden Witze gemacht, *jokes were told.*

Es wurde Witze gemacht, *there was joking* (*going on*).

The construction with the "retained object" (*i.e.* **Karten** above), may involve an accusative reflexive being thus retained:

Was uns keine Ruhe läßt, sind die Läuse . . . Da wird sich auf der Pritsche hin und her geworfen (Th. Plievier), *the lice give us no peace . . . there's a lot of tossing about on the bunks.*

(*e*) Verbs governing a dative (of advantage), such as **helfen, dienen, trauen,** etc., often use impersonal constructions in the statal passive (*v.* § 211), and the prepositional infinitive used as a modal verbal (*v.* § 250):

Beiden war geholfen gewesen, und nun war beiden nicht zu helfen (E. Kästner), *both had been helped, and now they were both beyond help* (lit., *both could no longer be helped*).

(*f*) The objective predicate may, in formal style, have a construction which is implicitly impersonal and passive; so

Ich glaube ihr damit geholfen, *I believe her* (*to have been*) *helped* (*in this way*),

may be regarded as an abbreviated form of:

Ich glaube (,daß) ihr geholfen (worden ist), *that she has been helped* [impersonal passive as in (*c*) above].

v. further, § 434 (*b*).

EXERCISE XLII

A. Translate into ENGLISH:

1. „Und es wallet und siedet und brauset und zischt,
   Wie wenn Wasser mit Feuer sich mengt."
   (A whirlpool in Schiller's ballad *Der Taucher*.)

2. Kraniche rufen am hinteren Rande (des Moores), es flüstert im trockenen Gras, und es weht ein wenig unheimlich und ist wie eine Wunde im Wald (E. Wiechert). 3. Aber ich sehe, bei Ihnen ist Platz. Zwar habe ich mein Dessert schon gehabt, aber wenn es Ihnen recht ist, nehme ich den Kaffee bei Ihnen. Oder verlangt Sie nach Einsamkeit? (Th. Mann). 4. Aber es bedurfte eigentlich der Worte nicht, die Sprache ihrer Gebärden belehrte unmittelbar (W. Bergengruen). 5. Die Wahrheit war an den Tag gekommen, wem war damit gedient? (E. Kästner). 6. Fabian in the Unemployment Exchange: Fabian las die Druckschriften, die an den Wänden hingen. Es war verboten, Armbinden zu tragen. Es war verboten, Umsteigebillets der Straßenbahn von den Erstinhabern zu übernehmen und weiter zu benutzen. Es war verboten, politische Debatten hervorzurufen und sich an ihnen zu beteiligen. Es wurde mitgeteilt, wo man für dreißig Pfennige ein ausgesprochen nahrhaftes Mittagessen erhalten konnte. Es wurde mitgeteilt, für welche Anfangsbuchstaben sich die Kontrolltage verschoben hatten. Es wurde mitgeteilt, für welche Berufszweige die Nachweisadressen und die Auskunftzeiten geändert worden waren. Es wurde mitgeteilt. Es war verboten. Es war verboten. Es wurde mitgeteilt (E. Kästner).

B. Translate into GERMAN, using impersonal constructions where possible:

1. It occurs to me that I have forgotten to turn off the light. 2. Everything has happened to him that can happen to a man. 3. When the day broke he saw that it was beginning to snow. 4. Gradually he realised that he had seen her before somewhere—or so it seemed to him. 5. She was very cold and hungry when she got home. 6. I don't like not knowing what is going on in my own home. 7. He felt giddy when he looked down from the church tower and there was a rushing noise in his ears. 8. There was a lot of laughing and talking as soon as the girls were left alone. 9. I am so sorry that you couldn't come. 10. He felt drawn to enter the church and to rest in its cool shadows.

CHAPTER XLIII

THE IMPERATIVE MOOD AND MODAL VERBAL

247. Forms of the Imperative

(a) General.—German has only two grammatically distinct forms of the imperative mood, the second singular and plural familiar (**du** and **ihr**): **Komm! Kommt!** The remaining personal forms are supplied by the subjunctive: **Man nehme vier Eier** (cooking recipe), *take four eggs* (v. there, especially §§ 273-4). Modal forms provide useful circumlocutions both for imperative and subjunctive: **Sie sollen gehen!** *Let them go!*

(b) Second person singular, **du** form.

This is formed from the infinitive stem in various ways:

(1) Strong verbs which change -e- to -i- or -ie- in the present indicative, **du** form, have the stem with this vowel change: **brich, gib, iß, nimm, sprich, stirb, triff, wirf; befiehl, lies.**

Note.—**Werde!** (NOT **wird!**) is the imperative in the sense *Become!* For the passive imperative (*Be . . .!*), v. § 212 (b). **Sein** has **sei! be!** (*e.g.* **sei stark!** *be strong!*). Cp. also **siehe!** below, (4).

(2) All other strong and weak verbs add -e to the stem:

falle, fahre, habe, kaufe, mache, entsage, wandle.

Note.—No apostrophe is used if this -e is elided [**sag!**, v. § 545 (c) (5)].

(3) But strong verbs in general are liable to be influenced by those in (1) to drop the ending -e: **beiß, komm, fahr, sing, wasch.** The distinction between the -e and the -e-less forms in strong verbs is often mainly one of euphony or style, the -e-less forms being common in speech, those in -e being felt as more elevated:

Hans, komm hier! tu das! lauf mal hin! *come here, do that, run along.*

Fahre hin, o Traum meiner Jugend! *Farewell, dream of my youth!*

Further, there is a certain reluctance to accept the change in pronunciation of a final consonant which would attend the abbreviation of certain forms as: **find, meid, scheid, schweig, steig.**

(4) Certain verbs, normally with vowel change as in (1), are in process of changing to a weak present, so that both forms may be found: **milk!** or **melke!**; **gebäre!** is possible besides **gebier!**

Note.—One verb may have both vowel change and -e form: **siehe!** often in the rhetorical sense: *lo and behold!* and when used for cross-references: **siehe S. 154**, *see p. 154* (abbreviated **s.**).

315

(5) A separable prefix has the usual end-position:

Sammle die Gaben Gottes ein!   *collect* (*harvest*) *the gifts of God!*

(*c*) Second person plural, **ihr** form.

This is formed by adding **-t** to the stem (with euphonic **-e-** inserted as noted § 9 and Appendix B), and is thus the same as the indicative, though without the pronoun: **Kommt Kinder!   Scheidet als Freunde! Versprecht es!   Vergeßt ihn!** *come children, part as friends, promise it, forget him.*

Note to (*b*) *and* (*c*).—Both second persons familiar may nevertheless, in emphatic contexts, take the personal pronoun following (cp. English, *Go you . . .*):

Handle du richtig! (E. Kästner), *do you act justly!*

Geht ihr voraus, wir kommen nach!   *You go on ahead, we will follow.*

(*d*) First and second person plural, polite form, **wir** and **Sie,** use forms which are identical with questions in the indicative: **Gehen wir!** *let us go!* **Stehen Sie auf!** *stand up!* These are in fact the subjunctive, as is shown by the one verb, **sein,** which has forms distinct from the indicative in these cases: **Seien wir!** *let us be!* **Seien Sie!** *be!* Note also the rare first person imperative: **ich sei . . .!** *let me be . . .!*

(*e*) The imperative of a first person singular or plural statement is peculiar in that an order issued to oneself often ceases to be peremptory, and becomes a wish or request to another (to be permitted to . . .): *Let us go!   Let me go!* The latter is not distinguishable from a normal request. The former—*let us go!*—because of the element of imperative force to those other than the speaker, is felt as a genuine imperative, and is expressed:

(1) By the subjunctive, as above (*d*): **Gehen wir!**

(2) By the imperative of **lassen,** according to the nature and number of the other persons in the **wir**-group:

Laß uns gehen! *let us go!* (one other, intimate familiar).

Laßt uns gehen! *let us go!* (several others, familiar).

Lassen Sie uns gehen! *let us go!* (one or several others, formal).

For **lassen** with second person object (**laß dich . . .**) *v.* imperative of **sein** [§ 273 (*d*) (1)].

(3) By the use of the modal form: **Wir wollen gehen!**

(*f*) The modal verbs are used as variants of the imperative as follows:

(1) **wollen,** first plural:

Wir wollen einen Ausflug machen! *let us . . .* [*v.* (*e*) (3)].

(2) **sollen**, second and third singular and plural:

du sollst gehen, ihr sollt nicht zu viel essen, sie soll mithelfen, Sie sollen kommen, sie sollen uns in Ruhe lassen, *you are to (must) go, you should not . . ., let her . . ., etc.*

(3) **mögen**, third singular and plural:

Er mag jetzt lesen, *let him read.*
Sie mögen eintreten, *let them enter.*

(4) And even **können**:

Reinhardt, du kannst beten! *Now, Reinhardt, say grace!*

(*g*) The following alternative forms are dealt with under § 248:

(1) past participle, (2) infinitive, (3) passive and impersonal passive, (4) non-verbal forms.

248. Uses of the Imperative

(*a*) General.—The imperative mood expresses a command of every degree of peremptoriness from the tentative request of a prayer to the bark of the sick-parade:

Ach neige, Du Schmerzensreiche, Dein Antlitz gnädig meiner Not!
(Gretchen's prayer to the Virgin in Goethe's *Faust*, Part I.)

Paarweise antreten! schrie Petrow. Einrücken ins Lazarett! (H. Fallada)
Fall in in twos, shouted P., quick march into the sick-bay!

It is not surprising, therefore, that the imperative forms proper and their immediate variants [§ 147 (*e*) and (*f*)] should play an indispensable but comparatively unobtrusive role within the wide variety of forms which may have imperative force. Some of these are given here, with an indication of their particular flavour.

(*b*) The **du** imperative is used, apart from familiar contexts proper:

(1) In all those further cases described in § 167, as when addressing:

the Deity: **Unser tägliches Brot gib uns heute,** *give us this day our daily bread.*

the public: **Bleibe gesund, lebe länger!** (poster), *keep well and live longer!*
a person, under one's breath:

Mache du deine eigene Sache, dann kümmere dich erst um die der anderen! murmelte er, *look after your own business first . . . he muttered.*

(2) In directions to a reader or imaginary audience:

siehe S. 76, *see p. 76;* **s. oben (unten),** *v. supra (infra).*

Die Kasacken leben heute dank dem Sowjetsystem in festen Siedlungen, lies Lehm- und Bretterbuden (newsp.), *live in stable settlements, which no doubt means mud and wooden huts.*

Er heißt Lewin, sprich Levisohn, *his name is Lewin* (*of course his real name is Levisohn*).

Er hat sage und schreibe zwei Jahre zur Arbeit gebraucht, *he spent two whole years* (pop., *believe it or not!*) *on the work.*

These may be regarded as absolute uses, not directed to anyone specifically; **lies** and **sprich,** as the examples show, usually introduce ironical asides.

(*c*) The indicative is used in the present or future:

(1) Present, when speaking to or as to a child:

Den Schluck trinkst du aus und gehst dann hübsch nach Hause und schläfst. Versprich mir's (H. Hesse), *now just drink that up and be good and go home to bed. Promise me!*

or when giving directions, especially local:

Sie fahren geradeaus, biegen links ab, und sind in zehn Minuten da, *drive straight on, turn left, and you are there in 10 minutes.*

(2) Future or modals, with a more peremptory tone:

Du wirst (or wirst du) sofort aufhören! *will you stop at once!* **Du sollst (or willst du) gleich aufhören!**

(*d*) The infinitive is widely used in commands and requests to an indefinite (public) audience, as well as to children:

Stuttgart! Nach Tübingen umsteigen! *change for Tübingen!*

Bitte nachschicken! *please forward.*

Einsendungen an die Redaktion adressieren, *all letters to the Editor* [*v.* the Fallada example in (*a*)].

Träume gut. Aber gleich einschlafen! (H. Fallada), *pleasant dreams, but go to sleep straight away, won't you!*

(1) As with the infinitive noun [§ 204 (*e*)], from which this form of the imperative is not always distinguishable, the infinitive is reduced to essentials, especially reflexive pronouns being omitted:

Alles ausziehen bis auf die Hosen! (W. Speyer), *all strip to shorts.*

Alles in zwei Gliedern aufstellen! (H. Fallada), *all fall in in twos.*

(2) The infinitive imperative may have the third person collective neuter subject **alles,** *v.* examples in (1). **Alles** and **jeder** also are not uncommon with the indicative imperative: **Alles hört auf mich! Jeder ist in fünf Minuten in Bett!** (cp. English: *Everyone listen to me!*).

(*e*) The past participle is used for more peremptory commands or warnings, especially those involving action or motion:

„**Lustig, Kinder! . . . Laßt's euch schmecken! Nur immer zugegriffen und getan, als wär't ihr zu Haus!"** (E. Langgässer), *help yourselves and do as you would at home!*

As such it is suitably used for military commands:

Angetreten! *Fall in!* **Abgesessen!** *Dismount!*

but gives place to the infinitive if the command becomes more explicit, especially when a subject is added [cp. (*d*) (1)]:

Paarweise antreten! Alles an die Maschine treten!

Note.—Both infinitive and past participle are used for musings and silent exhortations to oneself:

Was tut man mit unserem Globus? Man behandelt ihn mit Kamillentee . . . Abwarten und Teetrinken, denkt man . . . (E. Kästner), *better wait and drink tea, so people think.*

Also rein ins Bett und losgegrübelt (H. Fallada), *better climb into bed and think it over.*

(*f*) The passive, especially in the impersonal form, is used for sharp requests:

Keine Einrede! Es wird geblecht! *Pay up and no argument!*

So, und nun wird schlafen gegangen, marsch! (E. Wiechert), *come on, you boys, off to bed!*

(*g*) An isolated subordinate clause with **daß** is often used in warnings, especially to children:

Daß du nicht mit verdrecktem Anzug zurückkommst! *Mind you don't come back with your suit all filthy!*

The request may be supported by the adverb **ja**, accented (**Daß du já nicht dabei einschläfst!** *Mind you don't . . .*), or by the dative pronoun for the person interested (**Daß du mir já nicht mit verdrecktem Anzug . . .!** not translated).

(*h*) A non-verbal form may indicate an imperative:

Ins Bett! Auf! Her zu mir! (*to heel!*) **An die Maschine!**

249. The Modal Verbal (1). Infinitive

(*a*) The prepositional infinitive used in the predicate may acquire passive force and a certain modal meaning, corresponding in English to the senses *must, ought, can, need not,* etc.:

Die Karriere des Mannes war nicht aufzuhalten (E. Kästner), *the man's career was not to (could not) be stopped.*

The vast majority of cases are after **sein,** but a few other verbs with similar force may take the construction, especially **bleiben, stehen:**

Es bleibt noch zu sehen, ob er wirklich erscheint, *it remains to be seen, whether he will really appear.*

Du kamst mit Absichten hierher, die sich rascher erfüllt haben, als zu hoffen stand (E. Kästner), *hopes which have been fulfilled more quickly than might have been hoped.*

(*b*) English normally uses the passive infinitive after both *to be* and *to remain,* as above; but the use of *to be* for a modal verb is distinctly commoner in the negative than the positive: *he is not to be told, the play is not to be produced, the money is not to be sneezed at* (sense of *must, should*). But the wide use of the German modal verbal in the positive, with the force of *can,* and even in the negative (meaning *cannot*) is not paralleled in English, which has to use the explicit modal verb:

Dann ist nur der Schnee an den Fenstern zu hören (E. Wiechert), *only the snow on the windows can be heard.*

Ein System war nicht zu entdecken, der geringste Anhalt nicht zu finden (E. Wiechert), *a system could not be discovered, or the slightest clue found* (to a series of burglaries).

(*c*) Both languages often add an adjective (adverb) for *easy* (**leicht,** etc.) to this construction: *the child is easy to control,* **leicht zu regieren;** but as soon as the statement is amplified, English reverts to the modal and passive infinitive:

ein vergnügtes und problemloses Kind, das mit Lob und Schokolade leicht zu regieren ist (H. Hesse), *can easily be controlled . . .*

Vierhundertdreißig Mark sind nicht so sehr viel Geld, und das Ende war leichtlich auszurechnen (H. Fallada), *could easily be foreseen.*

and German frequently uses reflexive constructions:

der Wagen fährt sich leicht, das Kind läßt sich leicht führen, *is easy to drive, easily guided* (cp. § 180).

(*d*) Recently the construction "*to be*—adjective—active infinitive with passive force" has been extended in English to other adjectives, but still with the air of a neologism:

The reasons for the Victorian taste in Rabelais are not far to seek (book review in *The Times*) = **sind nicht weit zu suchen.**

(*e*) Otherwise the active infinitive with passive force is rare in English, and the passive form is usually an alternative: *the house is to let* (*to be let*), *he is to blame,* **das Haus ist zu vermieten, er ist (daran) schuld.**

(*f*) On the other hand, the construction is commoner as a following attribution: *he is the man to send, this is the point to discuss.*

For this German uses:

(1) The modal verbal infinitive in a relative clause:

> **die Frage, die zu besprechen ist.**

(2) The modal verbal present participle:

> **die zu besprechende Frage** (*v.* § 279).

(3) An explicit modal:

> **der Mann, der geschickt werden muß (sollte).**

Thus German has two modal verbals, the infinitive and present participle, while English has one corresponding construction, the infinitive, but used either in the predicate or the following attributive position.

250. Use of the Modal Verbal Infinitive

(*a*) The infinitive as modal verbal is like the passive in that the subject of the auxiliary verb is the object of the action of the infinitive/past participle:

> **die Tür wurde geöffnet** (passive), **war nicht zu öffnen** (modal verbal).

It differs in that there can never be an explicit agent (*e.g.,* **von seiner Frau**); the implied agent is **man**: **Man konnte die Tür nicht öffnen.**

(*b*) Similarly the subject of the auxiliary (and object of the action) is quite often a noun clause, pronoun or impersonal **es**, summing up a general situation:

> **Auf welche Weise sie zu ihrem Beruf gekommen war, war niemals aus ihr herauszubringen** (R. Musil), *how she had come to take up her work could never be discovered.*

> **Das ist nie wieder gutzumachen,** *can never again be put right.*

> **Es ist nicht auszudenken, auszuhalten,** *one just does not know what the answer is, how to stand it* (*in the long run*).

Note.—The modal force (*can,* etc.) explains the common occurrence of prefixes with durative force, as here **aus-.**

(*c*) Such impersonal subjects may be associated, as the direct object of the action, with another dative object of the verb:

> **Was er wollte, war ihm seit langem anzumerken** (H. Mann), *what he wanted had for long been clear* (lit., *was to be detected in him*).

> **Die Tante behauptete: „Es war ihnen anzusehen"** (H. Mann), *you could see it in their faces* (a coming engagement).

> **Seufzend gab ich es auf. Diesem Menschen war nicht beizukommen** (H. Hesse), *it was impossible to make an impression on this man.*

(*d*) Thus, as with the passive proper, the modal verbal infinitive with impersonal **es** subject provides a way of translating statements with modal verbs and a second verb which in German takes an object not in the accusative (*v.* § 213):

The man could not be helped, **Es war dem Mann nicht zu helfen,** or: **Dem Mann war nicht zu helfen.**

The name of a man must here be recorded, who . . ., **Es ist hier noch eines Mannes zu gedenken, der . . .,** or: **Eines Mannes ist hier noch zu gedenken, der . . .**

251. Modal Verbal Infinitive in Apposition

(*a*) The modal verbal infinitive may be loosely associated with another construction with **sein**:

Das Schloß ist nur Blech, eine Zuhalte, mit jedem Draht aufzutändeln (H. Fallada), *the lock is a makeshift one, could be opened with any piece of wire.*

So that by extension an apposition without **sein** is common:

(Sie) bog um die Ecke, mit zwei Kindern an der Hand, fremd geworden, kaum wiederzuerkennen (E. Kästner), *hardly recognisable.*

Bücher, an Jugendliche zu verschenken (book review title), *books, suitable as gifts for young people.*

(*b*) As the adjective (adverb) **leicht** may be added to qualify the modal verbal [*v.* § 249 (*c*)], so also **wie** often follows **anzusehen** in the sense *looking like, in appearance like*:

Die Pflanzen waren anzusehen wie ein Versprechen auf eine bessere Zeit (E. Langgässer), *seemed to her like a promise . . .*

This may similarly stand in simple apposition:

Herr Seidenzopf . . . etwa anzusehen wie ein Schnauzhund, so dicht ist sein Gesicht mit wolligen schwarzen Haaren bewachsen (H. Fallada), *looking something like a shaggy dog . . .*

252. The Prepositional Infinitive Noun

The construction **zum** with the infinitive noun may be used after the verb *to be* and similar verbs either with passive force (as with the modal verbal) or with active force:

(*a*) Passive force.

Die Teilnahme war ehrlich.   Es war nicht zum Aushalten (E. Kästner), *her sympathy was sincere, but quite insufferable (not to be suffered).*

This construction competes with the prepositional infinitive:

(1) In the predicate, *i.e.* as modal verbal:

es ist nicht auszuhalten, zum Aushalten.

(2) In the attributive position after pronouns, **etwas, nichts,** either in the predicate after **sein**:

da ist nichts zu fürchten, zum Fürchten, *nothing to fear, to be feared.*

or as the object of a transitive verb, especially **es gibt**:

hier gibt's etwas zu bewundern, zum Bewundern, *something to admire.*

This latter use, after a pronoun object, is one of a series of uses of the prepositional infinitive as objective predicate (*v.* § 366).

The infinitive noun following a pronoun may acquire concrete status:

Er hatte etwas zum Essen besorgt, *something to eat, something for (lunch,* etc.) [cp. infinitive noun, § 205 (*c*)].

(*b*) Active force.

War ein derartig goldenes Zeitalter überhaupt auszuhalten? War es nicht viel eher zum Blödsinnigwerden? (E. Kästner), *was such a golden age (Utopia) something one could stand? was it not a world fit only for morons?*

Here the passive and active (intransitive) force are clearly distinct. The sense of the latter is *enough to make one . . . (cause one to . . .).* Thus also:

es ist zum Heulen, zum Lachen, zum Verzweifeln, zum Sterben langweilig,
    enough to make you cry, laugh, despair, die of boredom.

Similarly with verbs synonymous with *to be enough*:

Ich bin auf meine Talente nicht eingebildet, sie reichen glatt zum Verhungern
    (E. Kästner), *my talents just about qualify me to starve.*

and in adverbial contexts:

ein Gummiband . . . zum Reißen gespannt, *stretched to breaking point.*

Note.—An alternative: **es ist, um blödsinnig zu werden,** *v.* § 203 (*c*).

(*c*) Both the above constructions demonstrate the general purposive force of the preposition **zu**, *v.* § 527. Thus when the preposition has strong purposive force it may govern a preceding noun/pronoun [as in (*a*) (2)] in an oblique case:

Im Inflationswinter hatte er kein Geld zum Heizen gehabt (E. Kästner) (= **womit er heizen konnte**), *no money with which to heat his room,* or:
                    for heating purposes.

Where the infinitive noun has active force, it does in fact often govern the situation **es** which is the subject; and this is sometimes, in informal style, made explicit: **es ist zum Dranverzweifeln,** *it is a situation to despair at.*

EXERCISE XLIII

A. Translate into ENGLISH:

1. Daily exercise in prison: Nun, am Tor zum Freihof, stehen zwei Wachtmeister, und wiederholen wie die Automaten: „Abstand nehmen! Es wird nicht gesprochen. Nehmen Sie Abstand! Wer spricht, kriegt eine Anzeige" (H. Fallada). 2. The new German Army, 1955: Bald schallen wieder die Trompeten zu dem Kommando: „Angetreten!" „Ich trete"—sagt der kluge Mann—„am liebsten meine Quickly an!" (Adv. for Moped in Simpl.). 3. Aufgepaßt! nicht zu viel geschwatzt, ihr Kinder! 4. Erst besinn's, dann beginn's (prov.). Erst bedacht, dann gemacht (prov.). 5. Der Bürger ist . . . seinem Wesen nach ein Geschöpf von schwachem Lebensantrieb, . . . leicht zu regieren (H. Hesse). 6. Wenn man die Höhe der Marmorklippen erstieg, war das Gebiet, darin er die Gewalt erstrebte, in seinem vollen Umfange einzusehen (E. Jünger). 7. Ich bin erst von 10 Uhr ab zu sprechen. 8. Daß er ein Gedanken- und Büchermensch war und keinen praktischen Beruf ausübte, war bald zu sehen (H. Hesse). 9. Über dem blattlosen Geäst der Stadtwaldbäume war der Himmel—ohne Sterne—mehr zu ahnen als zu sehen (H. Fallada). 10. Am Himmel stand eine kleine, einsame, schneeweiße Wolke, anzusehen wie ein verlaufenes Kaninchen (W. Bergengruen).

B. Translate into GERMAN, using modal verbals in Nos. 4-10 where possible:

1. Don't be cross, and when you go, close the door quietly. 2. Stop talking, children, while I am trying to telephone, and run and play in the garden. 3. Let us try again this year to keep the garden really tidy (three ways). 4. Come, laugh at yourself! There's nothing to cry about. 5. He sat in the cool little pub where the company was quite bearable. 6. There are no candles to be had in the whole town. 7. The poem was unintelligible. 8. It is easy to see why the car could not be repaired. 9. The child could be cheered up by any little joke. 10. His lectures were enough to make you die of boredom.

GERMAN—ENGLISH VOCABULARY

For a note on the contents of this Vocabulary, *v.* Preface.
For abbreviations used, *v.* List of Abbreviations.
Masculine and neuter nouns are strong [*i.e.* genitive in **-(e)s**], unless (as for weak and mixed nouns) a special genitive inflection is given before the plural ending.
Compound verbs are described as *sep.* or *insep.* only when the prefix with which they are compounded may be either [cp. § 88 (*c*), especially (3)].

A

abbrechen, *s.*, break off.
Abendessen, *n.*, -, supper.
abends, in the evening.
Abfahrt, *f.*, **-en,** departure.
abhandenkommen, *s.*, get lost.
abjagen, rob.
abliefern, deliver.
abnehmen, *s.*, lose weight, decrease.
abschalten, switch off.
abschließen, *s.*, lock.
Abspannung, *f.*, relaxation.
Abstand, *m.*, "e, distance.
Abstufung, *f.*, **-en,** degree.
Abwasser, *n.*, ", waste water.
abweichen, *s.*, deviate.
Achtung, *f.*, respect.
achtzig, eighty.
Acker, *m.*, ", ploughed field.
Admiral, *m.*, **-e,** admiral.
Affe, *m.*, **-n, -n,** monkey.
Ahn, *m.*, **-s & -en, -en,** ancestor.
ahnen, suspect presence of.
ähnlich, similar.
Ähre, *f.*, **-n,** sheaf of corn.
albern, silly.
Album, *n.*, **Alben,** album.
allerhand, all sorts of things.
allgemeinen (im), generally.
Altar, *m.*, "e & **-e,** altar.
Alter, *n.*, age.
Amerikaner, *m.*, -, American.
Amsel, *f.*, **-n,** blackbird.
Amt, *n.*, "er, office.
amüsieren, amuse.
an, *D./A.*, on, to.
an und für sich, in itself.
Ananas, *f.*, - & **-se,** pineapple.
ander-, other.
Anfang, *m.*, "e, beginning.
anfangen, *s.*, begin, do.
Anfangsbuchstabe, *m.*, **-ens, -en,** initial letter.
anfühlen (sich), feel.

angreifen, *s.*, attack.
Angst, *f.*, "e, fear.
ängstigen, frighten.
ängstlich, anxious(ly).
anhängen, sell (a pup).
anheben, *s.*, begin (to speak).
anhören (sich), sound.
anklopfen, knock.
Anlaß, *m.*, "e, occasion.
anlaufen, *s.*, touch (at a port).
Anmut, *f.*, grace, charm.
(an)säen, sow.
ansammeln (sich), collect.
Ansichtskarte, *f.*, **-n,** picture postcard.
Anspruch (in . . . nehmen), claim attention, preoccupy.
ansteigen, *s.*, rise.
anstellen, employ, appoint.
antreten, *s.*, fall in, kick-start.
Antwort, *f.*, **-en,** answer.
Anzeige, *f.*, **-n,** report.
anziehen, *s.*, attract.
Anzug, *m.*, "e, suit.
anzünden, light up.
Apfel, *m.*, ", apple.
Apostat, *m.*, **-en, -en,** apostate.
Apparat, *m.*, **-e,** camera, apparatus.
arbeiten, work.
Arm, *m.*, **-e,** arm.
arm, poor.
Armbinde, *f.*, **-n,** armlet.
armselig, miserable, needy.
arrangieren, arrange.
Arzt, *m.*, "e, doctor.
Aschenbecher, *m.*, -, ashtray.
Asiat, *m.*, **-en, -en,** Asiatic.
Assistent, *m.*, **-en, -en,** assistant.
Athlet, *m.*, **-en, -en,** athlete.
atmen, breathe.
auch, also.
auf, *D./A.*, on, on top of.
Aufgabe, *f.*, **-n,** homework, duty.
aufgeben, *s.*, give up.
aufhören, cease, stop.

Aufklärung, *f.*, enlightenment.
aufmerksam (machen), draw attention to
Aufmerksamkeit, *f.*, -en, attention.
Aufnahme, *f.*, -n, photograph.
aufpassen, watch, pay attention.
Aufräumen, *n.*, tidying up.
Aufsatz, *m.*, ⁻e, essay.
aufschieben, *s.*, postpone.
aufschreiben, *s.*, note.
aufsparen, save up.
aus, *D.*, out (of).
ausdrücken, express.
Ausflug, *m.*, ⁻e, excursion.
ausgedient, retired.
ausgesprochen, genuinely.
ausgezeichnet, exceptionally good.
Auskunft, *f.*, ⁻e, information.
ausreichen, suffice.
außerdem, moreover.
außerordentlich, extraordinary.
ausspannen, relax.
ausüben, practise.
Auswahl, *f.*, -en, selection.
auswendig, by heart.
Autokrat, *m.*, -en, -en, autocrat.
Automat, *m.*, -en, -en, slot-machine, automaton.

B

backen, *s.*, bake.
Bäcker, *m.*, -, baker.
Bäckerei, *f.*, -en, baker's shop.
Bad, *n.*, ⁻er, bath.
Bahn, *f.*, -en, course.
Bahnhof, *m.*, ⁻e, station.
bald, soon.
Balken, *m.*, -, beam, bar of wood.
Banane, *f.*, -n, banana.
Band, *m.*, ⁻e, volume.
Band, *n.*, ⁻er, ribbon.
Bank, *f.*, ⁻e, bench.
Bär, *m.*, -en, -en, bear.
bauen, build.
Bauer, *m.*, -s (-n), -n, peasant, farmer.
Bauer, *n.*, -, bird cage.
baufällig, tumbledown.
Baum, *m.*, ⁻e, tree.
Bayer, *m.*, -n, -n, Bavarian.
bebändert, beribboned.
Becher, *m.*, -, mug, tankard.
Becken, *n.*, -, basin.
bedenken, *irr.*, reflect.
bedeuten, mean, signify.
bedeutend, important.
(be)dienen, serve.
Bedienung, *f.*, service.

Bedienungsprozente, *pl.*, tip of 10%.
Bedrängnis, *f.*, -se, tight corner.
bedrückend, oppressive.
bedürfen, need.
Beere, *f.*, -n, berry.
Beet, *n.*, -e, flower bed.
befehlen, *s.*, *D.*, order.
begegnen, meet.
begehen, *s.*, commit.
beginnen, *s.*, begin.
begrüßen (sich), greet (one another).
beherbergen, shelter.
beherrschen, rule over.
bei, *D.*, by, near, beside.
beid-, both.
beißen, *s.*, bite.
beistehen, *s.*, *D.*, help.
bekannt, known.
bekommen, *s.*, get.
beleben (sich), come to life.
Bemerkung, *f.*, -en, remark.
bereits, already.
Bereitschaft, *f.*, readiness.
Berg, *m.*, -e, hill, mountain.
Beruf, *m.*, -e, profession.
Berufszweig, *m.*, -e, (type of) job.
berühmt, famous.
beschäftigt (mit), occupied (with).
Beschäftigung, *f.*, -en, occupation.
bescheiden, modest.
Beschreibung, *f.*, -en, description.
beschuldigen, *G.*, accuse (of).
besiedeln, settle.
besinnen (sich), *s.*, reflect.
Besitzer, *m.*, -, owner.
besser, better.
bestehen (in, aus), *s.*, consist (in, of).
Besuch, *m.*, -e, visit, visitor.
besuchen, visit.
Besucher, *m.*, -, visitor.
beteiligen (sich), take part.
beten, pray.
betreten, *s.*, enter.
betrunken, drunk.
Bett, *n.*, -en, bed.
beugen (sich), bend.
Bevölkerung, *f.*, -en, population.
bewähren (sich), last.
bewältigen, master.
Bewegung, *f.*, -en, movement, action.
beweinen, mourn.
beweisen, *s.*, prove.
bewußt, conscious.
Bibliothek, *f.*, -en, library.
biblisch, biblical.
biegen, *s.*, bend.
Biene, *f.*, -n, bee.
Bier, *n.*, -e, beer.

bieten, *s.*, offer.
Bild, *n.*, -er, picture.
billigen, approve.
Binse, *f.*, -n, rushes.
Bischof, *m.*, ˮe, bishop.
Bissen, *m.*, -, bite (of food).
bitte, please.
bitten, *s.*, ask for.
blamieren, let down (*coll.*).
blattlos, leafless.
bleiben, *s.*, stay.
bleich, pale.
Bleistift, *m.*, -e, pencil.
blicken, look.
Blinzeln, *n.*, winking.
bloß, only.
Blume, *f.*, -n, flower.
Blumensame(n), *m.*, -n (-), flower seed.
Boden, *m.*, ˮ & -, floor, ground, attic.
Bogen, *m.*, ˮ & -, arch.
Boot, *n.*, -e, boat.
böse, wicked, cross.
Bote, *m.*, -n, -n, messenger.
Braten, *m.*, -, roast meat.
brauchen, need.
brechen, *s.*, break.
brennen, *irr.*, burn.
Brief, *m.*, -e, letter.
Briefmappe, *f.*, -n, briefcase.
Briefmarke, *f.*, -n, stamp.
bringen, *irr.*, bring.
Brot (belegtes), open sandwich.
Bruder, *m.*, ˮ, brother.
Buch, *n.*, ˮer, book.
Buchhalter, *m.*, -, bookkeeper.
Buchstabe, *m.*, -ns, -n, letter (of alphabet).
büffeln, swot, study hard.
Bulgar(e), *m.*, -n, -n, Bulgarian.
bunt, many coloured, bright.
Bürger, *m.*, -, citizen.
bürgerlich, bourgeois.
Büro, *n.*, -s, office.
Büroangestellte, *m.*, *adj.-n.*, office worker.
burschikos, like a boy.

C
Charakter, *m.*, -e, character.
chemische Reinigung, *f.*, dry cleaner's.
Chor, *m.*, ˮe, choir (singing).
Christ, *m.*, -en, -en, Christian.
Clausur, *f.*, -en, enclosure.

D
Dachboden, *m.*, ˮ & -, attic.
Dämmern, *n.*, dusk.

Däne, *m.*, -n, -n, Dane.
danken, *D.*, thank.
dann, then.
Darlegung, *f.*, -en, exposition.
darstellen, represent.
Datum, *n.*, Daten, date.
Dauer (auf die), in the long run.
Deck, *n.*, -e, deck.
decken, cover, lay.
Demokrat, *m.*, -en, -en, democrat.
denken, *irr.*, think.
derb, rough.
Detektiv, *m.*, -e, detective.
deutsch, German.
Diamant, *m.*, -en, -en, diamond.
dicht, dense.
dick, fat, thick.
Dieb, *m.*, -e, thief.
dienen, serve, *D.*
Dienst, *m.*, -e, service.
Dienstag, *m.*, -e, Tuesday.
Dienstanweisung, *f.*, -en, instruction.
Dienstmagd, *f.*, ˮe, maid.
dieser, this.
Doktorand, *m.*, -en, -en, candidate for doctor's degree.
Dom, *m.*, -e, cathedral.
Donnerstag, *m.*, -e, Thursday.
Dorfkirche, *f.*, -n, village church.
Dorn, *m.*, -en, thorn.
Drache, *m.*, -n, -n, dragon [§ 52 (*b*)].
Drachen, *m.*, -, kite, "dragon" (human).
Drangsal, *f.*, anxiety.
dreißig, thirty.
dreiviertel, Dreiviertel, three-quarters.
dritt-, third.
drittens, thirdly.
drohen, *D.*, threaten.
drüben, over there.
Druckschrift, *f.*, -en, notice.
drunter und drüber, topsy-turvy.
duften, smell fragrant.
Düne, *f.*, -n, dune.
dunkel, dark.
dunkelgegerbt, dark-tanned.
durch, *A.*, through.
dürfen, *mod.*, to be allowed to.
Dutzend, *n.*, -e, dozen.

E
Ecke, *f.*, -n, corner.
edel, noble.
Ehre, *f.*, -n, honour.
ehrlich, honest.
Ehrlichkeit, *f.*, honesty.
Ei, *n.*, -er, egg.

Eiche, f., -n, oak tree.
eigen (zu . . . sein), own.
eigentlich, actually, really.
eilen, hurry.
Eindruck, m., ̈e, impression.
einfach, simple.
einige, a few, several.
einladen, s., invite.
einmal, once.
einmalig, unique.
einnehmen, s., take.
einnehmen (für), predispose (in someone's favour).
einrahmen, frame.
einsam, lonely.
Einsamkeit, f., solitude.
einschreiben, s., register.
einsehen, s., understand.
einstürzen, crumble.
eintönig, monotonous.
eintreffen, s., arrive.
eintreten, s., enter, occur.
Eintritt, m., -e, entrance.
einwecken, bottle.
einzeln, single.
einzig, solely.
Eis, n., ice.
eisgekühlt, cooled on ice.
eitel, vain.
Elefant, m., -en, -en, elephant.
Eltern, pl., parents.
Empfang, m., ̈e, reception.
empfinden, s., feel.
empörend, outrageous.
Ende, n., end.
Endstation, f., -en, terminus.
Engel, m., -, angel.
Engländer, m., -, Englishman.
entbehren, lack.
entdecken, discover.
Entdeckungsreise, f., -n, expedition.
Ente, f., -n, duck.
Enterich, m., -e, drake.
Entfernung, f., -en, distance, removal.
entgegenbringen, irr., show.
enthalten, s., contain.
entschließen, s., resolve.
entweder . . . oder, either . . . or.
Entwicklung, f., -en, development.
entzücken, delight.
entzückend, charming.
Enzian, m., -e, gentian.
Epos, n., Epen, epic poem.
Erdbeben, n., -, earthquake.
Erdbeere, f., -n, strawberry.
Erde, f., -n, earth.
Erfahrung, f., -en, experience.
erhalten, s., receive, maintain.

erhoben, raised.
erkennen, irr., recognise.
erklären, explain.
Erklärung, f., -en, explanation.
erlauben, allow.
erlauben (sich), permit oneself.
Erleben, n., experience.
Erleichterung, f., -en, relief.
Erlernung, f., learning.
ermüdend, tiring.
Ernte, f., -n, harvest.
Erntefest, n., -e, harvest festival.
ernten, bring in, harvest.
erreichen, reach.
erschrecken, s., be frightened.
erst, only.
erst-, first.
erstens, firstly.
Erstinhaber, m., -, first owner.
erstreben, strive for.
erwachen, wake up.
erwähnen, mention.
erwarten, expect.
erweisen, s., show.
erzählen, tell (story).
essen, s., eat.
Essen, n., food, meal.
Etage, f., -n, floor.
Expert(e), m., -en, -en, expert.

F

fabelhaft, extremely good, fine.
Fabrik, f., -en, factory.
Faden, m., ̈, thread.
fähig, G., capable of.
Fahne, f., -n, flag.
fahren, s., travel.
Fahrkarte, f., -n, ticket.
Fahrrad, n., ̈er, bicycle.
Fall, m., ̈e, case, fall.
fallen, s., fall.
falsch, false, faked.
fälschen, forge.
Fälschung, f., -en, forgery.
Familie, f., -n, family.
Farbbild, n., -er, colour photo.
Farbe, f., -n, colour.
Farbentönung, f., -en, shade.
fassen, hold, grip.
faul, lazy.
Faust, f., ̈e, fist.
Februar, m., February.
fechten, s., fight (duel, etc.).
Feder, f., -n, pen, feather.
Federbett, n., -en, feather bed.
Feierabendarbeit, f., -en, hobby, spare-
time work.

feierlich, impressive, ceremonious.
feiern, celebrate.
Feind, *m.,* **-e,** enemy.
Feld, *n.,* **-er,** field.
Felsen, *m.,* **-,** rock.
Fenster, *n.,* **-,** window.
Fensterscheibe, *f.,* **-n,** window pane.
Ferne Osten, der, *m.,* Far East.
fernliegen, *s.,* be far (from).
Fernsehapparat, *m.,* **-e,** television set.
Festspiel, *n.,* **-e,** festival (drama, music).
Festung, *f.,* **-en,** fortress.
Feuer, *n.,* **-,** fire.
feuerspeiend, erupting.
feurig, fiery.
finden, *s.,* find.
fischen, fish.
Flamme, *f.,* **-n,** flame.
Flasche, *f.,* **-n,** bottle.
flehen, appeal, beg.
Fleisch, *n.,* **-e,** meat.
Fleiß, *m.,* industriousness.
fleißig, industriously, hard.
Flickwerk, *n.,* **-e,** patchwork.
Fliege, *f.,* **-n,** fly.
fliegen, *s.,* fly.
fliehen, *s.,* flee.
Flughafen, *m.,* **˝,** airport.
Flugzeug, *n.,* **-e,** aeroplane.
flüstern, whisper.
folgen, *D.,* obey, follow.
fordern, demand.
Fortschritt, *m.,* **-e,** progress.
Fortsetzung, *f.,* **-en,** continuation.
Frachter, *m.,* **-,** cargo ship.
Franzose, *m.,* **-n, -n,** Frenchman.
Französich, French (language).
Frau, *f.,* **-en,** woman, wife.
frauenhaft, feminine.
Freihof, *m.,* **˝e,** open courtyard.
Freitag, *m.,* **-e,** Friday.
fressen, *s.,* eat (of or like an animal).
Freude, *f.,* **-n,** joy, pleasure.
freudig, happily.
Freund, *m.,* **-e,** friend.
Freundin, *f.,* **-nen,** friend (*f.*).
Friede(n), *m.,* **-n** [§ 52 (*b*)], peace.
Friedhof, *m.,* **˝e,** churchyard.
friedlich, peacefully.
frieren, *s.,* be cold, freeze.
frisch, fresh; **bei frischer Tat,** in the act.
froh, joyful.
fröhlich, cheerful, merry.
Frucht, *f.,* **˝e,** fruit.
früh, early.
Frühling, *m.,* **-e,** spring.
Frühstück, *n.,* **-e,** breakfast.

Fuchs, *m.,* **˝e,** fox.
Füchsin, *f.,* **-nen,** vixen.
Führer, *m.,* **-,** leader.
Füller, *m.,* **-,** fountain pen.
Füllfeder, *f.,* **-n,** fountain pen.
fünfzig, fifty.
Funke(n), *m.,* **-n** [§ 52 (*b*)], spark.
funkeln, sparkle.
für, *A.,* for.
furchtbar, frightful(ly).
Furore (machen), (make) a hit.
Fürsorge, *f.,* care, social work.
Fürst, *m.,* **-en, -en,** prince.
Fuß, *m.,* **˝e,** foot.
Fußballrasen, *m.,* **-,** football pitch.
Fußmatte, *f.,* **-n,** door mat.

G

Gans, *f.,* **˝e,** goose.
Gänserich, *m.,* **-e,** gander.
ganz, whole.
gänzlich, completely.
gar, well cooked.
Garage, *f.,* **-n,** garage.
Garten, *m.,* **˝,** garden.
Gast, *m.,* **˝e,** guest.
Gasthof, *m.,* **˝e,** inn, public house.
Geäst, *n.,* network of branches.
Gebärde, *f.,* **-n,** gesture.
gebären, *s.,* give birth.
Gebell, *n.,* barking.
geben, *s.,* give.
Gebiet, *n.,* **-e,** region, realm.
gebieten (über), be master (of).
Gebirge, *n.,* mountains.
Gebirgstal, *n.,* **˝er,** mountain valley.
Gebirgswelt, *f.,* **-en,** mountains.
Gebrüll, *n.,* roaring.
Geburtstag, *m.,* **-e,** birthday.
Gedanke(n), *m.,* **-en** [§ 52 (*b*)], idea.
gedeihen, *s.,* flourish.
Geduld, *f.,* patience.
geeignet, suitable.
Gefahr, *f.,* **-en,** danger.
gefährlich, dangerous.
Gefallen, *m.,* **-,** favour.
gefallen, *s., D.,* please.
Gefühl, *n.,* **-e,** feeling.
gegen, *A.,* against, towards.
Gegenteil, *n.,* **-e,** opposite.
Gehalt, *n.,* **˝er,** salary.
geheim, secret.
Geheimnis, *n.,* **-se,** secret.
gehen, *s.,* go.
gehören, *D.,* belong.
Geige, *f.,* **-n,** violin.
Geist, *m.,* **-er,** spirit, ghost.

gelangen, reach, arrive.
Geld, *n.*, money.
gelegen, situated.
Gelegenheit, *f.*, -en, opportunity.
Gemäldegallerie, *f.*, -n, picture gallery.
genau, exact(ly).
General, *m.*, "e & -e, general.
Geologe, *m.*, -n, -n, geologist.
Gepäck, *n.*, luggage.
geraten (gut), *s.*, turn out (well).
geräuschlos, noiselessly.
gern, gladly, like to.
Geruch, *m.*, "e, smell.
Gesang, *m.*, "e, song.
Geschäft, *n.*, -e, shop, business.
geschehen, *s.*, happen.
Geschenk, *n.*, -e, present.
Geschichte, *f.*, -n, history, story.
Geschichten machen, make a fuss.
Geschick, *n.*, skill.
geschickt, clever.
Geschirrwaschen, *n.*, washing up.
Geschmack, *m.*, taste.
geschmückt, decorated.
Geschrei, *n.*, shouting.
Geschütz, *n.*, -e, gun.
Geschwindigkeit, *f.*, -en, speed.
Geschwister, *n. pl.*, brother(s) and sister(s).
Geselligkeit, *f.*, -en, sociability, social occasion.
Gespenst, *n.*, -er, ghost.
gespreizt, spread out.
gesund, healthy.
gewahr werden, *s.*, notice.
Gewalt, *f.*, -en, power.
gewaltig, powerful, very much.
gewärtig, *G.*, prepared for.
Gewehr, *n.*, -e, rifle.
Gewimmel, *n.*, seething mass.
gewinnen, *s.*, win.
gewiß, certain(ly).
Gewißheit, *f.*, -en, certainly.
Gewitter, *n.*, -, thunderstorm.
gewöhnen (sich . . . an), get accustomed to
gewöhnlich, usually.
Gipfel, *m.*, -, peak.
Gitarre, *f.*, -n, guitar.
glänzen, sparkle, gleam.
Glas, *n.*, "er, glass.
glatt, smooth, slippery.
Glaube(n), *m.*, -n [§ 52 (*b*)], faith.
glauben, believe.
gleich, equal(ly), alike; at once.
gleichkommen, *s.*, *D.*, equal.
gleichtun, *s.*, *D.*, imitate.
Glocke, *f.*, -n, bell.

glorreich, glorious.
glücklich, happy.
Gold, *n.*, gold.
golden, gold.
gönnen (sich), treat (oneself).
gottseidank, thank goodness.
Graben, *m.*, ", ditch.
graben, *s.*, dig.
Grad, *m.*, -e, grade, degree.
Graf, *m.*, -en, -en, count.
Gräfin, *f.*, -nen, countess.
Grafschaft, *f.*, -en, county.
grandios, grandiose.
Granit, *m.*, -e, granite.
greifen, *s.*, grasp.
grob, rough.
Grönländer, *m.*, -, Greenlander.
Groschen, *m.*, -, penny (old coin).
groß, large, tall.
großartig, magnificent.
Großmutter, *f.*, ", grandmother.
Großstadt, *f.*, "e, metropolis.
Großvater, *m.*, ", grandfather.
Grund, *m.*, "e, reason.
Gruß, *m.*, "e, greeting.
Gulasch, *n.*, goulash.
Gummi, *m.*, -s, rubber.
Gunst, *f.*, "e, favour.
gut, good, well.

H

Haar, *n.*, -e, hair.
Hafen, *m.*, ", harbour.
Hahn, *m.*, "e, cock.
Haken, *m.*, -, hook.
halb, half.
Hälfte, *f.*, -n, half.
Hals, *m.*, "e, neck.
halten, *s.*, hold; halten (für), take (for).
Hammer, *m.*, ", hammer.
Hand, *f.*, "e, hand.
Handlung, *f.*, -en, action.
hängen, *tr.*, hang (up).
Hase, *m.*, -n, -n, hare.
Haselnuß, *f.*, -nüsse, cobnut.
Haß, *m.*, hatred.
Haube, *f.*, -n, cap.
hauen, hit.
Haufe(n), *m.*, -n [§ 52 (*b*)], heap, pile.
Haus, *n.*, "er, house.
Hausfrau, *f.*, -en, housewife.
Hausordnung, *f.*, domestic routine.
heben, *s.*, lift.
Heft, *n.*, -e, exercise book.
heftig, violent(ly).
hegen, cherish.
Heidekraut, *n.*, "er, heather.

Heim, *n.,* -e, home.
Heimat, *f.,* -en, home-country.
heiß, hot.
heißen, *s.,* be called, named; mean.
heizen, heat.
Heizung, *f.,* -en, heating.
Held, *m.,* -en, -en, hero.
helfen, *s.,* help.
hell, light (colour), bright.
Hemd, *n.,* -en, shirt.
Herbst, *m.,* -e, autumn.
Herr, *m.,* -n, -en, gentleman, sir.
herrlich, magnificent.
Herrschaften! goodness me!
Herrscher, *m.,* -, ruler, master.
herunter, down.
Herz, *n.,* -en [§ 52 (*a*)], heart.
herzlich, heartily.
heulen, howl.
heute, to-day.
hiesig, local.
Hilfe, *f.,* -n, help.
Hilferuf, *m.,* -e, cry for help.
Himmel, *m.,* -, sky, heaven.
Himmelbett, *n.,* -en, canopied four-poster.
himmelwärts, towards the sky.
hinfahren, *s.,* travel to a place.
hinreißend, enchanting.
hinter, *D./A.,* behind.
Hitze, *f.,* -n, heat.
hoch, hoh-, high.
hocken, squat.
hoffen, hope.
Hofrat, *m.,* ⁔e, councillor.
horchen (auf), listen (to).
hören, hear.
Horizont, *m.,* -e, horizon.
Hörspiel, *n.,* -e, radio-play.
hübsch, pretty.
Hubschrauber, *m.,* -, helicopter.
Huf, *m.,* -e, hoof.
Huhn, *n.,* ⁔er, chicken, fowl.
Hund, *m.,* -e, dog.
hundert, hundred.
hungrig, hungry.
Hut, *m.,* ⁔e, hat.

I

immer, always.
indem, as, while.
indisch, Indian.
Insekt, *n.,* -en, insect.
Inserent, *m.,* -en, -en, advertiser.
Interesse, *n.,* -n, interest.
irrig, mistaken, wrong.
Italiener, *m.,* -, Italian.

J

Jahr, *n.,* -e, year.
Jahreszahl, *f.,* -en, date (history).
Jahrhundert, *n.,* -e, century.
jammern, moan, complain.
Januar, *m.,* January.
Japaner, *m.,* -, Japanese.
jedesmal, every time.
jedoch, but.
jener, that.
Jesuit, *m.,* -en, -en, Jesuit.
jetzt, now.
Johannistag, *m.,* -e, midsummer day.
jüdisch, Jewish.
Juli, *m.,* July.
jung, young.
Juni, *m.,* June.
Juxartikel, *m.,* -, party novelty.

K

Kabine, *f.,* -n, cabin.
Kaffee, *m.,* -s, coffee.
Kaktus, *m.,* **Kakteen** [§ 90 (*c*)], cactus.
Kalb, *n.,* ⁔er, calf.
Kamerad, *m.,* -en, -en, comrade.
kämmen, comb.
Kampf, *m.,* ⁔e, fight.
Kanal, *m.,* ⁔e, canal.
Kandidat, *m.,* -en, -en, candidate.
Kaninchen, *n.,* -, rabbit.
Kapitel, *n.,* -, chapter.
Kartoffel, *f.,* -n, potato.
Käse, *m.,* -, cheese.
Kassa machen, be a box-office success.
Kasten, *m.,* ⁔, wardrobe.
Katastrophe, *f.,* -n, catastrophe.
katholisch, catholic.
kauen, chew.
kaufen, buy.
kaum, hardly.
Kautsch, *f.,* -en, couch.
keineswegs, not at all.
kennen, *irr.,* know.
Kenntnis, *f.,* -se, knowledge.
Kerze, *f.,* -n, candle.
Kette, *f.,* -n, chain.
Keuchhusten, *m.,* whooping cough.
Kiesel, *m.,* -, pebble.
Kind, *n.,* -er, child.
kindisch, childish.
Kino, *n.,* -s, cinema.
Kirche, *f.,* -n, church.
Kirsche, *f.,* -n, cherry.
Kissen, *n.,* -, cushion, pillow.
Kiste, *f.,* -n, chest.
Klage, *f.,* -n, complaint.
klar, clear.

Klause, *f.*, -n, hermitage.
kleben, stick.
Kleid, *n.*, -er, frock.
kleiden, suit, clothe.
Kleidungsstück, *n.*, -e, article of clothing.
Kleinod, *n.*, -ien, jewel.
klemmen, squeeze.
Kleptomane, *m.*, -n, -n, cleptomaniac.
klingeln, ring.
klirren, rattle (of glass, metal).
klopfen, knock.
Kloster, *n.*, ″, convent.
Knabe, *m.*, -n, -n, boy.
Knallbonbon, *n.*, -s, cracker.
knallen, go bang.
kneten, screw up, knead.
Knochen, *m.*, -, bone.
Knopf, *m.*, ″e, button.
Knotenstock, *m.*, ″e, club.
Köchin, *f.*, -nen, cook.
Kohle, *f.*, -n, coal.
Komet, *m.*, -en, -en, comet.
komisch, funny.
kommen, *s.*, come.
Komparse, *m.*, -n, -n, film extra.
Konditorei, *f.*, -en, café.
König, *m.*, -e, king.
können, *mod.*, to be able to.
Konservenbüchse, *f.*, -n, tin.
Konsonant, *m.*, -en, -en, consonant.
Konzert, *n.*, -e, concert.
Konzertsaal, *m.*, ″e, concert hall.
Kopf, *m.*, ″e, head.
körperlich, physically.
Kost, *f.*, food.
Kostbarkeit, *f.*, -en, treasure.
kostenlos, gratuitous.
köstlich, delicious.
Kostüm, *n.*, -e, costume.
krachend, with a crash.
Kragen, *m.*, -, collar.
krakelig, scrawly.
Krampf, *m.*, ″e, cramp.
Kranich, *m.*, -e, crane (bird).
Krankenschwester, *f.*, -n, nurse.
Kreis, *m.*, -e, circle.
kriegen, get.
Krug, *m.*, ″e, jug.
Küche, *f.*, -n, kitchen, cooking.
Kuchen, *m.*, -, cake.
Kuchenblech, *n.*, -e, baking sheet.
Kuh, *f.*, ″e, cow.
kühlend, cooling.
Kunde, *m.*, -n, -n, client.
Kunst, *f.*, ″e, art.
kurz, short(ly).
kürzlich, recently.

küssen, kiss.
Kutscher, *m.*, -, cabby.

L

lachen, laugh.
lächerlich, ridiculous.
Lade, *f.*, -n, drawer.
Laden, *m.*, -, shutter.
Laden, *m.*, ″, shop.
Lager, *n.*, -, camp.
Laken, *n.*, -, pall, sheet.
Lamm, *n.*, ″er, lamb.
landen, land.
Landkarte, *f.*, -n, map.
Landschaft, *f.*, -en, landscape.
Landungssteg, *m.*, -e, landing stage.
Langschläferei, *f.*, late rising.
langweilig, boring.
Lärm, *m.*, -e, noise.
lärmen, make a noise.
lassen, *s.*, leave.
Lastauto, *n.*, -s, lorry.
Laube, *f.*, -n, arbour.
lauschen, *D.*, listen to.
Laut, *m.*, -e, sound.
laut, loud(ly).
läuten, ring.
lauter, nothing but.
Leben, *n.*, -, life.
Lebensantrieb, *m.*, vitality.
Leber, *f.*, liver.
Leder, *n.*, -, leather.
leer, empty.
legen, lay.
lehnen, lean.
Lehrer, *m.*, -, teacher.
Lehrerin, *f.*, -nen, (woman) teacher.
Leib, *m.*, -er, body.
Leid(en), *n.*, -en (-), suffering.
leiden, *s.*, suffer.
leiden (nicht . . . können), dislike.
leid tun (sich), be sorry for (oneself).
leihen, *s.*, lend.
leise, soft.
Lektüre, *f.*, -n, reading.
lenken, lead, guide.
Lerche, *f.*, -n, lark.
lesen, *s.*, read.
letztens, lastly.
Licht, *n.*, -er, light.
Lichtmeß, *f.*, Candlemas.
lieben, love.
lieblich, pleasant.
Lieblingsunterricht, *m.*, favourite lesson.
Lied, *n.*, -er, song.
liefern, deliver.

Lift, *m.,* **-e,** lift.
lila, mauve.
Lilie, *f.,* **-n,** lily.
Linde, *f.,* **-n,** lime tree.
Lippe, *f.,* **-n,** lip.
Lob, *n.,* praise.
Loch, *n.,* ″**er,** hole.
Lohn, *m.,* ″**e,** wages.
Lokal, *n.,* **-e,** restaurant.
los und ledig werden, be rid of.
Löwe, *m.,* **-n, -n,** lion.
Löwin, *f.,* **-nen,** lioness.
Luder, *n.* **(armes),** (poor) devil.
Luft, *f.,* ″**e,** air.
lügen, *s.,* tell lies.
Lunge, *f.,* **-n,** lung.
lustig, merrily.

M

machen, make.
Macht, *f.,* ″**e,** power.
Mädchen, *n.,* **-,** girl.
Magd, *f.,* ″**e,** maiden, maid.
Magen, *m.,* **-,** stomach.
Mai, *m.,* May.
Major, *m.,* **-e,** major.
Mangel, *m.,* ″**,** lack.
Manieren, *f.,* *pl.,* manners.
Mann, *m.,* ″**er,** man, husband.
Mannschaft, *f.,* **-en,** team.
Mannschaftsführer, *m.,* **-,** captain of team.
Mantel, *m.,* ″**,** coat.
Marmorklippe, *f.,* **-n,** marble cliff.
März, *m.,* March.
Maßnahme, *f.,* **-n,** measure.
Mast, *m.,* **-en,** mast.
Match, *m.,* **-e,** match.
Matrose, *m.,* **-n, -n,** sailor.
mauerfest, firm as a rock (wall).
Maus, *f.,* ″**e,** mouse.
Medium, *n.,* **Medien,** medium.
Meer, *n.,* **-e,** sea.
Mehl, *n.,* **-e,** flour.
meinen, mean.
Meister, *m.,* **-,** master (of a trade).
mengen (sich), mix.
Mensch, *m.,* **-en, -en,** person, human being.
Menschen(s)kind! man!
messen, *s.,* measure.
Messer, *n.,* **-,** knife.
Meter, *m.,* **-,** metre.
Militärdienst, *m.,* military service.
Milliarde, *f.,* **-n,** milliard.
Million, *f.,* **-en,** million.
Mineral, *n.,* **-ien,** mineral.

Minute, *f.,* **-n,** minute.
mit, *D.,* with.
Mittag, *m.,* **-e,** noon.
Mittagessen, *n.,* **-,** lunch, dinner.
mitteilen, *D.,* inform.
Mittelmeer, *n.,* Mediterranean.
Mitternacht, *f.,* ″**e,** midnight.
Mittwoch, *m.,* **-e,** Wednesday.
Modell, *n.,* **-e,** model.
mögen, *mod.,* to like to.
Monat, *m.,* **-e,** month.
Mond, *m.,* **-e,** moon.
Monsun, *m.,* **-e,** monsoon.
Montag, *m.,* **-e,** Monday.
Mord, *m.,* **-e,** murder.
Morgenmesse, *f.,* **-n,** morning mass.
morgens, in the morning.
Motor, *m.,* **-en,** engine.
Mottorrad, *n.,* ″**er,** motor bicycle.
Möwe, *f.,* **-n,** seagull.
müde, tired.
Mühsal, *f.,* **-e,** difficulty.
Mund, *m.,* **-e &** ″**er,** mouth.
mündig, of age.
mündlich, oral.
munter, lively.
Museum, *n.,* **Museen,** museum.
Musikstunde, *f.,* **-n,** music lesson.
Muskel, *m.,* **-n,** muscle.
müssen, *mod.,* to have to.
Muster, *n.,* **-,** pattern.
mutig, courageous.
Mutter, *f.,* ″**,** mother.
Mütterverein, *m.,* **-e,** Mothers' Union.
Mütze, *f.,* **-n,** cap.

N

nach, *D.,* to, after, past.
Nachbar, *m.,* **-s (-n), -n,** neighbour.
nachfolgen, *D.,* succeed.
nachmachen, imitate.
nachmittags, in the afternoon.
Nachricht, *f.,* **-en,** news.
Nachruf, *m.,* **-e,** obituary.
Nacht, *f.,* ″**e,** night.
Nachteil, *m.,* **-e,** disadvantage.
Nachtisch, *m.,* **-e,** dessert.
nächtlich, nightly.
nachts, at night.
Nachweisadresse, *f.,* **-n,** permanent address.
Nagel, *m.,* ″**,** nail.
Nähe, *f.,* proximity (near).
naheliegen, *s.,* to be expected, be in character.
nähen, sew.
nahrhaft, nourishing.

Name(n), *m.,* **-n** [§ 52 (*b*)], name.
Narr, *m.,* **-en, -en,** fool.
Nase, *f.,* **-n,** nose.
neben, *D./A.,* beside, next to.
nebenan, next door.
Neffe, *m.,* **-n, -n,** nephew.
Neger, *m.,* **-,** negro.
nehmen, *s.,* take.
Nelke, *f.,* **-n,** carnation.
nennen, *irr.,* name, call.
Nerv, *m.,* **-en,** nerve.
Nest, *n.,* **-er,** nest.
neugeformt, newly formed.
neugereinigt, newly cleaned.
neugierig, curious.
Neuigkeit, *f.,* **-en,** news.
neunzig, ninety.
nichts, nothing.
nie, never.
Niederlassung, *f.,* **-en,** settlement.
niemand, no one.
noch, still.
Not, *f.,* **˝e,** need.
Note, *f.,* **-n,** mark, report.
nottun, *s.,* be necessary.
Novelle, *f.,* **-n,** short story.
Null, *f.,* **-en,** nought, cipher.
Nummer, *f.,* **-n,** number.
nun, now.

O

oben, above, up.
Ochs, *m.,* **-en, -en,** ox.
Ofen, *m.,* **˝,** stove, oven.
offen, open.
Offizier, *m.,* **-e,** officer.
ohne, without.
Ohr, *n.,* **-en,** ear.
Onkel, *m.,* **-,** uncle.
Oper, *f.,* **-n,** opera.
Opernhaus, *n.,* **˝er,** opera-house.
Orange, *f.,* **-n,** orange.
Ort, *m.,* **-e & ˝er,** place.
Ost(en), *m.,* East.
Ostern, *pl.* (§ 57), Easter.
Österreicher, *m.,* Austrian.
östlich, eastern.
Ostsee, *f.,* Baltic.

P

Paar, *n.,* **-e,** pair.
Päckchen, *n.,* **-,** packet.
Packet, *n.,* **-e,** parcel.
Papagei, *m.,* **-en, -en,** parrot.
Passagier, *m.,* **-e,** passenger (on boat).
Passant, *m.,* **-en, -en,** passer by.

Pastetchen, *n.,* **-,** meat pasty.
Pastor, *m.,* **-en, & -e,** pastor.
pechschwarz, pitch-black.
Pensum, *n.,* **Pensa,** allotted task.
Personal, *n.,* staff.
persönlich, personal.
Pfannkuchen, *m.,* **-,** pancake.
Pfeife, *f.,* **-n,** pipe, whistle.
Pferd, *n.,* **-e,** horse.
Pfingsten, *pl.* (§ 57), Whitsun.
Pflaster, *n.,* **-,** pavement, street.
Pflaume, *f.,* **-n,** plum.
pflegen, be accustomed to.
Pflicht, *f.,* **-en,** duty.
pflücken, pick.
Pförtner, *m.,* **-,** porter (doorkeeper).
Philologe, *m.,* **-n, -n,** philologist.
Philosoph, *m.,* **-en, -en,** philosopher.
Photograph, *m.,* **-en, -en,** photographer.
Photohelfer, *m.,* **-,** book of aids to photography.
Plage, *f.,* **-n,** scourge.
Plakat, *n.,* **-e,** poster.
Platte, *f.,* **-n,** dish.
Platz, *m.,* **˝e,** place.
plaudern, chat.
plötzlich, suddenly.
Poet, *m.,* **-en, -en,** poet.
Politik, *f.,* policy, politics.
Polizist, *m.,* **-en, -en,** policeman.
Pommer, *m.,* **-n, -n,** Pomeranian (person).
praktisch, practical.
Preuße, *m.,* **-n, -n,** Prussian.
prima, first-class.
Prinz, *m.,* **-en, -en,** prince.
Propfen, *m.,* **-,** cork.
Propfenzieher, *m.,* **-,** corkscrew.
Proselyt, *m.,* **-en, -en,** proselyte.
Prozent, *n.,* **-e,** percentage.
Prozeß, *m.,* **-e,** law suit.
Prüfung, *f.,* **-en,** examination.
prügeln (sich), have a fight.
Pudel, *m.,* **-,** poodle.
Punkt, *m.,* **-e,** point, full-stop.
Puppe, *f.,* **-n,** doll.

Q

Qual, *f.,* **-en,** torment.
Quittung, *f.,* **-en,** receipt.

R

Rabe, *m.,* **-n, -n,** raven.
Rad, *n.,* **˝er,** bicycle.
Radtour, *f.,* **-en,** cycle tour.
rasch, quickly.

rasen, rush.
Rat, m., counsel.
raten, s., intr., advise; tr., guess.
Ratschlag, m., "e, hint, advice.
Rätsel, n., -, riddle.
rauchen, smoke.
Raucherabteil, n., -e, smoking compartment.
rauh, rough.
Recht, n., -e, right.
recht, right.
Rechtsanwalt, m., "e, lawyer.
rechtzeitig, in good time.
Rede (zur . . . stellen), challenge.
reden, weak.
Reflektant, m., -en, -en, prospective customer.
regelmäßig, even.
Regenmantel, m., ", mackintosh.
Regierung, f., -en, government.
Regiment, n., -e, régime.
Regiment, n., -er, regiment.
regnen, rain.
Reich, n., -e, empire.
reich, rich.
reichen, reach, suffice.
reif, ripe.
Reise, f., -n, journey.
Reisebericht, m., -e, travel book.
Reiseführer, m., -, guide book.
reisen, travel.
reiten, s., ride.
reizend, charming.
Reklameplakat, n., -e, hoarding.
reklamieren, claim.
rennen, irr., run.
Reparatur, f., -en, repair.
Resultat, n., -e, result.
retten, rescue, save.
Rettungswagen, m., -, ambulance.
Reue, f., remorse.
Rhein, m., Rhine.
Rohmaterial, n., -ien, raw material.
Rolle, f., -n, part (in play).
Roman, m., -e, novel.
rosa, pink.
Rose, f., -n, rose.
rosten, rust.
rösten, fry, roast.
rot, red.
Rückkehr, f., return.
Ruderboot, n., -e, rowing boat.
Ruf, m., -e, call, reputation.
rufen, s., call.
Ruhe, f., quiet, rest.
Ruhetag, m., -e, day of rest.
ruhig, quiet(ly).
rührend, moving.

Rundfunk, m., wireless, radio.
Russe, m., -n, -n, Russian.
rüstig, fit, hale.

S

Saalschlacht, f., -en, rowdy fight indoors.
Sache, f., -n, thing.
säen, sow.
sagen, say.
Same(n), m., -n [§ 52 (b)], seed.
Sammlung, f., -en, collection.
Samstag, m., -e, Saturday.
sämtlich, all.
Satz, m., "e, sentence.
Sau, f., "e, sow.
sauber, clean.
sauer, sour, toilsome.
saufen, s., drink (of or like an animal).
saugen, s., suck.
sausen, rush.
Schach, n., chess.
Schachtel, f., -n, box.
schaffen, work, manage to do.
Schaffner, m., -, conductor (bus, tram).
schallen, (re)sound.
Schalter, m., -, counter, ticket office.
schändlich, shameful.
schätzen, value.
schäumen, foam.
Schauspiel, n., -e, drama, spectacle.
Schauspieler, m., -, actor.
Scheibe, f., -n, window pane.
Scheit, n., -e, piece of wood.
scheitern, founder, fail.
schenken, give a present.
Schi, m., - & -er, ski.
schick, chic.
schicken, send.
schieben, s., push.
schießen, s., shoot.
Schifahrer, m., -, skier.
Schiff, n., -e, ship.
Schilf, n., -e, reeds.
Schirm, m., -e, umbrella.
Schlacht, f., -en, battle.
Schlaf, m., sleep.
schlafen, s., sleep.
Schläfchen, n., -, nap.
Schlag, m., "e, blow.
schlagen, s., hit, beat, strike.
Schlagsahne, f., whipped cream.
schlau, sly, clever.
schlecht, bad(ly).
schließen, s., shut.
schließlich, in the end, finally.
schlimm, bad, naughty.

Schlimmste, *n.*, *adj.-n.*, the worst.
Schlips, *m.*, -e, tie.
Schlückchen, *n.*, -, a little drop.
Schlüssel, *m.*, -, key.
schmackhaft, tasty.
schmal, narrow.
schmecken, taste.
schmelzen, melt.
Schmerz, *m.*, -en, pain, grief.
schmücken, decorate.
schnalzen, click with tongue.
Schnaps, *m.*, ˝e, brandy.
Schnee, *m.*, snow.
schneiden, *s.*, cut.
schnellen, release suddenly, fling.
schnellfließend, swiftly-flowing.
Schnurrbart, *m.*, ˝e, moustache.
Schokolade, *f.*, -n, chocolate.
schon, already.
schön, beautiful.
Schönheit, *f.*, -en, beauty.
Schotte, *m.*, -n, -n. Scotchman.
Schottin, *f.*, -nen, Scotchwoman.
Schrank, *m.*, ˝e, wardrobe.
schreiben, *s.*, write.
schreien, *s.*, cry out.
Schriftsteller, *m.*, -, author.
Schriftzeichen, *n.*, -, written character.
schrillen, whistle, ring.
Schritt, *m.*, -e, step.
Schritt und Tritt (in), in step.
Schuh, *m.*, -e, shoe.
Schulaufgabe, *f.*, -n, homework.
Schuld, *f.*, -en, debt.
Schule, *f.*, -n, school.
Schüler, *m.*, -, pupil.
Schuster, *m.*, -, cobbler.
Schwäbin, *f.*, -nen, Swabian woman.
schwach, weak.
Schwägerin, *f.*, -nen, sister-in-law.
Schwalbe, *f.*, -n, swallow.
Schwarzbrot, *n.*, -e, rye bread.
schwatzen, chatter.
Schwede, *m.*, -n, -n, Swede.
Schweif, *m.*, -e, tail.
schweigen, *s.*, be silent.
Schwein, *n.*, -e, pig.
Schweiß, *m.*, sweat.
schwer, heavy, difficult.
Schwert, *n.*, -er, sword.
Schwester, *f.*, -n, sister.
Schwierigkeit, *f.*, -en, difficulty.
Schwimmbad, *n.*, ˝er, swimming bath.
Schwindler, *m.*, -, trickster.
schwören, *s.*, swear.
schwül, sultry.
sechzig, sixty.
See, *m.*, -n, lake.

See, *f.*, -n, sea.
Segen, *m.*, -, blessing.
sehen, *s.*, see.
sehenswert, worth seeing.
sehr, very.
Seidenmalerei, *f.*, painting on silk.
seit, *D.*, since, for (time).
Seite, *f.*, -n, page, side.
Sekretärin, *f.*, -nen, secretary.
selbstverständlich, as a matter of course.
selten, rare.
senden, *irr.*, send.
Sender, *m.*, -, wireless station transmitter.
Senf, *m.*, mustard.
setzen, place.
sicher, sure of, safe.
sichtbar, visible.
siebzig, seventy.
sieden, *s.*, boil.
Signal, *n.*, -e, signal.
singen, *s.*, sing.
sittlich, moral.
sitzen, *s.*, sit, serve time in prison.
skandinavisch, Scandinavian.
smaragd, emerald green.
sofort, at once.
sogar, even.
Sohn, *m.*, ˝e, son.
Soldat, *m.*, -en, -en, soldier.
sollen, *mod.*, to be expected to.
Sommer, *m.*, summer.
Sonnabend, *m.*, -e, Saturday.
Sonne, *f.*, -n, sun.
sonnig, sunny.
Sonntag, *m.*, -e, Sunday.
Sorge, *f.*, -n, anxiety, care.
Sorte, *f.*, -n, kind.
sowohl . . . wie, both . . . and.
sparen, save.
Sparsamkeit, *f.*, thrift.
spät, late.
später, later.
Spaten, *m.*, -, spade.
Spatz, *m.*, -en, -en, sparrow.
spazieren (gehen), go for a walk.
Spaziergang, *m.*, ˝e, walk.
Spazierstock, ˝e, walking stick.
speien, *s.*, vomit.
Spiegel, *m.*, -, mirror.
spiegeln (sich), be mirrored.
Spiel, *n.*, -e, game, play.
spielen, play.
Spielzeug, *n.*, -e, toy.
spinnen, *s.*, spin.
spiritistisch, spiritualist.
Sporn, *m.*, Sporen, spur.
Sportlehrer, *m.*, -, games master.

Sportplatz, *m.*, ˮe, playing field.
spotten, *G.*, jeer.
sprechen, *s.*, speak.
springen, *s.*, spring, crack.
Staat, *m.*, -en, state; finery (no *pl.*).
Staatskirche, *f.*, -n, state church.
Stammcafé, *n.*, -s, favourite café.
standhalten, *s.*, stand fast.
stark, strong, corpulent.
starten, start (race).
Statist, *m.*, -en, -en, (theatre) extra.
Stativ, *n.*, -e, tripod.
stattfinden, *s.*, take place.
stecken, stick.
stehen, *s.*, stand.
stehlen, *s.*, steal.
steigen, *s.*, climb.
steil, steep.
steinig, stony.
Steinkrug, *m.*, ˮe, beer tankard.
Stelle, *f.*, -n, post, job, place.
Stenotypistin, *f.*, -nen, shorthand-typist.
sterben, *s.*, die.
stets, always.
Steuer, *f.*, -n, tax.
Stimme, *f.*, -n, voice.
stöbern, rummage.
Stock, *m.*, ˮe, stick, floor.
Stoff, *m.*, -e, material.
stolz, proud.
stoßen, *s.*, push.
strafen, punish.
Strahl, *m.*, -en, beam (of light).
Strauch, *m.*, ˮer, bush.
Streichholz, *n.*, ˮer, match.
streiten (sich), *s.*, quarrel.
stricken, knit.
Strom, *m.*, ˮe, river (large).
Stube, *f.*, -n, room, sitting room.
Studienrat, ˮe (title of), secondary school teacher.
studieren, study.
Stuhl, *m.*, ˮe, chair.
Stunde, *f.*, -n, hour, lesson.
Sturm, *m.*, ˮe, storm.
stürzen, fall over, down, burst into.
Stute, *f.*, -n, mare.
suchen, look for.
Süden, *m.*, south.
Suppe, *f.*, -n, soup.
süß, sweet.

T

Tafel, *f.*, -n, board, table.
Tag, *m.*, -e, day.
Tagesanbruch, *m.*, dawn.
täglich, daily.

Takt, *m.*, -e, beat (rhythm).
Tal, *n.*, ˮer, valley.
Tannenbaum, *m.*, ˮe, fir tree.
Tante, *f.*, -n, aunt.
tanzen, dance.
Tanzlied, *n.*, song for dancing.
Tapete, *f.*, -n, wallpaper.
tapfer, brave.
Taschentuch, *n.*, ˮer, handkerchief.
Tasse, *f.*, -n, cup.
Tat, *f.*, -en, deed.
Tatar, *m.*, -en, -en, Tartar.
Tätigkeit, *f.*, -en, activity.
Tau, *m.*, dew.
tausend, das Tausend, *n.*, -e, thousand.
Tee, *m.*, -s, tea.
teilhaben (an), share (in).
telefonieren, telephone.
Telegraph, *m.*, -en, -en, telegraphist.
Tenor, *m.*, ˮe & -e, tenor.
Termin, *m.*, -e, date, closing date.
Tertianer, *m.*, -, fifth-former.
Teufel, *m.*, -, devil.
Theater, *n.*, -, theatre.
Thema, *n.*, -en & -ata, theme, subject.
Thymian, *m.*, thyme.
Tinte, *f.*, -n, ink.
Tisch, *m.*, -e, table.
Titel, *m.*, -, title.
Tochter, *f.*, ˮ, daughter.
Tod, *m.*, -e, death.
Todesnot, *f.*, agony.
tönen, sound.
Tor, *m.*, -en, -en, fool.
Torbogen, *m.*, -, archway.
Torte, *f.*, -n, sponge cake, open tart.
tot, dead.
Tourist, *m.*, -en, -en, tourist.
tradieren, hand down.
tragen, *s.*, carry, wear.
Transparent, *n.*, -e, streamer.
Traubenlese, *f.*, grape harvest.
Traum, *m.*, ˮe, dream.
träumen, dream.
traurig, sad.
treffen, *s.*, meet.
treten, *s.*, step.
Tribut, *m.*, -e, tribute.
Trieb, *m.*, -e, impulse, urge.
triefen, *s.*, drip.
trinken, *s.*, drink.
Tropen, *pl.*, tropics.
Trotz, *m.*, defiance.
trotzdem, in spite of this.
trotzen, *D.*, defy.
tüchtig, *adj.*, efficient, *adv.*, very much.
tun, *s.*, do.
Tür, *f.*, -en, door.

U

üben, practise.
über, *D./A.,* above, over.
Überbleibsel, *n.,* -, remnant.
überflüssig, superfluous.
überhaupt, in general, at all.
überraschen, *insep.,* surprise.
überschneiden (sich), *s., insep.,* inter-
   sect.
Übersetzung, *f.,* -en, translation.
überwinden, *s., insep.,* get over, defeat.
überzeugend, convincing.
Überzeugung, *f.,* -en, conviction.
üblich, usual.
Ufer, *n.,* -, river-bank.
Uhr, *f.,* -en, clock.
um, *A.,* round, about, around.
Umfang, *m.,* ⸗e, dimension.
umfangreich, large, spacious.
Umgang, *m.,* contact.
umgehen (mit), *s., sep.,* consort (with).
umsteigen, *s., sep.,* change (train, etc.).
unanfechtbar, indisputable.
unbekannt, unknown.
unendlich, infinitely.
unentdeckt, undiscovered.
unentwickelt, undeveloped.
unerforscht, unexplored.
unermüdlich, untiring(ly).
unerwartet, unexpected(ly).
unfehlbar, infallibly.
Ungar, *m.,* -n, -n, Hungarian.
Unglück, *n.,* -e, accident.
unheimlich, uncannily.
unmittelbar, immediately.
unter, *D./A.,* under, underneath.
unterhalten, *s., insep.,* entertain.
unterrichten, *insep.,* teach.
unterscheiden, *s., insep.,* distinguish.
Unterschrift, *f.,* -en, signature.
unvermögend, not wealthy.
unzimperlich, robust.
Urlaub, *m.,* -e, holidays.
Ursache, *f.,* -n, reason, cause.

V

Vater, *m.,* ⸗, father.
Ventil, *m.,* -e, valve, (air)-outlet.
Verabredung, *f.,* -en, date, appointment.
verächtlich, *adv.,* disdainfully, *adj.,*
   despicable.
verankert, anchored.
verboten (es ist . . .), (it is) forbidden.
verbringen, *s.,* spend (time).
verdauen, digest.
verdienen, deserve, earn.
Verdienst, *n.,* -e, merit.

Verdienst, *m.,* earnings.
verdient (sich . . . machen), acquire
   merit.
vergeßlich, forgetful.
vergleichen, *s.,* compare.
Vergnügung, *f.,* -en, pleasure.
Verkehr, *m.,* (social) relations.
verkehren (mit), associate (with), visit.
verklingen, *s.,* cease (of sound).
verlangen, *imp., A.,* want.
verlassen, *s.,* leave.
verlaufen, lost.
Verlegenheit, *f.,* -en, quandary.
verlesen, *s.,* read out.
verlieren, *s.,* lose.
Verlobung, *f.,* -en, engagement.
vermeiden, *s.,* avoid.
vermutlich, presumably.
verprügeln, beat.
verreisen, go on a journey.
verrückt, mad.
verschieben, *s.,* defer.
verschieden, various.
verschwenden, waste.
verschwinden, *s.,* vanish.
versehen, *s.,* service.
versprechen, *s.,* promise.
Verstand, *m.,* sense, reason.
verstummen, fall silent.
vertrauensvoll, confidently.
vertraut, familiar.
Verwandte, *m., adj.-n.,* relation.
verweigern, *D.,* deny, refuse.
verzeihen, *s.,* forgive.
verzichten, renounce.
verzweifeln, despair.
verzweifelt, desperately.
Veteran, *m.,* -en, -en, veteran.
Vetter, *m.,* -, cousin.
viel, much, a lot.
vielleicht, perhaps.
viereckig, square.
viertel, quarter.
Viertel, *n.,* -, quarter, district.
vierzig, forty.
Vogel, *m.,* ⸗, bird.
Vokabel, *f.,* -n, word, (*pl.*) vocabulary.
Volk, *n.,* ⸗er, people, nation.
Volkslied, *n.,* -er, folk song.
vollkommen, perfectly.
von, *D.,* of, from.
vor, *D./A.,* in front of.
vorbereiten, prepare.
vorbringen, *s.,* urge (reasons).
vorgehen, *s.,* advance, proceed.
vorig-, last.
vormittags, in the morning.
vorsetzen, serve (food).

vorstellen (sich, *D.***),** imagine.
Vorteil, *m.*, **-e,** advantage.
Vortrag, *m.*, **ᵁe,** lecture.
vorziehen, *s.*, prefer.

W

wachsen, *s.*, grow.
Wachtmeister, *m.*, **-,** guard.
Waffel, *f.*, **-n,** waffle.
Wagen, *m.*, **-,** car, cart.
wagen, dare.
Wahl, *f.*, **-en,** choice.
wählen, choose.
Wahrheit, *f.*, **-en,** truth.
wahrscheinlich, probably.
Wald, *m.*, **ᵁer,** forest.
Waldweg, *m.*, **-e,** forest path.
wallen, rush (water).
Walzer, *m.*, **-,** waltz.
Wand, *f.*, **ᵁe,** wall (of room).
wann? when?
warm, warm.
warten, wait.
warum? why?
was? what?
waschen, *s.*, wash.
Waschtag, *m.*, **-e,** washing day.
Wasser, *n.*, water.
weglegen, put away.
wehen, blow.
weiblich, feminine.
weichen, *s.*, yield, retreat.
Weihnachten, *pl.* (§ 57), Christmas.
weinen, weep.
Weißwurst, *f.*, **ᵁe,** type of sausage.
Welt, *f.*, **-en,** world.
Weltgeschichte, *f.*, world history.
Weltkrieg, *m.*, world war.
wenden, *irr.*, turn.
wer? who?
werben, *s.*, woo.
werden, *irr.*, become.
werfen, *s.*, throw.
Werk, *n.*, **-e,** work, task.
Wesen, *n.*, **-,** being.
Wetter, *n.*, weather.
wichtig, important.
wider, *A.*, against.
widmen, dedicate, devote.
wie? how?
wiederholt, repeatedly.
Wiesenblume, *f.*, **-n,** meadow flower.
wieviel? how much, many, what?
Wille(n), *m.*, **-n** [§ 52 (*b*)], will.
winken, wave.
Wirklichkeit, *f.*, **-en,** reality.
Wirtin, *f.*, **-nen,** landlady.

wissen, *irr.*, know.
witzig, amusing, witty.
wo? where?
Woche, *f.*, **-n,** week.
wohlbekannt, well known.
wohltätig, beneficial.
Wohnung, *f.*, **-en,** flat, accommodation.
Wohnungsamt, *n.*, **ᵁer,** billeting office.
Wohnzimmer, *n.*, **-,** living room.
Wolke, *f.*, **-n,** cloud.
Wolle, *f.*, wool.
wollen, *mod.*, to want/wish to.
Wort, *n.*, **-e** & **ᵁer** (§ 445), word.
wund, sore.
Wunde, *f.*, **-n,** wound.
Wunsch, *m.*, **ᵁe,** wish.
wünschen, wish.
Würfel, *m.*, **-,** dice.
Wurm, *m.*, **ᵁer,** worm.
Wurst, *f.*, **ᵁe,** sausage.
wütend, fuming, raging.
Wüterich, *m.*, **-e,** tyrant, ruthless man.

X

x-mal, umpteen times.

Z

Zahl, *f.*, **-en,** number.
zahlen, pay.
zählen, count.
zärtlich, tender.
„Zauberflöte", *f.*, "Magic Flute".
zehn, ten.
Zeichen, *n.*, **-,** sign.
Zeichenstunde, *f.*, **-n,** drawing lesson.
zeichnen, draw.
Zeit, *f.*, **-en,** time.
Zeitpunkt, *m.*, **-e,** point of time.
Zeitungsverkäufer, *m.*, newspaper vendor.
zerstören, destroy.
ziehen, *s.*, pull; migrate.
Ziel, *n.*, **-e,** goal, aim.
ziemlich, fairly.
Zigarre, *f.*, **-n,** cigar.
Zigarrenkiste, *f.*, **-n,** cigar box.
Zigarette, *f.*, **-n,** cigarette.
Zimmer, *n.*, **-,** room.
Zirkus, *m.*, **-se,** circus.
zischen, hiss.
Zitrone, *f.*, **-n,** lemon.
Zivilist, *m.*, **-en, -en,** civilian.
zögern, hesitate.
zoologischer Garten, *m.*, zoo.
zottig, shaggy.
zu, *D.*, to, for.

Zucker, *m.*, sugar.
Zug, *m.*, "e, train.
zugeben, *s.*, admit.
zugrunde gehen, *s.*, perish.
Zukunft, *f.*, future.
Zündholz, *n.*, "er, match.
zunehmen, *s.*, increase.
zurückprallen, start back.
Zustand, *m.*, "e, condition.

zustattenkommen, *s.*, come in useful.
zuverlässig, reliable.
zuweisen, *s.*, allot.
zwanzig, twenty.
zweifeln, doubt.
zweit-, second.
zweitens, secondly.
zwinkernd, twinkling.
zwischen, *D./A.*, between.

ENGLISH—GERMAN VOCABULARY

For a note on the contents of this Vocabulary, *v.* Preface.
For abbreviations used, *v.* List of Abbreviations.
Masculine and neuter nouns are strong [*i.e.* genitive in ‐(e)s], unless (as for weak and mixed nouns) a special genitive inflection is given before the plural ending.
Compound verbs are described as *sep.* or *insep.* only when the prefix with which they are compounded may be either [cp. § 88 (*c*), especially (3)].

A

about, über, *A.,* von, *D.*
abroad, im Ausland.
accident, der Unfall, ″e.
accordingly, demgemäß.
act, handeln.
action, die Handlung, -en.
address (letter), adressieren.
address (person), ansprechen, *s.*
admire, bewundern.
aeroplane, das Flugzeug, -e.
afford, sich (*D.*), leisten.
afraid (be), Angst haben.
afternoon, der Nachmittag, -e.
afternoon (in the), nachmittags.
against, gegen, wider, *A.*
age (century), das Jahrhundert, -e.
. . . ago, vor, *D.*
air, die Luft, ″e.
air force station, der Flugplatz, ″e.
air-port, der Flughafen, ″.
allowed to, dürfen, *mod.*
alone, allein, selbst.
alphabet, das Alphabet, -e.
Alps, die Alpen, *f. pl.*
already, schon.
always, immer.
American, der Amerikaner, -.
ancient, alt.
animal, das Tier, -e.
answer, die Antwort, -en.
answer, antworten, *D.*
anything (new), irgend etwas (Neues).
appear, erscheinen, *s.*
appearance (external), das Äußere, *adj.-n.*
apple, der Apfel, ″.
Arctic regions, die Arktischen Regionen, *f. pl.*
army, das Heer, -e.
arrange (a meeting), sich verabreden mit.
arrange, einrichten.
art gallery, die Gemäldegalerie, -n.

artist, der Künstler, -.
as soon as, sobald.
ash tree, die Esche, -n.
assemble, *intr.,* zusammenkommen, *s.*
at (time), um, *A.,* **(place)** in, bei, *D.*
at (a town), in, *D.*
(not) at all, garnicht.
at last, endlich.
at least, wenigstens.
at once, sofort.
atlas, der Atlas, Atlanten *or* Atlasse. [§ 91 (*b*)].
attack, angreifen, *s.*
attractive, hübsch.
August, August, *m.*
aunt, die Tante, -n.
Austria, Österreich, *n.*
Austrian, österreichisch.
autumn, der Herbst, -e.

B

bad, schlimm, schlecht.
bake, backen, *s.*
baker's (shop), die Bäckerei, -en.
ball, der Ball, ″e.
ball point pen, der Kugelschreiber, -.
bang (a door), zuschlagen, *s.*
bank (of river), das Ufer, -.
bar, die Stange, -n.
bark, bellen.
battle, kämpfen.
Bavarian, bayrisch.
bean, die Bohne, -n.
bear, aushalten, *s.*
beard, der Bart, ″e.
beautiful, schön.
beauty, die Schönheit, -en.
become, werden, *irr.*
bee, die Biene, -n.
beech, die Buche, -n.
beer, das Bier, -e.
beer-bottle, die Bierflasche, -n.
beggar, der Bettler, -.

341

begin, anfangen, *s.*
beginning, der Anfang, *ᵘ*e.
behind, hinter, *D./A.*
bell, die Glocke, -n.
belong, gehören, *D.*
beside, neben, *D./A.*
between, zwischen, *D./A.*
big, groß.
bind, binden, *s.*
biography, die Biographie, -n.
bird, der Vogel, *ᵘ*.
bird-migration, der Vogelzug, *ᵘ*e.
birthday, der Geburtstag, -e.
bishop, der Bischof, *ᵘ*e [§ 76 (c) (2)].
black, schwarz.
blackbird, die Amsel, -n.
Black Forest, der Schwarzwald.
book, das Buch, *ᵘ*er.
bored (be), sich langweilen.
boring, langweilig.
bottle, die Flasche,
boy, der Junge, -n, -n, der Knabe, -n, -n.
bread, das Brot, -e.
bread-and-butter (slice of), das Butter-
    brot, -e.
break (day), tagen. *imp.*
breakfast, das Frühstück, -e.
bring, bringen, *irr.*
bring up (topic), erwähnen.
broadcast, senden, *p.p.* gesendet
    [§ 551 (c)].
brother, der Bruder, *ᵘ*.
brown, braun.
brush, bürsten.
brush (paint), der Pinsel, -.
build, bauen.
bundle, das Bündel, -.
burn, *intr.*, brennen, *irr.*
burn, *tr.*, verbrennen, *irr.*
bus, der Autobus, -se.
business, das Geschäft, -e.
button up (garment), *refl.*, (sich, *D.*)
    zuknöpfen.
buy, kaufen.

C

café, die Konditorei, -en.
cage, der Käfig, -e.
cake, der Kuchen, -.
call, rufen, *s.*
Canada, Kanada, *n.*
canal, der Kanal, *ᵘ*e.
candle, die Kerze, -n.
cap, die Mütze, -n.
capable (of), fähig, *G.*
Cape of Good Hope, das Kap der
    Guten Hoffnung.

capital, die Hauptstadt, *ᵘ*e.
car, der Wagen, -.
careful(ly), vorsichtig.
carrot, die Karotte, -n, die Mohrrübe,
    -n.
carry, tragen, *s.*
castle ruin(s), die Schloßruine, -n.
cat, die Katze, -n.
catch, fangen, *s.*
catch (train), erwischen.
catechism, der Katechismus, -ismen.
cathedral, die Kathedrale, -n.
celebrate, feiern.
century, das Jahrhundert, -e.
certain, sicher, gewiß.
chapter, das Kapitel, -.
charming, reizend.
cheer (up), *tr.*, aufheitern.
cheerful(ly), fröhlich.
cheese, der Käse, -.
chess, das Schach(spiel).
chicken, das Huhn, *ᵘ*er.
child, das Kind, -er.
childhood, die Kindheit, -en.
child-psychologist, die Kinderpsycho-
    login, -nen.
Christian, christlich.
Christian name, der Vorname, -ns,
    -n.
Christmas, die Weihnachten, *f. pl.*
Christmas Eve, der Weihnachtsabend,
    -e.
Christmas (feast), das Weihnachtsfest,
    -e.
Christmas tree, der Weihnachtsbaum,
    *ᵘ*e.
church tower, der Kirchturm, *ᵘ*e.
cigarette, die Zigarette, -n.
cinema, das Kino, -s.
circus, der Zirkus, -se.
clap, klatschen.
class, die Klasse, -n.
clean, reinigen, putzen.
clear (away), wegräumen.
clever(ly), **(head)** gescheit, **(hands)**
    geschickt.
climate, das Klima, -s [§ 91 (a)].
climb, klettern.
clock, die Uhr, -en.
close (narrow), eng.
close (up), (zu)schliessen, *s.*
clothes, die Kleider, *n. pl.*
coffee, der Kaffee.
collapse, zusammenfallen, *s.*
collect, sammeln.
collected (of works), sämtlich-.
collection, die Sammlung, -en.
come (back), zurückkommen, *s.*

come (through), durchkommen, *s., sep.*
comedy, das Lustspiel, -e.
comical, komisch.
commemorate, gedenken, *irr., G.*
common, gemeinsam.
company, die Gesellschaft, -en.
compare, vergleichen, *s.*
complete(ly), vollkommen.
concept, der Begriff, -e.
concert, das Konzert, -e.
conference, die Konferenz, -en.
considerably, beträchtlich.
continue, *tr.,* weiterführen.
continually, dauernd.
convent, das Kloster, ".
convincing, überzeugend.
cook, der Koch, "e.
cook, kochen.
cool, kühl.
cooling, kühlend.
corner, die Ecke, -n.
cornflower, die Kornblume, -n.
correct, richtig.
cost, kosten.
costume (regional), die Tracht, -en.
council (church, etc.), das Konzil, -e *or* -ien [§ 91 (*d*)].
counsel, der Rat.
count, der Graf, -en, -en.
countess, die Gräfin, -nen.
count (on), rechnen (auf, *A*).
couple, das Ehepaar, -e.
courage, der Mut.
court, der Hof, "e.
cousin, der Vetter, -.
creep, kriechen, *s.*
cress, die Kresse.
criticise, kritisieren.
cross, böse.
crown, die Krone, -n.
cry (for help), der Hilferuf, -e.
cry, schreien, *s.,* rufen, *s.*
cry (weep), weinen.
cucumber, die Gurke, -n.
current, die Strömung, -en.
customer, der Kunde, -n., -n.
cut, schneiden, *s.*
cycle, das Fahrrad, Rad, "er.
cynic, de Zyniker, -.

D

dance, der Tanz, "e.
dance, tanzen.
dancer, der Tänzer, -.
dangerous, gefährlich.
dark, dunkel.
darkness, die Dunkelheit.

date, das Datum, -en [§§ 91 (*c*), 41 (*c*)].
date (appointment), die Verabredung, -en [§ 41 (*c*)].
day, der Tag, -e.
day (off), der freie Tag.
dead (the), die Toten, *pl., adj.-n.*
decorate, schmücken.
delegate, der Gesandte, -n, -n.
delicious, köstlich.
deliver (goods, etc.), abliefern.
deliver (letter), austragen, *s.*
desert, die Wüste, -n.
desk, das Pult, -e.
despair, die Verzweiflung.
details (further), Genaueres, *n., adj.-n.*
detective, der Detektiv, -e.
detective story, der Detektivroman, -e.
diamond, der Diamant, -en, -en.
dice, der Würfel, -.
dictate, diktieren.
differently, verschieden.
difficult, schwer.
direct(ly), direkt.
disappear, verschwinden, *s.*
discover, entdecken.
discuss, besprechen, *s.*
discussion class, das Kolloquium, -ien, [§ 91 (*c*)].
dishes, das Geschirr.
distinguish, unterscheiden, *s., insep.*
district, die Gegend, -en.
disturb, stören.
doctor, der Arzt, "e.
dog, der Hund, -e.
doorway, der Eingang, "e.
dozen, das Dutzend, -e.
drama, das Drama, -en [§ 91 (*a*)].
drawing, die Zeichnung, -en.
drawing lesson, die Zeichenstunde, -n.
drawn, feel, einen ziehen, *s., imp.*
dreadful, schrecklich.
dress, das Kleid, -er.
drink, trinken, *s.*
drive, fahren, *s.*
dry, trocken.
dull, langweilig, uninteressant.
dune, die Düne, -n.
dye, färben.

E

each, jeder, -e, -es.
earliest (at the), am frühesten.
early, früh.
earthquake, das Erdbeben, -.
Easter, Ostern, *pl.*
easy (easily), leicht.

edge, die Kante, -n.
edition, die Ausgabe, -n.
effort, der Versuch, -e.
egg, das Ei, -er.
either, beid-.
either . . . or, entweder . . . oder.
Elbe, die Elbe.
elegant, elegant.
elephant, der Elefant, -en, -en.
emigrate, auswandern.
employ, anstellen.
end, das Ende, -n, der Schluß, Schlüsse.
enemy, der Feind, -e.
England, England, n.
engraver, der Kupferstecher, -.
enjoy, geniessen, s.
enjoy (oneself), sich gut unterhalten,
   s., insep.
enough, genug.
entertaining, unterhaltend.
envelope, der Umschlag, "e.
Eskimo, der Eskimo, -s.
especially, besonders.
essay, der Aufsatz, "e.
even, sogar.
evening, der Abend, -e.
evening (in the), abends.
evening (this), heute abend.
every(one), jeder, -e.
everything, alles.
examination, die Prüfung, -en.
excellent, ausgezeichnet.
excitable, erregbar.
excitedly, aufgeregt.
exciting, aufregend.
excuse, die Entschuldigung, -en.
exhibit, ausstellen.
expect, erwarten.
expedition, die Entdeckungsreise, -n.
explain, erklären.

F

face, das Gesicht, -er.
fact, die Tatsache, -n.
fall, fallen, s.
fall asleep, einschlafen, s.
fall ill, erkranken.
family, die Familie, -n.
far (from), weit weg von, D.
fashion, die Mode, -n.
fast, schnell.
fate, das Schicksal, -e.
feast, das Fest, -e.
feel, fühlen.
fence, der Zaun, "e.
fetch, holen.
field, das Feld, -er.

film, der Film, -e.
finally, schließlich.
find, finden, s.
fine, schön.
firm, fest.
first-class, prima.
firstly, erstens.
fish, der Fisch, -e.
flow, fließen, s.
flower, die Blume, -n.
fly, die Fliege, -n.
fly, fliegen, s.
folk-song, das Volkslied, -er.
food, das Essen.
for, für, A., zu, D.
forbid, verbieten, s.
forcefulness, die Kraft.
foreign, ausländisch.
forest, der Wald, "er.
forget, vergessen, s.
forgetful, vergeßlich.
form, die Art, -en, die Form, -en.
former, jener.
fountain pen, die Füllfeder, -n.
fourth, viert-.
Frenchman, der Franzose, -n, -n.
freshly, frisch.
Friday, Freitag, m.
friend, der Freund, -e.
friend, die Freundin, -nen.
friends (make), sich befreunden mit.
frighten, beängstigen.
frightened, ängstlich.
from, von, aus, D.
front (in . . . of), vor, D./A.
front entrance, der vordere Eingang.
fruit, das Obst.
full (of), voll (von).
fun, der Spaß, "e.
funny, komisch.
furiously, wild.
furniture, die Möbel, n. pl.

G

garden, der Garten, ".
gardener, der Gärtner, -.
gardening, die Gartenarbeit.
general, der General, "e.
genuine, echt.
geologist, der Geologe, -n, -n.
German, der Deutsche, adj.-n.
German, deutsch.
get (become), werden, irr.
get (into), steigen (in, A.), s.
ghost, der Geist, -er; das Gespenst, -er.
giddy (feel), einem schwindlig werden,
   imp.

girl, das Mädchen, -.
girl-friend, die Freundin, -nen.
give, geben, *s.*
give (thought to), nachdenken (über, *A.*), *irr.*
give in, nachgeben, *s.*
give up, aufgeben, *s.*
go, gehen, *s.*
go away, weggehen, *s.*
go on (happen), vorgehen, *s.*
go on (working), weiterarbeiten.
go (to bed), schlafengehen, *s.*
goal, das Ziel, -e.
gold, golden.
good, gut.
gramophone, das Grammophon, -e.
grandmother, die Großmutter, ˝.
granite, der Granit, -e.
grapes, die Trauben, *f. pl.*
great, groß.
Greek, griechisch.
green, grün.
grey, grau.
ground, der Boden, der Grund.
grown up, erwachsen.
guess, raten, *s.*
guest, der Gast, ˝e.

H

hair, das Haar, -e.
half, halb, die Hälfte, -n.
hand (on the one . . . other), einerseits . . . ander(er)seits.
handle, behandeln.
happen, geschehen, *s.*
harbour, der Hafen, ˝.
hard (work . . .), fleißig.
hardly, kaum.
harvest, die Ernte, -n.
hat, der Hut, ˝e.
hate, hassen.
head, der Kopf, ˝e.
health, die Gesundheit.
healthy, gesund.
hear, hören.
heart, das Herz, -ens, -en [§ 52 (*a*)].
heat, die Hitze, -n.
heavy, schwer.
helicopter, der Helikopter, -.
help, die Hilfe.
help, helfen, *s.*
hide, *tr.,* verstecken.
hike, wandern.
hill-top, die Bergspitze, -n.
hire-purchase (on the), auf Raten, *f. pl.*
hock, der Rheinwein, -e.
hold, halten, *s.*
holiday, der Feiertag, -e.

holidays, die Ferien, *pl.,* der Urlaub.
home, das Heim, -e.
home (go), nach Hause (gehen).
honest, ehrlich.
hoof, der Huf, -e.
hope, hoffen.
horse, das Pferd, -e.
hospital, das Krankenhaus, ˝er.
hot, heiß.
house, das Haus, ˝er.
housewife, die Hausfrau, -en.
however, jedoch.
howling, heulend.
hundred, hundert, das Hundert, -e.
Hungarian, der Ungar, -n, -n.
Hungarian, ungarisch.
hungry (be), hungrig, Hunger haben.
hurry, eilen.

I

Iceland, Island, *n.*
icy, vereist, eisig.
ideal, ideal.
if, wenn.
ill, krank.
illness, die Krankheit, -en.
imitate, (es) gleichtun, *s., D.*
importance, die Wichtigkeit.
important, wichtig.
impression, der Eindruck, ˝e.
inconsiderate, rücksichtslos.
increase, zunehmen, *s.*
indeed, ja.
India, Indien, *n.*
inhabitant, der Einwohner, -.
injure, verletzen.
ink, die Tinte, -n.
inn, das Wirtshaus, ˝er.
innkeeper, der Wirt, -e.
inside, drinnen.
intelligent, intelligent, gescheit.
interest, das Interesse, -n.
interesting, interessant.
interrupt, unterbrechen, *s., insep.*
Iron Curtain, der eiserne Vorhang.
island, die Insel, -n.
Italian, der Italiener, -.
Italian, italienisch.
Italy, Italien, *n.*

J

January, Januar, *m.*
Japanese, der Japaner, -.
jet-plane, der Düsenjäger, -.
join, beitreten, *s., D.*
joke, der Witz, -e.

346   VOCABULARY

journey, die Reise, -n.
joy, die Freude, -en.
July, Juli, *m.*
jump, springen, *s.*
June, Juni, *m.*

K

keep word, worthalten, *s.*
kilometer, der Kilometer, -.
kind, die Art, -en.
king, der König, -e.
kitchen, die Küche, -n.
kitchen-table, der Küchentisch, -e.
knife, das Messer, -.
knock (at), klopfen an, *D.*
know, kennen, *irr.*

L

lack, entbehren, *G.*
lady, die Dame, -n.
lake, der See, -n.
land, landen.
landlady, die Wirtin, -nen.
landlord, der Mietsherr, -n, -en.
language, die Sprache, -n.
language (foreign), die Fremdsprache,
    -n.
last, letzt.
last (in time expression), vorig.
latter, dieser.
laugh, lachen.
laughter, das Gelächter.
lazy, faul.
lead, führen.
leaf, das Blatt, "er.
leap up, aufspringen, *s.*
learn, lernen.
least (not in the), nicht im geringsten.
leather, das Leder.
leave, verlassen, *s.*
leave (in will), hinterlassen, *s.*, *insep.*
lecture (9 o'clock), die Vorlesung, um
    9 Uhr in die V . . . gehen.
leg, das Bein, -e.
lend, leihen, *s.*
let down, blamieren.
letter (alphabet), der Buchstabe, -ns,
    -n [§ 52 (*a*)].
letter, der Brief, -e.
lettuce, der Salat, -e.
library (lending), die Leihbücherei, -en.
lie, lügen, *s.*
life, das Leben.
lift (telephone), das Telefon abnehmen,
    s.
lift (up), aufheben, *s.*

light, das Licht, -er.
like, mögen, *mod.*
like to, gern(e), *adv.*
lily, die Lilie, -n.
lime tree, die Linde, -n.
listen, zuhören, *D.*
literary, literarisch.
little, klein.
live, leben.
live (in house, etc.), wohnen.
lively, munter.
logical, logisch.
lonely, einsam.
long, lang(e).
long (as . . . as), solange (noch).
long for, sich sehnen (nach, *D.*).
look up (a fact), nachschlagen, *s.*
lose, verlieren, *s.*
lot (a), viel.
loudly, laut.
love, lieben.
low, nieder.
luggage, das Gepäck.
lunch, das Mittagessen, -.

M

manager, der Direktor, -oren, -oren
    [§ 90 (*a*)].
manuscript, das Manuskript, -e, die
    Handschrift, -en.
many-coloured, bunt.
march, marschieren.
market place, der Marktplatz, "e.
marriage, die Ehe, -n.
masonry, das Bauwerk, -e.
mast, der Mast, -en.
match, das Streichholz, "er.
matter, die Sache, -n.
mauve, lila.
meal, die Mahlzeit, -en.
mean, meinen.
meanwhile, indessen.
meat, das Fleisch.
medicine, die Medizin.
medieval, mittelalterlich.
meet, *tr.*, treffen, *s.*
meet, *intr.*, sich treffen, *s.*
meeting (gathering), die Versammlung,
    -en; (conference) die Sitzung, -en;
    (rally) das Zusammentreffen, -.
melody, die Melodie, -(e)n.
mend, stopfen.
messenger, der Bote, -n, -n.
middle, die Mitte.
midnight, die Mitternacht.
milk, die Milch.
million, die Million, -en.

mind, der Kopf, "e.
mirror, der Spiegel, -.
miss, versäumen.
missionary, der Missionar, -e.
misunderstand, falsch verstehen, s.
moment, der Augenblick, -e.
monastery, das Kloster, ".
Monday, Montag, m.
money, das Geld, -er.
monkey, der Affe, -n, -n.
month, der Monat, -e.
month (every), monatlich.
monument, das Denkmal, "er.
mood, die Stimmung, -en.
more, mehr.
morning, der Morgen, -, morgen.
most, adv., äußerst.
mother, die Mutter, ".
mountain, der Berg, -e.
mountain valley, das Gebirgstal, "er.
mouse, die Maus, "e.
muscle, der Muskel, -n.
museum, das Museum, pl. Museen
   [§ 91 (c)].
music club, der Musikverein, -e.
music lesson, die Musikstunde, -n.

N

name, der Name, -ns, -n [§ 52 (b)].
nap, das Schläfchen, -.
narrow, eng.
navigate, befahren, s.
near, bei, D., nahe, adj., D.; in der
   Nähe von, D.
neat, ordentlich, nett.
necessary, nötig, notwendig.
need, brauchen.
neighbour, der Nachbar, -n, -n
   [§ 52 (a)].
neither, kein- (von beiden).
nephew, der Neffe, -n, -n.
neutral, neutral.
never, nie.
nevertheless, jedoch.
new, neu.
news, die Neuigkeiten, f. pl.
newspaper, die Zeitung, -en.
next (day), ander-, nächst-.
next door, nebenan.
next to, neben, D./A.
niece, die Nichte, -n.
ninetieth, neunzigst-.
noise, der Lärm.
noon, der Mittag, -e.
noon (at), mittags.
North America, Nordamerika, n.
northern, nordisch.

note paper, das Briefpapier.
nothing, nichts.
nothing but, lauter.
notice (give), kündigen, D.
now, jetzt
number, die Zahl, -en, die Nummer,
   -n.
nut, die Nuß, Nüsse.
nutritive, nahrhaft.

O

oak, die Eiche, -n.
object, der Gegenstand, "e.
occasion, die Gelegenheit, -en.
occur (remember), einem einfallen, s.,
   imp.
October, Oktober, m.
of, von, D.
office (job), das Amt, "er.
office (place), das Büro, -s.
old(en), alt.
olive tree, der Olivenbaum, "e.
on, auf, D./A.
once, einmal.
only, nur.
open, öffnen, aufmachen.
opera, die Oper, -n.
or, oder.
orchard, der Obstgarten, ".
originator, der Urheber, -.
other, ander-.
other day, vor einigen Tagen.
otherwise, sonst.
outermost, äußerst-.
outpost, der Vorposten, -.
outside! (he)raus!
over, über, D./A.
own, eigen.
own, besitzen, s.

P

page, die Seite, -n.
paint, malen.
painter, der Maler, -.
paints, die Farben, f. pl.
pale-looking, bleich aussehend.
parents, die Eltern, pl.
park, der Park, -s.
park, parken.
pass, tr. (exam.), bestehen, s.
pass, intr. (of time), vergehen, s.
passer-by, der Passant, -en, -en
   [§ 76 (d)].
passport, der Paß, Pässe.
path, der Weg, -e.
patience, die Geduld.

pay, zahlen.
pea, die Erbse, -n.
peace, der Friede, -ns, -n [§ 52 (b)].
peasant, der Bauer, -n, -n [§ 52 (a)].
peel, schälen.
pen, die Feder, -n.
pen-name, der Deckname, -n [§ 52 (b)].
people, die Menschen, m. pl.; die Leute, pl.
per cent., das Prozent, -e.
performance, die Aufführung, -en.
periodical, die Zeitschrift, -en.
pet, das Haustier, -e.
philologist, der Philologe, -n, -n.
photograph, die Aufnahme, -n.
piano concerto, das Klavierkonzert, -e.
pick, pflücken.
pick up, aufheben, s.
picture, das Bild, -er.
piece, das Stück, -e.
pile, der Haufe, -ns, -n [§ 52 (b)]; der Berg, -e.
pink, rosa.
place, der Ort, -e.
place, stellen.
plain, einfach.
plan, planen.
platform, der Bahnsteig, -e.
play (drama), das Schauspiel, -e.
play, spielen.
play over (to, music, etc.), vorspielen, D.
please, bitte.
pleasure, das Vergnügen.
plentiful, reichlich.
plunder, plündern.
pocket, die Tasche, -n.
point, der Punkt, -e.
policeman, der Schutzmann, "er; der Polizist, -en, -en.
polish, polieren.
pond, der Teich, -e.
poor, arm.
Pope, der Papst, "e.
popular, beliebt.
position, die Lage, -n.
possible, möglich(st).
post (letter), einwerfen, s.
postman, der Briefträger, -.
potato, die Kartoffel, -n.
powerful, kräftig.
practice flight, der Übungsflug, "e.
pray, beten.
prefer, vorziehen, s.
prepare (oneself), (sich) vorbereiten.
present, das Geschenk, -e.
present, adj., gegenwärtig.
print, drucken.
prize, der Preis, -e.

probably, wahrscheinlich.
problem, das Problem, -e.
professor, der Professor, -oren, -oren [§ 90 (a)].
promise, versprechen, s.
properly, richtig.
public, das Publikum.
public house, das Gasthaus, "er.
publication, die Veröffentlichung, -en.
pull, ziehen, s.
pulpit, die Kanzel, -n.
punctually, pünktlich.
punish, strafen.
put (place), legen.

Q

question, fragen.
quick(ly), schnell.
quiet(ly), ruhig, still.
quite, ganz.
quite (a long time), ziemlich lange.

R

race, das Wettrennen, -.
rain, der Regen, regnen.
reach, erreichen.
read, lesen, s.
reading-lamp, die Leselampe, -n.
ready, bereit.
realise, einem klar werden, imp.
really, wirklich.
reason, die Ursache, -n; der Grund, "e.
recently, in letzter Zeit.
recite (by heart), auswendig sagen.
recognise, erkennen, irr.
record (gramophone), die (Schall-) Platte, -n.
red, rot.
refrain, absehen, s. (von, D.).
refresh, erfrischen.
regularly, regelmäßig.
rejoice (in), sich freuen, G.
rely (on), sich verlassen, s. (auf, D.).
remain, bleiben, s.
remember, sich erinnern, G.
rent, die Miete, -n.
repair, reparieren.
respect, achten.
responsibility, die Verantwortung, -en.
rest, sich ausruhen.
result (as a . . . of), infolge, G.
return, wiederkehren, sep.
return, die Rückkehr.
return (by), umgehend.
return ticket, die Rückfahrkarte, -n.

revolutionary, revolutionär.
revolver, der Revolver, -.
Rhine, der Rhein.
rich, reich.
riddle, das Rätsel, -.
ride (cycle), fahren, s.; (horse), reiten, s.
ring, läuten.
rise early, früh aufstehen, s.
river, der Fluß, Flüsse.
roar, brüllen.
Roman, römisch.
romantic, romantisch.
roof, das Dach, ″er.
room, das Zimmer, -.
rose, die Rose, -n.
round, um, D.; umher, herum, adv.
row (in theatre), der Rang ″e.
ruined, zerfallen.
run, laufen, s., rennen, irr.
runner, der Läufer, -.
rush, rasen.
rush (of water), rauschen.
rushing noise (there is a), es saust, imp.
Russian, der Russe, -n, -n, russisch.
rye-bread, das Schwarzbrot, -e.

S

sad, traurig.
safely, sicher.
sake (for her . . .), um ihretwillen.
salary, das Gehalt, ″er.
sand, der Sand.
sausage, die Wurst, ″e.
save, sparen.
say, sagen.
school, die Schule, -n.
scientist, der Naturwissenschaftler, -.
scold, schelten, s.
Scotland, Schottland, n.
sculpture, die Bildhauerkunst.
sea, das Meer, -e.
seashore, der Meeresstrand, -e.
season, die Jahreszeit, -en.
secondly, zweitens.
secret, das Geheimnis, -se.
secretary, die Sekretärin, -nen.
see, sehen, s.
seem, scheinen, s.
sell, verkaufen.
send, schicken.
serenade, die Serenade, -n.
serious(ly), ernst.
servant girl, das Dienstmädchen, -.
serve, servieren.
setting, der Hintergrund, ″e.
seventh, siebent-, siebt-.

several, einig-.
sew, nähen.
shadow, der Schatten, -.
shady, schattig.
sharp, scharf.
sheep, das Schaf, -e.
shine, scheinen, s.
shining, glänzend.
shoe, der Schuh, -e.
shoot, schießen, s.
shop, der Laden, ″; das Geschäft, -e.
shore, das Ufer, -.
short, kurz.
show, zeigen.
shut, schließen, s.
sick, krank.
side, die Seite, -n.
siesta (take a), Siesta halten, s.
sign, das Zeichen, -.
significant, bedeutend.
silence, zum Schweigen bringen, irr.
simple, einfach.
since, seit, D.; seitdem, adv.
siren, die Sirene, -n.
sister, die Schwester, -n.
sit down, sich setzen.
situation, die Lage, -n.
sleep, schlafen, s.
slippery, glatt.
slow(ly), langsam.
smoke, rauchen.
snap, die (Moment-)Aufnahme, -n.
snow, schneien, imp.
society, die Gesellschaft, -en.
softly, leise.
soldier, der Soldat, -en, -en.
solemn, feierlich.
someone (or other), (irgend) jemand.
sometimes, manchmal.
somewhere, irgendwo.
song, das Lied, -er.
soon (as . . . as), sobald.
sorry (be), einem leid tun, s. irr., imp.
sort, die Art, -en.
sort, aussortieren.
sorts (all), allerlei.
source, die Quelle, -n.
space, der Platz, ″e.
Spain, Spanien, n.
speak, sprechen, s.
speciality, die Spezialität, -en.
spectacles, die Brille, -n.
spinsterish, altjüngferlich.
spite (in . . . of), trotz, G.
spoil, verderben, s.
sports-car, der Sportwagen, -.
spring, der Frühling, -e.
square, der Platz, ″e.

350 VOCABULARY

stage, die Bühne, -n; **(open air)** die Freilichtbühne, -n.
staircase, die Stiege, -n.
stamp, die Briefmarke, -n.
stand, stehen, *s.*
station, der Bahnhof, ⁻e.
station (wireless), der Sender, -.
stay, bleiben, *s.*
steal, stehlen, *s.*
step down, niedersteigen, *s.*
stick, der Stock, ⁻e.
stick, kleben.
still, noch.
stop (talking), schweigen, *s.*
stork, der Storch, ⁻e.
story, die Geschichte, -n.
story (short), die Novelle, -n.
stove, der Ofen, ⁻.
strange, seltsam.
stranger, der Fremde, *adj.-n.*
street, die Straße, -n.
street-corner, die Straßenecke, -n.
strenuous, anstrengend.
strong, stark.
student, der Student, -en, -en.
stupidity, die Dummheit, -en.
suddenly, plötzlich.
sugar, der Zucker.
suit, der Anzug, ⁻e.
suit, passen, *D.*
summer, der Sommer, -.
summer night, die Sommernacht, ⁻e.
sunshine, der Sonnenschein.
supper, das Abendessen.
surround, umgeben, *s., insep.*
swallow, die Schwalbe, -n.
Swedish, schwedisch.
swiftly, schnell.
swim, schwimmen, *s.*

T

table (multiplication), das Einmaleins.
take, nehmen, *s.*
take part (in), teilnehmen, *s.* (an, *D.*).
take place, stattfinden, *s.*
talk, reden, sprechen, *s.*
talking, das Gerede.
tall, hoch (*infl.*, hoh-).
tea, der Tee, -s.
tea-time, die Teestunde.
teach, unterrichten, *insep.*, lehren.
teaspoonful, der Teelöffelvoll.
telephone, das Telefon, -e.
telephone, telefonieren.
tell a lie, lügen, *s.*
temperature, die Temperatur, -en.
temple, der Tempel, -.

Tennis, das Tennis.
terribly, furchtbar.
text, der Text, -e.
thank, danken, *D.*
thereupon, daraufhin.
thick, dick.
think, denken, *irr.*
third, das Drittel, -.
third, dritt-.
thirdly, drittens.
though, obzwar.
thousand, tausend, das Tausend, -e.
throw, werfen, *s.*
thrush, die Drossel, -n.
ticket (railway), die Fahrkarte, -n; **(theatre),** die Karte, -n.
tidy (keep), in Ordnung halten, *s.*
till, bis, *A.*
time, die Zeit, -en.
-times, -mal.
tired, müde.
to-day, heute.
together, zusammen, miteinander.
tomato, die Tomate, -n.
to-night, heute abend.
towards, gegen, *A.*
town, die Stadt, ⁻e.
toy, das Spielzeug, -e.
toy factory, die Spielwarenfabrik, -en.
train, der Zug, ⁻e.
travel, fahren, *s.*, reisen.
travel book, der Reisebericht, -e.
treasure, der Schatz, ⁻e.
tree, der Baum, ⁻e.
tremble, zittern.
trip, die Reise, -n.
triple, dreifach.
tropical, tropisch.
true (it is . . .), zwar.
trunk (elephant), der Rüssel, -.
try, versuchen.
Turk, der Türke, -n, -n.
turn (in), abwechselnd.
turn back, umkehren, *sep.*
turn off, abdrehen.
twice, zweimal.
twin, der Zwilling, -e.
type, der Typ, -en, die Art, -en.
Tyrol, Tirol, *n.*

U

ugly, häßlich.
uncertain, ungewiß.
unclouded, ungetrübt.
uncomfortable, unangenehm.
underneath, (dar)unter.
understand, verstehen, *s.*

undertake, unternehmen, *s.,* *insep.*
unexpectedly, unerwartet.
unfriendly, ungemütlich.
unity, die Einheit, -en.
university, die Universität, -en.
university library, die Universitäts-
bibliothek, -en.
unknown, unbekannt.
unlucky (be), Pech haben.
unparalleled, unerhört.
until . . . ago, bis vor, *D.*
upstairs, oben.
usually, gewöhnlich.

V

variety, die Auswahl, -en.
various, verschieden.
vegetables, das Gemüse, -.
very, sehr.
victim, das Opfer, -.
Vienna, Wien, *n.*
village, das Dorf, ̈er.
violin, die Geige, -n.
visit, besuchen.
vivid, lebhaft.

W

wake, wecken.
walk, gehen, *s.*
wall, die Wand, ̈e.
wander (about), herumwandern.
war, der Krieg, -e.
warning, die Warnung, -en.
wash, waschen, *s.*
waste, verschwenden.
watch, die Uhr, -en.
water, begiessen, *s.*
way, der Weg, -e.
weak, schwach.
wealth, der Reichtum, ̈er.
weather, das Wetter.
wedge (squash), quetschen.
Wednesday, Mittwoch, *m.*
weed, jäten.
weeds, das Unkraut.

week, *adv.* (*e.g.* **Monday week**),
Montag über acht Tage.
weep, weinen.
weight, das Gewicht, -e.
well, gut.
well kept, gut gepflegt.
Westphalia, Westfalen, *n.*
where? wo?
while away, vertreiben, *s.*
whistle, pfeiffen, *s.*
white, weiß.
whole, ganz.
wholesome, gesund.
whose? wessen?
wild, wild.
willow tree, die Weide, -n.
window, das Fenster, -.
wine, der Wein, -e.
winter's day, der Wintertag, -e.
wireless, das Radio, -s.
with, mit, *D.*
withdraw, entziehen, *s., D.*
woman, die Frau, -en.
wood, das Holz, ̈er.
wood (forest), der Wald, ̈er.
word, das Wort, -e *or* ̈er, Appendix
A.
work, die Arbeit, -en.
worker, der Arbeiter, -.
wrest, abringen, *s., D.*
write (to), schreiben, *s., D.*
write down, aufschreiben, *s.*

Y

year, das Jahr, -e.
year (every), jährlich.
yellow, gelb.
yet, doch.
yield (crop, etc.), ergeben, *s.*
young, jung.

Z

zoo, der zoologische Garten, ̈.
Zulu, der Zulu, -s.

PART TWO

CHAPTER XLIV

USE OF THE ARTICLES (1). BY SENSE

253. General

(*a*) Over a broad field the use of the article in German is similar to that in English. There is, however, sufficient difference to repay an attempt to classify some uses in which the languages diverge. Such differences are caused by:

(1) The meaning and use of the noun which the article precedes.

(2) The position and grammatical function of the noun in the sentence.

These two approaches, here and in Chapter XLIX respectively, are not quite mutually exclusive; but some overlapping may be useful. Only common nouns are considered in these chapters; for proper names of persons, places, etc., *v*. §§ 156 f. and 219 f.

(*b*) Before a German common noun:

(1) The definite article stands for one or more known or designated objects of a certain class:

Das Haus (*this house, the one we know of*) **ist unbewohnt,** *is uninhabited.*

Die Amerikaner konsumieren viel Kaugummi, *the Americans* (a group immediately recognised by this designation) *consume much chewing-gum.*

(2) The indefinite article stands for an unknown or undesignated object of a class which is otherwise known:

Es ist ein Schnitter, heißt der Tod, (title of folk-song), *there is a reaper whose name is Death.*

In einem fernen Lande lebte ein König, der hatte zwei Töchter, *in a distant country there lived a king* . . .

Note that the indefinite article (in spite of its name) refers to objects as "definite" as those described by the definite article, though they are not designated, and thus could not be located. Both articles are thus "individualising" in their force, compared with nouns before which:

(3) No article is used since no item or particle is even contemplated:

Nicht alles was glänzt ist Gold, *not all that glitters is gold.*

(*c*) The two main differences between the use of the articles in English and German are:

(1) When a noun becomes quite certain in its reference, either by reason of its abstract and indivisible nature (*beauty, science, silver*), or its unique reference (*Heaven, Parliament*), English omits the article, while German normally uses the definite article (**der Himmel, die Schönheit, die Wissenschaft, das Silber**) in a quasi-demonstrative manner (cp. § 65, definite article as a demonstrative).

(2) In a large number of descriptive or appositional contexts German uses no article, while English carries over the individuality of the subject into the form of the predicate by using the definite or indefinite article:

Essen—Lichtstadt des Westens, *Essen, the modern city of West Germany* (from a tourist folder).

Das ist Sache des zuständigen Amtes, *that is a matter for the appropriate authority.*

(*d*) Further, within the same field of sense or function of a noun there are always generalising or particularising factors:

(1) Generalising, and dispensing with the article, are all statements of general truth, proverbial sayings, and attempts to express something in a summary formula:

Proverbial: **Not bricht Eisen,** *necessity knows no master.*

Headlines: **Kanzlers Erklärung an Westmächte,** (*The*) *Chancellor's declaration to* (*the*) *Western Powers.*

Doublets: **Anfang und Ende,** *beginning and end;* **Ebbe und Flut,** *low and high tide.*

Commands: **Hände hoch!** *hands up!* **Schuhe ab!** *shoes off!*

(2) Individualising, and thus needing the article, are all statements which place a general idea in a specific context:

Sie haben die Not im Haus, *they are in need,* lit., *they have need in the house* [cp. example in (1)].

Sie hatte Kraft, zu wollen, und bekam die Kraft, es zu vollenden (E. Barlach), *she had* (*enough*) *strength to will, and was given the strength to succeed.*

This is particularly so when a following element, especially a genitive or relative clause, defines more closely the sense of the noun:

Milch ist gesund, *milk is health-giving;* **die Milch der Kuh ist gesund und schmackhaft,** *cow's milk is health-giving and tasty.*

For a relative clause, *v.* below, § 254 (*c*).

(*e*) Use of the article by sense:

(1) There are certain groups of common nouns which, by reason of their sense, present certain problems; they are: (i) nouns of unique reference, (ii) collective and abstract nouns, (iii) nouns of material.

(2) Common nouns not distinct by reason of their meaning may become representative of their class in certain other ways, *v.* § 257.

254. Nouns of Unique Reference

(*a*) Certain religious and philosophical concepts are of their nature singular; German uses the (definite) article, English omits it.

(1) Religious ideas:

das Elysium, Fegefeuer, Paradies, Schicksal, *Elysium, Purgatory, Paradise, Fate;* **der Himmel, die Hölle, die Vorsehung,** *Heaven, Hell, Providence;* **die Seligkeit, die (ewige) Verdammnis,** *blessedness, (eternal) damnation.*

(2) Conditions of human life:

die Geburt, die Jugend, die Ehe, das Alter, der Tod, *birth, youth, marriage, age, death;* **das Leben, die Zeit, die Ewigkeit, das Glück, das Unglück,** *life, time, eternity, happiness, unhappiness.*

Note.—English uses the article for the heavenly bodies, which are unique but material entities: **die Sonne, die Erde, der Mond,** *the sun, the earth, the moon.*

All religious and philosophical concepts may in German lose the article in a generalising context [cp. § 253 (*d*)]: **In deinen Armen ist Paradies!** *in your arms is Paradise;* or take the indefinite article as one of a class: **eine Hölle,** *a Hell;* **eine Ehe,** *a marriage* (and **eine Hochzeit,** *a wedding*); **ein Tod,** *a death* (cp. § 444).

(*b*) The singularity may, however, lie in a concrete reference:

der Vater, die Tante, das Karlchen, die Köchin, *Father, Aunt, Little Charlie, Cook.*

(*c*) **Gott,** *God,* is a noun of unique reference, both on the abstract and concrete (personal) plane. This noun may, however, be specified:

Der Gott, der Eisen wachsen ließ, der wollte keine Knechte (patriotic song), (*the*) *God, who made iron grow, made all men free.*

or may become one of a class in the sense "pagan god": **der (heidnische) Gott,** plural **Götter.**

255. Abstract Nouns

The definition of an abstract noun is difficult in any language, but the following classes may be distinguished:

(*a*) Abstracts proper, *i.e.* the names of qualities and conditions.

In general statements, including definitions, the article is used:

Die Arbeit bringt ihren Lohn, *work brings its reward.*

Ihn plagt der Geiz, *he is a victim of miserliness.*

But this group is very instable, and:

(1) Many proverbial and sententious statements omit the article:

Ordnung muß sein, *order is essential;* **Hochmut kommt vor dem Fall,** *pride comes before a fall.*

(2) Abstracts in everyday life vary between general and specific:

Der Arzt hat ihm Ruhe verordnet, *the doctor prescribed rest.*

Die Ruhe hat ihm nicht geholfen, *the rest (which he had) was no use.*

Härte wird bei ihm nicht anschlagen, *it is no use treating him strictly.*

Die Härte hat bei ihm nicht angeschlagen, *the strict treatment did not help matters in his case.*

Note that abstracts sometimes have plurals in an applied concrete sense: **Schönheiten,** *beauties;* **Unruhen,** *disturbances;* **Tiefen,** *depths;* **Tugenden,** *virtues* [*v.* § 444 (*c*) (2)].

(*b*) Actions or individual events are designated by many masculine verbal derivatives: **der Fall, Gang, Schlag, Sprung,** *fall, walk, blow, jump.* These acquire generalised force as types of human actions, as with crimes: **Einbruch wird schwer bestraft,** *housebreaking means a long sentence;* **Widerstand ist nutzlos,** *resistance is useless;* or individualised force in the sense of *a case of,* though here also their abstract sense often requires a second noun in apposition: **ein Mord, Fall von Mord,** (*case of*) *murder,* but in the plural only **Mordfälle, Mordtaten,** *murders* [cp. § 444 (*c*) (3)].

(*c*) Activities or general events:

Activities or general events normally take the article, but may omit it with generalising force:

(1) Subjects or fields of knowledge:

die Botanik, Geographie, Tierkunde, *botany, geography, zoology.*

But without the article: **er studiert Geschichte,** *studies history.*

(2) Public or economic activities:

der Ackerbau, *agriculture;* **das Bankwesen, Unterrichtswesen,** *banking, education;* **die (Handels-)Schiffahrt,** *(merchant) shipping.*

(3) Sports (*v.* § 206):

das Boxen, Rudern, Pferderennen, *boxing, rowing, horse-racing;* **der Ringkampf, die (Leicht-)Athletik,** *wrestling, athletics.*

(4) But infinitive nouns of more general reference are often on the border of infinitives, so that the article is absent (v. § 205):

Das Kochen macht mir Spaß, *I like cooking,* but: **Kochen macht Spaß,** *cooking is fun.*

Arbeiten ist Geschmacksache, *work is a matter of taste.*

Frühaufstehen war nie mein Fall, *I was never an early riser.*

(5) Similarly with other prefixes of general activity, as **-erei:**

die Schönrednerei, *giving fair words;* **die Fahrerei,** *travelling around.*

Er hat sich für die Bildhauerei entschieden, *decided to become a sculptor.*

Malerei und Bildhauerei waren der Architektur gegenüber [cp. § 258 (a) (1) below] **freier, selbstbewußter geworden,** *painting and sculpture had acquired confidence . . .*

(*d*) Divisions of time:

The names of the days, months, and seasons are more commonly found with the definite article in German than in English (v. § 57); thus also meals and meal times, etc.: **beim Frühstück,** *at breakfast;* **zum Kaffee einladen,** *to invite to coffee;* **das Semester dauert bei uns zehn Wochen,** *term lasts for ten weeks;* **nach der Abendandacht,** *after evening service.*

256. Collective and Material Nouns

These behave on the analogy of the other classes of noun they resemble.

(*a*) Collectives of unique reference vary, as do those under § 254, from abstract to concrete reference:

(1) Abstract collectives:

die Nachwelt, *posterity;* **die Natur,** *nature;* **das Altertum,** *antiquity;* **die Menschheit,** *humanity;* **die Gesellschaft,** *society;* **die Wissenschaft,** *science, scholarship;* **die Geschichte,** *history;* **die Kunst,** *art;* **die Sitte,** *custom.*

Distinguish **die Christenheit,** *Christendom,* and **das Christentum,** *Christianity;* but **das Papsttum,** *the Papacy.*

(2) Concrete collectives:

English accords the article-less form only to Parliament and Congress among legislative bodies, **das Parlament, der Kongreß.** The (German) Federal Parliament is **der Bundestag** and the (French) Chamber of Deputies, **die Abgeordnetenkammer.**

(*b*) Collectives of general reference may be:

(1) Collective groups which are also members of a class:

die Armee, Mannschaft, Nation, das Volk, *the Army, team, nation, people.*

But as an indefinite quantity the article is omitted:

meuterndes Volk, *people rioting;* **vor uns streckte sich ungastliches Gebirge,** *an inhospitable stretch of mountainous country* . . .

(2) An indefinite quantity of individuals: **die Leute,** *people* (as in: *they say* . . .); **die Ereignisse,** *events.*

(*c*) Names of materials often have no article in general statements: **Wasser besteht aus Wasserstoff und Sauerstoff,** *water consists of* . . .; but the article is almost as common: **der Wein erfreut des Menschen Herz,** *wine delights the heart of man;* it must be used [*v.* § 253 (*d*) (2)] when the noun is specified: **das Gold der Sonne.**

257. Nouns Representative of their Class

A common noun which has no specific abstract, collective or material content or uniqueness of reference may come to represent its fellows, and thus attract to itself the definite article in German, while English uses the indefinite article or unmodified plural.

(*a*) In general statements:

Der Mensch ist ein mit Vernunft begabtes Tier, *man is an animal possessed of reason.*

Dem Tüchtigen ist diese Welt nicht stumm, *a capable man will make sense of the world.*

(*b*) A person for a class:

Ich glaube im Namen aller beim Amerikaner Beschäftigten zu sprechen . . . (letter to Editor), *I think I can speak for all those employed by the Americans* . . .

(People look like animals) **Sie sehen da den Fisch und den Fuchs, den Hund, den Seehund, den Habicht und den Hammel** (Th. Mann), *you see fish, foxes, dogs* . . .

Der moderne Mensch wird in der Klinik geboren und stirbt in der Klinik: also soll er auch wie in einer Klinik wohnen (R. Musil), *modern man is born in (a) hospital* . . .

(*c*) A person as *epitome of* . . .:

Sie sind der geborene Spion, *you would make an ideal spy.*

Er war die Rücksicht selbst, *he was considerateness itself.*

und ihr glattgescheiteltes Haar trug dazu bei, daß das Bild der alten Jungfer schon fertig war (Th. Mann), *the picture of an old maid* . . .

(*d*) A person playing a role:

er spielt den Hamlet, *takes the part of Hamlet;* **den Retter, den Kasperl machen,** *to play the role of rescuer, the fool.*

das Haus, in dem ich den blaubefrackten Bediensteten spielte (Th. Mann), *in which I played the role of a blue-jacketed servant.*

258. The Definite Article in Specific Contexts

There are certain purely local factors which require the definite article where often none is needed in English:

(*a*) To show the grammatical case:

(1) With verbs or adjectives taking the dative:

In dieser Verwendung ist Gold dem Silber vorzuziehen, *for this use gold is to be preferred to silver.*

Unordnung ist der Ordnung feind, *disorder is the enemy of order.*

(2) With verbs or adjectives taking the genitive:

Als Kustos eines Privatmuseums bedurfte sie nicht einmal mehr der Phantasie (H. Kasack), *not even did she need (any) imagination.*

des Weines ungewohnt, *unused to wine.*

(3) With proper names without genitive inflection (**die Beurteilung des Erasmus,** cp. § 156); and to avoid opening a sentence with a concealed dative:

Dem Paracelsus erschien die ganze Welt als Gottes Schöpfung, *for P. the whole world was God's Creation.*

(*b*) In the appositional genitive, where the standard construction is the article corresponding to English *of;* thus in the

(1) partitive genitive: **Spuren der Skepsis,** *traces of scepticism;*

(2) partitive genitive of time: **Monate der inneren Vorbereitung,** *months of inner preparation;*

(3) genitive of attribution: **ein Nimbus des Respekts,** *an aura of respect;*

(4) genitive of apposition: **die Kunst des Kartenzeichnens,** *the art of map-making.*

The student can add innumerable examples from his reading.

Note.—Many appositional genitives are purely descriptive, and correspond to an attributive adjective in English: **ein Ding der Unmöglichkeit,** *an impossible thing, impossibility;* **eine Stadt der Huld und Anmut** (W. Bergengruen), *a graceful and pleasant town.*   (Cp. §§ 486 f.)

259. The Indefinite Article in Speculative Statements

(a) The indefinite article refers to a thing, etc., of a certain class, but not specifically designated [v. § 253 (b)]. Its existence may thus lie in the future, as in the statement **ein Bier!** to a waiter. German thus uses the indefinite article widely in cases where English requires *any, a possible*, etc.

Es ist eine falsche Ansicht—das haben wir alle erfahren—wer aber vermißt sich, einen ersten Stein zu werfen? *But who would presume to throw the first stone* (cp. John viii. 7).

(b) Abstract words may, of course, take the indefinite article as soon as their sense is sufficiently concrete for particularisation:

eine Beschäftigung, *an employment;* **mit einem Zurückwerfen des Kopfes,** *with a toss of the head;* **ich bat um einen Rat,** *I asked for (a piece of) advice.*

They may, however, when used with speculative force, take the indefinite article even when fully abstract and general:

Die Sache muß durch: an ein Versagen ist nicht zu denken, *(any possibility of) failure must not be contemplated.*

Sie sträubten sich gegen eine restlose Unterwerfung unter Luther oder Zwingli (W. Andreas), *resisted any prospect of complete submission to L. or Z.*

(c) Similarly an abstract word followed by a description of its nature may have the indefinite article:

Nein, er konnte niemand mehr ernähren—besonders eine Jugend nicht, die lebte, wie das Rad rollt (H. Mann), *especially young people who (as it seemed to him) had no more self-control than a rolling wheel.*

since an abstract (or collective) concept is still in some sense speculative until its nature has been indicated.

260. The Indefinite Article in Material Statements

(a) The indefinite article with a noun of material indicates in both German and English:

(1) A certain kind of the material:
   ein Salz, *a salt;* **ein Tuch,** *a (kind of) cloth* [v. § 444 (b)].

(2) A certain article made from the material:
   ein Glas, Blei, Holz, Tuch, Eisen, Stahl, etc., *a glass, lead,* etc.

(3) A portion of the material in common use:
   ein Bier, Kaffee, Tee; eine Milch; ein Stein; *a beer, coffee,* etc.

Note.—Austrian use goes further in the direction of applying a common noun to a portion than does standard German:

Hast du ein Geld?   *Have you any money?*

„**Es muß irgendwo ein Regen niedergegangen sein,**" sagte Melzer (H. v. Doderer), *somewhere there must have been a shower.*

(*b*) Both languages use nouns of portion:

a pot, cup, dish of tea; **eine Schale Tee, eine Kanne Kaffee, ein Glas Bier.**

But German perhaps more often uses the simple indefinite article of portion [as (*a*) (3) above], where English has a specific noun:

Er bereitete sich einen Tee, *made himself some (a pot of) tea.*

cp. **Man servierte uns einen Aufschnitt,** *they gave us a plate of meat.*

German never uses a noun of portion for the portion itself:

a loaf, **ein Brot;** *a crust,* **ein Stück Brot, eine Brotrinde;** *a glass,* **ein Glas (Bier, etc.);** *a nip,* **ein Gläschen (Branntwein, etc.).**

German never uses the verb as a derived noun standing for the portion:

Will you have a drink, bite?   **Wollen Sie etwas trinken, essen?**

Exercise XLIV

A. Translate into English:

1. Rosalie konnte sich am kurzgestielten Krokus erfreuen, der überall in den Vorgärten der Villen und im Hofgarten sproß (Th. Mann). 2. Wer läßt sich beim Spaniel, Dachshund, Pudel, beim schottischen Terrier oder beim gütevollen Bernhardiner den Wolf einfallen? (Th. Mann). 3. Er will überlegen sein, und hat doch irgendwo den Lakaien in sich (R. Guardini). 4. Er schleppte Teller, Messer, Gabel, Brot und Wurst und Keks herbei und markierte, während sie aß, den aufmerksamen Oberkellner (E. Kästner). 5. Ein Nimbus des Respekts umwölkte wie ein Heiligenschein alles, was mit dem Hoftheater auch nur in entferntester Beziehung stand (S. Zweig). 6. So töricht ist der Mensch geschaffen, ein Wesen der Halbheiten und der Vorbehalte (W. Bergengruen). 7. Er hörte gern eine freie Meinung, je drastischer und extremer, desto besser (Th. Fontane). 8. Jetzt schlug der Mann den Rock zurück und zeigte die Messingmarke. „Ich warne Sie vor einer Beamtenbeleidigung" (L. Frank). 9. Sie haben sich beim Schreiben des Aufsatzes Mühe gegeben? Geben Sie sich also die Mühe, ihn ein letztes Mal durchzusehen. 10. Böse Frau macht den Mann grau. Not kennt kein Gebot (prov.).

B. Translate into German:

1. Beauty is not always a sign of goodness.   2. The beginning and
the end of this play are striking; what you think of the middle is a matter
of taste.   3. Eternity is a concept which we cannot really understand.
4. He lost his father and mother in a railway accident.   5. Providence
sends us health and sickness in turn.   6. Hatred of (für) his brother made
him leave home and seek his fortune abroad.   7. Geography is really
my favourite subject, but I am having to study history and economics
as well.   8. The German tribes were first converted to Christianity by
Irish missionaries.   9. Modern woman has more leisure than her grandmother, but does she know what to do with it?   10. You would make an
ideal burglar; you open and close doors so softly.

CHAPTER XLV

PREPOSITIONS. GENERAL

261. General and Survey

(*a*) Prepositions represent one of the greatest difficulties for the learner of German. Not only is the field of prepositional usage proper inexhaustible, but prepositions enter into the use of a large number of verbs and adjectives. Full guidance can only be obtained from a reliable dictionary.

(*b*) Prepositions are usually presented in long lists by cases which they govern and in alphabetical order. This method duplicates the information to be found in any dictionary, and can never be as full. An attempt has been made in the following chapters to make a grammatical contribution to prepositional usage by grouping the idioms logically.

Fundamental to all prepositional usage are prepositions of place, followed closely by those of time. Local and temporal words are then used, with other specialised terms, in a wide range of figurative meanings: **nach Berlin** (place), **nach der Schlacht** (time), **nach seiner Ansicht** (conformity), **er sehnt sich nach Glück** (aim or end), etc.

Figurative expressions are commonly expressive of:

(1) Relations of quantity:

ich bin knapp an Geld, *short of money;* **er kam um genau eine Stunde zu spät,** *exactly an hour too late.*

(2) Logical relations, in which all the common adverbial senses are represented, as manner, means, result, purpose, thus:

Trotz seiner Hilfe geschah das Unglück, *in spite of . . .* (opposition, *i.e.* concessive).

Er wurde blaß vor Zorn, *white with anger* (cause).

(*c*) The groups above described are dealt with successively at Chapters LII (place), LVII (time and aggregation), LX and LXIII (logical relations). Refer to skeleton lists (by cases governed) in earlier §§ 18, 30, 188; and *v.* Index of Prepositions.

Before their uses are illustrated in detail, a few general comments may be made on the origin, form, position, and case government of prepositions. As the senses are given fully elsewhere, prepositions and smaller prepositional phrases quoted in these introductory paragraphs have not been translated.

262. Origin

Two broad groups may be distinguished:

(*a*) An older group consisting of the main prepositions of place and time, governing the commoner cases (dative, accusative), and derived largely from adverbs of place, *e.g.* **an, auf, durch, hinter, nach, über, um,** and also **mit, von.**

(*b*) A newer group, mainly governing the genitive, and expressing less common, especially local and logical relations, and of varied origin, thus:

(1) From nouns: **dank, kraft, laut, trotz, wegen, zeit;** with genitive inflection: **längs, mittels, zwecks,** etc.

(2) From adjectives: **nächst, unweit.**

(3) From adverbs: **abwärts, einschließlich, hinsichtlich, links.**

(4) From past participles: **ungeachtet, unbeschadet,** and one from a present participle: **während.**

(5) From prepositional phrases: **anstatt** or **statt** (from **an Statt**); thus also **infolge,** and recently **anhand, anstelle, aufgrund.**

Though numerically the largest group and constantly growing, the genitive group includes many rare senses, and an excessive use of prepositions with this case is considered a mark of poor (official) style.

263. Form

(*a*) The form of prepositions may be:

(1) Single words (including the commonest): **an, durch, nach, um.**

(2) Two or more terms, which may:

   (i) precede the noun as a unit: **bis an, bis auf, bis zu,** etc.;

   (ii) bracket the noun governed: **um seines Vaters willen.**

Note.—Single word prepositions compound with certain pronouns to form adverbs (**davon, wodurch, vordem**), or conjunctions, whether adverbial or subordinating (**nachdem, indessen, trotzdem**); or they may contract with the definite article (**im, vom, durchs,** etc.). *v.* §§ 224 f. and 303, etc.

(*b*) A succession of two prepositions as a unit is limited to combinations with **bis** as first element (**bis auf, bis zu**), or **von** as second element (**innerhalb von**). They take the case of the second word: **bis zum Bahnhof, innerhalb von vier Tagen.**

If two prepositions are distinct in sense and govern separate words it is considered poor style to allow them to come together: **mit vor Zorn** gerötetem Gesicht; eine Sammlung von in Stein gepreßten Pflanzen (E. Jünger, in whom this construction is common). They should be resolved, *e.g.* by using the relative: **auf mit Purpur überzogenem Thron = auf dem Thron, der . . . war.**

Distinguish this from the (permitted) case where the second preposition and its noun form a common phrase which is governed as a unit by the first: **das England von vor 100 Jahren; das Zimmer erinnerte an zu Hause; eine Gruppe von gegen 20 Männer(n)** [cp. § 267 (*b*)]. Three in a group: **eine Ladung von bis zu 10 000 t Weizen** [*v.* also (*e*) below].

(*c*) A prepositional bracket is a unit, though embracing the noun governed: **um seines Vaters willen.** As such it combines with a governed pronoun: **um seinetwillen** (*v.* § 197). A very few other expressions also tend to follow this pattern: **um Himmelswillen** [= um (des) Himmels willen]; **von Staatswegen** [= von (des) Staates wegen].

Um . . . willen, and **von . . . wegen** are the only two of this kind, but a few others compounded of preposition and noun may still be resolved into their component parts and bracket a noun in the genitive: **anstelle, anstatt, inmitten. Anstatt des Vaters,** *instead of the father;* **an Vaters Statt,** *in loco parentis;* **an seiner** (= poss. adj.) **Statt,** *in his place.*

(*d*) The above should be distinguished from other brackets in which a preceding preposition is completed and reinforced in its sense by a following:

(1) Directional or other adverb: **hin, her, los,** etc.:

neben ihm her, nach dem Walde hin, durch die Stadt hindurch, mit den Eltern zusammen, auf dem Dache oben, auf das Ziel los.

(2) Prepositions used with adverbial force: **an, auf, zu,** etc.:

vom Ei an, von Jugend auf, von mir aus, auf ihn zu.

The following adverb in (1) adds no significant element of sense, but that in (2) often transforms the meaning: **von mir aus,** *as far as I am concerned;* **auf ihn zu,** *towards him.*

The following adverb is often absorbed into the verb as a stable prefix: **über jemanden herfallen,** *to fall on* (*attack*) *someone;* **über etwas hinausgehen,** *to go beyond, exceed something;* but it may well remain separate: **weil das Kind hinter ihm her heulte,** *came howling behind him* (cp. § 88).

(*e*) The common English double prepositional construction with *from* and a local preposition, *from inside, from under, from behind,* etc., corresponds to the colloquial German **von unter, von hinter,** etc.

He fetched the case from under the bed, **er nahm den Koffer von unter dem Bett.**

But correct usage only allows a bracket as in (*d*) (1):

Er nahm den Koffer unter dem Bett hervor.

Compare also:

ein Wirtshaus, hinter dessen Fenstern heftige Tanzmusik erscholl
(H. Hesse), *an inn, from behind the windows of which* . . .

264. Position

Most prepositions precede the word governed, but some follow, and among these latter two groups may be distinguished:

(*a*) The case, genitive or dative, is genuinely governed by the preposition, which can often also precede, though occasionally with a change of case and/or meaning:

(1) These either precede or follow: **entgegen, gegenüber, nach, ungeachtet, wegen, zufolge:**

seiner Ansicht entgegen, seinem Haus gegenüber, ihrer Aussage nach, dem Wortlaut zufolge, des Wetters ungeachtet, der Leute wegen.
entgegen seiner Ansicht, etc.

Note.—**zufolge** before or after with change of case and sense, *v.* §§ 508-10.

(2) These only follow:

gewisser Umstände halber, seiner Mutter zuliebe, seinem Wunsch zuwider.

Distinguish two-part prepositions bracketing the noun, § 263 (*c*).

(*b*) The case, accusative, is still an adverbial accusative [of measure of distance, or time, *v.* § 264 (*a*)], or has developed out of this:

er fuhr die Straße entlang, die Themse hinauf, die Nacht hindurch; sie fiel die Treppe hinunter, ging den Bahnsteig auf und ab.

Standard practice is careful not to extend these uses, thus especially for movement *out of, away from.* Thus **er sah zum Fenster hinaus,** *out of the window;* but not usually: **sie glitt zum Bett hinaus,** *out of bed* (E. Langgässer), though Goethe has **den Saal hinaus. Er fuhr von zu Haus weg,** *from his home;* but not: **er fuhr dem Bunker fort,** *away from the air-raid shelter* (H. Fallada, also S. Andres).

265. Case. Dative and Accusative

(*a*) There are two problems of case government requiring comment:

(1) The use of the dative or accusative in prepositions of that class: **an, in, über,** etc.

(2) The use of the genitive and its partial replacement by other constructions, *v.* §§ 266, 267 (*a*), cp. also § 486 (*c*).

(*b*) The rule requiring the dative or accusative in contexts of position or motion respectively, with certain prepositions, raises problems of interpretation in both literal and figurative idioms.

Certain verbs, literal in sense, but in which motion is only part of a complex meaning, thus *to arrive, to disappear,* are rendered in German by a compound verb or other construction and a preposition in the dative: **wir kamen in der Stadt an,** *arrived;* **er verschwand in den (plur.) Schatten,** *disappeared;* but: **das Buch kam unter den Tisch zu liegen,** *landed up.*

Sein and the past participle of a transitive verb may be seen as representing either a state or the action from which that state resulted (cp. §§ 211, 212, statal passive):

(1) The dative is used with compound verbs, since the past participle is regarded as equivalent to an intransitive verb, not of motion:

Die neuen Methoden sind in den Schulen schon eingeführt, *have been introduced, are valid* (= **gelten in den Schulen**).

Sein Name ist auf der Liste (or in dem Buch) eingetragen, *is registered on the list* (= **steht auf der Liste**).

(2) Either case may occur with simple verbs, depending on their force, but the accusative is strikingly frequent:

Auf winzigen Eselchen sind große Lasten gelegt, und der Treiber sitzt auf der Last noch dazu (G. Hauptmann), *large burdens are laid on minute asses* (= **die Eselchen tragen . . .**).

Wir sind hinter einem Berg von Gepäck ins Boot gequetscht (G. Hauptmann), *we are squashed into the boat . . .*

Aber die Schranken sind zwischen die Menschen gesetzt (H. Risse), *but barriers are* (= *have been*) *laid between men.*

(*c*) In figurative senses, where the literal rule of position versus direction does not apply, it will usually be found that **auf** and **über** take the accusative, the others of this group the dative:

auf Ihr Wohl! *your health!* **er klagte über seinen Vater,** *about his father;* **er leidet an der Gicht,** *from gout;* **unter Hochrufen erschien der Präsident,** *greeted by vivats;* **ich werde mich vor ihm hüten,** *be on my guard against him.*

Compare **er stieß an die Tischkante** (lit., *collided with*); **er stieß sich an ihrem Benehmen** (fig., *took objection to*).

The rule is qualified by "usually", since the boundary of literal and figurative usage is not always clear:

Er ist lahm auf einem Bein, *lame in one leg.*

Über dem Warten verging mir die Lust zum Essen, *through waiting I lost my appetite to eat.*

(*d*) Nouns derived from verbs follow the original verbal case usage:

die Lage im Wald, *situation in the forest;* **ihre Furcht vor dem Gewitter,** *fear of the storm;* **die Fahrt ins Gebirge,** *journey into the mountains;* **ein Duft nach Veilchen und frischer Wäsche,** *a fragrance of violets and fresh laundry.*

But care is needed to detect those cases where English usage might mislead: thus **der Gedanke** is always followed by **an** with accusative:

der Gedanke an den Tod, *thought of death.* Also: **seine Wahl in den Ausschuß,** *election to;* **ein Kuß auf die Stirn,** *kiss on;* **auf ihren Gängen übers Land,** *during her walks in the country.*

266. Case. Dative for Genitive

The field of the genitive is being partly invaded by other constructions. In prepositional usage this is represented largely by the spread of the dative (full details passim under the prepositions). Thus certain prepositions take:

(*a*) Genitive before the noun, dative after: **zufolge, ungeachtet.**

(*b*) Genitive or dative before the noun: **längs, trotz, wegen.**

(*c*) Dative for genitive when the latter has no distinct case ending as in:

(1) Neuter singular: **trotz vielem, wegen manchem.**

(2) Plural: **innerhalb zwei Tagen, während vier Jahren.**

(*d*) Dative after **von** for genitive:

(1) With an isolated noun in which neither case alone would be distinctive: **innerhalb von vier Wochen, infolge von Stromkürzungen.**

(2) With a proper noun (of person or place), since these increasingly resist case endings: **seitlich von Wolfgang, unterhalb von Stuttgart.**

(*e*) Dative, or **von** with dative, for genitive with (personal) pronouns where the genitive forms (*v.* § 190) are increasingly avoided:

unweit von ihm, wegen uns, am Berg und nördlich davon.

Compare also § 486 (*c*) (**von** for genitive). ·

267. Anomalies in Case Government

(*a*) Non-inflection of governed noun.

Where the genitive inflection is not replaced by the dative, as above, it is often omitted, together with any inflected article, etc., preceding;

and this rather laconic style is followed by prepositions taking other cases, *e.g.* dative, in similar senses:

einschließlich Risiko, *including risk;* **zuzüglich Porto,** *carriage additional;* **wegen Einbruch,** *for house-breaking;* **infolge Absterben,** *through death;* **in puncto** (or **laut,** dat.) **Vertrag,** *according to contract;* **mangels Zuschuß,** *in the absence of an advance.*

The legal and commercial origin of this practice is clear; there are, however, some factors which have contributed to its spread:

(1) Similar uses with proper names, whether personal (**wegen Hans**), local (**südlich Frankfurt, Ecke Kaiserplatz**), temporal (**Mitte Januar**), or with common nouns used as proper names (**wegen Vater**).

(2) Other constructions difficult to inflect, *e.g.* doublets (**inmitten Kummer und Elend, trotz Nacht und Nebel**).

In all these cases the juxtaposition of preposition and uninflected noun is preferred to the other alternatives to the inflected genitive, *i.e.* **von,** etc. (*v.* § 266).

(*b*) Prepositions used as adverbs, conjunctions.

Many prepositions are derived from adverbs and can still be used as such, either in their original form or in an adverbial compound: **er ging durch den Wald, durch den Wald hindurch,** *right through;* **es ist zehn Uhr durch,** *gone ten.* Normally, however, such non-prepositional uses are confined to a position after the noun. In certain cases, however, a preposition may be used in a modified, non-prepositional role before the noun:

(1) **ab,** *from* (place and time), takes dative, but may be followed by an unrelated adverbial accusative (of time): **ab nächsten Sonntag;** cp. **nächsten Sonntag** (point-time), and **die Straße entlang** (adv. acc. of place).

(2) **außer,** *except,* may be a preposition or conjunction: **ich sah alle da außer ihm** (= prep., dat.), or **außer ihn** (= conjn., acc., object of verb).

(3) Terms of approximation with numerals normally govern their proper case: **mit an die zehn Soldaten,** *with some ten soldiers.* But **bis zu** may occur adverbially: **sie schickt mir bis zu zehn Briefen** (prep., dat.) **im Monat,** *up to ten letters,* or **bis zu zehn Briefe** (adv. = **ungefähr,** *approximately,* followed by accusative object). Thus also: **eine Gruppe von gegen 20 Männer(n),** *of about 20 men.*

Note.—The student is reminded that the avoidance of points of grammatical conflict may be a mark of good style.

EXERCISE XLV

A. Translate into ENGLISH:

1. Beim Tode seines Vaters erbte er eine Summe von über 100 000 Mark.   2. Das Europa von vor dem ersten Weltkrieg ist schon beinahe gänzlich verschwunden.   3. Der Geruch von neu gebackenen Kuchen erinnerte ihn plötzlich an zu Hause.   4. Als sie in die Bauernstube trat, kam ein alter zottiger Hund hinter dem Ofen zum Vorschein.   5. Wegen Mangel an geeigneten Räumen muß die geplante Filmvorstellung ausfallen.   6. Innerhalb vier Tagen wird sich wohl auch kein solcher Raum finden lassen.   7. Die alte Apfelfrau schimpfte noch lange hinter dem Studenten her.   8. Hauptsächlich der Kinder wegen wollten Brauns einmal aus der heißen Stadt hinaus.   9. Sie gehen erst diese Straße entlang, dann die erste links.   10. Alle Jahre, außer dieses, hatten sie einander an jenem Gedenktage gesehen.

B. Translate into GERMAN:

1. Until a week ago he had never given the matter a thought.   2. For the sake of his family he kept his job.   3. She went with him as far as the corner of the road.   4. George was ill on the day of the match, so another boy played instead of him.   5. The dog was running straight towards his car.   6. She took a folded paper from inside her handbag.   7. The sentry walked slowly up and down the edge of the wood.   8. Her longing for home made her return from New York to a small village in Ireland.   9. The thought of home haunted her continually.   10. In spite of sorrow and care he never forgot old friends.

CHAPTER XLVI

THE SUBJUNCTIVE MOOD

268. General. Force of the Subjunctive

(*a*) The indicative mood is the normal aspect of the verb, and its forms and uses have been demonstrated in previous lessons; it is the form of statement for what is believed or known to be a fact. The subjunctive mood, however, expresses a discrepancy between reality and some view or attitude taken up by the speaker, such as:

(1) A wish:

Er schicke mir sofort den Brief, *let him send me the letter at once.*

(2) The statement of another:

Man sagt mir, er sei krank, *they tell me he is ill.*

(3) A possibility:

Ich wußte seine Absicht, ohne daß er sie mir gesagt hätte, *I knew his intention without his having told me.*

Not all wishes, however peremptory, or statements, however credible, or possibilities, however probable, may be taken to be realised or true.

(*b*) As is shown by the above examples, the subjunctive has provided a convenient form with which to express two categories of statement which are formally quite distinct; the subjunctive expressing

(1) *a wish* supplies missing forms of the imperative [*v.* (1) above, and cp. § 247 (*a*) and (*d*)]; and that expressing

(2) *a possibility* is used to report the statements of others in a form which does not implicate the speaker [*v.* (2) above, and cp. §§ 304-5].

(*c*) In both these cases, the original force of the subjunctive, the expression of a discrepancy between fact and a view or attitude of the speaker, becomes secondary, and may disappear, as when:

(1) A wish and its fulfilment are identical [*v.* § 273 (*d*)]:

Gelobt sei Jesus Christus; in Ewigkeit, Amen! *Praise be to Jesus Christ; for ever and ever. Amen.*

Sei innig gegrüßt von Deiner Dich liebenden Mutter, *greetings* (lit., *be greeted*) *from your loving mother* . . .

(2) A view conforms to the real situation [*v.* §§ 305 (*c*) and 307]:

Ich wußte damals schon, daß er Kettenraucher sei, *I already knew then that he was a chain smoker.*

370

(d) On the other hand, the very sense of discrepancy, which is the force of the subjunctive, may be formalised, and may express in the past no more than:

(1) A regret about a past event of which the outcome is no longer in doubt [v. § 273 (e)]:

Ach, wäre ich nur gegangen! *If only I had gone (but I did not).*

(2) An attitude of caution or modesty towards the content of a statement, the actual truth of which is not in doubt (v. § 309):

Jetzt wären wir am Ziel! *Well, here we are, I suppose!*

Ich müßte eigentlich zwei Pfund haben. *What I really need (if I may mention it) is two pounds.*

269. The Subjunctive. Alternative Forms

(a) The proper grammatical forms of the subjunctive are often replaced by certain circumlocutions:

(1) The forms of the modal verbs, either:

In the indicative: **Sagen Sie ihm, er soll kommen,** *tell him to come.*

or: In the subjunctive: **Ich schrieb ihm, damit er zeitig kommen möchte,** *I wrote to him, so that he should come in good time.*

(2) The so-called periphrastic form of the subjunctive, *i.e.* the imperfect subjunctive of **werden**, in a subordinate clause:

Er hatte die Stirn zu behaupten, er würde unschuldig sein, *he was impudent enough to assert that he was innocent* (= **er wäre unschuldig**).

This use in a subordinate clause is popular and incorrect, but derives from the feeling that an unrealised possibility may be regarded as relating to the future (*i.e.* his innocence might be shown in the future to be in conformity with fact).   However:

(3) The periphrastic subjunctive in the main clause is the normal and legitimate way of expressing a condition (English *should* or *would*), since a future possibility may be interpreted as a present condition:

Ich würde das Haus kaufen, wenn ich das Geld dazu hätte, *I would buy the house if I had the money.*

[**würde** as a cautious statement of the future **werde**, cp. § 309, especially (c) (2)].

Note.—It is essential that the legitimate use of **würde** in the main clause of a conditional statement be distinguished from its improper use in the subordinate clause of a variety of statements.

(*b*) The indicative alternates with the subjunctive. Thus:

(1) A statement, especially one of reported speech, which normally takes the subjunctive, may have the indicative if the extent to which fact and statement (do not) tally ceases to be of importance:

> **Er behauptet, er sei krank,** *he insists that he is ill.*
>
> **Er meint, daß er krank ist,** *he thinks he is ill.*

Thus the preceding verb may prepare the ground for subjunctive or indicative.

(2) A statement, such as one of result, which in itself does not require the subjunctive, may do so if the content is unreal:

Er predigte, daß die Steine mitsangen, *he preached in such a manner that the very stones joined in and sang.*

Er hat kein solches Gesicht, daß man zu ihm Vertrauen hätte, *he has not the kind of face which would cause one to trust him.*

Note that, as in the first example, a statement, to be envisaged as real (rather than unreal), does not have to be highly credible.

(*c*) In general, it may be said that the subjunctive, though still widespread in its use, is being simplified by the elimination of special uses, the spread of the indicative, and the use of circumlocutions. But in accordance with recent tendencies towards a more literary and cultivated style, some forms and uses are at the same time being reactivated.

270. The Subjunctive. Indirect Speech

For the subjunctive of indirect or reported speech, *v.* Chapter L. Certain general rules concerning the use of the subjunctive are largely, though not entirely, relevant to that category of statement.

(*a*) Tenses. As noted in § 268 (*d*), the present and past subjunctive have come to be distinct, not only, or even primarily, in tense, but in force and meaning. Thus no rigid system or sequence of tense (e.g. *I am ill* . . . *He said he was ill* . . .) is possible. Reported speech especially makes a general practice of reporting a statement in the tense in which it was made:

Er behauptete, daß das Schaukeln des Dampfers ihn krank mache (pres. subj.), *he said that the pitching of the boat was making him ill.*

(*b*) The use of tenses, beyond this general principle, is a matter more of practice than of rule, and must be studied under the individual uses.

(*c*) A subjunctive in the main clause may entail a consequent subjunctive in a dependent clause, without there being any apparent independent justification for the latter:

Er sagte, daß er sich krank fühle, weil das Schiff so unruhig sei, *he said he felt ill because the ship was so unsteady.*

(*d*) In reported speech, and to some extent also in other uses of the subjunctive, the introductory subordinating conjunctions **daß** or **ob** [the latter in the group **als ob**, *v.* §§ 310 (*c*) and 312 (*a*)] may be omitted, and the subordinate statement made in main clause order:

Er sagte, er fühle sich krank, *he said he felt ill.*

Er sah aus, als wäre er krank, *he looked as if he were ill.*

271. The Forms of the Present Subjunctive

(*a*) The following endings are added to the infinitive stem; they are the same for weak and strong verbs, no change or mutation of vowel taking place:

(daß) ich mach-e, du mach-est, er (sie, es) mach-e;
wir mach-en, ihr mach-et, sie (Sie) mach-en.

Similarly: **(daß) ich gehe,** etc.; **(daß) er nehme,** etc.

The **-e-** of the forms for **du** and **ihr** (**-est, -et**) may distinguish the subjunctive from corresponding indicative forms, and thus are never elided:

Indicative: **du kommst, ras(es)t, hetzest, lädst, bist.**

Subjunctive: **(daß) du kommest, rasest, hetzest, ladest, sei(e)st.**

Indicative: **ihr liebt, rast, hetzt, ladet, seid.**

Subjunctive: **(daß) ihr liebet, raset, hetzet, ladet, seiet.**

(*b*) Note the present subjunctive of certain verbs:

(1) Irregulars:

haben; (daß) ich habe, du habest, er habe, wir haben, etc.

sein; (daß) ich sei, du sei(e)st, er sei, wir seien, etc.

werden; (daß) ich werde, du werdest, er werde, wir werden, etc.

tun; (daß) ich tue, (du tuest), er tue, wir tuen, etc.

(2) Stems in **-el** and **-er** usually elide the **-e-** of the stem, while retaining the characteristic **-e-** of the subjunctive ending:

(daß) ich wand(e)le, du wand(e)lest, er wand(e)le, etc.

(*c*) The contrast between indicative and subjunctive forms may be summarised thus: the subjunctive is distinct from the indicative:

(1) In the third person singular, always: **er singe, mache, schlafe.**

(2) In the second person singular and plural, commonly:

du schläfst/schlafest; ihr schlaft/schlafet;
du singst/singest; ihr macht/machet.

(3) In the first singular, first plural, third plural and second plural (polite), only in a few verbs. Thus **tun** has **tuen** (v. above), and the seven past present verbs have, in the first person singular, a different stem for indicative and subjunctive:

wissen, ich weiß, (daß) ich wisse;

dürfen, ich darf, (daß) ich dürfe, etc.

272. The Forms of the Past Subjunctive

(a) The same endings are added as for the present, but to the stem of the past tense; and vowel changes take place in certain verbs.

(daß) ich macht-e, du macht-est, er (sie, es) macht-e;

wir macht-en, ihr macht-et, sie (Sie) macht-en.

Similarly: **(daß) ich riet-e,** etc.

Vowel mutation in strong verbs takes place as follows:

(1) Any vowel which may be, is mutated:

(daß) ich trüge (cp. trug), **sänge** (cp. sang), **böge** (cp. bog).

(2) A few verbs with infinitive stem in short or long -e- [v. Appendix C, Class III (3)] take a mutated vowel different from that of the past indicative; but in all cases (except **sterben, verderben,** and **werben**) this is alternative to the regular mutated vowel. Thus:

beföhle (befähle); gölte (gälte); hülfe (hälfe);

stürbe, verdürbe, and **würbe** as the only forms.

Note.—These changed vowel forms are felt to have an archaic flavour but their continued retention is due partly to recent preference for distinctly literary forms, partly also to the convenience of distinguishing in sound between present and past subjunctive, thus **hülfe,** for **hälfe** which is not distinct from **helfe.**

(b) Note the past subjunctive of certain verbs and classes:

(1) Irregulars:

haben; (daß) ich hätte, du hättest, er hätte, wir hätten, etc.

sein; (daß) ich wäre, du wär(e)st, er wäre, wir wären, etc.

werden; (daß) ich würde, du würdest, er würde, wir würden, etc.

tun; (daß) ich täte, du tätest, er täte, wir täten, etc.

(2) Irregular weak verbs (v. § 77):

The **brennen** group reverts in the subjunctive to the present vowel -e- (for -ä-): **(daß) ich brennte,** etc.; the **bringen** group, on the other hand, retains the modified vowel: **(daß) ich brächte,** etc.

(3) Past present verbs (*v.* § 66):

These only mutate if the infinitive vowel is already mutated, thus:

(daß) ich dürfte, könnte, möchte, müßte, and also **wüßte;** but

(daß) ich sollte, wollte (infinitive **sollen, wollen**).

(*c*) The contrast between indicative and subjunctive forms in the past may be summarised thus:

(1) In all regular weak verbs, and in **sollen, wollen,** there is no apparent difference.

(2) All strong verbs, irregular weak verbs, and the other five past present verbs, have clearly distinct forms.

273. The Subjunctive of Will or Wish (1) in Main Clauses

The subjunctives of will and wish respectively are not clearly distinguishable in main clauses, the context largely deciding the degree of peremptoriness.

(*a*) The subjunctive of will provides for all the third persons the normal form of the imperative:

Er setze sich sofort mit seiner Firma in Verbindung, *he is to (let him, tell him to) get in touch with his firm at once.*

With the pronouns **wir, Sie,** the normal order is reversed, and these are regarded as straight imperative forms [*v.* § 247 (*d*)].

The imperative third person is common with formal (logical) demonstration:

Die Figur ABCD sei ein gleichwinkliges Viereck, *let the figure ABCD be a quadrilateral with equal angles.*

often with the indefinite pronouns **man, einer, jeder:**

Man nehme an, *let us assume;* **man achte auf die Folgen,** *note the results.*

„Nun seh' mal einer diesen Krischen Buddenbrook!" **schrie Konsul Döhlmann** (Th. Mann), *now just look at that fellow . . .*

(*b*) The subjunctive of wish introduces many expressions of pious desire: **Gott gebe, daß . . .,** *may God grant that . . .;* **Hol' ihn der Teufel,** *the devil take him,* etc.

(*c*) In general and for third person statements, straight order is rather more imperative (= will) than inverted or question order (= wish). This is seen in modal idioms, where:

(1) **sollen** may in the singular, and in the plural commonly does stand (in the *indicative*) for the imperative:

Er soll mich morgen anrufen, *let him call me up* . . . (= **er rufe** . . .)

Sie sollen nicht so viel Lärm machen, *they are not to make so much noise* (= **sie machen** . . .).

(2) while politer requests are couched in the *subjunctive* of **mögen** or **wollen:**

Er möge mich um sieben Uhr abholen, *would he please fetch me* . . .

Man wolle sich nicht so laut ausdrücken, *please do not express yourself so loudly.*

Compare **möge er diesen schweren Schlag überstehen,** *may he come through after this severe blow.*

(*d*) The appropriate forms of **sein** replace those of **werden** as the auxiliary for passive statements in the imperative and present subjunctive [*v.* § 212 (*b*)]:

(1) Second singular and plural, imperative, *be!*:

Sei gegrüßt von Deinem Dich liebenden Vater, *greetings from* (lit., *be greeted from*) *your loving father.*

Sei versichert, daß . . ., *be assured that* . . .

Seien Sie gesegnet . . ., *may you be blessed* . . .

Note.—Lassen, in the person appropriate to the person or persons addressed, and a dependent infinitive, is also used:

Laß dich, laßt euch, lassen Sie sich beschenken, *let yourself* (*yourselves*) *be given a present.*

For **lassen,** with first person plural object, *v.* § 247 (*e*) (2).

(2) Commonly in the third person impersonal, both in logical demonstration and pious ejaculation, (*let*) *be*:

bevor . . . **sei die Frage aufgeworfen,** *before* . . . *the question should* (*may*) *be considered* . . .

hier . . . **sei ein Wort gesagt, eine Erklärung versucht, eine Einschränkung gemacht,** *let me here say something, attempt an explanation, introduce a limitation.*

Gott sei's gedankt! *Thank God* (lit., *May God,* dative, *be thanked!*).

Wir sind fertig mit dem Mann, Wachtmeister . . . **Gott sei's getrommelt und gepfiffen** (H. Fallada). *Thank God and all the choirs of Heaven.*

Compare §§ 211-12 on the statal passive, of which this may be regarded as a further example.

(*e*) The present subjunctive in the above sections represents a request or desire not unlikely of fulfilment. The imperfect subjunctive, often with **doch**, in the general sense *if only*, expresses—

(1) A more tentative wish or one in which fulfilment is more remote, or even (in the perfect) practically excluded:

Käme er doch bald! *if only he would come.*

Möchte er bald schreiben, *if only he would write soon.*

Wollte Gott, wir wären schon zu Hause! *would to God we were . . .*

Hätte ich ihn nur gesehen! *if only I had seen him.*

Note.—F. Werfel says of these forms:

Doch wozu das? ,,Hätte`` und ,,wäre`` sind die grammatikalischen Formen unserer unfruchtbarsten Reue, *but what is the use! "If only" is but the expression of our most useless regrets.*

(2) A polite imperative:

Herr A. möchte zu mir ins Konferenzzimmer kommen. *Ask Mr A. to be so good as to . . .*

274. The Subjunctive of Will or Wish (2) in Subordinate Clauses

The following are illustrative of subordinate uses:

(*a*) Any of the uses in § 273 when grammatically subordinated:

Logical demonstration, with impersonal subject:

welche Möglichkeit vorläufig außer acht gelassen sei, *which possibility we may leave aside for the moment* (lit., *let it be . . .*).

Es roch nach Katzen, nach Holz, nach sauer gewordenem Kohl, wobei nicht an Sauerkraut gedacht werden wolle, denn danach roch es außerdem (W. Bergengruen), *under which the reader should not think of sauerkraut, for that smell was also present.*

Simple and pious wishes, often introduced by **daß** or **wenn** with the past subjunctive:

wenn die Sache, wovor uns Gott bewahre, einen solchen Ausgang nimmt, *if that is the way things will end, from which God preserve us . . .*

O daß ich schon ihre Antwort hätte . . . wenn er kommen möchte, *if only I had her answer . . . he would come . . .*

(*b*) A noun clause, as:

(1) Complement of a noun of explicit willing or wishing:

Mein Anliegen wäre (subjunctive of tentative statement, *v.* § 309), **daß Sie die Sache sofort in die Hand nähmen** (or **nehmen möchten/sollten**), *the kind of thing I should like is to see you take the matter under your own control at once.*

(2) Object of a verb of similar sense:

Ich wollte, es schriebe einmal jemand eine Natur- und Weltgeschichte des italienischen Kaffeehauses (W. Bergengruen), *I wish someone would write a natural and political history of the Italian café.*

This field is common ground with the subjunctive of indirect speech, *v.* further, § 354 (*c*).

Note.—After verbs of willing or wishing, an objective predicate may replace the subjunctive, with **haben, wissen,** or **sehen** in the subordinate clause:

Ich will alles bis Ende der Woche erledigt wissen, *I want everything to be dealt with before the end of the week* (for **daß . . . sei**).

Compare further § 218 (*c*) (**haben**) and § 434 (*e*) (objective predicate).

(3) Object of a verb expressing what is meet, right, proper, seemly, or deserving, especially **verdienen,** usually in apposition to **es** as the immediate object:

Er verdient (or verdiente, more tentative) **(es), daß man ihm die Einladung sofort absage,** *he deserves to have his invitation refused.*

(*c*) Any subjunctive use may entail the subjunctive in any further subordinate clause dependent on the first use [*v.* § 270 (*b*)]:

> **Ihr glücklichen Augen,**
> **Was je ihr gesehn,**
> **Es sei, wie es wolle,**
> **Es war doch so schön!**　　　(Goethe, *Faust II*).
>
> . . . *whatever it was* (lit., *let it be what it will,* subjunctive).

EXERCISE XLVI

A. Translate into ENGLISH:

1. Dieses Buch enthält die uns gebliebenen Aufzeichnungen jenes Mannes, welchen wir . . . den „Steppenwolf" nannten. Ob sein Manuskript eines einführenden Wortes bedürfe, sei dahingestellt (H. Hesse). 2. Sehnlich wünschte er, nichts mehr von sich zu wissen, Ruhe zu haben, tot zu sein. Käme doch ein Blitz und erschlüge ihn! Käme doch ein Tiger und fräße ihn! Gäbe es doch einen Wein, ein Gift, das ihm Betäubung brächte, Vergessen und Schlaf, und kein Erwachen mehr! (H. Hesse). 3. „Am liebsten möchtest du, daß wir uns hier ein für alle Male vergrüben und daß ich keinen Menschen mehr zu Gesichte bekäme!" (Th. Mann). 4. B.H. . . . wollte nicht, daß ich mich blamiere und als ein völlig Unwissender und Ungebildeter meinen neuen Zeitgenossen erscheine (F. Werfel). 5. „Jetzt wären wir so weit", meinte der Zahnarzt,

indem er den Bohrer behutsam in meinen Zahn drückte. 6. Sie antwortete, daß das Haus jetzt in Ordnung war, und daß man es jederzeit besehen könne. 7. „Mögen sie nur hereinkommen, die Kinder", sagte der Großvater, „du weißt ja, daß sie jederzeit zu mir dürfen".

B. Translate into German (§§ 273, 274 only):

1. May God grant you good health and may all your wishes come true. 2. I wish we had met a year ago. 3. Take three eggs and an equal weight of sugar and beat for ten minutes. 4. He is to eat three good meals a day and go to bed early. 5. Tell them they are not to smoke in the auditorium. 6. First of all a word should be said about the background to (= genitive) this question. 7. If only I could persuade him to see the truth of this argument. 8. It is proper that a son should support his old parents. 9. He deserves to be told the truth (use **man**). 10. Let everyone contribute the sum of ten marks, and we shall soon have the necessary sum.

CHAPTER XLVII

THE PRESENT PARTICIPLE. THE ENGLISH GERUND

275. The Present Participle. Adjectival Use

Revise §§ 37-9, 152 (*b*).

(*a*) The English participle, standing in immediate adjectival apposition after the noun, may fulfil either of two functions:

(1) Descriptive, in which some item of description is added:

A boy's face, gleaming with expectation, appeared at the window.

A beggar, dragging his feet through the snow, was enough to touch her heart.

(2) Determinative, in which the participle differentiates the noun from others of its kind:

The timber standing in his grounds (but no other timber) *is sold.*

The man standing in the corner (not elsewhere) *is my uncle.*

The respective intentions of these two uses above may be described briefly as colour (1) and clarity (2).

(*b*) The German participle can only be used in following, *descriptive* apposition, as in (1) above:

Das Gesicht eines Jungen, vor Erwartung glänzend, erschien im Fenster.

Ein Bettler, mit den Füßen durch tiefen Schnee schlurfend, genügte, um ...

Drunten im Städtchen ... war ein nett und anziehend ausgestatteter Delikatessenladen, Zweigniederlassung einer Wiesbadener Firma ... und den höheren Gesellschaftsschichten als Einkaufsquelle dienend (Th. Mann),

serving the better classes as a source of provisions.

(*c*) English, however, makes wide use of the following, *determinative* construction, using even an isolated participle in this manner:

The man standing (not sitting) *in the corner is my uncle.*

In all such cases, German must use other constructions, as:

(1) A relative clause:

der Mann, der in der Ecke steht ...

der Baumbestand, der sich auf seinem Gut befindet ... [*v.* (*a*) (2)].

(2) A complex inflected adjective (to be used with discretion):

der in der Ecke stehende Mann ...

der sich auf seinem Gut befindende Baumbestand ...

(3) An abbreviated prepositional phrase:

der Mann in der Ecke ..., der Baumbestand auf seinem Gut ...

(d) A preceding adjective-participle fulfils in German both the functions in (a) above: **glänzende Gesichter, die steuerzahlende Bevölkerung, radfahrende Bürger, eine liegende Körperstellung;** but in some cases English requires that the participle should follow:

Wolkenbrüche mit folgendem Landregen, *cloud-bursts, with rain following* (*followed by rain*).

276. The Present Participle.   Adverbial Use

(a) Wide use is made in English of a participial construction, in apposition to a noun or pronoun, and taking the place of an adverbial clause:

Walking down the street (= *as he walked*) *he stumbled and fell.*

Such constructions are widely descriptive of some form of attendant circumstance (= manner), but a more special note of time, cause, or means may sometimes be distinguished:

Time: *Saying this he walked out of the room.*

Manner: *Raising his hat he revealed hair going very grey.*

Cause: *Knowing you, I do not believe it.*

Means: *Practising daily he learnt quickly.*

English may use *as* and a finite verb, instead of the participle, for most of the above senses, but for means, *by* and a gerund (*by practising*) is required.

(b) The following German constructions may be recommended to translate the English appositional participle, in order of usefulness:

(1) Appropriate subordinating conjunctions, as:

Specific conjunctions for time (**als, indem,** etc.), cause (**da,** etc.); **indem,** or the pronominal adverb **dadurch** and the conjunction **daß,** for means [*v.* gerund below, § 278 (*f*)]:

Indem er das sagte . . . Als er das gesagt hatte . . ., etc.

(2) A prepositional phrase: **Nach diesem Ausspruch** (*Saying this*). **Beim Lüften des Hutes** (*Raising his hat*). **Durch tägliche Übung** (*By practising daily*).

(3) A simple **und** joining two equal statements is often enough, especially for manner:

Er lüftete den Hut und ließ stark ergrautes Haar sehen.
Er übte täglich und lernte schnell.

(c) The corresponding German participial construction is limited, being strictly applicable only to attendant circumstance, though within these limits heavily (perhaps excessively) used by certain descriptive writers:

Die Handlung, in hundert Szenen und Höllen führend, ist unmöglich, zerklüftet, heldenlos (K. Kraus), *the action, taking the reader (as it does) into* . . .

Sie griff, sich reckend, nach dem Kragen seines Staubmantels und mit der Zunge an den Lippen spielend, zog sie ihm den Gabardine herunter (S. Andres), *stretching up . . . her tongue playing* . . .

Der Hund stieß, mich entsetzt anstarrend, ein langes singendes Gewinsel hervor (F. Werfel), *staring at me with horror* . . .

sah er, wie der Schuster Nicola plötzlich von seinem Schemel auffuhr, auf dem er eine Zeitung lesend gesessen hatte (S. Andres), *reading a paper.*

Wie viele Vormittage habe ich hier versessen, Träumen und Gedanken nachhängend (W. Bergengruen), *pursuing my dreams and thoughts.*

(*d*) With ingenuity, a specific adverbial element of time, cause, etc., might be detected in the above examples. But their essentially descriptive nature is shown by the ease with which they can be converted into another construction not involving a specific conjunction [as in (*b*) (1)], such as:

A relative: **die Handlung, die** . . .

Simple coordination: **sie reckte sich und griff** . . .

                starrte mich entsetzt an, und stieß . . .

Prepositional phrase: **bei der Lektüre der Zeitung** . . .

Another appositional construction: **in Träumen versunken** . . .

(*e*) The distinction between a descriptive apposition with adjectival, and one with adverbial force is often hardly more than a matter of its position; thus the first example in § 275 (*b*) might be reworded adverbially as follows:

Das Gesicht eines Jungen erschien, vor Erwärtung glänzend, am Fenster.

(*f*) The isolated participle with adverbial force, followed by its own subordinate clause, is an English construction; in German it is either an idiosyncracy or a Gallicism:

Sie macht keine Theorie daraus . . . sondern nimmt es auf sich, glaubend, sie müsse (R. Guardini), *thinking that she must.*

Ich erschien pünktlich um vier Uhr, vergessend, daß sie eine Russin war und somit jenseits von Zeit und Pünktlichkeit (S. Zweig), *forgetting that she was a Russian* . . .

(*g*) It is clear, therefore, that, in preference to an attempted literal translation of the English by the German participle, the former should be dealt with on the lines of "subordination, coordination, or elimination" [cp. (*b*) above].

277. The Absolute Use of the Present Participle

(a) This has developed from the adverbial construction. In English it is strictly twofold:

(1) The unattached participle:

> *Considering the circumstances, you may go . . .*
> *Seeing that . . ., roughly speaking . . ., assuming that . . .*

(2) The absolute construction proper, in which the participle is not unattached, but has its own subject:

> *George being a friend of mine, I don't mind helping him.*

(b) The unattached present participle may be rendered into German by:

(1) A preposition (**in Anbetracht der Umstände . . .**, *considering . . .*) or the corresponding conjunction (**in Anbetracht dessen, daß . . .**, *seeing that . . .*);

(2) An unattached past participle:

Die Sache mit dem Brief betreffend . . ., *concerning that business . . .* (or **Was die Sache . . . betrifft/anbelangt . . .**).

Dies einleitend (Th. Mann), *this by way of introduction* (= **zur Einleitung**).

(3) An unattached past participle:

allgemein gesprochen, *generally speaking;* **angenommen, daß . . .** (or straight order without **daß**), *assuming that . . .*

(c) Certain unattached present participles are used as adverbs or degree adverbs:

> **Er gefiel mir ausnehmend gut,** *I liked him extremely well.*

Ich wurde eingehend über die Sache unterrichtet, *I was informed at length about the matter.*

Thus also **laufend**, *constantly*, and **beiliegend**, *enclosed*, the former a fashion-word, the latter commercial; many oppose their use, and adduce examples of possible ambiguity:

> **Stehengelassene Fahrräder werden laufend gestohlen,**

and **beiliegend** cannot avoid, on one view, being misrelated to either the writer or recipient of a letter:

> **Beiliegend schicke ich Ihnen (or erhalten Sie) unsere Preisliste.**

(d) The absolute construction proper, with adverbial sense (*George being . . . = as George is . . .*), is rare in English, and unknown in German, but *descriptive* apposition occasionally occurs:

Sein Kopf war breit und schwer, das schwarze Haar in die Stirn fallend, der gewaltige Bart bis zu den Augen wuchernd (E. Wiechert), *his black hair overhanging his forehead and the great beard growing up to his eyes.*

and adverbial apposition of accusative and *past* participle is very common (**Den Kopf gesenkt, ging er . . .**, *v.* § 350).

German often uses **bei** and a participle in the *attributive* position where English has an apposition of noun and *following* participle:

Mit dem Stundenschlage begann, bei fortspielender Musik, aus der größten Mitteltür die Prozession der Akteure sich hervorzubewegen (Th. Mann), *. . . the music continuing . . .*

278. The English Gerund and its Translation

Compare Chapter XXXVII, the Infinitive Noun.

(*a*) The English participle becomes a verbal noun (gerund) when it is used with nominal function: *singing is good for the soul, teaching by caning*, etc.

The English gerund may be rendered in German by any of the three kinds of verbal noun:

Sein Kommen hat uns alle hoch erfreut, *his coming was a great joy to us all.*

Er widmete sich dem Ankauf von Kunstgegenständen und ihrem Verkauf an Sammler, *he devoted himself to buying objets d'art and to selling them (their re-sale) to collectors.*

Die Absicht war gut, ihre Durchführung ließ aber zu wünschen übrig, *the plan was good, but the carrying out (its execution) was not satisfactory.*

(*b*) As a verbal form, the gerund may have a subject, object, or both. Here the various verbal nouns in the two languages differ:

(1) The gerund and the German infinitive noun may indicate the subject of the activity by a preceding possession adjective (**sein Kommen**, *his coming*, above); on the other hand, a possessive preceding other kinds of verbal nouns, German and English, is often, when the original verb is transitive, objective in force (**ihr Verkauf**, *their sale;* **ihre Durchführung**, *its execution*) [§ 207 (*d*)].

(2) The gerund demonstrates its verbal force by taking its object directly (*buying objets d'art*, above), while all forms of verbal noun in German have the nominal form of objective genitive (or **von** plus dative):

    der Ankauf und Verkauf von Büchern, *buying and selling books.*

    die Durchführung seiner Absicht, *his carrying out his plan.*

    beim Singen des Liedes, *while singing the song.*

(*c*) The English gerund, with or without its own object, may be governed, like any noun object, by a verb (*I like eating cabbage*), verb and preposition (*I aim at eating cabbage once daily*), an adjective with or without a preposition (*I am busy, tired of eating cabbage*), etc.

Such constructions may be rendered into German:

(1) By verb and adverb:

ich esse gern (*like*), **ungern** (*dislike*), **weiter** (*go on*), **nicht mehr** (*stop, have ceased*), **mit Vorliebe** (*prefer*) **Kohl** (*eating cabbage*).

(2) By a verbal noun (cp. above):

mit dem Sammeln beschäftigt, *busy collecting;* **für die Durchführung verantwortlich,** *responsible for carrying out;* **auf den Verkauf von Trödelwaren angewiesen,** *reduced to selling junk.*

(3) By a prepositional infinitive:

ich fange an (*start*), **höre auf** (*cease*), **ziehe (es) vor** (*prefer*), **Kohl zu essen** (*eating cabbage*).

(*d*) When the German construction involves the government of the gerundial idea by a preposition (**angewiesen auf,** *reduced to*) or in an oblique case (**müde** with genitive, *tired of*), and the gerund itself appears as a prepositional infinitive construction or other noun clause (**Kohl zu essen,** *eating cabbage*), the straightforward combination of these two elements is precluded by the fact that no German clause may be governed in an oblique case (relatives have special rules):

ich bin mit [Geld zu sammeln] beschäftigt.

In these cases a grammatical link is provided by the neuter pronoun **es,** usually compounded with the preposition in a **da-** group (cp. §§ 33, 223 f.), and acting as a stand-in for the clause, with which it is in apposition, and to which it points forward:

Ich bin *damit* beschäftigt, Geld zu sammeln, *busy collecting.*

Ich bin *darauf* angewiesen, Kohl zu essen, *reduced to eating.*

Ich bin es [genitive, *v.* § 192 (*c*)] müde, Kohl zu essen, *tired of eating.*

(*e*) When the gerundial object in English has its own subject, the possessive adjective is preferred to the pronoun object:

I remember his singing that song (not: *him singing . . .*).

German uses here the appositional construction as in (*d*) and a **daß** clause, rather than attempting to develop the possessive construction [*e.g.* **sein Singen,** as **sein Kommen** in (*a*)]:

Ich erinnere mich daran, daß er jenes Lied immer sang.

Ich bin es müde, daß er immer betteln kommt, *I am tired of his always coming begging* (not: *tired of him . . .*).

(*f*) The gerundial construction often has adverbial force, thus time (*after saying this*), manner (*without saying a word*), means (*by practising daily*), etc.

(1) Many such statements, especially of time, manner, are translated by a subordinating conjunction and clause (*v.* passim, Chapter XXV, etc.); but **ohne** and **anstatt,** where the subject does not change, may have the prepositional infinitive [*v.* § 203 (*b*)].

(2) The appositional construction, as in (*d*), is often used with **daß** or other conjunction:

Means: **Dadurch, daß er täglich übte, lernte er schnell,** *by practising daily he learnt quickly.*

Cause: **Das kommt daher, weil** (or **davon, daß**) **er immer zu viel ißt,** *that is due to his always over-eating.*

(3) The simplest construction is often a verbal noun:

Time: **Nach dem Verkauf seines Hauses . . .,** *after selling . . .*

Manner: **Beim Überqueren der Straße . . .,** *while crossing the road . . .*

Means: **Durch Übertreibung der ganzen Sache gelang es ihm . . .,** *by exaggerating the affair he managed . . .*

279. The Modal Verbal (2). Present Participle

Revise the Modal Verbal Infinitive, §§ 249 f.

(*a*) The attributive participle preceded by **zu** has, like the corresponding infinitive construction, modal and passive force:

Das zu verkaufende Haus wurde am Vormittag besichtigt, *the house (which was) to be sold, was viewed in the morning.*

This construction may only be used when the noun is the direct object of the participial verb, thus:

eine zu befolgende Vorschrift, *a regulation to be observed;* but: **ein Vorbild, dem man folgen sollte,** *a model to be followed.*

(*b*) As with the infinitive, the modal sense varies between *must, should,* and *can*; it is, however, stronger in the negative:

ein nicht zu übersehender Umstand, *a circumstance which must not be ignored.*

Through its modal force it may convey future sense:

bei einer später zu bestimmenden Gelegenheit, *on some occasion to be arranged later.*

(*c*) Apart from **nicht,** the modal passive participle may be preceded by simple extensions of the sense; but usage is very sensitive in what may *not* be said, and no general rule can be given:

ein unmöglich zu erwähnender Umstand, *a point impossible to mention.*

but not: **ein unnötig zu erwähnender Umstand,** *unnecessary to mention.*

Where the student is uncertain, a relative clause is always safe:

ein Umstand, den zu erwähnen nicht nötig ist.

(*d*) The modal passive participle may be used as an adjective-noun:

(eine) Ahnung, daß etwas zu Vollbringendes vor ihr lag (W. Bergengruen), *a feeling that something to be achieved lay before her.*

EXERCISE XLVII

A. Translate into ENGLISH:

1. Im überdachten Wandelgang gingen alte Nonnen betend langsam hin und her (L. Frank). 2. In weiten Bogen umkreiste ich meine Wohnung, stets die Heimkehr im Sinn, stets sie verzögernd (H. Hesse). 3. Der Pelerinenträger steuerte auf die Bank zu, ließ sich, eine Begrüßungsformel murmelnd, neben F. nieder . . . Er atmete keuchend, hatte ein Holzbein und ging an einem Stock (E. Kästner). 4. Batzkes Kopf tauchte immer wieder auf, spähend wie ein Fuchs sah das harte, böse Gesicht . . . über die Straße (H. Fallada). 5. Die Kirchen überragten in ungeheuren stummen Proportionen stadtbeherrschend die armseligen Häuschen (L. Frank). 6. Ich darf sagen, daß ich seine besondere Gunst genoß, und heranwachsend diente ich ihm häufig als Vorbild für seine Kunstgemälde (Th. Mann). 7. Der Schaffner legt salutierend die Hand an die Mütze (Th. Mann). 8. Eigentlich hatte er mehr als dreißig Jahre . . . einzig hier an diesem viereckigen Tisch lesend, vergleichend, kalkulierend verbracht (S. Zweig). 9. Ich habe das gern, auf der Treppe diesen Geruch von Stille, Ordnung, Sauberkeit, Anstand und Zahmheit zu atmen . . ., und habe es gern, dann über die Schwelle meines Zimmers zu treten, wo das alles aufhört (H. Hesse). 10. A trapeze act: Ein Schauer der Begeisterung überrieselte den, der es sah, und kalt trat es ihm ans Herze . . . Diese stets aufs Haar genau auszukalkulierende Knappheit der Bedingungen ließ erbeben (Th. Mann).

B. Translate into GERMAN:

1. Not seeing anyone in the shop he waited awhile and then left. 2. Fearing the worst he rang up the police. 3. The train was travelling at great speed, swaying dangerously. 4. Whistling loudly the messenger boy walked up to the house and rang the bell. 5. He had been sitting and gazing idly across the river for some time when (cp. § 126) he suddenly heard the splash of oars. 6. He busied himself in preparing his horse for the afternoon ride. 7. Collecting and mounting stamps was his wintertime hobby. 8. Instead of skiing in the winter you should spend your money on mountaineering in the summer. 9. Before writing his next book he spent a year travelling in the East. 10. The view from the mountain top was a sight not to be forgotten.

CHAPTER XLVIII

NOTES ON ADJECTIVE INFLECTION. RELATIVES

280. Non-inflection of Adjectives

Numerous set expressions with adjective and noun may still retain an earlier uninflected form when used in a homely, humorous, or archaising context.

Compounds of **gut** are especially common: **gut Freund sein,** *to be on good terms;* **auf gut Glück,** *haphazardly;* **ein gut Teil,** *a good portion.* A famous advocate of the care and purity of the language published two books, one called „**Gut Deutsch**" (1893), a later one, „**Gutes Deutsch**" (1918). A writer castigating specious originality in using the language writes: **Afferei heißt auf gut Deutsch solches Bestreben** (Mspr.).

Others are: **sich (bei jmdm) lieb Kind machen,** *to get into someone's good books;* **ein würdig Glied der Familie,** *a worthy member of the family;* **ein liebend Paar,** *a loving pair.*

281. Adjectives from Place-Names

(*a*) Adjectives may be formed from geographical proper names in two ways; using the endings:

(1) **-(i)sch,** often with modification of the vowel, and inflection: **badisch, sächsisch, rheinisch, römisch,** *of Baden, Saxon, Rhenish, Roman.*

This ending is found largely with the names of countries and larger divisions.

(2) **-er,** retaining the capital and not inflected: **Meißner Porzellan, der Münchner Föhn, die Washingtoner Regierungspolitik,** *Meißen Porcelain, the Munich Föhn* (warm wind), *the governmental policy of Washington.*

This ending is with names of towns. Towns in **-en,** etc., usually omit **-e-,** *v.* examples above, also **Basler, Zürcher.**

(*b*) The division of function is not, however, absolute, and some names have both forms:

badische Truppeneinheiten, Badener Wein, *troops, wine from Baden.*

schweizerische Kuckucksuhren, Schweizer Käse, *Swiss cuckoo clocks, cheese.*

eine kölnische Zeitung, der Kölner Dom, *a Cologne newspaper, the Cathedral at Cologne.*

(*c*) The undeclined form **Münch(e)ner** is originally the genitive plural of the inhabitants: **Münch(e)ner Weißwürste = Weißwürste der Münchener.**

Perhaps influenced by the group numeral ending -er (*v.* § 94), the form **Schweizer** is increasingly, and **Berliner** occasionally, to be seen without the capital: **in einer schweizer Klinik, eine berliner Firma.**

282. Adjectives from Personal Names
The ending **-(i)sch** is also used to convert personal names into adjectives.

(*a*) Commonly as **-sch** (NO apostrophe), retaining the capital, in the sense of *works by, originating from*: **die Mörikesche Dichtung,** *the poetry of Mörike;* **Schinkelsche Bauten,** *buildings by Schinkel;* **die Gesichter Riemenschneiderscher Figuren,** *the faces of figures by Riemenschneider.*
But the genitive is commoner: **die Dramen Schillers.**

(*b*) Commonly as **-isch,** with small initial, in the generic sense *of a certain kind*: **die lutherische Kirche,** *the Lutheran Church;* **homerisches Gelächter,** *Homeric laughter;* **eine galvanische Batterie,** *a galvanic battery.*
Compounds are also common: **ich litt Tantalusqualen,** *the tortures of Tantalus.*

283. Inflection of Foreign Adjectives
(*a*) There is nothing to prevent foreign adjectives as such from being inflected, if they can be suitably pronounced; thus **mokant, genant** (Fr. *mocking, annoying*), pronounced with end-accent but German end-consonants: **mit mokanter Stimme.** But the foreign look may be what is desired. Thus **chic** has become **schick** in the dictionaries, but fashion-advertisements prefer to write: **chicer Hänger** (*swagger-coat*) **mit Raglan-Schnitt,** and **chice Kleider für Schulmädchen.**

(*b*) Foreign colour-adjectives, however, in **-a,** and the one non-colour word **prima,** *first class,* are invariable:
prima Käse, *first-class cheese;* **lila Unterhosen,** *mauve underpants;* **rosa Briefpapier,** *pink note-paper.*
Popular language often inflects:
Verkaufen Sie die Socken? Die mag ich. Was wollen Sie haben für die Lilaen? (H. Fallada), *what will you take for the mauve ones?*
Compounds with a German element are, of course, inflected normally:
rosenfarben, rosenfarbig, *rose-coloured.*

284. Adjectives only Used in the Predicative Position
Certain adjectives are never used attributively before nouns:

(*a*) **voller,** *full of* [with following noun, *v.* § 192 (*g*)], and **alle,** *finished up* [*v.* § 85 (*c*)], show old but now invariable inflectional endings.

(b) The following adjectives, derived from nouns, and governing the genitive or dative: **er ist mir freund (feind)**, *friendly (inimical) towards* . . .; **ich bin dessen (or daran) schuld,** *guilty of* (but **schuldig** with accusative for a debt: **ich bin ihm ein Pfund schuldig,** *owe him*); **mir wurde angst um ihn,** *I became afraid for him.*

Note.—Derivative forms are often available for use in the attributive position: **ein ängstlicher Blick, eine freundliche Miene; freundlich** and **feindlich** also as degree adverbs before **gesinnt: ein uns feindlich gesinnter Kerl,** *unfavourably disposed towards us.*

(c) The following adjectives, commonly and closely associated with the verbs **gehen, sein, werden: allein,** *alone;* **eingedenk,** *mindful of;* **gar,** *done (cooked);* **kund,** *known (to);* **leid,** *a pity* (*e.g.* **es ist mir leid ums Geld**); **los,** *free (of);* **nutz,** *of use;* **quitt,** *quits* or *even;* **ansichtig, gewärtig, teilhaftig werden,** *to see, notice, benefit (from);* **ausfindig machen,** *to find out;* **verlustig gehen,** *to lose;* **barfuß,** *bare-footed;* **barhaupt,** *bare-headed,* etc.

Most of these govern the genitive (cp. § 192).

Note.—Some have developed derivative forms for use before nouns: **alleinig, barfüßig, nützlich.**

(d) Being refractory to inflection, such words may also not be compared; but if the sense allows, the periphrastic comparison with **mehr, am meisten** may be used, *v.* § 118 (b) (1).

For certain double adjectives of this kind, *v.* § 495 (a).

285. Differential Inflection of Adjectives

(a) Unless they belong to a special, uninflected class (cp. preceding paragraphs), two or more descriptive adjectives take the same inflection: **dieser gute alte Mann, guter alter Wein** (cp. § 46).

A very few adjectives have been recognised as having a status similar to that of limiting adjectives (*i.e.* **dies-,** etc.), and therefore, when no article is present, take strong endings while a second adjective is weak:

    folgender überraschende Brief, *the following surprising letter.*

    beiliegender kleine Beitrag, *the enclosed small contribution.*

    erwähntes neue Buch, *the (above) mentioned new book.*

(b) A rule of punctuation, seldom nowadays observed, requires parallel parts of speech (as two descriptive adjectives) to be separated by a comma: **dieser gute, alte Mann.** The absence of the comma then clearly indicates that the second adjective forms a general concept with the noun, qualified as a whole by the first: **dunkles bayrisches Bier.**

The first rule being largely ignored, there is a tendency to attempt to indicate the sense of the second case by differentiating between strong and weak endings, even where this is not strictly necessary: **in unmerklichem gradweisen Übergange** (F. G. Jünger), *by an insensible gradual transition* (*transition by insensible degrees*), **Fremdenzimmer mit fließendem kalten und warmen Wasser,** *with running hot and cold water.* This does not occur in the feminine or plural.

(*c*) Differential inflection, except in the very few cases noted at (*a*), is strongly opposed; but with certain adjective-noun groups, especially **(sein) Äußeres,** *external appearance,* it is common:

ein junger Priesterzögling von sehr gepflegtem Äußeren (G. Hauptmann),
of neat appearance.

(ich saß neben) einem portugiesischen Weinexporteur von rouéhaftem Äußeren (Th. Mann), *with the look of a roué.*

Similarly sometimes: **einige Angestellten, Elektrischen,** and **Parallelen,** etc. Cp. § 144A (*c*).

286. Adjective with Degree Adverb

(*a*) Certain standing expressions appear to be degree adverb and adjective, though they are in fact concealed compounds: **(ein) gut bürgerlicher Mittagstisch** (common advertisement for pension providing midday meals to casuals); **christlich katholische Sitten,** *Catholic custom.* It is common to hyphenate some groups of this kind: **die königlich-preußische Flagge,** *the Prussian Royal flag.*

(*b*) When there is a desire to subordinate a first adjective to a unit of second adjective and noun [cp. § 285 (*b*)], a method often preferred to differential inflection is to make the first a degree adverb: **nach dreitägig strengem Reinemachen** (S. Zweig), rather than **nach dreitägigem strengen Reinemachen.** This form avoids infringing a grammatical rule, but is spreading to cases which it would probably be more legitimate to regard as parallel adjectives:

(1) These may be genuine adverbs:

ein Dutzend glänzend fauler Birnen (H. Risse), *shiny bad pears;* **eine norddeutsch gehemmte Frau** (S. Zweig), *a woman with North German inhibitions.*

(2) These are probably concealed adjectives:

ein behaglich lustiges Gesicht (Th. Mann), *comfortable and cheerful face;* **das lässig häusliche Leben** (F. Werfel), *easy domestic life;* **jenes grandios entscheidende Ereignis** (F. Werfel), *that gigantic and decisive event;* **ein rapid erschrecktes „O "** (S. Zweig), *a sudden, surprised "Oh".*

287. Adjective After Personal Pronoun

(a) An adjective, with its noun, often follows a personal pronoun in apposition. The construction is wider than in English, where, especially with singular pronouns [v. (b) below], another construction is often necessary.

(b) An adjective after a plural pronoun is inflected weak, though the normal rule [§ 46 (a)] might seem to require a strong ending:

wir Modernen, *we moderns;* **wir halbwüchsigen Jungen, wir kleinen Gymnasiasten,** *half-grown youths, small schoolboys as we were;* **ihr alten Jakobiner,** *you old Jacobites.*

(c) After a singular pronoun the inflection is strong:

ich argloser Neuling, *I, unsuspecting greenhorn as I was . . .;* **einige Gäste verwunderten sich über uns ungleiches Paar,** *were surprised to see the incongruous pair that we made.*

288. Eigen,

after a possessive adjective, is uninflected, standing for an older neuter noun which has lost its initial capital:

. . . was sie an äußerem Besitz ihr eigen nannte, *such material possessions as she could call her own.*

289. The Dative with Adjectives and Adjective-participles

(a) Many adjectives govern the dative of the person or thing towards whom the activity is directed; the governed noun or pronoun usually precedes. They may be grouped according to the senses previously noted with verbs governing the dative (v. §§ 97 f., 171 f.):

(1) (Dis)similarity: **ähnlich,** *similar;* **gleich,** *equal;* **über,** *superior.*

(2) (Dis)advantage: **angenehm,** *pleasant;* **böse,** *at loggerheads (with);* **dankbar,** *grateful;* **eigen,** *peculiar (to);* **heilsam,** *of benefit (to);* **lieb,** *attractive (to);* **treu,** *faithful (to),* and many others.

Note the numerous synonyms for **gleich,** *a matter of indifference:* **Das ist mir ganz gleich, egal, einerlei, eins,** and (pop.) **wurst, schnuppe,** *that's all the same to me.*

(3) Local: **fern,** *far (from);* **nahe,** *near (to);* **zunächst,** *close by.*

(b) By origin these adjectives may be divided into:

(1) Adjectives proper: all those quoted above.

(2) Participles used as adjectives, in similar senses: **bekannt,** *known (to);* **ergeben,** *devoted (to);* **geneigt,** *inclined (to);* **überlegen,** *superior (to);* **verwandt,** *related (to).*

(3) Adjectives formerly nouns, as noted in § 284 (*b*).

(*c*) Most of the adjectives proper have a negative in **un-: unähnlich, undankbar, untreu, unfern.** Adjective-participles fluctuate between **un-,** as **unbekannt,** and the verbal negation **nicht,** as **nicht geneigt;** there may be different uses, as **ich bin ihm nicht verwandt,** *not related* (*to*)*;* but: **wir sind nicht verwandt** or **unverwandt,** *unrelated.*

(*d*) The dative government is in itself adequate to express the English prepositions *to* or *from*: **nahe dem Bahnhof,** *near to the station;* **der Heimat fern,** *far from home.* But local expressions may often also have a preposition: **nahe beim Bahnhof, fern von der Heimat.**

Non-local expressions tend, however, to have different senses when used with prepositions, thus:

(1) Dative for a person, **zu** with a thing:
ich bin ihm sehr geneigt, *well disposed to him;* **der Mensch ist zum Bösen geneigt,** *man inclines to evil.*

(2) Dative for attitude, **zu** for treatment:
das Kind ist mir sehr lieb, *the child is dear to me;* **sie war sehr lieb zum Kinde ihrer Schwester,** *she showed great affection for the child,* or *treated the child with . . .*

(*e*) Derivative adjectives with the endings **-lich** and **-bar,** expressing a passive potentiality, as **vergleichbar,** *comparable* (= that which can be compared), have the dative as an alternative to a preposition, especially **für: deutlich,** *clear* (to the senses); **undurchdringlich,** *impenetrable;* **unbemerkbar,** *unnoticeable;* **unsichtbar,** *invisible.*

(*f*) Many adjectives in set expressions with an impersonal subject, often understood, take the dative: **mir ist schlecht;** with mental processes and events, **zu Mute** (lit., *in the mind, feelings*) is often added: **mir war ganz sonderbar (zu Mute),** *I had quite a queer feeling* (*impression*). Compare fully Chapter XLII.

290. Welch- as Relative Pronoun and Adjective

(*a*) There is an alternative form of the relative, declined with endings like the definite article: **welcher, welche, welches,** etc.

This form is hardly used in spoken German, being markedly literary in style. It is the only form available for the infrequent relative adjective [*v.* (*b*) below]; but as a relative pronoun there are certain definite cases where **der** and not **welcher** should be used (*v.* § 291), but none where the reverse is true.

(*b*) **Welch-** as a relative adjective occurs with general or specific force:

(1) As a specific relative after a noun:

Er wollte dem Branntwein gänzlich abschwören, welches Vorhaben ich sofort unterstützte, *which plan I supported immediately.*

The genitive masculine, neuter, like that of **jed-,** etc. [*v.* § 146 (*b*)], is strong or weak:

Der Besitz eines eigenen Heimes, welches (welchen) Glückes ich wohl nie teilhaftig werden soll, *which pleasure will no doubt never fall to my lot.*

Thus also uninflected before the comparatives of **erst** and **letzt:**

welch ersterer . . ., welch letzterer . . ., *the former of which, latter of which.*

(2) As a general relative, introducing a concessive clause:

In welche Unternehmung er sich auch einläßt, stets hat er Glück, *whatever project he takes up, he is always successful.*

Note.—Biblical also as an indefinite relative *pronoun*:

Welchen der Herr lieb hat, den züchtiget er, *Whom the Lord loves he chastises* (= **Wen . . ., den . . .**).

291. Der and welch- as Relative Pronouns

(*a*) **Der,** and not **welch-,** must be used in certain cases:

(1) When a relative in the genitive singular or plural immediately precedes a noun on which it depends:

Die Frau, deren Hut mir so in die Augen stach, war seine Tante, *the woman whose hat . . .*

(2) With a pronoun antecedent, *v.* (*b*) below.

(3) In contracted correlatives, *v.* § 293 below.

(*b*) A pronoun antecedent, as **er** and other personal pronouns, **jeder, keiner, wer** (interrogative), etc., requires **der** as relative:

Er, der Schwindelgeschäfte betätigt hatte, warf sich als Sittenrichter auf, *he, who had carried on black-market dealings, claimed to make moral judgments.*

Wer, der in Arkadien war, sieht nicht mit Wehmut dahin zurück? *Who, of those who have been in Arcadia, does not look back to it with melancholy?*

Distinguish these statements carefully from:

(1) *he, who* as a general relative, which is **wer . . .,** and not **er, der . . .,** the latter referring to a specific person. But **wer . . .** may appear in the form **jeder, der . . .** or **keiner, der . . . :**

Jeder, der im Krieg gewesen ist, weiß, was Furcht bedeutet, *everyone who has been in a war knows what fear is* (= **Wer . . . weiß . . .**).

(2) **wer . . ., der . . .,** *whoever . . ., (he) . . .,* in which the **der** is a demonstrative, not a relative, and may be omitted, as usually in English, unless the case changes:

Wer das sagt, (der) lügt, *whoever says that, lies* [*v.* § 176 (*c*)].

(*c*) Some would suggest that **welch-** may be introduced as an alternative to **der** for variation:

(1) In successive relative clauses:

Either descending (called **Treppensatz,** "stair-case sentence", if it progresses beyond two links):

das offene Fenster, bei welchem das große Faß stand, an dem die Alten saßen und mit Weingläsern prosteten (E. Langgässer), *window by which stood the large barrel at which . . .*

Or in parallel order:

ein Buch, das mit so viel Liebe geschrieben wurde, und mit welchem die Kritiker so scharf umgegangen sind, *a book which . . . and which . . .*

(2) In a sequence of **der**'s as relative, demonstrative, article, etc.:

Die, welche die Kinder betreuten, waren ihrer Aufgabe ganz ergeben, *those who looked after the children . . .*

But most are unconvinced that this practice needs to be erected into a rule, and equally impressive are the cases where it is not observed:

Ihr wird er dienen, ihr und dem Werk, das sie von ihm fordert, das er in ihrem Namen vollenden darf (W. Bergengruen), *the work which . . . and which . . .*

292. Correlative Pronouns

Certain constructions combine an antecedent (pronoun or demonstrative) and a relative in the sense: *the one (the person), who . . .; that (the thing), which . . .* These are called correlatives. They indicate:

(*a*) A definite person or thing:

derjenige, welcher (der); der, welcher (der); er [and other pronouns, *v.* § 291 (*b*)], **der; solcher, der (welcher); derselbe, der.**

Der, welcher diesen Brief schrieb, war dem Wahnsinn nahe, *the person who wrote this letter was near to madness.*

In these expressions, the person or thing is definite, though it may be unknown; with **wer** the person is indefinite:

Derjenige, der das Fenster brach, soll für den Schaden aufkommen, *the person who . . .*

Wer ein Fenster brechen möchte, soll sich mit der Reparatursumme bei mir melden, *anyone who would like to break a window . . .*

Wer has specific force in one construction:

Wer nicht kam, war Eduard, *it was Edward who did not come (who didn't turn up but Edward?).*

(*b*) A definite or indefinite thing:

dasjenige, was; das, was; etwas [and other indefinite pronouns, *v.* § 177 (*b*)], **was . . .**

Dasjenige, was er unter Druck ausgesagt hat, darf ruhig übergangen werden, *what he said under pressure may be ignored.*

Note.—v. § 227 (*b*) for **das** as relative replacing **was**.

The general and indefinite relative **was** may be used for many of these statements, since the neuter terms themselves are already comparatively indefinite in force: **Was er unter Druck ausgesagt hat . . .**

(*c*) **Welch-** may be used for several expressions in (*a*) in replacement of the relative **der,** as shown above; but not after certain pronouns [*v.* § 291 (*b*)]. It is seldom used in expressions under (*b*).

293. Abbreviated Correlatives

(*a*) In noun clauses, acting as subject, object, or complement of the verb, the expressions for *the person(s) who, those who* [*v.* § 292 (*a*)] may be abbreviated to the one word **der,** etc. (not **welcher**):

(1) Subject: this construction is much influenced by the language of the Sermon on the Mount (Bergpredigt, Matt. v.):

Selig sind, die reines Herzens sind; denn sie werden Gott schauen. *Blessed are the pure in heart, for they shall see God.*

Die heute jauchzen—werden morgen klagen (K. Kraus), *those who rejoice to-day will weep to-morrow.*

(2) Complement:

Auf diesem Wege allein konnte er werden, der er gewesen war (W. Bergengruen), *become (again) the person he had been.*

(3) Object:

Liebet eure Feinde, segnet, die euch fluchen (Matt. v. 44), *Love your enemies and bless those that curse you.*

*Note.—*The noun clause is, according to rule, enclosed in commas, the abbreviated correlative occupying the place of the relative *within* the clause (cp. last example).

(*b*) The abbreviated correlative may often be replaced, especially in the subject construction, by the generalising **wer** without significant change of force:

Wer reinen Herzens ist . . .   Wer heute jauchzt . . .

But this is not possible when the plural is clearly specific, thus:
Die auf Steinen schlafen, *Those who sleep on stones* (title of book on the peoples of the East).

EXERCISE XLVIII

A. Translate into ENGLISH:

1. Ein unnütz Leben ist ein früher Tod (Goethe). Ein gut Gewissen ist das beste Ruhekissen (prov.). 2. Herrn Strickmüllers violett-rosa Gesicht erstrahlte in ehrlicher Freude (L. Frank). 3. So manches besprachen wir noch, bei mehreren Gläschen Benediktiner Likör und sehr guten ägyptischen Zigaretten (Th. Mann). 4. Aber wer dachte damals an Krieg? Wir jungen Mädchen gewiß nicht (G. von le Fort). 5. Der Bibliothekar, den ich argloser Neuling um Auskunft gebeten, murrte mich unfreundlich an (S. Zweig). 6. Der Verzweiflung nahe, blieb er dennoch seiner Pflicht treu. 7. Eine Woche verging, während welcher Ken Keaton zweimal bei Tümmlers zu Nacht aß (Th. Mann). 8. Er schloß sich denen an, die unter dem Namen Bummler bekannt waren, aber auch unter denen war er der, den es am wenigsten trieb (H. Böll). 9. „Das Himmelreich ist nahe herbeigekommen, junger Herr, aber nicht die auf den Thronen sitzen, werden es verkünden, sondern die im Schweiße ihres Angesichts ihr Brot verdienen" (E. Wiechert). 10. Die beiden Frauen saßen am Tisch und schälten Kartoffeln. Die eine war alt . . . Die neben ihr saß, sah verblüht und ältlich aus (H. Böll). 11. Local delicacies: Lübecker Marzipan, Frankfurter (Wiener) Würstchen, Aachener Printen, Berliner Weiße, Münchner Bier.

B. Translate into GERMAN:

1. Berlin doughnuts are a great favourite in Germany, and are always eaten on Shrove Tuesday. 2. They sell first-class quality woollen blankets at this store. 3. The children loved to walk barefoot in the summer. 4. It is a pity about (**um**) all that waste of time. 5. Mindful of my deep obligation to (**gegenüber**) you, I am sending you a copy of my book. 6. Loquacity is often characteristic of old age. 7. One day her small four-year-old daughter surprised her with the following curious remark . . . 8. You (**ihr**) young people have no nerves. 9. The person who picked up a diamond ring in the dance hall last night is requested to go to the office. 10. Those who laugh in the morning will weep before the evening (two ways).

CHAPTER XLIX

USE OF THE ARTICLES (2). BY FUNCTION

In many cases, under the influence of the function and position of the noun in the sentence, German varies from English practice, often showing no article where English has the definite or indefinite article. We may distinguish uses (1) in the predicate (§§ 294-6), (2) in adjectival apposition (§§ 297-9), (3) as object of the verb (§ 300), (4) set expressions (§ 301), and (5) omission of the article for brevity (§ 302).

294. General Predication

(*a*) When a noun in the predicate after **sein** attributes to a person some general quality, function, capacity, or calling, the attribution is felt as descriptive, and the noun stands unparticularised, without the indefinite article, which in English alternates with a descriptive adjective.

In unserem Zeitalter muß man vor allem Mensch sein, *in our age one must be before all else human* (*have the qualities of a human being*).

ich bin Junggeselle, Familienvater, Witwer, *I am a bachelor, the father of a family, a widower.*

er ist Architekt, Autodidakt, Briefmarkensammler, Langschläfer, Straßenkehrer, *an architect, a self-taught man, a stamp-collector, he sleeps late, is a street sweeper.*

The term **von Beruf** may be added in appropriate cases:

er ist Hausmakler von Beruf (von Beruf Hausmakler), *he is a house-agent by profession, his work is . . .*

(*b*) Similarly with nationality or religion, the adjective being also used:

er ist Deutscher, Däne, Neuseeländer, *he is a German, Dane, New Zealander* (also **deutsch, dänisch**).

The term **der Herkunft nach,** *by origin,* may be added.

er ist Protestant, Anglikaner, Katholik, *he is a Protestant, an Anglican, a Catholic* (also **protestantisch,** etc.).

Note.—Feminine attributions in (*a*) and (*b*) must, as a rule, have the feminine form: **sie ist Witwe, Innenarchitektin, Dänin, Katholikin.**

(*c*) As with **sein,** similarly with **werden:**

er wurde Soldat, König, Erster Minister, *he became a soldier, King, First Minister.*

Vater werden ist nicht schwer, Vater sein dagegen sehr (W. Busch), *it is less difficult to become a father than to be one.*

But if, with **werden,** emphasis is laid on the process of becoming, or a synonymous verb replaces **werden, zu** is added, which requires the article, thus **zum:**

Durch diese Schlacht wurde Napoleon zum größten Feldherrn der Zeit, *N. became the greatest general of the day.*

er wurde zum Premierminister ernannt, erwählt, *he was appointed, elected Prime Minister* (passive).

Die Arbeiterbewegung entwickelte sich zum ausschlaggebenden Faktor, *the Labour movement became a* (or *the*) *decisive factor.*

Das Gespräch scnaltete sich scharf um zum Verhör (S. Zweig), *the conversation changed its nature sharply and became an interrogation.*

295. Specific Predication

(*a*) In all predications without the article, as in § 294, the individual becomes secondary to the quality. But a predication may serve to raise the individual out of the mass, thus in statements of perception: **er wurde Soldat,** but: **der Mann da ist ein Soldat.** This, strangely, applies to scientific definition, as: **der Mensch ist ein Tier (ein Säugetier),** *an animal* (*mammal*), since this clarifies his whole nature; while **der Mensch ist Tier** would mean: *there is some animal quality about human nature.* But partial definitions, especially forms in **-er,** as: **der Elefant ist Pflanzenfresser,** *the elephant is herbivorous,* omit the article since they only inform us of a single quality, as is shown by the use of an adjective in English.

The use of the indefinite article in specific predication is best shown when expressions analogous to those in § 294, but indicating some form of exceptional status, *i.e.* an irregular, unusual, or notional quality, are used.

(*b*) Unusual (including disreputable) qualities.

er ist ein Esel, Dieb, Frauenfeind, *he is an ass, a thief, a woman-hater (misogynist).*

du bist ein Schatz, ein Engel, *you are a darling, angel.*

sie ist eine Perle, *she is a treasure* (of servants, etc.).

Absence of, or some irregularity in status requires an article or adjective:

er ist Protestant, but: **er ist konfessionslos, ein Gottgläubiger, ein Fanatiker,** *an undenominational non-believer* or *believer, a fanatic.*

er ist Herr des Hauses, *master of the house,* but: **er ist ein Pantoffelheld,** *he is hen-pecked.*

sie ist Witwe, but: **sie ist (unschuldig) geschieden,** *she is divorced (as the innocent party).*

Irregular status is constantly being regularised: **er ist Atheist, Agnostiker,** *an agnostic;* especially when used technically: **er ist ein Sadist** (schoolboy of master), **er ist Sadist** (doctor of patient).

Amateur status is normally protected: **ich bin ein Amateur;** but a connoisseur of the arts has relinquished it: **er ist Liebhaber der Künste.**

A notional attribution is a case of specific predication, as when R. Musil describes the nondescript modern man in the street:

Wofür würdest du ihn halten? Sieht er aus wie ein Arzt, wie ein Kaufmann, ein Maler, oder ein Diplomat? *does he look like a doctor, business man, painter, diplomat?* (*v.* further § 311).

(*c*) An adjectival qualification does not by itself change the statement from one of general to specific predication:

(1) A function or calling may be specialised:

er ist Arzt, Facharzt, langjähriger Kinderarzt, Facharzt im Ruhestand, *a doctor, specialist, experienced childrens' doctor, retired specialist.*

(2) A specific predication may be made more specific:

der Mann da ist ein amerikanischer Soldat, *an American soldier;* **der Mensch ist ein zweibeiniges Säugetier,** *a two-legged mammal;* **du bist ein kompletter Esel,** *a complete ass;* **ein verfluchter Amateur,** *a confounded amateur.*

(3) But an adjective may change a general to a specific predication:

sie war Braut, *she was engaged* (*fiancée*)*;* **sie war eine schöne Braut,** *a pretty bride* (not a necessary part of the function).

296. General Predication of Things

Certain predicative statements, not of persons, after **sein** and **werden,** do not have the article:

(*a*) Very commonly, statements of time and place [cp. § 244 (*b*)]:

Heute ist Versteigerung, Ausverkauf, *there is an auction, sale to-day.*

Um sieben Uhr ist Geschäftsschluß, *closing time is seven.*

Nürnberg war . . . Mittelpunkt geographischer Studien und Sitz einer Schule geworden, *had become a centre . . . and the seat . . .*

(*b*) Other statements:

Das ist Sache des zuständigen Amtes, Aufgabe des Staates, *a matter for the responsible authority, a task for* (*the task of*) *the State.*

Aber eine feine Tischlerei sage ich dir, einfach Klasse (H. Fallada), *a fine workshop, real class!*

297. General and Specific Apposition

(*a*) The distinction made between general predication (§§ 294, 296) and specific predication (§ 295) reappears in phrases in adjectival apposition, representing an abbreviated predication. Thus compare—

Ein stämmiger Fischer, Inhaber des Bootes, erschien und wollte bezahlt werden, *a thickset fisherman, the owner of the boat . . .,* **Markus, der Inhaber des Bootes, erschien und . . .**

Markus, a specific man, has the specific attribution; an unnamed fisherman has the general attribution, since nothing is relevant about him except that he appeared in his quality *as owner* of the boat.

Note.—Thus the conjunction **als,** preceding, always requires omission of the article, since the following noun is introduced solely as a functional attribution: **Markus, als Inhaber . . .** (cp. § 311).

(*b*) Examples:

(1) General, of persons (*v.* § 294):

Rheinländerin von Geblüt und Mundart, hatte Rosalie die Jahre ihrer Ehe in dem gewerbfleißigen Duisburg verbracht (Th. Mann), *a Rhineland woman by birth and dialect . . .*

(2) General, of things (*v.* § 296):

Allgemeiner Besitz des Erdteils (= Europa), hatte die Gothik in Deutschland ihr eigenes Gepräge gewonnen (W. Andreas), *the common heritage of Europe (though it was), the Gothic style . . .*

For apposition with concessive force, cp. § 240 (*b*).

(3) Specific (*v.* § 295):

Herr Bärens, ein eifriger Fünfziger mit leicht angegrauten Koteletten (H. Kasack), *an active man of fifty . . .*

298. Descriptive Phrases

(*a*) Many descriptive phrases, of adjectival or adverbial nature, introduced by a preposition, omit the article:

(1) Adjectival, commonly with **mit, von:**

ein Gebäude von schönem Aussehen, *of an attractive appearance;* **von alter Bauart,** *old-fashioned;* **an sonniger Stelle,** *in a sunny place.*

einen untersetzten beleibten Herrn mit rötlichem, ergrautem Backenbart, einer dicken Uhrkette auf der blau karierten Weste und offenem Leibrock (Th. Mann), *with reddish, greying side-whiskers . . . and his jacket open.*

(2) Adverbial, commonly with **mit:**

mit lässiger Gebärde, *with a nonchalant gesture;* **mit zorniger Miene,** *with an angry look.*

and also sometimes with others:

wie sie den Kopf über etwas schrägem Körper wendete (H. Broch), *turning her head above a (her) rather bent body.*

(*b*) Similarly descriptive phrases in the (adverbial) genitive:

Adverbial: **Der Matrose schwankte schweren Schrittes durch die dunkle Gasse,** *with a heavy gait . . .*

Adjectival: **„Hé, beauté", sagte Stanko zu mir, als ich, gescheitelten Haares und reinen Angesichts, in den Schlafraum hinüberkam** (Th. Mann), *my hair combed and with a clean face . . .*

(*c*) Dependent phrases in genitive or with **von** and dative:

(1) A number of compounds used in descriptive phrases are derived from the Saxon genitive [cp. § 486 (*b*)]:

Manneswort wird gehalten, *a man's word is kept* (= **eines Mannes Wort**). **ein von Meisterhand gemaltes Bild,** *painted by the hand of a master.*

(2) A following attributive genitive has the article:

er bekam den Rang eines Hauptmanns, den Titel eines Professors, den Posten eines Bibliothekars, *the rank of captain, title of Professor, the post of librarian.*

Also compounds: **er bekam den Professortitel.**

(3) In descriptive attributions, as *a devil of a boy,* usage varies:

ein Bild (Schrank) von einem Mann, *a picture (giant) of a man;* **ein Wunder von Gedächtnis,** *a miracle of a memory.*

299. Attributive Adjectives

There are a number of cases where attributive adjectives dispense with the article in German, which is required in English:

(*a*) The absolute superlative has no article in German, but the English translation may require one:

feinste Milchschokolade, *(the) finest milk-chocolate;* **Beispiele absonderlichster Art,** *examples of a (the) most peculiar kind;* **möglichste Sparsamkeit,** *the greatest possible economy.*

(*b*) The following are or may be used without the article:

alle (beide) Männer, *all (both) the men.*

erst, nächst, letzt with plurals, cp. § 55 (*a*).

dieser (jener), *the former (latter);* also **ersterer, letzterer.**

folgend-, beiliegend-, erwähnt-, etc., *v.* § 285 (*a*); and the pronominal form: **folgendes,** *the following.*

Many proverbial statements, as:

Eigner Herd ist Goldes wert, *a hearth of one's own is worth its weight in gold.*

300. Nouns Associated with Verbs

(*a*) Many German idioms, in which a noun is the direct or prepositional object of the verb, have shed the article:

Atem holen, *to draw breath;* **Maß halten,** *to observe moderation;* **Schritt halten,** *to keep pace.*

The corresponding English idioms have also often been thus abbreviated; but many have retained:

(1) The indefinite article:

Lust haben, *to have a (good) mind;* **Hand anlegen,** *to take a hand;* **Kopfweh haben,** *to have a headache;* **Familie haben,** *to have a family (children).*

(2) The possessive adjective:

den **Mund halten,** *to hold one's tongue;* **goldene Hochzeit feiern,** *to celebrate one's golden wedding.*

(*b*) Such expressions often become standing locutions, omitting the article, by reason of the capacity of the infinitive noun (and also of the infinitive used as imperative), cp. § 204, to strip off unnecessary elements. Thus:

(das) Bahnfahren, but still: **mit der Bahn fahren,**
   Mundhalten! but still: **den Mund halten,**
(das) Zeitunglesen, but still: **die Zeitung lesen,**
(das) Pferdereiten, but still: **ein Pferd reiten.**

Such abbreviations may produce new compound verbs (*v.* § 542):

radfahren, *to ride a cycle, to cycle;* **kehrtmachen,** *to make a (right about) turn;* **kopfstehen,** *to stand on one's head.*

(*c*) From time to time new formations are produced on the analogy of ones already formed, and may or may not become general:

Welche Sommerferien an der See, wenn man im Kurhause wohnte, badete und Esel ritt! (Th. Mann), *rode on donkeys* (cp. **Auto fahren**).

Sonst war nur der Mann mit dem Jägerhut noch da, trank Bier und las Zeitung (H. Böll), *drank beer and read the paper* (cp. **Bier trinken**).

301. Set Expressions

Among expressions so common as to have become formulas, there are numerous cases of the omission of the article, which is often retained in the corresponding English expression.

(*a*) Doublets and other enumerations:

der Einfluß von Sonne und Mond auf Ebbe und Flut, *the influence of sun and moon on high and low tide.*

Religion, Vaterland, Familie, Staat waren mir entwertet und gingen mich nichts mehr an (H. Hesse), *religion, country, family, state* . . .

(*b*) Prepositional Phrases:

(1) Of movement:

zu Lande, Wasser, Pferde as in English, but: **nach Norden, Süden,** *to the North, South, Northwards.*

(**im**) **Galopp, Schritt, Trab reiten,** *to ride at a gallop, to gallop,* etc.

(2) Of purpose, numerous idioms with **zu**:

zum Essen, Kaffee, Abend eingeladen, *invited to a meal, tea, supper;* **zur Not,** *at a pinch;* **zum Beispiel,** *for example;* **zum Spaß,** *for a joke;* **zur Abwechslung,** *for a change.*

zum Feinde machen, *to make an enemy* (*of*); **zum Freunde (Manne) haben,** *to have as a friend* (*husband*); **zum Dichter geboren,** *born a poet.*

(3) Others:

im Augenblick, im Nu, *in a moment;* **in der Lage,** *in a position.*

(*c*) Some distributives and other numerals have the definite article for English indefinite:

fünfmal das Jahr, *a year* (*in the year*); **ein Schilling das Pfund,** *a shilling a* (*the*) *pound;* **die gute Hälfte,** *a good half;* **eine gute Feder ist schon der halbe Gedanke,** *half the thought.*

302. Brevity

When economy of statement is required, articles are almost the first elements to go:

(*a*) Headlines and announcements:

Anmeldung erfolgt Alte Universität, *students should report to the Old University building.*

Junge Sängerin macht Karriere, *young singer makes good.*

Abfahrt 14.15, *departure 2.15;* **Durchgehen gestattet,** *passage permitted.*

(*b*) Commands:

Gewehr über! *shoulder arms!* **Hut ab!** *hat off!* **Eintritt verboten!** *no entry!* **Türe zu!** *close this door!*

(c) Laconic speech:

Auf dem Korridor traf er S.—Clemens hielt ihn auf. „Wohl ziemliches Theater hier?" S. hob verlegen die Schultern. (H. Kasack.) *Pretty to-do here?*

(d) Certain agent nouns, associated with functions, are often treated as quasi-proper names, omitting the article:

Kläger, *the plaintiff;* **Schreiber (dieser Zeilen),** *the writer (of these lines);* **Verfasser (des vorliegenden Buches),** *the author (of the present book).*

This use is generally regarded as characteristic of "clerks'" style.

303. Contraction of the Definite Article

(a) The definite (not the indefinite) article undergoes, by practice rather than strict rule, certain contractions with prepositions. Usage, rather than grammatical rule, decides what contractions are permitted and in what circumstances.

Modern German only tolerates normally contractions with:

(1) **dem,** masc. and neut. dat.; commonly: **am, beim, im, vom, zum;** less commonly: **aufm, hinterm, überm, vorm.**

(2) **das,** neut. acc.; commonly: **ans, aufs, fürs, ins.**

(3) **der,** fem. dat., only **zur.**

(b) Contraction is normal in certain contexts:

(1) All kinds of set expressions:

am Sonntag, am 10. Juli, Ihr Brief vom 1. September; am Meer; im Augenblick; zum Tode, zur Genüge, zum Vorteil.

(2) Neuter infinitives and similar verbal nouns:

am Singen, *singing;* **beim Kartoffelschälen,** *peeling potatoes;* **es ist zum Sattwerden,** *it makes one fed up* [v. § 205 (c)].

(3) The adverbial superlative: **am schönsten** (v. § 117; but **aufs beste** may be resolved, v. § 162).

(4) Two nouns bracketing the preposition and article:

Frankfurt am Main (place-name); **Gasthaus zur Sonne,** *the Sun Inn;* **Herkules am Scheidewege,** *the Trial of Hercules.*

(c) Factors preventing contraction:

The article may not contract if it has some demonstrative force. Thus: **zur Zeit,** *at the time;* **zu der Zeit,** *at that time.* For this reason the relative **der,** etc., having developed from the demonstrative, may never contract [v. § 95 (a)]. A following relative clause may be purely descriptive, and thus permit a contraction in the antecedent:

Im Schlaf, den er so lange entbehrt hatte, fand er Vergessen und Heilung, *in sleep, which he had so long lacked* . . .

But it may clarify the antecedent, and thus prevent contraction:

In dem Schlaf, der ihm nach Aussage des Arztes den Tod bringen sollte, fand er Vergessen und Heilung, *in that sleep which the doctor had said would* . . .

With a superlative there may be a distinct difference of sense:

Im ältesten Manuskript, das ich gelesen habe . . ., *in the oldest MS. (and I have read it)* . . .

In dem ältesten Manuskript, das ich . . ., *in the oldest of the MSS. which I have read* . . .

Exercise XLIX

A. Translate into English:

1. Er wurde Politiker, Parteimitglied, Führer einer Bewegung, Reichskanzler, endete sein Leben aber als ein von allen Verfolgter und Verworfener. 2. In drei Wochen ist Maskenball (H. Hesse). 3. Hochzeiten und Begräbnisse waren nicht Sache der Betroffenen, sondern gleichsam kommunale Ereignisse (E. Wiechert). 4. Der in Berlin geborene Wilhelm Speyer, einer unserer elegantesten und lebendigsten Erzähler . . . (publisher's blurb). 5. Auf dieser Bank, ein Bild des Behagens, saß der alte Stechlin in Joppe und breitkrempigem Filzhut (Th. Fontane). 6. Dann erst begreifen wir, wie sehr es schon ein Glücksfall für uns Menschen ist, wenn wir in unseren kleinen Gemeinschaften dahinleben, unter friedlichem Dach, bei guten Gesprächen und mit liebevollem Gruß am Morgen und zur Nacht (E. Jünger). 7. Schön war er, das war nicht zu leugnen, schön von Wuchs und schön von Gesicht (H. Hesse). 8. Prospekt und Probeheft schickt auf Wunsch gern der Verlag (adv.). 9. Feuersäulen standen rings in der Luft . . . Auf leeres Pflaster fiel schwarzer Regen, der gewaschener Ruß war (H. Mann). 10. Spring in Florence: Es riecht nach Feuchtigkeit, Erde, jungem Jahr, bitter und kräftig (W. Bergengruen).

B. Translate into German:

1. He is a doctor, but he doesn't look in the least like a doctor. 2. He died at (**bei**) an advanced age. 3. Charlie Chaplin and his wife alight from the train at Waterloo (newsp. caption). 4. Little Jackie had

to tidy his toys every evening.   5. My fiancée is a nurse by profession, but I hope she will also prove a good cook.   6. Helena, the mother of the Emperor Constantine, was, they say, an English Princess.   7. With a scornful laugh he threw the bill on the table.   8. On his mother's side he is of Jewish origin.   9. The following report appeared in the evening papers . . .   10. Has he any relatives in Berlin?

CHAPTER L

SUBJUNCTIVE OF PROBABILITY. INDIRECT SPEECH

304. General.   Indirect Speech

(*a*) The second main use of the subjunctive is that which represents a statement as plausible, possible, or even probable, but not necessarily as fact.

The widest use of this subjunctive is that known as the subjunctive of indirect speech, in which:

(1) A statement is reported as that of another person, the speaker not committing himself:

Er sagte, er sei unschuldig, *he said he was innocent.*

(2) A question is reported without indicating whether the answer received was positive or negative:

Ich fragte, ob er unschuldig sei, *I asked whether he was (were) innocent.*

(*b*) In all cases of reported speech (and analogous verbs, *v.* § 305) the opening conjunction **daß,** or **ob** in the group **als ob** [*v.* §§ 310 (*c*) and 312] but NOT **ob** alone (as after **fragen**), may be omitted, and the reported statement given in main clause order:

Er sagte, daß er unschuldig sei, or **sagte, er sei unschuldig.**

(*c*) The sequence of tenses in indirect speech is notably different from that in English (thus **sei** . . . *was*, above); *v.* § 306.

305. Subjunctive of Probability

(*a*) The subjunctive of probability, in noun clauses, is described by a well-known German rule as following on verbs of **Denken, Meinen, Sagen.** Such verbs are better exemplified under the three headings:

(1) Report: type verb **sagen:**

antworten, behaupten, erfahren, erklären, erzählen, gestehen, hören, leugnen, etc.

(2) Opinion: type verb **meinen:**

ahnen, annehmen, denken, sich einbilden, fühlen, glauben, etc.

(3) Anticipation: type verb **hoffen:**

erwarten, fürchten, vermuten, zweifeln, etc.

Note.—All the above are followed by **daß,** except **zweifeln,** which has **daß** or **ob** (*doubt that* . . ., *whether* . . .).

408

(*b*) It is clear from these examples that the force of this subjunctive is partly:

(1) For report and opinion (indirect speech proper), the detachment of the person speaking from the statement reported:

er sagt, er sei arm; er sagte, er sei arm geworden.

(2) For anticipation (and opinion), the uncertainty of the outcome:

Ich hoffe, daß er kommt, *I hope* (and am optimistic) *that he will come.*

Ich hoffte, daß er käme (kommen würde), *I hoped that he was coming (would come).*

and since it must now be known whether he did in fact come, the statement is deliberately non-committal, and thus in the subjunctive.

(*c*) The subjunctive is a mood, not a meaning. Thus none of the above verbs is bound to take the subjunctive in all cases. The indicative will thus be used when either (i) there is no reason not to accept the statement of another, or (ii) the outcome of a situation is no longer or hardly in doubt:

Er meldet, daß sein Vater mit dem 9-Uhr-Zug gekommen ist, *reports that his father . . .*

Jedermann glaubt, daß er bald kommen wird, *everyone believes . . .*

Given this condition, it is clear that the subjunctive will be:

(1) Less common after the first than the second and third persons:

Ich glaube, ich muß ihn besuchen, *I think I must visit him* (cp. **er glaubt, er müsse . . .,** *thinks he must*—but need he?).

(2) More common in the past than the present:

Er meint, er muß seine Mutter besuchen, *he thinks he must . . .* (speaker not interested in the probability of the case).

Er meinte, er müsse (müßte) seine Mutter besuchen, *he thought he ought to . . .*

since here the indicative: **er meinte, er mußte . . .** (*thought he had to . . .*) would immediately indicate that he in fact did do so.

(*d*) There is no rule covering the subjunctive after **wissen,** since the modality of statements with this verb varies widely. But the present tendency is to apply strictly the rule of certainty v. uncertainty:

Ich wußte, daß mein Bruder schon wieder zu Hause war, *knew that . . .*

Ich weiß nicht, ob er der rechte Mann dafür sei, *do not know whether (= doubt if . . .).*

306. Tenses in Indirect Speech and Probable Statements

(a) Indirect speech reported in the present tense stands mainly in the same tense as the original statement:

Direct: Sie sagt: „Er lügt (hat gelogen, wird lügen)", etc.

Indirect: Sie sagt, er lüge, habe gelogen, werde lügen, etc.

The exceptions are the past and pluperfect tense of the reported verb:

Direct: Sie sagt: „Er log (hatte gelogen, als . . .)."

Indirect: Sie sagt, er habe gelogen (als . . .).

Thus a statement made directly in the past, perfect, or pluperfect in German appears in all cases in the perfect when reported. This may confuse the time sequence, unless secondary subordinations make this clear:

Sie behauptet, sie habe geschlafen, als ich ins Zimmer trat, *she declares that she **had been** sleeping when I entered the room*, or: *was sleeping when . . .*

Sie behauptet, sie habe das Geld bezahlt, ehe ich sie daran erinnerte, *she declares that she **had** paid the money before . . .*

The alternative to this would be a past form of the subjunctive which was not distinguishable from an uncompleted conditional (*v.* §§ 426-7):

Sie sagt, er lüge, *that he lied*, or:

> *that he would lie* (wenn er dadurch Geld bekommen könnte, *if he could thereby . . .*).

Sie sagt, er hätte gelogen, *that he had lied*, or:
> *that he would have lied* (wenn . . ., *if . . .*).

(b) The same confusion with the conditional would arise if, when the reporting verb was placed in the past, the subordinate verb suffered the corresponding transposition of tense known as "sequence of tenses (in indirect speech)", as happens in English:

Direct: Sie sagt: „Er lügt (hat gelogen)", etc.

Indirect: Sie sag*te*, er lüge (hätte gelogen), etc.
> *She said he lied (had lied), but also:*
> *She said, he would lie . . . (would have lied), etc.*

Thus the practice has grown up in indirect speech in German for all other tenses of the *reporting* verb to follow the present in not influencing the tense of the *reported* verb:

Sie sagt (sagte, hat gesagt, etc.), er lüge, *She says (said, has said, etc.), that he lies (lied, has lied, etc.).*

The only exception to this is where, in the first person or any person of the plural, the present tense form does not show the subjunctive, and the corresponding past tense form does; in this case the latter is preferred:

Direct: **Sie sagten: „Wir haben geweint"... „Wir werden kommen",**

Indirect: **Sie sagten, sie hätten geweint . . ., sie würden kommen,**

rather than: **Sie sagten, sie haben geweint . . ., sie werden kommen.**

This may lead to the otherwise rare case, a past subjunctive following a present: **Sagen Sie ihm, ich käme schon,** *tell him I am coming.* For other **ich**-forms, *v.* last example, § 308, and Note there.

(*c*) Those verbs otherwise analogous to indirect speech, as **hoffen, fürchten,** etc. (*v.* § 305), but in which the subjunctive renders the uncertainty of the outcome, are not subject to the ambiguity of the past subjunctive, and thus retain the sequence of tenses much more commonly:

Er sagte, er sei gekommen (werde kommen), um mich zu besuchen.

Ich hoffte, er wäre gekommen (würde kommen), um mir das Geld zu bezahlen, *that he had come (would come) . . .*

In these cases also the past subjunctive fulfils the positive function of clearly indicating the unreality or improbability of the assumption, or the cautious or tentative tone of the statement [cp. §§ 268 (*d*) and 309-10], a condition which may also apply to verbs of indirect speech proper:

Ich kann nicht sagen, daß der „Entschluß" mein Leben stark verändert hätte (H. Hesse), *I cannot assert that this "decision" greatly changed my life* (= **zweifle, ob . . .**), for **habe.**

Dem Burschen aber träumte, er ginge über das Lager auf dem früheren Exerzierplatz der französischen Militärverwaltung (E. Langgässer), *the boy dreamed that he was walking . . .*, for **er gehe . . .**

(*d*) An indirect statement relating to the present may have present or future force (cp. §§ 67-8):

Er sagt (hofft), daß sie geht, *he says (hopes) that she is going (will go).*

Thus a reported statement in the past may, and a verb of anticipation often does have the force of future in the past:

he said that they were going (i.e. *would be going, wanted to go*).

Two of the forms otherwise current [*v.* (*b*) and (*c*)] are peculiarly unsuited to bringing out this future force:

(1) The unchanged present of reported speech:

Er sagte, daß sie gehe, *he said that she was going.*

(2) Any form in the subordinate clause which does not show clearly the subjunctive:

Er sagte, daß sie gehen, *he said that they were going.*
Er hoffte, daß sie gingen, *he hoped they were going.*

In both these cases, the form **würde,** as used with the conditional [*v.* §§ 236 and 426], should be used for clarity:

Er sagte (hoffte), daß sie gehen würden, *that they would go (be going).*

Note.—But **würde** must not be used in subordinate clauses where this sense of future or future in the past is absent, cp. § 269 (*a*).

307. Indirect Speech in Attributive Clauses

The subjunctive of indirect speech occurs also in attributive clauses after a noun which derives from or is analogous to a verb of communication:

Zum Glück kam jetzt die Meldung, daß das Essen bereit stehe (H. Hesse), *fortunately there now came the message that dinner was ready.*

(er) gab dem Mann der Kasse ein Zeichen, daß das Eintrittsgeld entfalle, und drehte die Kreuz-Barriere für mich unter freundlichen Begrüßungsworten (Th. Mann), *he gave the man at the cash-desk a sign that the entrance-fee was waived . . .*

308. Concealed and Transferred Subjunctive of Indirect Speech

(*a*) A verb of reporting may be understood in the context, and the subjunctive otherwise appear to be unmotivated:

(1) In direct clauses:

„Ein Herr K. möchte Sie sprechen. Sie wüßten Bescheid" (H. Fallada), *a Mr K. would like to see you; (he says) you know what it is about.*

(2) In subordinate clauses:

Die Athener verurteilten Sokrates zum Tode, weil er die Jugend verderbe, *because (as they said) he corrupted young people.*

So gaben sie mir ein Eselchen mit und einen Treiber, der die kürzeren Bergpfade kenne (Erhart Kästner), *and a driver, who (they said) knew the short cuts in the hills.*

(*b*) The subjunctive of indirect speech may be carried over into a further subordinate clause depending on the first subordinate statement:

mit dem Bemerken, ich könne damit machen, was ich *wolle* (H. Hesse), *with the comment that I could do what I wanted with it.*

sagte mir, daß man ihm den Besuch unseres Hauses verboten habe, weil es nicht ehrbar bei uns *zugehe* (Th. Mann), *that he had been forbidden to visit us because we were not respectable* [cp. also verderbe, in (*a*) (1)].

The English reader is apt to be disconcerted if such clauses are multiplied, and especially if a transferred subjunctive leads:

Aber mein Onkel sagte, daß ich solche Langeweile auf dieser Erde *empfände*, das komme nur daher, weil ich ein Dummkopf *sei* und meinem Herzen nicht recht *gäbe* (S. Andres), *said that the fact that . . . was because . . .*

Note.—The past subjunctives in the first and last examples above, wüßten, empfände, and gäbe are substituted for the present forms wissen, empfinde, gebe, in accordance with the rule in § 306 (*b*), last paragraph.

309. Probability in Main Clauses

(*a*) The subjunctive is used in main clauses to make a tentative statement, and thus conveys:

Surprise:

Was! Er wäre schon da! *What! (Can it be true that) he has come already!*

Satisfaction at an unexpected event:

Das wäre nun gottseidank vorbei! *Well, that's finished, thank Heavens!*

A polite request:

Könnten Sie mir bitte den Koffer tragen? *Could you carry my case for me?*

Caution:

Er dürfte sich getäuscht haben, *he may well have made a mistake.*

(*b*) Modal verbs are common in this use (as above), also wünschen:

Ich wünschte, ich wäre schon wieder zu Hause, *I wish that . . .*

and sein, especially with the adverb beinahe:

Er wäre beinahe umgefallen, *he almost lost his balance.*

The sense *ought to* is rendered in the present sense by müßte or sollte:

Sie müßten (sollten) endlich mal vorwärtskommen, *you ought (by rights) to be improving your position.*

and in the past by müßte . . . haben or hätte . . . sollen:

Jetzt verdiene ich nur noch kalten Kaffee. Ich müßte schon gefrühstückt und gebadet haben (Th. Mann), *I ought really to have breakfasted and bathed long ago.*

Compared with this, the second form expresses a possibility more irrevocably missed: Sie hätten mich benachrichtigen sollen, *ought to have* (but did not, the matter being now closed).

Distinguish from all these forms the expression of present modality in the indicative, with dependent infinitive in the perfect: **er kann (muß, soll) schon geschrieben haben,** *he has probably (must have, is said to have) written already;* such statements are not more tentative than is implied by the nature of the modal verb itself.

(*c*) The subjunctive of tentative statement in main clauses is entirely in the past (*v.* above) even when the sense is in the (narrative) present:

Das Boot wäre umgeschlagen, der Mann muß nach dem Ruder greifen (H. Mann), *the boat almost overturns and the man has to* . . .

It may often be regarded as suggested by a verb understood, thus:

(1) A verb of reported speech:

„Du kannst nicht länger warten?—Deine Fahrt nach Köln wäre so wichtig?" (H. Mann), (*you pretend that*) *your trip to Cologne is so important?*

(2) A suppressed condition:

Ich möchte gern ins Ausland gehen (wenn ich das Geld hätte, etc.), *I should like to go abroad (if I had the money).*

310. Probability in Subordinate Clauses

(*a*) Many clauses introduced by **daß,** but not depending on the verbs in § 305, may have the subjunctive because they envisage a proposition independently of its realisation.   They are:

(1) Noun clauses, subject or object of a verb, etc.:

Dann und wann seufzte jemand darüber, daß seine Frau mit dem Kaffee warte (Th. Mann), *sighed at the thought that his wife was waiting* . . .

(2) Attributive clauses after a noun:

Wenn der Soldat ausrückt, so rechnet er mit der Wahrscheinlichkeit, er komme nicht zurück (Th. Plievier), *he accepts the probability that he will not return.*

(3) Clause in apposition to an impersonal subject:

Es ist billig (erforderlich, Zeit, etc.), daß man die beiden zusammenbringe, *it is fair (necessary, time) that they should be brought together.*

(*b*) The degree of (im)probability may affect the decision for subjunctive or indicative:

Es ist möglich, daß er morgen mit dem Zug kommt, *it is possible* . . .

Es ist unmöglich, daß er sie kenne, *it is impossible that he should* . . .

Thus also after nouns of probability as **Wahrscheinlichkeit** (above), **Meinung, Ansicht,** etc.

But the subjunctive may still be used if the statement is only entertained notionally (*v.* Th. Mann, above), or if the content of the statement is to be isolated from the manner in which it is asserted:

Sie spricht ihre Überzeugung aus, daß er uns nicht enttäuschen werde, *her conviction that he will not disappoint us.*

(*c*) After verbs of seeming and feeling, and similar nouns, a more intangible note may be struck, either:

(1) By using the past subjunctive after the present [*v.* §§ 268 (*d*) and 309 (*c*)]:

Mir scheint, daß wir ein gut Stück vorangekommen wären, *it appears to me that we have made good progress.*

or (2) By using **als ob** [or **als** with inversion, cp. § 270 (*c*)] and the past subjunctive, even after a present:

Es will mir vorkommen, als ob wir keine Antwort zu erwarten hätten, *it almost seems to me as if we need not expect an answer.*

Thus after similar nouns: **Eindruck, Gefühl,** etc.:

Sie hatte die Empfindung, als stände sie auf einem sehr hohen Berg (S. Andres), *she had the feeling that she was . . .*

Note.—This construction is distinct from the use of **als ob** for manner, cp. § 312 (*b*).

EXERCISE L

A. Translate into ENGLISH:

1. Er bildet sich ein, sein Gesundheitszustand habe sich in letzter Zeit verschlechtert. 2. Ich habe nie gehört, daß sie geklagt hätte (F. Thiess). 3. Sein Vater hatte ihm diese bequeme Beamtenstellung verschafft und die Drohung damit verknüpft, daß er ihm seine Geldunterstützung entziehen werde, wenn er sie nicht annehme (R. Musil). 4. Ein alter Baumeister pflegte zu sagen, daß, wer bauen wolle, zuerst die Vollkommenheit der menschlichen Figur erkannt haben müsse, denn in dieser seien die tiefsten Geheimnisse der Proportion verborgen (Th. Mann). 5. Clemens half der Ärztin beim Einsteigen in seinen Wagen und hätte beinahe ihren Sommermantel in der Tür eingeklemmt (H. Kasack). 6. Invitation to a Bull-fight: Wie immer empfing er mich mit vieler Herzlichkeit, lobte mich für meine Anhänglichkeit an sein Institut und machte mir dann folgende Eröffnung: Heute, Samstag, sei der Geburtstag des Prinzen Luis-Pedro, eines Bruders des Königs. Aus diesem Anlaß sei auf den morgigen Sonntag, nachmittags drei Uhr, eine Corrida de toiros, ein Stierkampf, dem der hohe Herr beiwohnen werde,

in der großen Arena am Campo Pequeno angesetzt, und er, Kuckuck, gedenke mit seinen Damen und Herrn Hurtado das volkstümliche Schauspiel zu besuchen. Er habe Karten dafür, Plätze auf der Schatten- seite, und er habe auch einen für mich. Denn er meine, es treffe sich ausgezeichnet für mich als Bildungsreisenden, daß mir, gerade noch bevor ich Portugal verließe, Gelegenheit geboten sei, hier einer Corrida beizuwohnen. Wie ich darüber dächte? (Th. Mann).

B. Translate into GERMAN, using the indicative where you think it is justified:

1. The doctor doubted whether he could reach the sick man in time. 2. He hopes that she will accept his proposal of marriage, but he has considerable doubts. 3. Why does he deny that he is in debt? 4. England expects every man to do his duty. 5. They declared that they had not heard any suspicious sounds in the house that night. 6. Tell him I have already bought the tickets; he is to come to platform 8 at once. 7. With the suggestion that I should telephone again later, he left my house. 8. It is out of the question that such a mediocre essay should win the prize. 9. It seems as though spring were on its way at last. 10. He offered me some snuff from his little gold box; that would do me good, he said

CHAPTER LI

CONJUNCTIONS AND STATEMENTS OF COMPARISON, MANNER, MEANS

311. Comparison, General. Als and Wie

(*a*) "Statements of manner" is a wide term, covering aspects of comparison, attendant circumstance, and even result, etc., *v.* references *passim* in following paragraphs.

Revise § 121, conjunctions of comparison.

(*b*) Comparisons may be of manner (this paragraph), or of degree (§ 313, below). Statements of manner are introduced, with predicative function, by **als** or **wie,** not exactly corresponding to the English *as* and *like*. These are distinguished as follows:

(1) **als** indicates an assumption of identity.

(2) **wie** indicates a comparison short of identity.

The predicate contexts in which these are used are: (i) after a verb; (ii) as the predicative complement of the subject or object; (iii) after an adverb; further, (iv) basically the same distinction is made between **als ob,** *as if,* and **wie wenn,** *as when,* conjunctions introducing subordinate clauses (§ 312).

(*c*) After verbs:

Er kam, als Husar verkleidet, auf den Ball, *he came to the ball dressed as a hussar* (an assumption of identity for a purpose).

Er kam wie ein Dieb in der Nacht, *he came like a thief in the night* (a comparison short of the assumption of identity, even for a limited purpose).

(*d*) As predicative complement:

(1) Subjective, often equivalent in English to a straight statement of identity:

Düsseldorf und Köln vermitteln als einzige Ämter Mannequins! (newsp.), *D. and C. are the only Labour Exchanges to provide mannequins!*

(cp. **Düsseldorf und Köln, wie auch andere Ämter . . .,** *like other Labour Exchanges . . .*).

(2) Objective:

Wir werden die Sache als erledigt betrachten, *consider the matter as closed* (which it is).

Man behandelte ihn einfach wie ein Tier, *like (as one would) an animal* (which he was not).

Note.—**Als,** expressing identity between preceding subject (or object) and a following noun predicate causes the latter to omit the article: **als Husar ; wie,** expressing a comparison with an otherwise quite different object, retains the indefinite article: **wie ein Dieb, wie ein Tier.** Identity may be affirmed by a following clause: **als der Lügner, der er war.** A comparison may appear as an identity without being so: **Gesprochen wie ein Mann!** *spoken like a man!* Cp. § 297 (*a*).

(*e*) After adverbs:

(1) Comparisons of degree use both **als** and **wie** (*v.* § 121):

Er schreibt schlechter als, (nicht) so schlecht wie Sie, *worse than, as (not so) badly as you.*

(2) But a genuine comparison of manner must use **wie:**

Er schreibt schlecht wie Sie, *he writes badly—as do you also.*

312. Clauses of Comparison of Manner

(*a*) Basically the same distinction as noted in § 311 (*b*) is made, in clauses, between comparisons in which:

(1) An appearance is measured against fact:

he looks as if he were ill.

German uses: **als ob, als wenn,** or **als** with inversion [cp. § 270 (*c*)]; the **als** asserts the identity, the subjunctive the uncertainty concerning its truth:

Er sieht aus, als ob er krank wäre (als wäre er krank).

(2) A fact is illustrated by a comparison:

her looks melted as when snow sweeps down the mountainside.

German uses: **wie wenn,** the **wie** asserting that a genuine comparison is made between independent phenomena, the indicative, that the second event has real existence independently of the analogy drawn with the first.

(*b*) Comparison of appearance.

This is used after many expressions of appearing, seeming, pretending:

Es war ihm, als ob (als wenn) er bald in Tränen ausbrechen müßte, *he felt as if he might burst into tears . . .*

Er ging neben seinem Schwips her, und tat, als kennten sie einander nicht (E. Kästner), *he walked beside his tipsiness and pretended they were not acquainted.*

Sometimes, incorrectly, **wie wenn** is used:

Er sieht aus, wie wenn er (an Sauberkeit und Ordnung) nicht mehr gewöhnt wäre und es entbehrt hätte (H. Hesse), *as if he had long lacked cleanliness and order.*

The incorrect periphrastic **würde** is also common, especially in the South:

wie wenn man ihm von einer Seelenwanderung erzählen würde (R. Musil), *as if someone were telling him about transmigration of souls.*

Such clauses may be felt as reported speech, and both conjunctions omitted: **mir ist, ich wäre . . . ihm war, er höre . . .,** *it seems to me (seemed to him) as if . . .*

They are, in fact, a conditional comparison (cp. §§ 426 f.):

Er sieht aus, als (er aussehen würde,) wäre er krank.

Like others [cp. § 308 (*b*)], this subjunctive may be transferred:

Da eine unübersehbare Menge diesem Ziel nachjagte, war mir, als versäume ich etwas, wenn ich nicht mitliefe (H. Risse), *it seemed to me that I would miss something if I did not run too.*

(*c*) Comparison of illustration.

In diesem Augenblick versinkt die Straße unter ihnen . . ., wie wenn man bei einer Berg- und Talbahn im Lunapark plötzlich in die Tiefe geht (B. Werner), *at this moment the road sinks under them, as when one suddenly drops on the switch-back railway.*

Both comparison of appearance and of illustration are heavily used in descriptive and narrative contexts, but the former then employs the force of the subjunctive to suggest an unreal, even a fantastic comparison:

Er hatte die Siebzehnjährigen geschunden und schinden lassen als bezöge er von Tod und Teufel Tantieme (E. Kästner), *he had flayed, and driven others to flay these seventeen year olds, as if in the pay of Death and the Devil.*

(*d*) Comparisons of appearance may be abbreviated to a non-finite part of the verb (participle or infinitive construction), **wie** being here used:

ein hoher Blumen-Teppich, in dem die Rinderherden langsam weideten, wie schwimmend im bunten Schaum (E. Jünger), *as if swimming in the brightly coloured foam.*

Ein zartes, reines und wie auf Porzellan gemalt blasses Abendrot . . . (Th. Mann), *as if painted on porcelain.*

Er langte aus, wie um mir einen entscheidenden Schlag zu versetzen . . ., *he lunged, as if to give me the decisive blow . . .*

(*e*) Comparison of similarity.

So wie (also **sowie**) introduces a comparison of manner which asserts the essential similarity of both parts of the statement, the relation being one either of cause and effect:

So wie wir ihn gestalten, wird der Staat sich entfalten, lit., *as we build it, so the State will develop* (postal cancellation used for civic education, 1954).

or of event and descriptive illustration:

So wie im Bergland ein dichter Nebel die Wetter kündet, ging dem Oberförster eine Wolke von Furcht voraus (E. Jünger), (*just*) *as in the mountains thick mist precedes storms, the Chief Forester* (= *tyrant*) *was preceded by a cloud of fear.*

So wie and its clause may either lead or follow (*e.g.* **dem Oberförster ging . . ., so wie . . .**); **so** and **wie** may also stand in separate clauses [cp. **so daß** and **so . . . daß**, § 202 (*b*)]:

„Wozu das Konditionale, Mama? Offenbar steht es so mit dir, wie du sagst. Du liebst!" (Th. Mann), *why the conditional, Mother? It is clearly as you say: you are in love!*

Wie die Alten sungen (old form), **so zwitschern auch die Jungen**, lit., *as the old birds sang, the young ones twitter* (= *children take after their parents*).

When **so wie** introduces a descriptive statement, it is equivalent to **wie wenn**, as in (*c*): **Wie wenn im Bergland . . .**, in the Jünger example.

(*f*) Comparison in relative clauses, with **wie** and repetition of the pronoun standing for the antecedent, *v.* § 233.

313. Clauses of Comparison of Degree

The subordinating conjunctions introducing comparisons of degree are:

(*a*) Comparison of equality and inequality.

Als and **wie**, besides introducing phrases of comparison (cp. § 311), may also introduce clauses of comparison expressing (in)equality; these are usually abbreviated:

Equality: **Der Vorschlag ist ebenso zweckmäßig als (er) gelegen (ist),** *the suggestion is as useful as it is timely.*
             (Also: **nicht weniger . . . als . . .**, *not less . . . than . . .*)

Inequality: **Nichts könnte mir ferner liegen, als eine solche Absicht (mir fern liegt),** *nothing could be further from my thoughts than such an intention.*

The second part of the comparison may take the form of a construction with the (prepositional) infinitive:

Nichts könnte mir ferner liegen, als eine solche Absicht zu hegen, *than to harbour such an intention.*

Was konnte ich anders tun, als die Verabredung absagen? *What could I do but cancel the appointment?*

(*b*) Comparison of extent or restriction.

The full conjunctions **insofern, als . . ., (in)soweit, wie . . .**, are usually abbreviated [as other conjunctions with **so-**, *v.* § 125 (*c*)] to **sofern, soweit**:

Sofern er das wirklich gemeint hat, täuscht er sich sehr, *in so far as he really meant it, he is quite wrong.*

Soweit ich die Lage überblicken kann, haben wir bis Weihnachten Zeit, *as far as I can survey the situation, we have time till Christmas.*

Daß is used, especially in the common expression: **Nicht, daß ich wüßte,** *not that (as far as) I know (of).* **Was** is used in the absolute participial construction [*v.* § 277 (*b*)]: **Was das anbelangt (anbetrifft),** *as far as that goes . . .*, and in many descriptive statements as:

da die Leute ohnehin hasteten, was ihre Lungen hergaben (H. Broch), *as they were in any case racing along to the fullest extent of their lungs.*

(*c*) Comparison of proportion.

A comparison expressing a proportionate increase or decrease (English, *the more . . ., the more . . .; the less . . ., the less . . .*, etc.) may use various double conjunctions:

Im selben Maße wie er Erfolg hatte, schwand sein Selbstvertrauen, *in the same degree as his success grew, his confidence waned.*

Je mehr er büffelt, desto mehr (or **umso mehr**) **fürchtet er, durchzufallen,** *the more he swots, the more he fears he will fail.*

Wir werden gelobt und getadelt, je nachdem wir fleißig oder faul sind, *we are praised and blamed according to whether we work or are lazy.*

Je nachdem, wie das Wetter ist, werde ich mich entscheiden, *I shall make my decision according to how the weather is.*

Note.—**Das ist je nachdem.** *That's according.*

„**Sehr wohl**", **entgegnete der Mann mit allduldsamem Lächeln, das ihm um so leichter fallen möchte, als sein Trinkgeld enorm war** (Th. Mann), *with a patient smile, which came to him the more easily as his tip was huge.*

Unsere deutschen Wörter auf -ung sind um so weniger schön, je länger und komplizierter sie sind (E. Schairer), *the less attractive, the longer and more complicated they are.*

314. Statements of Attendant Circumstance

(*a*) Statements of manner with the most general force, *i.e.* attendant (or absent) circumstance, seldom appear in a subordinate clause proper, since **indem,** *as*, has largely gone over to statements of means (*v.* below, § 315), *v.* examples under time [§ 123 (*d*)].

On the other hand, a large number of other statements, including subordinate clauses of other kinds, have secondary force of manner.

(*b*) Clauses of result, including:

(1) **anstatt daß, ohne daß,** or **anstatt** and **ohne** with the prepositional infinitive, expressing negative result, and taking the indicative or subjunctive [cp. §§ 202, 203, and 359 (*b*)].

(2) **daß,** in a descriptive statement:

Er redete, daß kein Ende war, *without ceasing* [*v.* § 202 (*d*) (*e*)].

(*c*) Constructions in apposition, with adjectival or adverbial force:

(1) Absolute accusative:

Sie gingen . . ., den frischen Salzwind im Gesicht . . . (Th. Mann), *they walked . . ., the fresh salt wind in their faces . . .*

(2) Adverbial genitive:

wie er breiten Rückens dasaß (F. Werfel), *as he sat there with his broad back.*
während sie federnden Schrittes daherging (S. Andres), *while she walked on with light, springy step . . .*

(3) Many present participles, *v.* § 276, and some past participles, *v.* § 357.

(*d*) Noun clauses, especially those with anticipatory constructions in **da-** [cp. § 278 (*f*)] translating an English gerund, but especially **dabei, daß** (or **wie**):

Georg ertappte sich dabei, wie er vor sich hinpfiff (B. Werner), *George discovered himself whistling quietly.*

(*e*) Prepositional phrases, *v.* **an, bei, unter,** etc., §§ 503-6.

314A. Compound Adverbs in -weise

(*a*) The noun form **-weise** (**die Weise,** *manner*) compounded with nouns and adjectives produces a very large number of adverbs, many of which are adverbs of manner:

(1) With nouns the suffix has often distributive force: **paarweise,** *in pairs,* **schrittweise,** *step by step;* but it also stands for other adverbial groups, especially **als . . .** (*by way of . . .*): **beispielsweise,** *as an example,* **vergleichsweise,** *comparatively,* standing for **als Beispiel, im Vergleich:**

Die Teuerung wurde schrittweise schärfer (H. Broch), *the food-shortage became steadily worse.*

(das) Städtchen, in welchem ich mich gastweise aufhielt (W. Bergengruen), *in which I was staying as a guest* (= *residing*).

(2) With adjectives it represents a "sentence adverb", often translated into English by *it is . . . that*:

Merkwürdigerweise ist mir dieses Wort in Erinnerung geblieben (G. von le Fort), *it is a strange thing, that . . .*

Man muß gerechterweise zugeben, daß . . . (newsp.), *as a matter of common justice, one must admit . . .*

Er wollte nicht verbotenerweise fotografieren (H. Kasack), *did not want to take photographs where it was forbidden.*

Forms in **-weise** may not be used as simple adverbs, since the adjective itself is adequate for this (cp. § 11); thus for: **Wir gehen ja naiverweise stets von der Annahme aus, daß wir in unserm eignen Haus allein Meister seien** (C. G. Jung), it would be better to write: **Wir gehen stets von der naiven Annahme aus . . .**

(*b*) Compounds formed under (1), but *not* under (2), have come to be used fairly widely as adjectives: **eine schrittweise Verbesserung,** *a gradual improvement,* **ein probeweiser Ansatz,** *a trial start;* but the noun with which the compound is associated must be a verbal noun, to preserve the adverbial force of the compound, *i.e.* noun in **-ung,** infinitive noun, or verbal derivative (cp. § 193); thus *not* (as written in another context by the East German Duden, which itself recognises this rule):

Wichtig sind auch die paarweisen Pronomen wie dieser und jener, *the contrasted pronouns, such as* **dieser** *and* **jener,** *are also important.*

(*c*) The separated form: **ungerechter Weise, komischer Weise,** an adverbial genitive [cp. § 314 (*c*)], is not now used; but a preceding preposition requires the nominal form: **in besonderer Weise.**

315. Statements of Means

(*a*) **Indem** has now generally the force of means; it renders, not *as,* but the gerundial construction which also appears as **dadurch, daß . . .** [cp. § 278 (*f*)]:

Indem er künstliche Belebungsversuche anstellte, konnte der Arzt ihn noch retten, *the doctor managed to save him by applying artificial respiration* (**dadurch, daß er . . .**).

As with **durch,** other prepositions commonly used with the force of means or instrumentality (**an, bei, mit,** etc.) may appear in gerundial compounds:

Sie werden ihn daran erkennen, daß er eine rote Nelke im Knopfloch trägt, *you will recognise him by his wearing . . .*

(b) Appositional constructions are less prominent than with attendant circumstance [v. § 315 (c)]; one finds an occasional:

(1) Adverbial genitive, especially in expressions of place:

Er führte uns immer nächsten Weges aus der Stadt heraus (S. Andres), *led us out of the town by the nearest route.*

(2) Present participle:

Sie griff, sich reckend, nach dem Kragen seines Staubmantels (S. Andres), *v.* § 276 (c),

but these are hardly distinguishable from statements of manner.

316. Interrogative Adverbs of Manner and Means

(a) Manner. **Wie?** *how?* and, more explicitly, **auf welche Weise?** *in what manner,* or, more explicitly for degree, **inwiefern (inwieweit),** *how far? to what extent?* are the interrogative adverbs of manner.

Wie? both direct and indirect, may correspond to English *what?*:

Wie war die Vorstellung? *What was the performance like?*

Er wußte nicht, wie ihm geschah, *he did not know what was happening to him.*

Wie ist Ihr Name? *What is your name?* **Wie meinen Sie?** *What do you mean?* **Wie bitte?** *What did you say?*

Wieso? serves to query an answer: *How is that? What do you mean?* but it has invaded the field of the direct question of reason (**warum?**) though incorrectly and against opposition:

Wieso ging er nicht sofort nach Hause? *Why was it that he did not . . . ?*

(b) Means. There is, as in English, no specific interrogative adverb of means, **wie?** *how?* being used. But a compound may serve to foreshadow the answer expected:

Womit hat er das Fenster gebrochen? *What did he . . . with? How . . . ?*

Woran wird er uns erkennen? *How will he recognise us?*

EXERCISE LI

A. Translate into ENGLISH:

1. Sie wurde für schuldig erklärt und als eine Ehrlose, Recht- und Mittellose aus allen Gemeinschaften gestoßen (E. Wiechert). 2. Die Rot-Schwänzchen fütterten die zweite Brut, die hungrig zirpte, als würden Messerchen gewetzt (E. Jünger). 3. Lärm und Johlen der Klasse verstummten, als höbe eine eiserne Wand sich auf und verberge Gebärde, Ton und jegliches Dasein (E. Wiechert). 4. Je länger und näher wir an dem nördlichen Rande von Korfu hingleiten, um so fieberhafter wird das

allgemeine Leben an Deck (G. Hauptmann).   5. Er setzte den Weg fort
und ertappte sich dabei, daß er in jedes Hutgeschäft schielte (E. Kästner).
6. Und dann lachte der Schwarzbart, daß die Gläser klirrten (E. Wiechert).
7. Da spaziert der junge Kaiser Franz Joseph inkognito durch idyllische
Wälder, verliebt sich in ein braves Kind des braven Volkes, . . . und
fährt, feuchten Auges, doch tapfer lächelnden Mundes, wieder davon
(newsp. film review).   8. Auf der Bank saß Teta, den Hund Wolf zu
ihren Füßen, diesen ältesten und grimmigsten Veteranen der Meute von
Grafenegg, gefürchteten Wächter und geschworenen Feind aller Briefträger (F. Werfel).   9. Sie sprach mit lebhafter und stoßweiser Bewegung
des Unterkiefers (Th. Mann).   10. Loss of meaning in the modern world:
Was ist also abhanden gekommen?—Etwas Unwägbares. Ein Vorzeichen.
Eine Illusion. Wie wenn ein Magnet die Eisenspäne losläßt und sie
wieder durcheinandergeraten. Wie wenn Fäden aus einem Knäuel
herausfallen. Wie wenn ein Zug sich gelockert hat. Wie wenn ein
Orchester falsch zu spielen anfängt (R. Musil).

B. Translate into GERMAN:

1. He spoke to her as a sensible elder brother, but she burst out
laughing like a schoolgirl. 2. I am not making as many mistakes in
German as I used to earlier on. 3. No-one nowadays can act tragic
parts as Eleonore Duse did. 4. It looks as if he had forgotten the appointment (two ways). 5. In so far as I had understood his lecture I told the
others about (**über**) it. 6. She went with a glad heart to bring them the
good news. 7. To what extent did you commit yourself? 8. She saw
him leaning against a lamp-post, his hands buried deep in his pockets.
9. By dieting strictly he succeeded in reducing his weight. 10. The more
we are together the merrier we shall be.

CHAPTER LII

PREPOSITIONS OF PLACE

317. Ab, dat.; *from*, usually commercial or official style: **ab unserem Werk, ab Hafen, ab hier;** a bracket [*v.* § 263 (*d*)] is recommended: **vom Werk ab, vom Lager aus, von hier aus.**

Old dative plural: **das Buch ist mir irgendwann abhanden gekommen,** *got lost*, cp. § 173 (*b*). *v.* also § 390.

318. An, dat., acc.; expressing local contact or close association, especially with a side surface, while **auf** expresses super-imposition.

(*a*) Position. *At, to, on, by, against*, etc.

an der Wand (*on*), **am Tisch** (*at*), **am Zaun** (*by*), **an der Wand lehnend** (*against*).

Distinguish **am Abhang, auf dem Gipfel,** *on the* (*flank, top of*) *mountain;* **an Deck,** *on deck*, **auf dem Deck lagen Taue; an Land gehen,** *to land*, **aufs Land gehen,** *to go to the country*.

Austrians put **an** for **auf: der Kaffee steht am Tisch.**

Distinguish **am Himmel,** *in the sky*, **im Himmel,** *in Heaven.*

An may indicate a line, rather than a surface, of contact: **an der Grenze,** *at* (*along*) *the border*, **am Rande,** *at the edge* (*limit*), and in place names: **Zell am See.**

Thus also after **direkt: direkt an der Straße, am Wasser, am Abgrund.**

Figurative. **Sie hängt sehr an der Mutter** (*attached to*), **er hielt an seinem Vorsatz fest** (*held to*), **am Tode** (*near to*), **die Sache liegt uns allen am Herzen** (*close to*).

(*b*) Motion. *At,* (*on*)*to, towards*, etc.

er setzte sich an den Tisch (*at*), **lehnte die Leiter an** (*gegen, against*) **die Mauer, steckte den Ring an** (*on*) **den Finger;** cp. **er zog die Jacke an.**

An indicates goal, recipient, limit: **Jeder Weg führt an ein gutes Ziel** (R. Musil), **Jagdscheine werden an Amerikaner ausgestellt** (newsp.), **an den Garten anstoßend** (*bordering on*). Thus **er begleitete mich an die Tür** is more formal, since more intended, than **zur Tür.** Thus also **er legte ihm eine Binde an die Stirn,** but **die Hand auf die Stirn,** where both actions are intended, but **an** is more permanent than **auf.**

Figurative. **Die Reihe kommt an mich, die Erbschaft fiel an ihn, er denkt nie an sich selbst, schreibt nie an seine Mutter, ich knüpfte an seine Worte an, die Arbeit stellt große Anforderungen an uns.**

319. Auf, dat., acc.; expressing local contact with an upper surface, super-imposition.

(*a*) Position. *On, upon.*

das Essen auf dem Tisch, der Hut auf dem Kopf, die Wetterfahne auf dem Dach, ein Schiff auf hoher See, auf Flügeln des Gesanges.

Rest or activity in a position which is exposed, either through being elevated, unenclosed, or enclosed but public, often has **auf** for English *in*: **auf dem Gute,** (*up*) *at the Hall,* **auf der Kanzel,** *in the pulpit;* **auf dem Felde, Lande, Markte; auf der Post, Schule, auf der Insel Norderney.**

Distinguish **auf der Universität** (of students), but **an** for staff, and **in** for *in* the building. **Er geht in die Schule** (*attends*), **um neun Uhr zur Schule** (*to school*), **im Herbst geht er aufs Gymnasium** (the next educational stage, a public action).

Distinguish **er arbeitet auf dem Felde** (*in the fields*), **er fiel im Felde** (*in the field*).

A house stands **direkt an der Straße,** one meets people **auf der Straße,** an event happens **auf offener Straße;** but a specific addition, as name, number, etc., requires **in: ich wohne in** (or **an**) **der Hauptstraße, traf ihn in einer Nebenstraße, das Unglück geschah in der Münchener Straße.**

Figurative: **auf der Stelle, ich bin auf dem Wege dazu, ich bin auf Ihrer Seite, kenne mich auf meinem Gebiete aus, halte mich auf dem Laufenden, bestehe auf meinem Rechte, die Verwechslung beruhte auf einem Irrtum.**

(*b*) Motion. *On, onto.*

das Essen kommt auf den Tisch, ich gehe auf die Post, das Fenster geht auf die Straße, wir müssen uns auf den Weg machen.

Figurative, terms for relying on: **ich verlasse mich auf Sie, er schwört auf Karbolsäure, auf ihn ist kein Verlaß.**

Auf, figurative, quickly acquires the sense of aim or goal, even when the subject is inanimate: **ich bin auf den Namen** (*under the name*) **Willi getauft, er kommt immer auf** (*to*) **die Minute, Ableitungen auf -er (wie Bäcker),** *derivatives in,* **der Frack ist auf Seide gearbeitet,** *done in* (*lined with*).

320. Auf und ab, after noun in acc.; *up and down.*

er schritt den Bahnsteig auf und ab, cp. § 142 (*a*).

321. Aus, dat.; *out of, from*; movement from inside, or from a point of origin.

wir fuhren aus der Stadt, das Mädchen aus der Fremde, er tat es aus Versehen (cp. § 198), **das weiß ich aus bitterer Erfahrung.**

322. Außer, dat., and **außerhalb,** gen., *outside.*

Außerhalb has local sense: **außerhalb der Stadt, des Hauses,** but often **vor der Stadt, hinter dem Hause.**

Außer has figurative sense: **er geriet außer Rand und Band,** *lost control of himself,* **außer Betrieb,** *out of order, not working,* **ich war ganz außer mir,** *beside myself,* **außer der Reihe,** *out of (regular) order,* **außer Dienst,** abbreviated **a.D.,** *retired,* of official and military ranks.

Außer, with expressions of motion, is found: (i) sometimes with accusative, after **setzen: außer allen Zweifel setzen,** *to put beyond doubt,* **außer Kurs, Tätigkeit setzen;** (ii) with genitive, only in **außer Landes gehen,** *to leave the country* (often of banishment).

323. Bei, dat.; *near* or *close to, by*; but without contact (= **an**).

er stand dicht bei der Fähre, but **das Haus stand dicht an der Fähre,** *next to the ferry;* also vicinity in addresses: **Haunshofen bei Diemendorff,** or in battles: **die Schlacht bei Fehrbellin.**

Association with a person, their house, work, profession: **er ist bei einem Tischler in der Lehre** (*apprenticed to*), **ich hörte bei Kraus** (*went to K.s lectures*), **hier bei Prof. Schmidt** (*this is Prof. S.s house*—on telephone), **ich will bei ihm vorsprechen** (*call on*), **sich bei einer Firma beteiligen** (*have an interest in*), **bei einer Unternehmung mitwirken** (*collaborate in*).

Er ist schon bei Jahren und kaum mehr bei Kräften, *well on in years and no longer so strong.*

324. Bis, acc.; *to, up to*; as far as a limit of place.

wir fuhren bis Frankfurt zusammen, and often with fare-stages: **ich fuhr bis Schillerstraße, stieg dann aus.**

Combinations [all with accusative, *v.* § 263 (*b*)]: **das Wasser reichte uns bis an die Knöchel, bis über die Schwelle. Bis auf** is inclusive of the limit if literal: **wir kamen bis auf die Mettalm** (*reached*), but exclusive if figurative: **wir schafften es bis auf die letzte Meile** (*except for*).

325. Durch, acc.; *through.*

der Hund sprang durch den Reifen; figurative: **seine Klage ging mir durchs Herz;** combined: **er bahnte sich einen Weg mittendurch (querdurch) das Gedränge,** *slap through the crowd;* **sie sprachen alle durcheinander,** *all at once, confusedly.*

Distinguish from the following adverb: **meine Schuhe (Kleider) sind durch,** *worn out;* **der Zug ist durch,** *has gone through.*

326. Entlang, after noun in acc., dat.; **längs,** gen.; both *along*.

Accusative when movement is between two sides, dative (but also accusative) when along one side: **er taumelte die Straße entlang,** *down the street,* **der Häuserreihe entlang,** *along the house-fronts;* **wir fuhren den Fluß entlang,** *down* (in a boat), **dem Fluß entlang,** *along* (in a car). Also **entlang dem Ufer, längs des Ufers (dem Ufer), am Ufer entlang.** Thus statements of position are common with the dative: **Erlen stehen dem Bach entlang (säumen den Bach).**

The position after the noun indicates adverbial force [*v.* § 142 (*a*)], which may lead to compounding, **an** taking over the prepositional role: **als sie hinter ihrem Vater an dem Weizenschlag entlangging** (E. Wiechert).

327. Gegen, acc.; *towards*; both of direction and movement.

der Abhang des Tales senkte sich gegen die Talmulde, *dipped down towards the valley;* **das Haus liegt gegen Süden (hin),** *faces South*.

328. Gegenüber, dat.; *opposite*; before or after the noun.

gegenüber dem Bahnhof, dem Bahnhof gegenüber; before a place-name, may have **von: direkt gegenüber von Bonn liegt Beuel;** a governed pronoun must precede: **ich setzte mich ihm gegenüber.**

329. Hinter, dat., acc.; (*from, to*) *behind, beyond*.

(*a*) Position.

hinter dem Gebäude liegen Wirtschaftsräume, was steckt eigentlich dahinter? jetzt haben wir das alles gottseidank hinter uns.

The sense *from behind*, though indicating motion, requires dative, not accusative, as the directional force is absorbed by an adverbial compound [cp. § 263 (*e*)]:

Er zog einen alten Filzhut hinter dem Kleiderständer hervor, *from behind* (coll. also **von hinter dem . . .**).

Hinter Rohrbach liegt Sulzbach, *beyond Rohrbach . . .*

(*b*) Motion.

er führte uns hinter das Hauptgebäude; figurative: **jetzt müssen wir uns wirklich dahinter setzen** (*shoulder to the wheel*), **mich sollst du nicht hinters Licht führen!** (*take in, deceive*).

330. In, dat., acc.; *in(to)*; position in or motion into a place.

Uses of **in** are so numerous that only a few which differ from English idiom can be mentioned:

(*a*) Position.

im **Herzen** (*at*), im **Augenblick** (*at the moment*), im **Alter von** (*at*), in einer **Entfernung von** (*at*), im **Trab** (*at a trot*), im **Durchschnitt** (*on an average*), wir **kommen um zehn Uhr in Berlin an,** *arrive at* or *in Berlin;* das **Maximilianeum in München,** *at* or *in Munich* (cp. **zu**).

(*b*) Motion.

ins **Gefängnis kommen,** *to be sent to prison,* and often **in** for *to,* of regular attendance at an institution: ins **Kino, Theater, in die Kirche, Schule gehen.** Er ist in die **Türkei,** *has gone to Turkey.*

Figurative: **sich in jemanden verlieben,** *fall in love with,* in etwas **einwilligen,** *fall in with* (*a suggestion*).

With verbs indicating an activity not specifically of motion, German often has an accusative of result when English sees the relation as one of position: er **zeichnete mit dem Schirm Kreise in den Sand,** *in the sand;* even er **nickte ins Zimmer** would be: *he nodded to the people in the room.* But: er **verschwand im Nebel,** *disappeared into the mist* [*v.* § 265 (*b*)].

331. Inmitten, gen.; *in the midst of, among.*

Inmitten der Menge stand ein langer, grauhaariger Mann.

When governing a pronoun, the preposition should be resolved [cp. § 263 (*c*)]: **in ihrer** (poss. adj.) **Mitte,** *in the midst of the crowd, of it.*

332. Nach, dat.; *to(wards), in the direction of.*

The goal must be non-personal (especially place-names) and at some distance: **wir fuhren nach London, Deutschland, der Schweiz** (or **in die Schweiz**). **Zu** is used with nearness of goal: **er ging zur Tür, zur** (or **in die) Kirche,** or **fuhr bis Endstation;** also person as goal: **sie reiste über ganz Europa zur Mutter.** Both prepositions: **sie fuhr zur Mutter nach Rom,** where English admits only one goal and converts the other: *to Rome to see her mother.* Names of place close by often avoid both: **wir radelten bis Epping hinaus,** *cycled as far as Epping.*

Nach with persons is often goal, but figurative, without actual contact **ich ging nach dem Gasmann,** *went to fetch* (or *order*), **ich telefonierte nach dem Arzt,** *telephoned for the doctor.*

333. Nächst, dat., *close to,* the superlative of **nahe,** *near.* Literary style for (**gerade) bei.**

sein Haus liegt nächst der Haltestelle (= **gleich nach** or **gleich vor**), *close to,* almost the same as English *next* (*to*).

334. Neben, dat., acc.; *beside.*

(*a*) Position.

das Kind saß neben der Mutter, sie ging neben dem Pfluge her; figurative: neben Geschichte studiert er auch Englisch, thus das Nebenfach, *subsidiary subject.*

A common figurative sense is that of missing (the mark): seine Kugel ging neben dem Ziel vorbei, commonly in the adverbial compound prefix danebengehen, -hauen: mit seinen wohlgemeinten Hilfsversuchen haut er immer furchtbar daneben, *he's always putting his foot in it.*

(*b*) Motion.

sie setzte sich neben ihn (but neben ihm hin); ein Witz, der danebenging, *a joke that didn't come off.*

335. Über, dat., acc.; *over, above.*

(*a*) Position.

die Wolken lagen über dem Städtchen, ein Geschäftsmann grübelt über seiner Einkommenssteuererklärung (newsp.), *sits and ponders . . .*

Figuratively, über easily acquires time force: (er verbrachte) Tage über dem Mikroskop und Tage über Gedichten (E. Wiechert), and causal force: über der Betrachtung der Gesichter vergaß ich zu antworten (F. Werfel), *through studying the faces . . .*

(*b*) Motion.

Apfelsinenschalen, über die man ausgleitet, . . . liegen niemals da, wenn man hinsieht (Th. Mann). Also authority: er schwang das Lineal über seine Schulkameraden wie ein Zepter. In a bracket with adverb: sie fiel über mich her (*attacked*), fiel über den Tisch hin (*fell across*).

336. Um, acc.; *around, about.*

der Herrscher zog eine Mauer um das Städtchen (herum), um den König (*about*) waren lauter selbstsüchtige Männer.

337. Unter, dat., acc.; *under(neath), below, among.*

(*a*) Position.

unter dem Dach hervor schauten halbflügge Vögelchen, es gibt nichts Neues unter dem Himmel, in der Schule war ich unter ihm (*below*), beim Militär wieder unter ihm (*under his authority*), unter den Briefmarken war eine wertvolle, *among.* Figurative: unter Greiffuß versteht man einen Vogelfuß zum Greifen, *by . . . we understand.*

(*b*) Motion.

er streckte die Füße unter den Tisch, warf Geld unter (*among*) **die Menge, brachte neue Gebiete unter die Herrschaft seines Gebieters.**

338. Von, dat.; *from*; point of departure, origin.

von Frankfurt nach Heidelberg, Grüße von Haus zu Haus, Adalbert von Chamisso; ich gratuliere vom Herzen, *hearty congratulations.*

339. Vor, dat., acc.; *before, in front of.*

(*a*) Position.

sie trafen sich vor dem Bahnhof; here, as often, **vor** is used where English has *outside* or *near*: **ein kleines Haus vor der Stadt,** *on the outskirts,* **die Insel liegt vor der Küste,** *close to,* compare **das Vorgebirge,** *promontory.* **Ich schwöre vor Gott, er erschien vor Gericht, das Schiff ging (lag) vor Anker,** (*lay*) *anchored.*

(*b*) Motion.

das Taxi fuhr vor den Bahnhof und hielt, *drove up to;* as with **in,** but differing from **über,** a following prefix or directional particle changes the case to dative: **der Wagen fuhr vor dem Bahnhof an.**

Distinguish from the following adverb: **der Wagen fuhr vor,** *drew up.*

Figurative: **(sich) kein Blatt vor den Mund nehmen,** *to speak one's mind.*

340. Zu, dat.; *to, at, in,* etc.

Distinguish **zu** and **an** (*v.* § 318), the latter being more formal, intended, also distant: **ich wandte mich zu ihm,** *to him* (to speak, etc.), **ich wandte mich an ihn,** *to him* (for help, advice, etc.).

Distinguish **zu** and **in,** of well-known institutions in places. **In** is the general term: **der Prater in Wien, zu** more formal and used of a few unique monuments: **der Dom zu Köln, das Völkerdenkmal zu Leipzig,** as also of hotels: **(Gasthaus) zum Wilden Mann,** and chemists: **Apotheke zum Bären.**

Zu is much used in bracketing expressions:

(1) As the first element in expressions of entry and exit: **es ritten drei Reiter zum Tore hinaus,** *out of* (*by*) *the gate* (folk song), **er sah zum Fenster hinaus,** *out of,* **er kam zur Türe hereingetaumelt,** *in by* (*at*). But not of unconventional modes of entry and exit: **der Vogel fiel durch den Schornstein ins Zimmer; mit der Tür ins Haus fallen,** *to barge in* (lit., *bring the door in with one*).

(2) As the second (adverbial) element in expressions of goal or direction: **nach Süden zu, auf mich zu;** here the dative with following

zu is regularly used for *towards, facing*: **sie fuhren dem Walde zu, das eine Fenster—der Straße zu**— ... [*v.* § 263 (*d*)].

Figuratively, **zu** often becomes the term of an activity: **man brachte ihn zu Bett, bringt seine Gedanken zu Papier** (*get down on*), **macht etwas zu Geld** (*turn into*), **eilt einem zu Hilfe** (*to someone's assistance*), **steht zu seinem Wort** (*stands by*), etc., *v.* also § 205 (*c*) and § 527.

341. Zwischen, dat., acc.; *between.*

(*a*) Position.

Like *between*, **zwischen** can mean (i) the action of a third between two or more things, or (ii) a relation between two or more things themselves: **zwischen mir und meinem Bruder gibt's drei Jahre, zwischen den Donnerschlägen hörte man das Schreien eines Kindes, zwischen uns kam es zum Bruch**; even (iii) a singular noun, if collective, may stand after **zwischen: es wächst viel Unkraut zwischen dem Weizen.** Cp. **unter,** § 411.

(*b*) Motion.

Der Polizist schob sich zwischen die sich raufenden Männer.

When *between* is intensified to the sense of *through*, **zwischen** may be bracketed with **hin, durch,** or **hindurch,** according to the degree of perfective force required, the case being dative: **der König schritt zwischen den Reihen hin, der Wagen fuhr zwischen den hurrarufenden Reihen hindurch.**

342. Genitive Prepositions of Relative Place

(*a*) Apart from some noted above (*v.* **außerhalb,** etc.), many prepositions express some aspect of relative place and govern the genitive: **abseits,** *to one side* (*of*), **auf-** and **abwärts,** *up* and *down* (*from*), usually *upstream*, etc., as **stromabwärts, stromaufwärts, ober-** and **unterhalb,** *above* and *below*, **diesseits** and **jenseits,** *on the near, far side*, **links** and **rechts,** *on the left, right* (*of*), **nördlich,** etc., *to the north,* etc. (*of*), **seitlich** or **seitwärts,** *to the side* (*of*), **unfern** and **unweit,** *not far* (*from*).

(*b*) The link with the governed noun, represented by English *of* or *from*, is in German the genitive case: **unweit der Stadt;** but in all these forms, **von** is also used less formally: **unweit von der Stadt.**

But **von** becomes the general idiom:

(1) Before proper nouns, of place or person: **abwärts von Heidelberg, seitlich von Hans;** or pronouns: **westlich von uns** [*v.* § 266 (*d*), (*e*)].

(2) When the sense emphasises *from* rather than *of*:

Abseits von der Verkehrsstraße . . . **lag das stattliche Sommerhaus** (H. Kasack), (*hidden*) *away from the main road* . . .

EXERCISE LII

A. Translate into ENGLISH:

1. Wir entsannen uns bestimmter Bettler an bestimmten Straßenecken, zu bestimmten Stunden und bei bestimmtem Sonnenstande (W. Bergengruen). 2. Ich hängte Hut und Mantel an die Garderobe (H. Risse). 3. Das große graue Schulgebäude, bis unters Dach mit Kindersorgen angefüllt . . . (E. Kästner). 4. Die Bombe war den meisten Menschen von Citta morta sozusagen gerade in die richtige Entfernung gefallen— nicht zu nah und nicht zu weit (S. Andres). 5. Ich strecke mich auf das saftige Grün der Terrasse unter die zahllosen Gänseblümchen aus (G. Hauptmann). 6. Er starb auf hoher See und wurde fern der Heimat im Meer bestattet. 7. Als Hans Carossa auf der Universität Leipzig Medizin studierte, hörte er bei Trendelenburg Kolleg. 8. Inmitten der ihm fremden Gesichter erblickte er auf einmal ein wohlbekanntes. 9. Noch lange winkte sie zum Fenster hinaus, als er schon zwischen den hohen Häusern verschwunden war. 10. Das Häuschen des Fährmanns lag jenseits des Stroms und dicht am Walde.

B. Translate into GERMAN:

1. After they had settled in Berlin they often went out to the Wannsee to bathe. 2. She liked to have all her familiar little things round her. 3. He stopped his car opposite to the prison gates outside the town. 4. What can you see at a distance of 500 metres without your glasses? 5. When he was old he preferred to live apart from society. 6. To the east of the city of Vienna there is a wide plain on which many battles have been fought. 7. He looked sternly at the class from beneath his bushy eyebrows. 8. He walked in front of the brass band and over his shoulder shouted directions to the musicians at the back. 9. I found her sitting on the kitchen floor amongst her pots and pans. 10. To the left of the town hall is the street leading to the theatre.

CHAPTER LIII

343. Impersonal Es in Apposition

Refer to Chapter XLII, especially § 243.

Es may stand in anticipation of a following noun or pronoun, or noun clause, etc. (subject or object); its function is purely grammatical and it is commonly omitted when the order justifies this.

(*a*) Anticipating a noun or pronoun subject, **es** acts as a formal introduction to the sentence; a plural noun or indefinite pronoun (personal pronouns may not be used here) attracts the verb into the plural:

Es ist ein Unglück passiert, *an accident has happened.*

Es sind alle schon da, *all have come.*

Inversion causes the construction to revert to normal:

Gestern ist ein Unglück passiert. Bald waren alle da.

German **es** may correspond to English *there* [cp. also § 244 (*a*)]; but the latter is more restricted in its use:

Es erschien ein Mann hinten im Garten, *there appeared a man* . . .

Es wurde ein Film vorgeführt . . ., *a film was shown* . . .

Es weiß niemand, ob . . ., *no one knows* . . .

On the other hand, English may use *there* after a leading adverb, while **es** is here omitted:

Yesterday there happened . . . (cp. example above).

(*b*) Anticipating a noun clause or infinitive construction, **es** either stands for the proper subject, as in (*a*), or provides a brief explicit object for a verb or adjective to govern:

(1) Anticipating the subject:

Es ist nicht möglich, daß wir heute den Ausflug unternehmen, *it is not possible for us to* . . .

Es lohnt sich sehr, diesen Ausflug zu unternehmen, *it is well worth while our undertaking* . . .

Inversion does not require omission of **es**, since the subject is still delayed; but it may be omitted:

Bei diesem Wetter lohnt (es) sich ganz besonders, den Ausflug zu machen.

Gut ist, daß er den Kognak hat . . . (H. Fallada), *a good thing that* . . .

Similarly in subordinate clauses:

Sie . . . sehen kein Ziel vor Augen, für das sich zu leben lohnt (H. Kasack), *no aim for which it is worth while living.*

435

But **es** must be omitted when the subject actually precedes:

Den Ausflug zu machen lohnt sich bei diesem Wetter ganz besonders.

(2) Anticipating the object; here practice is not uniform:

Er vermied (es), mit ihm zu sprechen, *he avoided speaking to him.*

Ich bin es herzlich satt, seine Bücher immer lesen zu müssen, . . . daß er mir immer noch auf der Tasche liegt. *I am tired of having to read . . ., of his continuing to depend on me.*

but **es** is the more liable to omission, especially before infinitive constructions, the closer it stands to the real object of the verb (cp. first example above). Thus also:

Ich weiß, daß er morgen kommen wird, *I know that . . .*

Ich weiß es sicher, daß er morgen kommen wird, *I know for certain that . . .*

(*c*) This latter use must be clearly distinguished from:

(1) Infinitive, etc., constructions following verbs not properly transitive in force, and thus not needing a specific object:

Ich glaubte, ihn zu kennen . . ., daß er kommen würde.

Ich hoffte, ihn begrüßen zu dürfen . . ., daß ich ihn sehen würde.

(2) Impersonal **es** which is part of the idiom or a summary of the situation (often with back-reference), thus:

Der Handwerker hat es von Haus aus leichter als der Beamte, gut deutsch zu sprechen, *finds it easier to . . .* (cp. **er hat es leicht**).

Er hat es darauf abgesehen, sich nützlich zu machen, *he made a special point of being useful* (the anticipatory role falls to **darauf**).

Viele kannten den Polen, wenige aber gaben es (back-reference) **zu oder liebten es** (anticipatory), **von ihm zu sprechen** (W. Bergengruen), *but few admitted it or liked speaking of him.*

344. Es as Emphatic Pointer

(*a*) As in English, though to a much more restricted degree, the impersonal **es** may be used in a quasi-anticipatory fashion with the intention of isolating an element of a sentence for emphasis:

Es ist mehr als dreißig Jahre her, daß ich diese Geschichte gelesen habe, *it is more than thirty years ago that . . .*

The element emphasised may be:

(1) The subject; the rest of the sentence becomes a relative clause:

Die Angst ist es vor allem gewesen, die mich von Kind an beherrscht hat (H. Risse), *it was fear especially which . . .*

(2) An adverb; the rest becomes a clause with **daß** or **als**: *v.* above, and: **es war gegen Abend, als wir ankamen,** *it was . . . when . . .*

(*b*) Since the intention is to emphasise, the emphatic element, subject, or adverb, often leads, as in (1) above. But a following **es** cannot be omitted, *v.* (1) again, as it provides an essential link between the two parts of the sentence.

345. Impersonal Es Summarising a Situation

Es may act as a convenient summary of a general situation or inexplicit content; in this role it is partly idiomatic, and partly required by formal grammar. It may be the subject, object, or complement of a verb; as subject it is commonly also present in English, but not otherwise.

(*a*) Many idiomatic uses require **es**:

es geht nicht, *it's no good;* **es kam zu schweren Unruhen,** *serious disorders broke out;* **Väter haben es schwer,** *fathers have a difficult time (of it);* **er hat es faustdick hinter den Ohren,** *he's a sly one;* **es wurde mir zu dumm,** *I got sick of it.*

In demonstrative contexts, personal names, etc., may, as in English, be predicated of **es: es ist Inge, es ist der Gasmann.** A following plural attracts the verb into its number: **es waren Schmidts.** But a following pronoun, especially in the first and second person, imposes both number and person on the verb, and displaces **es** from leading position, though **es** remains the subject, as in English:

ich bin es, *it is me;* **bist du's?** *is it you?* **wir waren's,** *it was us.* Cp. § 480 (*c*).

(*b*) German, unlike English, prefers not to leave a verb in the air, with an object or predicate understood, and in these cases supplies **es** to represent the implicit content:

Sind Sie fertig? Ja, ich bin's. *Are you ready? Yes, I am.*

[Distinguish this from **ich bin's,** in (*a*), *it's me.*]

Sind Sie geheilt? Ich glaube es, weiß es aber nicht. *Are you cured? I believe so, but do not know.*

Ach, lieber Freund, was für ein Dilemma! Ich muß reisen und will es nicht; habe mich verpflichtet zu reisen—und kann es nicht (Th. Mann), *. . . and do not want to . . . and cannot.*

Compare **es** for reference back in last example of § 343 (*c*) (2).

Note.—A following dative object renders **es** optional:

Glauben Sie (es) mir, *believe me;* **ich glaube (es) ihm aufs Wort,** *I believe implicitly in what he says.*

(c) In accordance with the use described in (b), situation es is required in certain subordinate clauses of comparison:

(1) Of degree [v. § 313 (a)] with **als**:

der nächste Krieg, der wohl noch scheußlicher sein wird, als dieser es war (H. Hesse), *more horrible than the last one was.*

Note.—But not when abbreviated by omission of the verb: **scheußlicher als der letzte.** Compare **er kommt sobald als möglich,** or **als es möglich ist.**

(2) Of similarity [v. § 312 (e)] with **wie**:

Zeiten, in denen das flüchtige Obdach aufgeschlagen wurde, wie der Zug der Herden es gebot (E. Jünger), *as the movements of the herds required.*

Compare § 233 (relative clause, *such as*).

Note.—But certain simple subordinate clauses of comparison, introduced parenthetically, may omit **es,** as they often omit **wie** also: **wie folgt,** *as follows;* **wie sich denken läßt,** *as may be imagined;* cp. **soweit bekannt ist,** *as far as is known.*

(der Preis), den aber ich, versteht sich, bar erlegte (Th. Mann), *the price, which of course I paid in cash.*

Compare **er benahm sich nicht, wie es sich schickte,** *he did not behave as was proper*; **er benahm sich, wie sich schickte, tadellos,** *he behaved, as was proper, faultlessly.*

346. Impersonal Es, Final Comments

Basically, no use of the impersonal **es** may be isolated from other uses. Thus **es** in apposition to a following subject or object is essentially similar to situation **es** when it refers back to an implicit content; this is clear when both occur:

Ich begreife es nicht, daß er sowas sagen konnte, möchte es aber nicht leugnen, *do not understand . . ., but do not deny it.*

Further, many dative verbs are essentially impersonal in their use, and analogous to those of sensation [v. § 245 (c)], but are also often used in anticipatory constructions:

es passiert mir oft (zu . . .); es gefällt uns (daß . . .); es ist mir egal (ob . . .); es fiel mir ein (daß . . .).

es schickt sich nicht, *it* (situation) *is not appropriate.*

es schickt sich nicht, daß . . ., *it* (anticipatory subject) *is not appropriate that . . .*

Lastly, even **es** with the sole function of grammatical anticipation may acquire something of the elemental force of other uses of **es** [cp. § 224, esp. (d)]; thus v. Exercise XLII, A. 6, concluding sentences, where **es** represents the inscrutable voice of authority.

347. The Past Participle in Appositional Constructions

(*a*) Many past participle constructions, though in apposition to a noun or pronoun, and thus adjectival in function, are in fact adverbial in force, and correspond to an adverb proper or subordinate clause. As the adverbial relationship is not explicit (cp. also § 276, present participles), such appositions may be variously interpreted. Subject to this limitation, participles may correspond to:

(1) Simple adverbs of, *e.g.* place, manner:

Mir benachbart saß . . . eine dreiköpfige Gruppe von Herrschaften (Th. Mann), *near me sat . . .* (= **in meiner Nähe**).

Gebeugt, eine Hand nach guter Servierschule auf dem Rücken, bot ich meine Schüsseln an (Th. Mann), *bending slightly . . . I offered . . .* (= **in gebeugter Stellung**).

(2) A causal relationship (often also the opposite, *i.e.* concession, *though* for *because*, cp. § 201):

Für ein nicht gelehrtes Publikum verfaßt, füllt dieses Buch eine fühlbar gewordene Lücke aus (newsp.), *written (as it is) for a general public . . .*

(3) Often, a subordinate clause of (preceding) time:

Ein schweres Lungenleiden . . .; genesen, konnte er dann im Weltkrieg ein Kommando übernehmen (S. Zweig), *after he had recovered . . .*

(*b*) While the sense is often adverbial, the force of the past participle in apposition is either passive (with transitive verbs, *e.g.* **verfaßt,** above), active (with intransitive verbs, *e.g.* **genesen,** above), or reflexive (as with **gebeugt,** above, cp. **sich beugen**). Those with active or reflexive force are sometimes explained as abbreviated forms of the perfect present participle: **(sich) gebeugt (habend), genesen (seiend)**; this shows why, in time contexts, the active (intransitive) past participle usually indicates preceding time, thus compare:

genesen, konnte er dann im Weltkrieg . . . (= **nachdem . . .**),

genesend, wollte er dann im Weltkrieg . . . (= **als . . .**).

(*c*) It is normally participial constructions *preceding* the noun or pronoun to which they are in apposition which have specific adverbial force. Those following have either adjectival force:

„Hab' ich dich gefragt?", schrie er, schon wieder aufgebracht (E. Kästner), *he cried, already again in a rage.*

or that of a simple adverb of manner:

Sie war unbemerkt eingetreten, *she had entered unnoticed.*

348. The Past Participle in Attributive Use with Adverbial Force

(*a*) Even the past participle preceding the noun as an attributive adjective may have the force of a subordinate adverbial construction:

so wie die Sehne vom allzu straff gespannten Bogen springt (E. Jünger),
as the bow-string snaps if (or *when*) *it is pulled too taut.*

though the commoner sense is that of a relative clause with the force of preceding time:

Bücher mit eingelegten Papierzeichen (H. Hesse), *books with slips of paper*
(*which had been*) *inserted.*

(*b*) Constructions with **nach** often have adverbial (time) force:

nach bestandenem Kampfe, *after the battle had been fought and won;*
nach geschehener Abmachung, *after agreement had been reached.*

In such constructions the noun is either the object (**den Kampf bestehen**) or the subject (**die Abmachung geschieht**) of the participial sense, thus corresponding to the passive or active force, respectively, of the participle used in apposition [*v.* § 347 (*b*)].

When the noun itself is one of time and the force passive, the construction is normal in both languages:

Nach angenehm durchzechter Nacht kommt Maler Mendinger gegen acht Uhr früh in sein Atelier . . . (Simpl.), *after a pleasantly dissipated night . . .*

349. The Past Participle in the Predicate

(*a*) Apart from its use with auxiliaries to form tenses and the passive voice (*v.* there), the past participle often supplies a further description of the subject in the predicate (subjective predicate), especially after quasi-auxiliary verbs:

Das Papier flog unbesehen in den Papierkorb, *flew unexamined . . .*
Die Bäume standen erstarrt, *stood rigid with cold.*
Das Kätzchen lag zusammengerollt, *lay rolled up.*

Such constructions have the force (as here: passive, intransitive reflexive) of their respective verbs, as noted above [§ 347 (*b*)].

(*b*) In the predicate after **kommen,** the past participle of a verb of motion (intransitive) has *present* participial and adverbial force, indicating manner of movement or arriving:

er kam gelaufen, geeilt, herangeritten, hereingeschneit, *he came running, hurrying, riding up, turned up (unexpectedly).*

Der Unfallwagen kam mit lautem Heulton vorm Krankenhaus angefahren
(Simpl.), *came driving up with its siren sounding . . .*

(1) A descriptive verb, not of motion, has here the present participle, as in English: **er kam pfeifend,** *came along whistling;* and similarly the present participle of a verb of motion will express a circumstance attendant on the arrival rather than the manner of progression itself: **er kam tanzend,** *he came (and was) dancing, danced on the way.*

(2) Within these limits, however, the verb of motion need not be intended literally (cp. **hereingeschneit,** above and):

Träume kamen ihm und rastlose Gedanken aus dem Wasser des Flusses geflossen, aus den Sternen der Nacht gefunkelt, aus den Strahlen der Sonne geschmolzen . . . (H. Hesse), *flowed from the river, flashed from the stars, and melted into him from the sun's rays.*

350. The Past Participle in the Adverbial Accusative Construction

This construction is partly appositional (as § 347), and partly absolute (as § 351).

(*a*) Accusative in appositional construction.

A past participle from a transitive verb, apparently in apposition to the subject, may be preceded by an accusative:

Z. faltete die knochigen Hände, den lächelnden Blick auf seine Frau gerichtet (E. Wiechert), *his smiling look directed to his wife.*

Allein, diesen klaren Gedanken in Sicherheit gebracht, gehe ich noch einen Schritt weiter (Th. Mann), *this clear idea established . . .*

Such constructions may be considered from two points of view:

(1) Appositional participle with its own object [a present participle being understood, as in § 347 (*b*), thus: **gerichtet habend, gebracht habend**]; or:

(2) An adverbial accusative [cp. **den Hut unter dem Arm . . .,** cp. § 314 (*c*) (1)] with a past participle with passive force (= *this clear idea having been established*).

The first view (1) sees the participle as active in force, and looks back to § 347; the second (2) sees it as passive, and looks forward to the absolute use in § 351.

(*b*) Adverbial accusative absolute:

When the sense of the participle cannot be related to any stated subject the construction becomes absolute and the accusative is the adverbial accusative:

Wohl ein Dutzend Teilnehmer, mich eingeschlossen, kamen im ganzen zusammen (Th. Mann), *including me.*

Und all das erwogen, drängt sich mir die Frage auf . . . (Th. Fontane), *taking all that into consideration, the question remains . . .*

Cp. § 277 (*b*) (absolute present participle).

Thus many expressions of logic (*e.g.* **gesetzt den Fall,** *supposing*) and calculation (**eingeschlossen,** above; **Provision eingerechnet, nicht eingerechnet, ungerechnet,** *inclusive* or *exclusive of commission*).

Note.—Some idioms are single words, especially those in **un-** corresponding to English absolute present participle: **unberufen,** *touch*(*ing*) *wood,* **ungescherzt,** *joking apart,* **ungewollt,** *unwillingly,* **unverweilt,** *immediately* (lit. *not waiting*).

351. The Past Participle in Absolute Constructions

(*a*) The past participle is often used, especially in proverbial and other pithy expressions, in a nominal context (subject, object, complement of a verb), or in verbless statements, to express the general sense of the verb apart from the specific sense of the past participle:

Das ist zu viel verlangt, ein bißchen hochgerechnet, *that's expecting too much, putting it a bit high.*

Aber ich gebe die Hoffnung nicht auf, das wäre doch gelacht, mein Lieber! (E. Kästner), *that would be ridiculous* (*a matter for ridicule*).

Wie gewonnen, so zerronnen, *easy come, easy go.*

Gelernt ist gelernt, *what you know you don't forget.*

Jung gefreit, hat niemand gereut, *marry early, never regret.*

(*b*) Some regard this use as the equivalent of the (prepositional) infinitive [*e.g.* **das heißt zu viel verlangen,** or **verlangt haben,** cp. § 151 (*a*)]; but the analogy to the imperative [cp. § 248 (*e*)] is also strong:

„**Wenn die fünf Minuten um sind, pfeif' ich meinen Pfiff. Und dann heißt's angeschwirrt . . .**" (H. Fallada), *and then you come double quick my boy.*

And many proverbial statements may be regarded as a presupposition, expressed vividly as an imperative, followed by a forecast of the result (cp. **Jung gefreit,** above, and):

Mitgefangen, mitgehangen! *Let yourself be caught with bad company, and you'll share their fate!*

(*c*) The basic force of the absolute past participle is therefore, probably, a vivid participation in an experience more closely related to the imperative than to the infinitive:

Da stieß sein Fuß an, im Dunkel des Fußbodens.   Was lag hier ?   Herumgerissen den Kerl:—Sterny! (H. Mann), *what was this? over with the fellow—Sterny!*

And a woman who admiringly watches a man driving reflects: **Sichere Eleganz der Lenkung, korrektes Stoppen vor aufglühenden roten Lichtern und rasch Vorteile wahrgenommen: in Lücken geschlüpft, sich vorsichtig vorgedrängelt** (H. Böll), *advantages quickly taken, slipping into gaps, easing forward carefully.*

Exercise LIII

A. Translate into English:

1. Es darf nicht sein, daß ein unschuldiger Mann für ein Verbrechen büßt, das andere begangen haben (L. Frank). 2. „Sie begreifen es, aber Sie lehnen ab, es zu begreifen!" (H. Risse). 3. Sie liebte nicht, Gemeinsames zu tun in einem großen Kreise . . . Aber sie liebte es, ein paar Schritte hinter dem Vater herzugehen, wenn er über die Felder ging (E. Wiechert). 4. Ja,—sagte die Dame—aber Sport sei doch roh. Gewiß,—beeilte sich Ulrich, es zuzugeben—Sport sei roh . . . (R. Musil). 5. (Ich) versuchte ihm zuzublinzeln, so wie Mitwisser von Geheimnissen es untereinander tun (H. Hesse). 6. Ihre einzige Freude fand sie im baren Geld, das sie zäh zusammenraffte, um nicht, alt geworden, im Armenhaus noch einmal das bittere Brot der Gemeinde würgen zu müssen (S. Zweig). 7. Nach beendeter Mahlzeit begaben sich die Gäste ins Spielzimmer. 8. Bettler, mit zwei alten Getreidesäcken bekleidet, den einen unter den Achseln um den Leib geschlungen, den andern über die Schultern gehängt, wie ein Umschlagetuch, sprechen die Inhaber ärmlicher Laden um Gaben an (G. Hauptmann). 9. In einer Verhandlungspause wurde ich ungewollt Zeuge folgender Unterhaltung zwischen zwei Rechtsanwälten . . . (Simpl.). 10. Proverbial: Aufgeschoben ist nicht aufgehoben. Unverhofft kommt oft. Unverzagt hats oft gewagt.

B. Translate into German, using past participle constructions in Nos. 6-10 when possible:

1. It is completely unnecessary, and even ridiculous, to get excited about a thing like that. 2. She avoided thinking of the inevitable result of her action. 3. They disdained to give me any sort of answer. 4. Above all, it was the man's face that attracted me from the beginning. 5. I think I can come to the party to-night, at least I hope so. 6. I caught a glimpse of him as he sat in the first-class carriage, leaning back comfortably. 7. The thief, confronted with his confederates, persisted in the statement that he had already made. 8. I came down in the cable railway with the others, and when we had arrived below we parted. 9. After she had got back from her voyage she began writing her novel. 10. Suddenly a large black dog came jumping up at me.

CHAPTER LIV

SUBJUNCTIVE OF INDIRECT QUESTION, COMMAND, EXPECTATION

352. Indirect Questions

(*a*) The rules for indirect statements (*v.* §§ 304 f.) apply analogously to indirect questions, both as regards mood and tense:

Wer sind Sie? Er fragt, wer ich bin. Er fragte, wer ich sei (wäre).
Kommen Sie? Er fragt, ob er kommt. Er fragte, ob er komme (käme).

The subjunctive is uncommon after a present tense in the main clause, thus **bin, kommt,** above.

(*b*) The interrogatives introducing indirect questions are: the pronouns **was,** *what,* **wer,** *who;* and the adverbs **ob,** *whether,* **wann,** *when,* **wie,** *how,* etc. But while the use of **ob** is common with **fragen** and its synonyms (**sich überlegen,** *to consider,* **jemandem etwas überlassen,** *to leave the decision to,* etc.), it is also common with **wissen,** *to know* (*whether*), **vergessen,** *to forget* (*whether*)*;* and the other interrogatives have uses with many verbs [as **erfahren,** *to learn,* **sich erinnern,** *to remember,* *v.* § 353 (*b*) below] which are only technically associated with indirect questions. Thus many examples belonging to the subjunctive of indirect question in the wider sense bear an even fainter resemblance to actual indirect questions than in the analogous cases of indirect statement (*v.* § 305).

(*c*) As with indirect statements, certain subjunctive forms in indirect questions are based on analogy and extension:

(1) A clause in apposition to a noun of questioning (cp. § 307):

Die ganze Frage, ob und wann er komme, ist noch nicht geklärt worden, *the whole question, whether and when he will come, is not yet settled.*

(2) The subjunctive is transferred to a subordinate clause [cp. § 308 (*b*)]:

(er) fragte, ob ich keinen Wein trinken wolle (ind. qu.), **zu dem er mich einlade** (H. Hesse), *he asked whether I would not drink some wine, which he would stand me.*

353. Wider Contexts of Indirect Question

(*a*) Noun clauses, subject or object of a verb, which are introduced by one of the interrogative particles [cp. § 352 (*b*)], and are envisaged as propositions independently of their truth, or about which there is some uncertainty, are formally associated with indirect questions and take the subjunctive (cp. analogous indirect statement, § 305):

Subject: **Wer sein Besucher gewesen sei, ist mir noch immer unklar,** *it is still unclear to me who his visitor was* (*may have been*).

Object: **Ich hatte noch gewisse Zweifel, ob der Vater es sei, der ihn besucht habe** [transferred, *v.* § 352 (*c*)], *I still had certain doubts whether it was his father who had visited him.*

(*b*) Similarly, the analogy to indirect questions suggested by the use of the interrogative particles has caused the subjunctive to be widely used in noun clauses (object) after verbs of perception and knowing, as **sehen, erfahren, vernehmen, wissen,** though there may be no doubt of the substance of the clause; but there is also much critical opposition to this:

als er hörte, wer ich wäre (H. Risse), *when he heard who I was.*

(**er**) **erinnerte sich, wo er wäre und wie er hierher gekommen sei** (H. Hesse), *remembered where he was and how he had got here.*

354. Indirect Commands

(*a*) There are two senses in which the term "indirect command" may be understood:

(1) The reporting, in indirect speech, of a command:

Command: *Come!* Report: *He said I should come.*

(2) The reporting of a command, with a verb of command used in the main clause:

Command: *Come!* Report: *He told* (*instructed*) *me to come.*

English uses *to tell* in this context, and distinguishes it from *to say* in context (1).

(*b*) Indirect statements and questions are recognised by their verbs (**sagen** and **fragen**) or their introductory particles (**daß, ob,** the interrogatives). But an indirect command introduced by **sagen** and **daß** [*v.* (1) above] would be quite unrecognisable unless some appropriate modal word (*should*, above) distinguished it from the corresponding simple statement. German uses the modal **sollen:**

Kommen Sie! Sie ließ ihm sagen, daß er kommen solle, *said he was to come.*
Sie sagte mir, ich sollte (solle) kommen, *told me to come.*

[Distinguish **Sie sagte mir, daß er komme (käme),** *told me he was coming, would come.*]

(*c*) With a specific verb of request in the main statement [*v.* (2) above], a wider selection of modals is used; thus **sollen** after **sagen,** *to tell* (*someone to . . .*), **mögen** or **wollen** after **bitten** and synonyms:

Hören Sie auf mit dem Klavierspielen! Ich sagte ihm, er solle mit dem Klavierspielen sofort aufhören. *I told him to stop* . . .

Ich bat ihn, er möge (wolle) bedenken, daß sein Klavierspielen meinem Kunstempfinden zuwider sei, *I asked him to bear in mind that his playing was an insult to my artistic feelings.*

But certain verbs of explicit request use other constructions:

(1) Verbs of explicit willing (**wollen, verlangen,** also **bitten**) take **daß** and the subjunctive of purpose, cp. § 357 (*b*).

(2) Verbs of explicit command or veto (**befehlen, gebieten, verbieten**) have a prepositional infinitive construction, which may be alternative to the use of a modal as above:

er befahl ihm wegzufahren (or er solle wegfahren); man gebot ihr, sich zu entfernen; sie verbot ihm, anwesend zu sein.

Note.—The prepositional infinitive has, by exception [cp. § 370 (*b*) (1)], the logical subject of the dative object of the main verb (**ihm, ihr**).

(*d*) As a direct command is always in the present (*Come!*), the time of an indirect command is always parallel to the tense in which it is reported (*He said I was to come*) and problems of sequence of tense (as in indirect statements, *v.* § 306) seldom arise. Thus in the past it is seldom necessary to distinguish between the reporting of a direct command (**Kommen Sie!**) and of a statement couched in the *ought* form (**Sie sollten kommen**), cp. examples in (*b*) and (*c*).

In the present, **sollen** is always used in the indicative [cp. § 352 (*a*)]: **sagen Sie ihm, er soll kommen,** *tell him to come,* but this should be distinguished from the communication of a wish, which has the subjunctive in its own right [cp. § 273 (*c*)]:

Sagen Sie ihm, er möge kommen, *tell him I wish him to come.*

When the force of the subordinate clause is that of a wish, the past tense is often used to convey it politely:

Sie bat mich, ich möchte doch bitte nichts davon verlauten lassen, *she asked me to be so good as not to let anything be known.*

Similarly in the past, **sollte** may be less peremptory than **solle,** as in English *should* as against *was to* (*He said I was to come*).

355. Concealed and Oblique Subjunctives of Indirect Speech

(*a*) As with indirect statements [*v.* § 308 (*a*)] the verb **fragen** may be understood before a subjunctive of indirect question, etc.; the sense is often nearer that of **sich fragen,** *to wonder*:

Die Reiter sagte, sie gehe jetzt. Aber ehe sie es vergesse: ob denn niemand wisse, wo der junge Labude wohne (E. Kästner), *the woman Reiter said she was now going. But before she forgot it, she would like to know if anyone could tell her where L. lived* (**vergesse** and **wohne** are transferred subjunctives).

Ja, fuhr sie fort, wen denn so ein Mensch angehe, so ein hohler, eitler Schwätzer (S. Andres), *yes, she continued, she wondered who cared a rap about a man like that* . . .

(*b*) Equally common in much descriptive writing is the practice of concertina'ing the sense of a verb of indirect statement, question, or request with a descriptive verb, so that the subjunctive appears to depend on that verb:

(1) Indirect statement, with sense of *asserting*:

plötzlich wieder in der Wohnung ihrer Eltern erschien und Sturm läutete, sie wolle den gräßlichen Menschen nicht mehr sehen . . . (S. Zweig), *and roused the house with her protests that* . . .

(2) Indirect question, with sense of *asking*:

wie eines Tages die der Schwindsucht fast erliegende K.I. der Stieftochter vorgeworfen habe, warum sie nicht helfe . . . (R. Guardini), *asked her reproachfully, why she was not helping* . . .

(3) Indirect request, with sense of *telling* . . . *to*:

Danach winkte er die Kellnerin herbei, sie solle ihm einen Kaffee bringen (F. Thiess), *called the waitress and asked her for a coffee.*

(*c*) Often the descriptive verb is one of enquiry or perception, and the sense understood is *to see if*, etc.; this use provides a convenient transition between the subjunctive of indirect speech and that of expectation (below):

Dort (= **an der Endstation) wollten sie sich umschauen und in die Weite schnuppern, wohin es sie weiterziehe** (S. Andres), *look around and see where they felt like going next.*

356. Subjunctive of Expectation (Purpose and Result)

(*a*) The subjunctives of purpose and result are based on the common factor that an expectation that something will be achieved (purpose) or will materialise (result) is not for that reason a certainty; or that some possibility that is open to one (purpose) or which may happen (result) may not in fact be seriously contemplated:

Purpose: **Er bat um die Adresse seiner Retterin, damit er ihr seinen Dank abstatte** (R. Musil), *so that he might thank her.*

Result: **Zu gewaltig war das Frohlocken in ihrem Herzen, als daß sie
hät.e länger sitzenbleiben können** (F. Werfel), *too great was
her feeling of exultation for her to be able to remain seated
any longer.*

(*b*) Statements both of purpose and result often take the indicative
when expectation gives way to certainty, and especially in time relations
other than the past:

Purpose: **Ich telegraphiere nach Köln, daß man mich morgen von der Bahn
abholt,** *I'll send a wire to Cologne for them to . . .*

Result: **Ich bin so froh, daß ich nicht mehr sitzenbleiben kann,** *I am so
pleased that . . .*

(*c*) Most clauses of purpose, and many of result, may be converted
into a prepositional infinitive construction (with or without **um**), if they
share the subject with the main clause:

Purpose: **Er bat um die Adresse seiner Retterin, um ihr seinen Dank
abzustatten,** *so as to thank her.*

Result: **Sie war zu froh, um länger sitzenbleiben zu können,** *too happy to
be able . . .*

357. Subjunctive of Purpose (Verbs)

(*a*) The force of purpose may be expressed by either:

(1) An explicit verb of willing (**wollen,** etc.) or expectation (**warten,**
etc.), or

(2) A specific conjunction, especially **daß** or **damit,** (*so*) *that, v.* § 358.

(*b*) Noun clauses after verbs of willing, etc.

Daß-clauses which are the objects of verbs expressing various aspects
of willing and wishing, as **bitten, raten, sorgen (für), verlangen, wollen,** or
the opposite aspects of preventing, as **verhindern, verhüten, vermeiden,
nicht wollen,** etc., may convey a certain force of purpose directed to the
furthering or prevention of some event:

Ich werde dafür sorgen, daß er die Nachricht zeitig genug bekomme, *see
that he gets the information in time.*

Ich wollte verhindern, daß er einschlafe, *prevent him from falling asleep.*

A positive purpose is common ground with the subjunctive of will or
wish [cp. § 274 (*b*) (2)]; a negative aim brings out the force of purpose
even more clearly (example above).

Note.—An infinitive or other construction may be possible:

Ich wollte ihn daran verhindern, einzuschlafen, or **ihn am Einschlafen
verhindern,** *prevent him from . . .*

(*c*) Adverbial clauses after verbs of waiting, etc.

The subjunctive after **warten, daß** (or **bis** or **ob**) combines a purposive action and an expected result:

Nachmittags saß er in einem großen Zeitungsverlag und wartete, daß Herr Z. Zeit fände (E. Kästner), *waiting till Mr Z. should find time* (or **wartete, bis . . .**).

Man wollte erst abwarten, ob noch was übrigbliebe, *they decided to wait and see whether anything was left over.*

English, when it does not use a prepositional infinitive (*waited for Mr Z. to find time*), may indicate expectation in past contexts by *should* or the subjunctive: *should find time till the house were sold . . .* The indicative in German turns expectation into actual event: **(er) wartete, bis Herr Z. Zeit fand.**

The insertion of *to see whether* in certain English versions (*v.* last example) shows the common ground between this use and that described in § 355 (*c*).

Note.—*v.* also § 362 (conjunctions of time).

358. Subjunctive of Purpose (Conjunctions)

(*a*) The standard conjunction of purpose is **damit** [as that of result is (**so**) **daß**, *v.* § 359 (*a*)], with the subjunctive or, in less formal style, the indicative or a modal (*e.g.* **können**); but with a subject common to main and subordinate statement, **um . . . zu** takes its place:

Teta beschloß: dieser Neffe soll mein Vermittler werden, damit mir der Himmel nicht verloren gehe (F. Werfel), *so that I shall not lose my eternal reward* (less formal: **geht**).

Die Dame bot sich besorgt an, ihn irgendwohin zu fahren, damit er Hilfe fände (R. Musil), *so that he might find help* (less formal: **finden konnte**).

For **um . . . zu,** *v.* Musil example in § 356 (*a*) and (*c*), and §§ 371 f.

When purpose is expressed by verbs of serving, sufficing, and needing (**dienen, reichen, brauchen,** etc.), **damit** is required for the change of subject expressed by the English formula *for . . . to be . . .* (cp. the corresponding **um . . . zu** construction, § 373):

Sie hatte geglaubt, man brauche nur zu sagen: „Ihr Antrag ehrt mich, aber ich kann ihn nicht annehmen,“ damit alles erledigt sei (Th. Mann), *she thought she need only say . . . for everything to be settled.*

Note.—**Damit** may be used with absolute force [corresponding to **um . . . zu,** *v.* § 376 (*b*)]:

Erstens ist euer Altersabstand natürlich unpassend, damit ich nicht sage: anstößig (H. Mann), *the difference in your ages is unsuitable, not to say objectionable.*

(*b*) **Daß** is used as a synonym for **damit,** in clauses of purpose with the subjunctive:

Sie küßte ihn und zog ihn an den Tisch, daß er ihre Vorbereitungen zum Abendessen bewundere (E. Kästner), *for him to admire* . . .

The indicative is used less formally [*v.* first example § 356 (*b*)] but more commonly indicates result [*v.* §§ 202 and 359 (*c*) below].

359. Subjunctive of Result (Manner)

(*a*) The subjunctive of result is found in adverbial clauses of manner (*v.* here), degree (*v.* § 360), and time (*v.* § 362); further in some relative clauses (*v.* § 361).

The standard conjunction of result in adverbial clauses is **daß,** in many different combinations; the subjunctive (as distinct from the indicative, *v.* § 202) is used where the result is expected or envisaged, rather than stated to have happened, *v.* § 356 (*a*). It thus occurs mainly in clauses of manner which have negative or restrictive force.

(*b*) Clauses of result with:

(1) Negative force; these may envisage:

A result which did not happen, commonly after (**anstatt daß** and) **ohne daß:**

Ein Tag nach dem anderen verstrich, ohne daß ich der Vorladung Zouzous Folge geleistet hätte (Th. Mann), *without my having obeyed the invitation of Zouzou.*

Or one which did not "not happen", the so-called excluded negative with **daß nicht:**

eine Sonne, deren Kraft freilich nicht mehr so groß war, daß nicht . . . im Landschaftszimmer schon der Ofen geknistert hätte (Th. Mann), *whose power was no longer so great for the stove not to be alight.*

(2) Restrictive force; these envisage an exception as sole condition for a certain action:

Nach nichts wollte er trachten, als wonach die Stimme ihm zu trachten beföhle, bei nichts verweilen, als wo die Stimme es riete (H. Hesse), *he wished to desire nothing but what the voice (might) bid him desire* . . .

(*c*) Clauses of results without negative or restrictive force normally take the indicative, even if improbable [cp. § 202, especially (*e*) (1)], but **daß** or **so daß** is often associated with the subjunctive of tentative statement (*v.* § 309) in the subordinate clause, thus in:

(1) Expressions of desire:

Oft war sie so müde, und die Beine brannten so höllisch, daß sie sich am liebsten mitten im Menschenstrom auf das Pflaster gesetzt hätte (F. Werfel), *so tired that she would have liked to . . .*

(2) Expressions of approximation, with **fast**:

Trauer befiel sie, daß sie fast auf dem Fleck hingesunken wäre, *sorrow came over her such that she almost . . .*

(*d*) Clauses of negative or restricted result may often be abridged to **um . . . zu** [cp. § 203 (*b*)]; thus the latter example in (*b*) (1) might end:
. . . so groß war, um das Ofenfeuer unnötig zu machen.

360. Subjunctive of Result (Degree)

(*a*) A form of excluded result, with the subjunctive, is common after a statement of degree (including a comparative) and the conjunction **als daß**:

Er ist zu empfindlich, als daß er diese Behandlung leicht vergessen könnte, *too sensitive to be able to . . .* [and cp. example in § 356 (*a*)].

Das Haus ist teurer, als daß wir es ohne Überlegung übernehmen könnten, *dearer than we could contemplate without thinking it over.*

(*b*) This form is commonly abridged to **um . . . zu**:

Er ist zu empfindlich, um diese Beleidigung leicht zu vergessen,
and this is the form in which the excluded negative, amounting to a positive statement [cp. second example, § 359 (*b*) (1)] usually occurs:

Er ist zu empfindlich, um eine solche Behandlung nicht ernst zu nehmen, *too sensitive not to . . .*

361. Subjunctive of Result (Relative Clauses)

(*a*) Relative clauses indicating the expected qualities of a hypothetical antecedent often contain a subjunctive; this is normally closer to result than purpose, but the context may suggest the latter:

Result: **Wo gibt's in der ganzen Welt einen Beruf, der einem Glück und Befriedigung brächte** (less formal: **bringen könnte**), *which would (could) bring one . . .*

Purpose: **Er suchte einen Lebensberuf, der ihm Glück und Einkommen brächte,** *a calling which would bring him . . .*

The indicative occurs when there is a probability that the requirement will be satisfied:

Ich möchte einen Geldbeutel haben, der zwei Fächer hat, *I should like a purse with two compartments* (in a shop).

(b) The subjunctive of expectation in relative clauses, because of its speculative quality, is commonly the past subjunctive, even after a verb in the present [v. first example in (a)]:

Es gibt schlechterdings keinen bedeutenden Gedanken, den die Dummheit nicht anzuwenden verstünde (R. Musil), *not a single important idea which the stupid cannot (could not) also use.*

After a past tense verb, the fulfilment of the speculative quality may be felt to lie in the future (in the past), so that the force is conditional; v. examples under (a), and:

Von der Göttin Fortuna verlangte er einen Geldbeutel, der nie leer würde (= werden würde), *which would never become empty* [cp. indicative example in (a)].

(c) The hypothetical nature of the statement is often reflected in its form, *i.e.* a negative statement [v. first example in (b)], a wish (v. Exercise XLVI, A. 2), or a rhetorical question [v. first example in (a)].

A rhetorical question may even require this subjunctive in a main clause, when the sense combines antecedent and relative:

Welcher Schüler hätte seinen Vater nicht schon mit der Frage „Was ist das?" in Verlegenheit gebracht (newsp.), *where is the schoolboy who has not embarrassed his father . . .?*

362. Subjunctive of Expectation in Time Clauses

(a) Clauses introduced by certain temporal conjunctions may take the subjunctive if the (future) event is envisaged hypothetically; those with **bis, sobald,** etc., have force of purpose, those with **bevor, ehe,** etc., that of (negative) result:

(1) Purpose, v. § 357 (c) for example of **warten, bis . . .,** and:

Sobald er schlecht und recht mit dem langweiligen Humanismus zu Rande gekommen sein würde, wollte er das Polytechnikum besuchen (Th. Mann), *as soon as he was finished with the boring grammar school course he was going in for technical training.*

(2) Result:

Seiner Mutter wollte er seinen Plan eröffnen, ehe sie ihn durch den Vater erführe, *before she learnt of it from his father.*

Both forms take the indicative in less literary statements.

(b) As with other subjunctives of expectation [cp. § 361 (b)], the periphrastic form **würde** is in order [as in example in (1)] because of the conditional force of most of these statements.

Exercise LIV

A. Translate into English:

1. Sie fragte eine Dame, ob in der Nähe vielleicht die Lanzelotstraße liege.—Es sei die Parallelstraße. Sie fügte dem Dank für die Auskunft hinzu: dann kenne sie sich aus und wisse Bescheid (H. Kasack). 2. Und sie fragte ihn auch noch, ob er Tanzunterricht nehmen werde, und er, sofort mit protestierender Stimme, was sie ihm zumute? Ob er sich denn . . . in der Gangart von Lackschuhnegern und fetthüftigen Inflationisten bewegen solle? (S. Andres). 3. . . . die glorreichen Zeiten, wo eine Gräfin Thun sich vor dem großen Dämon (= Beethoven) auf die Knie warf, er möge den „Fidelio" nicht von der Oper zurückziehen (S. Zweig). 4. Und nun saß ich warm und blickte ungeduldig durch die blauüberflossenen Scheiben, wann es dem lästigen Regen belieben würde, sich ein paar Kilometer weiter zu verziehen (S. Zweig). 5. Karlemann, der mit der Urweisheit einer ägyptischen Katze herunterschaute, was sich unten bei den Menschen begab (W. Speyer). 6. So wühlt er appetitlos in der Schüssel, ob sich vielleicht ein Stückchen Schweinefleisch hinein verirrt hat—aber nichts (H. Fallada). 7. „Feinhals, gehen Sie aufs Dach, ob Sie etwas sehen können" (H. Böll). 8. Dies hier ist ein erstes Kapitel, welches verhindern soll, daß vorliegendes Werkchen mit einem Zweiten Kapitel beginne (F. Werfel). 9. (Er) konnte sich keiner Zeit seines Lebens erinnern, die nicht von dem Willen beseelt gewesen wäre, ein bedeutender Mensch zu werden (R. Musil). 10. Es fehlte nur noch, daß ich den Zug versäumt hätte.

B. Translate into German, using the subjunctive where you think appropriate:

1. He asked whether dinner was ready, as he had to watch something on television in half an hour's time. 2. My supposition that he had been the thief proved correct. 3. He suddenly remembered that it was Tuesday, and that this was the day of the trial. 4. His father told me that he was to live at the University in such a way as not to make any debts in future. 5. When the great man arrived he begged his hosts not to reveal his presence to anyone outside the family. 6. He complained a good deal about the noise: who on earth could sleep with cars rushing by at all hours? 7. She had always wanted to find out why he made such a great secret of their money matters. 8. He decided to wait until all the other passengers had got into the bus and then he would give the signal. 9. They worked hard and saved a lot of money so that they should have a carefree old age. 10. He was so happy that he would have liked to sing for joy as he walked along by the river.

CHAPTER LV

THE INFINITIVE AND INFINITIVE CONSTRUCTIONS

Revise §§ 107-8.

363. The Infinitive in Nominal Roles

(a) The infinitive as the subject, object, or complement of a verb appears variously as the simple and prepositional infinitive:

Stiefel und Beinkleider über Füße und Beine ziehen war hier eine turnerische Tätigkeit (G. Hauptmann), *to put on one's boots and trousers over feet and legs was a gymnastic exercise.*

Zu beten erfüllte sie mit einer kühlen Heiterkeit (H. Böll), *praying filled her with a cool serenity.*

(b) The simple infinitive often occupies the leading position as:

(1) The (preceding) object of **es gibt nicht**:

Uns also in den Rücken fallen gibt es nicht (S. Andres), *there's to be no squealing on this job* (one gangster to another).

(2) A form identical with the infinitive noun [cp. § 205 (a)]:

Tiefschürfen ist nicht Sache des modernen Menschen (newsp.), *deep reflection is not something which modern man indulges in.*

or a following position as:

(3) The complement of **heißen**:

Deutsch sein heißt: aufs Ganze gehen (H. Mann), *to be German is to go all out for an object.*

(c) In the leading position the prepositional infinitive is less usual than the simple infinitive, and may often be regarded as an emphatic inversion of the appositional form with **es** [v. § 343 (b)]:

Nein, Sekretärin zu spielen, war nicht ihres Amtes (H. Kasack). *No, it was none of her business to play the secretary* (= **es war nicht . . .**).

Zu sagen, daß sie glücklich waren, genügt nicht. Sie triumphierten (H. Mann), *to say they were happy is not adequate, they were triumphant* (= **es genügt nicht . . .**).

Similarly, the prepositional infinitive as complement of **sein** is perhaps less common in the straightforward form:

Ihre einzige Sorge (ihre erste Pflicht) war, die alte Mutter in ihrem Lebensabend zu versorgen, *her one care (first duty) was to . . .*

than with impersonal **es** leading and linking subject and complement:

Es war ihre einzige Sorge, die alte Mutter . . .

364. The Infinitive in Appositional and Dependent Constructions

(*a*) The prepositional infinitive is the rule in all constructions in apposition to a noun or pronoun (except a demonstrative, *v.* § 365), or dependent on a verb or adjective.

Thus constructions in apposition to:

(1) **es,** either subject or object, *v.* § 343 (*b*), including many where **es** is understood, *v.* there and § 363 (*c*) above.

(2) A noun:

würgte ihn die Scham, von heut auf morgen ein armer Mensch zu sein (H. Kasack), *oppressed by the shame of his sudden descent into poverty.*

Note.—Brief appositions are often alternative to an infinitive noun or a compound: **die Kunst zu reiten, die Kunst des Reitens, die Reitkunst; der Versuch, sie wiederzusehen, der Wiedersehensversuch.**

(*b*) Constructions dependent on:

(1) A verb, *v.* § 107 (*d*), and, for preceding constructions, second example in § 363 (*c*).

(2) An adjective, cp. § 107 (*c*):

„Wie aufrichtig betrübt war ich, mein Fräulein, Sie zu verfehlen!" (Th. Mann), *how disappointed I was to miss you!*

The dependent construction often precedes for emphasis [*v.* § 363 (*c*)]:

Aber es war immer nur Sympathie und Freundlichkeit, was er fand . . . sein Leben zu teilen war niemand gewillt und fähig (H. Hesse), *no one was ready and able to share his life.*

The infinitive dependent on an adjective is close to the modal verbal [*v.* § 249 (*c*)], and the sense may be passive:

Italienisch ist leicht zu lernen, *is easy to learn (can easily be learnt),* = **eine leicht zu erlernende Sprache,** cp. § 279.

Solche Versuche sind nicht hoch anzurechnen, *should not be estimated very highly.*

Note certain alternative constructions: **bereit, den Auftrag zu übernehmen,** or **zur Übernahme des Auftrages bereit; müde zu leben,** or **müde des Lebens** [cp. § 192 (*e*) and (*f*)]; **wert zu erwähnen,** or **erwähnt zu werden,** *worth mentioning (being mentioned),* **des Erwähnens wert, erwähnenswert** [cp. § 192 (*c*)].

(c) The dependent or appositional infinitive may itself take a relative pronoun as object (*the meal which he was too tired to eat*). To prevent it from standing isolated after the end of the relative clause (. . . **zu müde war, zu essen**), it is in accepted practice placed further forward:

(1) In informal and usual practice, before the governing verb:

. . . **die er zu müde zu essen war.**

(2) In literary and formal style, after the relative:

die Bürde, die auf sich zu nehmen nichts verlocken konnte—als die Liebe! (S. Andres), *a burden which nothing but love could tempt him to take upon himself.*

This construction may often be re-construed as a new prepositional infinitive subject consisting of relative and infinitive:

Nun, wozu hier Worte verlieren, wozu Dinge aussprechen, welche zu wissen sich für jeden Denkenden von selbst versteht, welche zu äußern jedoch nicht Sitte ist? (H. Hesse), *things which it is normal for every thoughtful man to know, but not the thing for him to express.* (New subjects: **welche zu wissen, welche zu äußern.**)

But on any interpretation the construction is oblique.

365. The Simple Infinitive in Constructions with Demonstrative Force

(a) As a general rule (cp. §§ 363-4):

(1) The simple infinitive occurs in leading (especially subject) constructions, while

(2) The prepositional infinitive is the rule in following and dependent constructions.

(b) Thus the simple infinitive occurs where the construction acquires some force independent of the grammatical structure of the sentence, as when:

(1) It is summed up (whether as subject or object) by a preceding or following demonstrative:

In der Vergangenheit leben wollen, das sind Betisen (W. Bergengruen), *to want to live in the past is foolish.*

Eine Stunde nachdenken, eine Weile in sich gehen . . .—sieh, das will niemand (H. Hesse), *to reflect for an hour, for a time, that's what no one wants to do.*

Es dauerte lange, bis ihm die höchste Lebensfülle dies bedeutete: Bauer sein (W. Muschg on Gotthelf), *until he saw the highest meaning in life in being a peasant.*

(2) An infinitive follows and is in apposition to a noun, and has emphatic, even quasi-imperative force [cp. **Bauer sein** above and § 248 (d)]:

Parole: sich durchschlagen! *Our motto is—through at all costs!*

Ergebnis: ein Jahr Französisch nachlernen (newsp.), *the result—a year's French to be caught up.*

(3) A course of action is reflected upon:

Den Kaiser um Begnadigung angehen, nun ja . . . (H. Mann), *petition the Emperor for pardon? . . . well, he supposed he could.*

Von Müllhaufen zu Müllhaufen wandern, welch ein unbegreiflich Los der Erbärmlichkeit! (G. Hauptmann), *to wander from one rubbish heap to another, what a wretched lot!*

and cp. § 376 (*a*) (absolute uses).

366. The Infinitive Construction with Relative Force

(*a*) A prepositional infinitive following a noun or pronoun, after *to be* or *to have*, and with relative force, is common in English: *he is the man to ask, he has nothing to do, have you anything to write with?*

It is more restricted in German, occurring only after certain pronouns (**etwas, nichts**); after nouns relative clauses should be used [*v.* § 249 (*f*)], but cp. also § 373 (*c*).

(*b*) The prepositional infinitive may follow certain pronouns: **er hat nichts zu tun, haben Sie etwas zu lesen?, da ist nichts zu fürchten** (or **zum Fürchten**), cp. § 252 (*a*).

The force of this infinitive is (1) passive if related to the pronoun (cp. *nothing to be done*), but (2) active if related to the (logical) subject (cp. *nothing—for one—to do*).

Thus if the infinitive governs the pronouns through a preposition (*something with which to write*), this complication is often ignored [under (2) above]:

„**Haben Sie übrigens etwas zu schreiben bei sich?**" (Th. Mann), *something to write with?*

and in the idiom: **meine Herren, es gibt nichts zu lachen!**

But it is better to relate the infinitive explicitly to the first subject by inserting **um** [cp. § 375 (*a*)]:

eine stattliche weiße Katze . . .; **ich hatte nichts, um sie zu bewirten** (W. Bergengruen), *I had nothing to feed her with.*

(*c*) This use is occasionally found, with active force, after other expressions:

Aber, geht es im großen schief (= **mit der Welt**), **dann ist doch niemand mehr da, die Katastrophe zu bejammern** (W. Bergengruen), *if things go wrong on a large scale there will be no one left to complain.*

**Er beteuerte, stets . . . sei er der Erste, sich ihr (= der Kirche) zu unter-
werfen und zu widerrufen** (W. Andreas), *that he would be the first to submit
and recant.*

(*d*) Analogous to the above senses is the special use of the prepositional infinitive as a predicative complement after certain quasi-auxiliary
verbs, mainly transitive; the force is active or passive according to the
viewpoint [cp. (*b*) above]:

Dort bekomme ich nur Klagen zu hören, *I only hear complaints there.*

Seine Arbeit läßt viel zu wünschen übrig, *his work leaves much to be desired.*

and the common idiom **haben (finden) viel auszusetzen (an),** or **haben
viel einzuwenden (gegen),** *to have (find) much to object to (in):*

(sie) hatte aber noch eine Menge an meinem Äußeren auszusetzen (H. Hesse),
found a lot wrong with my appearance.

Intransitive: **daß er die Balance verlor, . . . und auf den Fußboden zu
sitzen kam** (E. Kästner), *landed up on the floor.*

Note.—This is the nearest use of **haben** to the English idiom *to have to*
(= *must*), with which it is never quite identical:

An diesem Erlebnis . . . hatte Johannes lange zu denken und zu grübeln
(E. Wiechert), *J. had to* (= **mußte**) *think of this experience for a long time,
as he had a lot of thinking to do about* (**an**) *it.*

367. The Infinitive in Statements of Comparison

(*a*) The infinitive follows **als** in certain statements of comparison
introduced by a negative (**nichts, nicht(s) anders als . . .**), or a comparative
(**lieber als . . .**).

(*b*) With a negative, **können** often occurs and may suggest the simple
infinitive:

Hier kann man nicht anders, als glauben (R. Guardini), *here one can only
believe* (= **man kann nur, muß glauben**).

(*c*) But with **tun, tun können,** or a comparative adjective, the prepositional infinitive is used:

**haben wir halbwüchsigen Jungen Jahre nichts getan als Bücher, Bilder,
Musik, Philosophie zu diskutieren** (S. Zweig), *did nothing for years but
argue about . . .*

**Lieber Herr, nichts liegt mir ferner, als diese Bürgerlichkeit und Ordnung
etwa verlachen zu wollen** (H. Hesse), *nothing is further from my thoughts
than to . . .*

368. The Infinitive Governed by a Preposition

(a) The only prepositions which may introduce or govern the **zu** and infinitive construction are **(an)statt, ohne** [English *instead of, without,* and the present participle, *v.* § 203 (*b*)], and **um,** (*in order*) *to, v.* § 108 and below §§ 371 f.   When the preposition marks a change of subject, German has **(an)statt daß, ohne daß** and subordinate clause, English the full gerundial construction [*v.* § 202 (*f*)];   **um** then becomes **damit** [*v.* §§ 202 (*b*) and 358 (*a*)].

(b) All other prepositions govern the infinitive construction indirectly, through a compound adverb of the form **da(r)-,** as **darauf,** etc. [*v.* § 278 (*d*)], with a subordinate clause for change of subject [§ 278 (*e*)].

Note.—(1) **Dazu** has a special use, *v.* §§ 108 (*c*) and 372 (*d*); (2) the combined construction of purpose *for . . . to . . .* (*it is hopeless for him to expect . . .*) must be resolved into a subordinate clause [cp. § 358 (*a*)]:

Damit sein Plan gelingt, muß er alle Kräfte anspannen, *for his plan to succeed he must make every effort.*

except in the few cases where **für** governs a personal object in its full sense (cp. § 451):

Es ist für ihn schwer, . . . zu . . ., *it is difficult for him to . . .*

369. The Infinitive Governed by a Verb

(a) With the exception of those verbs which require the simple infinitive (*v.* §§ 63 and 109), any verb taking a dependent infinitive requires it with **zu.**   But many German verbs [*e.g.* those of certain mental processes, *v.* § 107 (*e*) (2)] permit a dependent infinitive in German while taking *that* and a clause in English, or vice versa.

(b) Again, in the objective predicate construction (noun or pronoun object and prepositional infinitive, cp. § 433), verbs of thinking and saying are used widely with the infinitive in English while needing **daß** and a clause in German, thus:

(1) Saying: to admit, announce, declare, prove, report, etc.
We declared him to have deserved the prize, **wir erklärten, daß . . .**

(2) Thinking: to believe, expect, like, prefer, want, etc.
We like you to come in time, **wir erwarten, daß . . .**

Note.—(i) German often permits a simple alternative with a preposition [cp. § 435 (*a*) (2)], often valuable when rendering the English passive of this form: *the wages were believed to be adequate,* **man hielt den Lohn für ausreichend; es wurde dafür gehalten, daß die Löhne völlig ausreichten.**
(ii) The only remnant in German of this use is a limited range of idioms

with an adjective, and **sein** understood: **ich glaube ihn glücklich,** *believe him to be happy;* **wir vermuten ihn tot,** *assume him to be dead.*

370. The Logical Subject of the Prepositional Infinitive

(*a*) The infinitive is, as its name states, a non-finite part of the verb; it cannot therefore have a grammatical subject. But its action must be relatable to some (logical) subject, and this may be specific or general.

(*b*) Specific subject. The infinitive, if dependent, is normally assumed to refer to the grammatical subject of the main statement [cp. § 107 (*f*)]:

Ich bin jetzt in der Lage, ein neues Haus zu kaufen, *I am now in a position to buy* . . .

(1) But by accepted usage it may relate to the (accusative or dative) object of the main verb:

Ich bat ihn, bald zu kommen, *asked him to come soon,*

Ich riet (befahl) ihm, schleunig zu gehen, *advised (ordered) him to* . . .

(2) Infinitives with **(an)statt, ohne** may not, however, thus refer to an object; if the subject is other than that of the main verb, a clause takes their place [*v.* § 202 (*f*)].

Note.—But they may take as logical subject a preceding logical subject:

Ich riet *ihm,* in die Stadt zu *fahren,* ohne auf mich zu *warten.*

(*c*) General subject. The infinitive is related in most other cases to the general sense of the context:

(1) In nominal functions, cp. examples in § 363 and cp. § 343 (*b*).

(2) In apposition to nouns or pronouns, cp. examples in § 364 (*a*), and (*b*) above, and: **es ist Zeit, sich schlafen zu legen,** *time to go to bed.*

(3) In absolute constructions, *v.* § 376.

Note.—Both the simple and prepositional infinitive may refer to a generalised unstated object of a preceding verb, thus:

Ich ließ einschenken, *I ordered (them) to fill the glasses* (cp. § 215).

Ich bitte zu bedenken, daß . . ., *I would ask (you) to consider* [cp. § 377 (*e*)].

and a preceding object is often that of the *dependent* verb:

Ich bitte, das zu bedenken; ich ließ Wein einschenken [§ 215 (*b*)].

371. Statements of Purpose with Zu and Um . . . Zu

(*a*) The preposition **zu,** through long formal association with the infinitive, no longer expresses explicitly the force of purpose or intention, which has been transferred to the prepositional group **um . . . zu . . .** Thus theoretically one might expect:

(1) **zu** (alone) in contexts not expressive of purpose [*e.g.* § 363 (*c*)], or where the intentional force is already adequately expressed by a governing noun, adjective, or verb:

versuchen (gewillt, der Wunsch), Geld zu verdienen.

(2) **um . . . zu . . .** in the sense *in order to*, where purpose might not otherwise be inferred from the sense of the main statement:

A. beschleunigte seinen Schritt, um zum Bahnhof zu gelangen (H. Broch), *quickened his pace to reach the station . . .*

(*b*) However, the endless shades of meaning requiring expression by only two forms (**zu** or **um . . . zu . . .**), and the fact that **zu** is not entirely without purposive force, nor **um . . . zu . . .** entirely concerned with expressing purposive force, leads to considerable fluctuations in usage. English also does not distinguish precisely between *to, so as, in order to*, etc. Some comments on outstanding points are offered in §§ 372-4.

372. Zu in Purposive Contexts

(*a*) Usage is particularly uncertain with verbs of action and motion, which often take **zu** where **um . . . zu . . .** might be expected:

Da zog er die Jacke aus und sprang, das Kind zu retten, hinterher (E. Kästner), *jumped in after the child to rescue it.*

die alte Dame, die nun ihrerseits die Hand ausstreckte, sie ihm zur Begrüßung zu reichen (H. Broch), *stretched out her hand to give it him in greeting.*

Thus often where **gehen** or **kommen** are used in a semi-auxiliary function (cp. English *to go and see, to come and look*, etc.):

Frau Lux ging in die Stube, den Hut zu suchen (L. Frank), *went to look for her hat.*

Such verbs may also take the simple infinitive, cp. § 109, especially (*b*) (2).

(*b*) Similarly in descriptive passages where intention can only be imputed, or an apparent intention suggested:

Es war, als senkte sie (= die Wolkendecke) sich immer tiefer herab, sich mit der emporsteigenden Straße zu vereinigen (H. Broch), *sank ever lower to join the rising road.*

(*c*) Given the implicit intention, waiting or inaction may equally dispense with **um**:

Konfetti hagelte, Papierschlangen hüllten sie ein, und sie saßen stocksteif, diese Zier nicht zu zerreißen (H. Fallada), *and they sat stiffly unmoving so as not to tear these decorations.*

(*d*) Many verbs and adjectives with purposive force, *e.g.* expressing (i) intention, (ii) sufficiency [for these two *v.* § 108 (*c*) and § 373 below], or (iii) using for or serving a purpose (as **benutzen, dienen, gehören**) are or may be followed by the adverbial compound **dazu**, which points to the following infinitive construction; it is quite distinct from the **zu** of the infinitive proper, and may precede either **zu** or **um . . . zu . . .** constructions.

Die Hilfsverben dienen als Kopula dazu, andere Wortarten zum Prädikativum zu machen (Duden), *auxiliary verbs serve to make other parts of speech into predicates.*

373. Statements of Sufficiency, etc., with Um . . . Zu . . .

(*a*) Expressions indicating that a certain amount, degree, length of time, etc., is (in)sufficient to achieve a certain purpose or result are commonly, but not necessarily, followed by **um . . . zu . . .** Among the commoner expressions are:

(1) Verbs of needing and sufficing, as quoted and exemplified in § 108 (*b*).

(2) Adverbs of degree, as **zu,** *too,* and **so,** *so*:

zu bequem, um tanzen zu lernen, *too lazy to learn to dance.*

Nicht so taub bin ich geworden, um nicht zu hören das Brausen der Bomber . . . (F. Werfel), *I am not so deaf as not to hear . . .*

(3) Time expressions of the form (*only*) *waiting for . . . to . . .*:

Die Straßenwände wankten wie Kulissen, hinter denen etwas auf das Stichwort wartet, um herauszutreten (R. Musil), *swayed like scenery behind which something was only waiting for the word to emerge . . .*

(*b*) The sense of conformity between a given cause and effect is

(1) Prominent in many examples under (*a*), thus:

wandernde Wolkenschatten, die der Sonne bedurften, um als solche empfunden zu werden (F. Thiess), *which need the sun (if they are) to be recognised as such.*

(2) Most clear after **müssen,** which posits a necessary condition if a certain effect is to happen:

Menschen sind nun einmal ungläubige Thomasse, die erst sehen müssen, um glauben zu können (F. Thiess), *who have to see (if they are) to believe.*

(3) And may apply to certain nouns, especially **Mittel** and **Weg(e),** *ways* and *means,* where it has the force of a relative:

ein vorzügliches Mittel, um Schmerzen zu stillen (H. Hesse), *an excellent remedy for pain (with which to relieve pain).*

Ich wollte nach Hause, aber . . . da wäre keine Mama gewesen, um den dummen Buben zu trösten (H. Hesse), *but I would have found no mother there to console (who could console) the silly boy* [cp. § 366 (c), first example].

(c) Finally, in negative statements, **um . . . zu . . .** may be used for an effect which is excluded, a limit expressly not reached:

Denn Schwermut und Heiterkeit sind ja . . . aufeinander zugeschaffen, freilich nicht, um sich aufzuheben (W. Bergengruen), *melancholy and cheerfulness are interrelated—though not to the degree that they cancel each other out.*

(d) The above statements show how **um . . . zu . . .** may measure the degree appropriate to effect a given result, and is therefore only in one aspect of its use properly intentional in force.

374. Um . . . Zu . . . with Verbs of Action and Motion

(a) Constructions with **um . . . zu . . .** are often used to add vividness to the sequence of events in narrative style; it is often difficult to distinguish this use from that of genuine intention. Thus in:

Und wenn er einmal die kleine Klara auf die Knie genommen hatte, um ihr vielleicht eines seiner drolligen Lieder vorzusingen (Th. Mann), *had taken her on his knee and sung one of his funny songs—*

the second event might seem intended in the first; but the continuation:

so konnte er plötzlich stillschweigen, um dann die Enkelin zu Boden zu setzen und sich abzuwenden, *he often suddenly fell silent, and then set his grandchild down and turned away—*

dispels this impression.

(b) This non-intentional use of **um . . . zu . . .** in narrative is often criticised, and it is easy to select examples which may be made to appear ridiculous:

Nach ihrer Vereinigung trennten sie sich, um nie einander wiederzusehen (H. Mann), *never to see each other again* (as it happened; though—such is the drama of human life—they were oblivious of it then).

But in the light of the uses of **um . . . zu . . .** to express a certain conformity in cause and effect (*v.* § 373), it cannot be denied that many effective writers justifiably use the form in narrative style to suggest a certain conformity in human affairs which is (1) superior to the knowledge of man (example above), or (2) at least to that of some men:

in einem Variété-Theater, wo . . . ein Zauberkünstler jemandes goldene Uhr in einem Mörser zerstampfte, um sie dann einem völlig unbeteiligten Zuschauer . . . wohlbehalten aus der hinteren Hosentasche zu ziehen (Th.

Mann), *pounded up someone's gold watch in a mortar—and then (to everyone's surprise) drew it undamaged from . . .*

375. Logical Subject of the Infinitive with Um . . . Zu . . .

(a) Specific subject (cp. § 370).   The action of the infinitive is strictly related to the subject of the main verb; if it is to be related to any other subject (thus the object of the main verb), a subordinate clause with **damit** [v. § 358 (a)] or **als daß** (v. § 360) should be used.

(b) General subject.   The infinitive after **um . . . zu . . .** may relate to the general sense of the context:

(1) In apposition to a noun, v. examples in § 373 (b).

(2) In absolute constructions, v. § 376 (b).

376. Absolute and Abbreviated Infinitive Constructions

(a) The simple infinitive is used unrelated:

(1) In direct and indirect questions with a modal verb (especially **sollen**) understood:

Na, wozu Lärm machen und die Leute beunruhigen! (H. Hesse), *why make a fuss and disturb people* (= **soll man**).

Auf der Straße überlegte er, wohin sich wenden (H. Broch), *he considered where he should go* (= **er sich wenden sollte**).

(2) In absolute constructions, where the thought is too generalised to have finite form:

Nicht auf den Lorbeeren ausruhen (newsp. heading to an article on Germany's economic achievements), *No resting on the nation's laurels!*
Moment . . . Mal horchen, was sich in der Weltgeschichte tut (E. Kästner, a comment in a newsp. office), *Let's see what's happening in world history.*

The above two uses are not clearly distinct, and many brief statements may be explained under either: **Was da tun?** *what can we do?* **Herr Ober! Bitte zahlen,** *waiter, the bill please;* cp. also § 365 (b).

(b) Many absolute statements with **zu,** and especially **um . . . zu . . .,** are parenthetical comment: **die Wahrheit zu reden,** *to tell the truth;* **seltsam zu sagen,** *strange to say;* **um die Dinge beim Namen zu nennen,** *to call things by their right names;* **um kurz zu sein (um das Ergebnis gleich vorwegzunehmen),** *to cut a long story short,* etc.

(c) In informal or vivid speech a construction with **zu** or **um . . . zu . . .** may be replaced by simple coordination:

Die ist imstand und steckt ihr ganzes Vermögen in den Koffer zwischen die Hemden . . . dachte Herr S. (L. Frank), *she's capable of putting her whole fortune into the trunk between her chemises.*

EXERCISE LV

A. Translate into ENGLISH:

1. „Das Leben lieben und zugleich die Menschen verachten, das geht selten gut aus," sagte F. (E. Kästner). 2. Sich zum Schatten und Echo eines anderen machen, ist eines denkenden Menschen unwürdig und macht lächerlich (F. G. Jünger). 3. Kürze soll eine Tugend sein, aber sich kurz fassen, heißt meistens auch, sich grob fassen (Th. Fontane). 4. Ein breites Lächeln ging in seinen Zügen auf, das ein Grinsen zu nennen ich mich scheue, denn es war verhüllt schmerzlich (F. Werfel). 5. Was hatte er hier in dieser Stadt, in diesem verrückt gewordenen Steinbaukasten, zu suchen? (E. Kästner). 6. Fräulein M. läuft eilig in der Schreibstube von Platz zu Platz, zu sehen, wo das Hamburger Adreßbuch liegt (H. Fallada). 7. An solchen Tagen mußte man auf die Marina (= coastal strip) blicken, um zu ahnen, was Leben heißt (E. Jünger). 8. Bei jedem ungewöhnlichen Geräusch hinter der Tür seiner Zelle klopfte ihm das Herz, um nur müder zu schlagen, wenn nichts erfolgte (H. Mann). 9. Er sprang in die Küche hinauf, schickte Teresa in sein Zimmer, das Köfferchen aufzuräumen, und . . . (S. Andres). 10. Und dann saßen sie wieder stumm da, die Lampe brannte still weiter, und sie wußten wieder nicht, wovon reden (H. Fallada).

B. Translate into GERMAN, using infinitive constructions when possible:

1. His remarks cannot be taken seriously. 2. She said many other things that day which he was too excited to take amiss. 3. Wise shopping and good cooking—that is only a small part of a housewife's responsibility. 4. "He wants to talk to you personally."—"But there's nothing to talk about," grumbled the other. 5. He would be the last man to commit an injustice of this kind. 6. In addition to his fear he had to suffer great physical pain because of the cold. 7. He had much fault to find with the new assistant who had been sent to work in the shop. 8. They expected the train to get them there punctually. 9. The porter was considered to be responsible and to have failed in his duty. 10. Why waste money and make yourself miserable?

CHAPTER LVI

THE GOVERNMENT OF THE VERB

377. The Object of the Verb. Transitive Verbs

(*a*) The general division of verbs, in respect of their objects, into transitive (with object in accusative), and intransitive (with no object or one in the dative), needs in some degree to be modified:

(1) A transitive verb may be used with (specific or general) object understood, *v.* below;

(2) Intransitive verbs may take certain special objects, *v.* § 378.

(*b*) Certain unstated specific objects are clear from the situation:

Sie machte auf, schloß hinter sich ab (= **die Tür**), **legte ab** (= **Mantel und Hut**), *she opened, closed the door, took off her hat and coat.*

Darf ich Ihnen einschenken? (= **Tee**, etc.), *may I give you another cup?*

Darf ich kassieren? (= **Geld**), *will you settle the bill?* (from waitress).

(*c*) Certain general and indefinite objects:

(1) Direct polite address (**Sie,** or the polite third person form: **die Herrschaften**):

Darf ich nach links (ins Zimmer) bitten? *would you please come to the left* (*into the room*)—often from a servant, guide.

(2) Unspecified persons (**Leute, Gäste,** etc.):

Baronin Kirchenmaus—verarmter Adel—hatte zum Tee eingeladen (Simpl.), *Baroness Churchmouse—an impoverished aristocrat—had people to tea.*

(3) People in general [**die Menschen, einen**—*v.* § 60 (*b*)]:

Die Liebe bringt auf Ideen und Gefahren (H. Mann), *love is a serious and a dangerous matter.*

Note.—Dative verbs also appear thus: **ich gratulierte (ihm),** *I congratulated him,* cp. § 98 (*a*) (2).

(*d*) Such verbs would, in English, often have appropriate non-personal objects: *to offer one's congratulations* (above); **einladen,** *to issue invitations;* **haben Sie bestellt?** *have you given your order?* (waitress).

(*e*) The unstated (general) object may be the logical subject of a following infinitive: **ich bitte einzutreten,** *please come in* [*v.* § 370 (*c*) Note].

378. The Object of the Verb. Intransitive Verbs

An intransitive verb may be accompanied by noun objects in varying degrees cognate with its meaning, and elucidating more fully the verbal sense.

(*a*) General cognate sense. **Er schlief den Schlaf des Gerechten,** *the sleep of the just;* **sie starb einen milden Tod,** *a peaceful death.*

and especially the cognate objects of **gehen,** etc., as: **seinen Weg gehen,** *to go one's way;* **einen langen Weg kommen,** *to (have) come a long way,* and:

Ein Dampfer geht zwischen uns und der Küste gleichen Kurs (G. Hauptmann), *is keeping the same course* . . .

(*b*) Specific cognate sense of mode of progression or activity. **Schlittschuh laufen,** *to skate;* **Eisenbahn fahren,** *to go by rail;* **Wache stehen,** *to stand on guard.*

These are usually abbreviated from a phrase (**mit der Eisenbahn**), and may be in process of joining the verb as a prefix (**radfahren,** *to cycle,* but still: **ich fahre Rad**), §§ 88 (*d*) and 300 (*b*).

(*c*) The accusative of result, *v.* § 386.

(*d*) English also has:

(1) A cognate accusative of a part of the body, e.g. *he stamped his foot, v.* § 384 (*b*).

(2) An intransitive verb used factitively, where German requires **lassen** and a dependent infinitive: *to run the* (*bath*)*water,* **das Badewasser laufen lassen;** *to curdle the milk,* **die Milch gerinnen lassen.** It was almost certainly an English communiqué that caused a reporter to write:

Man wird . . . Männer, Frauen und Kinder aus Berlin herausfliegen (newsp.), *fly out of Berlin* (= **herausfliegen lassen, transportieren**).

(*e*) The analogy with a transitive verb of similar sense (as **herausfliegen = transportieren**) accounts for some occasional forms:

Nach einer Stunde frühstückte man einige Schinkenbrötchen und trank Portwein dazu (Th. Mann), *breakfasted off* (= **aß zum Frühstück**).

379. The Genitive Object

(*a*) Normal genitive object, *v.* § 189.

Note.—Earlier the genitive was used with partitive force after *e.g.* verbs of consumption, as **essen, trinken** (cp. § 192, partitive force after adjective): **Wer dieses Wassers trinkt, den wird wieder dürsten** (Joh. iv. 13);

and more recently with causal force: **Hungers sterben,** *to die of hunger* (cp. § 517, **an**).

(*b*) The adverbial accusative in a cognate sense after verbs of motion [*v.* § 378 (*a*)] has its counterpart in an adverbial genitive still common in formal language: **seines Weges gehen,** *to go on one's way.*

380. The Dative Case
Revise §§ 97 f. and 167 f.

(*a*) The sense of (dis)advantage or communication usually present in a verb with dative object does not exclude non-personal objects:

Von uns andern lebt jeder nur dem Augenblick und sich selbst (H. Mann), *each one lives for the moment and for himself.*

But a number of verbs may take a personal object in the dative and/or a non-personal one in the accusative:

befehlen, gebieten, *to command:* **er befahl ihm, . . . zu . . .; der Befehls-haber befahl einen Rückzug,** *ordered a retreat.*

glauben, *to believe:* **ich glaube Ihnen; das kann ich (Ihnen) nicht glauben,** *I can't believe that.*

sagen, *to tell:* **Sagen Sie mir die Wahrheit!**

helfen, nützen, schaden may take a neuter pronoun object, **es, nichts, etwas, was: das hilft etwas, schadet nichts, was nützt das? ich kann es nicht helfen,** *I can't do anything about it.*

(*b*) Alternatively a dative verb may take a personal object in the accusative in special contexts:

(1) In a more material, external sense than the dative:

Der Junge ahmt seinem Vater nach, *imitates his father* (= emulates), **ahmt die Mutter nach,** *imitates* (= parodies speech, gait, etc.).

But the presence of an accusative non-personal object transfers the personal object, even in the external sense, to the dative:

Der Junge ahmt ihr den Gang nach, *imitates her gait.*

Hast du den Schneider bezahlt? *paid* (*off*), **Hast du dem Schneider den Anzug bezahlt?** *paid the tailor for the suit.*

Note.—**versichern** in this case takes accusative and genitive [*v.* § 383 (*b*)]:

ich versichere Ihnen, daß . . ., *assure you that . . .;* **ich versicherte ihn des Gegenteils,** *assured him of the contrary.*

(2) In the context of result [*v.* § 386 (*b*)]:

Berittene Polizei wartete hinter der Sperrkette darauf, zur Attacke befohlen zu werden (E. Kästner), *were waiting to be brought in to attack.*

(c) **Rufen,** and other verbs of communication (**klingeln, schreien, winken,** etc.), have several constructions illustrating the above statements [v. also § 172 (b)]:

(1) A personal gesture, a following prefix and dative:

sie rief ihm Zärtlichkeiten zu, schrie ihm Verwünschungen nach, *called out endearments to him, shouted abuse after him.*

(2) Simple communication, dative:

sie rief ihrem Jungen, klingelte dem Diener, *called, rang (for).*

(3) More peremptory communication, accusative (of result):

sie rief den Jungen ins Haus, winkte den Wagen heran, *beckoned up.*

381. Nouns with the Dative

(a) Apart from verbs, and adjectives [v. §§ 289 and 392 (b) below], nouns also sometimes have the dative; this may be one of two forms:

(1) The dative of a verb understood:

Ehre seinem Andenken, *honour to his memory* (= sei, *be paid*);

eine Schmach der Gesellschaft (R. Musil), *an insult to society* (= **eine der Gesellschaft angetane Schmach**).

„Dem Vaterland sein letzter Gedanke", rühmte der Nachruf (H. Mann), *his last thought was for his country, as the obituary said* (= **galt**).

(2) The dative of reference or interest (cp. § 382):

Er war mir Bruder und Mann zugleich, *both a brother and husband to (for) me,* cp. also § 284 (b) (**er war mir freund, feind**).

(b) In neither case may the dative be properly said to be governed by the noun.

382. The Dative of Interest or Reference

(a) The dative may stand in a more general sense than that of the dative verbs proper, and in association with other verbs, to indicate the person or thing to which the action of the verb is referred, or who is directly or indirectly interested in this action. This dative, though not clearly distinct from the narrower verbal dative, is not properly governed by the verb at all, but is a function of the whole sentence, and thus is often called "sentence dative". It is known in English only in the very restricted form of the (Shakespearean) ethical dative: *he that kills me some six or seven dozen of Scots at a breakfast* (*I Henry IV*, II, 4). Modern English omits it in translation or uses a possessive adjective, v. examples below.

(*b*) Reference.

So war das Reich, das um die Marmor-Klippen dem Blick sich rundete (E. Jünger), *spread out for the eye to see.*

Allen, die mir Schüler waren und Freunde wurden, *to all who were my pupils and became my friends* (book dedication).

A preposition is often alternative, as in the special case of the adjectives from verbs by suffixes **-bar, -lich, -sam** [**dem Auge sichtbar,** *v.* § 289 (*e*)]; but there may be a distinction of sense: **die Jacke ist für mich** (when first inspected), or **mir** (when wearing it) **zu groß.**

(*c*) Interest.

Er brannte sich eine Zigarre an (E. Kästner), *lit a cigar,* and cp. first example in § 380 (*a*). The sense is often of deprivation:

Schon das Jahr darauf starb ihm die Frau (H. Mann), *his wife died.*

The "ethical dative" may be considered as expressing emotional rather than material interest; any dative pronoun may occur, but the first person is common:

Schöne Düsseldorfer, setzte sie hinzu, seien sie ihr alle vier! (Th. Mann), *they were fine Düsseldorf people!* (never to have seen a local sight). (She said: **Ihr seid mir . . .!**).

(*d*) Relation to the person.

The dative by which an event is related to the person in whom it occurred, or to another person, may be regarded as partaking of both the dative of reference and of interest. Uses are numerous, but three may be distinguished:

(1) An internal event related to a part of the body:

kalter Schweiß brach ihm aus, *broke out on him;* **ich wußte nicht, wo mir der Kopf stand,** *whether I was on my head or my feet;* **mir lachte das Herz im Leibe,** *my heart jumped with joy.*

Der Richter stutzte, obwohl eine Stirnader ihm anschwoll (H. Mann), *although a vein started swelling on his forehead.*

(2) A reflexive action, with the reflexive pronoun as dative of reference: **sich** (dat.), **den Fuß verstauchen,** *to sprain one's foot* [cp. § 184 (*b*)—Note (2), (3)].

(3) A communication of feeling to another, as with the verbs **erregen, erwecken,** *to arouse* (*in someone*), **Eindruck machen,** *to produce an impression* (*on someone*):

Gereiztheit war es offenbar, was meine Gegenwart ihr erregte (Th. Mann), *it was clearly irritation that my presence aroused in her.*

der **Eindruck, den sie ihm machte** (H. Mann), *the impression she made on him.*
Cp. also § 385 (actions to the body).

383. Verbs with Double Object

(*a*) Many verbs are used with two objects, usually in different cases, and commonly referring to the person and the thing affected by the action. Many such expressions are given in the special sections on actions to the body (§ 385), objects of result (§ 386), and the objective predicate (§§ 149 f.). The various possibilities of double objects may, however, be summarised here:

VERBS	OBJECT OF THE PERSON	THE THING	REFERENCE
Giving, Saying, etc.	Dative	Accusative	§§ 16, 99, 171.
Legal and Logical, etc.	Accusative	Genitive	(*b*) below.
Various.	Accusative	Prepositional	(*c*) below.
Various.	Dative	Prepositional	(*d*) below.
Various.	Accusative	Accusative	(*e*) below.

The first, personal object, may in all classes be a reflexive pronoun (*v.* schematic table, § 184). The personal object normally precedes the impersonal object, *v.* examples below (but for the first class *v.* fully § 16).

(*b*) Accusative and genitive verbs are of widely differing sense, but include many verbs expressive of legal and logical relations, as:

(1) Removal or deprivation: **berauben, entkleiden,** *to deprive* (*of*); **entlasten, erleichtern,** *to relieve* (*of*); **entwöhnen,** *to break* (*of a habit*); **sich entledigen,** *to get rid* (*of*).

(2) Mental processes, such as verbs for *to accuse* (**anklagen, beschuldigen**), and *to convict* (**überführen**); **überzeugen,** *to convince;* **versichern,** *to assure* [*v.* § 380 (*b*) (1), Note]; **sich vergewissern,** *to assure* (*convince*) *oneself.*

Many such verbs increasingly use a preposition for the genitive:

Man verwies ihn des Landes (aus dem Lande), *he was banished from the country;* **sie hat ihn des Rauchens (vom Rauchen) entwöhnt,** *broken him of (the habit of) smoking.*

(*c*) Accusative and prepositional verbs include:

(1) A few primary ones: **bitten um, fragen nach,** *to ask for, about:* **Zwischendurch fragte Z. seinen Sohn nach seinen Tagesaufgaben** (E. Wiechert), *now and then (at breakfast) Z. asked his son about his schoolwork.* and an increasing number which are transferring from (*b*), above, as **erinnern an** (instead of genitive).

(2) Many other verbs when used for actions to the body, § 385 (*a*).

(*d*) Dative and prepositional verbs include:

(1) A few primary ones: **berichten über/von,** *to report about;* **raten zu,** *to advise* (*something*); **gratulieren zu,** *to congratulate* (*on*):

ich rate (Ihnen) zu einer guten Zigarre, *I advise* (*you to smoke*) *a good cigar.*

But **beglückwünschen zu** takes accusative of the person, as in (*c*).

(2) Many other verbs when used for actions to the body, § 385 (*b*).

(3) **helfen** when used with prepositional phrases of result, § 386 (*b*).

(*e*) Double accusative verbs are abandoning this for other constructions [especially dative and accusative, cp. § 380 (*d*)], through a desire to differentiate the case of the two objects. But (in spite of controversy and many infractions of the rule) the double accusative is still correct after **kosten,** *to cost,* and **lehren,** *to teach*:

es kostete mich Mühe, er lehrte ihn Deutsch, *it cost me some trouble, he taught him German.*

Lehren is supported in this construction by the fact that the non-personal object is often an infinitive, and thus indistinguishable from the infinitive noun (**er lehrte ihn Singen/singen**); those who are uncertain often use **unterrichten: er unterrichtete ihn im Englischen.**

A few verbs take a double accusative in certain contexts only:

(1) **bitten** and **fragen** with a neuter pronoun:

Was hat er Sie gefragt? Eins möchte ich dich bitten.

(2) **führen,** etc., with an adverbial accusative [cp. § 378 (*a*)]:

Er führte den blinden Mann den Weg zurück, *led the blind man back.*

384. Actions of or with the Body

(*a*) Actions of or with the body, or close extensions of the body, as clothes, food, instruments, etc., always have the definite article in German, while English consistently uses the possessive or the noun alone:

er schloß die Augen, *his eyes,* **hielt den Mund,** *his tongue* (*peace*), **erschien mit dem Hut in der Hand,** (*his*) *hat in* (*his*) *hand;* **haben Sie schon zu Abend gegessen?** *have you had your* (pop.) *supper?*

Extensions of the person include many immaterial entities:

er verlor das Leben, das Gleichgewicht, den inneren Frieden, das Bewußtsein, *he lost his life, his balance, his peace of mind, consciousness.*

When the action becomes reflexive *to* the body, the dative reflexive is added to an accusative: **das Kind hat sich die Augen wundgerieben,** *inflamed its eyes by rubbing* [*v.* § 386 (*c*)].

Objects only shed the possessive when they are actually associated with the person [cp. § 382 (*b*), last example], thus:

Wo ist mein Glas, meine Zigarette, meine Jacke? *Where is . . .?* But:

Er hob das Glas, *raised his glass,* **machte sich die Jacke schmutzig,** *dirtied his jacket,* and:

Heute morgen hatte ich zur Zigarette . . . (Th. Mann), *over my cigarette . . .*

The number may differ from English in distributive contexts:

> **Viele Soldaten verloren dabei das Leben,** *lost their lives.*

Note.—*One's own* is always: **eigen; auf eigene Verantwortung,** *at one's own risk,* **jeder hat eine eigene Meinung,** *each has his own view.*

(*b*) An action with a part of the body or a close extension in an instrumental sense may take the direct object in English, but needs a prepositional object (**mit**) in German:

er nickte mit dem Kopf, *nodded his head;* **sie winkte mit dem Taschentuch,** *waved her handkerchief;* **der Hund wedelte mit dem Schwanz,** *wagged his tail.*

(*c*) **Fahren** is used for a rapid or semi-involuntary action, with literal or figurative force, followed by **mit**:

Sie fuhr mit der Hand in die Tasche, *she felt quickly in her handbag* (or: *her hand went to her handbag*).

„Da fahren wir drein!" **grollte der General** (H. Mann), *we shall have a word to say there!* (lit., *intervene decisively*).

(*d*) A mutual action between two or more persons needs **sich** only if there is no accusative object, or if the verb governs the dative primarily:

sie liebten sich, *loved (each other),* **wechselten die Plätze,** *changed places,* **gaben sich die Hand** [distributive sense, *v.* (*a*)], *shook hands.*

Cp. also § 183 (*a*) (2) (reciprocals).

385. Actions to the Body or Person of Another

(*a*) After certain verbs, especially but not entirely those of a violent nature (*to beat,* etc.), the object of the action is the whole person, which is represented by a noun or pronoun in the accusative:

der Vater schlug das Kind, *hit the child,* **die Schlange biß ihn,** *bit him;* **die Kavallerie schlug mit der flachen Klinge auf die Demonstranten,** *belaboured the demonstrators with . . .*

A preposition introduces the part of the body involved:

er küßte sie auf die Stirn, *kissed her on the forehead;* **sie stieß ihn in die Seite,** *nudged him;* **er faßte ihn am Arm,** *grasped his arm.*

ihre Brüder, die sich ein Vergnügen daraus machten, sie in die Nase zu beißen, . . . sie an den Zöpfen zu ziehen (E. Langgässer), *to bite her nose and pull her plaits.*

Note the cases governed, with accusative of motion predominating.

(*b*) Other actions are felt to be directed primarily towards a certain part, the whole person being involved only indirectly, and thus in the dative; the part of the body may be governed:

(1) In the accusative:

er küßte ihr die Hand, *kissed her hand;* **die Kugel nahm ihm glatt die Nase weg,** *took his nose right off.*

(2) Or through a preposition:

das Wasser reichte ihnen bis an die Knöchel, *reached their ankles;* **das Wort kam ihm auf die Zunge,** *was on his tongue;* **er las ihr sein Schicksal vom Auge ab,** *read his fate in her eyes* [*v.* § 384 (*a*), distributive].

(*c*) If the action is reflexive, the same distinction is observed:

(1) Direct: **er schlug sich (vor den Kopf),** *struck himself (his forehead).*

(2) Indirect: **er kämmte sich das Haar,** *combed his hair,* **schnitt sich in den Finger,** *cut his finger,* cp. § 184, Note (3).

(*d*) English has the two forms under (*a*) above: *kissed her* (*on the forehead*), but under (*b*) has only form (1): *kissed her hand,* and on the whole prefers to use throughout this direct action to a part of the body, the interest of the person as a whole appearing in the possessive.

(*e*) The distinction between forms (*a*) and (*b*) may be summarised:

(1) The accusative of the person is more general and direct, the dative more specific and indirect, thus cp.:

er griff ihn am Arm, *grasped his arm* (to arrest his attention, etc.), **er griff ihm an den Arm,** *grasped at his arm* (*e.g.* to remove an insect).

(2) Statements with the dative of the person show a preponderance of (i) figurative expressions: **er fällt seinem Vater auf die Tasche,** *depends* (*financially*) *on his father;* (ii) involuntary actions: **er fuhr ihr über das Haar,** *ran his hand over her hair;* (iii) actions by inanimate objects: **der Stein schlug ihm auf den Kopf,** *fell on his head;* (iv) perfective actions: **man schlug ihm den Kopf ab,** *struck off his head.*

386. The Accusative and Predicate of Result

(*a*) Many normal accusative objects come into existence only as a result of the activity of the verb, thus often with **schneiden:**

das Gras schneiden (normal); Stroh, Gesichter schneiden, *to cut straw,
make faces* (result); Holz schneiden (either sense).

Similarly an adjective predicated of an object may indicate a resultant
condition:

sie klopfte ihn wach, *knocked him up;* er wischte die Schuhe im Grase
rein, *wiped his boots clean in the grass.*

The adjective as predicate of result may, if sufficiently intimately
associated with the verb, become a prefix [cp. § 88 (d)]:

man hat ihn totgeschlagen, *killed him,* totgefahren, *run him over;* but:
sie hat mich halbtot geredet, *nearly talked me into the grave.*

The predicate of result is a form of the objective predicate (*v.* §§ 149 f.
and 433 f.). An intransitive verb may take an object or objective
predicate of result (thus above reden), and a transitive verb may take a
new object not otherwise possible (thus above fahren, schneiden, and):

Mittags aß er den Teller leer.   Sie war so froh darüber, als habe ein Hund
den Napf sauber gefressen (E. Kästner), *ate the plate clean.*

(b) An especially vivid form of the predicate of result is obtained by
replacing the adjective by a prepositional phrase or adverb of direction:

Sie tanzten die Konkurrenz glatt an die Wand (Simpl.), *they danced all
opponents off the floor.*

This is the normal case with all verbs which otherwise take the dative
[*v.* § 98 (b) and examples in § 380 (c), (d)] with the important exception of
helfen and its compounds, which remain unchanged:

F. . . . half der Dame vom Trittbrett (E. Kästner), *helped the lady down
from the running-board.*

Er verhalf ihm zu einer großen Karriere, *helped him to a great career.*

(c) Reflexive expressions are prominent with predicates of result:

Dann zitterten sich die Tannen langsam still (S. Zweig), *the firs trembled
into silence* (adjective as predicate).

Er schlief sich in ein Traumland hinüber (W. Speyer), *fell off to sleep into a
world of dreams* (prepositional phrase and adverb).

Er lief und lief und rannte sich den Kummer an den Stiefelsohlen ab
(E. Kästner), *he walked his sorrow off with his shoe-leather* [prepositional
phrase and adverb; the direct object is here Kummer, and the reflexive is
dative of interest, *v.* § 382 (d)].

(d) Analogous to expressions of result are certain direct adjectival
objects of tun and synonyms (sich stellen, sich geben), in the sense to
pretend; also markieren (pop.) with a following noun:

Frau H. tat beleidigt (E. Kästner), *took on a hurt tone;* **er stellte sich schlafend, gab sich überzeugt,** *he pretended to be sleeping, to be convinced;* **er markierte erfahren, den Lebemann,** *he put on an air of experience, man of the world, man about town.*

EXERCISE LVI

A. Translate into ENGLISH:

1. Friede ernährt, Unfriede verzehrt (proverb). 2. Er ritt Rennen, duellierte sich und unterschied nur drei Arten von Menschen: Offiziere, Frauen und Zivilisten (R. Musil). 3. Er war grauhaarig und schon in dem Alter, da einem mit Gottes Willen manches Haar vom Haupte und mancher Sperling vom Dache fällt (W. Bergengruen). 4. . . . drei lebendige Äffchen, die die Zähne fletschten, einander Flöhe suchten, grinsten und spektakelten (S. Zweig). 5. Außerdem war er falsch. Er schwänzelte um meine Eltern herum und sprach ihnen in schamloser Weise nach dem Munde (Th. Mann). 6. Er geriet an einem der Antiquariatstische über einen Auswahlband von Schopenhauer, blätterte und las sich fest (E. Kästner). 7. Soll ich dir sagen, woran mein Leochen gestorben ist? . . . Er hat sich zutode gesoffen! (W. Bergengruen). 8. The Writer's Post Bag: Ich seufze, nicht maßvoll, vielmehr unmäßig, und ich beginne.—Drucksachen, Verlags- und Redaktionskorrespondenz, Prospekte, Ansichtskarten, Kataloge, Zeitschriften, Korrekturen, Honorarabrechnungen, behördliche Aufforderungen, Ansinnen und Mahnungen. Ich soll beitreten, mitarbeiten, befürworten, bevorworten, lesen, loben, spenden, verzichten, bestellen, zahlen, kondolieren, gratulieren, rezensieren, abonnieren, subskribieren, mich versichern lassen, kaufen und in der Lotterie spielen. Und ob ich mich noch erinnere, daß wir zusammen in der Schule waren? (W. Bergengruen).

B. Translate into GERMAN:

1. He took a glass and a bottle of rum from the cupboard. "May I pour you out [a drink]?" he asked. 2. Will you please put down [your hat and coat] in the hall. 3. Is it time for me to serve [the meal]? 4. The Post Office is going to run a new telephone line out to this suburb. 5. It was so many years since he had seen his brother that they had become strangers to one another. 6. Why have I grown a moustache? Perhaps to increase my importance. 7. He had a monocle fixed in his left eye and in his hand he carried a walking stick. 8. The Three Wise Men from the East each returned to his own country by another way. 9. There came a time when he had to clean his own shoes and brush his own clothes. 10. The boy next to him suddenly pulled his sleeve to attract his attention.

CHAPTER LVII

PREPOSITIONS OF TIME AND AGGREGATION

The prepositions of time, and those of aggregation (material and quantity), are arranged under appropriate subheadings interpolated among the paragraphs.

Prepositions of time may be divided into (i) point-time, (ii) time from, (iii) time before and after, (iv) same time, (v) time during, (vi) time to(wards) which.

Prepositions of Point-time: An, Um, Zu

387. An, dat.; *at, in, on*; is in normal use for *time when*:

am Abend, Montag, 10. (zehnten) Juni, es ist an der Zeit, *it is time (that).* Apposition: **(am) Dienstag, *den* 4. (vierten) August.** Sometimes for **zu,** *at* (of a festival): **an** or **zu Ostern, an Mariä Himmelfahrt** (S. Andres).

An, with accusative of time, only after **bis, bis an seinen Tod,** cp. § 324.

388. Um, acc.; *at*; varies in precision according to the following word: **um Weihnachten,** *at* (*about*) *Christmas,* **um vier Uhr,** *at* (*precisely*) *four o'clock.*

389. Zu, dat.; *in, at, for.* **Zu** replaces **um** if a specific moment is not indicated, thus: **um fünf Uhr, um diese Zeit,** but **zu jeder Stunde** (*at*), and is itself replaced by **bei** for attendant circumstance: **bei jeder Gelegenheit** (*on*). **Am Neujahrstag,** but **zu Anfang des Jahres; zu Ostern** is more precise than **um Ostern. Zuerst, zunächst, zuletzt, zum ersten Male,** *at first, next,* etc. **Wir essen um Mittag,** *at noon,* **erst am Abend,** *not till the evening;* but **wir essen zu Mittag, zu Abend,** *we have lunch, dinner* (*supper*), without indicating a time.

Both **zu** and **auf** indicate time towards which (*v.* **auf**): **in der Nacht zum (or auf den) 1. Januar;** but **zu** is more determined, **auf** more expectant, thus: **von gestern zu heute sind die Baumwipfel grün geworden,** *between yesterday and to-day;* **von heut auf morgen wollte er das Haus samt Zubehör verkauft wissen!** *wanted to have the whole place sold up at a day's notice.*

Zu replaces the criticised commercial term **per: wir erwarten Erfüllung des Vertrages per 1. (= zum ersten) April,** *by the first of April.*

Note.—**Anfangs** and **ausgangs,** *at the beginning, end,* with genitive; better **am (beim) Anfang, Ausgang (Juli, des Sommers).**

Prepositions of Time from Which: Ab, Seit

390. Ab, dat.; usually commercial or official style (*v.* § 317), especially with an isolated noun/adverb: **ab Sonntag, ab morgen.** A bracket [*v.* § 263 (*d*)] is recommended: **von Sonntag (morgen) an. Ab sofort** is tautologous for **sofort.** South German writers still use the dative: **ab diesem Tage erzählten die Briefe immer von René** (H. von Doderer). **Ab** is often followed by accusative: **ab 10.** (zehnten) **Juni, ab kommenden Dienstag;** this is probably not a governed, but an adverbial accusative; better: **vom 10. Juni (vom nächsten Dienstag) an.**

391. Seit, dat.; *since, for.* **Seit Wochen besuchen sie uns nicht mehr,** *they have not visited us for weeks,* cp. § 67 (*c*); **seit Mittwoch.**

Prepositions of Time Before and After: Vor, Nach

392. Vor, dat.; *before (to)* a point of time: **er kam vor der Zeit,** *before (his) time,* **(um) Viertel vor fünf,** *quarter to; ago* with a period of time: **vor zwei Jahren.**

Distinguish the adverbial use: **Meine Uhr geht vor,** *is fast.*

393. Nach, dat.; *after,* **nach Weihnachten,** or after a period has elapsed: **(erst) nach Tagen, Monaten (sah ich ihn wieder),** *days (months) later . . .*

Prepositions of the Same Time: Bei, Über, Unter

394. Bei, dat.; *at (the time, occasion of):* **beim leisesten Geräusch fährt er aus dem Schlaf,** *at the least sound;* **ich lernte ihn bei einem Pfadfindertreffen kennen,** *at (on the occasion of) a scout rally.* **Bei** is common with the infinitive noun [*v.* § 205 (*c*)].

Distinguish: **wir erreichten unseren Bestimmungsort am Abend** (*time when*) but **noch bei Tage** [*while day(light) lasted*].

Also **anläßlich** or **gelegentlich,** with genitive, *on the occasion of;* better **bei,** with dative, or **beim Anlaß, bei der Gelegenheit,** with following genitive.

Also **über,** dat., **über dem Lesen bin ich eingeschlafen,** *over my book . . .* [cp. § 335 (*a*)].

395. Unter, dat.; *during.* The sense is some indefinite time *during . . . ,* and thus distinct from **bei** (two coincident events) and **während** (two coterminous periods). Thus: **unter der Woche gehen wir oft zu ihm hinüber,** *of a weekday;* **während der Mahlzeit spielte das Orchester,** *throughout.* In practice, **unter** for time and authority [*e.g.* **unter Ludwig (des) XIV. Regierung,** *under Louis XIV*] often coincide, thus: **Sie** (= **die**

Löwen) hockten widerspenstig zögernd unter seinen Zurufen auf den fünf herumstehenden Taburetts nieder (Th. Mann), *during and in obedience to his words of command.*

Old genitive: **unterdessen,** *meanwhile.*

Preposition of Time During: Während

396. Während, gen.; *during.* The general term for two events which are indefinitely coterminous: **während der Vorstellung darf nicht geraucht werden.** But time how long is the (adverbial) accusative, not **während,** as French *pendant*: **ich lebte fünf Jahre im Ausland.**

With dative only colloquially: **während dem Regen standen wir unter.** But both cases in old compounds: **währenddessen, währenddem,** *meanwhile.*

Prepositions of Time Within or Through Which: Binnen, In, Durch, Über, Zeit

397. Binnen, dat.; *within.* Originally with the genitive (= **innerhalb**) as **binnen eines Monats,** but the dative was adopted to show the case in plural expressions, as **binnen zwei Tage(n),** on analogy of **in zwei Jahren,** *v.* § 266 (*c*), and this is now the rule: **binnen wenigen Wochen,** or **innerhalb weniger Wochen.**

Also **in**: **in den letzten Jahren,** *of recent years;* **er geht nun ins siebzigste Jahr,** *is entering his . . .*

398. Durch, acc.; *throughout.* **Durch so viele Jahre ist er niemals bei mir gewesen;** but commonly as following (compound) adverb: **so viele Jahre hindurch,** *throughout . . .;* **zehn Uhr durch,** *gone ten,* cp. § 325.

399. Über, acc.; *in, over.* **Morgen über acht Tage** (or **in acht Tagen**), *to-morrow week.* **Übers Jahr sind wir nicht mehr hier,** *in a year.* **Ich will das Buch über den Sonntag lesen,** *over the week-end.*

Duration: **er blieb über Nacht, über den Winter,** but: **den Tag, die Nacht, das Jahr über.**

400. Zeit, gen.; *during (the whole of),* only in the expression: **zeit meines (seines,** etc.) **Lebens,** often abbreviated to **zeitlebens,** used for both past and future: *all my (his) life, for as long as I (shall) live.*

Prepositions of Time To(wards) Which: Auf, Für, Bis

401. Auf, acc.; *for,* of general prospective time.

Es geht auf 10 Uhr, Mittag; es ist Viertel (auf) vier; ich komme nur auf einen Sprung vorbei, *for a brief visit;* **auf zwei Worte!** (Th. Mann), *a word with you;* eine Beschäftigung auf Dauer, *with prospects.* In invitations, auf is for the time, day, zu is for the meal: auf halb acht Uhr, auf Dienstag abend, zum Abendessen eingeladen sein. But the most lively expectation is the dish, and here auf takes precedence over zu: daß Herr G. zum nächsten Sonntag auf einen Kalbsbraten gebeten sci (Th. Mann), *for next Sunday, to eat . . .*

Idioms: sich freuen, hoffen auf, *to look forward to, hope for.*

Auf and für compete: auf (für) den Fall, daß . . ., *in case . . . [against the possibility,* cp. § 236 (c)]; but für is commoner in informal style: ich ging für (auf) zehn Tage an die See, and für could replace time or day in invitations (above). But if the expectation is lively, auf is preferred: dieses köstliche Land wird nun auf Wochen hinaus . . . für mich eine Heimat sein (G. Hauptmann).

402. Bis, acc.; *until, by.* With inflected (bis nächste Woche, bis 1. = ersten Mai), or non-inflected (bis Sonntag, heute, zwei Uhr, Ostern, bis wann?) nouns or adverbs; or with both: bis Mittwoch, den 2. September. In double prepositions: bis an den Abend, bis zum Tag, bis gegen 4 Uhr, bis tief ins Neue Jahr, bis vor (nach) Weihnachten. Usually the question whether the limit is exclusive or inclusive (*v.* § 324) does not arise, but bis *mit* makes inclusive sense clear: bis mit (den) 10. Dezember, or bis einschließlich (den) 10. Dezember; the case remains the accusative, but the dative is found in the popular form: bis und mit (dem) 10. Dezember.

Prepositions of Material, Source or Origin: Aus, Von

The prepositions of aggregation are concerned with material, quantity, and amount, etc.

403. Aus and von, dat.; *of, from*; source or origin.

Aus is the primary term of origin: eine Melodie aus der „Zauberflöte"; wir haben Besuch aus der Schweiz, *a guest from Switzerland* (but: er ist heute von der Schweiz gekommen); er erinnerte mich an Einzelheiten aus unseren früheren Gesprächen. Thus often with verb of origin (entstehen aus, *to derive from*), change of state (erwachen aus, *to awake from*), and logical inference (daraus ersehe ich . . ., *infer;* daraus erhellt . . ., *follows*).

Von rapidly loses its force of origin (vom Bäcker kaufen), and acquires the sense of separation (ein Blatt vom Kalender reißen), distinction (vom Vater verschieden), or dependence (von den Eltern abhängig sein). But genuine original force is preserved in: in der Nacht klirrte es leise wie vom Fensterriegel oder dem Schloß einer Tür (E. Wiechert), *as if caused by . . .*

Thus **aus** is dynamic, **von** static: **der Regen kommt vom Himmel, das Wasser quillt aus der Erde; der Mann von der Behörde, der Mann aus dem Gefängnis; ich weiß das aus guter Erfahrung, ich weiß es nur vom Hörensagen.**

Social origin may thus give impetus (**aus**) or status (**von**), as:

Sie sind also—aus guter Familie—bei uns Adligen sagt man einfach „von Familie"; aus *guter* Familie kann nur der Bürgerliche sein (Th. Mann),

a distinction not possible in English.

404. Aus and von, dat.; *of, out of*; material.

Von indicates a uniform material: **der Tisch ist von Holz, ein Ring von Eisen zog sich um die Armee;** it suggests utilisation rather than transformation: **von Lumpen kann man nichts machen; aus Lumpen läßt sich Papier machen.**   Thus numerals, having no organic unity, require the partitive force of **von: ein Dorf von 1000 Einwohnern, ein Heer aus verschiedenen Waffengattungen.**   **Aus** is thus used: (i) where there has taken place a process of fashioning (**Broschen aus Elfenbein**), or of organic development (**es wird noch ein Mann aus ihm werden**); or (ii) the components are notably disparate (thus **zusammengesetzt aus**, *compounded of*), as: **das Programm stellte einen seltsamen Salat aus Puccini und Vater Strauß dar; Abhänge aus gelbem Lehm und Geröll,** *yellow loam and loose stones;* or (iii) the unity is figurative: **Erdbeben aus Papier,** *a paper earthquake* (in a newsp. office).

Note.—Material as cause: **Kinder starrend von Schmutz,** *stiff with filth, v.* §§ 522-3.

Prepositions of Exclusion, Inclusion, Exchange: (An)statt, Außer, Für, Gegen, Mit, Ohne, Unter, Von

405. (An)statt, gen.; *instead of.*   **(An)statt des Brotes bekam er einen Stein.**   **Statt** may take dative colloquially, or when the genitive is not distinct: **denn statt etwas Schrecklichem kam Rollo** (= dog) **auf sie zu** (Th. Fontane).   Compound adverb: **stattdessen,** *instead.*

An (gen.) **Stelle,** *in the place of,* has recently become **anstelle,** and thus joined **anstatt.**   Both prepositions are resolved back into their components: (i) commonly when governing a pronoun: **an meiner Statt, an seiner Stelle würde ich . . .,** with possessive for the pronoun; (ii) sometimes with a noun: **an seines Herrn Stelle,** *in his master's place,* and in set expressions as **an Kindes Statt adoptieren,** *to adopt, v.* § 263 (*c*).   But with original force: **An die Stelle des Vaters trat die Mutter,** *took the place of the father.*

Anstatt as conjunction, *v.* § 406.

406. Außer, dat.; *except, besides.* **Sie waren alle da, außer ihm,** *except him;* **sie bekommen außer dem Lohn noch zwei Wochen Urlaub,** *besides their wages.* Compound: **außerdem,** *in addition.*

Anstatt and **außer** may be used as conjunctions, linking without governing: **das Buch gab ich ihm anstatt ihr** (dat.), **ich sah alle außer ihn** (acc.), *v.* § 267 (*b*) (2).

407. Für, acc.; *for.* **Ich kaufte das Buch für 4 DM.** But price is also used to indicate quantity: **Ich hätte gern für 50 Pf. Kochsalz,** *50 Pf.s worth of . . .* **Wir haben keinen Wagen, dafür können wir uns aber anderes leisten,** *but instead we can afford other things.*

Note.—For **um** and **für** in statements of price, *v.* also § 526.

408. Gegen, acc.; (*in exchange*) *for, against.* **Das Geld gebe ich nur gegen Quittung ab,** *against a receipt;* **verbrauchten Wagen gegen neuen Fernsehapparat zu tauschen gesucht** (adv.), *would exchange . . . for . . .*

409. Mit, dat.; (*together*) *with.* **Zu verkaufen: Nähmaschine mit Zubehör,** *with kit.* **Nebst, samt, mitsamt,** all with dative, are occasional forms, but only of a natural (especially human) association, and often with an ironic note: **Frau B., nebst Kindern; es erschien die ganze Familie, mitsamt Dienern und Gepäck,** *with servants, bag and baggage.*

Mit, as adverb, means *one of a party:* **das Kind will überall mit dabei sein,** *in on everything;* **und dabei essen Sie derartig viel, daß ich davon mit satt werde** (E. Kästner), *I feel satisfied from just looking on.* Thus it may (i) tone down an exclusive statement: **er war mit der Beste** (= **unter den Besten**) **seiner Klasse,** *one of the best,* **mitverantwortlich für den Unfall,** *not without responsibility;* (ii) become a verbal prefix: **Darf ich mitfahren?** *may I have a lift?;* or (iii) a noun prefix: **ein Mitläufer,** *fellow-traveller.*

410. Ohne, acc.; *without.* **Ohne Ende,** *endless(ly),* **ohne Zweifel,** *without doubt,* **ohne Umstände,** *without standing on form.* **Ohne ihn hätte ich nichts erreicht,** *but for him.* **Wir haben schon zehn Pfund Obst, ohne die Pflaumen** (= **außer den Pflaumen**), *without counting.* **Das ist nicht so ganz ohne,** *it's not at all bad.* Compounds: **ohnedies, ohnedem; ohnehin,** *in any case;* **zweifelsohne,** *doubtless.*

Sonder, acc., in sense of **ohne,** in survivals:

Es wurde erzählt, natürlich aus freier Faust heraus und sonder Zensur (E. Barlach), *without censorship* (children telling stories in bed).

Compound: **ohne-, sondergleichen,** *without a parallel.*

411. Unter, dat. and acc.; *among.* May be followed by varying number: (i) plural: **in Zivil gekleidete Polizisten mischten sich unter die Zuschauer,** and may have partitive force: **unter allen Schülern der Beste;** (ii) dual: **unter uns gesagt,** *between ourselves;* (iii) singular, if the noun is collective: **unter der Menge,** *among the crowd;* **viel Spreu unter dem Weizen,** *much chaff among the corn;* **unter anderem,** abbreviated **u.a.,** *inter alia.*

412. Von, dat.; *from, of.*

From the sense of source (*v.* § 403) comes separation: **die Flöhe gehen vom Tier herunter,** *leave the (dead) animal.* Thus, further, the partitive (= *some, a part of*): **sie schenkte ihm vom Tee ein; ich verkaufte viele von meinen Büchern; von** (= **unter**) **allen Schülern der Beste.**

413. Genitive Prepositions. Inclusion and exclusion would not be complete without a note on the genitive group, mainly in **-lich,** or from past participles, used largely for stating prices: **der Preis versteht sich einschließlich (ausschließlich) Porto, Versandkosten,** *inclusive (exclusive) of carriage, carriage free.* Non-inflection in the singular [as here **Porto,** *v.* § 267 (*a*)], and the use of the dative in the plural [**einschl. vier Gästen,** *v.* § 266 (*c*)] is common. But the desire to make mail-ordering simple leads to the popular euphemistic term **portofrei,** *post-free.*

Such words are also used as adjectives (**zusätzliche Kosten,** *additional expenses*), in absolute expressions (**den Versand eingerechnet, ungerechnet,** *with, without carriage*), or as adverbs (**Pensionspreis 10 DM. inkl.** = **inklusive alles,** *inclusive, all included*).

For the prepositional role, **mit** and **ohne** are also pressed into service: **5 DM. ohne Überweisungsgebühr,** *without cost of remittance,* **8.80 mit Bedienung,** *with service charge,* or simply: **mit;** and the following colloquy may be heard when the bill is presented: **Ist das schon mit? Nein, das ist ohne.**

Prepositions of Limit, Up to or Beyond Which: Auf, Bis Auf, Bis Zu, Über, Unter

414. Auf, acc.; *to, at,* etc. **Ich würde den Schaden auf 100 Pfund taxieren,** *estimate at;* **Geld auf Abruf,** *money at call.*

For **bis auf,** *v.* § 324.

415. Bis zu, dat.; *up to.* **Eine Garantie bis zum Betrag von . . .** But when followed by a numeral, **bis zu** may be regarded as an adverb of approximation, not affecting the case: **die Maschine liefert bis zu 1000 Exemplare** (acc. object) **pro Stunde.** Cp. § 267 (*b*) (3).

416. Über, dat., acc.; *beyond.*

(*a*) Dative: **Das Geschäft liegt über der Straße,** *over the road.*

(*b*) Accusative: **Mann über Bord!** *overboard;* **das geht über meine Kräfte, meinen Verstand,** *is beyond me;* **sie sprach über ihre Gewohnheit dem Weine zu,** *beyond her custom;* **das Kind war über alle (über die) Maßen frech,** *impudent beyond all bounds.* The former German national anthem: **Deutschland, Deutschland über alles, Über alles in der Welt,** was said to belong here (**Dem Deutschen geht sein Vaterland über alles),** rather than under § 454 (**herrschen über,** *i.e.* other nations) as was popularly assumed.

416A. Unter, dat.; *below.* **Unter fünf Glas Bier kommt man nicht in Stimmung. Die Leistungen der Kandidaten sind unter aller Kritik** (colloquial: **Kanone),** *worthless,* lit., *fall short of any standard.*

Prepositions of Increase and Decrease: An, Um, Zu

417. An, dat.; *in respect of.* Expresses the partitive sense after very many adjectives, verbs, nouns, and pronouns: (i) adjectives: **jung an Jahren, an weltlichen Gütern arm, reich bedacht;** participles: **er ist mir an Stärke gewachsen** (*equal*), **überlegen** (*superior*); (ii) verbs: **an Weisheit (Macht) zunehmen, abnehmen,** *to increase, decrease in;* (iii) nouns: **ein gewisses Maß an Glück,** *measure of happiness,* **ein Minimum an Einkommen,** *minimum of income;* but **ein Quantum von Arbeit, ein Betrag von Geld;** (iv) pronouns: **zuviel an Ehre,** also following: **an der Geschichte ist kaum etwas Wahres,** *hardly anything true in* . . .

Thus with nouns and pronouns, **an** competes with **von,** even in the case of the objective genitive, thus: **die Industrie verbraucht Rohstoffe,** *consumes raw materials,* **die Entwicklung der Industrie hat zu einem Riesenverbrauch an Rohstoffen geführt,** *enormous consumption of.*

418. Um, acc.; used of loss or consumption: **er kam ums Leben,** *lost his life,* **hat sich um sein Vermögen gebracht,** *lost his fortune.* Adverb: **meine Zeit ist um,** *finished.*

419. Zu, dat.; (*in addition*) *to.* **Zum Preis kommen noch die Versandkosten; nehmen Sie Milch oder Zitrone zum Tee?** *in your tea;* **das werden wir zu den Akten legen,** *file away,* fig., *shelve.* Compounds: **dazu, zudem,** *moreover.* **Hinzu kommt noch eine Mark Steuer,** *there is one mark in tax to be added.* This use is close to that indicating a goal, point of intention: **Zum Mittagessen nehmen wir kein Brot,** cp. § 527.

Prepositions of Measurement: An, Gegen, Um, Von, Zu, etc.

420. Approximation: **An, gegen, um,** all acc.; *about.*

Er wohnte an die zehn Jahre in Berlin [note the article, and cp. § 267 (*b*) (3)].

Es waren gegen 1000 Mann auf dem Paradeplatz.

Um 500 Zuhörer waren in dem Saale versammelt, cp. § 388.

Note.—These prepositions, being synonyms of the adverbs **ungefähr, zirka,** *about, approximately,* etc., might also be regarded as adverbs, without influence on the case, though this normally only happens with **gegen: Der Bundespräsident gratulierte gegen hundert Preisträgern persönlich.** Cp. example in § 422, below.

421. Measure of Difference: **Um,** acc.; *by.* In various contexts: (i) with **zu** and an adjective: **er kam um einen Bruchteil einer Sekunde zu spät,** *too late by . . .;* (ii) with a comparative: **er ist um einige Jahre älter als ich,** *older by . . .;* (iii) after a verb: **er hat sich um einen Schilling verrechnet,** *miscalculated by . . .;* (iv) before an adverb: **sie sind um einige Meilen zurück,** *a few miles behind.*

Um in this sense plays an important role before clauses: (1) of result: **ich kam zu spät, um ihn noch zu Hause anzutreffen,** *too late to . . .* [*v.* (i) above]; (2) of comparison: **je mehr er in mich drang, umso mehr entzog ich mich,** *the more . . ., the more . . .* [*v.* (ii) above]. Cp. §§ 203 (*a*), 313 (*c*).

Sometimes **bei: bei weitem die Schönste war Hedwig,** *prettiest by far.*

422. Apposition of Quantity, etc.: **Über,** acc., **von, zu,** dat.; *for, of, at.*

Eine Quittung über zwei Mark, *receipt for.*

Ein Dorf von einigen 500 Einwohnern; eine Frau von gegen [*v.* § 267 (*b*) (3)] **vierzig Jahren; ein Mann von zwei Meter Höhe.**

Note.—The adverbial phrase of distance, *at a distance of,* is **in, aus,** or **bei** according to context: **das Haus lag in einer Entfernung von . . .; aus einer solchen Entfernung kann man nichts erkennen; bei solchem Abstand** (*at such a distance*) **kann man kaum was erkennen.**

Ein Bleistift zu 50 Pf.; wir verrechnen Ihnen die Kohlen zum Selbstkostenpreis, *charge at wholesale price;* **zu 5% läßt sich das noch machen; das Jahr besteht aus 7 Monaten zu 31 Tagen usw.; die Waren sind zum größten Teil schon verkauft,** *for the large part.*

423. Distributive: **à, zu, pro, auf.**

At (of price): **à, zu: zwei Zigarren zu 30 (Pf.) und eine à 50.**

For (of a unit): **pro Pfund 50 Pf.; das Pfund 50 Pf.**

10% = 10 prozent, or **10 vom Hundert** (abbrev. **p.c.** or **v.H.**).

$10^0/_{00}$ = **10 pro mille,** or **10 vom Tausend** (abbrev. **p.m.** or **v.T.**).
10 Mark pro Woche, but **einmal in der Woche,** *once a week.*

Per: **auf,** acc.: **Der Gewinn beträgt 100 Mark, macht auf den Kopf zehn Mark,** *10 marks per head;* **auf einmal,** *(all) at once.*

In: **zu,** dat.: **die Menschen kamen zu Tausenden angerannt,** *in thousands;* **er verkauft seine Eier zu Dutzenden** (also **in Dutzenden,** and **dutzendweise**), *in dozens.*

Cp. also § 241 (*c*).

Prepositions of Response, Succession

424. Auf, acc.; *on, to.* Expresses a free response, rather than a determined sequence: **der Hund hört seinen Namen,** *hears,* but **hört auf den Namen Willi,** *responds to;* or, if determined, the sequence is psychologically interesting: **auf Winter folgt Sommer, auf Leid folgt Freud, auf Regen Sonne.** „Vorn" und „hinten" sind Ortsangaben auf die Frage „Wo?", *adverbs of place (given) in answer to the question "where?"*

Thus **auf** may express: (i) expectation: „Ja", **antwortet K. und sieht, wo das Wechselgeld auf seinen Hunderter bleibt** (H. Fallada), *and looks for the change from his note;* but when in his pocket it becomes: **das Wechselgeld von dem Hunderter** (partitive); (ii) conformity: **ich bin seinem Vorbild gefolgt,** but: **ich habe es nur auf seinen Wunsch (hin) getan,** *in response to his wish;* (iii) cause: **Sieben auf einen Schlag,** *seven (flies) at one blow* (*Grimm's Fairy Tales*). Cp. further § 524.

425. A sequence of events of a uniform nature: **Für, um,** acc., *after.*
Jahr für Jahr verbringt er seine Ferien in Deutschland, *year after year;* **Wort für Wort,** *word for word;* **einen Tag um den andern,** *one day after another.*

Otherwise, the preposition is suggested by the sense:
Brief nach Brief schickte ich an ihn ab, Woche um Woche verstrich, aber es kam keine Antwort, *letter after letter, week after week.*
Der Maack schreibt (Adressen) wie eine Maschine. Hundert auf Hundert türmt sich dort, Stöße über Stöße (H. Fallada), *hundred upon hundred, pile upon pile.*

Exercise LVII

A. Translate into English:

1. Von dem Holz könnte man einen Hühnerstall bauen. Aus dem Holz läßt sich allerlei Schönes machen. 2. Nichts geht mir über ein gutes Buch. Probieren geht über Studieren. 3. An Charakter ist sie

ihm gleich, an Talent ihm weit voraus. 4. Jeder Mensch bedarf der Kleidung und Nahrung; mein Bedarf an Kleidung ist für diesen Sommer schon gedeckt. 5. Dies ist eine der Ursachen weshalb ich . . . zeit meines Lebens ein Träumer blieb (Th. Mann). 6. Auch aßen wir gern geröstete Kastanien und junge Nüsse zum neuen Wein (E. Jünger). 7. Wein auf Bier, das rat' ich dir, Bier auf Wein, das laß sein! (prov.). 8. Auf das Zureden der beiden Freunde schüttelte sie nur den Kopf (B. Werner). 9. In einer Mischung aus Gruseln und Verzauberung zieht sie den Kopf tief in die Schultern (B. Werner). 10. In diesem Augenblicke wurde der Himmel nachtschwarz, wie von einer schweren Gewitterwolke (B. Werner).

B. Translate into GERMAN:

1. I shall be glad to see you at three o'clock, or indeed at any time after this. 2. We invited her for Friday evening for a cup of coffee. 3. From New Year's Day we shall be going to the theatre at least once a week. 4. Our visitors from London stayed till late in the afternoon on the following day. 5. This cake is made of flour, sugar, butter, and eggs, that is, from the best ingredients obtainable. 6. He exchanged his stamp collection for a second-hand camera. 7. He would have sold his car for 10,000 marks, but his friend was only prepared to go up to 8,000 marks. 8. Farmers complained that it was impossible to sell milk at this price. 9. During his illness he read incessantly; his wife brought one book after another (= book after book) from the library. 10. He also did jigsaw puzzles by the dozen.

CHAPTER LVIII

THE SUBJUNCTIVE OF CONDITION AND CONCESSION. PARTICIPLES AND THE OBJECTIVE PREDICATE

Revise §§ 236-40.

426. The Subjunctive of Condition

(a) Conditions are either:

(1) Open conditions, *i.e.* the statement of an event which has actually or may still come about [*v.* § 236 (*a*) (1)], or

(2) Unreal conditions, *i.e.* the statement of an event about which there is some improbability.

In either case the main statement states the result of the conditional statement, upon the realisation of which it depends.

Unreal conditional statement:

Wenn er es täte, freute ich mich, *if he did it* (*were to do it*), *I should be pleased.*

(b) The various possibilities of tense sequence are:

(1) Both verbs are in the past subjunctive, the form for tentative or unreal statements (*v.* § 309):

> **Wenn er es täte, freute ich mich** (formal or literary use).

(2) The main clause has the subjunctive in the periphrastic form **würde**:

> **Wenn er es täte, würde ich mich freuen** (informal, spoken use).

(3) The periphrastic form **würde** is used in both clauses:

> **Wenn er es tun würde, würde ich mich freuen** (popular use).

(c) Alternative forms:

(1) A second periphrastic form, often used in the conditional clause, informally but quite correctly, is the imperfect of **sollen**:

> **Wenn er es tun sollte, würde ich mich freuen** (cp. *were to do it*).

(2) As with all conditional statements [cp. § 236 (*b*)] the preceding (sometimes following) conditional clause may omit the conjunction and take question order; the main clause is then usually introduced by a particle:

> **Täte er es, dann** (or **so**) **freute ich mich.**

(3) Any of the conjunctions noted in § 236 (*c*) may stand for **wenn,** the condition envisaged being one stage more remote than the corresponding indicative; the subjunctive is always the past, but need not entail a subjunctive in the main clause:

Angenommen, er hätte das Geld gestohlen, was würden wir dann tun?
(was tun wir dann?), cp. example in § 236 (c) (3).

(d) Negative Conditions. There is no special requirement of the subjunctive in negative conditions, either after **wenn nicht,** *unless,* or **außer wenn,** *unless* in the special sense *except* [cp. § 236 (d)]. But it is used in two cases:

(1) **außer wenn** following a main statement in the conditional subjunctive:

Ich würde nicht hingehen, außer wenn er mich darum bäte [or **außer er**
bäte mich darum, v. (c) (2)], *I would not . . . unless he were to . . .*

(2) The special set expression **es sei denn (wäre denn), daß . . .,** meaning *unless (if not),* which is inserted with this force into conditional sentences, whether negative or positive, and whether open or unreal conditions:

Ich werde (würde) nicht hingehen, es sei (wäre) denn, daß er mich darum
bittet (bäte, bitten sollte), *I shall (should) not go unless . . .*

Ich werde (würde) hingehen, es sei (wäre) denn, daß er mir es verbietet
(verböte, verbieten sollte), *I shall (should) go unless . . .*

In either case, the final **daß** may be omitted and direct order used [**er bittet mich . . .,** v. § 270 (c)].

This is the only case where the present subjunctive is used in a conditional statement; the form **es sei (wäre)** is, however, not actually a conditional, but a disjunctive concessive [cp. § 429 (c)].

427. Concealed, Abbreviated, and Transferred Conditionals

(a) The conditional is the only form of the subjunctive which normally involves a subjunctive form in the main, as well as in the subordinate statement. It is therefore possible to regard the main clause subjunctive as the subjunctive of tentative statement [cp. § 309 (c)], and the subordinate form as depending on this. Thus many tentative statements with the subjunctive are concealed conditionals:

Du glaubst hoffentlich nicht, daß ich nicht gern bei euch bin, Papa . . . ich
müßte ja Schläge haben, es wäre die höchste Undankbarkeit! (Th. Mann),
it would be the height of ingratitude (if I were to take up such an attitude).

(b) In other cases a concealed subjunctive is present in another form:

(1) As a phrase:

In dem Fall würde ich kommen; unter Umständen möchte ich ihn sehen;
ich könnte das unter einer Voraussetzung übernehmen, *in that case, under*
certain circumstances, on one condition.

(2) As a prepositional infinitive construction:

Es wäre sehr angenehm, bei diesem Frühlingswetter eine Auslandsfahrt zu unternehmen, *it would be very pleasant (if we were) to* . . .

(c) The conditional subjunctive, like other forms [cp. § 270 (*b*), etc.], is transferred to any other dependent subordinate clause:

Nicht lange, so überlegte das Kind, dann würde wieder der (erste) Flieger über den Himmel ziehen, dem die anderen folgten (E. Langgässer), *the first plane would appear, and others would follow.*

428. Final Comments on the Subjunctive

(*a*) Before considering the subjunctive of concession, we may conclude the general comments on the subjunctive.

The intrusive and objectionable periphrastic **würde** in the subordinate subjunctive clause, occurs, apart from the conditional [*v.* § 426 (*b*) (3) above], also commonly in clauses of reported speech and manner:

Reported Speech: **Er hatte die Stirn zu behaupten, er würde unschuldig sein,** *that he was innocent* (= **er wäre**), *v.* § 269 (*a*) (2).

Manner: **Er stellte sich an, als würde er mit der Sache nichts zu tun haben,** *as if he had nothing to do* . . . (= **als hätte er** . . .), *v.* § 312 (*b*).

But this must be distinguished from the legitimate use of **würde** in subordinate clauses with other functions:

In Amerika verbrennt man Getreide und Kaffee, weil sie sonst zu billig würden (E. Kästner), *because they would otherwise become too cheap* (past subj. of **werden,** *to become*).

Wer bei einem Techtelmechtel mit einem Russen betroffen würde, der stünde unweigerlich an der Wand (Th. Plievier), (*he said*) *if anyone were discovered parleying with a Russian, he would be shot* (past subj. of **werden,** the passive auxiliary).

These may clearly be distinguished in that they do not have the conditional conjunction (**wenn**, etc.).

(*b*) A special case of the transferred subjunctive, but quite common, is when it is isolated through its controlling clause having become a prepositional infinitive construction:

Zeugen, die erklärten, niemals etwas an ihm bemerkt zu haben, was auf Unzurechnungsfähigkeit schließen ließe (R. Musil), *that they had never noticed anything* (= **daß sie** . . . **hätten**) *which indicated lack of responsibility for his actions.*

429. The Subjunctive of Concession

(*a*) The subjunctive of concession, like the indicative (*v.* §§ 238 and 239), has two forms, a milder (or connected) and a firmer (or disjunctive) form; these correspond respectively to the English forms: *even if . . .* and *whatever (whoever),* etc.

(*b*) The normal concessive subjunctive is a strengthened condition, **wenn** becoming **wenn auch** (or **auch wenn**), as *if* becomes *even if*:

Wenn er es auch täte, würde ich mich nicht freuen [cp. § 238 (*a*)].

With this there may be, and is commonly associated:

(1) Direct (not inverted) order in the following main clause:

Wenn er es auch täte, ich würde mich nicht freuen.

(2) Omission of conjunction in the leading subordinate clause:

Täte er es auch, ich würde mich nicht freuen.

(*c*) The disjunctive concessive subjunctive may be regarded as two independent statements juxtaposed firmly (even harshly) without any explicit connection.   Thus the statement:

However lazy the boy may be, I shall teach him grammar,

would appear in the following two parts:

(1) A statement of the situation, in the form of a weakened subjunctive of will or wish (i.e. *let him be never so lazy . . .*), or conditional statement without the conjunction:

Der Junge sei (or sei er, ist er, mag er . . . sein) noch so faul . . .

(2) A statement of determination:

. . . ich werde ihm die Grammatik beibringen.

(*d*) The view in (*c*) explains a number of features of the concessive, especially in its disjunctive form, which differ from a normal conditional even when strengthened:

(1) The variety of possibilities open to the leading (concessive) clause, *e.g.* subjunctive or open (indicative) condition under (*c*), and any strengthened interrogative (**was, wer . . . auch,** etc.) under (*b*).

(2) The separation between the two parts of the statement, so that the second may follow paratactically [**ich würde** in (*b*)], or remain in the indicative after a preceding subjunctive [**ich werde** in (*c*)].

(3) The exuberance of the particles often found in the concessive statement:

Und wenn Sie mir *auch noch so* hart zusetzen, ich tu's nicht! *No matter how insistently you press me, I will not do it!*

(*e*) The concessive subjunctive is used in a number of set expressions: **Es koste, was es wolle,** *whatever it costs . . .;* **es komme, was da kommen mag,** *whatever comes . . .;* **es sei (wäre) denn, daß . . .** [*v.* § 426 (*d*) (2)], and

Und ist nicht sie (= **die Gewalt**) **das ewige Pendel, das die Zeiger vorwärtstreibt, sei es bei Tage, sei es in der Nacht?** (E. Jünger), *the eternal pendulum driving the hands of the* (*human*) *clock, whether by day or by night?*

430. Anomalies in the Present Participle

(*a*) The present participle has, in general, present time, active force, and in adjectival use refers to its noun as the subject of the action; in fact, however, usage is slightly wider than this:

(1) The time may, in appropriate contexts, be past or future; thus the adverbs **gestern** or **morgen** could be added to the following statement without disturbing the form of the participle:

Die (gestern, morgen) in der Stadt spielenden Artisten verlangen eine Gehaltserhöhung, *the artists playing* (*who played . . ., will be playing . . .*) *in the town are asking for a rise in salary.*

Note.—The use of the modal verbal participle for a future active is incorrect (**die morgen in der Stadt zu spielenden Artisten,** cp. English *who are to play . . .*). Correct use is shown in the standard notice on German railway stations:

Der um 1015ʰ fahrplanmäßig aus Richtung München ankommende Zug wird voraussichtlich . . . Minuten Verspätung haben, *the train scheduled to arrive from Munich at 10.15 a.m. is delayed by . . . minutes.*

(2) The force is never passive, as English *a boiling fowl,* cp. *a good milker,* and (pop.) *the book is reprinting.* But cp. § 180 (*c*) for the use of the reflexive with passive force, *e.g.* **diese Schuhe tragen sich gut,** *are hard wearing.*

(3) The subject may occasionally be a logical general subject rather than the noun associated with a participle-adjective, *e.g.* **eine sitzende Lebensweise,** *a sedentary way of life,* **zu nachtschlafender Zeit,** *at night.*

(*b*) Nevertheless, sporadic attempts are made to devise participles with time explicitly differing from the present, thus:

(1) Past time, with the auxiliary **habend:**

nachdem die vom Westen sich abgesetzt habenden Divisionen nur teilweise die vorgesehenen Stellungen bezogen hatten (Th. Plievier), *the divisions which had disengaged in the West* (for **sich absetzenden,** to avoid confusion of time).

(2) Future time, with the auxiliary **werdend:**

die Zeit aufzuheben, alles gewesene, seiende und sein werdende Leben als gleichzeitig anzusehen (H. Hesse), *to eliminate time and see all past, present and future life as contemporary.*

(3) More successful is the use of the modal participles **wollend, sollend,** for future time: **der sein sollende Witz,** *alleged joke,* and commonly in the expression **nicht enden wollend,** *prolonged*:

Ein nicht enden wollender Beifall belohnte die Artisten für ihre Bemühungen, *applause which, it seemed, would never end . . .*

Cp. § 478 (*e*), (*f*) (modal verbs).

431. Anomalies in the Past Participle

(*a*) The adjectival use of the past participle (with noun or in the predicate) is regarded as analogous to its verbal use in the predicate, thus:

(1) Passive in force with transitive verbs:

ein gefällter Baum, *felled tree;* **ein Gesandter,** *ambassador* (lit., *man sent*); **das Haus lag zertrümmert,** *lay in ruins* (cp. **man hat den Baum gefällt, den Mann gesandt, das Haus wurde zertrümmert**).

(2) Active, but perfective in force, for intransitive verbs which take **sein** as auxiliary:

ein eingestürztes Gebäude, *collapsed building;* **der teure Verstorbene,** *our dear deceased;* **die Blume lag verblüht,** *lay faded* (cp. **das Gebäude ist eingestürzt, er ist verstorben, die Blume ist verblüht**).

and the participle may only refer to the noun or pronoun to which it is attributed or predicated.

(*b*) Attempts are made to extend explicitly the scope of the past participle, in respect of:

(1) Anterior time in the passive participle, with the auxiliary **gewesen**:

Diese Worte . . . richteten sich in Wirklichkeit gegen seinen dreimal verheiratet gewesenen Vater (Th. Fontane), *against his father, who had been* (not *then was*) *married three times* (= **sich dreimal verheiratet hatte**).

(2) Participle conjugated with **haben,** *v.* § 432.

(3) Relation of participle to subject, thus in the common (though criticised) term: **die angefragte Firma,** *the firm about which you enquire;* and **10,000 bescherte Kinder** (newsp. headline), *10,000 children receive* (not *have been given as*) *Christmas presents.*

432. The Past Participle with Active Force

(*a*) The adjectival past participle has active force by established idiom in many expressions not in accordance with § 431 (*a*):

(1) From intransitives which, as verbs, take **haben**:

der gediente Soldat, *soldier who has served;* **der gelernte Tischler,** *skilled joiner;* **der Geschworene,** *juryman (one who has taken the oath);* **der Bediente,** *servant (=* **Bedienende**), etc.

(2) From reflexives:

ein erklärter Liebhaber, *declared suitor;* **ein Verirrter,** *person lost;* **er lebte zurückgezogen,** *lived a retired life;* etc.

(3) Negatives in **un-**, both from (1) and (2):

Darunter sind auch viele ungediente junge Leute (newsp.), *many (volunteers for the new German Army) who have had no military service.*

ungewaschen, ungefrühstückt, *not having washed, breakfasted.*

and the common term **ungewollt,** *unwitting(ly),* which perhaps owes its use to the rareness of the present participles of modal verbs.

(*b*) Extensions of these accepted idioms are much criticised, largely because of the possible resulting confusion with the (opposite) passive sense, as in § 431 (*a*) (1) above, thus **die stattgefundene (stattgehabte) Unterredung, Versammlung,** *which has taken place;* **der Unterzeichnete wird in den nächsten Tagen bei Ihnen vorsprechen,** *the undersigned;* **die früher bestandene Vorschrift,** *which was earlier valid* (but **die nunmehr bestandene Prüfung,** *examination now passed,* is correct). The correct form would be to change the construction: **die abgehaltene Versammlung, der Unterzeichnende, die früher gültige Vorschrift,** etc.

433. The Objective Predicate.   General

(*a*) Certain verbs may take a direct object, and a second accusative or predicative element, of which the first is the logical subject:

er glaubte sich verloren, *believed himself lost;* **ich weiß sie in guten Händen,** *know her to be in good hands;* **ich sehe diese Maßnahme als wertlos an,** *regard this measure as useless.*

Note.—English uses a similar construction, or inserts *to be.*

(*b*) Such constructions contain three elements of interest:

(1) The verb, which is commonly one of knowing, perceiving, naming, wearing, etc.: **wissen, finden, nennen, tragen,** etc.

(2) The objective predicate, which may be a pronoun (personal or reflexive), noun, adjective (including participles), adverb, genitive or prepositional phrase, or infinitive.

Note.—The objective predicate may have certain special force: (i) passive force in the infinitive, *v.* §§ 149 f.; here the first object, if general (**man,** etc.), is commonly omitted, cp. §§ 215 and 216; (ii) force of result, *v.* § 386.

(3) The mode of connection between direct and predicative object, which may be (i) by immediate juxtaposition, or (ii) through a conjunction or preposition, **als, für,** or **zu.**

434. The Objective Predicate with Direct Connection

Past participles predominate in this construction, the sense being often perfect [*v.* first example in (*a*) below].

(*a*) Knowing: **wissen,** also **denken, glauben, meinen:**

sie wußte den Beifall verdient, *knew the applause to have been deserved;* **ich wußte die Gartenpforte offen,** *knew the gate to be open;* **er meinte sich in den Herbst zurückversetzt,** *imagined himself to be back in the autumn.*

Note.—This use is literary, less formal style requiring a subordinate clause with **daß.**

(*b*) Perception: **finden, sehen, (sich) fühlen:**

er fühlte sich beobachtet, unverstanden, *he felt himself to be observed, misunderstood;* **er sah sich verlassen, geliebt,** *saw himself abandoned, loved;* **ich habe seinen Namen im „Figaro" erwähnt gelesen,** *saw his name mentioned.*

als ich damals in das Oratorium trat und meine Mitbrüder dicht knieend und wartend fand (S. Andres), *found my brothers kneeling and waiting.*

Note.—A past participle objective predicate may occasionally be derived from a dative verb without disturbing the construction: **er fühlte sich geschmeichelt,** *felt flattered.* In formal style, the preceding object may be regarded as governed by the past participle (whose subject is then general and understood, cp. §§ 215 and 216): **ich wußte ihm geholfen,** cp. § 246 (*f*).

(*c*) Naming and abusing: **nennen, schelten, schimpfen:**

er nennt sich Baron, *calls himself (a) Baron;* **er hat den Chef der Armee einen Mörder geschimpft,** *called the Army Commander a murderer.*

Gewisse Snobs schelten California eine mit künstlicher Üppigkeit überzogene Wüste (F. Werfel), *describe C. abusively as . . .*

(*d*) Having and wearing: **haben, tragen:**

Auch der zweite dieser imponierenden Berghirten hat drei Mäntel übergeworfen (G. Hauptmann), *has thrown over his shoulders* (later: **trägt . . . über die Schultern gehängt**) [cp. § 151 (*d*)].

**machte ohne weiteres klar, daß man für eine Partie auf dem Wasser sich
weiß zu tragen hatte** (H. von Doderer), *had to wear white.*

Note.—**Haben** with the past participle is identical in form, but not in
force, with the normal perfect tense.

(*e*) **Wissen, sehen,** and **haben** (cp. § 218), depending on **wollen,** provide,
with appropriate past participles as objective predicate, a variant of the
passive:

**er wollte die Sache erledigt wissen, die Frage behandelt sehen, alles genau
erklärt haben,** *he wanted the matter to be cleared up, the question to be
dealt with, everything to be explained in detail* (and *v.* example in § 389).

435. The Objective Predicate with Prepositional, etc., Connection
Adjectives and nouns predominate in this construction.

(*a*) Many verbs are followed by **als** or **für** and an objective predicate
agreeing with the accusative of the direct object; the choice of **als** or **für**
is largely a matter of idiom:

(1) **als** after **ansehen, beschreiben, empfehlen, sich erweisen, sehen,**
etc.: **er erwies sich als tüchtig,** *turned out to be capable;* **ich betrachte ihn
als minderwertig,** *regard him as of inferior quality.*
**Herr Bendix Grünlich, den wir alle als einen braven und liebenswürdigen
Mann kennengelernt haben** (Th. Mann), *have got to know as . . .*

(2) **für** after **halten, erklären,** etc.:
　　ich hielt ihn für schuldig, *considered him to be guilty.*
**wenn er mit etwas ungeschickter aber zorniger Geste alle Adligen für
Idioten und Elende erklärte** (Th. Mann), *declared all aristocrats to be . . .*
　　But: **sich (bereit, etc.) erklären,** *to declare oneself (ready,* etc.).

(*b*) **Zu** is used after verbs of making (into), taking (as), etc.: **machen,
nehmen, befördern,** *to promote,* **wählen,** *to elect,* **haben,** *to have (as);*
the predicate (usually of result) is always a noun, which may be preceded
by an article:

sie wählten ihn zum Vorstande, *elected him Chairman;* **der Kaiser schlug
den Jüngling zum Ritter,** *dubbed him Knight;* **er nahm sie zur Frau,** *took
her to wife.*

**ein Graben, der die von ihm durchschnittene Landzunge zu einer kleinen
Insel machte** (G. Hauptmann), *made . . . into a small island.*

Note.—**machen** without **zu** only with adjectives, and then rare:
geltend, ungeschehen, nervös machen, *to make valid (assert rights), to cancel*
(lit. *make non-existent*), *to make nervous, irritate;* cp. also § 294 (*c*)
(werden zu).

436. The Objective Predicate after Reflexives: Als, Wie

(a) The objective predicate, if a noun or pronoun, whether predicated directly or through the conjunction **als,** of the object proper, has the same case, the accusative; thus after a reflexive and **als** it agrees formally with the reflexive pronoun:

Ich bekenne mich als warme*n* Hundefreund (Th. Mann), *I confess to being a great lover of dogs.*

Er fühlte sich durchaus als Einzelne*n*, als . . . krankhafte*n* Einsiedler (H. Hesse), *he felt himself to be entirely isolated, a morbid hermit.*

(b) Perhaps more commonly, however, the **als**/noun phrase may be related to the subject, involving no change of sense, but requiring the nominative:

Er fühlte sich nicht als *ein* Held, nicht als *ein* Feige*r* (E. Wiechert), *he did not feel that he was either a hero or a coward.*

Unter den zahlreichen Gästen der Argans habe ich mich niemals als eine*r* unter vielen betrachtet (F. Werfel), *I have never considered myself to be one of the crowd.*

(c) The nominative construction is further suggested by the analogy of **wie,** which properly compares rather than asserts an identity (cp. § 311) and thus relates to the subject:

Zwischen den geputzten, feiertäglichen Menschen . . . ließ ich mich wie ein Prälat beschauen (F. Werfel), *I exhibited myself like a prelate* (which he was not).

and is in any case preferred colloquially to **als**:

„Du hast dich also wie ein dummer Junge betragen?" fuhr der Lotsen- kommandeur Morten an (Th. Mann), *you have behaved like a silly boy.*

437. The Passive of the Objective Predicate

(a) The first (direct) object of the objective predicate construction may become the subject of a passive statement:

(1) The predicate being an adjective:

er wurde bewußtlos, schlafend gefunden, *found unconscious, asleep;* **er wurde gefangen genommen** [cp. § 48 (b) (2)]; **das Buch wurde totgeschwiegen,** *the object of a conspiracy of silence;* **diese Maßnahme wird als wertlos angesehen,** *is considered to be useless.*

(2) The predicate being a noun; this then becomes:

(i) Nominative, if predicated simply, or with **als**, of the new subject:

er wurde Graf genannt, ein Feigling gescholten, *he was called Count, a coward;* **er wurde als ein tüchtiger Mann bezeichnet,** *he was described as a capable man.*

(ii) Accusative or dative, if predicated through the prepositions **für** or **zu,** respectively:

er wird für einen tüchtigen Mann gehalten, *considered to be . . .;* **der Junge wurde zum Klassenvorsteher ernannt,** *was appointed monitor.*

(*b*) Reflexive expressions have no passive form.

EXERCISE LVIII

A. Translate into ENGLISH:

1. Und diese Spannung wäre unerträglich geworden, wenn nicht in demselben Moment, fast ohne daß ein Tropfenfall vorhergegangen wäre, der Regen herniedergebrochen wäre, daß das Wasser im Rinnstein schäumte und auf dem Bürgersteig hoch emporsprang (Th. Mann). 2. Sein Klingeln klang kurz und scharf, als schlüge man eine Scheibe ein oder als würde [*v.* § 428 (*a*)] man aus dem Elf-Meter-Raum einen Fußball hart ins Tor schießen (H. von Doderer). 3. Die Leute hätten (reported speech) gesagt, sie würden ihn eher totschlagen, als zusehen, daß ihr ein Haar gekrümmt werde (E. Wiechert). 4. The poet to a would-be poetess: Wäre ich ein Gott, es kostete mich nur ein Handumdrehen . . . Ich täte, was Sie von mir erhoffen: ich öffnete Ihnen das Tor zum Tempel des Ruhmes—(wie Sie sich das so vorstellen) (W. Bergengruen). 5. Rabener sah Liane an, aber sie ließ sein Lächeln unerwidert (H. Mann). 6. Denn er leugnete seine Taten nicht, er wollte sie als Unglücksfälle einer großen Lebensauffassung verstanden wissen (R. Musil). 7. Die Tat, die Kirillof sich auferlegt fühlt, ist eine religiöse (R. Guardini). 8. Ich empfinde die Seekrankheit als einen empfindlichen Racheakt (Poseidons) (G. Hauptmann). 9. Harry Haller hatte sich zwar wunder-voll als Idealist und Weltverächter, als wehmütiger Einsiedler und als grollender Prophet verkleidet, im Grunde aber war er ein Bourgeois (H. Hesse). 10. Proverbial: Soll die Ehe lang bestehen, sei blind das Weib und taub der Mann. Die Pfanne schilt den Topf Schwarzmaul.

B. Translate into GERMAN:

1. If the subject consists of several nouns and pronouns, the verb is (stands) in the plural. 2. I think the rain has come just at the right moment; we should collapse if we had to continue working in this heat.

3. He had expected that the stage would open the door for him to fantastic adventures, in which he would figure as the hero.   4. I heard the farmer say that potatoes would not grow well unless they got both rain and sun. 5. Even if we were to arrive before 5 o'clock we might not find him at home.   6. I was told that the man was a skilled electrician and he couldn't even mend a fuse.   7. The child at last felt itself understood and loved. 8. He described himself as an idealist and a prophet, but in reality he was nothing but a political opportunist.   9. They appointed him secretary of their group, and declared him responsible for all the arrangements which had to be made.   10. She did not feel like a person who has just had bad news, but like someone in a happy dream.

CHAPTER LIX

NOUNS. THEIR GENDER, NUMBER, ACCIDENCE, STRESS

In conclusion, a brief summary is given of some rules of gender, of certain anomalies of gender, number, inflection, and emphasis in nouns, and of stress in complex words and word groups.

438. Gender According to Meaning. Animates
Revise §§ 2, 7.

(*a*) Where any principles governing gender can be discerned at all, they are (1) of meaning, (2) of form, or (3) of analogy.

Except as modified by the special statements made below, the name of an animate being is masculine or feminine according to sex; thus especially words connoting family or biological relations: **die Mutter, der Sohn,** etc.; **der Stier, die Kuh,** etc.

In the animal world, certain biological terms have wide application to different species: **der Bock,** male of many game animals, as **Hasenbock, Rehbock; der Bulle, die Kuh,** male and female of many larger animals, as elephants, and of certain marine mammals, as whales.

Neuter are:

(1) **Das Weib,** and terms for the young of humans or animals, whether specific: **das Kind, Füllen,** *foal,* **Kalb,** *calf;* or general: **das Junge des Löwen,** *lion-whelp,* **sie bekommt bald ein eigenes Kleines,** *a baby.*

(2) Nouns with neuter suffixes, as for humans: **das Fräulein, das Onkelchen;** and **das Männchen, Weibchen,** for the male or female of any species of animal or bird, conveying no limitation of size (thus: **das Männchen des Elefanten**).

(*b*) Nouns not indicating family relationship among humans, and among animals, birds, etc., the names of species proper, do not follow natural gender: **der Mensch, die Waise,** *orphan;* **der Wolf, die Ziege, das Pferd.**

But among animals closest to man as a countryman, hunter, naturalist, natural gender may be variously distinguished.

(1) Male and female names distinct from generic name: **das Pferd, der Hengst, die Stute; das Huhn, der Hahn, die Henne,** etc.

(2) Generic name shared with one sex, the other distinguished by suffix or compound, etc.: (i) **der Wolf, die Wölfin,** less commonly the

reverse: **die Gans, der Gänserich;** (ii) **die Katze, der Kater; das Schaf, der Widder; die Ziege** (fem. also **Zicke**), **der Ziegenbock.**

With terms which permit neither of these methods of differentiation (as especially birds), **Männchen** and **Weibchen** must be used: **das Männchen der Schwalbe, das Weibchen des Adlers.**

439. Gender According to Meaning. Inanimates

(a) Masculine are the names of days, months, and seasons (v. § 57) of winds (**der Föhn**), points of the compass (**der Süden**), mountains (**der Brocken**), precious and semi-precious stones (**der Achat, Rubin**). So also many West German rivers [v. § 219 (b)], and foreign rivers, especially the larger (as **der Kongo**, after **der Strom**), and foreign mountains (**der Mount Everest**). Also a number of plants: **der Flachs, Hafer, Mais, Weizen.**

But in descriptive compounds, especially for mountains, the second component confers gender: **der Kaiserstuhl, die Zugspitze, das Matterhorn.**

(b) Feminine are the names for trees (**die Pappel**), most plants (**die Kartoffel**), flowers (**die Tulpe**), fruits (**die Birne**, but **der Apfel**); and numerals (v. § 54). Also most rivers in Germany and (Central) Europe: **die Mosel, Donau, Elbe, Oder, Weichsel;** and others with an apparent feminine ending: **die Themse, Wolga.**

(c) Neuter are the names of minerals (**das Silber, das Eisen**, but **der Stahl**), and of natural and political geographical areas which do not take the article [v. § 219 (c) (1)]. Further, all nouns from other parts of speech, whether adjectives (unless relating to persons, v. §§ 143-4, 185-7), infinitives (v. § 204), or minor parts of speech and syntactical fragments [v. §§ 131 (c), 447].

But these may have: (1) masculine gender (for both sexes) if standing for persons (**der Tunichtgut,** *ne'er-do-well,* **der Störenfried,** *busybody*); (2) grammatical gender (for either sex) if standing for persons by metonymy (**der Lahmfuß,** *lame person,* **die Rothaut,** *Redskin*).

440. Gender According to Form

(a) Nouns derived from verbal stems, strong or weak, and with or without a vowel change, are:

(1) Mostly masculine if monosyllables (**der Biß, Gang, Tanz,** etc.), or disyllables [v. § 194 (c)]; but some are feminine [**die Schur,** cp. **Schafschur; die Ausfuhr,** etc., v. § 194 (f)]; and **das Schloß,** *lock,* **das** (or **der**) **Floß,** *raft,* are neuter.

(2) Feminine if disyllables in -e: **die Falle, Mache, Sprache, Stiege** [as are many similar non-derivatives with concrete sense, v. § 40 (b) (1)].

502 GENDER OF NOUNS BY FORM, ANALOGY

(b) Nouns formed with the collective, etc., prefix **Ge** . . . (e) may be neuter, masculine, or feminine, v. § 194 (e).

(c) Suffixes:

(1) Masculine are words with the agent suffix **-er** (or **-ler, -ner**), as **Bäcker, Tischler**; the instrumental suffix **-el**, as **Klöppel** (for these two suffixes, v. § 24); and with some others [**König, Frühling**, etc., v. § 194 (b) (1) (ii)].

(2) Feminine are a large number of suffixes with abstract or collective force, i.e. **-ei** (or **-erei, -elei**), **-heit** or **-keit, -schaft**, and **-ut** (**Armut**), the action suffix **-ung** (cp. English -ing), the abstract-collective **-t** (**die Kunst, Macht**), and the personal ending **-in** (for further examples of all these, v. § 40); further, abstract nouns from adjectives in **-e** (**Süße**), which often duplicate other endings (**Süßigkeit**, also **Schnelle, Schnelligkeit**), and from verbs in **-e** [v. (a) (2) above].

(3) Neuter are words with the diminutive suffixes **-chen** and **-lein** (v. § 24), the collective suffix **-icht** (**das Dickicht**), and fraction words in **-tel** [from **Teil**, v. § 79 (a)].

Note.—The following suffixes are shared: (i) **-nis** and **-sal**: the commonest words are neuter, **das Gefängnis, Schicksal**, but some are feminine, v. § 40, and some fluctuate; but **-sel** words (**das Rätsel**, v. § 24) are almost all neuter; (ii) **-tum**: neuter and masculine, v. § 194 (d); (iii) **-at**: masculine and feminine, **der Monat, die Heimat** [but v. § 441 (d), Note, below, for nouns from French]; (iv) for masculine and neuter foreign suffixes, v. § 76.

441. Gender According to Analogy

(a) It is clear from the statements in § 439 that the gender of groups of words is often influenced by the analogy of the class word, as **der Föhn** (= Wind), **der Fox** (= Tanz). This principle operates widely in suggesting genders for words where no other guide is possible; and in causing change of gender from one arrived at on other principles.

(b) The gender is suggested by a class noun understood, thus:

(1) For foreign words: **der Scirocco(wind); der Boston(tanz); das Tennis(spiel)**.

(2) For proper names, whether geographical: **der Mosel(wein), die Brasil(zigarre), der Emmentaler** (**Käse**); or personal: **die Junkers-(maschine)**, abbrev. **Ju**, and similarly **die Condor** (another plane), **die Gabelsberger (Stenographie)**, v. § 159 (d).

Note.—The same principle applies, in reverse, with adjective-nouns taking the gender of a noun understood, *e.g.* **die Rechte** (= **die r. Hand**), *v.* § 143 (*d*) (3).

(*c*) The gender is suggested by a synonym, thus:

(1) For foreign words: **der Fog** (= **dicker Nebel**).

(2) For syntactical fragments, etc., otherwise neuter: **der Lugaus (Luginsland)**, *watchtower* (= **Wartturm**); **der Saufaus**, *toper* (= **Säufer**), **der Mittwoch** (= other days in **-tag**).

(3) For words of difficult origin, as feasts, *v.* § 57 (*d*).

Note.—Quasi-proper names, *i.e.* planets, ships, newspapers, are often given genders by analogy, cp. § 235.

(*d*) Foreign words. The basic rule is to retain any gender the noun may have had in the original language, thus **das Kloster** (Lat. *claustrum*), *v.* passim under declension of foreign nouns. But analogy also operates:

(1) Unchecked in *e.g.* borrowing from English, which has no genders: **das Beefsteak** (= **Rindfleisch,** a poor analogy!), **der Dreß** (= **Anzug**).

(2) To bring about changes of gender by analogy of (i) sense: **Europa** (Lat. fem.), neuter after names of countries, **das Dutzend** (Fr. fem.) after **das Hundert,** etc.; (ii) form: words in **-er** to masculine (**der Keller,** Lat. neut., **der Puder,** Fr. fem.), words in **-e** and **-el** to feminine (**die Kanzel, Bibel,** both Lat. plurals; **die Etage, Rhone,** both Fr. masc.).

Note.—French masculine words in *-at, -ment* often become neuter after an obscure analogy: **das Etat, Resultat, das Ressentiment** [for latter, *v.* § 130 (*b*) (2)].

442. Gender of Compound Nouns

(*a*) These have, by rule, the gender of the last component; but analogy causes some differentiation:

(1) Those in **-mut** (**der Mut,** *courage,* generally *state of mind*) are masculine and feminine, differentiation having taken place roughly between the more vigorous and the milder qualities: **der Hochmut, Übermut; die Anmut, Demut,** etc.

(2) Those in **-teil** (**der Teil,** *part*), are generally masculine: **der Anteil, Vorteil;** but **Teil** is still often neuter in the sense of *portion* (cp. **ein gut Teil, sie hat das bessere Teil erwählt),** and some follow this gender: **das Abteil, Gegenteil,** especially those reflecting the sense of *portion*: **das Altenteil, Erbteil,** both terms connected with inheritance.

(b) There are numerous misleading analogies with compounds; thus **die Armut** is not connected with **-mut,** nor **das Urteil** with **-teil; die Antwort** is not neuter, nor is **die Heirat** masculine; **das Interesse** is not feminine, being derived from a compound Latin infinitive.

443. Singular and Plural Number of Nouns

(a) Certain nouns occur only in the plural form, mainly because of their meaning; they are called **Pluraliatantum** ("only plurals"):

(1) Words of classical origin in **-ien** and **-en,** as: **Ferien, Naturalien, Personalien, Utensilien; Annalen** and words for animals (**Herbivoren**) or plants (**Orchideen**); here a German compound usually replaces the missing singular, and often the group name: **der (die) Pflanzenfresser, Knabenkraut(pflanzen).**

(2) Illnesses, as **Blattern, Masern, Pocken,** etc.; **Auslagen, Einkünfte, (Un)Kosten, Spesen; Effekten, Gliedmaßen; Alpen** [but **die Alp(e),** *high meadow in Alps*], **Niederlande; Gebrüder, Geschwister** (illogical plurals of earlier collective singulars); **Leute** [cp. § 445 (c)], **Eltern.**

Distinguish **Leute, Menschen, Personen.** **Leute** is unspecified and miscellaneous people: **die Leute sagen . . . (man sagt),** *people (they) say . . .* **Menschen** is also unspecified people, usually of indefinite number, but in a situation which can be generalised: **viele Menschen standen umher** (*a crowd*), **die Menschen glauben immer . . .,** *people* (*men*, by reason of human nature) *believe . . .* **Personen** is specified people, often numerically definite: **vier Personen waren im Zimmer.**

(b) A number of very common words are singular in German, plural in English:

der Gewinn, *winnings;* **der Hafer,** *oats;* **der Inhalt,** *contents;* **das Hauptquartier,** *headquarters;* **die Kaserne,** *barracks;* **der Lohn,** *wages;* **das Mittel,** *means;* **das Mittelalter,** *Middle Ages;* **die Nachricht,** *news;* **das Protokoll,** *minutes;* **der Rückstand,** *arrears;* **der Schadenersatz,** *damages;* **Westindien,** *the West Indies.*

Further, (1) collective words compounded with **-werk,** etc., as **Feuerwerk,** *fireworks* [*v.* § 444 (b) (4)], and (2) "pair" words, as: **die Brille, Hose** (also plural), **Schere, Zange,** *pair of spectacles, trousers, scissors, tongs;* and **das (der) Pyjama,** *pyjamas.*

Most of these have their plurals, which appear in English either (i) in the same form, **die Treppe, Treppen,** *stairs;* or (ii) with the appropriate group words: **Brillen,** *pairs of spectacles;* **Löhne,** *rates of pay.* Such summarising terms are also useful in the singular: **eine Nachricht,** *item (piece) of news* (cp. **ein Glück,** *stroke of luck*).

(c) Some words, while singular in English, may have either number in German, thus **die Auskünfte, Fortschritte, Geschäfte, Haare,** *information, progress, business, hair,* are as common as the singular; **das Geschäft** may be *business* (*premises*); **die Kenntnisse** is common in compounds: **ich habe nur Schulkenntnisse im Englischen,** *a school-knowledge of English.*

444. Nouns with no Plural or Variant Forms in Plural

(a) Nouns indicating an undifferentiated collective (**der Adel**), a material (**die Butter**), or an abstract concept (**der Tod**), cannot in themselves take plural number. This rule may be absolute (**der Adel**), or modified in practice in that a particularised sense of the noun is indicated by:

(1) A normal plural: **Tode,** *deaths* (*kinds of death*).

(2) A plural of an analogous compound: **das Glück,** *fortune;* **Glücksfälle,** *strokes of fortune, windfalls.*

(b) Material collectives normally have no plural:

Butter, Einkommen, Eis, Gold, Hafer, Inhalt, Kaffee, Laub, Milch, Obst, Putz, Rauch, Sand, Tau, Staub, Stroh, Vieh, Wild, etc.

But (1) analogous plurals may be formed through compounds:

Putzsachen, *finery;* **Kohlköpfe,** *cabbages;* **verschiedene Kaffeesorten** or **Tucharten,** *various coffees, cloths.*

(2) Two simple plurals may exist, that with mutation tending towards a concrete (object) sense, that without mutation having more abstract ("type") force: **die Tücher,** (*household*) *cloths,* **Tuche,** (*types of*) *cloth;* **die Hörner,** *horns* (*on the animal*), **Horne,** (*kinds of*) *horn.*

(3) Plurals in **-sorte** are commoner in commerce than in science (**ätherische Öle, tierische Eiweiße**) or general use (**aromatische Tees**); there is now even a fashion for the simple plural, resisted only by **Butter, Kaffee, Zucker;** the distinction is preserved in:

Für diese Zigarettensorte verwenden wir nur feinste mazedonische Tabake (newsp. adv.), *for this brand . . . only the finest tobaccos.*

(4) Certain words are commonly used to form the second component of a singular collective, which often requires the plural or a group noun in English: **die Konkursmasse,** *assets of a bankrupt,* **das Takelwerk,** *ropes, rigging,* **der Gebäudekomplex,** *group of buildings,* **das Bienenvolk,** *swarm of bees.*

(c) Abstract nouns normally do not form a plural; this limitation applies:

(1) Absolutely in the case of the neuter adjective noun [**das Un-angenehme**, *v.* § 143 (*b*)], since the plural form can only refer to persons; but only

(2) Relatively to (i) the infinitive noun [**die Andenken**, etc., *v.* § 208 (*b*) (1)], and (ii) many abstract terms which form a simple plural with particularisation of sense: **Größen**, *important people*, **Schönheiten**, *beautiful women* or *aspects*, **Hoffnungen**, (*specific*) *hopes*, etc.

(3) Relatively also to those abstracts which form plurals with (i) analogous suffixes: **Räubereien**, *robberies*, **Liebschaften**, *loves*, **Kümmernisse**, *cares*, **Streitigkeiten**, *conflicts;* or with (ii) compounds in **-fall**, *event*, **-tat**, *act:* **Gewalttaten** (**Gewalttätigkeiten**), *acts of violence*, **Unglücksfälle**, *misfortunes*.

Various forms above may be differentiated, thus: **Tode**, *kinds of death*, or *deaths* (figurative, e.g. *a thousand deaths*), but **Todesfälle**, *cases of death* (*i.e.* people dying). A selection of differentiated plurals is included in Appendix A.

(4) A multiplicative plural singular [cp. § 154 (*b*)] in **-fach** is often used in legal language with plural force: **er kam wegen mehrfachen Betruges vor Gericht**, *was charged with several acts of fraud* (but: **er setzte seine Betrügereien ungehindert fort**, *continued his frauds unchecked*).

445. Differentiated Plurals in Concrete Nouns

(*a*) Many words, not specifically abstract or collective in sense, unite several senses under the same singular form, but differentiate these either by gender, or by plural form, or both; a selection is included in Appendix A.

(*b*) Of these, a number of masculine and neuter nouns have a contrasted plural in (i) mutation and **-er,** which is felt to indicate richness and variety, as against (ii) the **-e** or **-en** plural, which is a less concrete (sometimes poetical) extension of the singular sense: **die Länder**, *countries*, **Lande** (poet.), *lands:* **die Wörter**, *words* (unconnected, thus rich in variety, *e.g.* **Schimpfwörter**, *abuse*), **Worte**, *words* (in connected discourse, thus with less individual force). Compare, at Appendix A, **Ort, Ding, Mensch**; and **Mann** below.

(*c*) **Der Mann** has, apart from the archaic **Mannen**, *vassals*, two plurals used in compounds:

(1) **-männer**, where the reference is general (**Ersatzmann**, *stand-in*, **Strohmann**, *straw-man*), or specifically male (**Staatsmann**, *statesman*, **Steuermann**, *helmsman*).

(2) **-leute,** where the reference is to an occupation or status (**Bergleute, Geschäftsleute**), or at least not specifically male (**Edelmann, Edelfrau, Edelleute,** *nobility*).

Thus a word may be differentiated in the plural: **Ehemann,** *husband,* **Ehefrau,** *wife,* **Ehemänner,** *husbands,* **Eheleute,** *man and wife,* or *married people.*

446. Inflection of Complex Nouns

(*a*) Normally, compound nouns have the inflection and plural of the second component only. But certain compounds of adjective and noun are given interior inflection: **der Hohepriester, des Hohenpriesters,** *High Priest* (Bibl.); sometimes **die Langeweile, der Langenweile, aus Langerweile** (but **das hat noch lange Weile,** *that can wait*); **der Armesünder, des Armensünders, zwei Armesünder,** lit., *poor sinner,* earlier restricted to *person condemned to death,* now widened again to *person in the dumps* (*v.* below).

(*b*) Adjective/noun groups of this kind compounded with a further noun raise certain problems:

(1) Reference of the adjective if this is separated from the compound noun: **das geheime Stimmrecht,** *right to secret franchise* (not, as apparently, *secret right to the franchise*); cases of transferred reference of the adjective with humorous result were earlier popularly quoted: **ein geräucherter Fischhändler,** *a smoked fish-dealer,* but most compounds of this kind are immediately clear and unexceptionable.

(2) Internal inflection, if all three components are compounded: **das Armesündergesicht,** *woeful mien;* it is now considered preferable to compound fully, omitting the inflection: **der Armsünderkarren,** *tumbril,* **eine Rotkreuzschwester,** *Red Cross sister,* or at least not to inflect: **in einer solchen Armeleutestube;** but a few may still inflect: **in der Saurengurkenzeit,** *in the silly season.*

447. Nouns Formed from other Parts of Speech

(*a*) There is not a single part of speech or syntactical fragment which may not be converted to nominal use. A selection is quoted below. By standard convention such words are neuter, but there are exceptions [*v.* § 441 (*c*) (2)]. They are either invariable, or take strong declension, with genitive in **-s,** plural in **-s** [cp. § 131 (*c*)] or **-e.**

(*b*) Nouns formed from other parts of speech.

(1) Adjectives, *v.* §§ 143 f. and 185 f.

(2) Verbs: *v.* §§ 204-9 (infinitive nouns), and § 143 (adjectival participle-nouns); past participles: **ein Unentschieden,** (*football*) *draw,* **ein Eingesandt (an eine Zeitung),** *a letter,* etc., *to the Editor;* finite form: **Hartes Muß der Entsagung,** *the harsh necessity of renunciation* (chapter heading).

(3) Pronouns: *v.* § 167 (*c*) (1); **das ländliche Einerlei,** *monotony of country life;* **das Nichts,** *negation, Nirvana.*

Sie, die sonst zu aller Welt demütig in der dritten Person spricht, holt ein nacktes und hartes Du aus ihrem Innern hervor (F. Werfel), *fetches a naked, hard "Du" from deep within her.*

(4) Prepositions: **das Für und Wider** (or **Gegen**), *the pros and cons.* **Die Sandrock spielte . . . ihr Gegenüber glatt nieder** (H. von Doderer), *played her opponent off the court* (used without distinction of sex, in sport, war, negotiations, etc.).

Er hat sich erst in späteren Jahren das „von" zugelegt, *only later did he assume the particle of nobility.*

(5) Adverbs: **die Vielfalt des Außen,** *variety of the world;* **der schwebende Augenblick des Jetzt,** *fleeting present moment;* **die Ferne des Einst,** *remoteness of the past.*

Mit Restaurieren und Renovieren und Aufpolieren machen wir aus dem Gestern ein falsches Heute (H. Kasack), *we make out of* (*things of*) *the past a false present.*

(6) Other parts of speech, thus interjections:

merkwürdig vokalische Urlaute . . . ein gedehntes, fast erschrockenes „Ah" und „Oh" hingerissener Bewunderung und dann wieder ein rapid erschrecktes „Oi" oder „Oiweh" (S. Zweig).

(*c*) Nouns formed from syntactical fragments, etc.

(1) Syntactical fragments: **das Gang-und-Gäbe** (Th. Mann), *accepted custom;* **ein Stelldichein,** *rendezvous;* **ein Zuhause,** *place to live.*

Alles kam darauf an, den richtigen Augenblick wahrzunehmen. Ein Zufrüh konnte ebenso wie ein Zuspät alles verderben (W. Bergengruen), *to act too soon might be as fatal as to act too late.*

(2) Fragments of speech: **er rief ihr ein „Guten Morgen" zu** (*not* masculine); **nicht einmal ein Dankeschön,** *not even a word of thanks;* the opening words of prayers: **das letzte Ave Maria;** distinguish **das Paternoster** (= **Vaterunser,** *Lord's Prayer*) and **der Paternoster,** *lift on the chain link system* (gender by analogy from **der Aufzug**).

„In der Tat . . .", sagte er und dieses In der Tat war genau so lang wie sein linker goldgelber Backenbart (Th. Mann), *this "Indeed" was as long as . . .*

448. Stress of Compound and Complex Words

(*a*) As a general rule, German words, including compounds and derivatives, are front-stressed, thus: **das Hóchhaus, die Réinemachefrau, zwéistimmig, hóchflutähnlich, síebzehn,** etc.

Clearly recognisable broad groups of exceptions are, *e.g.*:

(1) Nouns with foreign end stress, *v.* passim in §§ 76, 89 f., 130. Also some foreign abstract and collective suffixes, as in **Prominénz, Theoríe, Generalität, Frisúr;** but -ik varies, both in its concrete and collective sense: **Katholík, Musík,** but **Téchnik, Botánik,** and **Mathematík** or **Mathemátik.**

(2) Verbs with inseparable prefixes [*v.* § 88 (*b*)], and nouns and adjectives derived from these (*v.* § 193, nouns; adjective: **versándbereit**).

Certain other recognisable groups, however, have what may be termed: (i) equal stress (on two components); (ii) second stress (on the second of two or more components); (iii) end stress (on the last of any number of components).

(*b*) Equal stress, especially in nouns and adjectives, where the first component does not modify the sense, but is rather:

(1) A descriptive addition, *e.g.* with colours: **grásgrün,** *grass-green* (but cp. **Gráshalm**).

(2) An intensifier, *e.g.* **húndemûde,** *dog-tired,* **ein Mórdskérl,** *devil of a fellow* (but cp. **Húndehütte, Mórdtat**).

(*c*) Second stress obtains where a second component is felt still to be the main bearer of the meaning, especially when:

(1) An inflectional relationship obtains: **die Muttergóttes** (but **die Góttesmutter**); **die Langewéile** (but **die Lángweile**); **die Rotekréuzschwester** (but **die Rótkreuzschwester**), cp. § 446.

(2) The first element is (i) a fraction: **eine Viertelstúnde, ein Achtelpfúnd** (but **Halb-** is stressed: **ein Hálbjahr, Hálbpfund**); or (ii) a numeral which quantifies the following noun: **das Zweikámmersystem,** *bi-cameral system,* **die Dreifélderwirtschaft,** *three-field agriculture* (but **der Dréispitz,** *three-cornered hat,* and **der Dréimaster,** *three-master,* do not quantify the corners or masts); note also **das Jahrhúndert, Jahrtáusend.**

(3) Names of feasts when compounded from days of the week: **Aschermíttwoch, Ostersónntag** (but: **am ersten Pfíngstfeiertag**).

Note.—Official and military titles formed with **General-, Ober-,** or **Unter-,** vary greatly in stress, and should be looked up in a dictionary.

(*d*) End stress obtains in many compounds in which the principle of association is less the modification of one component by a preceding one (das Hóchhaus, a kind of house), than a series of externally related items (das Abecé, *the ABC*). As none of these items is felt to attract the accent, group unity is conferred by making the appropriate stress of the last one the group stress. Such compounds include:

(1) Compound numerals: **dreihundertundzéhn**; points of the compass (**Nordnordóst**); many adjectives of colour (**schwarzweißrót**, of a flag), of national and political groups (**deutschschwéizerisch, deutschnationál**), and their corresponding nouns (**der Deutschamerikáner, Schleswig-Hólstein**).

But in the attributive position, end stress may give way to secondary front stress: **fúnfundzwanzig Männer, die schwárzweißrote Fáhne.**

(2) Numerous onomatopoeic formations: **Kladderadátsch** (= **Krach!** title of a satirical newspaper); **das Abrakadábra,** *abracadabra;* **etepetéte,** *finicky.*

(3) Many syntactical fragments: **das Einmaléins,** *multiplication table;* **ein Lebehóch,** *a vivat;* but a leading verb often assumes front stress, reflecting the natural stress of the connected statement: **der Túnichtgut, Lúginsland; das Vergíßmeinnicht.**

(4) Finally, many adverbs and particles in compound, though not all for the same reason: **davón, heréin; durcháus, zuvór; nachdém, indéssen; anstélle** (but **ánstatt**); **zugrúnde(gehen),** etc.; **stromáb, tagáus tagéin; allerhánd, unterderhánd; schlechterdíngs,** etc.

But the requirements of group rhythm and emphasis may shift this. **Davón,** but: **dávon sagte er mir níchts. Wovón,** but: **er sprach vom Besuch . . . Wóvon sprach er? Überáus,** but: **ein úberaus schöner Ánzug. Allerhánd,** but: **állerhand Léute.**

448A. Rhetorical and Rhythmic Stress

Word-stress, as described in § 448, may be affected by factors of emphasis, contrast, and group rhythm.

(*a*) Emphasis may cause shift of stress:

(1) Occasionally, *e.g.* on to a suffix: **Ich sage Ihnen, es ist einfach furchtbár! Heillós!** But group rhythm may replace the accent in the adjectival position: **ein héilloses Durcheinánder!**

(2) Permanently in some cases, especially adjectives in **-lich, -ig,** though these suffixes do not take the stress themselves: **hauptsáchlich, vorzúglich, wahrháftig,** cp. **Háuptsache, Vórzug, wáhrhaft.**

Distinguish **ein áußerordentlicher Professor,** regular title for holder of certain kind of non-established Chair; but **ein außerórdentlicher Mann.** Cp. English *éxtraordinary (confessor), extraórdinary man.*

(*b*) Contrast may shift the stress on to a differentiated syllable; thus **Subjékt, Objékt** may be front stressed: **das Súbjekt, nicht das Óbjekt.** This principle has no doubt speeded up assimilation of **Síngular, Plúral,** to German front stress. It has, however, caused confusion with the inseparable prefix **miß-,** *v.* § 472 (*d*).

(*c*) Group rhythm often influences stress, especially in words in the attributive position before nouns (*v.* passim § 448, here, and § 448B), and in (normally end stressed) foreign words used as appositions of title: **Generál,** but **Géneral von Fálkenstein; Bäckeréi,** but **Bǎckerei Úlmenhorst; Theoríe,** but **die Théorie Héisenberg(s).**

448B. Stress of Adjectives with Prefix Un-

This group is caught, in respect of its stress, between conflicting requirements.

(*a*) Normally, and by general rule, such words conform to the front stress of nouns with nominal prefix: **úngefähr, únwissend,** as **Únsitte, Úntiefe,** etc. But two groups are felt to have verbal force and take their stress elsewhere:

(1) Adjectives in **-bar, -lich, -sam,** when passive in force, have emphatic accent [*v.* § 448A (*a*) (2)], *i.e.* the root syllable is stressed even when the original verb is separable: **unaufháltsam, unausfúhrbar unverzéihlich,** etc.

(2) Past participles, in which the verbal action is stressed and the meaning passive, may have stress appropriate to the verb: **unbeséhen, ununterbróchen, unvolléndet.**

(*b*) The prefix **un-** can, however, even in the two groups in (*a*), never be deprived of secondary stress, and a slight shift in the rhetorical or rhythmical accent of the statement will develop this, giving the word two equal stresses, or a strong leading stress, with secondary stress on the syllable appropriate under (*a*):

(1) Emphatic stress in adjectives in **-bar,** etc.:

    únverzéihlich, únaufháltsam, únausfúhrbar or **únáusfúhrbar.**

(2) Group stress normally requires a past participle used in the attributive position to take the adjectival front stress, even when elsewhere (in the predicate) it may take verbal stress:

Seine Macht war unumschränkt, but: **er besaß únumschränkte Gewalt. Sie redete ununterbróchen,** but: **eine únunterbrochene Folge von Gemeinplätzen.**

    Cp. **seine Anwesenheit blieb unbemérkt,** but: **er war únbemerkt eingetreten.**

(c) The difference between verbal and adjectival stress in past participles in **un-** leads to differential stress between two apparent synonyms or two senses of the same word:

únvermählt, *single* (a state), **unveréhelicht,** *unmarried* (a lack), **úngezogen,** *naughty* (children), **ungezógen,** *not drawn* (lot), **únerhört,** *disgraceful* (behaviour), **unerhört,** *unheard* (petition).

(d) In some adjectives, not past participles or passive in force, stress is shifted away from the leading syllable for emphasis:

unéndlich, unmöglich, unstérblich, etc.

Exercise LIX

A. Translate into English:

1. Er griff in eine große Blechbüchse und füllte die Waagschale mit Zwieback . . . Wir steckten die hellbraunen Zwiebäcke in die Tasche (E. Kreuder). 2. Ich kann keinen Shimmy tanzen, und auch keinen Walzer und keinen Polka und wie die Dinger alle heißen (H. Hesse). 3. Wenn ich aber nach beendeter Kurzweil meine schale und nichtige Alltagskleidung wieder angelegt hatte, so befiel mich . . . ein Gefühl unendlicher und unbeschreiblicher Langerweile (Th. Mann). 4. Der in unserer Sprache am meisten gebrauchte Buchstabe ist das e (H. Reimann). 5. Durch über ein Jahrtausend war die christlich-kirchliche Lehre Maßstab für Wahr und Falsch, Richtig und Unrichtig (R. Guardini). 6. Der Quittungsblock erschien, Geld wechselte seinen Besitzer, ein höfliches „Danke auch. Guten Tag" (H. Fallada). 7. Third-rate modern plays: Stücke von Dichterlingen in Kafkaterstimmung, die häufig auf dem Bahnhof spielen, wobei irgendwer irgendwie auf irgendwas wartet (Simpl.). 8. Translate and explain the following combinations: die reitende Artilleriekaserne, der saure Essigfabrikant, eine unverheiratete Beamtenwohnung; die philosophische Doktorwürde, der deutsche Sprachunterricht, das Bürgerliche Gesetzbuch. 9. Translate and explain the following compounds: silberne Hochzeiter, Lebendgewicht, Begleiterscheinung, eine Gemischtwarenhandlung, ein Gebrauchtwagenhändler, spätes Eheglück. 10. Proverbial: Gehgemach und Lebelang sind Brüder. Tummeldich hat den Hals gebrochen, Langsam lebt noch.

B. Translate into German:

1. She had learnt to realise that people can die many deaths in the imagination. 2. A fresh north-wester sprang up early in the afternoon. 3. Two Junkers and a large four-engine Condor were circling over the

deserted airfield.   4. Great was the pleasure of the young ne'er-do-wells when they had played a successful trick on their schoolmaster.   5. The ascent of the Jungfrau had always been one of his dearest ambitions as a mountaineer.   6. As I knocked I heard an impatient "Come in".   7. With a brief "If you please" the maid showed the visitor into the drawing room.   8. His great interest in my project was the opposite of what I had expected.   9. I need a new pair of scissors for this work; you can put them down to expenses.   10. The monotony of his long flow of technical words began to get on my nerves.

CHAPTER LX

PREPOSITIONS OF LOGICAL RELATION I

Considered here are prepositions expressing general logical relations, comparison and identity, and opposition.

Prepositions of General Logical Relation: An, Auf, Für, Gegen(über) Mit, Über, Um, Von, Vor, Zu

449. An, dat.; *at, on, of,* etc.

An may express the sense of *about*: **das Unerträglichste aber an Schwabing sind die Gäste selbst;** *at* (*in*): **ein Lehrer an einer Schule, teilnehmen an einer Firma; der Kummer frißt (nagt) einem am Herzen;** *to* after words derived from verbs: **(er wurde zum) Verräter an seinem Lande,** *became a traitor to* . . ., **Dienst am Volk,** *service to the community* (**verraten, dienen** with dat.).

Analogous to the partitive use of **an** (*v.* § 417), and reflected in various examples above, is that in which it links a verb to the noun on or through which, as a material, the verbal activity is realised. Two aspects may be distinguished:

(1) The activity is obliquely, not immediately, directed towards the object, so that (i) the object remains unconsumed, uncompleted, **man arbeitet an einem Buche; ein Gesicht, als trüge dieser Mensch an einer auferlegten Buße** (H. von Doderer), *labouring at an imposed penance;* or (ii) the relation is indirect: **der Kummer nagt am Herzen** (but **der Hund nagt den Knochen**), **ich roch an der blutigen, grellen (Jazz)- Musik** (H. Hesse), *smelt at, savoured* (but **den Braten riechen**); cp. **an etwas schnuppern,** *to sniff.*

(2) The object provides the occasion of the activity, that through which it is realised, and thus the cause: **an einer Lage verzweifeln,** cp. **er litt an Gicht** (occasion), **starb an der Schwindsucht** (cause); **sich an seinem Feinde rächen,** *to revenge oneself on one's enemy* (and **die Rache am Feinde**); **er wurde an seinem Kinde zu einem stilleren, besseren Menschen,** *through* (but without active cooperation); **sehr hübsche Fälschungen, an denen es fünfhundert Mark Belohnung zu verdienen gibt** (E. Wiechert), *which might be the occasion of earning* . . . (*for information leading to* . . .).

450 Auf, dat.; *in.* In descriptive phrases *in respect of*, analogous and often alternative to **an: er ist schwach am Leibe** (but **im Kopf**), **klein an** (or **von**) **Gestal�, blind auf** (or **an**) **einem Auge, taub auf einem Ohr** (**beiden Ohren**).

451. Für, acc.; *for.* There are so many uses that only a few can be given. The relationship between the subject and the outside world is assessed in respect of its benefit or otherwise. **Die Luft ist für mich gesund, vorteilhaft, wohltätig; die Gesellschaft erwies sich für sie als verderblich; für mich ist das (un)wichtig, (un)wesentlich.** The subject may be responsive or not: **ich bin für Natureindrücke (un)empfänglich, tot für die Welt; das Volk ist noch nicht reif für die Freiheit.** The subject may act to the profit of another: **für jemanden (etwas) werben, kämpfen, arbeiten, sich entscheiden.**

Benefit and (dis)advantage are the sphere of the dative of interest [*v.* § 382, especially (*c*)]; thus many uses of **für** are alternative with the dative, thus (as above): **die Luft ist mir gesund, den Eindrücken der Natur offen;** also **der Schmeichelei (or für Schmeichelei) zugänglich.** The dative may express an immediate feeling, reaction, **für** an ultimate (dis)advantage: **die strenge Behandlung war mir schmerzlich, ich erkannte aber nachher, daß sie für mich von Vorteil war.**

When concerned for the benefit of another, a person may be more actively (**für**) or more generally (**um**) involved: **die Mutter sorgt für ihren Sohn; sie ist besorgt (or bange) um ihn.**

Für also intersects the sphere of personal reaction expressed by **gegen: er war blind für (gegen) die Fehler seiner Schüler, unempfindlich für (gegen) Tadel;** thus accessibility (cp. **Natureindrücke, Schmeichelei,** above) shades off into inaccessibility.

452. Gegen, acc., and **gegenüber,** dat.; *towards.*

An attitude taken up towards another person or thing, or a treatment meted out consciously and intentionally, is expressed, after many adjectives, by **gegen: er war gegen uns freundlich, gut, falsch, großmütig, gefühllos.**

As with **für, gegen** is closely related to the sphere of the dative: **wir waren ihm (gegen ihn) dankbar, gnädig.** But the dative is distinct in many more subtle, less overt relationships: **er war gegen uns gut,** *good to us,* **er war uns gut,** *liked us;* and the force of the dative of reference [*v.* § 382 (*b*)] may cause the sense to be the opposite of **gegen: er war gegen uns streng (gleichgültig),** *strict with (indifferent to) us,* but: **er war uns zu streng** means that *he was too strict for us* (= for our liking), and **er war uns gleichgültig** means that he was indifferent as far as we were concerned, i.e. *we were indifferent to him.*

When feelings give place to actions, **gegen** is close to **mit** and **zu: sie war gut gegen die Kinder (or zu den Kindern),** *good to;* **sie war gut mit den Kindern,** *good with,* or *on good terms with.*

These examples show that **gegen** stands for both positive and negative attitudes; **wider** is used of actual opposition: **seine Liebe für mich** (zu usually for things: **seine Liebe zur Natur**), **gegen seine Freunde,** but **sein Haß gegen** or **wider alles, was ihn an den Vater erinnerte.**

Gegenüber is used, in figurative contexts, where the relation is indirect: **gegenüber seinen Schulkameraden ist er weit im Hintertreffen,** *in relation to his school-fellows he is far behind.* But the sense of indirectness has been applied in the sphere of **gegen** less on lines of meaning than of syntax, so that: (i) though adjectives are commonly used with **gegen** (*v.* above), (ii) verbs and nouns, especially those expressing *to behave, behaviour,* take **gegenüber: seinem Vater gegenüber verhielt er sich immer untadelig,** *towards his father,* **sein Benehmen gegenüber seiner Braut war erfüllt von . . . Zartgefühl** (Th. Mann), *behaviour towards . . .*

453. Mit, dat.; *with.* Expresses, in so many uses that only a few can be given, a close relationship or association between persons or things. In the sphere of association (*v.* §§ 499, 505, manner and means), usage in the two languages is quite close; but in that of general relations German has a number of unfamiliar idioms.

Wie war die Sache mit ihm? *that business about him?* **Mit ihm geht's bergab,** *he's sinking* (various senses). **Ich bin mit ihm verwandt, verlobt, bekannt,** *related, engaged to him, know him.* **Dieser Plan ist kaum mit dem anderen vergleichbar,** *comparable with, to.* (Both **verwandt** and **vergleichbar** may take the dative.) **Sie war mit ihm im gleichen Alter,** *of the same age as he.* **Er befaßt sich, beschäftigt sich mit Ornithologie,** *is engaged on.* **Die Dame mit dem roten Hut,** *in the red hat.* **Ich, mit meinen fünfzig Jahren . . .,** *I, at my age . . .*

454. Über, acc.; *about, concerning.* From the literal sense of place above (*v.* § 335), **über** comes to mean control or authority (**herrschen über,** acc.), then mental activity intentionally directed towards an object, whether remaining in the sphere of thought (**über etwas nachdenken, grübeln,** *to ponder on*), or issuing in general action (**erröten, klagen, lachen, scherzen über**), or specific action (**lesen, schreiben über**). Thus with nouns expressing the subject of intellectual products: **ein Buch, Vortrag, Vertragstext über . . .**

After adjectives, especially past participles (**über etwas froh, traurig, bekümmert sein**), the subject is more passive, so that **über** indicates less the object of the attitude than its cause (*v.* § 521).

Von, with its partitive force, expresses not the main object of mental activity, but a matter partially or indirectly touched upon: **Eben lese ich ein Buch über Geologie; darin liest man von Gesteinsschichten, landschaftsbildenden Kräften, usw.**

455. Um, acc.; *about, of, for,* etc. **Wir trauern, weinen um den lieben Freund, sind in Sorge (in Unruhe, bange) um ihn; es ist schade um das Geld,** *a pity about the money.* **Es ist etwas Schönes um die Jugend (Liebe),** *what a wonderful thing is . . .*

Um is less purposive than **über,** and again less partitive than **von: er schreibt ein Buch über . . .** (*about*), **im Buche handelt es sich um . . .** (*the subject is . . .*), **dort handelt der Verfasser von . . .** (*the author deals with . . .,* i.e. *devotes some space to . . .*). Thus after nouns, especially in headings and book titles, **um** describes something uncertain in extent, or ill-defined in nature, but crystallising round a person or thing: **Prozeß um Sauerbruchs „Memoiren",** and **Diskussion um Bert Brecht,** are newspaper headings, **Der Streit um den Sergeanten Grischa,** the title of a war book by A. Zweig.

Wissen demonstrates these senses, corresponding generally to news (**von**), knowledge (**über**), and experience or wisdom (**um**): **Was wissen Sie von seinen finanziellen Angelegenheiten?** *What do you* (*happen to*) *know . . .?* **Was wissen Sie über Beethoven?** *What have you learnt . . .?* **Der Dichter weiß um die letzten Geheimnisse des Lebens,** *the poet has knowledge* (though fragmentary and uncertain) *of . . .* (The last use is much overdone in pretentious writing.)

456. Von, dat.; *of, about.* Introduces the object of an activity which is intentional but imperfectly concentrated: **er sprach von seinen Erlebnissen, träumt von dem erhofften Glück, die Backfische** (*flappers*) **schwärmen von Filmstars** (cp. **über, um** above). It gives the subject of a poem, etc.: **das Lied vom Winde, das Märchen vom Schneiderlein** (but **ein Buch über Bismarck**). It links several forms of descriptive apposition: **ein Mann von Ehre, eine Frau von Geschmack; ein Baum von einem Kerl, ein Bild von Mädchen,** *a giant of a man, picture of a girl;* **bucklig von Gestalt,** or, more commonly, preceding the adjective: **von herrlichem Wuchs, von gutem Benehmen.**

457. Vor, dat.; *to, of,* etc. Closely related to the literal sense of appropriate behaviour before (in the presence of) someone, are uses with verbs of subjection to, guarding against, or of definite aversion from: **kriechen, sich schämen, sich fürchten, zurückschrecken vor jemandem** (**etwas**), *to cringe to, be ashamed before, afraid of, recoil from;* **man muß sich vor ihm hüten, in acht nehmen,** *be cautious in dealing with him.*

Among the few attitudes of confidence are: **ich bin bereit, meine Handlungen jederzeit vor ihm zu verantworten,** *to answer for . . .;* **ich habe alle Achtung vor ihr,** *a great respect for her.*

458. Zu, dat.; *to, towards, about.* Expresses generally the direction of an attitude or relation, usually with an element of addition (*v.* § 419) or aim (*v.* § 527): **Zu Ihrem Plan möchte ich folgendes vorschlagen . . . ; er hat leider noch nicht dazu Stellung genommen (sich dazu geäußert),** *given his opinion of . . .;* **zur Liebe befinde ich mich gerade in einem gespannten Verhältnis,** *relations are at the moment strained;* **die Jugend hat einen Hang zum Müßiggang,** *an inclination to idleness;* **er sprach zu mir** (usually **mit mir**), **war nett zu mir.**

459. Genitive Prepositions. A number of grudgingly admitted prepositions with the genitive may be avoided if the corresponding noun phrase (shown in brackets) is used: **angesichts des Todes,** *in the face of* (**im Angesicht des Todes,** but *considering* must be: **angesichts der Gefahr**); **bezüglich** and **hinsichtlich,** *with regard, reference to* (**in Bezug auf, mit Hinsicht auf,** acc.); **namens,** *in the name of,* and **seitens,** *on the part of* (**im Namen, von Seiten,** gen.); **zu(un)gunsten** or **zu (Un)Gunsten,** *to the* (*dis*)*advantage of* (better, **zum Vorteil, zum Nachteil,** gen.).

As earlier noted [*v.* § 405 (i)], genitive prepositional phrases of this kind when governing a pronoun take the possessive adjective rather than the genitive proper: **in** (or **vor**) **seinem Angesicht, in seinem Namen, zu ihrem Vorteil;** but: **in Bezug (mit Hinsicht) auf ihn,** with accusative.

Prepositions of Comparison and Identity

460. Für, acc.; *for, as.* **Für einen Ausländer spricht er gut Deutsch,** *for a foreigner.* After certain verbs, **für** links the direct object and objective predicate in a statement of identity (**ich halte ihn für einen klugen Mann**); it is alternative to **als,** a conjunction used in the same manner with other verbs, *v.* fully §§ 433 and 435.

461. Gegen, acc.; *against, compared with.* **Gegen die Gelehrten früherer Jahrhunderte sind wir alle Ignoranten,** *compared with.* **Der Lebensstandard ist gegen früher ganz unglaublich gestiegen.** Cp. also **gegenüber,** § 452.

462. Mit, dat.; *with, to.* **Die Verhältnisse auf dem Lande sind mit denen in der Stadt kaum vergleichbar,** *comparable with,* cp. also § 453.

463. Neben, dat.; *compared with.* **Czako war ein guter Sprecher, aber er verschwand neben seiner Partnerin** (Th. Fontane), lit., *disappeared beside, was quite overshadowed by . . .*

464. Unter, dat.; *by*. **Was verstehen Sie unter „Koexistenz"?** *understand by* . . . (but: **was meinen Sie mit . . .?** *mean by* . . .). Cp. also § 337 (*a*) (place).

465. Von, dat.; *of*. Cp. § 456 for various forms of descriptive apposition used as statements of identity.

466. Vor and **nach,** dat.; *before, after*. **Vor allem möchte ich folgendes betonen . . .,** *especially;* **er hat vieles vor seinem minder befähigten Bruder voraus,** *many advantages over*. **Er war nach dem Kaiser der mächtigste Mann Frankreichs,** *after the Emperor*.

In statements of relative priority, those with more local force use **voraus** (cp. example above) and **hinter,** for *before* and *after*: **Dem Kaiser voraus ging sein erster Würdenträger,** *before the Emperor*, **in der Reihenfolge ihres Auftretens kamen die Kurfürsten unmittelbar hinter (nach) dem Kaiser,** or **hinter dem Kaiser her,** with emphasis on both local order and precedence.

467. Zu, dat.; *to*. **Der Wein verhält sich zum Bier wie der Witz zur Zote,** *wine is to beer as wit is to bawdy*.

Prepositions of Opposition

468. Für, acc.; *against*. It is a man-made view which considers what is *good against* his enemies (as remedies for diseases, poison for pests), to be *good for* them: **Haben Sie ein Mittel für Kopfweh? Das Gift kann ich für Mäuse empfehlen.** Nowadays, **gegen** is preferred: **ein Mittel gegen Halsschmerzen,** especially with the sense *to use*: **dieses Pulver läßt sich gegen allerlei Ungeziefer anwenden.** But still: **ich muß für meine Kopfschmerzen etwas tun.**

A thing is sometimes exaggeratedly desired *in exchange for* life itself: **weil sie für ihr Leben gern Speiseeis aß,** cp. *would give her ears for . . .;* the negative is: **ich kann ihn für den Tod nicht ausstehen,** *not for the life of me* . . .

Für and **vor** were earlier not clearly distinguished, thus **Gnade für (vor) Recht ergehen lassen,** *to temper justice with mercy*, may be read as **für** (*instead of*) or **vor** (*give precedence to*).

469. Gegen and **wider,** acc.; *against*. In the general sense of opposition, hostility, resistence, there is little to choose between **gegen** and **wider,** though **gegen** is commoner: **gegen (wider) die Abmachung, gegen (wider) die Gewalt ihrer eigenen Gefühle; das geht gegen (wider) den Strich,** *against the grain*. Cp. also § 447 (*b*) (4).

But each has certain idioms in which it only is used, thus only **gegen** in: **in Sachen Müller gegen Müller** (*contra*, *V*., legal), **gegen die Liebe wächst kein Kraut** (prov., *v.* **für** above); in adverbial compounds: **ich bin entschieden dagegen;** with many verbs, as: **Berufung einlegen gegen,** *to appeal against,* **haben Sie etwas dagegen einzuwenden?** *anything to object?*

Wider is often more of internal conflict, as: **er tat es wider Willen;** but this may be just a matter of construction: **er tat es gegen seine eigene Überzeugung;** thus also **wider besseres Wissen,** but **gegen seine eigene bessere Einsicht.**

470. Entgegen and **zuwider,** dat.; *against.* **Zuwider,** *averse to.*

Entgegen precedes or follows the noun, **zuwider** only follows: **entgegen meinen Wünschen, meinen Wünschen entgegen (zuwider).** **Zuwider** is stronger, and as such is always used for inner repugnance: **dieser Mensch ist mir zuwider,** *repels me.*

Both may be used as end-position adverbs, and as such may join the verb as prefixes: **der Minister trat mit Entschiedenheit dem neuen Mißbrauch entgegen,** *determinedly opposed;* **ein solcher Handelsbrauch dürfte dem Gesetz zuwiderlaufen,** *probably infringes the law.*

Zuwider- in compounds has strong figurative force, and is almost limited to the two compounds **zuwiderlaufen** (*v.* above) and **zuwiderhandeln: Wer dem Verbot zuwiderhandelt, wird bestraft,** *infractions of the prohibition will be punished* (distinguish: **wer dem Verbot zuwider handelt,** *anyone who, against the prohibition, takes any action* . . .).

Entgegen, having both senses *towards* and *against,* may in compounds convey cooperation or opposition: (i) **entgegenkommen,** *to oblige, meet halfway,* is always positive; (ii) **entgegentreten, -stehen,** and **-setzen** are always negative (cp. **die entgegengesetzte Ansicht,** *the opposite view*); (iii) **entgegengehen** is neutral.

471. Trotz, gen. or dat.; *in spite of.*

Both **trotzen,** *to defy,* and **zum Trotz,** *in defiance of,* take the dative: **er trotzte seinem Meister, tat es seinem Meister zum Trotz.** Thus also did **trotz** earlier; but the analogy of **wegen,** complementary in sense, and of **ungeachtet,** almost identical, led to the use of the genitive in **trotz** also, and this is now common and correct. The dative with **trotz** is thus both older and less formal than the genitive, quite different from the dative with **wegen** (§ 516), which is a popular neologism.

There is some division of labour between the genitive and dative. Thus standing idioms, especially with indefinite pronouns, usually take the dative: **trotz allem, trotz alledem** (and in the old compound: **trotzdem,** adverb and conjunction); and the genitive is also often avoided where its use would lead to a multiplication of -s endings: **trotz dem Ernst seines Vorhabens;** but the genitive is common with strong adjectives: **trotz gelegentlichen Einspruchs,** especially in the plural: **trotz widerholter Versuche.**

EXERCISE LX

A. Translate into ENGLISH:

1. „Ida!" sagte sie zu Mamsell Jungmann, an der sie eine vertraute Freundin besaß . . . (Th. Mann). 2. Der Schmerz über den Verlust (eines Toten) sänftigt sich; nie aber verläßt uns die leise Stimme des Vorwurfs über das, was wir bei seinen Lebzeiten an ihm versäumten und zu versäumen gezwungen waren (W. Bergengruen). 3. Plötzlich fiel mir das Erlebnis vom Abend wieder ein, mit der rätselhaften Spitzbogentür, mit der rätselhaften Tafel darüber, mit den spöttisch tanzenden Lichtbuchstaben (H. Hesse). 4. Wie machst du es, daß du mit Fünfzig noch immer wie mit Fünfundzwanzig ausschaust? (F. Werfel). 5. „Und doch wissen Sie im Grunde, daß Ihr Abscheu vor dem Experiment kein Beweis gegen sein Gelingen ist" (Th. Mann). 6. (Er) zupfte immer wieder am Stiel der weißen Camelie, die er im Rockaufschlag trug (B. Werner). 7. Ich hätte dem Baron seine vier Jahre, die er älter war, ums Leben gern abgekauft (F. Thieß). 8. Er denkt edel von jedermann; über keinen Menschen hört man ihn klagen. 9. Gegen den Strom der eilig fortschreitenden Menschen konnten wir kaum ankommen. 10. Gegen den Geschmack dieses Gorgonzolakäses läßt sich nichts einwenden, für mich ist aber so was vollkommen unverdaulich.

B. Translate into GERMAN:

1. He worked at his large oil painting every morning, and by the progress he was making he realised that it would be finished by the autumn. 2. He found a yearly trip to the South of France of great benefit for his health. 3. Animals are seldom cruel to their young, but care for them as best they can. 4. Stop that man in the blue raincoat! 5. At present he is busy on a new scheme for importing ivory. 6. I could not help laughing at the child's solemn account of his adventures. 7. Ibsen's "Ghosts" deals with problems in which we in the twentieth century are no longer interested. 8. As he had no passport he was counted amongst the stateless refugees. 9. Nowadays there are drugs for every ache and pain. 10. In going abroad at this time he acted against the advice of his doctor and in the face of his own instinct.

CHAPTER LXI

VERBS, COMPOUND AND MODAL
AGREEMENT OF NUMBER AND PERSON

472. Plurality of Prefixes. Miß-, Ob-

Revise § 88.

(*a*) Some compound verbs have two prefixes. The combination of two inseparable prefixes being unknown, the possible combinations (in order of frequency) and their behaviour are as follows:

(1) Separable-inseparable: **anerkennen**, *to recognise*, has normally separation of the first prefix: **ich erkenne . . . an, habe anerkannt, glaube anzuerkennen.**

(2) Inseparable-separable: **sich überanstrengen**, *to over-exert oneself*, is inseparable: **überanstrengte, überanstrengt** (but sometimes, by analogy with **angestrengt, überangestrengt**).

(3) Both separable: **unterabteilen**, *to subdivide*, separates to the extent of admitting **-ge-** and **-zu-**, **unterabgeteilt, unterabzuteilen**, but avoids other forms.

(*b*) In fact, however, for the first and commonest group, either (1) forms other than the infinitive (**anvertrauen, vorenthalten, vorverlegen**) or the past participle (**ausverkauft**, *sold out*) are avoided; or (2) as with **anerkennen**, unseparated forms are increasingly used: **auf diese Weise anerkannte er . . .** (H. Hesse); but **anzuerkennen.**

(*c*) The conjugation of such verbs as a unit (apart from telegraphic convenience) is not entirely unjustified, since it is probable that some of them at least were formed, not through normal accretion of prefix to simple verb (**verkaufen** plus **aus**), but by back-formation from verbal nouns, thus **der Ausverkauf**, *bargain sale*, **die Überanstrengung**, *over-exertion*, **die Unterabteilung**, *subdivision;* or at least that the analogy of the verbal noun has caused a second formation, as: **anerkennen** (sep.), giving **die Anerkennung**, giving **anerkennen** (insep.). So **ich leiste (für etwas) Gewähr**, *undertake a guarantee*, becomes **die Gewährleistung**, *guarantee*, which (in spite of criticism) has returned in the limited (non-personal) sense: **diese Maßnahme gewährleistet den Erfolg.**

(*d*) **Miß-** is an unaccented, inseparable prefix, with pejorative force, thus contrasting negatively with simple verbs (**deuten, mißdeuten**, *to misinterpret*), or compounds with **ge-** (**gefallen, mißfallen**, *to displease*); thus past participle: **mißdeutet, mißfallen.**

False analogy of two kinds may, however, cause it to be regarded as accented, and thus as separable in the past participle: (1) the contrast of the verbal prefix **miß-** with its positive opposite, and the analogy of similar verbs with **fehl**, separable prefix: **fehlschießen,** *to miss,* **fehlschlagen,** *to fail* (= **mißlingen,** opposite of **gelingen**); and (2) the analogy of nouns with the corresponding (accented) nominal prefix **Miß-,** as **Mißachtung,** *disrespect,* from **Achtung.**

Thus, in addition to **mißdeutet,** there are two incorrect past participles, **mißgedeutet** (as separable compound), and **gemißdeutet** (as indirect compound, *v.* § 474). And among other irregular but accented forms are: **mißgelaunt,** *bad-tempered,* **mißgebildet,** *misshapen,* **miß(ge)artet,** *malformed,* all in common use as participial adjectives, cp. **die Mißlaune, Mißbildung, Mißart.**

(*e*) The opposite tendency not to separate **ob-,** giving forms as: **mir obliegt** (for **mir liegt ob**), *it is my duty;* **ihm hatte die Ausbildung jener . . . Kompanie oblegen** (E. Kästner), *he had been responsible for . . .* (for **obgelegen**), is however resisted as incorrect.

473. Verbs from Other Parts of Speech

(*a*) Verbs may be formed from other parts of speech, *e.g.* (1) from adjectives and nouns with verbal prefix: **verlangsamen,** *to slow up,* **beglückwünschen,** *to congratulate,* **sich verabschieden,** *to take one's leave;* (2) from nouns directly, whether common nouns: **robben,** *to crawl,* **tränen,** *to weep* (eyes), **weihnachten,** *to draw near to Christmas;* foreign nouns: **handikappen,** *to handicap;* proper names: **röntgen,** *to X-ray,* **lynchen,** *to lynch,* etc.

(*b*) Such words may be anything from old-established words to nonce formations, as when Bergengruen reproaches a correspondent for writing poetry in nineteenth-century style:
Hätten Sie wenigstens gerilkt, gewerfelt, geböllt . . ., *if only at least you had adopted the* (*modern*) *style of Rilke, Werfel, Böll.*
According to strict rule they are conjugated as compound or simple weak verbs: **wir verlangsamten das Tempo, wurden dadurch gehandikapt,** etc.

474. Verbs Indirectly Compounded from Nouns

(*a*) Certain verbs from compound nouns may, however, appear to be genuine compound verbs, formed from simple verb and prefix: **handhaben,** *to handle* (from **die Handhabe,** *handle, grip*); **ratschlagen,** *to take counsel* (from **der Ratschlag,** *counsel*); also certain others loosely compounded from two elements: **lobpreisen** (probably from **Lob und Preis singen**).

Strict rule requires in these, as in other modern verbal formations [v. § 473 (a) (2)], simple, weak forms: **handhabte, gehandhabt,** etc. Under the analogy of verbal compounds, however, such "indirectly compounded verbs" develop irregular forms of various kinds, which have won varying degrees of acceptance.

(b) The leading syllable is unstressed, and (1) the **ge-** of the participle is lost: **frohlócken, frohlóckt,** *exulted,* beside: **fróhlocken, gefróhlockt;** and even, in addition, (2) the second element is conjugated as a simple strong verb, thus: **man willfúhr ihm,** *humoured him,* beside: **man willfáhrte ihm.**

(c) The leading syllable is stressed, but the analogy of the simple weak verb causes intrusion of **-ge-** (and **-zu-**); this is now accepted practice with *e.g.* verbs in **not-** (emergency action), as **notlanden, nottaufen,** *to land, baptise in an emergency.* These are perhaps by back-formation from **die Notlandung, Nottaufe,** and have forms: **ich notlande, notlandete, bin notgelandet (habe notgetauft).**

(d) The leading syllable is stressed, but the analogy with the simple strong verb causes conjugation as a completely separable verb; this is now accepted practice with *e.g.* verbs in **wett-** (competitive activity, cp. **um die Wette laufen,** *to race*). They are perhaps by back-formation from nouns: **der Wettlauf, das Wetturnen,** etc., and have benefited from the example of **wettmachen,** *to make even,* which has always been separable. Thus: **wettlaufen, wettreiten, wettschwimmen, wetturnen,** etc., **ich lief,** etc., **wett, bin (habe) wettgelaufen,** etc. But **wetteifern,** *to compete,* is regular: **wetteiferte, gewetteifert.**

475. Other Verbal Forms by Back-Formation from Nouns

(a) Back-formation from nouns (cp. above, §§ 472 and 474) has probably given rise to certain other isolated verbal forms:

(1) Certain infinitives (only), from infinitive nouns, thus: **kunststopfen,** *to mend invisibly,* **sackhüpfen,** *to (take part in a) sack race,* **strafexerzieren,** *to do punishment drill.* Stages of formation: **das Stopfen,** *darning,* **das Kunststopfen, kunststopfen.**

(2) Certain past participles, from verbal nouns in **-ung,** thus: **uraufgeführt,** *given a first performance,* **spiralgeheftet,** *bound on "spiral" system,* **zwangsverschleppt,** *(compulsorily) deported,* from: **die Uraufführung, Spiralheftung, Zwangsverschleppung.**

(b) Any attempt to conjugate such forms would, in (1), lead to the difficulties noted in § 474, and, in (2), often present a manifest impossibility

because of the association of nominal and verbal prefix, as **urauf-,
zwangsver-**.

Compare analogous English forms, from nouns in *-er* (agent) or
-ing (verbal): *to bird-watch, hitch-hike, house-keep, sleep-walk.* Newspaper report: *a new plane has been test-flown* (from *test-flight*).

476. Modal Verbs (and Wissen). Conjugation, Constructions

Revise §§ 63 and 66.

(*a*) The imperative is hardly possible, except for **wolle!** *will!* and
wisse! wissen Sie, *know!*

The present participle is rare in its simple form, and usually occurs:
(1) as a participial adjective, with dependent infinitive and future force
[cp. § 430 (*b*) (3)]: **das nichtendenwollende Gelächter,** *prolonged laughter;*
ein die Einsätze lohnen sollendes Geschäft, *a business which should repay
the money invested;* and (2) in compounds, as **vermögend,** *well off,*
wohlwollend (mißwollend), *benevolent, favourably (unfavourably) disposed.*

(*b*) The dependent infinitive is often omitted in certain senses:

(1) Verbs of motion: **du sollst nach Hause; die Sache muß in Satz**
(E. Kästner), *must go into print;* **wollen Sie zu mir?** *are you looking
for me?* The past participle is regular [against § 66 (*b*) (2)]: **am
Vormittag haben sie zur Kirche gemußt** (H. Fallada), *had to go to Church.*

(2) tun, heißen: **Was kann ich für Sie? Was soll das?**

(3) With general force (cp. § 377):
Sicher durfte sie es nicht [es as (*c*) (1)]. **Aber sie glaubte, zu müssen**
(R. Guardini), *believed she had to.*

Compare also second example in § 253 (*d*) (2).

(*c*) Apart from their use with a dependent infinitive, the modal verbs
may commonly stand:

(1) With impersonal (situation) es as object, standing for the dependent
infinitive and any object of that infinitive:
**Kannst du das beweisen? Ja, ich kann es. Das kann ich (= das beweisen).
Wollen Sie mir den Gefallen tun? Ich will's, darf es aber nicht (= den
Gefallen tun).**

(2) With a noun clause as object [mainly **können;** cp. also (*b*) (2)
above]:
Ein Mann muß können, was er will (H. Fallada); **wer nicht kann, was er
will, muß wollen, was er kann** (prov.).

Wollen may take **es** and a **daß**-clause in the sense *to bring it about that*:

Ein unerwarteter Zufall wollte es, daß diese Begegnung nie stattfand, *it was due to an unexpected event that this meeting never came about.* Cp. **In den Pausen des Essens, so wollte es wahrscheinlich die Sitte, hielten . . . längliche Reden** (F. Werfel), *for such was apparently the custom.*

(3) But only **können** and **wollen** are used with a direct noun object: **er kann gut Deutsch,** *knows German well;* **er kann alle Vogelstimmen** (E. Wiechert), *can imitate all birds' cries.* Distinguish **können,** for skill, from **wissen,** for knowledge of facts, and **kennen,** for knowledge of existent things: **er weiß alle Vogelstimmen** (from books), **kennt alle . . .** (*can recognise*); only **wissen** can add the adverb **auswendig** (*by heart*).

Ich will nur sein Bestes, *I only want to serve his best interests.*

(*d*) **Können** and **wissen** may be used with the adverbs **aus, ein** (which do not compound with them), in the sense *to be at one's wits' end*: **verzweifelte Eltern, die nicht mehr ein noch aus wissen** (newsp.). **Der** high pressure salesman **ist einer, der den armen Käufer so unter Druck setzt, daß dieser nicht mehr recht aus kann** (newsp.), *can think of no excuse.*

(*e*) Nominal forms. (1) All modal verbs have the infinitive noun: **das Müssen, Wollen,** etc.; **das Können** has the specific concrete sense of *skill, capacity*: **über sein Können besteht gar kein Zweifel, aber . . .** (2) Several have verbal derivatives: **die Kunst, die Macht** (from older force of **mögen**). (3) Finite forms as nouns: **(das) Soll und Haben,** *debit and credit,* **das Soll und das Muß,** *duty and necessity* [cp. **Muß** also § 447 (*b*) (2)]; **das (Jahres-)Soll,** *quota of production,* much used in Communist vocabulary.

477. Negatives of Modal Verbs

Several modal verbs may have a full or a reduced negative:

(*a*) Müssen. (1) Full negative, a veto: **du mußt das nicht tun** (also **du darfst, sollst nicht . . .**); or compulsion of an opposite: **hier muß etwas nicht stimmen,** *there must be something wrong here.* (2) Reduced negative, absence of compulsion: **wir *müssen* ihn nicht empfangen,** *we don't have to see him* (also: **brauchen nicht**).

(*b*) Wollen. (1) Full negative, a refusal: **nein, meine Suppe will ich nicht essen! er *will* nicht hören,** *won't listen* (rather than *doesn't want to hear*). (2) Reduced negative, lack of desire: **ich will nicht hoffen, daß . . .,** *I hope that . . . not . . .*

478. Senses of Modal Verbs

Some of the more common of the special senses of modal verbs are given below.

(*a*) **Dürfen** always indicates permission, a right or liberty, but against the background of non-permission; a right or entitlement may be **können: Die Kinder dürfen im Garten spielen; in diesem Lande darf man offen seine Meinung sagen; hier kann man tun, was man will; der Richter kann die Öffentlichkeit ausschließen,** *it is open to* . . .

In restrictive contexts, **dürfen (nicht, nur)** means *need(s)* (*not, but, only*): **Wer den Schaden hat, darf für den Spott nicht sorgen** (prov.), *he who is in trouble need not be surprised when he is blamed into the bargain.*

(*b*) **Können.** Apart from the normal sense of capacity, power, the commonest secondary force is that of probability (= *may*):
Kann amtlich geöffnet werden, *may be opened in transit* (label attached by postal authorities to registered parcels).

In this sense, **er kann es getan haben,** *may have done it,* is distinct from **er hätte es tun können,** *might have done it* [but did not, cp. § 309 (*b*)].

(*c*) **Mögen.** Apart from the wide general use of probability expressed by English *may,* **mögen** also corresponds to the adverb *probably*:
Sie mochte die Mitte der Dreißig kaum überschritten haben, *was probably hardly past her mid-thirties.*

An inclination may be negated: **ich mag nicht gehen,** *am not keen on going;* but an improbability requires another modal: **das mag wohl sein,** *may well be,* but: **das kann (darf) nicht sein,** *cannot be* (*is improbable*).

(*d*) **Müssen.** As with English *may* (**mögen**), a limitation of *must* is its present force and lack of a suitable past; suitable forms are supplied by *have to, is obliged to, cannot but,* etc., but in a past narrative even these may fail:
Es war gegen halb 12 Uhr; die Badegäste mußten sich noch am Strande befinden (Th. Mann), *the summer visitors were, no doubt* (*he thought*) . . .

(*e*) **Sollen.** Apart from the normal sense of a duty or commitment laid on one by a person or circumstances, **sollen** commonly expresses future sense:
Regungslose Sekunden, dem, der stürzen sollte, lief Grausen den Rücken entlang (H. Mann), *the man about to fall (from his post)* . . .

Thus it is widely used for the (otherwise lacking) future participle [*v.* § 475 (*a*)] and future infinitive:

Das Einsteigen in die verschiedenen Gefährte schien sich schnell und ohne Störung vollziehen zu sollen, als . . . (Th. Fontane), *it seemed that getting into the vehicles was going to cause no difficulty when . . .*

(*f*) **Wollen** normally expresses the undetermined volition of the subject; it is therefore complementary to **sollen,** and with it often expresses future sense. Secondary senses have both a personal and non-personal subject:

(1) With personal subject, meaning:

to claim: **2200 Herzfachärzte aus 50 Ländern wollen sich mit ihrer Hilfe** (= an international language) **verständigt haben** (newsp.), *claim to have understood each other.*

to expect: **Die Gegenwartskrise ohne eine vorherige Erneuerung des Geistes ökonomisch lösen zu wollen, ist Quacksalberei** (E. Kästner), *to expect to solve the present crisis on economic lines . . .*

to be likely (about) to: **in Fällen, wo trotz ihren Gebrechen die Neigung eines jungen Mannes sich ihr hatte zuwenden wollen** (Th. Mann), *seemed likely to turn her way . . .*

Compare the common idiom: **er wollte eben . . ., als,** *was about to . . . when . . .*

(2) With non-personal subject, meaning:

should be, with the statal passive infinitive **sein:**

Dies Aufblühen ihrer Seele und Sinne . . . wollte verhehlt und verschwiegen sein (Th. Mann), *was of such a nature that it had to be . . .*

the adverb *almost, nearly,* with **(er)scheinen:**

Auch Genf wollte mir als ein südlicher Boden erscheinen (W. Bergengruen), *almost appeared to me as Mediterranean soil.*

Thus, without personal volition, **wollen** expresses the natural tendency or requirements of a thing's proper nature.

(*g*) **Wissen** is much changed in force by the contexts in which it appears: **wissen Sie noch . . .?** *do you remember?* **Das weiß ich nicht mehr,** *I have forgotten (that)*; and, for instance, with **wollen** as governing verb:

und will nicht wissen, daß der Wolf zuzeiten sein bestes Teil ist (H. Hesse), *and refuses to recognise that the wolf (in him) . . .*

mit einer langen Peitsche von eingelegter Arbeit, die, wie man wissen wollte, der Schah von Persien ihm geschenkt hatte (Th. Mann), *which, as people asserted . . .*

Cp. also § 434 (*e*) (variant of passive).

479. Modal Verbs and the Subjunctive

Modal verbs are widely used as subjunctive substitutes, thus cp. §§ 269 (*a*) and 273 (*c*) (will and wish), § 354 (indirect commands), § 426 (*c*) (conditional clauses), etc.; and also each verb in the Index.

480. Verbal Agreement.   Subject and Predicate

The verb agrees with its subject in number and person.   This may raise some problems, since, with the wide possibilities of inversion in modern German, it is often not clear which part is subject, and which is predicate.

(*a*) After a singular general pronoun, as **wer,** and the neuter forms **es, das, dies, jenes, was,** etc., a plural noun confers plural number on the verb:

Es zogen drei Burschen wohl über den Rhein (German folk song).
Es sind vier Jahre her, daß ich ihn nicht gesehen habe, *it is four years since . . .;* **Wer sind diese Menschen?   Was waren seine Worte?**

The rule covers also certain special cases, where:

(1) A singular pronoun follows with collective force:

Welche amüsanten und behaglichen Stunden waren das . . .! (Th. Mann), where the verb formally agrees with **das,** not with **Stunden.**

(2) Two pronouns are formally singular, the second collective:

Wer sind diese „Man"? (R. Guardini), *who are these people referred to as "man"?*

(3) Two pronouns, etc., with a following plural noun in apposition:

Es sind das alles spätere Fragen (Th. Mann), *those are all questions for later.*

(*b*) The above rule is applied by custom also where two nouns are concerned, one in the plural:

„Der beste Trost, der uns bleibt, sind die Freunde" (E. Mörike), *our best consolation is our friends.*

Note.—English observes the rule in (*a*): *who are . . .? what are . . .? there are . . .,* but does not normally use singular pronouns with collective force (**das,** etc.).   In (*b*) the number of the verb follows the subject as written, but it is often preferable to lead with the plural noun: *our friends are our best consolation.*

(*c*) A following personal pronoun attracts the verb into its number *and* person against a preceding noun or (non-personal) pronoun:

Der Autor, über den Sie schimpfen, bin ich.   Das Volk sind wir.   Das waren wir; was werden wir sein?

But the impersonal **es** always follows a personal pronoun: **ich bin's,** *it's me;* **wir waren's,** *it was us;* **bist du's?** *is it you?*

481. Number After Collective and Abstract Nouns

(*a*) Collective nouns. German has no plural of sense after a singular collective, as in English: *the team want to go home,* **die Mannschaft will nach Hause.** But collectives of quantity (with their associated plural nouns) as **Anzahl, Haufen, Menge, Reihe, Schar, Volk,** may be followed by a singular or plural verb according to whether the sense is felt to be that of the singular collective or of the following plural noun: **ein Haufen Volk stand an der Ecke;** but: **eine Menge Leute waren da,** and: **Eine Reihe Verben werden durch eine Präposition mit ihrem Objekt verbunden** (E. German Duden), *a number of verbs are* . . . (note the distributive singular **Objekt).**

This principle may apply to a collective compound:
Hühnervolk, braunes und schmutzig weißes, irrten zwischen den Rädern herum (E. Langgässer), *some fowls were wandering around* . . .

(*b*) Numerals raise some difficulties. **Über tausend Stück Vieh kamen um** (a number, not a collective). **Ein Viertel der Studenten arbeitet** (but **drei Viertel arbeiten**) **zu Hause** (number according to first part of fraction). Genuine collectives fluctuate [as in (*a*)]: **es kamen rund ein Dutzend Kinder.** Compare also § 60 (*b*) (multiplication), and § 60 (*d*) (percentages).

(*c*) Abstract nouns. In themselves abstract nouns have no bearing on the number of the verb; but a noun may be considered in a formalised (abstract) sense different from its concrete (plural) sense, and require a singular verb: **Götter ist der Plural von Gott. Klare Geldverhältnisse heißt reines Gewissen** (H. Fallada), *tidiness in money affairs means* . . . Compare the singular predicate of occupation: **seine beiden Brüder wurden Arzt** [*v.* § 294 (*a*)].

(*d*) Compare § 168 (*d*) for the third person plural of politeness.

482. Number and Person with Plurality of Subjects

(*a*) A plurality of subjects, unless affected by rules given in § 481, take a plural verb: **Jäger und Hunde waren schon da.** But if different grammatical persons are concerned (*i.e.* with at least one pronoun subject), a problem of person and number arises.

(*b*) If the force is conjunctive (*both* . . . *and* . . .), the subjects form a joint (plural) number for the verb, the persons being given preference in the order: first, second, third person:

Der Lehrer und ich waren da (= wir, first person); du und mein Bruder seid beste Freunde (= ihr, second person).

The joint subject may be expressed: du und ich, wir kennen uns.

(c) If the force is disjunctive (not . . . but . . ., . . . but not . . ., either . . . or . . .), the verb agrees with the nearest subject:

Du nicht wir sind das gewohnt; entweder ich oder er hat es zu tun;

but it may be better to avoid this by writing: du, nicht wir, bist das gewohnt, or by saying: du bist das gewohnt, nicht wir.

(d) Weder . . . noch . . . fluctuates between (b) and (c):

Weder meine Mutter noch ich hatten wohl allzuviel darüber nachgedacht (H. Risse), neither my mother nor I had . . . (= wir hatten).

richtig betrunken aber habe weder ich noch sonst jemand ihn gesehen (H. Hesse), neither I nor anyone else has . . . (= ich habe).

483. Plural Subject with Distributive Pronoun

(a) As in English (we each of us think . . .), a plural pronoun subject may be followed in German by a singular distributive pronoun, without affecting the number of the following verb; but the distributive may not precede the verb: wir glauben jeder, daß . . .

(b) A following (direct, prepositional) object may have the distributive singular in both languages:

Sie nahmen auch jeder einen Stuhl in die Hand, oder stützten sich nur auf die Lehne (Th. Fontane), they each took a chair . . . or leaned on the back of one.

but German is more careful to maintain a following possessive in the singular, often by postponing the distributive till after the main statement:

W. und die Bildhauerin suchten das Mädchen an sich zu ziehen, jeder auf seine Seite (E. Kästner), each to his (or her) own side.

EXERCISE LXI

A. Translate into ENGLISH:

1. Die hat ein Atelier und bildhauert, wenn man ihr glauben darf (E. Kästner). 2. Abfälle und Gemüseblätter und verfaulte Melonen, alles was da unten (im schwarzen Wasser) herumsuppte, schlaffe Wellen eines schweren süßlichen Todeshauches (H. Broch). 3. 62 Millionen Amerikaner sozialversichert (newsp. headline). 4. Genasführt bin ich auf alle Fälle, dachte die Frau und seufzte (E. Langgässer). 5. In diesen

ihren harten und abgearbeiteten Händen unruhete der Wille, etwas zu unternehmen (F. Werfel). 6. „Glaubst du, daß der ‚Wullenwewer‘ zu Hafen kann, Buddenbrook? Was für ein Hundewetter" (Th. Mann). 7. Während Vasco da Gama sieben Monate benötigte, um Indien zu erreichen, erfüllte Genosse Kolumbus dieses Soll schon in knappen drei Monaten (Simpl.). 8. Man schien es (= das alte Schloß) seinem gänzlichen Verfall überlassen, auch nichts an seine Stelle setzen zu wollen (Th. Fontane). 9. Children on holidays: Die eine Quelle der Beglückungen war das Meer, die zweite waren die Pferde (W. Bergengruen). 10. Die beiden jungen Mönche . . . hielten jeder eine brennende Kerze in der Hand (F. Werfel).

B. Translate into GERMAN:

1. He had always detested fish, but had failed to eliminate it from the menu. 2. The pilot was forced to make an emergency landing [*v.* § 474 (*c*)]. 3. I wanted to take my coat to be invisibly mended [*v.* § 475 (*a*)]. 4. The man who inhabits this room might well be an actor, thought K. 5. It was to have been a festive occasion and ought to have been a success. 6. This is a house in which you cannot appear at dinner except in evening dress. 7. Those who can, do; those who can't, teach (G. B. Shaw). 8. The young girls each wore a posy of violets. 9. "Is that you?" asked Marie, as she pointed to my name at the bottom of a short story in a magazine. 10. What amused me most were the monkeys wearing spectacles on their noses.

CHAPTER LXII

APPOSITION AND AGREEMENT OF NOUNS

484. Apposition of Nouns. Direct Apposition

(*a*) The modification of a noun or pronoun by a following (sometimes preceding) word, phrase, or clause, is an extensive practice in any language, and has here been variously treated, *v.* § 174 (titles), § 265 (*d*) (prepositional phrase), §§ 307 and 310 (clauses), § 364 (infinitive construction), etc.

Certain special problems of agreement occur when a noun or pronoun is followed by a noun in various kinds of apposition, *i.e.* direct (**der Monat Mai**), indirect (**Schopenhauer als Philosoph**), or in the genitive, whether subjective (**die Liebe der Eltern**), objective (**die Beschenkung der Kinder**), or partitive (**genug des Wartens**).

(*b*) Direct apposition. There are two possibilities:

(1) The noun in apposition follows in the same case (and, if possible, gender and number): **mein Bruder, der Briefträger; Friedrich der Große** [cp. § 174 (*c*)]; **die Dame, Besitzerin eines großen Gutes . . .**; but a title following a name in an address or on a title-page is usually uninflected: **Herrn Dr Hans Seemann, Privatdozent an der Universität Heidelberg; . . . von Dr H. Seemann, Korrespondierendes Mitglied . . .**

Such appositions must be enclosed in commas unless they are accepted appellations (**der Große; Nathan der Weise**, but: **Nathan, ein weiser Jude, . . .**).

(2) The noun in apposition, which is a proper name, whether personal (**der Fall Maurizius**), or of place (**die Stadt München**), or a common noun used as a proper noun (**der Schnitter Tod, Stunde Null**), remains uninflected whatever the case or number of the preceding word:

„Fräulein, geben Sie mir doch mal die Akten Stadelmann", *give me the Stadelmann file.*

ein stämmiger Herr vom Typ Bulldogge (H. Mann), *of the bulldog type.*

Note that *ostrich* is usually **der Vogel Strauß** (**eine Kolonie des Vogel Strauß**—Simpl.), to distinguish from other senses (*v.* Appendix A); plural, **die Strauße.**

Place-names in geographical expressions sometimes precede in compound (**das Riesengebirge**), or as adjectives (**der Bengalische Meerbusen**), sometimes follow (**die Insel Wight**). In no case does the English *of* (cp. the Isle of Wight) correspond to a genitive in German

Compare also § 235 (*d*) (2) (apposition of title of book etc.).

485. Indirect Apposition with Als

(a) A phrase introduced by **als** may have one of four functions:

(1) Subjective predicate: **er gilt als geschickter Arzt,** *is reputed to be a clever doctor,* **ich als dein Vater . . .,** *I, your father . . .*

(2) Adverb (esp. of manner): **er handelte als geschickter Rechtsanwalt und erfahrener Menschenkenner,** *as a skilful lawyer and . . .*

(3) Objective predicate: **er bezeichnete ihn als seinen einzigen Freund,** *described him as* (*said he was*) *his only friend.*

(4) Appositive: **er bat ihn als seinen einzigen Freund,** *asked him as* (*in the capacity of*) *his only friend.*

In (1) and (3) the **als**-phrase completes the sense, in (2) and (4) it is a descriptive addition to a statement.

(b) As regards agreement, all uses normally require the **als**-phrase to agree with its reference noun or pronoun in case: **Mir als erfahrenem Arzt sagen Sie das?,** etc. But non-agreement may be necessary to distinguish the adverbial from other senses:

(1) Time: **ein arbeitsames Leben, aus dem ihn aber als Student der Theologie der Tod hinwegriß,** *from which he was taken by death while still* (not: *in his,* or *death's capacity as . . .*) *a theological student.*

(2) Manner: **die Verdienste Lessings als Gründer des modernen deutschen Dramas,** *the achievement of Lessing as founder* (**Gründer** relates to verbal noun **Verdienste: Lessing machte sich als Gründer . . . verdient**).

An incorrect use of the dative in appositional phrases following the genitive has become surprisingly common:

Sie (= die Nonnen) werden . . . zur Erkenntnis der Erde als einem Tal unerschöpflichen Jammers geführt (E. Langgässer), *to see the earth as a vale of tears.*

486. The Attributive Genitive and its Replacement by Von

(a) Perhaps the commonest form of following (sometimes preceding) apposition is the attributive genitive, expressing a wide variety of ideas: (1) possession or origin: **der Wagen meines Vaters, die Tür des Hauses, die Werke Schillers;** (2) description: **eine Miene äußerster Milde, für die Dauer einer Minute, die Zeit der Entdeckungen;** (3) partitive: **ein Viertel der Studenten, einer seiner Briefe, viel Aufhebens;** (4) verbal activity, whether subjective: **das Schreien der Kinder,** or objective: **der Verkauf des Hauses.**

Over a wide field, almost all these forms are alternative to other constructions, as (i) an adjective: **der väterliche Wagen,** (ii) a compound noun: **die Entdeckungszeit, der Hausverkauf,** or (iii) **von** with the dative, *v.* below.

(*b*) A noun or pronoun in the genitive: (1) normally follows its noun of reference: **die Macht der Liebe,** but (2) precedes it if it is (i) a proper name: **Georgs Uhr, Frankreichs Weine,** or (ii) a common noun, then known as the "Saxon genitive", in set expressions, and in more formal, often ironical style:

die gewaltigen Sierren, die vielleicht noch keines Menschen Fuß erklomm (F. Werfel), *perhaps never yet climbed by foot of man.*

(*c*) **Von** with the dative is used instead of the genitive:

(1) Often before names of places: **die Hauptstadt von England, eine Ansicht von Rom;** always if they end in a sibilant: **die Straßen von Paris.**

(2) Before nouns which would otherwise not show the case: **ein Sammler von Kunstgegenständen; die Schönheit von Goethes Gedichten.**

(3) Before two nouns to avoid a double genitive: **die Rolle von Tells Knaben Walter;** eine Nachricht vom Vater des Kindes (*of the*); **der Gegensatz von Bindung und Freiheit.**

(4) Before nouns commonly uninflected, as numerals: **eine Gruppe von 10 Menschen** [cp. (2)], adverbs: **die Zeitung von gestern,** phrases: **der Anblick von zu Hause** (but: **der Mangel eines Zuhause),** and to avoid the genitive of the personal pronoun: **die Situation von uns beiden, ein Freund von mir** (also: **einer meiner Freunde).**

(5) Before a word separated from its governing noun, especially leading: **er aß von beiden Kuchen (von beiden Kuchen aß er) ein Stück.**

(6) Sometimes to distinguish an originator from the subject or owner of a work of art: **ein Werk von Goethe,** *by,* **ein Bild Bismarcks,** *of* or *owned by,* **ein Bild von ihm,** *by* or *of him,* **eines seiner Bilder,** *a picture of his,* or *by him.*

(7) After a noun of descriptive apposition, where both terms are equated: **ein Schrank von einem Mann,** *v.* § 456.

(8) Before a word regarded as a word, not as a meaning: **Götter ist der Plural von Gott; von Tau gibt's nur die Einzahl.**

(9) In familiar S. German use: **das Büro von meinem Bruder.**

(10) When the sense approximates to any of the specific prepositional uses of **von,** as origin or separation: **eine Nachricht von seinem Vater, eine Ausnahme von der Regel, der Wirt vom Goldenen Löwen;** partitive: **ein Rest von Ehre, eine Reihe von Tatsachen;** general relation: **die Kunde von neuentdeckten Erdteilen, deine Idee von der Gefahr des Geldes;** for many such uses, *v.* Index under **von.**

487. The Partitive and the Partitive Genitive

(*a*) The partitive idea is now expressed in three different ways: (1) by the (original) genitive: **der Worte sind genug gewechselt,** *enough words;* (2) by **von** with the dative: **von seinen Freunden kenne ich nur wenige,** *few of his friends;* (3) by simple apposition: (i) after indefinite pronouns: **viel Geld, etwas Wertvolles;** (ii) after many expressions of weight and measure: **ein Glas Bier,** *v.* § 241 (*b*); (iii) in many time expressions: **Anfang April,** *v.* § 59 (*b*).

The genitive is being replaced by other constructions, but it still has many characteristic uses.

(*b*) After indefinite pronouns, as with all expressions of quantity (*v.* § 241) the genitive is the rule with more developed expressions, especially in the plural: **viele seiner Bekannten,** but the singular has simple apposition: **wenig Geld, zuviel Ruhm, mehr Ansehen** [cp. §§ 100 f. and 146 (*d*)]. But the genitive is still used in certain (singular) set expressions: **Manns genug,** *man enough (to),* **(Un)Glücks genug,** *(mis)fortune enough,* **zuviel des Guten,** *too much of a good thing,* **(ohne) viel Aufhebens (Federlesens),** *(without) much fuss,* etc. And **von** (often in adverbial compounds) is required before pronouns: **wenige von ihnen, genug (mehr) davon, keiner von allen.**

(*c*) After **was,** interrogative, the neuter inflected adjective is used with partitive force, in the sense *what (of a certain kind):*
Aber sag' jetzt: was war denn heut abend Besonderes los, daß ˅ . . .? (H. Hesse), *what was particularly the matter this evening?*

Sometimes also: (1) with a noun: **was Wunders** (usually **was Wunder**), **wenn . . .,** *what cause is (was) there for surprise, if . . .;* (2) with **alles,** an untranslatable expletive: **Ach, was sagen die Menschen nicht alles,** *what people do say!* or, more ironical: **was wollen die Menschen nicht alles wissen!** *the things people (claim to) know!*

(*d*) After cardinals, ordinals, and comparatives and superlatives, both the genitive and **von** are common, but **von** has more partitive force, the genitive more that of priority: **zwei von meinen Schülern, die zweite dieser Schallplatten, die beste seiner Reden, das Beste von seinem Werk.**

(*e*) **An** is used with partitive force after: (1) a pronoun or noun of indefinite quantity [cp. (*b*) above]: **ein Geringstes an Arbeitsverpflichtung,** *a minimum of,* **ein Zuviel an Glück,** *an excess of,* cp. also § 417; and (2) after **was** used as general relative [cp. (*c*) above]:
Alles was die Erde hat an Begehrenswertem (H. Mann), *all that the world offers of desirable things.*

(*f*) **Unter** is used after indefinite pronouns: **viele unter seinen Anhängern;** and in expressions of priority of excellence: **die intelligenteren unter den Studenten,** cp. (*d*) above and § 411.

488. Other Partitive Constructions

(*a*) The leading partitive. In the partitive constructions, the word denoting the whole, or the material from which a part is taken, may precede the partitive word, often leading the statement:

Solcher unbeantworteter Fragen gibt es Hunderte, *there are hundreds such . . .*

Der Schlafzimmer im zweiten Stockwerke waren zu wenige (H. von Doderer), *there were too few . . .*

Er hat der Steckenpferde einen ganzen Zirkus voll (book review), *the author rides a whole stable of hobby-horses.*

The construction is common with words of amount: **die Menge, die Fülle;** and the order is often retained when an uninflected noun has replaced the explicit genitive:

Dafür aber gab's Gründe die Menge (F. Werfel), *there were reasons enough* (note the order) *for this* (*state of affairs*).

In China soll man Dienerschaft die Fülle haben. Ein europäischer Junggeselle hat ihrer (as above) **ein Dutzend** (Th. Mann), *servants in superfluity . . . a round dozen of them.*

(*b*) The independent partitive. A number of partitive constructions are used without being preceded by a pronoun or noun of quantity; the partitive phrase is (rarely) the subject, (more often) object or complement of the verb:

(1) Complement:

Nein, Sekretärin zu spielen, war nicht ihres Amtes (H. Kasack), *was not part of her duties,*

and compare such traditional expressions as the Biblical:

So gebet dem Kaiser, was des Kaisers ist . . . (Matt. xxii. 21), *the things that are Caesar's . . .*

and **er lebte des Glaubens, daß . . .,** *lived in the belief, that . . .*

The negative is not unknown: **sie erkannte, daß dort nicht mehr ihres Bleibens war,** *that there was no remaining there for her.*

Compare genitive after certain verbs [§ 379 (*a*)].

(2) Object:

Sie hätte dann am liebsten von allen vorhandenen Speisen auf einmal gegessen (R. Musil), *eaten* (*some*) *of all the dishes at once.*

damit beschäftigt, sich von seinem Vichy-Wasser einzuschenken (Th. Mann), *busy pouring out some of his Vichy water.*

489. The Subjective and Objective Genitive. Transitive Force

(*a*) The genitive after verbal nouns derived from transitive verbs may have either subjective or objective force, both in the noun and in any associated possessive: **die Liebe der** (subj.) **Eltern, die Stadt München und ihre** (obj.) **Verwaltung, sein** (subj.) **Gewahrwerden ihrer Schwäche** (obj.).

The verbal noun in **-ung** is strongly active in force, so that: (1) when standing alone, a preceding possessive is always objective: **seine Ermordung,** *his being murdered* (unless the sense has become nominal, thus **ihre Verwaltung,** above, could also be: *its*—subjective—*administration*); thus often with a relative: **dieser Umstand, dessen Erwähnung . . .,** *the mention of which;* (2) but a following genitive is objective, and converts the possessive into subjective force: **ihre Erwiderung seiner Grüße;** (3) thus till recently an infinitive noun was not allowed with a following objective genitive if a verbal noun in -ung were available: **die Erschlagung der Gefangenen;** but now **das Erschlagen** is accepted.

(*b*) In uncertain contexts the subjective and objective genitives may be explicitly distinguished by appropriate choice of:

(1) Preposition; thus (i) subjective, the agent word **durch: seine Errettung durch den Arzt,** and (ii) objective, often those of inclination towards or against: **die Liebe zur Natur, der Haß gegen die Behörden, der Angriff auf die feindliche Stellung.**

(2) Noun compound; thus (i) many are objective, **die Tierliebe, der Menschenhaß,** and (ii) some are subjective, **die Vaterliebe.**

(3) Adjective: subjective, **die ärztliche Beratung,** *advice from* (*by*) *a doctor.*

490. The Subjective and Objective Genitive. Intransitive Force

The genitive after verbal nouns which derive from intransitive verbs taking a dative object or no object has only subjective force:

(*a*) Dative verbs. **Die Hilfe (der Beistand) des Arztes; der Widerstand der germanischen Stämme; die Entsagung des Dichters.**

Objective force may only be expressed by an appropriate preposition: **Dank an Schlesien** (book title); **diese erste Gabe Rilkes an mich** (S. Zweig), cp. **eine Bitte an jemanden haben; der Widerstand gegen die Eroberer,** *resistance to;* double object: **der Arzt . . . mit seinem Vorwurf der Schizophrenie** (dir. obj.) **gegen mich** (indir. obj.) (H. Risse), *with his accusation of . . .* (*levelled*) *against me.*

Noun compounds are only possible in a few established cases: **der Gottesdienst, die Thronentsagung, etc.**

Attempts to use the genitive are fraught with difficulty:

Sofort nahm er wahr, daß die Stadtbahnzüge in der entgegengesetzten Richtung seines eigenen Zieles (fuhren) (E. Langgässer), *in the opposite direction to his own goal* (= **in der seinem Ziel entgegengesetzten Richtung**).

(*b*) Verbs with no object. **Die Auferstehung des Herrn, das Singen der Vögel, das Erröten des Mädchens, der Sprung der Katze.**

Note.—Verbal nouns from verbs with prepositional objects normally take the same construction, and may not take a genitive of either force: **seine Furcht vor der Krankheit** [cp. § 265 (*d*)]; double object: **die Bezeichnung des Kanzlers** (dir. obj.) **als** (prep. obj.) **Handlanger der Westmächte.**

491. Grammatical and Natural Gender. Female Persons

(*a*) In the use of feminine forms for nouns of persons, German goes much further than English, which adopts various alternatives: **Bäuerin,** *peasant-woman,* **Lehrerin,** *woman-teacher,* **Bäckerin,** *baker's wife,* **Erzieherin,** *governess,* **Innenarchitektin,** *interior decorator.*

There are, however, certain limitations in the use of feminine forms (whether in **-in** or otherwise) in reference to female persons.

(1) A number of words have no feminine forms: **der Backfisch, Kerl, Mensch, Dienstbote, Krüppel, etc.**; among occupations: **der Ingenieur, Tischler**; words in -ling: **der Lehrling, Liebling, etc.**

Der bekannte Hollywooder Star Zsa Zsa Gabor (newsp.); **das Mädel, ein blonder, sechzehnjähriger Fratz** (S. Zweig), *a blond little thing.*

(2) Even when feminine forms are available, they may well not be used: (i) in general statements: **„Ein Arzt lernt seinen Patienten erst allmählich kennen", sagte sie** (*i.e.* **die Ärztin**) (H. Kasack), and in general predicates: **Die dicke Bäckersfrau war Herr und Meister im Hause** [cp. § 294 (*a*)]; (ii) with general pronouns: **Und so scheu war sein Gehaben, daß (es) ihr als einzigem auffiel** (W. Bergengruen), and with adjective-nouns: **ihr Verhalten . . ., das auf den Sehenden, auf Anna also, peinvoller wirkte, als . . .** (Th. Mann), *had a more unhappy effect on the onlooker, Anna, than . . .*

(*b*) For titles, the feminine form is, according to official ruling, to be used where available: **die Direktorin X., Frau Regierungsrätin Z.**; but there is a marked disinclination to extend the range of these: **Frau Kultusminister Teusch, Frau Amtmann Y.** Partly, the courtesy title **Frau** is felt to indicate clearly enough the association of sex and professional status, since it has ceased to be used with the title of a husband [cp. § 175 (*b*)].

(*c*) Personifications, whether concrete or abstract, with feminine gender, are found with either form of predication:

Bremerhaven erwartet „United States", Trägerin (but later: **der Träger)
des „Blauen Bandes"** (newsp.), *holder of the Blue Ribbon.*

Die Wissenschaft muß stets auf der Hut sein, aus sich eine Närrin zu machen
(F. Werfel), *careful not to make a fool of itself.*

(*d*) Certain neuter nouns or diminutives may also indicate female persons: **das Geschöpf, Kind, Luder, Mensch** (pop.), **Weib, Wesen; das Mädchen, Fräulein, Mütterchen, Töchterlein.** Grammatical and natural gender fluctuate in: (1) a later pronoun, **sie, es**; (2) a possessive: **Ihr(e) Fräulein Braut** [cp. § 175 (*c*)]; (3) a proper name: **das** (or **die) Annerl.**

492. Grammatical and Natural Gender. Male Persons

(*a*) Male persons may be designated by: (1) feminine nouns: **die Majestät, Memme, Ordonnanz, Polizei, Wache,** or (2) neuter nouns: **das Faktotum, Luder, Herrchen, Männlein, Wesen.**

Grammatical gender in a following personal or possessive pronoun is seldom observed, except (and this always) for **Majestät: (die) Majestät ist ungeduldig, daß man sie warten läßt,** but: **Ich frage die Ordonnanz, was sein Asthma macht** (G. Benn), *I ask the orderly how his asthma is.*

(*b*) Masculine terms may be predicated of abstract concepts of masculine or neuter gender: **das Unglück war sein Los, das Leiden sein Gefährte,** *suffering his companion.*

493. General Neuter Category

The neuter singular, either as pronoun or adjective-noun, is used in various contexts for an undifferentiated or collective idea, or one consisting of items of mixed gender:

(*a*) Adjective-nouns [cp. also §§ 144 and 438 (*a*), young of animals]: **„Da fährt sie hin, Bethsy".—„Ja, Jean, das Erste, das davongeht"** (Th. Mann), *the first (child) to leave (marry).*

(*b*) Pronouns:

(1) **das,** demonstrative [*v.* § 32 (*b*)], **was,** indefinite relative [*v.* § 176 (*d*)], and **welches,** interrogative, may refer to collective ideas, including persons: **die Frage, welches die Parteien im Konflikte sind** (F. G. Jünger), *which are the two parties in conflict.*

(2) The indefinites **alles, beides, (ein) jedes, eines, einziges,** etc., and **unsereins** [*v.* passim, and especially § 147 (*a*)]:

psychologisch-moralische Exerzitien, denen die Brautleute, jedes für sich, unterworfen wurden (F. Werfel), *to which the engaged couple, each separately, was subjected.*

494. Inflectional Agreement in Nouns

(*a*) Nouns used in certain contexts may be nominative or uninflected:

(1) Those felt to be names or titles:

seitdem es hoffähig ist, Christ zu spielen (E. Schaper), *to pretend to be a Christian* (but: **den Christen spielen**).

Den hochwürdigen Pater Exorzist nehme ich selbstverständlich aus (F. Werfel), *I except the Reverend Father Exorcist.*

(2) Those felt to be concealed quotations:

In diesem folgenden Jahre fällt der Höhepunkt ihres Lebens.—Der äußere Höhepunkt sollte man wohl sagen, aber . . . (H. von Doderer), *one should say "the external climax" . . .*

The colon, with its demonstrative force [*v.* § 539 (*d*)], often acts as a concealed quotation mark:

Fog, engl. (für: dicker Nebel), m. (entry in Duden).

But strict agreement is required if some part of the noun (*e.g.* the article) falls outside the quoted section:

dies Herz—ich weiß, du sprichst und hörst nicht gern vom „Herzen"— aber . . . (Th. Mann), *you do not like the "heart" being talked of.*

And cp. § 235 (*d*) (titles of books, etc.).

(3) Double forms connected by **und** may be (i) non-inflected: **das Vertrauen zwischen Herr und Diener, die Hilfsbereitschaft von Mensch zu Mensch; vom Herz zur Feder ist ein entsetzlich langer Weg** (H. Broch); or (ii) inflected as a unit: **der Besitz eigenen Grund und Bodens.**

(*b*) Grammarians would prefer to allow the use of two prepositions governing different cases only before words not normally inflected: **von und über Goethe, Infinitive mit oder ohne zu** (Duden); but writers often prefer to place an inflected noun in the case required by the nearest preposition [cp. § 482 (*c*)]:

Die Häuser dieser Stadt waren . . . nicht über, sondern tief in die Erde hineingebaut (F. Werfel), *not above ground but deep in the earth,*

especially as some recommended alternatives [**sondern tief in dieselbe,** cp. § 230 (*a*) (2)] are not preferable.

495. Inflectional Agreement in Adjectives

(a) Certain groups of adjectives are also not inflected. For single adjectives, v. § 280 (set expressions), § 283 (foreign words), etc.

In certain double forms, only the second is inflected [cp. § 494 (a) (3) above]: (1) occasionally normal doublets, whether repetitive for emphasis: **welch tief tiefe Erfahrung** (F. Werfel), or joined by **und: das süß und eiskaltcremige Tränklein** (F. Werfel); more commonly (2) certain double forms which, though commonly only used in the predicate (cp. § 284), are increasingly found in the attributive position:

(ich ging) in eines der wenigen gang und gäben Lokale essen (G. Benn), *went to eat at one of the few frequented places* [cp. also § 447 (c) (1)].

Warum konnte der Mensch nicht auf eine klipp und klare Frage eine ebenso klipp und klare Antwort geben? (H. Broch), *to a clear question a clear answer?*

(b) Three degrees of closeness of association of two colours are possible: **ein blaurotes (= violettes) Tuch; eine schwarz und weiße (or schwarzweiße) Kuh,** *a checked cow;* **eine schwarze und eine weiße Kuh,** two monotone cows. For flags the full compound is preferred: **die schwarzrotgoldene Fahne** (but the noun is: **die Fahne Schwarz-Rot-Gold**). Compare also **die englische und die deutsche Sprache** (*the English and the German languages*), but **ein englisch-deutsches Wörterbuch.**

(c) Complex numerals may be conjunctive or disjunctive:

(1) Conjunctive, especially with **ein, hundert,** etc., as first element: **an ein und demselben Tage, ein Opfer ein und desselben Verhängnisses, einundeinehalbe Stunde, ein um das andere neue Viertel Wein** (H. Kasack), **in zwei und einem halben Jahr, Tausend und eine Nacht,** but **Erzählungen aus den Tausendundein Nächten.** Thus the alternatives are separation with non-inflection of **ein** when leading, the noun agreeing with the second element; or compounding, with a plural noun: **in zweieinhalb Jahren.**

(2) Disjunctive: **ein oder zwei überflüssig gewordene Zimmer** (H. Broch), **ein oder zwei der Königssöhne** (S. Andres), **mit zwei gegen eine Stimme** (newsp.). The numeral remains separated, and the noun has the number of the last element.

(3) Complex forms with the iterative suffix **-mal (Mal)** [v. § 154 (c)] are commonly compounded if singular, but separated (sometimes compounded) if plural: **mit einemmal(e), zum erstenmal, ein anderesmal, ein einzigesmal; einige Male** (or **einigemale**), **viele, zahllose Male.** Compare also § 79 (fractions).

EXERCISE LXII

A. Translate into ENGLISH:

1. Nun, Gundermann ging, ohne viel Abschied und Aufhebens, um das Fest nicht zu stören (H. von Doderer). 2. Da . . . fiel mir stückweis ein, was ich Seltsames die Nacht geträumt hatte (S. Andres). 3. Die Leute haben nachgewiesen, was alles in der Braunkohle steckt. Man glaubt nicht, was alles drin steckt (Th. Mann). 4. Seine bräunliche Männerpracht . . . war Gegenstand der Schwärmerei aller Mädchen und Frauen der Gesellschaft, der Verhimmelung durch Gänse und Puten (Th. Mann). 5. A German on English spelling: „Eure Rechtschreibung ist eine Versündigung am gesunden Menschenverstand". 6. „Hast du denn keine Frau, keinen Schatz?" . . . „Einen Schatz habe ich schon, aber er wohnt nicht hier, ich sehe ihn nur selten, wir kommen nicht sehr gut miteinander aus" (H. Hesse). 7. Der Fünf-Uhr-Teetisch etwa zeigte immer zweierlei Getränk auf dem hübschen, gläsernen Wagen, Kaffee oder Tee, je nachdem, wie eines grad gelaunt war (H. von Doderer). 8. „Herr Pablo", sagte ich zu ihm, der mit einem dünnen schwarz und silbernen Stöckchen spielte . . . (H. Hesse). 9. The rising generation: Die Eltern hatten ihre großen Kinder an unpassender Vertraulichkeit so wenig hindern können, wie an jeder anderen falschen Auffassung des Lebens. Das schloß freie Kameradschaft und ließ sich nicht dreinreden. Das ging zusammen „groß aus" . . . Das bummelte wie es Geschäfte machte, ohne Maß und Gewissen (H. Mann).

B. Translate into GERMAN:

1. The romantic old town of Heidelberg has a special place in our affection. 2. What is the national dish of Germany? Some might say a plate of sauerkraut with fried sausages. 3. In the art exhibition at the end of March there was a landscape by Winston Churchill. 4. He has painted many of these in the course of his long and busy life. 5. We have fruit in large quantities in the garden, and ample time and energy to pick it. 6. Their love of music helped the refugees in these difficult years of their exile. 7. She says that she wants to be either a nurse or a social worker but not a governess. 8. She was a poor, frail little creature of about twelve years old. 9. The relationship between the brother and sister in that family was not a good one. 10. With one or two long strides he reached the edge of the cliff and looked over.

CHAPTER LXIII

PREPOSITIONS OF LOGICAL RELATION II

The Agent Relation: Von, Durch

496. Von, dat., and **durch,** acc.; *by.* Both introduce an agent, by or through whom (which) an action is completed, but **durch** is more indirect (*through* rather than *by*): **die durch den Verkehr verursachten Bauschäden müssen behoben werden,** *caused by the traffic;* **der vom Wagen überfahrene Mann war ein Fremder,** *run over by the car.*

Thus **durch** is always used (i) when the agent is mentioned elsewhere, and then becomes means: **Durch andauernden Fleiß kann man viel erreichen,** *by diligence;* and (ii) when such an agent is presupposed as a planning intelligence, as with mathematical statements: **vier (dividiert) durch zwei macht zwei; die Stadt wird durch die Hauptstraße in zwei gleiche Teile getrennt.**

Thus **von** is common for the immediate agent in the passive: **die Königin wurde vom Erzbischof gekrönt;** and in many past participles with passive force, in so far as **durch** is not preferred: **von Licht geblendet, vom Heer belagert.**

But verbal nouns in **-ung** and otherwise from transitives take **durch** to indicate the agent [for subjective genitive, *v.* § 489 (*b*)], **von** or the genitive having here objective force: **die Besetzung, die Einnahme (unserer Gebiete) durch den Feind.** But if a passive participle is present, **von** may be used: **die vom Feinde durchgeführte Besetzung.** With the passive participle, however, **von** may have separative force, so that **durch** is needed: **die Stadt wurde von feindlichen Truppenteilen gesäubert,** *cleared of* (cp. §§ 403 and 412), but **durch feindliche Truppenteile,** *cleared by.*

Both **durch** and **von** are close to the sense of means (instrument), and may be alternative to **mit: der Abhang war mit (von) Bäumen bestanden; die Stadt ist durch eine Mauer (mit, von einer Mauer) umgeben.**

Prepositions of Means, including Instrument: An, Bei, (Durch); Mit, Mittels, etc., Per, etc.

497. An, dat.; *by, with* (*the aid of*). **Ich konnte ihn nur an seiner Stimme erkennen,** *recognise him by;* cp. § 449, and **bei** and **mit** below.

498. Bei, dat.; *by.* **Die Gelegenheit beim Schopf ergreifen,** *time* (*opportunity*) *by the forelock;* **ich nannte ihn beim Namen,** *by name,* **nahm ihn beim Wort,** *at his word.* But in concrete, literal senses **an** is perhaps commoner than **bei: ich griff ihn beim (am) Arm,** but: **Jener Jüngling**

führt seine Gefährtin nicht am Arm, nicht an der Hüfte, sondern an der Schulter (Simpl.).

For **durch** in expressions of means, *v.* § 496, and below, § 499.

499. Mit, dat.; *with, through.* The standard preposition expressing means in the instrumental sense, and closely related to the wider senses of inclusion (*v.* § 409) and attendant circumstance (*v.* § 505). Thus **mit ein bißchen Verstand kommt man durch Stadt und Land** has all three senses; cp. English *how*, which asks both *by what means?* and *in what manner?* **Der Arbeiter arbeitet mit Werkzeugen, der geistige Arbeiter mit seinen Hilfsmitteln, der Hundezüchter mit Milde oder Drohungen.** Non-physical (or more indirect) means is the special sphere of **durch: Durch Milde muß man sein Ziel erreichen, nicht mit der Peitsche.**

Mit, like **an** (§ 449) and **von** (§§ 403 and 522) often has partitive force of the object (material) by or through which the action is carried out: **Er prahlt mit seinen Erlebnissen,** *boasts of,* **ich muß es mit meiner Zeit sehr genau nehmen,** *be very sparing of,* **er geht äußerst sparsam mit seinem Gelde um,** *is economical with.* **Man begann mit einer Ouvertüre und endete mit der Nationalhymne.**

500. Mittels, vermittels, gen.; *by means of.* **Kraft, vermöge,** gen., *by virtue of.* These are clearly distinguished in that **(ver)mittels** is the technical or instrumental means, **kraft** and **vermöge** the natural means: **die Schaufensterscheiben wurden vermittels Steinwurfes zertrümmert** (Th. Mann), *with stones;* **ein Stein fällt vermöge der ihm anhaftenden Schwerkraft zu Boden,** *by virtue of its mass.*

Natural means or resources may be used for an exterior object, either (i) technical, **mittels: ein Pendel wird mittels Schwerkraft in Bewegung gesetzt,** *set in motion through (by using) its gravity attraction;* or (ii) intensification of natural means, **kraft,** *by dint of:* **kraft seiner angeborenen Eigenschaften,** and also **kraft seines enormen Fleißes kam er in der von ihm gewählten Laufbahn schnell voran,** *by virtue of his gifts, by dint of industry.*

501. Per, via, über, all acc.; *by, via.* All are used with means of communication: (i) forms of transport: **per Rad, Post, Bahn, Schiff, Frachtdampfer;** (ii) route taken: **via Hamburg, per Adresse Herrn Werner Schmidt,** *care of Mr W. S.* (**p.a.,** *c/o*).

Per and **via** are criticised for their foreign (Latin) origin and commercial use (**via** is, in fact, an adverb, meaning *on the way*), and may be replaced by (1) **mit der Post,** etc., and (2) **über Hamburg, bei Herrn W. S.** But there is no sign of the displacement of the two favourites: **per Anhalter fahren,** *to hitch-hike,* **per Du sein,** *to be on Du terms (with),* cp. § 167 (*c*).

502. Zu, dat.; *by, on.* As means of progression, the only common idiom now using **zu** is **zu Fuß gehen**; in more elevated style also **zu Pferd** and **zu Schiff**; other means take (i) other prepositions: **im Wagen (Auto), mit der Bahn (dem Dampfer), per Lastauto (Frachtdampfer,** *v.* § 501) **fahren**; or (ii) compound nouns: **das Seefahren, eine Landreise** (for **zu See,** etc.).

Prepositions of Attendant Circumstance: An, Auf, Bei, Mit, Unter

503. An, dat.; *at, occupied in.* **Auf,** acc.; *at.* Only a brief reference is needed here to the use of: (i) **an,** also **bei,** with infinitive nouns: **sie war am (beim) Fußbodenschrubben** [*v.* § 205 (*c*)]; (ii) **an,** with the adverbial superlative: **die Vögel singen am lieblichsten bei Tagesanbruch** [*v.* § 117 (*a*)]; (iii) **auf,** with the absolute adverbial superlative: **sie sang aufs lieblichste,** *most charmingly* [*v.* § 162 (*b*)]. In all these cases, contraction of article and preposition must be used.

504. Bei, dat.; *at, with, by,* etc. This, the widest used of all prepositions of attendant circumstance, occurs in numerous idioms: **bei Tage, bei Lichte besehen, bei der Arbeit, bei seiner Ankunft, bei schönem Wetter, bei der allgemeinen Lage.**

As with all loose adverbial appositions [cp. § 201 (*a*)], phrases with **bei** easily develop special logical relations, especially of opposition; some are: (i) condition: **bei Bestellung des Gesamtwerkes ermäßigt sich der Preis um 10%,** *if the whole work is ordered;* thus with stated penalties: **es ist bei Geldstrafe verboten,** *under pain of fine;* (ii) concession: **beim besten Willen kann ich das nicht zugeben,** *with (in spite of having) the best will in the world;* **bei alledem = trotz alledem,** *with (in spite of) all that.*

As in English, solemn affirmations are made *by*: **bei Gott, beim Himmel!**

505. Mit, dat.; *with.* This is the preposition most widely used for accompanying circumstance of personal gesture, appearance, clothing, etc.: **eine alte Frau, mit der Brille auf der Nase** ...

As such it is often alternative to phrases in adverbial apposition, genitive or accusative, from which it is not easily distinguished: (1) **mit** is more informal than the adverbial accusative, but in casual modern style the two are almost interchangeable: **Will, mit Nägeln im Mund, den Hammer in der Hand, hatte ... herumgehämmert** (H. Böll), *with nails in his mouth and a hammer in his hand;* (2) the adverbial genitive is used primarily of immediate gestures of the body, while **mit** is (i) more peripheral (clothes, etc.): **mit abgezogener Kappe, geneigten Hauptes,** ...

stand er vor dem Blinden (H. Broch), *with cap off and head bent;* or (ii) more intentional: **abgewandten Gesichts oder mit einem lächelnden Blick in die Augen** (Th. Mann), *with averted face or smiling into the other's eyes.* **Mit** is never used with a noun and *following* adverb (adjective), as in English, cp. *(with) cap off* (above), but requires in such cases the full attributive participle; cp. **mit aufgepflanztem Bajonett,** *with bayonets fixed.*

506. Unter, dat.; *with, in, accompanied by.* The circumstances introduced by **unter** are even more intentional than those with **mit,** and especially more occasional and intermittent: **ein Programm phantastischer . . . aber mit leichtem Lächeln und unter Kußhänden vollbrachter Leistungen,** *carried out with a (constant) smile and with (continual) kissing of hands to the public.* **Unter** derives here from the time sense (*v.* § 395), and is thus (i) always of events in time (*while . . . ing*): **während Tony unter Stillschweigen und appetitlos ihren Kaffee trank** (Th. Mann); and (ii) always of the same subject as the main verb, thus in the last example, *in silence,* not *amid silent members of the family.* This distinguishes it from **bei,** which (1) being derived more directly from force of place (*v.* §§ 323 and 394) is used in both time and place contexts (**bei Tag, bei der Lage**); and (2) is commonly used of an attendant circumstance unrelated to the action of the subject, indeed, often appearing to be *mis*related (cp. **Bei Bestellung . . .,** example in § 504).

The most striking illustration of these two points is the common use of **unter** with a verbal noun, especially in **-ung: das Hotel hatte ich in aller Stille . . . unter verachtungsvoller Zurücklassung meiner Livree und gleichmütigem Verzicht auf meine letzte Monatslohnung verlassen** (Th. Mann), *leaving my livery behind and relinquishing my month's wages.* One of the objections to the abuse of this construction in official language is that it so often misrelates the verbal noun: **die Formulare sind unter Beilegung aller einschlägigen Belegscheine auszufüllen,** *please complete the forms and enclose all relevant documents.*

The time force of **unter** may explain why the expression: **unter diesen Umständen (Verhältnissen),** *under these circumstances,* has never been challenged by those wishing to substitute a logically more correct preposition (*in*). Note also: **unter dieser Bedingung,** *under (with) this condition.*

Prepositions of Conformity

507. Auf Grund, aufgrund, gen.; *on the basis of.* Till recently only separate: **ich fand sie ganz so, wie ich sie mir auf Grund ihres Briefes vorgestellt hatte** (W. Bergengruen), *on the evidence of her letter;* now increasingly compounded.

508. Gemäß, zufolge, gen. or dat.; *in accordance with.* Both may precede, usually with the genitive, or follow, always with the dative: **gemäß seines Auftrags, seinem Auftrag gemäß; zufolge des Gesetzes, dem Gesetz zufolge.** Compounds: **demzufolge,** adv., *accordingly* [but: **dem zufolge,** relative, *v.* § 225 (*c*)]; **standesgemäß,** *in keeping with one's social station.*

509. Infolge, zufolge, gen.; *in consequence of.* These only precede (thus enabling some distinction to be made with **zufolge** in § 508): **Infolge (zufolge) des besonders schönen Wetters bestehen ausgezeichnete Ernteaussichten.** Before plural nouns also **zufolge, infolge von** [*v.* § 266 (*d*)].

510. Laut, gen., dat., **nach,** dat.; *according to.* **Laut,** derived [like **kraft,** *v.* § 262 (*b*)] from the noun of like form (**nach Laut des . . .,** *according to the tenor of . . .*) normally takes the genitive: **laut des abgeschlossenen Vertrages,** *according to contract,* but the analogy of **nach** has caused the spread of the dative: **130 000 verschiedene deutsche Wörter gibt's laut neuem Mackensen,** *according to the new M. (dictionary),* and an isolated following noun is always uninflected: **laut Gesetz, laut Schreiben vom 10. Oktober.**

Nach precedes or follows: **nach dem Vertrag, dem Vertrage nach.**

Zufolge, following, with dative, has been extended, though against opposition, from *in accordance with* to *according to,* especially in newspaper reports: **einer Meldung der ,,Neuen Welt" zufolge;** better: **nach einer Meldung.**

Compound: **demnach = demzufolge,** *accordingly.*

511. Nach, dat.; *like* (of appearance). A wide extension of the above sense (§ 510) has taken place to express an imagined conformity, or inferred similarity, including the compound **danach:**

Die Lokale sahen alle nach Fremdenfang und Nepp aus (H. Fallada), *all the eating houses looked as if they were out to catch and fleece the stranger.*
Gutes Wetter im Anzuge, meinst du? Es sieht nicht danach aus, *it doesn't look like it.*

With sense impressions, especially **riechen, von** may introduce an identifiable (material) impression, **nach** a subtler, more reminiscent one: **hier riecht's von Hunden,** *smells of dog,* but:
Es riecht hier bei uns nach Sauberkeit und Ordnung und nach einem freundlichen und anständigen Leben (H. Hesse), *an atmosphere of . . .*

Prepositions of Motive, Reason: Aus, Halber, etc., **(Ob), Um . . . Willen, Wegen**

512. Aus, dat.; *for, from.* **Aus welchem Grunde hat er seinen Wagen verkauft? Aus Ungeduld, Unwissenheit . . . Er tat es aus freien Stücken,**

of his own free will.   The reason may be a conscious motive, against **vor** of unconscious motive: **er sparte aus Geiz, sie errötete vor Scham.**

513. Halber, -halb, -halben, gen.; *on account of, for the sake of.* The different forms, which always follow and are usually compounded, have become specialised in use: (i) **halber** after nouns: **des Beispiels halber,** *so as to give an example,* and compounded: **ehrenhalber,** *honoris causa,* **studienhalber,** *for purposes of study;* (ii) **-halb** in composition with demonstratives and interrogatives: **deshalb, weshalb;** (3) **-halben** in composition with personal pronouns: **seinethalben, ihrethalben.**   Cp. § 197 (*b*).

514. Ob, dat. or gen.; *on account of.*   Now seldom used, *v.* § 516 below.

515. Um . . . willen, gen.; *on account of, for the sake of.*   **Er tat es um seiner Mutter willen, um des poetischen Tones willen,** *for his mother, to achieve that poetic note.*   Compounded with pronouns: **um ihretwillen, um dessentwillen,** *v.* § 197 (*a*).   Now commonly compounded with certain nouns: **um Gotteswillen, um(s) Himmelswillen!** both *for Heaven's sake!*

516. Wegen, gen. (dat.); *on account of, because of.*   **Wegen** almost always involves an element of personal motive, distinct from the impersonal sense of consequence, of **infolge;** the latter may often be used for **wegen,** though with loss of force: **er ist wegen seiner bergsteigerischen Leistungen bekannt,** *known for,* but **infolge seiner . . .,** *known as a result of.*   But in: **eine Zeugin wurde wegen Nichterscheinens vor Gericht vernommen,** the noun **Nichterscheinen** is more than the cause, it is also the offence.

Wegen may even be intention or aim: **1350 Fahrstuhlführer traten wegen Lohnforderungen in den Streik** (newsp.), *in pursuance of;* **eines Tages suchte ich wegen eines Sprichwortes im „Deutschen Sprichwörter-Lexikon",** *was looking for;* **Weisungen wegen Verhaltens im Straßenverkehr,** *instructions about suitable behaviour.*

Wegen takes the genitive correctly, but sometimes the dative in colloquial use, especially when the genitive is not distinct: **wegen etwas anderem; und alles wegen fünf Tagen (Urlaub),** *v.* § 266 (*c*).   It follows the noun rarely (and only with the genitive): **des schlechten Wetters wegen.**   Informally, **wegen** may govern a pronoun in the dative: **wegen uns,** but stricter style requires a compound: **unsertwegen** [*v.* § 197 (*b*)]. An isolated noun may stand uninflected, especially in legal style: **wegen Landfriedensbruch,** *for disturbance of the peace.*

Ob, with genitive, is occasional (and older) in the sense of **wegen: sie sahen keinen Grund zu entschuldigendem Lächeln ob dieser Maskerade** (Th. Mann).

Von . . . wegen, with genitive, in set expressions means (i) *on the part of, by the authority of,* as **von Staats wegen;** or (ii) *by virtue of* (natural reason, conviction, etc.), as **von Verstandes wegen.** Even feminine nouns take the genitive **-s** by analogy: **von Gesinnungs wegen, von Obrigkeits wegen.**

Prepositions of Cause

517. An, dat.; *of.* The causal force of **an** develops out of the partitive idea (*v.* § 449), thus especially causes of illness, death: **er leidet, erkrankte, starb an der Schwindsucht, ist krank an der Lunge.** Mental suffering is usually **unter: er leidet unter seiner Unfähigkeit,** *suffers at the thought of;* and causes of illness not specifically medical use many other prepositions: **sie wurde krank durch Einbildung, von der schlechten Luft, vor unerfüllter Liebe, infolge übermäßiger Arbeitsanstrengung;** *v.* these passim.

518. Dank, dat.; *thanks to.* **Dank den Bemühungen aller konnte das Stück noch aufgeführt werden,** *thanks to the efforts of all . . .*

519. Durch, acc.; *through, as a result of.* The means by which something happens is often the cause: **durch seine Leistungen bekannt geworden,** especially with reflexives: **er zeichnete sich durch Fleiß und Intelligenz aus,** *by (as a result of)*; cp. § 496.

520. Mangels, gen. (dat.); *in default of,* expressing the idea of a negative cause, is almost limited to phrases such as **mangels der Beweise** (or with dative: **mangels Beweisen) freigesprochen,** *discharged for lack of evidence.* Non-official speakers prefer the noun phrase: **aus Mangel an Beweisen,** or a positive cause: **wegen Kohlenmangels** (for **mangels Kohlen) geschlossen.**

521. Über, acc., dat.; *at.* The object of mental activity, in more passive statements, easily becomes the cause (cp. § 454): **sie dachte über die Sache nach** (*thought over*), **und weinte über die Aussichtslosigkeit ihrer Lage** (*and wept at,* i.e. *because of*). This happens normally when from finite verb the construction changes to an adjective, and especially a past participle: **über etwas glücklich, erstaunt, beschämt sein** (cp. *unhappy at* or *over*). **Wegen** may be alternative: **ich bin böse auf ihn wegen seiner (über seine) Haltung.**

The dative may indicate cause with a few verbs operative in time contexts: **ich erwachte über dem Lärm, vergaß ihn über der Fülle der Arbeit** [cp. § 335 (*a*)].

522. Von, dat.; *with, by, through*. As the agent sense in **durch** leads to causal force, so the combined agent and partitive force in **von**: **von Regen durchnäßt, von Kraft strotzend**. Thus with (i) adjectives: **müde vom Gehen, schwarz von Menschen**; (ii) past participles: **von Zorn entbrannt**; (iii) verbs: **von Stipendien leben, vom Lärm erschallen**. **Diese Musik troff von Sentimentalität** (H. Hesse); **prangend von Kraft und Gesundheit** (H. von Doderer); **es fällt keine Eiche vom ersten Streiche** (prov.).

523. Vor, dat.; *with, for*. As with **von**, so also **vor** occurs widely with causal force after (i) adjectives: **blaß vor Schrecken, fast tot vor Freude**; (ii) verbs: **vor Wut kochen, vor Ehrgeiz sprühen, vor Begeisterung klatschen**. As **von** is used of outer and material cause, **vor** indicates inner and motivating cause, and some nice distinctions can be drawn: **er bebte vor Furcht, sie bebte von** or **vor Lachen**, *shook with;* **er war steif vor Kälte, das Kleid war steif von Goldfaden**, *stiff with*. **Er war sehr wirr, vor Freude zugleich und vom Wein** (Th. Mann), *confused with joy and the wine*. The old past participle **trunken** reflects, in its idiom, this distinction: **trunken von Wein, Liebe, Wonne, von/vor Begeisterung**, but only **vor Freude**.

Prepositions of Purpose

524. Auf, acc.; *at, to, on*, etc. A vast number of idioms use **auf** to indicate a direction of an activity of the mind or body. Some groups may be distinguished (cp. also § 401):

(1) Aiming at: **auf jemanden (etwas) schießen, schimpfen, zeigen**.

(2) Attending to: **auf . . . blicken, achten**; **auf** is more reflective than normal perceptive processes: **er blickte ihn an, auf die Stadt hinunter; er hörte ihn**, *heard him*, **hörte ihn an**, *listened to him*, **hörte auf sein Klagen**, *lent his ear to*.

(3) Direction of the feelings: **stolz auf etwas sein, Hunger auf etwas haben; neidisch, böse auf jemanden sein**.

(4) Something at stake: **eine Frage auf Leben und Tod, auf Sonnenschein wetten, eine Prämie auf umsichtiges Fahren**, *premium on*.

(5) An intended result: **auf eine Wirkung berechnet sein, auf jemandes Gesundheit trinken, auf Abenteuer hinausgehen**.

(6) A criterion: **der Schaffner prüfte meine Fahrkarte auf ihre Gültigkeit**, *to establish whether it were valid.*

Auf in many of these senses may have a following adjective: **das Barometer steht auf beständig**, *shows fine weather;* **eine auf alt gefälschte Truhe** (H. Kasack), *made to look old;* **er krempelte das altehrwürdige Kaffeehaus auf nobel um** (S. Zweig), *had it "poshed up"*.

525. Nach, dat.; *at, after, for.* As **auf** indicates the object aimed at, so **nach** gives the end desired: **er ist auf Erfolg aus, nach Reichtum begierig, hinter dem Gelde her.**

Nach thus indicates either (i) a greater indirectness in the process, thus with verbs of searching for, **nach Wahrheit forschen, nach der Gesundheit fragen, nach Effekt haschen, nach Essen schreien;** often as an adverbial prefix: **sie gruben den Bodenschätzen nach;** or pursuit without immediate success: **sie setzten dem Diebe nach, streben** and **trachten nach;** (ii) a greater proportion of desire in the intention, so with adjectives of desire: **geizig, gierig, lüstern nach.**

526. Um, acc.; *for,* etc. Synonyms of *to beg, request,* etc., commonly take **um: er bat um seine Freiheit, hielt um ihre Hand an, suchte um Gnade nach.** **Um** expresses the aim with **zu** and the infinitive: **er tat es, um zu Geld zu kommen** (cp. prepositional infinitive).

Um is a more final, hypothetical aim than **auf** or even **nach,** and is approached with greater circumspection: **er strebte nach Erfolg,** but **war um seinen guten Namen bestrebt,** *was mindful of.* Thus also **um,** in the price (to be) paid, is more hypothetical than **für: er tat es nur um das Geld** (money the deciding motive); **er tat es nur für Geld** (there was no other motive). Thus also hyperbole of price: **um nichts (alles) in der Welt,** *nothing would lead me to . . ., I would give anything for . . .;* **um jeden Preis,** *at any price.* Cp. §§ 407 and 474 (*d*) (**um die Wette . . .**).

527. Zu, dat.; *to, for.* The fundamental sense of the widely used **zu** and infinitive construction is aim or purpose: **ich hoffe, Sie bald wieder zu sehen,** or result: **es gelang mir, sie noch abzupassen;** both senses often with **um: er betrat das Geschäft, um Zigarren zu kaufen** (purpose), **er kam zu spät, um die richtige Marke zu bekommen** (result). Cp. §§ 372 and 373. Thus also many verbs of becoming: **die Arbeit wurde ihm zur Qual,** or producing a result: **er wurde zum Vorstand gewählt,** or of a situation developing: **sein Sohn fiel ihm zur Last, die Ehre wurde ihm zuteil.** Cp. further § 435 (*b*).

The common use of **zu** with the infinitive is reflected in its use with the infinitive noun; commonly (i) passive uses are purposive: **Wasser zum Trinken** (*for drinking, to be drunk*), and (ii) active uses are of result: **es war zum Totlachen** (cp. § 252). The two uses may be regarded as identical if the general purposive force of **zu** is borne in mind: *the water (the situation) is of such a nature that one can drink it (must die of laughing).*

Many idioms with **zu** depend on verbal actions, often in the form of nouns expressing a point intended or arrived at: (1) nouns in **-ung:**

zur Erholung an die See reisen; other verbal nouns: zum Verkauf anbieten, zur Wahl vorlegen; (2) adjectives of suitability: zu einem Beruf geeignet, zur Reise aufgelegt; (3) invitation to eat, drink: sie lud uns zu einer Tasse Kaffee ein, holte Wein und Kuchen zum Empfang, trug uns zum Abendessen auf.

527A. Zwecks, gen.; *for the purpose of, with a view to.* Only in official and journalistic language, often with unmodified noun: Akademiker sucht junge Dame aus gutem Elternhaus . . . zwecks Heirat (or: späterer Ehe) kennenzulernen (newsp.).

Prepositions of Condition, Reservation

528. Condition.

Many prepositions, especially those of manner, may acquire conditional force, thus: auf Probe kaufen, *subject to examination;* bei schlechtem Wetter fällt der Ausflug aus, *if the weather is bad;* ohne Hut dürfen die Damen die Kirche nicht betreten, *without hats;* unter dreißig Minuten bin ich nicht fertig, *unless I am given thirty minutes.*

The only common preposition specifically of condition is im Falle (with genitive): im Falle der Nichtbezahlung einer Rate wird der Vertrag hinfällig, *in case of non-payment* . . ., more commonly as a subordinating conjunction: im Falle, daß . . ., as is always the case with unter der Bedingung, daß . . ., *on condition that* . . . [*v.* § 236 (*c*)].

529. Reservation.

Official language has produced some choice genitive prepositions (all normally preceding) expressing reservation; the commonest are: unbeschadet (schon bestehender Rechte), *without detriment to;* ungeachtet/ unerachtet (später entstehender Bauschäden), *notwithstanding, without reference to;* vorbehaltlich (der Rechte Dritter), *subject to.* Occasionally the first two follow with the dative, as in the following notice posted in a particularly louche night-club:

Den idealen Absichten des Unternehmens ungeachtet sind die Konsumkosten sofort zu begleichen (E. Kästner), *notwithstanding the idealist aims of the establishment* . . .

EXERCISE LXIII

A. Translate into ENGLISH:

1. Die Schwaben sind schon vermöge ihrer Mundart denkbar ungeeignet, mit einer schönen Frau länger als zehn Minuten zu flirten

(F. Thiess). 2. Die natürliche Bewegungsart des Menschen (war) das Gehen zu Fuß, das Fahren zu Wagen, zu Schlitten oder im Eisenbahnwaggon, in selteneren Fällen auch das zu Wasser (W. Bergengruen). 3. Niemand darf meinen, der Degenstock sei ein Spielzeug, wenn der Fall danach war, hat er seine ernste Brauchbarkeit erwiesen (W. Bergengruen). 4. „Nun ja", sagte er, „ich komme wegen des Zimmers, das Sie zu vermieten haben" (H. Hesse). 5. Neulich hat jemand vorgeschlagen, das Brot von Staats wegen ins Haus zu liefern, genau wie das Leitungswasser (E. Kästner). 6. Kinder betteln mit Fröhlichkeit, starrend von Schmutz . . . (G. Hauptmann). 7. In diesen Wochen sprühte Viola von Eifer, Ehrgeiz und Energie (H. Kasack). 8. Das Neutrum . . . steht bei den Verkleinerungen auf -chen und -lein (East German Duden). 9. Die bürgerliche Welt, eine Gesellschaft zur gegenseitigen Assekuranz . . . (B. Werner). 10. Die zwei Kriminalbeamten waren in Anzug und Gebärde einander zum Verwechseln ähnlich (L. Frank).

B. Translate into GERMAN:

1. The harbour was separated from the sea by a long dike which was washed over by the waves when (use prep. phrase) there was a storm. 2. The ship he was to command was in good repair and smelt strongly of paint and tar. 3. He was glad about the change in the weather and decided to make an early start by means of the favourable south-west wind. 4. By means of much patience she had at last made friends with her difficult neighbours. 5. The evening passed quickly in (*not* **in**) pleasant conversation and moderate drinking. 6. Has he acted in accordance with the captain's instructions? It doesn't look like it. 7. He had taken out an insurance on his life with my firm. 8. He was arrested for theft, and convicted of robbery; the sentence was (= **lautete auf,** acc.) two years' hard labour. 9. The man pointed to his companion who was dropping with fatigue. 10. Not for all the world would I undertake this job again.

CHAPTER LXIV
PUNCTUATION

530. The Full Stop

(*a*) All completed and independent statements, unless requiring the question mark or exclamation mark (*v.* these), end, as in English, with a full stop. Parts of complete statements used as headings, titles of books, chapters, articles, and names on envelopes, letter-heads, etc., do not now usually take a following stop.

(*b*) The stop stands after numerals to distinguish the ordinal from the cardinal [*v.* § 41 (*b*)].

(*c*) The stop follows abbreviations of words which are to be spoken in full: **Frankfurt a.M., Verf., dergl., ü.d.M. (über dem Meeresspiegel)**; with several words often only after the last letter: **usw.**

But it is omitted after certain groups of this kind, *i.e.* coins (**15 DM**), weights and measures (**20g, 1000m**), points of the compass (**SO, NNW**), and chemical elements (**Ag, Silber**). Cp. also § 112 (*b*).

(*d*) There is no stop after abbreviations which are spoken as such, whether as initials (especially political parties, **CDU, SPD,** and other similar forms: **DGB, LKW**), or in a shortened form of the word itself (**die Vopo, Volkspolizei**).

531. The Semi-colon

(*a*) The semi-colon both links and separates two parts of a sentence, acting as a means of articulation. Thus it often precedes: (1) adversative conjunctions, as **aber, indessen, dennoch, trotzdem, hingegen**; (2) the more emphatic conjunctions of cause, as **darum, deshalb,** and sometimes [especially in biblical style, *v.* § 540 (*a*)] **denn**; (3) enumerations, with **erstens, zweitens, der erste, der zweite.**

Im Walde ging es um. Was es war, wußte niemand; aber etwas Gutes war es nicht (H. Löns).

Thus also when adversative force is implicit:

Dann blinzelte eine Laterne auf, eine kleine, schwache Laterne, die irgend jemand in der Hand hielt, der längs der Schneise ging; er vermochte nicht zu unterscheiden, ob hüben, ob drüben (E. Schaper).

(*b*) For the semi-colon in periods, *v.* colon, § 540. The semi-colon was much more widely used in the nineteenth century, and is now being progressively replaced by the simple comma.

532. The Question Mark

(*a*) The question mark is used after direct questions (**Wer ist wer?** *Who's who?*), including those reported (**„Woher?" fragte er**), abbreviated (**Wohin? Was tun?**), or used in the context of another kind of statement (**Die Frage wer? ergibt das Subjekt, die Frage wen? das Objekt**).

(*b*) But it is incorrect after exclamations in question form (*v.* § 533, below), or after indirect questions; thus NOT:

Immer noch bleibt die Frage zu beantworten, von welcher Art die Religiosität der kommenden Zeit sein werde? (R. Guardini).

533. The Exclamation Mark

(*a*) The exclamation mark indicates a general rise in the tone of a statement, and is thus used:

(1) After exclamations proper (**O weh!**) including those in the form of rhetorical questions (**Was haben wir da nicht alles erfahren!**).

(2) In polite direct address, as in letter openings (**Sehr geehrter Herr Oberstadtdirektor!**), and in wishes (**Fröhliche Weihnachten!**), but not in closing formulas of letters (**Herzliche Grüße**, etc.).

Note.—In modern usage the comma is preferred to the exclamation mark in letter openings.

(3) In expressions of wish and command, not generally (**Du sollst nicht stehlen**), but in those with an exclamatory (**Hau ab!**) or exhortatory (**Treten Sie ein! Bitte!**) tone; also in commands to the public: **Nicht überholen! Achtung, Dampfwalze! Schule!**

(*b*) In an otherwise objective narrative, an exclamation mark may represent:

(1) An abbreviated aside to the reader:

Die Technik der Verwertung von Schutt zu Bauzwecken hat seit 1945 in Deutschland (Bombentrümmer!) erhebliche Fortschritte zu verzeichnen.

(2) An ironical aside to the reader:

Er sagt nie: ich bin dreiundsiebzig oder vierundsiebzig; nein: um die siebzig herum! (S. Andres).

534. The Comma in Simple and Compound Sentences

(*a*) The comma separates parallel elements simply juxtaposed, in the simple and compound sentence:

dieses fünfzigjährige, zahnlose, hinkende, hautüberzogene Skelett . . . (L. Frank); **ich kam, sah, siegte** (*veni, vidi, vici*); **das glaube ich nicht, es ist kaum möglich.**

or, similarly, when joined by an adversative conjunction:

die Ware ist gut, aber teuer; ich wartete, doch kam er nicht.

(*b*) The comma is omitted in the simple sentence when parallel elements are linked by **und** or **oder** or their synonyms [**wie, sowie, entweder . . . oder . . .**, etc., *v.* § 69 (*c*)], or **als** and **wie** as conjunctions of comparison: **wir hatten Butter, Brot und Käse; entweder er oder ich muß gehen; du bist älter als ich.**

(*c*) In the compound sentence:

(1) The comma is omitted, as above, if one element is shared by the two statements: **wir öffneten die Büchse und aßen den Inhalt** (= **wir**); **ich war schon und er wurde betrunken** (= **betrunken**).

(2) But not otherwise: **ich war schon betrunken, und er wurde es; du bist älter, als ich es bin; entweder er räumt das Haus, oder es gibt Krach!**

(*d*) Adjectives separately attributed of the noun are, by rule, distinguished by the comma from those attributed in descending order: **ein langer, dunkler, schwarzbärtiger Mann; eine nette alte Jungfer** (cp. *a nice old maid*); this rule is much disregarded [*v.* § 285 (*b*)], but its observance may avoid ambiguity: **im Jahre . . . erschien die erste, wöchentliche Zeitung** (*the first newspaper*, which was a weekly), or **die erste wöchentliche Zeitung** (*the first weekly newspaper*, others having preceded).

535. The Comma with Parentheses and Apposition

Parenthetical and appositional elements are generally separated from the rest of the statement by a comma or commas.

(*a*) Appositional elements, cp. participial constructions (§§ 275-7 and 347-50), and nouns in apposition [§ 484 (*b*) (1)].

Apposition of the vocative: **Du, Vater, kennst mich besser!**

Apposition of nouns may dispense with the comma when the apposition becomes an appellation [cp. § 484 (*b*) (1)], thus (i) name and title: **der Lehrer, Schmidt, kam mit** (or **der Lehrer Schmidt**); (ii) maiden-names: **Frau Müller geb. Schmidt erschien.**

Explanatory appositions with the exemplifying conjunctions **als, wie, und zwar**, etc. (*v.* § 112), require preceding commas; but **wie** often omits: **Zeitungen wie Constanze, der Spiegel, wenden sich an ein besonderes Publikum.**

(*b*) Parenthetical elements, such as interjections (**Oh, wie schön!**), emphatic **ja** or **nein** (**Nein, das geht nicht**), reduced independent statements

(bitte, Gott sei dank, wie bekannt, versteht sich), and leading adverbial, especially adversative, conjunctions [**Trotzdem, Dennoch, Übrigens,** *v.* § 75 (*c*), and below, §§ 537 (*b*) (5) and 539 (*d*) (2)].

Parenthetical commas should be used sparingly; in particular, it is quite wrong to treat the following elements as parenthetical:

(1) Single adverbs not in a leading position, as in the English practice: *he did not, luckily, want to accept.*

(2) Elements in the attributive adjective position, which appear to be an afterthought (**je nach dem, sehr verschiedenen Preis der Ware**), or are governed in an oblique case (**die, meinen Ausführungen zugrunde liegenden Erfahrungen,** C. G. Jung).

536. The Comma in Complex Sentences

The comma serves to articulate the complex sentence by separating subordinate constructions from, and marking their limits against, the main statement.

(*a*) Contracted constructions, as:

(1) Participial constructions in adjectival and adverbial apposition, *v.* §§ 275 f., 347 f.

(2) Prepositional infinitive constructions, *v.* § 107 (*b*), etc.

Note.—An unmodified prepositional infinitive must be separated if it is itself a governing construction:

Ich schrieb ihm in der Absicht, zu erfahren, ob unsere Verabredung verschoben werden konnte.

The (prepositional) infinitive construction in leading position in a nominal role has no following comma (*v.* examples, § 363), unless it is summed up by a following demonstrative (§ 365).

(3) Elliptical main statements, represented by an adjective, adverb, or noun:

Wunderlich, was der Mensch alles schlucken kann (H. Hesse).

(*b*) One or more subordinate clauses, especially adverbial (§§ 113 f.), relative (§§ 95 and 176), noun clauses, etc.

As with simple sentences, *v.* § 534 (*b*), the comma is dispensed with before a coordinating conjunction linking two parallel subordinate constructions: **der Mann, der uns gestern besuchte und uns Lotterielose verkaufen wollte.** But the comma is required:

(1) Between subordinations of different order: **der Mann, der uns gestern besuchte, weil er uns Lotterielose verkaufen wollte** . . .

(2) Between subordinations linked otherwise than by **und** or **oder** (mainly adversatively): **die Stadt, wo er seine erste Jugend verbracht hatte, an die er aber keine angenehmen Erinnerungen behalten hatte . . .**

(3) Between a subordination and the continuation of the main statement: **ich wurde vom Mann angerufen, der . . . wollte, und mußte ihn leider auf einen anderen Tag bestellen.**

537. The Dash

(*a*) Between direct statements, where no fresh paragraph is used, the dash indicates a change of person: **"Was möchtest du?"—"Dich sprechen".**

(*b*) Elsewhere, the single dash is used to suspend the sense, (1) with interruptions: **"Was möchtest—" "Dich sprechen", unterbrach sie ihn;** (2) with suggestive but incomplete statements: **"Du gehst ins Bett, oder—";** (3) to arouse expectation before a final statement, especially a contrast: **er ging—und kam nicht mehr;** (4) to introduce an afterthought or extension of the sense: **um den Frieden zu bewahren—wenn das ein echter Friede ist, der . . .;** (5) with slight demonstrative force, instead of a comma after a leading adverb, especially adversative: **Indes— Immerhin— Allein— .**

(*c*) The double dash is a more striking form of parenthesis: **Und irgend etwas—war es die Größe, die Kleidung, der Gang gewesen—hatte ihn an den Diakon erinnert** (E. Schaper).

538. Dispositional Marks

Certain marks of parenthesis have almost no grammatical or rhetorical function, but serve to clarify the disposition of a statement:

(*a*) Brackets (parentheses) are used, as in English, for parenthetical additions, especially of an explanatory nature, and are thus alternative to commas or the double dash:
Der Strichpunkt (früher: Semikolon) ist mehr als ein Beistrich und weniger als ein Punkt (H. Reimann).

(*b*) Quotation marks [for form *v*. Introduction, § 6 (*c*)] precede and follow a passage of direct speech; and are also used, by extension, for (1) the names of ships, books, plays, etc., *v*. § 235; (2) a word, etc., quoted by a speaker as not representing his own view: **ich werde ihm sein "Memme" mit Zinsen zurückzahlen;** or even with ironic intent: **einen solchen "Frieden" möchten wir nicht haben;** (3) a reference to something to be understood in a figurative sense: **zum Geburtstag bekam sie eine Puppe; man hätte sehen sollen, wie sie ihr "Kindchen" herzte, hinsetzte, an- und auszog.**

Note.—Emphasis proper is achieved by spacing, rather than by the use of quotation marks, *v.* example below in § 539 (*d*) (1).

(*c*) Square brackets, and single quotes, are used when a second set is required within a first group.

539. The Colon

(*a*) The colon is, in modern German, used much more widely than the semi-colon, and much more expressively than the comma, which is generally limited to logical functions. The colon is a rhetorical mark of punctuation, whose basic function is to announce or point to something following, and is thus used in contexts of (1) quotation, (2) explanation, or (3) demonstration. A large number of uses may be distinguished, shading off one into the other.

(*b*) Quotation.

The colon introduces a direct quotation, with or without an explicit verb of reporting: **Er sah sie an: „Was machst du hier?"** (The quotation is an independent statement and requires an initial capital.) Extensions of this use are: (1) internal quotation, often replacing single quotes [*v.* § 538 (*c*)]: **„Wenn ich sage: nein, ist es nein!" brauste der Bursche** (E. Langgässer); (2) constructive speech or thought, with or without the verbs **wissen, denken,** etc.: **Er wußte: er hatte gefehlt, er mußte büßen** (W. Bergengruen); (3) correction of the speaker's own words: **„Geschlechter- und Abstammungskunde ist mein Steckenpferd—besser gesagt: meine Profession"** (Th. Mann).

(*c*) Explanation.

The colon clarifies, elucidates, enumerates: **Es wird sehr langweilig werden: Konferenzen, Phrasen, Kompromisse,—und wieder ein Krieg** (S. Andres). **Sehen Sie, hier ist gerade von Lungenödem die Rede, auf deutsch: Stickfluß** (Th. Mann).

In contexts where the thought is moving forward, the second, explanatory element may be: (1) the reason for the first (or an inference from it): **Das erste Mal war ein älteres Ehepaar aus Duisburg dabei, Verwandte Rosaliens: die Frau war eine Cousine von ihr** (Th. Mann); (2) a descriptive interpretation: **ein Totenkopf mit gekreuzten Knochen grinste: Achtung. Lebensgefahr** (E. Langgässer); (3) something perceived: **sie blickte ihn an: eine wollene Kappe ging ihm bis auf die Brauen und bedeckte Stirn, Schläfen und Ohren** (E. Langgässer).

(*d*) Demonstration.

The colon directs the reader's attention (1) after a demonstrative: **Und wie damals in Mitau klammerte sich sein verstörter Geist an den e i n e n Gedanken: zu Suzon** (woman's name) (W. Bergengruen);

(2) after a single-word pointer, leading the sentence, thus many writers start sentences with **Wohlgemerkt: Überhaupt: Trotzdem:** as: **Vor allem: Leopold war frei** (F. Werfel); (3) after a noun pointer, as when a brief announcement is displayed: **Parole: Sieg; Fleiß: genügend** (school-report); **Ort der Handlung: eine mitteldeutsche Stadt; Zeit: 16. Jahrhundert** (before a play); **Die Maschine steht startbereit. Also Stichtag: der siebzehnte** (H. Kasack); (4) after a word announcing a summing up: **Summa: der Friede blieb erhalten** (H. von Doderer); **Denn wahrhaftig: es schien ihm an nichts zu fehlen** (E. Langgässer).

A striking degree of laconism may be achieved. Thus, where a narrator has started a conversation with a fellow-traveller, the latter, after a lengthy exchange, remembers to introduce himself: **Übrigens: Kuckuck** (Th. Mann), *My name, by the way, is Kuckuck.*

On the other hand, the whole demonstrative force may be absorbed in suggesting a situation of heightened intensity. Thus, when a dentist announces the cost of an operation: **Er legte den Zettel vor sich hin, rauchte und sagte ganz plötzlich: „Erschrecken Sie nicht: es wird zwölfhundert Mark kosten"** (H. Böll).

Irony may also be conveyed, as when a lawyer is said to have amassed a fortune: **am Geschäft, die Fehltritte anderer vor dem, wie man sagt: unerbittlichen Gesetz zu verteidigen** (S. Andres).

(*e*) A colon is not required if a specific term, especially an exemplifying conjunction [*v.* §§ 112, 535 (*a*)], takes over the role of announcing the following statement.

540. The Colon and Semi-colon in the Period

(*a*) The colon is not uncommon in a rhythmical role between the two halves of a statement which are balanced, both in sense and in style: **Und was für Schaden auch die Bösen tun mögen: der Schaden der Guten ist der schädlichste Schaden** (Nietzsche).

The greatest collection of such rhythmical statements, the Bible, now, though not entirely suitably, uses the semi-colon in many German versions: **Selig sind, die da Leid tragen; denn sie sollen getröstet werden** (Matt. v. 4); cp. *Blessed are they that mourn: for they shall be comforted* (Revised Version).

(*b*) Related to this rhythmical use is that before the final statement in a period, the preceding parallel subordinate clauses being often separated by semi-colons: **Wo dir Gottes Sonne zuerst schien; wo dir die Sterne des Himmels zuerst leuchteten; wo seine Blitze dir zuerst seine Allmacht offenbarten: da ist deine Liebe, da ist dein Vaterland** (E. M. Arndt).

Such periods are also now uncommon, but the colon still may have rhythmical force, as in the following, where it enables the construction to be changed in mid-sentence:

Neben ihm lärmten und krakeelten die Billardspieler, liefen die Marköre und rasselte das Telephon: man scheuerte den Boden, man heizte den Ofen, er merkte nichts davon (S. Zweig).

Exercise LXIV

A. Study the following sentences and state a reason for each mark of punctuation:

1. Ein erklärter Tantenliebhaber, habe ich von Jugend an ein Gefühl für den Charme ganz alter Damen gehabt (W. Bergengruen). 2. Da lag mein alter Bursche, Familienvater, fünf Kinder, weißbandagiert auf einer Trage (B. Werner). 3. Rodin sculpting: Dann wurden die Hände zögernder. Sie schienen erkannt zu haben: es gab für sie nichts mehr zu tun (S. Zweig). 4. Er fragte, seit wann ich in der Stadt sei (ich log: seit einigen Tagen) und warum ich ihn nicht aufgesucht hatte (H. Hesse). 5. Er schrak auf: wie ein Totenschädel, bleich und käsig, schlotterte das verknöcherte Gesicht über der hageren, schwarzen Gestalt (S. Zweig). 6. Vogelstimmen zucken und perlen hinter ihr durch den Wald, aus dem Himmelsgewölbe hängt es wie eine Kette aus Kristallkugeln, durch die ein gläserner heller Klang von oben nach unten zieht: Lerchen! (S. Andres). 7. Aber deine politischen Seelenführer—ja, die sollte man, paß auf, was ich sage: aufhängen sollte man sie, richtig aufhängen! (S. Andres). 8. ,,Einmal machte er mir eine Szene, bei der er beinahe weinte . . . ich bitte Sie: ein Mann, der weint . . .'' (Th. Mann). 9. ,,Sensation: Opel Kapitän, Baujahr 1949—2800 Mark!'' (adv.). 10. ,,Schlau warst du immer—'', sagte der Bursche wütend. ,,Na, also'', schloß sie gelassen ab. ,,Was: also?'' (E. Langgässer).

B. Punctuate the following sentences:

1. Deutscher Herkunft wie der Name sagt aus dem Gothaischen stammend gleich Dir liebe Mama und aus gutem Hause wenn auch natürlich nicht von Familie ist er Paläontolog seines Zeichens und lebt urportugiesisch vermählt seit langem in Lissabon Begründer und Direktor des hiesigen Naturhistorischen Museums (Th. Mann) 2. Georg rief der Vater indem er sich die Pfeife in der Hand übrigens eine die er sich erst vor einigen Tagen erstanden hatte im Fensterrahmen sehen ließ bring mir etwas Tabak mit du weißt welchen meine eigene Marke die andren alle kann ich nicht rauchen die qualmen so

CHAPTER LXV
ORTHOGRAPHY

541. The Capital Letter Initial

(*a*) A capital letter is used in German at the beginning of every complete and independent statement, and, by extension, of all headings, as in English; and further for:

(1) Every noun; and every other part of speech used as a noun, whether (i) by general rule: the infinitive (*v.* § 204, and especially § 205), adjectives (§§ 143 f. and 185 f., and those from personal and place names, §§ 281-2), possessive pronouns [§ 170 (*c*)], and numerals [§ 54 (*a*), and those in -**er**, § 94]; or (ii) by special formation from any part of speech (*v.* § 44); or (iii) an adjective [§ 144A (*b*)] or numeral [§ 54 (*b*)-(*e*)] standing for a noun understood.

(2) Proper names, whether personal (§§ 156 f.), or of place (§§ 219 f.), or those called quasi-proper names (§ 235).

(3) Words used in certain other special contexts, *v.* below (*c*).

(*b*) Many adjectives are used in proper names, whether geographical, historical, or institutional: **das Schwarze Meer, der Dreißigjährige Krieg, das Rote Kreuz, der Norddeutsche Lloyd, das Auswärtige Amt.**
Only usage decides whether similar terms are or have become common nouns, losing the capital: **die Alte Pinakothek** (in Munich), **das alte Museum** (um die Ecke); **die Olympischen Spiele, olympische Ruhe; der Bayrische Wald, bayrische Biere.** Thus also with adjectives from personal names in -(**i**)**sch: die Platonischen Schriften, platonische Liebe.** Titles are not uniform: **Geheimer Rat, ordentlicher Professor.** For obvious reasons capitals are less common before personal names than before common nouns: **der Heilige Stuhl,** but **der heilige Paulus; die Deutsche Mark** (since 1948), but **der deutsche Michel.** In adjectives from persons a distinction is often made in the closeness of association between the person and the noun thus described: **die Lutherische Bibelübersetzung,** but **die lutherische Kirche** (Duden); perhaps also **das Linnésche System (der Pflanzen),** but **das kopernikanische Weltensystem.**

(*c*) Adjectives, etc., used in certain special contexts:

(1) Pronouns, possessive adjectives and pronouns used in direct address, either always [**Sie,** etc., *v.* §§ 8 (*a*), 25 (*a*), 170 (*d*)], or on certain more formal occasions (*v.* §§ 167-8); or similar words used in reference to or by Royal and Papal persons [**Wir,** § 168 (*b*), **Seine Majestät,** etc.].

(2) Adjectives or ordinals used as appellations: **der Große Kurfürst, Karl der Kühne,** cp. § 174 (*e*).

(3) Adjectives and numerals may be used with unique reference, as the equivalent of a proper name: **ich rechnete mich als Ewigen Gast zum Hause** (F. Werfel, the Permanent Guest, an institution); **er dachte das Wort Ewig in seiner vollen Kraft und Bedeutung** (H. Böll); **dieser Achtzehnte August,** *this 18th August;* or simply for emphasis: **(im Mittelalter) fielen Glaube und Wissen in Eins zusammen** [cp. § 54 (*a*) (1), **Erst** and **erst**].

542. The Loss of the Noun Capital

(*a*) Nouns lose their capital initial when used as other parts of speech, especially as adverbs (of time, § 59, superlatives of manner, § 165, etc.), as prepositions [*v.* § 262 (*b*) (1) and (5), also §§ 405 and 459], as indefinite pronouns (*v.* § 148); and when used in close association with verbs, becoming adverbs, adjectives, or prefixes, *v.* § 88 (*d*) and (*b*)-(*d*), below.

(*b*) Many verbs, especially the commoner, **sein, werden, tun, machen,** etc., take a noun as their object, prepositional object, complement, etc., and develop a joint sense with this noun or noun phrase: **(jmdm) angst machen, nottun; stattfinden; (jmdm) freund, feind, wohl, weh(e) sein; in acht nehmen, zu eigen machen; zugrunde gehen, zuteil werden,** etc.

Such nouns become either predicative adjectives [after **sein,** etc., *v.* § 284 (*b*) and (*c*)]; or objective prefixes [**stattfinden,** cp. § 88 (*d*)]; or remain in their adverbial function in a prepositional group, sometimes combining as a prefix (**überhandnehmen**). All these stages are individual to each idiom; but the criterion for the loss of the nominal force is that such words answer to an adverbial question: **Was tun Sie? Ich halte haus** (*not:* **was halten Sie?**). **Wie steht er zu Ihnen? Er ist mir freund** (*not:* **was ist er Ihnen?**).

(*c*) Many verbs take a prepositional object which is abbreviated to a direct noun object and develops with the verb a joint sense: **radfahren** (= **auf dem Rad fahren**), **maschineschreiben** (= **mit der Maschine schreiben**). Many are verbs of progression (**fahren, laufen, reiten**), but there are also **schreiben, spielen, stehen,** etc. The object is often cognate [cp. § 378 (*b*)]. Loss of capital and combination as a prefix happen together; the criterion is commonness of use and isolation from similar expressions; thus: **kehrtmachen, kopfstehen,** but **Klavier spielen** (cp. **gut Klavier spielen**), **Gefahr laufen** (cp. **große Gefahr laufen**). For some verbs there is probably an intermediate state in which the verb is combined only in the infinitive, and, perhaps, past participle: **radfahren, ich fahre Rad, bin radgefahren.**

If this is so, it is due to the influence of the infinitive noun (**Radfahren**) on the infinitive, cp. § 475 (*a*) (1).

(*d*) Noun objects of the attributive present participle are compounded, losing their capital, if the joint unit represents a habitual or characteristic activity: **der aufsichthabende Arzt**, but **Bonbons spendende Opas** (H. Böll); **Respekt gebietend**, but **vertrauenerweckend**; **beifallklatschende Zuschauer**, but **Pfui-rufende**. The decision to compound is often a personal one. Cp. also § 38 (*c*).

543. Division of Words by Syllables (Syllabification)

The rules for division of words by syllables, for carrying over to a following line, are complicated, but carefully observed.

(*a*) Simple words. The principle of division is intended to follow the natural division of words in slow articulation, *i.e.* a following syllable must begin with a consonant: **al-le, tob-te, äu-ßer-te**.

(1) A single consonant, after a long vowel, joins the following syllable: **Lie-be, hö-ren, nä-hen, mu-tig**.

(2) Two consonants after a short vowel divide, thus double consonants: **bel-len, Was-ser** (-ck- becoming -kk-, **Dek-ke**); and also the groups: **chs, dn, dt, gn, ng, nk, pf, sp, tsch, tz**, as **Och-sen, Fin-ger, Wes-pe**, etc.

(3) But certain groups are indivisible, and join the following syllable after either long or short vowel: **ch, sch, ß; st, z** (= ts); **ph, th**; thus **rä-chen, Ta-sche, schie-ßen, Ka-sten**.

(4) Three consonants lose the last to the following syllable: **Kämp-fer, lisp-le**; or the last two if they constitute any of the groups in (3): **sech-ste**, cp. also **Prit-sche**.

(5) Two distinct vowels or vowel groups divide: **hau-en, klei-ig, Trau-ung, Mau-er, schrie-en**; where these are abbreviated from three identical vowels (as **Seen** from **See-en**), the third vowel is not normally restored on division (**Se-en**), but some prefer to do so (**See-en, Armee-en** or **Arme-en**).

(6) The following are not divided: (i) monosyllables: **Pfund, tanzt, rauh**; (ii) disyllables, where division would produce an isolated vowel: **Ahorn, Uhu**; but diphthongs may be isolated: **Au-ge, äu-ßern, Ei-ter**.

It may be noticed that the above rules often cause different forms of the same word to be divided differently, thus: **Kopf, Köp-fe; prel-len, prell-te; kämp-fen, kämpf-te; Wech-sel, Wechs-ler; fin-ge-re, fing-re; ge-stern, gest-rig; sechs, sech-se, sech-ste**.

(*b*) Compound words are divided into their component parts, and this should normally be preferred to division along syllabic lines [as (*a*) above]: **Haus-tür, Gläs-chen, früh-stücken**; this includes prefixes, and suffixes beginning with a consonant: **ver-äppeln, Wachs-tum**; but suffixes beginning with a vowel take the last consonant with them: **Köni-gin, Zeh-rung, Ab-tei.**

Particles with inserted -r- by rule leave this with the first syllable: **dar-auf, wor-um**, as **her-ein.**

In cases where compounding has brought three identical consonants together, of which one has been omitted (thus: **Schallaut**, for **Schall-laut, programmäßig**, for **programm-mäßig**), this is restored on division: **Schiff-fahrt.** But this does not happen when one of two -hh- has been omitted from an abstract noun derived from an adjective, so **Rauheit** (for **Rauh-heit**) becomes **Rau-heit**; nor for two consonants representing three in certain words: **den-noch, Mit-tag, Drit-tel.**

(*c*) Foreign words are divided in the same way as German words: **Stro-phe, Bal-lon, Ten-nis, Inter-esse, Mikro-skop**; but

(1) the special groups represented by **l** or **r** following **b p d t g** or **k**, and the group **gn**, are not separated: **Pu-bli-kum, Ka-plan, Ma-gnet**, etc.; and

(2) two distinctly pronounced vowels or vowel groups (not representing a possible German sequence) may be separated: **na-iv, Oze-an, kre-ieren, Spermatozo-on, Individu-um.**

(*d*) Place-names are divided in the same way as normal German words: **Ber-lin, Heidel-berg, Salz-ach**; but too much thought need not be given to whether and how a word is compounded, thus **Grün-au**, but **Streh-le-nau.**

544. Compounds and the Hyphen

The hyphen is normally not used in compounds; but there are certain special classes of words where it is used to assist clarity.

(*a*) When two compounds have one element in common, it may be omitted in one of them, the hyphen taking its place: **Möbel- und Teppich-firmen, aus- und eingehen, ein- oder zweimal; Gepäckabgabe und -ausgabe, treppauf und -ab.** This form is commonest in nouns and verbs, and should not, especially in adjectives, be over-used; thus **schul- und dienstfrei**, but not usually (as in G. Keller) **ein frucht- und dankbarer Boden.** Note (above) that the full compound has no hyphen (**eingehen**), and a separated second component has no capital (**-ausgabe**).

(*b*) Certain difficult noun groups require the hyphen: (1) to separate three similar vowels (**die Hawaii-Inseln**), but not dissimilar (**das Seeufer**); (2) to avoid ambiguity, thus **Grün-Dung** is not **Gründung**, and **Ur-Teil** not **Urteil**; (3) to divide a compound of more than three components (**Arbeitslosenversicherungs-Gesetz**), unless reasonably manageable (**Eisenbahnfahrplan**); (4) to articulate compounds of which one part is a letter (**O-Beine, K.-o.-Schlag, Binde-s**), abbreviation (**LKW-Ersatzteile**), numeral/noun group (**Vier-Sterne-General, 12-Pf-Marke**), or other difficult combinations (**die Januar-Februar-Nummer, das In-die-Augen-Starren, das Ave-Maria**, etc.). But some numeral groups are written together: **ein Viertelliterglas**; and adjectives related to these groups of nouns do not take the hyphen: **obeinig, 20jährig**.

(*c*) Certain adjectival compounds take the hyphen to show that the components retain their separate force: **die deutsch-englische Verständigung, die römisch-katholische Kirche, die nord-südliche Achse** (but **die nordöstliche Richtung**), eine **blau-rote Fahne** (but **blaurot**, *purple*), cp. § 495 (*b*).

(*d*) In many compounds of place or personal names: **München-Gladbach, das Arndt-Gymnasium**, eine **Böhm-Kirche** (by the architect), **das Goethe-Schiller-Archiv, die St.-Georgs-Kirche** (better: **St. Georgskirche**). Such words are generally compounded when they are regarded as a compound common noun: **Röntgenstrahlen, Tantalusqualen, Schillerdenkmal, Lutherbild**.

Street names are either (1) compounded: **Marktplatz, Luthergasse, Kurfürstendamm**; (2) separated with a non-inflected first element in -**er**: **die Handschuhsheimer Landstraße**, or an inflected adjective: **Langer Weg, am Langen Weg**; or (3) compounded with a hyphen if more complex, especially if including a fuller personal name: **Georg-Ebers-Straße, Geschwister-Scholl-Platz**.

(*e*) Many reputable writers, however, in cases where a final component is associated with two or more preceding components which form a unity, prefer a simple hyphen linking the last two elements: **Adalbert Stifter-Gesellschaft, Herz Jesu-Bild, Hors d'oeuvre-Platte, Non Stop-Bücherei** (series of cheap reprints), **der à la mode-Kavalier** (Th. Mann), **ein Hopalong Cassidy-Heft** (H. Böll), **das Ende der Vogel Strauß-Politik** (newsp.).

545. The Apostrophe

(*a*) The apostrophe is used to show that a vowel, normally written and spoken, has been ommitted; this is commonly unaccented -**e**-: **ich hatt' einen Kameraden**; less commonly -**i**-: **wen'ge**; sometimes other elements: **'nen Garten, 's Mädchen, 'raus**, etc.

As such omissions follow the natural elisions of speech, the rule is an attempt to maintain the regularity of orthography against the variability of the spoken language; thus some writers drastically reduce the cases where they observe the rule (**wenns regnet, raus!**), but retain it to avoid ambiguity (**tanzt'**, different from **tanzt**).

(*b*) The apostrophe is used:

(1) With elision of following **es** to **'s**: **ich will dir's geben**; but **es sagens viel** (W. Bergengruen).

(2) After names ending in sibilants [but not -sch, *v*. § 156 (*b*) (2)] to show the missing genitive -s: **Aristoteles' Schriften**, but **Buschs Gedichte**. Avoidance is often preferable: **die Irrfahrten des Odysseus**.

(*c*) The apostrophe is not used:

(1) In contractions of article and preposition: **ins Haus, beim Bach**.

(2) In the genitive or plural of abbreviated nouns: **LKWs, GIs**.

(3) In the short forms of adjectives in -e: **müd, öd**.

(4) In the endings with -e- elision, *i.e.* -er-, -el-, -en-: **andre, unsern, offne**; **ich öffne, stammle**, etc., *v*. § 47 (*a*).

(5) In imperatives, even if the -e form is possible: **bring, sag, schreib**, *v*. § 247 (*b*).

(*d*) In certain cases distinctions must be made:

(1) Nouns ending in -e may omit this without apostrophe in traditional double groups: **Hab und Gut, Freud und Leid**; but not otherwise: **ohne Fried', ohne Freud'**; but **in Reih'n** (correct, older) or **in Reihn** [modern, analogy of **stehn**, *v*. (3) below].

(2) Adjectives in -isch and -ig may omit -i- with apostrophe: **rhein'sche Sagen, ew'ger Friede**; but analogous derivatives from names have no apostrophe: **die Hegelsche Philosophie**.

(3) Verb forms omitting final -e require apostrophe: **ich hab', hätt' er, sie könnt'**; but all other forms elide without a sign: **stehn, wir schrien** (for **stehen, schrieen**); **du bläst, er lädt**, *v*. Appendix B.

Exercise LXV

A. Study and translate into English the following sentences:

1. Der Verfall des Sprachstils läßt sich mit beinahe jedem x-beliebigen Zitat aus einem modernen Roman beweisen. 2. „. . . faux-frais!" wiederholte er mit grimmigem pariserischen Gurgel-r (Th. Mann).

3. Ein Mottorrad kam die leere Straße entlang, oarmig, obeinig donnerte er die Perspektive herauf (R. Musil).   4. Mit einem 6 : 3, 6 : 3, 6: 0-Sieg über E. B. stellte T. U. gestern innerhalb einer Stunde Dänemarks Davispokal-Sieg über Deutschland sicher (newsp.).   5. Wand-Klapp-Bett, ein- und zweischläfrig (newsp. adv.).   6. Ein beträchtlicher Vorschuß tut mir bitter not—zur Not genügt ein kleinerer.   7. Old and new fashion: Bei Torcks steht wohl alles schon Kopf (W. Bergengruen, 1926).   Er kann glücklicherweise nicht klavierspielen (H. von Doderer, 1951).   8. Department of non-coordination: Weite Welt-Bücherei (catalogue of Franckh, publisher). Weite-Welt-Bücherei (catalogue of Kosmos-Bücher, the firm producing the series).   9. Eine junonische Gestalt, homerisches Gelächter, ein herkuleischer Körperbau, sokratische Weisheit, ein spartanischer Lebenswandel, drakonische Maßnahmen.

B. Divide the following words if possible:

Sauerampfer, Dampfer; Christen, christlich; hassen, häßlich; Geographie, Erdkunde; München, münchnerisch; Brennerei, Brennessel; Plankton, Heraklit; Ozon, Oolith.

CHAPTER LXVI

CONJUGATION OF STRONG AND IRREGULAR VERBS

546. General

(*a*) A List of all Strong and Irregular (weak) Verbs at present current in German is at Appendix D. It contains: (1) strong verbs proper, (2) irregular weak verbs (*v.* § 77), (3) the seven past present verbs (the modal verbs and **wissen,** *v.* §§ 63 f.), and (4) the irregular auxiliaries **haben** (weak), **sein** and **werden** (strong), and the irregular strong verb **tun.**

(*b*) The weak conjugation is that of the vast majority of verbs in the language, *i.e.* all verbs other than the limited group of strong verbs, and including all new verb formations (cp. § 473). The group of strong and irregular weak verbs is thus subject to constant pressure to adopt regular weak forms, the opposite process, verbs of weak conjugation becoming strong, being much less common.

(*c*) Thus the List shows, in many cases, both strong and weak forms. Those in brackets are less common forms, being usually an older one going out of use: **triefte (troff),** but sometimes a newer one not yet established. In other cases, no preference is implied: **schliß/schleißte.** The same distinction applies to the choice of variant vowels in the past subjunctive: **gölte (gälte); schwömme/schwämme** [cp. § 272 (*a*)].

However, the bracketed alternative inflections for the second person singular imperative [**weich(e)!,** cp. §§ 247 (*b*) and 545 (*c*) (5)], and for the second and third persons singular present [**du reiß(es)t,** etc., *v.* Appendix B], are not intended to suggest any priority of use.

(*d*) In general, the relative frequency of competing forms for a given tense or mood of any verb is a complex matter in which meaning, tense, style, area, and personal linguistic habits all play a part, and all such distinctions must be highly tentative.

(*e*) All compound verbs, with few exceptions, behave like their corresponding simple verbs: **fahren, fuhr; befahren, befuhr;** there is thus no need to multiply entries in the List. But certain compounds which show some preference for strong or weak forms differing from that of the simple verbs are mentioned, either in the List or in the paragraphs below: **erschrecken,** cp. **schrecken; verschollen,** cp. **schallen.**

(*f*) Rules for the insertion or omission of euphonic **-e-** in the present tense forms of strong and weak verbs are given summarily at Appendix B, and a conspectus of vowel changes in strong verbs at Appendix C.

547. Replacement of Strong and Irregular Forms by Weak Forms

(*a*) The replacement of strong and irregular forms by regular weak forms is caused by:

(1) The general tendency towards the weak conjugation, *v.* § 546.

(2) The special tendency towards adopting the weak forms of a corresponding factitive verb, *v.* § 549.

(3) The analogy of other verbs of similar and historically related senses, which are weak, *e.g.* **backen,** *v.* § 551 (*e*).

(*b*) The following are some of the verbs in which this process is happening: **backen, sich befleißen** (weak, **sich befleißigen**), **dünken, gleißen, glimmen, klieben, klimmen, melken, schallen, schnauben, schrauben, schwören, senden, speien, spleißen, stecken, stieben, wenden, zeihen;** the strong verb **sprießen** is being replaced by the weak verb **sprossen.**

(*c*) The order in which this commonly happens is: (1) present and imperative (by abandoning the vowel change); (2) past tense and past participle; but (3) the special role of the past participle as a predicative and attributive adjective often causes it to retain a strong form when the verb has otherwise become entirely weak or ceased to be used, or to retain certain archaic forms, *v.* § 552.

(*d*) Partly the cause, and partly the result of the above process, is the differentiation of senses between strong and weak, *v.* § 551; and an accidental result may be the better differentiation of one verb from another strong verb, *e.g.* **triefen** and **schwären,** where the weak past participles **getrieft** and **geschwärt** are preferable to the earlier strong forms **getroffen** and **geschworen,** which could be confused with the past participles of **treffen** and **schwören.**

(*e*) In a few cases there is contamination of the weak by the strong forms, *e.g.* **laden,** *to invite, v.* § 551 (*e*).

548. Factitive Verbs

(*a*) Many verbs have acted as parent verbs for a derived form known as a factitive (or causative), having the sense of "bringing about in an object the action" described by the parent verb: **sitzen,** *to sit;* **setzen,** *to place* (put into a static position). Many of these pairs of verbs have analogues in English: **fällen,** *to fell,* from **fallen,** *to fall;* **tränken,** *to water* (animals), cp. *drench,* from **trinken,** *to drink.*

Factitive verbs may have the same infinitive as the parent verb: **quellen (quellen);** but commonly show vowel change, as those above; and occasionally consonantal change, *v.* **beizen, leiten, reizen, stecken,** below.

Usually the parent verb is intransitive and strong, and the factitive transitive and weak [v. (b) below]; but other relations may hold [v. (c), (d) below], and in these cases there is often a greater divergence of meaning between the related forms.

Most factitives are thus fairly distinct, both in sense and in conjugation, from their parent verbs (this paragraph); but in some cases interaction of forms has taken place (§ 549).

(b) The original verb is intransitive, the factitive transitive: **dünken** (**denken**), *to seem*, **löschen** (**er-löschen**), *to put out* (fire), *slake* (lime), etc., **führen** (**fahren**), *to lead*, **fällen** (**fallen**), *to fell*, **flößen** (**fließen**), *to instil* (courage, **einflößen**), *float* (logs), etc., **quellen** (**quellen**), *to swell up* (by water), **rennen** (**ge-rinnen**), *to curdle* (milk), etc., cp. *rennet* (and distinguish from **rennen**, weak irregular, *to run, race*), **ersäufen** (**ersaufen**), *to drown* (animals), **erschrecken** (**erschrecken**), *to frighten*, **ertränken** (**ertrinken**), *to drown*, **säugen** (**saugen**), *to suckle* (cp. der Säugling), **schicken** (**ge-schehen**), (*to make happen*, becoming) *to send*, **schrecken** (**schrecken**), *to frighten, cool suddenly* (*e.g.* **ein Ei abschrecken**), **schwellen** (**schwellen**), *to swell* (sails, etc.), **schwemmen** (**schwimmen**), *to wash away*, **sengen** (**singen**), (*to make sing* or *sizzle*, thus) *to singe*, **senken** (**sinken**), and **versenken** (**versinken**), *to sink*, **setzen** (**sitzen**), *to place*, **sprengen** (**springen**), *to gallop* (horse), *blow up* (fort), etc., **stäuben** (**stieben**), *to scatter, strew*, **stänkern** (**stinken**), *to cause dissension* ("*raise a stink*"), **triefen**, also **träufeln** (**triefen**), *to pour out in drops*, **tränken** (**trinken**), *to water* (animals), **weichen** (**weichen**), *to make soft* (*soak*).

(c) Both original verb and factitive are transitive: **beizen** (**beißen**), *to stain* (wood), *corrode* (metal), **leiten** (**leiden**), (*to make pass through*, from older sense of *suffer*, hence) *to lead*, **reizen** (**reißen**), *to irritate*, **schleifen** (**schleifen**), *to drag, raze* (defences).

(d) The original verb has both intransitive and transitive force; the factitive either specialises the transitive sense: **beugen** (**biegen**), *to bend* (the will or the knee); or replaces it in the parent verb: **drängen** (**dringen**), the transitive sense of **dringen** only remaining in some set expressions: **eine dringende Gefahr, gedrungene Gestalt** (cp. **eine gedrängte Übersicht**).

The factitive may develop both intransitive and transitive force: **stecken** (**stechen**), *to put* (stick) or *be put*, **wenden** (**winden**), *to turn* (cp. § 77); or the factitive may develop purely intransitive force: **schellen** (**schallen**), (*to cause to sound*, hence) *to ring* (for service, etc.).

Note.—**Dünken**, from **denken**, with strong forms and accusative object, though only fragmentary in use (**mich dünkt, mich deuchte**, past subjunctive, *I should think*), has developed a weak past, and may, after the analogy of **scheinen**, take a dative object (**mir dünkt, mich dünkte**).

549. Interaction of Weak and Factitive and Strong or Irregular Forms
Interaction often takes place between a verb and its factitive:

(*a*) A strong intransitive accepts weak forms: **hangen** is being displaced in infinitive and present by **hängen,** *to hang:* **die Töchter hängen an der Mutter; triefen,** throughout by its weak form [*v.* § 547 (*d*)]; and of the compounds of **schrecken,** at least **zurückschrecken** is often weak: **sie schreckte zurück,** *started back.*

(*b*) A weak factitive accepts strong forms: **schleißen,** *to wear out,* especially in its compound form, **verschleißen (verschlissene Kleider); schmelzen,** *to melt* or *smelt,* is often strong: **das Standbild wurde eingeschmolzen; wägen,** *to weigh* (consider words, actions, used in formal style), has, at least in its compounds **abwägen, erwägen,** accepted the strong forms of **wiegen.**

550. Simple and Compound Verbs
(*a*) In the relations between strong and weak forms a not uncommon process is the replacement of a simple strong intransitive (sometimes transitive) verb by an inseparable compound of analogous sense, especially with the prefixes **er-** (= a beginning), or **ver-** (= an ending); the sphere of the simple verb then becomes more exclusively weak and factitive:

(1) Intransitives: **bleichen,** *to turn pale, lose colour,* has largely given place to **erbleichen,** weak, *to turn pale,* and **verbleichen,** strong, *to lose colour:* **sie erbleichte, verblichene Farben;** and both are used, strong, in the figurative sense, *to die:* **Unser teurer Verblichener,** *our dear deceased* (in obituary notices), leaving **bleichen** to express the factitive sense, *to bleach.*

Löschen, *to be extinguished,* is now replaced by **erlöschen,** and **löschen** is left as the factitive verb, *to put out.*

Schrecken, *to be frightened,* has given place to **erschrecken,** and **schrecken,** especially in compounds (**abschrecken,** etc.), is mainly factitive, influencing also the intransitive compounds (**zusammen-, zurückschrecken**) towards weak forms.

(2) Transitive: **verbergen,** *to hide,* has replaced **bergen,** in that sense, so that the simple verb now usually means *to save, salvage.*

(*b*) A compound verb, if it has the strong or irregular weak forms at all, will take those of its parent simple verb [*v.* § 546 (*e*)]; but when simple verbs are in the process of changing from strong to weak it should never be assumed that all compounds of such verbs are at the same point of transition, or, in fact, are changing at all.   Compare examples above, and

schallen, which is becoming weak, while **erschallen,** *to ring out,* retains more strong forms (**der Ruf ist erschollen,** *has gone out*), and **verschallen,** now only represented in the past participle: (**der Forschungsreisende ist im Urwald) verschollen,** *lost,* may only be strong.   Compare also **schrauben** (§ 552).

551. Differentiation of Sense in Strong and Weak Forms

(*a*) A common and, for the student, satisfactory situation is when the strong and weak forms of a verb are used for fairly distinct senses:

VERB		STRONG SENSES	WEAK SENSES
bewegen,	tr.	*to move* (the will), *induce.*	*to move* (objects), or *stir* (the emotions).
hauen,	tr.		*to hew* (wood), *chastise* or *beat up* (persons).
	intr.	*to direct a blow* (which does not connect).	

(*b*) A verb may be strong in its main or primary sense, and weak in secondary, derived, or modern senses:

sieden,	tr.	*to cook by boiling.*	*to raise*⎫ *to boiling point*
	intr.		*to rise* ⎭ (not cooking).
schaffen,	tr.	*to create.*	*to produce, bring along.*
	intr.		*to work, be busy.*

Note.—The fourth sense of **schaffen,** *to bring about, cause* (as order out of disorder), partakes of both main and secondary senses, and thus varies: **er schaffte (schuf) Ordnung, Abhilfe.**

(*c*) A verb may be strong or weak in its primary sense, but weak only in secondary, special senses:

VERB		MAIN SENSE		WEAK SENSES
melken,	tr.	*to milk* (strong, weak).		*to fleece.*
senden,	tr.	*to send*	,, ,,	*to broadcast* (radio).
wenden,	tr.	*to turn*	,, ,,	*to turn* (a coat, etc.).
	intr.			*to turn.*
scheren,	tr.	*to shear*	,, ,,	*to concern,* (refl.) *bother oneself, clear out.*
weben,	tr.	*to weave*	,, ,,	
	intr.			*to be astir, active.*

(*d*) The main, strong conjugation may have become a remnant, and be overshadowed by secondary, weak uses:

VERB	STRONG SENSES	WEAK SENSES
pflegen, tr.	*to occupy oneself with* as: **die Kunst pflegen;** thus: *to take counsel:* **Rats** (gen.) **pflegen.**	*to care for:* **einen Kranken pflegen,** and (intr.) *to be in the habit of.*

(*e*) The differentiated senses of a verb may at a later stage begin to interact, thus **laden** and **backen** could at one time be differentiated thus:

laden, tr.	*to load.*	*to invite.*
backen, tr.	*to bake.*	
intr.	*to bake.*	*to cake* (*stick, e.g.* snow).

But *to invite* has acquired strong forms (**er lud mich ein**), and *to load,* at least colloquially, some weak forms (**er ladet das Gewehr**); and *to bake,* tr., perhaps under the influence of the other sense, is now increasingly weak (**sie backte den Kuchen**).

(*f*) Differentiation of sense may involve a distinction of force:

(1) Between a strong intransitive, and a weak transitive, *v.* under factitives, § 548 (*b*), and various verbs above, (*a*)-(*e*).

(2) Between a strong literal sense, and a weak figurative sense; thus for **gären,** intr.: **das Bier hat gegoren,** *fermented,* **es gärte im Volk,** *there was unrest;* and perhaps **glimmen,** intr.: **das Feuer glimmte** (older, **glomm**) **unter der Asche,** *glimmered,* but only: **die Hoffnung glimmte noch in seinem Herzen,** *was still alive.*

552. Differentiation of Sense in the Past Participle

As noted above [§ 547 (*c*)], the past participle is the form which retains most persistently any special strong form, or distinct sense; thus **schrauben,** *to screw,* is in its primary sense usually weak, but sometimes strong; but **geschraubt,** *affected* (*e.g.* language), is only weak, and **verschroben,** *affected* (of persons), *cranky,* is only strong. Various possibilities may be set out as follows:

(*a*) The one verb **mahlen,** *to grind,* is weak throughout, but has *only* the strong past participle **gemahlen.**

(*b*) A number of verbs are now largely or entirely weak, but have a strong past participle in addition to the regular weak form. This is used in special, figurative, or archaic senses, and occurs commonly in the (predicative or) attributive adjective form, and in certain set contexts of which one is quoted for each participle below: **der bedungene Lohn,** *stipulated;* **ein beklommenes Herz,** *oppressed;* **ein gedungener Mörder,** *hired assassin;* **eine gedrungene Gestalt,** *thick-set* [transitive, *v.* § 548 (*d*)];

mit gefaltenen (also gefalteten) Händen, *folded;* nach gepflogenem Rat, *having taken counsel* [*v.* § 551 (*d*)]; gesalzene Preise, Witze, *excessive, seasoned;* geschrotenes (now geschrotetes) Korn, *coarse-ground;* gespaltene Hufe, *cleft* (of ruminants); ein verhohlener Blick, *surreptitious;* mit unverhohlener Freude, *frank, open;* eine verworrene Lage, (objectively) *confused* (cp. er war im Augenblick verwirrt, momentarily and subjectively *confused*); ein verwunschenes Schloß, *charmed* (under a spell).

(*c*) Occasionally it is the weak form which is, to a large extent, isolated in its use: gesinnt (from der Sinn), *holding certain views* (*e.g.* fortschrittlich gesinnt), cp. gesonnen (from sinnen), *having a certain intention* (*e.g.* ich bin nicht gesonnen . . .*, not inclined*); verderbt, *morally corrupted* (*e.g.* ein verderbter Mensch), cp. verdorben (from verderben), *spoilt*, intransitive or transitive (*e.g.* seine verdorbene Gesundheit, verdorbene Speisen).

(*d*) The past participle is also, in general, the special refuge of exceptional and anomalous forms, *e.g.*:

(1) Older forms without ge-, especially in compounds: hausbacken, *prosaic* (lit., home-made), trunken, *drunk* (*v.* § 523), mit neuwaschenem Antlitz (Th. Mann), *with face just washed.*

(2) Older forms with different consonants, vowels: gediegen, *genuine,* sterling (from gedeihen), erhaben, *elevated, sublime* (from erheben), bescheiden, *modest* (from sich bescheiden, *to moderate one's requirements*).

(3) Past participles from verbs no longer in use: (auf)gedunsen, *bloated* (face), unbescholten, *of good character*, verwegen, *bold, jaunty.*

Note.—The forms war, gewesen, now used as past and past participle of sein, are from the disused strong verb wesen, now only: (i) in the participles: anwesend, *present*, abwesend, *absent*, and the infinitive noun, das Wesen, *creature, being*, and compounds: das Sanitätswesen, (military) *medical services;* (ii) wesen, weak, *to have existence* (of a superior being), only in the present; verwesen, *to decay*, weak.

(4) Past participles with anomalous force: gelegen, without passive force: das hochgelegene (= hochliegende) Schloß; also ich bin geboren, *was born.*

553. Archaic and Humorous Forms

Certain forms are used traditionally for archaic or humorous effect; they are either genuine old strong forms, or analogous formations from weak verbs: frug (fragte), gerochen (gerächt), genossen (geniest); (alles) was da fleucht und kreucht (fliegt und kriecht), *all that flies and creeps* (= all animal nature); und der Räuber hub an und sagte . . .*, spoke up and said . . .;* wie die Alten sungen, so zwitschern die Jungen (prov.), etc.

Note.—**Frug** (for **fragte**) is now quite common in less educated usage, without specific archaic or humorous flavour.

EXERCISE LXVI

Translate into ENGLISH, noting the uses of the verbs:

1. Er versenkte sich in seine Aufgabe; bald drängten sich aber die Ereignisse des Tages wieder vor sein Bewußtsein. Als ich ihn antraf, saß er in seinen Gedanken versunken. 2. Nach Erhalt der Nachricht zeigte sie sich sehr bewegt; ich fühlte mich aber nicht bewogen, ihr meine Hilfe anzubieten. 3. Durch achtzig Jahre hindurch schuf Goethe an seinem Lebenswerk. Da aber Pilatus sahe, daß er nichts schaffte, . . . nahm er Wasser, und wusch die Hände . . . (Matt. xxvii. 24). Er hat sich einen Wagen angeschafft. Was haben wir nicht in den Tagen geschafft! 4. Das schert mich nicht! Ich scherte mich gar nicht drum! Scheren Sie sich auf der Stelle fort! 5. Mein Blut siedete direkt bei diesem Ausspruch des hartgesottenen alten Sünders. 6. Er meinte, er hätte den Schlüsselbund in die Tasche gesteckt, aber bei seiner Rückkehr stak er noch in der Tür. 7. The pretentious writer: Im selben Augenblick, wo er zur Feder greift, geschieht eine Veränderung mit ihm: er schraubt sich hinauf, Richtung Wolken. Was dabei herausspringt, ist entsprechend geschraubt. Oder verschroben (H. Reimann). 8. Political Glossary, Party Whip: Fraktionszwang: die einzige Möglichkeit, Gleichgesinnte zu gleicher Gesinnung zu bringen (Simpl.). 9. Wenn ich am Morgen um sieben oder halb acht Uhr mit neuwaschenem Antlitz das Speisezimmer betrat, so fand ich die Gesellschaft noch . . . bei Kaffee und Likören versammelt (Th. Mann). 10. Wie könnte ich alle Tiere nennen und loben, die das Museum zur Anschauung brachte, die Vögel, die nistenden weißen Reiher, die grämlichen Käuze, den dünngestelzten Flamingo, die Geier und Papageien, das Krokodil, die Robben, Lurche, Molche und warzigen Kröten, kurz, was da kreucht und fleucht! (Th. Mann).

APPENDIX A

DIFFERENTIATION OF NOUNS BY GENDER, FORM, SINGULAR, PLURAL

Refer to §§ 444 and 445.

Note.—Forms for the plural are shown, where relevant, in brackets.

der Akt (-e), *act* (drama), *nude study,* cp. **Aktstudie; die Akten,** plur., *documents, file of papers* (Lat. *acta*), cp. **Aktentasche,** sing. **die Akte,** better: **das Aktenstück.**

der Atem, plur. **die Atemzüge,** *breaths.*

der Ball (ᵉe), *ball* (both senses); **der Ballen (-),** *bale.*

der Band (ᵉe), *volume;* **das Band,** *bond* (**Bande**), *ribbon* (**Bänder**); **die Bande (-n),** *band* (of people), especially derogatory.

die Bank, *bench* (**Bänke**) including **Sandbank, (Banken)** *bank* (financial).

der Bau, *building* (**Bauten**), *animal's earth warren* (**Baue**).

der Bauer (-n), *peasant;* **das Bauer (-),** *birdcage.*

das Bestreben, plur. **Bestrebungen,** *efforts.*

der Bogen, *sheet of paper* (**Bogen**), *bow* or *arch* (**Bogen** or **Bögen**).

der Bruch (ᵉe), *break;* **das Bruch** (ᵉe), *marshy land area.*

der Bund, *alliance* (**Bünde,** also **Bündnisse,** from neut. sing.), *bundle* (**Bunde**), also **das Bündel.**

der Chor, *choir* (singers), *chorus* (singers or song) (**Chöre**); **der** (also **das**) **Chor,** *choir* (chancel) (**Chore** or **Chöre**).

das Ding, *thing* (**Dinge**), (fam.) *thing, child, girl* (**Dinger**).

der Doppel (-), *double* (of a person); **das Doppel (-),** *copy, double* (tennis); **der** or **das Double (-s),** *double* (in film); **die Dublette (-n),** *duplicate* (in a collection), cp. **Doppelstück.**

der Druck, *printing* (*e.g.* **Neudrucke**), *pressure* (*e.g.* **Händedrücke**), *v.* § 194 (*c*).

der Effekt, *effect, impression* (**Effekte**), *effect* (property), especially *securities* (**Effekten**), as in **Effektenbörse,** *Stock Exchange.*

die Ehre, plur. **Ehrenbezeigungen,** *marks of politeness,* sometimes (especially military) **Ehrenbezeigungen,** *honours.*

der Ekel, *disgust,* **das Ekel,** *objectionable person.*

der Erbe (-n), *heir;* **das Erbe (-n** or **Erbschaften),** *inheritance.*

die Erkenntnis (-se), *insight,* (right) *judgment;* **das Erkenntnis (-se),** (legal) *judgment.*

der Faden, *thread* (**Fäden**), *fathom* [**Faden,** *e.g.* 4 **Fadentief,** § 241 (*a*)].

der **Fleck** (-e), *spot*, as **Ölfleck**; der **Flecken** (-), *village, small town*, as **Marktflecken**; but also **Flecken** for **Fleck** but not the reverse.

der **Flur** (-e), especially **Hausflur**, *entrance hall;* die **Flur** (-en), especially **Feldflur**, *meadow.*

die **Furcht**, plur. **Befürchtungen**, *fears.*

der **Gefährte** (-n), fem. die **Gefährtin**, *companion;* das **Gefährt** (-e), *vehicle*, especially horse-drawn.

der **Gehalt** (-e), *content*, as **Goldgehalt**; das **Gehalt** (¨er), *salary.*

das **Gesicht**, *face* (**Gesichter**), *vision* (**Gesichte**).

das **Glied** (-er), *member* (of body), also die **Gliedmaße** (-n).

das **Glück**, plur. **Glücksfälle**, *strokes of fortune*, § 444 (*a*).

der **Harz**, geographical region, das **Harz** (-e), *resin.*

der **Heide** (-n), *heathen;* die **Heide** (-n), *heath.*

das **Horn**, *horn* (on the animal, **Hörner**), (kind of) *horn* (**Horne**).

der **Hut** (¨e), *hat;* die **Hut** (-en), *guard*, as **Nachhut**.

der **Kiefer** (-), *jaw* (bone); die **Kiefer** (-n), *pine* (tree).

das **Korn**, *corn* (grain, **Körner**), (kind of) *corn* (**Korne**); der or das **Korn** (tot of) *spirits* (distilled from grain).

der **Kunde** (-n), *customer;* die **Kunde**, *knowledge*, as **Volkskunde**.

der **Laden** (¨), *shop, shutter*, but latter sometimes plur. die **Laden**, as **Fensterladen**.

der **Laib** (-e), *loaf of bread, a cheese;* der **Leib** (-er), *body.*

das **Land** (¨er), *country;* **Lande** is (1) special: die **Niederlande, Rheinlande**, (2) compound: die **Eilande**, (3) poet.: die **deutschen Lande** (*lands*), die **Lande der Kunst** (*realms*).

das **Leben**, plur. often die **Menschenleben**, *lives*, *v.* § 208 (*b*) (3).

das **Licht** (-er), *light*, sometimes **Lichte** for *candles* (**Wachslichte**, etc.), but also **Lichter**.

die **Liebe**, plur. **Liebschaften**, *loves.*

der **Lohn** (¨e), *wage, reward*, plur. also **Belohnungen** (*rewards*), **Lohnsätze**, *wages* (rates).

-mann, in compounds, plur. **-männer, -mannen, -leute**, *v.* § 445 (*b*).

die **Mark**, *mark* (coin), plur. (**sechs**) **Mark** (or **Markstücke**); die **Mark** also *March* (geogr.), and das **Mark**, *marrow.*

die **Maß**, *half-litre fluid measure;* das **Maß**, *measure* (general); plur. of both **Maße** (but **zwei Maß Bier**); also **Maßen** in certain idioms: **über die** (or **alle**) **Maßen**, *immoderate(ly).*

der **Mast** (-e or -en), *mast* (ship); die **Mast** (-en), *fattening* (of cattle), (fattening) *cattle food.*

der **Mensch** (-en), *human being;* das **Mensch** (-er), *wench.*

der **Moment** (-e), *moment* (of time); das **Moment** (-e), *momentum, factor* (for consideration).

der Raub, plur. **Räubereien** (general), **Raubüberfälle** (legal), *robberies.*

der Mord, plur. **Morde** or **Mordtaten,** *murders, v.* § 255 (*b*).

der Morgen, *morning, acre;* **das (Heute und das) Morgen,** *to-morrow, the future.*

die Niete, (losing) *number in a lottery, cipher* (person); **der (das) Niet (-e),** also **die Niete,** *rivet.*

die Not, plur. **Nöte,** *distress,* **Notwendigkeiten,** *needs, necessities.*

das Obst, plur. **Obstsorten,** (kinds of) *fruit(s),* cp. § 444 (*b*) (3).

der Ort, *place* (in general, **Orte**), *settled area* (between village and town in size, **Örter,** also **Ortschaft**); **das Ort (⁻er)** (mining), *end of gallery,* as **vor Ort arbeiten,** *at the coal-face.*

der Osten, *East* (point of compass); **der Ost,** *East,* occasional (**Ost und West**), postal (**Berlin Ost**), poet. for *East wind* (**Ostwind**).

das Produkt, *product* (**Produkte**), *produce* (**Produkten**), as **Produktenbörse,** *Produce Exchange.*

der Quell (-e), poet. and occasional for **die Quelle,** *source, spring.*

der Regen, plur. **Regenfälle, Niederschläge, Regenzeit** (period), *rains.*

das Regiment, *régime* (**Regimente**), *Regiment* (**Regimenter**).

der Reis (-e, kinds of), *rice;* **das Reis (-er),** *twig, offshoot.*

der Rest, plur. **Reste,** *remains,* **Rester** (in the shop: **Restbestände**), *remnants* (of material).

der Ruin, *decay,* (economic) *ruin;* **die Ruine,** *ruin* (building, etc.).

die Runde, *round* (canon), *round* (of drinks), (to go) *the round;* **das Rund** (*e.g.* **des Himmels**), *round shape, circle;* also **die Runda (-en),** and **das Runda (-s),** (regional) *round-song, v.* § 186 (*a*).

der Same, plur. **Samen,** *seeds* (undifferentiated), **Sämereien,** *seeds* (assorted, from seed merchant).

die Sau, plur. **Sauen** (*wild-sows*), **Säue,** also **Sauen** (*domestic sows*), only **Säue** in Bibl. and proverbial usage: **Man muß die Perlen nicht vor die Säue werfen** (cp. Matt. vii. 6).

der Scharlach, *scarlet colour* or *fever,* latter sometimes **das Scharlach** (= **-fieber**).

der Schild (-e), *shield* (defence); **das Schild (-er),** (shop) *sign, label, panel* in general.

der Schmuck, plur. **Schmucke, Schmucksachen,** *jewelry.*

die Schnur, plur. **Schnüre,** *braids, ropes* (pearls, etc.), **Schnuren,** *strings* (not specific, also **Schnüre**).

der Schock (-e or **-s),** *shock;* **das Schock (-e),** *5 dozen,* or an indefinite (large) number (**ein ganzes Schock Kinder**).

der Schurz (-e), *apron* (when worn by men, either occupationally, cp. **der Lederschurz,** or domestically); **die Schürze,** *apron* (when worn by women), or, by metonymy, *a woman* (**den Schürzen nachjagen**).

das **Schwarz,** *black* (colour), as in **Schwarz gekleidet;** der **Schwarze,** *black* (man); das **Schwarze (-n),** *black* (spot), as ins **Schwarze treffen,** *to hit the bull;* die **Schwärze,** *black* (colour), especially printer's ink, *v.* § 187 (*b*).

der **See (-n),** *lake;* die **See (-n),** *sea.*

das **Spektakel,** *spectacle* (to see); der **Spektakel (der Lärm),** *shindy* (to hear).

der **Sproß (-e** or **-en),** *shoot* (plant), *scion* (family); die **Sprosse (-n),** *rung* (ladder), *freckle* (**Sommersprosse**).

die **Steuer (-n),** *tax;* das **Steuer (-),** *helm, steering wheel, joystick.*

der **Stift (-e),** for **Bleistift, Lippenstift,** etc.; das **Stift (-e** or **-er),** *convent,* etc., or *charitable foundation for ladies of rank.*

der **Strauß,** *ostrich* (**Strauße,** also weak **Straußen;** sing. often der **Vogel Strauß),** *posy* or *skirmish* (**Sträuße**).

der **Streit,** plur. **Streite,** usually **Streitigkeiten,** *disputes.*

der **Tau,** *dew;* das **Tau (-e),** *rope.*

der **Teil (-e),** *part;* das **Teil (-e),** *portion, v.* § 442 (*a*) (2).

der **Tod,** plur. **Tode,** usually **Todesfälle,** *deaths,* § 444.

der **Tor (-en),** *fool;* das **Tor (-e),** (carriage) *door, gate, goal* (in sport).

der **Trost,** plur. **Tröstungen,** *consolation.*

der **Trug,** plur. **Trugbilder,** *phantoms.*

der **Trupp (-e** or **-s),** *band, group of unorganised people, animals,* plur. (mil.), die **Stoßtrupps;** die **Truppe,** *troops* (mil., collective), *troupe* (theatrical).

das **Tuch,** plur. **Tücher,** *cloths,* as **Taschentücher, Tuche** (types of) *cloth.*

der **Verdienst (-e),** *earnings;* das **Verdienst (-e),** *merits, desert.*

das **Vergnügen,** plur. die **Vergnügungen,** *pleasures, entertainments.*

der **Verrat,** plur. **Verrätereien,** *treacheries.*

die **Verteidigung,** plur. **Verteidigungswerke,** *defences* (defence works).

der **Verzug,** plur. **Verzögerungen,** *delays.*

die **Wehr,** *defence;* das **Wehr,** (river) *dam, weir.*

das **Wort,** plur. **Worte,** connected *words,* **Wörter,** non-connected *words, v.* § 445 (*b*). **Worte über Wörter** (book title), *Words about Words.*

der **Wurm ("er),** *worm;* sing. also (pop.), das **Wurm,** (helpless) *babe.*

der **Zank,** plur., **Zänkereien,** *squabbling.*

der **Zeh (-en),** occasional for die **Zehe,** *toe, clove* (of garlic).

das **Zeug,** *material,* das **Zeugs** (fam.), "*stuff*", der **Zeuge (-n),** *witness.*

APPENDIX B

INSERTION AND OMISSION OF -E- IN PRESENT TENSE VERB FORMS

For convenience of pronunciation an -e- is sometimes inserted or omitted in certain present tense verb forms.

1. Weak Verbs

(*a*) An -e- may be inserted between stem and ending in the **du, er, ihr** forms, *i.e.* before -st, -t; this happens especially when the stem ends in:

(1) A dental, before -t, and usually before -st:

er (ihr) redet, betet, rettet; du redest, betest, rettest.

(2) A sibilant (-s, -sp, -ss, -sch, -x, -z) before -st:

du fischest, rasest, reizest;

but not before -t:

er (ihr) fischt, rast, reizt.

(3) Certain liquids (-m, -n-) in certain consonantal groups:

before -st: **du atmest, begegnest, zeichnest;**
before -t: **er (ihr) atmet, begegnet, zeichnet;**

but not after the double consonants -mm-, -nn-:

du flennst, hemmst; er (ihr) flennt, hemmt;

and not after other liquids:

du qualmst, lernst; er (ihr) qualmt, lernt.

(*b*) On the other hand, an -e- is normally omitted, especially in speech, when stems ending in the suffixes -el, -er precede the ending -e or -en:

(1) Before -en, the -e- of the ending:

wir handeln, wandeln, wandern.

(2) Before -e, the -e- of the stem:

ich handle, wandle, wandre.

2. Strong Verbs

(*a*) An -e- may be inserted between stem and ending in the cases described in § 1 (*a*), especially (1) and (2):

(1) But only in those verbs which do not change or mutate the vowel:

du preisest, schließest, sitzest; er (ihr) leidet, schneidet.

(2) No -e- being inserted if such change takes place:

du lädst, hältst, trittst; er lädt.

Note.—**Ihr** forms, having no vowel change, behave according to (1):

ihr ladet, haltet, tretet.

(*b*) But if a consonantal cluster thereby arises which includes two letters of (nearly) identical nature, the opposite method of contraction is adopted to ensure ease of pronunciation:

(1) Always with change of vowel and a double -t-:

er hält, ficht, gilt, schilt, tritt, for **er hält-t, ficht-t,** etc.

(2) Commonly with change of vowel and double -s-:

du liest, ißt, wächst, schmilzt, for **du lies-st, iß-st,** etc.

(3) Often, especially in conversation, when no change of vowel takes place, with double -s-:

du preist, schließt, sitzt, instead of **du preis-est,** etc.

(And always in the past-present verbs: **du weißt, mußt.**)

(4) But never in similar verbs, with double -t-:

er bietet, reitet, schreitet, cp. (*a*) (1), above.

APPENDIX C

VOWEL CHANGE IN STRONG VERBS

1. Present Tense

(*a*) General Statement. Of strong verbs, some are regular (vowel unchanged) in the present tense, thus: **ich singe, rufe, schließe, schneide; er singt, ruft,** etc. But in some cases **-e-** becomes **-i-** or **-ie-**, and **-a-**, **-au** and **-o-** (the last two being fairly uncommon) normally mutate, in the second and third persons singular.

(*b*) Detailed Statement.

(1) Short **-e-** to **-i-**:

ich spreche, du sprichst, er spricht, wir sprechen, etc.

Thus also: **bergen, bersten, brechen, (er-)schrecken, essen, fressen, fechten, flechten, gelten, quellen, schelten, schmelzen, stechen, sterben, treffen, verderben, vergessen, werben, werfen;** and also: **(er-)löschen.**

But NOT: **stecken,** and not usually: **melken.**

(2) Long **-e-** to **-ie-**:

ich sehe, du siehst, er sieht, wir sehen, etc.

Thus also: **befehlen, empfehlen, geschehen, sehen, stehlen;** and also: **gebären.**

But NOT: **geben, heben, stehen, weben; schwären, gären;** and not usually: **scheren.**

Occasionally long **-e-** becomes short **-i-**: **geben, er gibt;** and two verbs of this group double the stem consonant: **nehmen, er nimmt; treten, er tritt.**

(3) **-a-** to **-ä-**:

ich schlafe, du schläfst, er schläft, wir schlafen, etc.

Thus also: **blasen, braten, fahren, fallen, fangen, graben, halten, hangen, laden, lassen, raten, schlagen, wachsen, waschen.**

But NOT: **schaffen, schallen; mahlen, salzen, spalten.**

(4) **-au-** to **-äu-**:

ich laufe, du läufst, er läuft, wir laufen, etc.

But only: **laufen, saufen;** and NOT: **hauen, saugen, schnauben, schrauben.**

(5) **-o-** to **-ö-**:

ich stoße, du stößt, er stößt, wir stoßen, etc.

But NOT: **kommen.**

Note.—The exceptions noted above are due partly to the incursion of weak forms, which often starts in (and may go no farther than) the present, cp. § 547.

2. Past Tense and Past Participle

Six classes may be distinguished.

(*a*) Class I.

(1) ei/i/i (- ˘ ˘). Ex.: **beißen, biß, gebissen.** Also: **gleichen, gleiten, greifen, reißen, reiten, schreiten, streiten;** and, with consonantal change: **leiden, schneiden.** Summary: verbs in **-ei-** and a voiceless consonant (**-ch, -f, -ß, -ss, -t**).

(2) ei/ie/ie (- - -). Ex.: **bleiben, blieb, geblieben.** Also: **leihen, scheiden, scheinen, schreiben, schreien, schweigen, steigen, verzeihen.** Summary: verbs in **-ei-** and a voiced consonant (**-b, -d, -g, -r, -h**), or no consonant following the stem vowel.

(*b*) Class II.

ie/o/o.   There are two patterns of vowel quantity:

(1) (- ˘ ˘). Ex.: **schießen, schoß, geschossen.** Also: **fließen, gießen, genießen, kriechen, riechen, schließen, triefen;** and, with consonantal change: **sieden.** Summary: verbs in **-ie-** and a voiceless consonant.

Also: **fechten (focht, gefochten), klimmen, saufen, erlöschen.**

(2) (- - -). Ex.: **biegen, bog, gebogen.** Also: **fliegen, fliehen, frieren, schieben, stieben, verlieren, wiegen, ziehen.** Summary: verbs in **-ie-** and a voiced consonant.   But **bieten (bot, geboten)** with unvoiced consonant.

Also: **heben (hob, gehoben), weben, saugen, schwören.**

(*c*) Class III.

(1) i/a/u/ (˘ ˘ ˘). Ex.: **finden, fand, gefunden.** Also: **binden, gelingen, klingen, singen, sinken, trinken, zwingen.** Summary: verbs in **-i-** and the consonantal groups **-nd-, -ng-, -nk-.**

(2) i/a/o (˘ ˘ ˘). Ex.: **spinnen, spann, gesponnen.** Also: **beginnen, gewinnen, schwimmen.** Summary: verbs with **-i-** and **-mm-** or **-nn-.**

Also: **gelten.**

(3) e/a/o.   There are three patterns of vowel quantity:

(i) (˘ ˘ ˘). Ex.: **helfen, half, geholfen.** Also: **sterben, verbergen, werfen.** Summary: verbs with **-l-** or **-r-** and a consonant.

(ii) (˘ - ˘). Ex.: **sprechen, sprach, gesprochen.** Also: **brechen, erschrecken, treffen.** Summary: verbs with **-r-** preceding the stem vowel.

(iii) (- - -).   Ex.: **stehlen, stahl, gestohlen.**   Also: **befehlen, empfehlen.** Summary: verbs with **-eh-.**   Also: **gebären.**

Also: **kommen** and **nehmen,** as (ii): **kam, gekommen; nahm, genommen.**

(*d*) Class IV.

e/a/e.   There are two patterns of vowel quantity:

(1) (˘ - ˘).   Ex.: **essen, aß, gegessen.**   Also: **fressen, messen, vergessen.** *Note.*—**ge-g-essen** as irregular past participle.

(2) (- - -).   Ex.: **geben, gab, gegeben.**   Also: **geschehen, lesen, sehen, treten.**

Also: three verbs with **-i-** or **-ie-** in the infinitive stem: **sitzen [saß, gesessen,** as (1)]; **bitten (bat, gebeten),** and **liegen,** as (2).

Distinguish the following verbs, similar in sense and/or appearance: **bitten** (str.), **bieten** (str.), **beten** (wk.); **liegen** (str.), **legen** (wk.), **lügen** (str.); **sitzen** (str.), **setzen** (wk.).

(*e*) Class V.

a/u/a.   There are two patterns of vowel quantity:

(1) (- - -).   Ex.: **fahren, fuhr, gefahren.**   Also: **graben, laden, schlagen, tragen.**

(2) (˘ - ˘).   Ex.: **backen, buk, gebacken.**   Also: **schaffen, wachsen, waschen.**

Note.—**stehen, stand, gestanden,** with changed stem.

(*f*) Class VI.

a/ie/a.   There are two patterns of vowel quantity:

(1) (¯ ¯ ¯).   Ex.: **schlafen, schlief, geschlafen.**   Also: **blasen, braten, raten.**

Also, with other long vowels or diphthongs in the infinitive, to which the past participle returns: **stoßen, rufen; hauen, heißen, laufen.**

(2) (¯ ˘ ¯).   Ex.: **fallen, fiel, gefallen.**   Also: **halten, lassen;** and, with short vowel in the past: **fangen (fing, gefangen),** and **hangen.**

Note.—**gehen, ging, gegangen,** with changed stem.

APPENDIX D

CONJUGATION LIST OF STRONG AND IRREGULAR VERBS

(With Alternative Regular Weak Forms)

Refer to Chapter LXVI.

The forms of the verb are set out in the order: (1) infin. and meaning; (2) second and third pers. sing. pres.; (3) second pers. imp. (for variant forms, *v.* § 247); (4) first pers. past; (5) first pers. past subj.; (6) past part., and aux., if **sein**.

backen, intr., tr., *to bake;* (intr., weak) *to cake* (snow, etc.). § 551 (*e*)
    bäckst, bäckt; back(e)! backte/buk; backte (büke); gebacken.
bedingen, tr., *to condition, require; to stipulate.*
    bedingst, bedingt; beding(e)! bedingte (bedang); bedingte; bedingt/ bedungen [§ 552 (*b*)].
befehlen, intr., tr., *to command.*
    befiehlst, befiehlt; befiehl! befahl; beföhle (befähle); befohlen.
sich befleißen/befleißigen, refl., *to apply oneself (to).* § 547 (*b*)
    befleißigst, befleißigt; befleißige dich! befliß/befleißigte; beflisse/ befleißigte; beflissen/befleißigt.
beginnen, intr., tr., *to begin.*
    beginnst, beginnt; beginn(e)! begann; begönne (begänne); begonnen.
beißen, intr., tr., *to bite.* § 548 (*c*)
    beiß(es)t, beißt; beiß(e)! biß; bisse; gebissen.
beklommen, past participle, *v.* § 552 (*b*).
bergen, tr., *to hide, conceal; to save, secure.* § 550 (*a*)
    birgst, birgt; birg! barg; bärge (bürge); geborgen.
bersten, intr., *to burst.*
    birst (berstest), birst (berstet); birst (berste)! barst; bärste (börste); geborsten.
bescheiden, tr., *to inform, summon, v.* **scheiden.**
bescheiden, past participle, *v.* § 552 (*d*).
unbescholten, past participle, *v.* § 552 (*d*).
bewegen, tr., *to move* (lit. and fig.); *to persuade, induce.* § 551 (*a*)
    bewegst, bewegt; beweg(e)! bewegte/bewog; bewegte/bewöge; bewegt/ bewogen.
biegen, intr., tr., *to bend.* § 548 (*d*)
    biegst, biegt; bieg(e)! bog; böge, gebogen.

bieten, tr., *to offer.*
> **biet(e)st, bietet; biet(e)! bot; böte; geboten.**

binden, tr., *to tie, bind.*
> **bind(e)st, bindet; bind(e)! band; bände; gebunden.**

bitten, tr., *to ask, request.*
> **bitt(e)st, bittet; bitt(e)! bat; bäte; gebeten.**

blasen, intr., tr., *to blow.*
> **bläs(es)t, bläst; blas(e)! blies; bliese; geblasen.**

bleiben, intr., *to remain.*
> **bleibst, bleibt; bleib(e)! blieb; bliebe; (ist) geblieben.**

bleichen, intr., *to turn pale, lose colour.*   § 550 (*a*)
> **bleichst, bleicht; bleich(e)! bleichte (blich); bleichte (bliche), (ist) gebleicht/geblichen.**

braten, intr., tr., *to roast, bake.*
> **brätst, brät; brat(e)! briet; briete; gebraten.**

brechen, intr., tr., *to break.*
> **brichst, bricht; brich! brach; bräche; (intr., ist) gebrochen.**

brennen, intr., tr., *to burn.*
> **brennst, brennt; brenne! brannte; brennte; gebrannt.**

bringen, tr., *to bring.*
> **bringst, bringt; bringe! brachte; brächte; gebracht.**

denken, intr., *to think.*   § 548 (*b*)
> **denkst, denkt; denke! dachte; dächte; gedacht.**

dingen, intr., tr., *to bargain; to hire, engage.*
> **dingst, dingt; ding(e)! dingte (dang); dingte (dänge/dünge); gedungen, § 552 (*b*) (gedingt).**

(auf)gedunsen, past participle, *v.* § 552 (*d*).

dreschen, intr., tr., *to thrash, thresh.*
> **drisch(e)st, drischt; drisch! drasch/drosch; dräsche/drösche; gedroschen.**

dringen, intr., *to penetrate, crowd, press.*   § 548 (*d*)
> **dringst, dringt; dring(e)! drang; dränge; gedrungen.**

dünken, tr. [§ 548 (*b*) and Note], *to seem, appear* (with acc. dat.).
> **dünkst, dünkt; no** imperative; **dünkte (deuchte); dünkte (deuchte); gedünkt (gedeucht).**

dürfen, aux., *to be allowed, may* (permission).
> **darfst, darf; dürfe! durfte; dürfte; gedurft/dürfen [§ 66 (*b*)].**

empfehlen, tr., *to recommend.*
> **empfiehlst, empfiehlt; empfiehl! empfahl; empföhle (empfähle); empfohlen.**

erbleichen, intr., *to grow pale, lose colour.*   § 550 (*a*)
> **erbleichst, erbleicht; erbleich(e)! erbleichte/erblich; erbleichte/erbliche; (ist) erbleicht/erblichen.**

erhaben, past participle, *v.* § 552 (*d*).

erkiesen (erküren), tr., *to choose, select.*

    erkies(es)t, erkiest; erkies(e)! erkor (erkieste); erköre (erkieste); erkoren (erkiest).

erlöschen, intr., *to be extinguished, go out.*   §§ 548 (*b*), 550 (*a*)

    erlisch(e)st, erlischt; erlisch! erlosch; erlösche; (ist) erloschen.

ersaufen, intr., *to drown* (of an animal), *v.* **saufen.**   § 548 (*b*)

erschrecken, intr., *to be frightened.*   §§ 548 (*b*), 550 (*a*)

    erschrickst, erschrickt; erschrick! erschrak; erschräke; (ist) erschrocken.

ertrinken, intr., *to drown, v.* **trinken.**   § 548 (*b*)

erwägen, tr., *to consider, v.* **wiegen.**   § 549 (*b*)

essen, tr., *to eat.*

    ißt/issest, ißt; iß! aß; äße; gegessen.

fahren, intr., *to go, travel* (in a vehicle).   § 548 (*b*)

    fährst, fährt; fahr(e)! fuhr; führe; (ist) gefahren.

fallen, intr., *to fall.*   § 548 (*b*)

    fällst, fällt; fall(e)! fiel; fiele; (ist) gefallen.

falten, tr., *to fold,* weak, except for an additional strong past participle, **gefalten** [§ 552 (*b*)].

fangen, tr., *to catch.*

    fängst, fängt; fang(e)! fing; finge; gefangen.

fechten, intr., *to fight, fence.*

    fichtst, ficht; ficht! focht; föchte; gefochten.

finden, tr., *to find.*

    find(e)st, findet; find(e)! fand; fände; gefunden.

flechten, tr., *to plait, weave.*

    flichtst, flicht; flicht! flocht; flöchte; geflochten.

fliegen, intr., *to fly.*

    fliegst, fliegt; flieg(e)! flog; flöge; (ist) geflogen.

fliehen, intr., tr., *to flee, fly.*

    fliehst, flieht; flieh(e)! floh; flöhe; (intr., ist) geflohen.

fließen, intr., *to flow.*   § 548 (*b*)

    fließ(es)t, fließt; fließ(e)! floß; flösse; (ist) geflossen.

fressen, tr., *to eat* (of or like an animal).

    frißt/frissest, frißt; friß! fraß; fräße; gefressen.

frieren, intr., tr., *to feel* or *make cold, freeze.*

    frierst, friert; frier(e)! fror; fröre; (intr., *became ice,* **ist) gefroren.**

gären, intr., *to ferment.*   § 551 (*f*)

    gärst, gärt; gär(e)! gor/gärte; göre/gärte; (hat, ist) gegoren/(hat) gegärt.

gebären, tr., *to bear* (children).

    gebierst, gebiert; gebier! [gebär(e)!] gebar; gebäre; geboren [§ 552 (*d*)].

geben, tr., *to give.*
> gibst, gibt; gib! gab; gäbe; gegeben.

gebieten, intr., tr., *to command,* v. **bieten.**

gedeihen, intr., *to thrive, prosper, make progress.*
> gedeihst, gedeiht; gedeih(e)! gedieh; gediehe; (ist) gediehen [§ 552 (d)].

gehen, intr., *to go, walk.*
> gehst, geht; geh(e)! ging; ginge; (ist) gegangen.

gelingen, intr., *to succeed* [impersonal, v. § 245 (c)].
> gelingt; no imperative; gelang; gelänge; (ist) gelungen.

gelten, intr., *to be valid, worth.*
> giltst, gilt; gilt! galt; gölte (gälte); gegolten.

genesen, intr., *to recover* (from illness).
> genes(es)t, genest; genes(e)! genas; genäse; (ist) genesen.

genießen, tr., *to enjoy.*
> genieß(es)t, genießt; genieß(e)! genoß; genösse; genossen.

gerinnen, intr., *to coagulate,* etc., v. **rinnen.**   § 548 (b)

geschehen, intr., *to happen* (impersonal, v. §§ 243 f.).
> geschieht; no imperative; geschah; geschähe; (ist) geschehen.

gewinnen, intr., tr., *to win, gain.*
> gewinnst, gewinnt; gewinn(e)! gewann; gewönne (gewänne); gewonnen.

gießen, intr., tr., *to pour.*
> gieß(es)t, gießt; gieß(e)! goß; gösse; gegossen.

gleichen, intr., tr., *to resemble, make equal.*
> gleichst, gleicht; gleich(e)! glich; gliche; geglichen.

gleißen, intr., *to glitter.*   § 547 (b)
> gleiß(es)t, gleißt; gleiß(e)! gleißte/gliß; gleißte/glisse; gegleißt/geglissen.

gleiten, intr., *to glide, slide.*
> gleitst, gleitet; gleit(e)! glitt; glitte; (ist) geglitten.

glimmen, intr., *to burn faintly, glimmer, smoulder.*   § 551 (f)
> glimmst, glimmt; glimm(e)! glimmte (glomm); glimmte (glömme); geglimmt (geglommen).

graben, intr., tr., *to dig.*
> gräbst, gräbt; grab(e)! grub; grübe; gegraben.

greifen, intr., tr., *to grasp, seize.*
> greifst, greift; greif(e)! griff; griffe; gegriffen.

haben, tr. and aux., *to have, possess.*
> hast, hat; hab(e)! hatte; hätte; gehabt.

halten, intr., tr., *to hold; to last; to stop,* etc.
> hältst, hält; halt(e)! hielt; hielte; gehalten.

hängen (hangen), intr., *to hang.*   § 549 (a)
> hängst, hängt; hang(e)!/häng(e)! hing; hinge; gehangen.

hauen, intro., tr., *to deliver a blow, hit, hew* (wood, etc.). § 551 (*a*)
   haust, haut; hau(e)! hieb/haute; hiebe/haute; gehauen/gehaut.
heben, tr., *to lift, heave.*
   hebst, hebt; heb(e)! hob (older, **hub**); **höbe (hübe); gehoben.**
heißen, intr., tr., *to mean, be called, bid.*
   heiß(es)t, heißt; heiß(e)! hieß; hieße; geheißen.
helfen, intr., *to help.*
   hilfst, hilft; hilf! half; hülfe (hälfe); geholfen.
kennen, tr., *to know* (personally).
   kennst, kennt; kenn(e)! kannte; kennte; gekannt.
kiesen (küren), tr., *to choose.*
   **kies(es)t/kürst, kiest/kürt; kies(e)!/kür(e)! kieste/kor/kürte; kieste/
   köre/kürte; gekoren.**
klieben, intr., tr., *to split* (= **spalten**). § 547 (*b*)
   kliebst, kliebt; klieb(e)! klob/kliebte; klöbe/kliebte; gekloben/gekliebt.
klimmen, intr., *to climb.* §§ 547 (*b*), 552 (*b*)
   **klimmst, klimmt; klimm(e)! klomm/klimmte; klömme/klimmte;
   (ist) geklommen/geklimmt.**
klingen, intr., *to (re)sound.*
   klingst, klingt; kling(e)! klang; klänge; geklungen.
kneifen, tr., *to pinch.*
   kneifst, kneift; kneif(e)! kniff; kniffe; gekniffen.
kommen, intr., *to come.*
   kommst, kommt; komm(e)! kam; käme; (ist) gekommen.
können, aux., tr., *to be able, can* (capacity, possibility).
   kannst, kann; könne! konnte; könnte; gekonnt/können [§ 66 (*b*)].
kriechen, intr., *to creep, crawl.*
   kriechst, kriecht; kriech(e)! kroch; kröche; (ist) gekrochen.
laden, tr., *to load, fill; to invite.* § 551 (*e*)
   lädst/ladest, lädt/ladet; lad(e)! lud/ladete; lüde/ladete; geladen.
lassen, tr., *to let, allow;* aux., with infin., *to cause, have* (something done).
   läßt/lässest, läßt; laß!/lasse! ließ; ließe; gelassen.
laufen, intr., *to run.*
   läufst, läuft; lauf(e)! lief; liefe; (ist) gelaufen.
leiden, intr., tr., *to suffer.* § 548 (*c*)
   leidest, leidet; leid(e)! litt; litte; gelitten.
leihen, tr., *to lend, borrow.*
   leihst, leiht; leih(e)! lieh; liehe; geliehen.
lesen, intr., tr., *to read, select.*
   lies(es)t, liest; lies! las; läse; gelesen.
liegen, intr., *to lie.*
   liegst, liegt; lieg(e)! lag; läge; gelegen.

lügen, intr., *to tell lies.*
> lügst, lügt; lüg(e)! log; löge; gelogen.

mahlen, intr., tr., *to grind,* weak, except for the past participle, which is strong: **gemahlen** [§ 552 (*a*)].

meiden, tr., *to avoid.*
> meidest, meidet; meid(e)! mied; miede; gemieden.

melken, tr., *to milk;* (weak, fig.) *to fleece.*   §§ 547 (*b*), 551 (*c*)
> melkst (milkst), melkt (milkt); melke! (milk!); melkte (molk); melkte (mölke); gemolken (gemelkt).

messen, tr., *to measure.*
> mißt/missest, mißt; miß! maß; mäße; gemessen.

mögen, aux., tr., *to like, be inclined (to), may, might* (possibility, inclination).
> magst, mag; möge! mochte; möchte; gemocht/mögen [§ 66 (*b*)].

müssen, aux., *to have (to), be compelled, must* (compulsion).
> mußt, muß; no imperative; mußte; müßte; gemußt/müssen [§ 66 (*b*)].

nehmen, tr., *to take.*
> nimmst, nimmt; nimm! nahm; nähme; genommen.

nennen, tr., *to name.*
> nennst, nennt; nenn(e)! nannte; nennte; genannt.

pfeifen, intr., tr., *to whistle, pipe.*
> pfeifst, pfeift; pfeif(e)! pfiff; pfiffe; gepfiffen.

pflegen, intr., tr., *to occupy oneself with; to tend, care for; to be accustomed (to).*   § 551 (*d*)
> pflegst, pflegt; pfleg(e)! pflegte (pflog); pflegte (pflöge); gepflegt [gepflogen, § 552 (*b*)].

preisen, tr., *to praise.*
> preis(es)t, preist; preis(e)! pries; priese; gepriesen.

quellen, intr., *to spring forth, gush out.*   § 548 (*b*)
> quillst, quillt; quill! quoll; quölle; (ist) gequollen.

raten, intr., tr., *to advise.*
> rätst, rät; rat(e)! riet; riete; geraten.

reiben, intr., tr., *to rub.*
> reibst, reibt; reib(e)! rieb; riebe; gerieben.

reißen, intr., tr., *to tear.*   § 548 (*c*)
> reiß(es)t, reißt; reiß(e)! riß; risse; gerissen.

reiten, intr., tr., *to ride.*
> reit(e)st, reitet; reit(e)! ritt; ritte; (intr., ist) geritten.

rennen, intr., *to run, race.*
> rennst, rennt; renne! rannte; rennte; (ist) gerannt.

riechen, intr., tr., *to smell.*
> riechst, riecht; riech(e)! roch; röche; gerochen.

ringen, intr., *to wrestle.*
　ringst, ringt; ring(e)! rang; ränge; gerungen.
rinnen, intr., *to run, flow.*　　　　　　　　　　§ 548 (*b*)
　rinnst, rinnt; rinn(e)! rann; ränne (rönne); geronnen.
rufen, intr., tr., *to call* (vocally).
　rufst, ruft; ruf(e)! rief; riefe; gerufen.
salzen, tr., *to salt, season,* weak, except for an additional strong past
　participle: **gesalzen** [§ 552 (*b*)].
saufen, intr., tr., *to drink* (of or like animals).
　säufst, säuft; sauf(e)! soff; söffe; gesoffen.
saugen, intr., *to suck.*　　　　　　　　　　　　§ 548 (*b*)
　**saugst, saugt; saug(e)! sog (saugte); söge (saugte); gesogen
　(gesaugt).**
schaffen, intr., tr., *to create; to bring about, avail; to bring* (up, to, from);
　to work, be busy.　　　　　　　　　　　　　§ 551 (*b*)
　**schaffst, schafft; schaff(e)! schuf/schaffte; schüfe/schaffte; geschaffen/
　geschafft.**
schallen, intr., *to sound.*　　　　　　　§§ 548 (*d*), 550 (*b*)
　schallst, schallt; schall(e)! schallte (scholl); schallte (schölle); geschallt.
scheiden, intr., tr., *to depart, separate.*
　scheidest, scheidet; scheid(e)! schied; schiede; (intr., ist) geschieden.
scheinen, intr., *to seem, shine.*
　scheinst, scheint; schein(e)! schien; schiene; geschienen.
schelten, intr., tr., *to scold.*
　schiltst, schilt; schilt! schalt; schölte (schälte); gescholten.
scheren, tr., *to cut, shear;* (weak) *to concern;* (refl., weak) *to concern
　oneself, to clear off.*　　　　　　　　　　　§ 551 (*b*)
　**scherst (schierst), schert (schiert); scher(e)! schor/scherte; schöre/
　scherte; geschoren/geschert.**
schieben, intr., tr., *to push, shove.*
　schiebst, schiebt; schieb(e)! schob; schöbe; geschoben.
schießen, intr., tr., *to shoot, emerge suddenly.*
　schieß(es)t, schießt; schieß(e)! schoß; schösse; (intr., ist) geschossen.
schinden, tr., *to skin, flay, oppress.*
　**schind(e)st, schindet; schind(e)! schund (schindete); schünde;
　geschunden.**
schlafen, intr., *to sleep.*
　schläfst, schläft; schlaf(e)! schlief; schliefe; geschlafen.
schlagen, intr., tr., *to hit.*
　schlägst, schlägt; schlag(e)! schlug; schlüge; geschlagen.
schleichen, intr., *to slink, creep.*
　schleichst, schleicht; schleich(e)! schlich; schliche; (ist) geschlichen.

schleifen, tr., *to grind* (sharpen); *to drag; to raze.*   § 548 (*c*)
  schleifst, schleift; schleif(e)! schliff/schleifte; schliffe/schleifte;
  geschliffen/geschleift.

schleißen, intr., tr., *to tear, split; to wear out.*   § 549 (*b*)
  schleiß(es)t, schleißt; schleiß(e)! schliß/schleißte; schlisse/schleißte;
  geschlissen/geschleißt.

schließen, intr., tr., *to close, shut.*
  schließ(es)t, schließt; schließ(e)! schloß; schlösse; geschlossen.

schlingen, tr., *to swallow, devour; to wind, tie.*
  schlingst, schlingt; schling(e)! schlang; schlänge; geschlungen.

schmalzen, tr., *to treat* or *cook with fat,* weak, except for an additional
  strong past participle: geschmalzen.

schmeißen, tr., *to fling, smite.*
  schmeiß(es)t, schmeißt; schmeiß(e)! schmiß; schmisse; geschmissen.

schmelzen, intr., *to melt.*   § 549 (*b*)
  schmilz(es)t, schmilzt; schmilz! schmolz; schmölze; (ist) geschmolzen.

schnauben (schnieben), intr., *to snort.*   § 547 (*b*)
  schnaubst, schnaubt; schnaub(e)! schnaubte (schnob); schnaubte
  (schnöbe); geschnaubt (geschnoben).

schneiden, intr., tr., *to cut.*
  schneid(e)st, schneidet; schneid(e)! schnitt; schnitte; geschnitten.

schrauben, tr., *to screw.*   § 552
  schraubst, schraubt; schraub(e)! schraubte (schrob); schraubte
  (schröbe); geschraubt (geschroben).

schrecken, intr., *to be frightened.*   §§ 548 (*b*), 549 (*a*), 550 (*a*)
  schrickst, schrickt; schrick! schrak; schräke; (ist erschrocken).

schreiben, intr., tr., *to write.*
  schreibst, schreibt; schreib(e)! schrieb; schriebe; geschrieben.

schreien, intr., tr., *to cry out, shriek.*
  schrei(e)st, schreit; schrei(e)! schrie; schriee; geschrie(e)n.

schreiten, intr., *to stride, step.*
  schreit(e)st, schreitet; schreit(e)! schritt; schritte; (ist) geschritten.

schroten, tr., *to grind coarsely,* weak, except for an additional strong past
  participle: geschroten [§ 552 (*b*)].

schwären, intr., *to fester.*   § 547 (*d*)
  schwärst, schwärt; schwär(e)! schwärte (schwor); schwärte (schwöre);
  geschwärt (geschworen).

schweigen, intr., *to be silent.*
  schweigst, schweigt; schweig(e)! schwieg; schwiege; geschwiegen.

schwellen, intr., *to swell.*   § 548 (*b*)
  schwillst, schwillt; (schwill!); schwoll; schwölle; (ist) geschwollen.

schwimmen, intr., *to swim, float.*   § 548 (*b*)
    schwimmst, schwimmt; schwimm(e)! schwamm; schwömme/schwämme; geschwommen.

schwinden, intr., *to dwindle, disappear.*
    schwind(e)st, schwindet; schwind(e)! schwand; schwände; (ist) geschwunden.

schwingen, intr., tr., *to swing.*
    schwingst, schwingt; schwing(e)! schwang; schwänge; geschwungen.

schwören, intr., tr., *to swear* (affirm solemnly).
    schwörst, schwört; schwör(e)! schwur/schwor; schwüre; geschworen.

sehen, intr., tr., *to see.*
    siehst, sieht; sieh!/siehe! sah; sähe; gesehen.

sein, intr., and aux., *to be.*
    bist, ist; sei! seien Sie! war; wäre; (ist) gewesen.

senden, tr., *to send.*   § 551 (*c*)
    send(e)st, sendet; send(e)! sandte/sendete; sendete; gesandt/gesendet.

sieden, intr., tr., *to boil, cook by boiling.*   § 551 (*b*)
    sied(e)st, siedet; sied(e)! siedete/sott; siedete/sötte; gesiedet/gesotten.

singen, intr., tr., *to sing.*   § 548 (*b*)
    singst, singt; sing(e)! sang; sänge; gesungen.

sinken, intr., *to sink.*   § 548 (*b*)
    sinkst, sinkt; sink(e)! sank; sänke; (ist) gesunken.

sinnen, intr., *to think, muse;* (past participle) *of a mind, an opinion,* v. § 552 (*c*).
    sinnst, sinnt; sinn(e)! sann; sönne (sänne); gesonnen/gesinnt.

sitzen, intr., *to sit, be sitting.*   § 548 (*b*)
    sitz(es)t, sitzt; sitz(e)! saß; säße; gesessen.

sollen, aux., *to be said to, shall, should* (will), *is to, ought* (duty).
    sollst, soll; solle! sollte; sollte; gesollt/sollen [§ 66 (*b*)].

spalten, intr., tr., *to split,* weak, except for an additional strong past participle: **gespalten** [§ 552 (*b*)].

speien, tr., *to vomit, spit* (fire, etc.), *emit.*   § 547 (*b*)
    spei(e)st, speit; spei(e)! spie (speite); spiee (speite); gespie(e)n.

spinnen, intr., tr., *to spin.*
    spinnst, spinnt; spinn(e)! spann; spönne (spänne); gesponnen.

spleißen, intr., tr., *to split.*   § 547 (*b*)
    spleiß(es)t, spleißt; spleiß(e)! spliß (spleißte); splisse (spleißte); (intr., ist) gesplissen (gespleißt).

sprechen, intr., tr., *to speak.*
    sprichst, spricht; sprich! sprach; spräche; gesprochen.

sprießen, intr., *to sprout.*   § 547 (*b*)
    sprieß(es)t, sprießt; sprieß(e)! sproß; sprösse; (ist) gesprossen.

springen, intr., *to jump, spring.*　　　　　　　　　　　§ 548 (*b*)
　　springst, springt; spring(e)! sprang; spränge; (ist) gesprungen.
stechen, intr., tr., *to sting, stab.*　　　　　　　　　　§ 547 (*b*)
　　stichst, sticht; stich! stach; stäche; gestochen.
stecken, intr., tr., *to be sticking* (in), *remain; to stick* (in), *put.*
　　　　　　　　　　　　　　　　　　　　§§ 547 (*b*), 548 (*d*)
　　steckst, steckt; steck(e)! steckte (stak); steckte (stäke); gesteckt.
stehen, intr., *to stand.*
　　stehst, steht; steh(e)! stand; stände (stünde); gestanden.
stehlen, tr., *to steal.*
　　stiehlst, stiehlt; stiehl! stahl; stähle (stöhle); gestohlen.
steigen, intr., *to mount, climb.*
　　steigst, steigt; steig(e)! stieg; stiege; (ist) gestiegen.
sterben, intr., *to die.*
　　stirbst, stirbt; stirb! starb; stürbe; (ist) gestorben.
stieben, intr., *to fly off/up* (as dust, sparks, etc.).　　§§ 547 (*b*), 548 (*b*)
　　stiebst, stiebt; stieb(e)! stob (stiebte); stöbe (stiebte); (ist) gestoben.
stinken, intr., *to stink.*　　　　　　　　　　　　　§ 548 (*b*)
　　stinkst, stinkt; stink(e)! stank; stänke; gestunken.
stoßen, intr., tr., *to push, thrust.*
　　stöß(es)t, stößt; stoß(e)! stieß; stieße; gestoßen.
streichen, intr., tr., *to wander; to stroke; to cross out.*
　　streichst, streicht; streich(e)! strich; striche; gestrichen.
streiten, intr., *to contend, quarrel.*
　　streitst, streitet; streit(e)! stritt; stritte; gestritten.
tragen, intr., tr., *to carry, wear.*
　　trägst, trägt; trag(e)! trug; trüge; getragen.
treffen, tr., *to meet, hit.*
　　triffst, trifft; triff! traf; träfe; getroffen.
treiben, intr., tr., *to move* (not under control), *drift; to drive.*
　　treibst, treibt; treib(e)! trieb; triebe; getrieben.
treten, intr., *to step, tread.*
　　trittst, tritt; tritt! trat; träte; (ist) getreten.
triefen, intr., *to drip.*　　　　　　　　　　　　§§ 547 (*d*), 548 (*b*)
　　triefst, trieft; trief(e)! triefte (troff); triefte (tröffe); getrieft (getroffen).
trinken, intr., tr., *to drink.*　　　　　　　　　　　　§ 548 (*b*)
　　trinkst, trinkt; trink(e)! trank; tränke; getrunken [§ 522 (*d*)].
trügen, intr., *to deceive* (of nature, not by intent).
　　trügst, trügt; trüg(e)! trog; tröge; getrogen.
tun, intr., tr., *to do,* etc.
　　tust, tut; tu(e)! tat; täte; getan.

verbergen, tr., *to hide,* v. **bergen.** §550 (*a*)

verbleichen, intr., *to lose colour, die,* v. **bleichen.** §550 (*a*)

verderben, intr., tr., *to spoil, corrupt.*

    verdirbst, verdirbt; verdirb! **verdarb; verdürbe; verdorben** [**verderbt,** § 552 (*c*)].

verdrießen, tr., *to vex.*

    verdrieß(es)t, verdrießt; verdrieß(e)! **verdroß; verdrösse; verdrossen.**

vergessen, tr., *to forget.*

    vergißt/vergissest, vergißt; vergiß! **vergaß; vergäße; vergessen.**

verhehlen, tr., *to conceal* (fig.), weak, except for an additional strong past participle: **verhohlen** [§ 552 (*b*)].

verlieren, intr., tr., *to lose.*

    verlierst, verliert; verlier(e)! **verlor; verlöre; verloren.**

vermessen, tr., *to measure, survey;* refl., *to presume,* v. **messen.**

verschwinden, intr., *to disappear,* v. **schwinden.** § 548 (*b*)

versinken, intr., *to sink,* v. **sinken.** § 548 (*b*)

verwegen, past participle, v. § 552 (*d*).

verwirren, tr., *to confuse, muddle,* weak, except for an additional strong past participle: **verworren** [§ 552 (*b*)].

verwünschen, tr., *to curse,* (*bewitch*), weak, except for an additional strong past participle [§ 552 (*b*)].

wachsen, intr., *to grow.*

    wächs(es)t, wächst; wachs(e)! **wuchs; wüchse; (ist) gewachsen.**

waschen, tr., *to wash.*

    wäsch(es)t, wäscht; wasch(e)! **wusch; wüsche; gewaschen.**

weben, tr., *to weave;* (weak) *to be active.* § 551 (*c*)

    webst, webt; web(e)! **webte (wob); webte (wöbe); gewebt (gewoben),** § 552 (*d*).

weichen, intr., *to yield, give way.* § 548 (*b*)

    weichst, weicht; weich(e)! **wich; wiche; (ist) gewichen.**

weisen, intr., tr., *to direct, point, show.*

    weis(es)t, weist; weis(e)! **wies; wiese; gewiesen.**

wenden, intr., tr., *to turn.* § 551 (*c*)

    wendest, wendet; wend(e)! **wandte/wendete; wendete; gewandt/ gewendet.**

werben, intr., tr., *to strive, canvas* (for); *to enlist.*

    wirbst, wirbt; wirb! **warb; würbe; geworben.**

werden, intr., *to become,* and aux. (v. future and passive).

    wirst, wird; werde! **wurde; würde; geworden/worden** [§ 210 (*a*)].

werfen, tr., *to throw.*

    wirfst, wirft; wirf! **warf; würfe; geworfen.**

wesen, intr., strong and weak, v. § 552 (*d*).

wiegen, intr., tr., *to weigh.*   § 549 (*b*)
    wiegst, wiegt; wieg(e)! wog; wöge; gewogen.

winden, intr., tr., *to twist, wind.*   § 548 (*e*)
    windest, windet; wind(e)! wand; wände; gewunden.

wissen, intr., tr., *to know* (how), *be able* (*to*).
    weißt, weiß; wisse! wußte; wüßte; gewußt.

wollen, aux., tr., *to want, wish, will* (desire).
    willst, will; wolle! wollte; wollte; gewollt/wollen [§ 66 (*b*)].

zeihen, tr., *to accuse* (= **beschuldigen**).   § 547 (*b*)
    zeihst, zeiht; zeih(e)! zieh (zeihte); ziehe (zeihte); geziehen.

ziehen, intr., tr., *to pull, draw.*
    ziehst, zieht; zieh(e)! zog; zöge; gezogen.

zwingen, tr., *to force, compel.*
    zwingst, zwingt; zwing(e)! zwang; zwänge; gezwungen.

APPENDIX E

GERMAN GRAMMATICAL TERMS

TERMINI TECHNICI DER GRAMMATIK. FACHAUSDRÜCKE DER SPRACHLEHRE

INTRODUCTORY NOTE

(*a*) The following Index gives the commonest terms used in German for grammatical concepts and relations. In most cases, two or more words are current:

(1) The international term, of Latin origin. These are those normally used in English, and exist in two forms: (i) fuller, with Latin endings, and (ii) shorter, without these; thus: **Futur(um), Partizip(ium), Genitiv(us).** Normally such endings are adjectival, a noun being understood: for **-um** words, *Nomen* (*word, part of speech*), etc., as **(nomen) adjectivum, (nomen) numerale, (verbum) futurum**; for **-us** words, *Casus* (*case*), etc.: **(casus) genitivus.** The plurals follow the principles given for the mixed (classical) declension, §§ 90-2; thus: **Genus (Genera), Kasus** (invar.), **Partizip (Partizipien), Verbum (Verba), Verb (Verben), Numerale (Numeralia,** or **-ien).** Purely Latin terms are also still current, as **dativus ethicus** and **consecutio temporum.**

(2) One or more German compounds, usually of standard words, devised as substitutes for the terms in (1), of which one is commonly widely accepted. Thus from **-wort** comes **Hauptwort (Hauptw., Hw.), Zeitwort (Zeitw., Zw.)**; from **-form** comes **Nennform, Tat- und Leideform (des Verbs)**; from **-lehre** comes **Sprachlehre,** etc. The plural of all **-wort** compounds is **-wörter** [*v.* § 445 (*b*)].

(*b*) As might be expected, the German forms are preferred in primary schools, while the Latin terms are used predominantly in grammar school and university. Those in favour of the German forms consider that they are more helpful in teaching grammar to younger pupils, and that their use should enable German grammar to liberate itself from ways of grammatical thought derived from, but only suitable to, the classical languages. On the other hand, the arguments against such forms are that (i) they make international exchange more difficult; and (ii) they are subject to arbitrary change and extension as the result of personal theories and predilections; thus **Dingwort** (beside **Hauptwort), Tätigkeitswort** and **Tuwort** (beside **Zeitwort), Grundform** and **Nominalform** (beside **Nennform)**; and the terms for the tenses are legion. In the List below, many such peripheral forms are placed in brackets after the main, accepted German term.

(c) The student is advised to use the short, Latin forms. But some familiarity with the various German forms is essential, since the grammatical "double-speak" described above (and illustrated in the title to this Appendix) is widely spread.

abstract (opp. concrete) *noun:* **das Abstraktum, begriffliche Hauptwort, (Gedankendingwort).**

accusative (*case*): **der Akkusativ(us), 4. Fall, Wenfall.**

active (*mood*): **das Aktiv(um), die Tatform, (Tätigkeitsform, Tuform).**

adjective: **das Adjektiv(um), Eigenschaftswort (Ew.), Beiwort.**

adverb: **das Adverb(ium), Umstandswort (Uw.).**

adverbial adjunct (*phrase*): **das (lokale, etc.) Adverbiale, die Umstandsbestimmung (des Ortes, etc.), die Lokalbestimmung, etc.;** *v.* under place, time, etc.

adverbial clause: **der Adverbial-, Umstandssatz;** *v.* under place, etc.

adverbial compounds: **adverbiale Verbindungen, Zusammensetzungen.**

agreement: **die Übereinstimmung, Kongruenz.**

apostrophe: **der Apostroph, das Auslassungszeichen,** *v.* orthography.

appellative (*i.e.* common noun): **das Appellativ(um), der Gattungsname.**

apposition: **die Apposition, Beifügung;** *appositive:* **der Beisatz, Zusatz.**

article (*indefinite, definite*): **der Artikel, das (unbestimmte, bestimmte) Geschlechtswort.**

attendant (*absent*) *circumstance:* **der begleitende (fehlende) Umstand.**

attributive: **das Attribut, die Beifügung;** (adj.) **beifügend; ein beigefügtes Adjektiv, Partizip.**

attributive clause: **der Attribut-, Beifügesatz.**

auxiliary verb: **das Hilfsverb, Hilfszeitwort (opp. Vollverb).**

brackets (*round, square*): **die Parenthesen, (runde, eckige) Klammern.**

capital, small (*initial*) *letters:* **große, kleine (Anfangs-)Buchstaben.** Rules for their use are: **die Groß- und Kleinschreibung,** *v.* orthography.

case (of the noun): **der Kasus (invar., sing. and plur.), der (Beugungs-, Deklinations-)Fall (des Hauptworts);** they have names [**der Nominativ(us)**], substitute names (**der Werfall**), and are numbered (**der 1.,** spoken **erste Fall,** etc.); further, the nominative may be: **casus rectus, unabhängiger Fall,** as distinct from a **casus obliquus, abhängiger Fall,** *oblique case;* and an oblique case governed by a preposition may be **der Verhältnisfall,** without specific reference to the case.

cause, adverb of: **das kausale Adverb, Kausaladverb, die Umstandsbestimmung des Grundes, die Kausalbestimmung;** *adverbial clause of:* **der Kausalsatz.**

clauses, v. under specific names.

collective noun: **das Kollektiv(um), der Sammelname.**

colon: **das Kolon, der Doppelpunkt.**

comma: **das Komma, der Beistrich;** for decimal point, *v.* § 80 (*a*); inverted commas, *v.* quotation marks.

common noun, v. **appellative.**

comparison, adverbial clause of: **der Komparativ-, Vergleichssatz.**

comparison (of adjs., advs.): **die Komparation, Steigerung (der Ew. und Uw.);** *positive,* **der Positiv, die Grundstufe;** *comparative and superlative,* **der Komparativ, Superlativ,** or **die 1. (= erste), 2. Steigerungsstufe,** or **die Mehrstufe** and **Meiststufe (Höchststufe);** *to compare:* **steigern.**

compound: **das Kompositum, die Zusammensetzung;** *compound nouns, verbs:* **zusammengesetzte Hauptwörter, Zeitwörter,** etc.

concession, adverbial clause of: **der Konzessiv-, Einräumungssatz.**

concrete (opp. *abstract*) *noun:* **das Konkretum, gegenständliche Hauptwort, (Sachdingwort).**

condition, adverb of: **das Adverb, die Umstandsbestimmung der Bedingung, die Konditionalbestimmung;** *adverbial clause of:* **der Konditional-, Bedingungssatz.**

conditional: **der Konditional (-is), die Bedingungsform.**

conjugation: **die Konjugation, Beugung, Abwandlung (des Verbs);** *to conjugate:* **konjugieren, beugen, abwandeln.**

conjunction: **die Konjunktion, das Bindewort (Bw.);** the following terms are self-explanatory: **subordinierend, unterordnend; koordinierend, gleich-(neben-, bei-) ordnend; adversativ, entgegensetzend; kausal, begründend; konsekutiv, folgernd; kopulativ, anreihend,** etc.

contraction (of prep. and art.): **die Verschmelzung, die Zusammenziehung.**

copula (verb *to be,* etc., opp. **Vollverb;** *v.* auxiliary): **die Kopula, das Satzband, die Formaussage.**

dash: **der Gedankenstrich;** *double dash:* **der zweiteilige Gedankenstrich, Schaltstrich** (i.e. *parenthesis dash*).

dative (case): **der Dativ(us), 3. Fall, Wemfall;** *ethical dative:* **dativus ethicus.**

declaratory statement (distinguish *command, question,* etc.): **der Aussagesatz** (distinguish **Befehlssatz, Fragesatz,** etc.).

declination, declension: **die Beugung, Abwandlung (des Hauptworts in die vier Fälle); die Fallbeugung,** etc.; **die Deklination;** *to decline:* **deklinieren, beugen, biegen, abwandeln.**

demonstrative (pronoun): **das Demonstrativ(um), Zeigewort; das Demonstrativpronomen, hinweisende Fürwort.**

diminution, diminutive (form, suffix): **die Diminution, Deminution,** and **-e-** or **-i-** also in the following: **das Diminutiv(um), die Diminutiv-, Verkleinerungsform, -silbe.**

602 GRAMMATICAL TERMS

elliptical statement: die Ellipse, der Auslassungssatz.

exclamation (mark): der Ausruf; der Ausrufesatz; das Ausruf(e)zeichen, Ausrufungszeichen.

factitive, causative (verb): das Faktitiv(um), Kausativ(um), verbum faktitivum, bewirkendes Zeitwort, Bewirkungswort.

feminine: weiblich; (gender) das Femininum.

finite verb: verbum finitum, die Personalform des Verbs, das Verb in konjugierter Form.

foreign (borrowed) *word:* das Fremdwort.

future tense: das Futur(um), 1. Futur, die 1. Zukunft.

future perfect tense: das Futurum exaktum, 2. Futur, die 2. Zukunft, vollendete Zukunft.

gender: das Genus (plur. Genera), Geschlecht, *v.* masculine, etc.

genitive (case): der Genitiv(us), 2. Fall, Wesfall.

government: die Rektion; *to govern:* regieren; *case governed:* der Richtfall.

hyphen: der Bindestrich; *carry-over hyphen* [*v.* § 544 (*a*)]: der Ergänzungs- bindestrich; *v.* orthography.

hypotaxis: die Hypotaxe, Unterordnung; untergeordneter Satz.

imperative (mood): der Imperativ, die Befehlsform (Beff.); (statement) der Befehlssatz; this and der Wunschsatz, *statement of wish,* are forms of Aufforderungssatz, *exhortation.*

impersonal verb: das unpersönliche Verb; often echte u. V.n are distinguished from those which may be used otherwise, cp. § 243, and reflexive verbs.

indefinite pronouns (man, etc.): das Indefinitpronomen, unbestimmte Fürwort; *indefinite adjectives (numerals)* (viel, etc.): das unbestimmte Numerale.

indicative (mood): der Indikativ, die Wirklichkeitsform (Wirkl.).

indirect (reported) speech: die indirekte, abhängige, (nichtwörtliche) Rede.

infinitive: der Infinitiv, die Nennform, Grundform (des Zeitworts); *simple, compound:* einfach, zusammengesetzt; *simple, prepositional:* reiner I., I. mit (ohne) zu; the infinitive with or without zu is also known as der nichterweiterte I., that with further adjuncts being der erweiterte I.; German distinguishes verbum infinitum or die Nominalformen des Verbs, *i.e.* infinitive and participles, from verbum finitum (*v.* finite verb).

infinitive construction: Infinitivgruppe, -satz.

infinitive noun: der substantivierte Infinitiv.

inflection: die Flexion, Beugung (des Hauptworts, etc.); die Flexions- endungen; die Formenlehre; *to inflect* is, for noun and verb, beugen, biegen, abwandeln (*v.* declination, conjugation), for adjectives usually flektieren.

(in)separable prefix, verb: das (un)abtrennbare Präfix, die (un)abtrennbare Vorsilbe; das (un)trennbare Verb.

interjection: die Interjektion, das Ausrufungswort, Ausrufewort; das Empfindungswort (Gefühlswort).

interrogative (pronoun, adverb): das Interrogativ(um), Fragewort; das Interrogativpronomen, fragende Fürwort, Fragefürwort; das Frageadverb.

(in)transitive verb: das (in)transitive, (nicht)zielende Zeitwort.

main (opp. subordinate) *clause:* der Hauptsatz.

manner, adverb of: das Adverb, die Umstandsbestimmung der Art und Weise, die Modalbestimmung (including in German: attendant circumstance, comparison, means, *q.v.*); *adverbial clause of:* der Modalsatz.

masculine: männlich; (gender), das Maskulinum.

means, adverb of: das modale Adverb, Modaladverb, die Umstandsbestimmung des Mittels; die Instrumentalbestimmung; *adverbial clause of:* der Instrumentalsatz.

modal auxiliaries: die modalen Hilfsverben; note that Modal- in adverbial contexts refers to manner, *q.v.*

mood (of the verb): der Modus (plur. Modi), die Aussageweise, Aussageform (des Zeitworts), *i.e.* imperative, indicative, subjunctive, *q.v.*

negation, negative: die Verneinung, die Neinform.

neuter: neutrum, sächlich; (gender), das Neutrum.

nominative (case): der Nominativ(us), 1. Fall, Werfall; *v.* case.

noun: das Substantiv(um), Hauptwort (Hw.), (Dingwort).

noun (subject, etc.) *clause:* der Subjekt-, Gegenstandssatz; der Objekt-, Ergänzungssatz; der Prädikativ-, Aussagesatz.

number: der Numerus (plur. Numeri), die Zahlform; *v.* singular, etc.

numeral: das Numerale (plur. -lia, -lien), Zahlwort; *cardinal,* die Kardinal-, Grundzahl; *ordinal,* die Ordinal-, Ordnungszahl; *fraction,* der Bruch, die Bruchzahl; *ordinal adverb* (-ens), das ordnende Zahladverb; *iterative* (-mal), die Wiederholungszahl; *multiplicative* (-fach), die Vervielfältigungszahl.

object: das Objekt, Ziel (eines transitiven Verbs), die (Satz-)Ergänzung; *direct, indirect:* das direkte, indirekte Objekt, or das Hauptziel, Nebenziel, (das Nahziel, Fernziel); *prepositional:* das Präpositionalobjekt, Verhältnisziel; *dative, accusative:* das Dativ-, Akkusativobjekt, das Wemziel, Wenziel, or die (Satz-)Ergänzung im Wemfall, Wenfall.

order (of words): die Wortstellung, Wortfolge; (of clauses) die Satzfolge; *normal, inverted:* die gerade (normale), ungerade Wortfolge, Inversion, Umstellung; *leading, second, end position* (of the verb): die Anfangs-, Zweit-, Endstellung (des Verbs).

orthography: die **Orthographie, Rechtschreibung;** *the right spelling:* die **richtige Schreibweise;** *a spelling error:* ein **Rechtschreibfehler, Fehler in der R.**; apart from the field of correct spelling, orthography comprises in German: die **Groß- und Kleinschreibung,** rules for capital, small (initial) letters; die **Satzzeichenlehre, Zeichensetzung,** *punctuation;* die **Wortzeichenlehre,** (rules for) apostrophe, hyphen.

parataxis: die **Parataxe (-xis), Nebenordnung;** nebengeordneter Satz.

parenthesis: die **Parenthese;** (clause), der **Schaltsatz.**

part of the sentence (subject, object, etc.): das **Satzglied,** der **Satzteil;** distinguish *part of speech* (noun, verb, etc.): der **Redeteil,** die **Wortart.**

particle: die **Partikel,** der **unveränderliche (unflektierbare) Redeteil,** das **Redeteilchen;** cp. die **Vergleichspartikeln als, wie,** *particles of comparison.*

participle: das **Partizip(ium),** das **Mittelwort (Mw.).**

participle construction: die **Partizipialgruppe, -konstruktion;** der **Partizipialsatz.**

passive (voice): das **Passiv(um),** die **Leideform (des Verbs).**

past participle: das **Partizipium Perfekti, Partizip Perfekt, Perfektpartizip,** das **2. Mittelwort (Partizip),** das **Mittelwort der Vergangenheit.**

past-present verb: das **Präteritopräsens** (plur. -entia, -entien).

past tense: das **Imperfekt(um), Präteritum;** die **1. (dauernde) Vergangenheit, Mitvergangenheit (Mitv.);** die **erzählende Vergangenheit.**

perfect tense: das **Perfekt(um),** die **2. Vergangenheit;** sometimes die **vollendete Gegenwart.**

period: die **Periode,** der **Großsatz, Gliedersatz;** pejorative, der **Schachtelsatz.**

person, first, second, third: die **erste (sprechende),** zweite **(angesprochene),** dritte **(besprochene) Person.**

personal pronoun: das **Personalpronomen, persönliche Fürwort.**

place, adverb of: das **lokale Adverb,** das **Lokaladverb,** die **Umstandsbestimmung des Ortes,** die **Lokalbestimmung;** *adverbial clause of:* der **Lokal-, Ortssatz.**

pluperfect tense: das **Plusquamperfekt(um),** die **3. Vergangenheit, Vorvergangenheit;** sometimes die **vollendete Vergangenheit.**

plural: der **Plural (Pluralis),** die **Mehrzahl (Mz.);** noun only in plural [*v.* § 443 (*a*)]: das **Pluraletantum** (plur. **Pluraliatantum**).

possessive: das **Possessiv(um), Possessivpronomen, besitzanzeigende Fürwort.**

predicate: das **Prädikat,** die **Satzaussage.**

predicative: das **Prädikativ(um), Prädikatsnomen, Aussagewort,** die **Sinnaussage;** (adj.) **prädikativ, aussagend.**

prefix: das **Präfix(um),** die **Vorsilbe.**

preposition: die Präposition, das Verhältniswort (Vw.), (Vorwort).

present participle: das Partizipium Präsentis, Partizip Präsens, Präsenspartizip, das 1. Mittelwort (Partizip), das Mittelwort der Gegenwart.

present tense: das Präsens, die (Zeitform der) Gegenwart (Gegw.).

print, Gothic: die Fraktur(schrift); *Latin:* die Antiqua.

pronoun: das Pronomen, Fürwort (Fw.).

pronominal adverb: das Pronominaladverb, Umstandsfürwort.

proper name: das Proprium, der Eigenname; *personal:* der Personenname; *geographical and place:* der erdkundliche Name, Ortsname.

punctuation (marks): die Zeichensetzung, die (plur.) Satzzeichen; (rules for), die Satzzeichenlehre.

purpose, adverbial clause of: der Final-, Absichts-, Zwecksatz.

question: die Frage, der Fragesatz; *indirect:* die indirekte Frage; *order:* die Fragestellung; *question mark:* das Fragezeichen.

quotation marks: die (plur.) Anführungszeichen (unten, oben).

reflexive pronoun: das reflexive Pronomen, Reflexivpronomen, rückbezügliche Fürwort; *reciprocal:* das reziproke Pronomen, wechselbezügliche Fürwort.

reflexive verb: das reflexive Verb, rückbezügliche Zeitwort; often echte r. V.n are distinguished from those which may be used otherwise, unechte (gelegentliche) r. V.n, cp. § 179, and impersonal verbs.

relative pronoun, clause: das Relativ(um), das Relativpronomen, das (rück)bezügliche (or zurückweisende) Fürwort, Bezugsfürwort; der Relativ-, Beziehungssatz; *antecedent:* das Beziehungswort.

result, adverb of: das Adverb, die Umstandsbestimmung der Folge, die Konsekutivbestimmung; *adverbial clause of:* der Konsekutiv-, Folgesatz.

semi-colon: das Semikolon, der Strichpunkt.

singular: der Singular (-is), die Einzahl (Ez.); noun only in the singular (v. § 444): das Singularetantum (plur. Singulariatantum).

stop, full: der Punkt.

stress accent: die Betonung; eine (nicht) betonte Silbe.

subject: das Subjekt, der Satzgegenstand.

subordinate (opp. main) *clause:* der Nebensatz, but *subordination* is Unterordnung, not Nebenordnung, which is *parataxis, q.v.*; for kinds of subordinate clauses, *v.* time, place, etc.; according to their degree of completeness, the following are often distinguished: (i) eingeleitete Nebensätze, with conjunction, relative, etc.; (ii) verkappte Nebensätze, with conjunction, etc., omitted; (iii) verkürzte Nebensätze, infinitive and participle constructions.

suffix: das Suffix, die Nachsilbe.

subjunctive (mood): der Konjunktiv(us), die Möglichkeitsform (Mögl.).

syllabification: die Silbentrennung.

syntax: **die Syntax, Satzlehre; die Wortfügung, der Satzbau.**

tense: **das Tempus** (sing. invar., plur. **-ora**), **die Zeit, die Zeitform, (Zeitstufe);** *sequence of tenses:* **consecutio temporum, die Zeitenfolge.**

time, adverb of: **das temporale Adverb, Temporaladverb, die Umstandsbestimmung der Zeit, die Temporalbestimmung;** *adverbial clause of:* **der Temporal-, Zeitsatz.**

verb: **das Verb(um), Zeitwort, (Zw.), (Tätigkeitswort, Tuwort, Tw.).**

voice: **das Genus** (plur. **Genera**) **verbi, die Handlungsform des Verbs,** *i.e.* active, passive, *q.v.*

word-formation: **die Wortbildung;** *to derive:* **ableiten;** *derivative:* **(ein) abgeleitet(es Hauptwort, etc.);** *derivative affix:* **die Ableitungssilbe.**

writing, Gothic: **die deutsche Schrift** (also **Kurrentschrift**), *Latin:* **die Lateinschrift, Rundschrift.**

INDEX OF PREPOSITIONS

Abbreviation: ST. = Synoptic Table, see pp. 608-9.

For Classes listed below, cp. § 261	an	auf	aus	bei	durch
CASE (v. §§ 18, 30, 265, 267)	D./A.	D./A.	D.	D.	A.
1. PLACE..	318	319	321	323	325
2. TIME..	58 387	58 389 401		389 394	398
3. AGGREGATION: Source, Origin			403		
Material			404		
Exclusion, Inclusion, Exchange					
To and beyond a limit		414			
Increase and Decrease	417				
Measurement	420	423		421	
Response, Succession		424			
4. LOGICAL RELATIONS: General	449	450			
Comparison, Identity					
Opposition					
Agent Relation					496
Means, including Instrument ..	497			498	499
Attendant Circumstance.. ..	503	503		504	
Conformity					
Motive and Reason			512		
Cause	517				519
Purpose		524 526			

FIFTEEN COMMON PREPOSITIONS

für	gegen	mit	nach	über	um	unter	von	vor	zu
A.	*A.*	*D.*	*D.*	*D./A.*	*A.*	*D./A.*	*D.*	*D./A.*	*D.*
	327		332 (142)	335	336	337	338	339	340
58 401			393	394 399	387	395		392	387 389
							403		
							404		
407	408	409 413				411	412		
				416		416A			
					418				419
	420			422	420 421		422		422 423
425					425				
451	452	453		454	455		454 456	457	458
460	461	462	466			464	465	466	467
468	469								
							496		
		499		501					502
		505				506			
		510 511 (264)							
				521			522 523	523	
526			525		526				527

INDEX

v. also Index of Prepositions.

610

PRINTED IN GREAT BRITAIN BY UNIVERSITY TUTORIAL PRESS LTD, FOXTON
NEAR CAMBRIDGE